D1238214

The Definitive Guide to MySQL5

Third Edition

Michael Kofler
Translated By David Kramer

Apress®

The Definitive Guide to MySQL 5

Copyright © 2005 by Michael Kofler

ISBN (pbk): 1-59059-535-1

Printed and bound in the United States of America 9 8 7 6 5 4 3 2 1

Trademarked names may appear in this book. Rather than use a trademark symbol with every occurrence of a trademarked name, we use the names only in an editorial fashion and to the benefit of the trademark owner, with no intention of infringement of the trademark.

Lead Editor: Jason Gilmore
Translator and Editor: David Kramer
Editorial Board: Steve Anglin, Dan Appleman, Ewan Buckingham, Gary Cornell, Tony Davis,
    Jason Gilmore, Jonathan Hassell, Chris Mills, Dominic Shakeshaft, Jim Sumser
Associate Publisher: Grace Wong
Project Manager: Beth Christmas
Copy Edit Manager: Nicole LeClerc
Assistant Production Director: Kari Brooks-Copony
Production Editor: Laura Cheu
Compositor: Linda Weidemann, Wolf Creek Press
Proofreader: April Eddy
Artist: Kinetic Publishing Services, LLC
Interior Designer: Van Winkle Design Group
Cover Designer: Kurt Krames
Manufacturing Manager: Tom Debolski

Distributed to the book trade worldwide by Springer-Verlag New York, Inc., 233 Spring Street, 6th Floor, New York, NY 10013. Phone 1-800-SPRINGER, fax 201-348-4505, e-mail orders-ny@springer-sbm.com, or visit http://www.springeronline.com.

For information on translations, please contact Apress directly at 2560 Ninth Street, Suite 219, Berkeley, CA 94710. Phone 510-549-5930, fax 510-549-5939, e-mail info@apress.com, or visit http://www.apress.com.

The source code for this book is available to readers at http://www.apress.com in the Source Code section.

Contents at a Glance

PART 1 ■■■ Introduction

PART 2 ■■■ Administrative Tools and User Interfaces

PART 3 ■■■ Fundamentals

PART 4 ■■■ Programming

PART 5 ■■■ Reference

PART 6 ■■■ Appendixes

Contents

PART 1 ▪▪▪ Introduction

PART 2 ■ ■ ■ Administrative Tools and User Interfaces

PART 3 ■■■ Fundamentals

PART 4 ▮▮▮ **Programming**

PART 5 ■■■ Reference

PART 6 ■■■ **Appendixes**

About the Author

MICHAEL KOFLER earned his Ph.D. in computer science at Graz Technical University. He has written a number of successful computer books on topics such as Visual Basic, Linux, Mathematica, and Maple. Kofler is also the author of *Definitive Guide to Excel VBA, Second Edition*, published by Apress.

About the Translator

DAVID KRAMER earned his Ph.D. in mathematics at the University of Maryland, and his M.A. in music at Smith College. For many years he worked in higher education, first as a professor of mathematics and computer science, and later as a director of academic computing. Since 1995 he has worked as an independent editor and translator. He has edited hundreds of books in mathematics and the sciences and has translated a number of books in a variety of fields, including *The Definitive Guide to Excel VBA*, by Michael Kofler; *Cryptography in C and C++*, by Michael Welschenbach; and *Enterprise JavaBeans 2.1*, by Stefan Denninger and Ingo Peters, all published by Apress; *Luck, Logic, and White Lies*, by Jörg Bewersdorff; *The Game's Afoot! Game Theory in Myth and Paradox*, by Alexander Mehlmann; and the novel *To Err Is Divine*, by Ágota Bozai.

Preface

MySQL is the most widely used database system in the Open Source sector. There are many reasons why this is so:

- MySQL is fast.

- MySQL is stable.

- MySQL is easy to learn.

- MySQL runs on popular operating systems (Windows, Linux, Mac OS X, various flavors of Unix).

- MySQL applications can be created in a great variety of programming languages (such as C, C++, C#, Java, Perl, PHP, Python, VB, and VB.NET).

- MySQL is extensively documented on the Internet, and there are many books on the subject available.

- MySQL is available for many applications free of charge (GPL license).

- Since the licensing restrictions of GPL are unacceptable for many commercial applications, there are reasonably priced commercial licenses and optional support contracts.

MySQL is on the verge of repeating in the database market the success achieved by Linux in the operating system sector. In combination with PHP or Perl, MySQL is increasingly used as the database system for web sites. (A favorite combination is Linux + Apache + MySQL + Perl or PHP. Such systems are called "LAMP systems" for short.) MySQL is not just for small web sites; it is used by large firms with huge amounts of data, such as Yahoo!, Slashdot, and NASA.

What Does This Book Offer?

This book provides a complete application- and example-oriented introduction to the database system MySQL. No previous knowledge of SQL or database design is assumed.

The introductory part of the book begins with an extensive introduction on installing MySQL, Apache, PHP, and Perl under Windows and Linux. We also consider the installation of components that are used in combination with MySQL. Building on this, our first example will show the basic use of MySQL and PHP.

The second part of the book introduces the most important administrative tools and user interfaces: *mysql, mysqladmin, mysqldump;* the programs MySQL Administrator, MySQL Query Browser; and finally phpMyAdmin. The latter program is particularly well suited for off-site administration using a web browser. A separate chapter shows how Microsoft Office, Sun StarOffice, and OpenOffice can be used to access MySQL databases.

Part 3 provides a large amount of background material on the database language SQL, the proper design of databases, stored procedures, MySQL's access system, and on many other topics on administration (such as backups, logging, and replication).

In Part 4, "Programming," we emphasize the language PHP: In a long chapter you will learn about techniques of programming. A number of example programs show how to use the interfaces *mysql* and *mysqli* (new in PHP 5). We deal with other programming languages, too, with chapters devoted to Perl, Java, C, Visual Basic 6, as well as VB.NET and C#.

We end the main text with a reference section (Part 5) that provides an overview of the SQL commands of MySQL, the commands and options of the administrative tools, and the functions of important programming interfaces (PHP, Perl, C, Java, ADO.NET).

Finally, there are several appendices, comprising (A) a glossary of terms, (B) information on the example files for this book (available at `www.apress.com`), and a bibliography with suggestions for further reading.

In combination with the example databases and programs, this book should provide a good foundation for the development of your own database applications. In this I wish you much fun and success.

What Is New in This Third Edition?

This edition is an extensive revision of the second edition. Most of the changes relate to changes in the MySQL server from version 4.1 to version 5.0. But there is also much that is new in areas surrounding MySQL, including new programming interfaces (e.g., *mysqli* in PHP 5) and new administrative tools. The most important new developments are collected in the following list.

Changes from MySQL 4.1 to 5.0

- Support for Unicode and other new character sets (additions and changes throughout the book).
- Views (a new section in Chapter 8).
- *INFORMATION_SCHEMA* tables (a new section in Chapter 9).
- Sub*SELECT*s (a new section in Chapter 10).
- Improved password authentication and additional privileges for access administration (Chapter 11).
- GIS functions (new Chapter 12).
- Stored procedures and triggers (new Chapter 13).
- New ways of administering InnoDB tables (a new section in Chapter 14).
- Various new SQL commands, functions, and data types (changes and additions in the entire book, with a reference in Chapter 21).
- Various new options for the MySQL server and its administrative tools (additions and changes in the entire book, with a reference in Chapter 22).

Changes in Surrounding Areas

- MySQL Administrator and MySQL Query Browser (new Chapter 5).
- Many new functions in phpMyAdmin (new Chapter 6).
- Database interface in OpenOffice/StarOffice (three new sections in Chapter 7).
- The object-oriented interface *mysqli* in PHP 5 (new Chapter 15, reference in Chapter 23).
- New functions in the C-API (Chapter 18, reference in Chapter 23).
- New ADO.NET driver Connector/Net (Chapter 20, reference in Chapter 23).

What Does This Book Not Offer?

Several chapters in this book deal with the programming of MySQL applications in a variety of programming languages, such as PHP, Perl, C, Java, and Visual Basic. These chapters assume that the reader is familiar with the specific programming language. (There is simply no room in this book to offer an introduction to a number of programming languages.) In other words, you will profit from, say, the PHP chapter in this book only if you are already familiar with the programming language PHP.

Example Programs, Source Code

The source code for all of the examples is available at `www.apress.com` in the `downloads` section.

In the longer program listings in this book you will find at the beginning of the example a comment line that specifies the file name appearing in the example files on the web site, for example,

```
<!- php/titleform.php ->
```

To save space, sometimes only the most interesting passages in the program code are printed.

Versions

The functionality of MySQL and of the programs, programming languages, and libraries placed in its environment changes with every new version—which sometimes appear weekly. The following summary indicates which versions I have worked with (explanations of the various names will appear at appropriate places in the book):

Apache: Version 2.*n*.

Connector/J: Versions 3.1.7 and 3.2.0.

Connector/ODBC (formerly MyODBC): Version 3.51.11.

gcc: Version 3.3.

Java: Versions 1.4.2 and 1.5.0.

Linux: MySQL and other programs were tested for this book under Linux and Windows. Under Linux, the distributions Red Hat Enterprise 4 and SUSE Professional 9.2 and 9.3 beta were used.

Microsoft Office: Office 2000.

Microsoft Visual Basic, VBA, ADO: Visual Basic programs were developed and tested with VB6, VBA6, and ADO version 2.8.

Microsoft Visual Basic .NET, C#, ADO.NET: Information presented is based on Visual Studio 2005 beta (.NET Framework 2.0).

Microsoft Windows: All tests under Windows were carried out with Windows XP SP2. The information given should also, in principle, be valid for Windows 2000 and for future versions of Windows.

MySQL: Version 5.0.3.

OpenOffice: Version 2.0 beta.

Perl: Version 5.8.

PHP: Versions 5.0 and 5.3.

phpMyAdmin: Version 2.6.1.

Notation

- SQL commands and functions, as well as methods, classes, and key words in SQL, C, Java, PHP, Perl, VB, etc., generally appear in italic (e.g., *SELECT*, *mysql_query*).

- Unix/Linux user names also appear in italic (e.g., *root*, *mysql*).

- MENU COMMANDS USE CAPS AND SMALL CAPS (e.g., FILE | OPEN).

- File and directory names use a monospace font (e.g., `/usr/local` or `C:\Windows`).

- Programs and programming commands are in the monospace font as well (e.g., `mysql` or `cmd.exe`).

- Program listings and command line input also appear in the `monospace font`.

SQL commands are generally written in *UPPERCASE* letters. This is not a syntactic necessity, but merely a typographical convention. MySQL does not distinguish between uppercase and lowercase in interpreting SQL commands.

In specifying Windows directories, we will often not write out the absolute path, since it depends in any case on the particular installation. We observe the following conventions:

`Windows\` means the Windows directory (e.g., `C:\Windows` or `D:\WinNT4`).

`Programs\` means the directory under Windows for program installation (e.g., `C:\Programs` or `D:\Program Files`).

`Mysql\` means the MySQL installation directory (e.g., `C:\Program Files\Mysql`).

Commands

Many commands will be presented in this book. We will be moving back and forth between the Unix/Linux and Windows conventions. The following two commands are equivalent:

```
root# mysqladmin -u root -h localhost password xxx
> mysqladmin -u root -h localhost password xxx
```

In each case we have given the system prompt (root# for Unix/Linux and > for Windows). You type in only what follows the prompt (here in **boldface type**). Under Unix/Linux it is possible to divide long inputs over several lines. The lines are separated by means of the backslash symbol \. We shall often use this convention in this book. The following command thus corresponds to the command above:

```
root# mysqladmin -u root -h localhost \
      password xxx
```

In each case, *xxx* is to be replaced by the relevant text (in this example by your password). I have indicated that *xxx* is dummy text by the use of a slant font.

Abbreviations

I have attempted in this book to make as little use of abbreviations as possible. However, there are several abbreviations that will be used repeatedly without being introduced anew in each chapter:

ADO	Active Data Objects (Microsoft database library).
ADO.NET	ADO for .NET (incompatible with ADO!).
BLOB	Binary Large Object (binary data block).
GIS	Geographical information system.
GPL	GNU Public License (important license for Open Source software).
HTML	HyperText Markup Language (format for describing web documents).
InnoDB	Not an abbreviation, but the name of a company that has developed a special table format for MySQL (InnoDB tables).
ISP	Internet Service Provider.
MySQL	The name of the company that developed the database system MySQL.
ODBC	Open Database Connectivity (interface for database access, particularly popular under Windows).
PHP	PHP Hypertext Preprocessor (a scripting programming language for HTML pages).
RPM	Red Hat Packet Manager (a format for Linux software packages).
SQL	Structured Query Language (database programming language).
URL	Uniform Resource Locator (Internet address of the form http://www.company.com/page.html).
VB	Visual Basic (programming language).
VBA	Visual Basic for Applications (programming language within the Microsoft Office package).
VBA.NET	Visual Basic for Applications (programming language within the Microsoft Office package).

PART 1

■ ■ ■

Introduction

CHAPTER 1

■ ■ ■

What Is MySQL?

This chapter begins with an overview of the most important concepts from the world of databases and then delves into the possibilities and limitations of MySQL. What is MySQL? What can it do, and what is it unable to do?

In addition to describing the central functions of MySQL, we shall also discuss fully the issue of licensing MySQL. When is one permitted to use MySQL without payment, and when is a license required?

What Is a Database?

Before we can answer the central question of this chapter, namely, *What is MySQL?* you and I must find a common language. Therefore, this section presents a rudimentary database glossary, without going into great detail. (If you have already had significant dealings with relational databases, you can skip the next couple of pages in good conscience.)

There is scarcely to be found a term that is less precise than *database*. A database can be a list of addresses residing in a spreadsheet program (such as Excel), or it can be the administration files of a telecommunications firm in which several million calls are registered daily, their charges accurately calculated, monthly bills computed, and warning letters sent to those who are in arrears. A simple database can be a stand-alone operation (residing locally on a computer for a single user), while others may be used simultaneously by thousands of users, with the data parceled out among several computers and dozens of hard drives. The size of a database can range from a few kilobytes into the terabytes.[1]

In ordinary usage, the word "database" is used to refer to the actual data, the resulting database files, the database system (such as MySQL or Oracle), or a database client (such as a PHP script or a program written in C++). Thus there arises a great potential for confusion as soon as two people begin to converse on the subject of databases.

Relations, Database Systems, Servers, and Clients

A *database* is an ordered collection of data, which is normally stored in one or more associated files. The data are structured as *tables*, where cross references among tables are possible. The existence of such *relations* among the tables leads to the database being called a *relational database*.

Let us clarify matters with an example. A database might consist of a table with data on a firm's customers (name, address, etc.), a table with data on the products the firm offers, and finally, a table

---

[1] It all started with the megabyte, which is about one million bytes. A terabyte is 1024 gigabytes, which in turn is approximately one thousand megabytes. The prefix "mega-" comes from the Greek for "great," or "large," while "giga-" is derived from the Greek word for "giant." In turn, "tera-" is from the Greek word for "monster." It would appear that numbers once regarded as large, gigantic, or even monstrously huge have become part of our everyday vocabulary.

containing the firm's orders. Through the table of orders it is possible to access the data in the other two tables (for example, via customer and product numbers).

MySQL, Oracle, the Microsoft SQL server, and IBM DB2 are examples of *relational database systems*. Such a system includes the programs for managing relational databases. Among the tasks of a relational database system are not only the secure storage of data, but also such jobs as the processing of commands for querying, analyzing, and sorting existing data and for storing new data. All of this should be able to take place not only on a single computer, but over a network as well. Instead of a *database system* we shall often speak of a *database server*.

Where there are servers, there are clients. Every program that is connected to the database system is called a *database client*. Database clients have the job of simplifying the use of the database for the end user. No user of a database system in his or her right mind would wish to communicate directly with the database server. That is much too abstract and inconvenient. (Let programmers worry about such direct communication!) Instead, the user has a right to expect convenient tables, listboxes, and so on to enable the location of data or to input new data.

Database clients can assume a variety of forms, and indeed, they are often not recognized by the user as database programs at all. Some examples of this type of client are HTML pages for the display and input of messages in an on-line discussion group, a traditional program with several windows for managing addresses and appointments, and a Perl script for executing administrative tasks. There is thus wide scope for database programming.

Relational Versus Object-Oriented Database Systems

Relational databases have dominated the database world for decades, and they are particularly well suited for business data, which usually lend themselves to structuring in the form of tables. Except for the following two paragraphs, this entire book discusses only relational databases (though we shall not always stress this point).

Another kind of database is the *object-oriented database*. Such databases can store free-standing objects (without having to arrange them in tables). Although in recent years there has been a trend in the direction of object-oriented programming languages (such as Object-Store, O2, Caché), object-oriented databases have found only a small market niche.

Note that relational databases can be accessed by means of object-oriented programming languages. However, that does not turn a relational database into an object-oriented one. Object-oriented database systems enable direct access to objects defined in the programming language in question and the storage of such objects in the database without conversion (persistency). It is precisely this that is not possible with relational database systems, in which everything must be structured in tables.

Tables, Records, Fields, Queries, SQL, Index, Keys

We have already mentioned tables, which are the structures in which the actual data are located. Every line in such a table is called a *data record*, or simply *record*, where the structure of each record is determined by the definition of the table. For example, in a table of addresses every record might contain *fields* for family name, given name, street, and so on. For every field there are precise conditions on the type of information that can be stored (such as a number in a particular format, or a character string with a predetermined maximum number of characters).

The description of a database consisting of several tables with all of its fields, relations, and indexes (see below) is called a *database model*. This model defines the construction of the data structures and at the same time provides the format in which the actual data are to be stored.

Tables usually contain their data in no particular order (more precisely, the order is usually that in which the data have been entered or modified). However, for efficient use of the data it is necessary that from these unordered data a list can be created that is ordered according to one or more criteria. It is frequently useful for such a list to contain only a selection of the data in the table. For example, one could obtain a list of all of one's customers, ordered by ZIP code, who have ordered a rubber ducky within the past twelve months.

To create such a list, one formulates *queries*. The result of the query is again a table; however, it is one that exists in active memory (RAM) and not on the hard drive.

To formulate a query one uses SQL instructions, which are commands for selecting and extracting data. The abbreviation SQL stands for *Structured Query Language*, which has become a standard in the formulation of database queries. Needless to say, every producer of a database system offers certain extensions to this standard, which dilutes the goal of compatibility among various database systems.

When tables get large, the speed at which a query can be answered depends significantly on whether there is a suitable *index* giving the order of the data fields. An index is an auxiliary table that contains only information about the order of the records. An index is also called a *key*.

An index speeds up access to data, but it has disadvantages as well. First, every index increases the amount of storage on the hard drive necessary for the database file, and second, the index must be updated each time the data are altered, and this costs time. (Thus an index saves time in the reading of data, but it costs time in entering and altering data. It thus depends on the use to which the data are to be put whether an index is on the whole a net plus or minus in the quest for efficiency.)

A special case of an index is a *primary index*, or *primary key*, which is distinguished in that the primary index must ensure a *unique* reference to a record. Often, for this purpose one simply uses a running index number (ID number). Primary indexes play a significant role in relational databases, and they can speed up access to data considerably.

MySQL

MySQL is a relational database system. If you can believe many diehard MySQL fans, MySQL is faster, more reliable, and cheaper—or, simply put, better—than any other database system (including commercial systems such as Oracle and DB2). Many MySQL opponents continue to challenge this viewpoint, going even so far as to assert that MySQL is not even a relational database system. We can safely say that there is a large bandwidth of opinion.

- The fact is that there is an ever increasing number of MySQL users, and the overwhelming majority of them are quite satisfied with MySQL. Thus for these users we may say that MySQL is good enough.

- It is also the fact, however, that MySQL still lacks a number of features that are taken for granted with other database systems. If you require such features, then MySQL is (at least for the present) not the database system for you. MySQL is not a panacea.

Next we shall examine some of the possibilities and limitations of MySQL.

Features of MySQL

The following list shows the most important properties of MySQL. This section is directed to the reader who already has some knowledge of relational databases. We will use some terminology from the relational database world without defining our terms exactly. On the other hand, the explanations should make it possible for database novices to understand to some extent what we are talking about.

Relational Database System: Like almost all other database systems on the market, MySQL is a relational database system.

Client/Server Architecture: MySQL is a client/server system. There is a database server (MySQL) and arbitrarily many clients (application programs), which communicate with the server; that is, they query data, save changes, etc. The clients can run on the same computer as the server or on another computer (communication via a local network or the Internet).

Almost all of the familiar large database systems (Oracle, Microsoft SQL Server, etc.) are client/server systems. These are in contrast to the *file-server systems*, which include Microsoft Access, dBase, and FoxPro. The decisive drawback to file-server systems is that when run over a network, they become extremely inefficient as the number of users grows.

SQL compatibility: MySQL supports as its database language—as its name suggests—SQL (Structured Query Language). SQL is a standardized language for querying and updating data and for the administration of a database.

There are several SQL dialects (about as many as there are database systems). MySQL adheres to the current SQL standard (at the moment SQL:2003), although with significant restrictions and a large number of extensions.

Through the configuration setting sql-mode you can make the MySQL server behave for the most part compatibly with various database systems. Among these are IBM DB/2 and Oracle. (The setting sql-mode changes some of the syntax conventions, and performs no miracles. More details are to be had in Chapter 14.)

A readable and entertaining article on the topic of how MySQL differs from other current database systems can be found at http://sql-info.de/mysql/gotchas.html.

SubSELECTs: Since version 4.1, MySQL is capable of processing a query in the form

```
SELECT * FROM table1 WHERE x IN (SELECT y FROM table2)
```

(There are also numerous syntax variants for sub*SELECT*s.)

Views: Put simply, views relate to an SQL query that is viewed as a distinct database object and makes possible a particular view of the database. MySQL has supported views since version 5.0.

Stored procedures: Here we are dealing with SQL code that is stored in the database system. Stored procedures (SPs for short) are generally used to simplify certain steps, such as inserting or deleting a data record. For client programmers this has the advantage that they do not have to process the tables directly, but can rely on SPs. Like views, SPs help in the administration of large database projects. SPs can also increase efficiency. MySQL has supported SPs since version 5.0.

Triggers: Triggers are SQL commands that are automatically executed by the server in certain database operations (*INSERT, UPDATE,* and *DELETE*). MySQL has supported triggers in a limited form from version 5.0, and additional functionality is promised for version 5.1.

Unicode: MySQL has supported all conceivable character sets since version 4.1, including Latin-1, Latin-2, and Unicode (either in the variant UTF8 or UCS2).

User interface: There are a number of convenient user interfaces for administering a MySQL server.

Full-text search: Full-text search simplifies and accelerates the search for words that are located within a text field. If you employ MySQL for storing text (such as in an Internet discussion group), you can use full-text search to implement simply an efficient search function.

Replication: Replication allows the contents of a database to be copied (replicated) onto a number of computers. In practice, this is done for two reasons: to increase protection against system failure (so that if one computer goes down, another can be put into service) and to improve the speed of database queries.

Transactions: In the context of a database system, a transaction means the execution of several database operations as a block. The database system ensures that either all of the operations are correctly executed or none of them. This holds even if in the middle of a transaction there is a power failure, the computer crashes, or some other disaster occurs. Thus, for example, it cannot occur that a sum of money is withdrawn from account A but fails to be deposited in account B due to some type of system error.

Transactions also give programmers the possibility of interrupting a series of already executed commands (a sort of revocation). In many situations this leads to a considerable simplification of the programming process.

In spite of popular opinion, MySQL has supported transactions for a long time. One should note here that MySQL can store tables in a variety of formats. The default table format is called MyISAM, and this format does not support transactions. But there are a number of additional formats that do support transactions. The most popular of these is InnoDB, which will be described extensively in this book.

Foreign key constraints: These are rules that ensure that there are no cross references in linked tables that lead to nowhere. MySQL supports foreign key constraints for InnoDB tables.

GIS functions: Since version 4.1, MySQL has supported the storing and processing of two-dimensional geographical data. Thus MySQL is well suited for GIS (geographic information systems) applications.

Programming languages: There are quite a number of APIs (application programming interfaces) and libraries for the development of MySQL applications. For client programming you can use, among others, the languages C, C++, Java, Perl, PHP, Python, and Tcl.

ODBC: MySQL supports the ODBC interface Connector/ODBC. This allows MySQL to be addressed by all the usual programming languages that run under Microsoft Windows (Delphi, Visual Basic, etc.). The ODBC interface can also be implemented under Unix, though that is seldom necessary.

Windows programmers who have migrated to Microsoft's new .NET platform can, if they wish, use the ODBC provider or the .NET interface Connector/NET.

Platform independence: It is not only client applications that run under a variety of operating systems; MySQL itself (that is, the server) can be executed under a number of operating systems. The most important are Apple Macintosh OS X, Linux, Microsoft Windows, and the countless Unix variants, such as AIX, BSDI, FreeBSD, HP-UX, OpenBSD, Net BSD, SGI Iris, and Sun Solaris.

Speed: MySQL is considered a very fast database program. This speed has been backed up by a large number of benchmark tests (though such tests—regardless of the source—should be considered with a good dose of skepticism).

Limitations of MySQL

Many of the shortcomings listed in this section can be found on the to-do list of the team of MySQL developers, or have already been implemented.

Tip The documentation for MySQL is not at all silent on the subject of shortcomings or missing features. There is a quite readable section in the MySQL documentation on the topic "How standards-compatible is MySQL?" There you will find extensive information on the points at which MySQL fails to comply with current standards. Often, a reason for the shortcoming is provided, and sometimes as well some pointers on how to get around the difficulty: http://www.mysql.com/doc/en/Compatibility.html.

- When MySQL is used with standard tables (table type MyISAM), then *locking*, that is, the temporary blocking of access to or alteration of database information, is in operation only for entire tables (*table locking*). You can circumvent the *table-locking* problem by implementing transaction-capable table formats, such as InnoDB, that support *row locking*.

- In using MyISAM tables, MySQL is not able to execute hot backups, which are backups during operation without blocking the tables with locks. Here again, the solution is InnoDB, though here the hot backup function is available only in the form of a commercial supplement.

- Many database systems offer the possibility of defining custom data types. MySQL does not support such functionality, nor is any currently planned.

- MySQL has up to now ignored the general XML trend. It is not clear when MySQL will support direct processing of XML data. Numerous commercial database systems offer considerably more functionality in this area, and even the SQL:2003 standard provides for a host of XML functions.

- MySQL is in fact a very fast database system, but it is very limited in its usability for real-time applications, and it offers no OLAP functions. OLAP stands for online analytical processing, and refers to special methods for the management and analysis of multidimensional data. OLAP-capable database systems are often called data warehouses.

- MySQL supports, since version 5.0, stored procedures and triggers, but these functions have not yet fully matured (this applies especially to triggers) and do not yet have the same stability and plenitude of functions offered by commercial database systems.

- Similar restrictions hold as well for the GIS functions introduced in version 4.1. Commercial database systems offer in some cases considerably greater functionality.

MySQL Version Numbers

Even for connoisseurs of MySQL it is a bit of a challenge to keep track of which version of MySQL is current and which functions are contained in which versions. This section provides some information on MySQL numbering.

As of January 2005 there are four main versions being worked on by the MySQL development team:

- **MySQL 3.23.*n*:** The first version of this series, 3.23.0, was published in August 1999. Since 3.23.32 (January 2001) MySQL 3.23.*n* has been considered stable. The current version is 3.23.58. Although MySQL 3.23 does not contain many of the innovations of recent years, it is the version most in use among Internet providers. There will be no further extensions to MySQL 3.23.*n*. New versions will only fix discovered errors or security holes.

- **MySQL 4.0.*n*:** The first version of this series, 4.0.0, was published in October 2001. Since March 2003 (4.0.12) MySQL 4.0.*n* has been considered stable and is now recommended for production use. The current version is 4.0.23. As with MySQL 3.23, new versions appear only to correct bugs.

- **MySQL 4.1.*n*:** The first version in this series (4.1.0) has been available for download since April 2003. Since October 2004 (version 4.1.7), MySQL 4.1.*n* has been considered stable and is recommended for production use.

- **MySQL 5.0.*n*:** The first version in this series (5.0.0) has been available since December 2003 for download. The current version is 5.0.2, which, however, has alpha status and is therefore not recommended for production use. It is expected that MySQL 5.0.*n* will be stable by the time this book is published.

Alpha, Beta, Gamma, Production (Generally Available)

MySQL versions are identified by the attributes *alpha*, *beta*, *gamma*, and *production*:

- **Alpha** means that the version is in the throes of the development process and that new functions and even incompatible changes are to be expected. Although an alpha version is not published until it contains no known errors, it is highly probable that many undiscovered errors still lurk within. Loss of data during testing of an alpha version is quite possible! Alpha versions are of interest only to developers who wish to try out the latest features of MySQL.

- **Beta** means that this version is largely complete, but it has not been thoroughly tested. Major changes are not expected.

- **Gamma** means that the beta versions have become more or less stable. The goal now is to discover errors and resolve them.

- **Production or Generally Available (GA)** means that MySQL developers have the impression that the version is mature and stable enough that it can be used for mission-critical purposes. According to the MySQL documentation, in production versions, only corrections, and no new functionality, are to be expected. However, this has not always held true in the past, and even with stable versions substantial changes have been made. Of particular note is the case of MySQL 3.23.*n*. After the version had been declared stable (3.23.32), there came general support for InnoDB and BDB tables (3.23.34), and later, integrity rules for InnoDB tables (3.23.44). Furthermore, many minor extensions were introduced. As a rule, MySQL developers are pleased with such extensions, but at the same time, compatibility problems among different production versions can arise.

In practice, this means that a new MySQL version (that is, *n.n.*0) always has the status *alpha*. With higher version numbers, the status rises to *beta*, *gamma*, and finally, *production*.

Normal MySQL users should use exclusively MySQL versions that have the status *production*. If you are developing web applications, you should find out which version your Internet service provider is using. (Since Internet service providers are concerned with maintenance and stability, they are not generally keen on using the latest version, preferring earlier versions, which may not contain many of the functions of the newer versions.)

Tip If you want to experiment with a development version that is not yet available in compiled format (and thus has not even reached alpha status), instructions on downloading and compiling the source code can be obtained at `http://dev.mysql.com/doc/mysql/en/installing-source.html`.

MySQL Functions Ordered by Version Number

It is not always the easiest thing in the world to determine which particular database version can be used with which version of MySQL. Of course, the version number often reveals when a function first became officially available, but it often happens that thereafter, significant changes to the function are made or bugs fixed, so that a stable implementation occurs only several versions later. Note as well that certain functions are available only for particular table formats.

Table 1-1 ventures a glance into the future. The entries are based on information contained in the MySQL documentation as of spring 2005.

The projections into the future come, naturally, without warranty of any kind. In the past, it frequently occurred that particular functions became available earlier or later than originally projected.

Table 1-1. *MySQL Functions Past and Future*

Function	Version
Replication	3.23
Full-text search in MyISAM tables	3.23
Transactions with BDB tables	3.23.34
Transactions with InnoDB tables	3.23.34
Referential integrity for InnoDB tables	3.23.34
DELETE and *DELETE* across several tables	4.0
UPDATE across several tables	4.0
UNION (unite several *SELECT* results)	4.0
Query cache (speeds up repeated SQL commands)	4.0
Embedded MySQL library	4.0
Encrypted connections (Secure Socket Layer, SSL)	4.0
Hot backup for InnoDB (commercial add-on product)	4.0
GPL for client libraries (previously LGPL)	4.0
Sub*SELECT*s	4.1
Unicode support (UTF8 and UCS2 = UTF16)	4.1
GIS support (*GEOMETRY* data type, R-tree index)	4.1
Prepared Statements (SQL commands with parameters)	4.1
ROLLUP extension for *GROUP BY*	4.1
Better password encryption in the mysql.user table	4.1
Individual InnoDB tablespace files for each table	4.1
VARCHAR columns with more than 255 characters	5.0
Genuine *BIT* data type	5.0
Stored procedures (SPs)	probably 5.0
Triggers (automatic execution of SQL code)	5.0/5.1
Views	5.0
Space-saving InnoDB tablespace format	5.0/5.1
New schema management (data dictionary, *INFORMATION_SCHEMA* database)	5.0
FULL OUTER JOIN	probably 5.1
Referential integrity for MyISAM tables	probably 5.1
Fail-safe replication	probably 5.1
Hot backup for MyISAM tables	probably 5.1
Column-level constraints	probably 5.1
Views	probably 5.1
XML support	planned, but no date given
User-defined data type	not currently planned

The information for the table was drawn from the following pages of the MySQL documentation:

```
http://dev.mysql.com/doc/mysql/en/roadmap.html
http://dev.mysql.com/doc/mysql/en/todo.html
http://dev.mysql.com/doc/mysql/en/news.html
```

MySQL Licensing

One of the most interesting features of MySQL is the license. MySQL is an open source project. That is, the complete source code of MySQL is freely available. Since June 2000 (that is, since version 3.23.19) the *GNU Public License* (GPL) has been valid for MySQL. It is thus ensured that MySQL will continue to be freely available in the sense of the open source idea. (For commercial applications of MySQL there is a second, commercial license available in addition to GPL. More on this later.)

Rights and Duties with Respect to the GPL

Open source is often incorrectly interpreted to mean "without cost." It is indeed true that GPL software can be used without payment of fees, provided that one adheres to certain conditions. However, the open source idea goes much further:

- Since the source code is freely available, when there are problems, you are not at the mercy of a software vendor.

- When problems arise, you can perhaps attempt to repair the problem yourself or to implement features that are lacking. Furthermore, you can appeal to the developers' group for help.

- You can be certain that the program code has been read by many developers and does not contain any unsavory surprises (such as so-called back doors such as the database system Interbase had for many years, whereby access to every Interbase database was possible via a hard-coded password).

- You are permitted to alter GPL products, and indeed sell the resulting new programs.

At the end of this list of GPL merits there are a few demerits (for commercial applications). If you wish to use a GPL program as the basis for a commercial product, you must again make your own source code freely available, in the sense of GPL, with the changes made. This is seldom something that developers of commercial products wish to do.

In general, then, every program that is derived from GPL software exists under the terms of GPL. (GPL is, so to speak, transmitted.)

Tip Further information on the open source idea, the full text of GPL, and explanations can be found at the following addresses:

```
http://www.gnu.org/copyleft/gpl.html
http://www.opensource.org/osd.html
```

Use of MySQL with an Open Source License

The following list collects the different situations in which one may freely use MySQL in the sense of GPL:

- MySQL can be used without cost if an application is locally developed and not used commercially. It is only when the resulting solution is to be sold to customers that the question of licensing comes into play. This rule is expressed on the MySQL home page as follows: *Free use for those who never copy, modify, or distribute.*

- MySQL can be used freely within a web site. If you also develop a PHP application and install it with your Internet service provider, you do not have to make your PHP code freely available in the sense of GPL.

- Likewise, an Internet service provider may make MySQL available to its customers without having to pay MySQL license fees. (Since MySQL is running exclusively on the ISP computer, this application is considered internal.)

- Finally, MySQL can be used free of charge for all projects that themselves run under the GPL or comparable free license. (If you have developed a new free e-mail client for Linux, say, and wish to store e-mails in a MySQL database, you may do so without further ado.)

Use of MySQL with a Commercial License

In the sense of GPL the following uses are prohibited:

- You may not change or extend MySQL (that is, the database server) or sell the new version or product thus created without simultaneously making the source code of your changes freely available. You are thus prohibited from developing a new database system based on MySQL if you are not prepared to make your extensions freely available to the MySQL community in the sense of GPL.

- It is forbidden to develop a commercial product, such as a bookkeeping program, that is geared toward MySQL as the database without making the code available in the open source sense.

If the limitations of the GPL are not acceptable to you as a commercial developer, then you may sell your product (program) together with a commercial MySQL license. This can prove worthwhile because MySQL remains available to you even if you are unable or unwilling to make your code available in the sense of GPL.

The firm MySQL offers commercial licenses for consumers (that is, purchasers of their database applications) in two formats:

MySQL Network: Here the buyer obtains the right to run one *MySQL Pro Certified Server* with InnoDB support for one year. (A server is considered to be one computer, regardless of the number of CPUs.) There is no limitation on the number of clients that can access the server. The program *MySQL Network* also contains access to special compiled server versions that are said to be particularly stable, e-mail and telephone support, as well as various other services. Updates to the MySQL server (even for versions 4.0 and 5.0, etc.) are free during the period of the program.

Classic Commercial License: Since the introduction of the program *MySQL Network* the once common normal licenses have become hard to find. (Use the last link of the following list.) Classic MySQL licenses have no time limit, but are restricted to a particular principal server version. (If you have a license for version 4.0, you must apply for a new license for version 5.0.) The cost is quite reasonable in comparison to commercial database systems (currently $295 for a license without InnoDB support and $595 for a license with InnoDB support, with a significant reduction starting at ten licenses).

The advantage of the program *MySQL Network* is in the additional services and the free update option. Classic licenses are cheaper, on the other hand, once the MySQL server has been installed and should just run.

Tip Further information on licensing MySQL can be found at the following web sites:

```
http://www.mysql.com/company/legal/licensing/
http://www.mysql.com/network/
https://order.mysql.com/
https://shop.mysql.com/?sub=vt&id=software
```

Commercial Licenses for Client Libraries (Connector/ODBC, Connector/J, etc.)

In addition to the actual MySQL server, the MySQL company offers client libraries that are necessary for the development of application programs (there are additional drivers that have been developed outside of the firm MySQL, such as the PHP driver):

C-API: Application interface for C programming

Connector/C++: Library for C++ programming

Connector/J: JDBC driver for Java programming

Connector/MXJ: J2EE MBean driver for Java programming

Connector/NET: .NET driver primarily for programming under Windows

Connector/ODB: ODBC driver for all programming under Windows

Like MySQL, these drivers are available under GPL. Many MySQL client libraries, such as the JDBC driver Connector/J, used to be available in earlier versions under LGPL (lesser Gnu public license), which implies fewer restrictions for commercial applications. The situation changed, however, with version 4.0.

If you wish to use these drivers in commercial applications, the following rule is in force: If MySQL client programs access a MySQL-licensed server, then this server license is valid for the client libraries. It is thus usually unnecessary to obtain licenses for the use of client libraries, because the client libraries are automatically included with the server license.

However, if you develop and sell a commercial program but do not deliver it together with MySQL and leave the installation of the MySQL server and its licensing to the customer, then you must obtain licenses for the client libraries used in your program.

Explicit licensing of the client library is seen by the MySQL company as an exception, since as a rule, the server is licensed. Commercial licensing of the client library actually represents nothing other than a protection of the MySQL company's commercial interests. They want to avoid the situation in which commercial developers get around having to obtain a commercial license simply by not providing the MySQL server. The customer then loads the GPL version of the MySQL server from the Internet and believes that all is right with the world. In such a case the MySQL company would receive nothing for the development of a commercial MySQL product.

Client Licenses for the PHP Project, F(L)OSS Exception

Since MySQL 4.0, the GPL license for client libraries has led to problems with some other open source projects. For example, the PHP project is not subordinate to GPL, but to another open source license that is considerably more liberal and contains fewer restrictions for commercial applications. If PHP were to provide the MySQL client library under GPL, the GPL would have to hold for the entire PHP project. PHP developers were not agreeable to this. MySQL therefore defined an exception that permitted the PHP project to make the MySQL client library part of PHP.

For other open source projects that do not use the GPL license, MySQL has defined the FLOSS or FOSS license exception. FLOSS stands for *Free/Libre and Open Source Software*. (On the MySQL website the exception is often abbreviated FOSS.) Open source projects that exist under a license that is part of the FOSS exception are permitted to integrate the MySQL client library into their code without the GPL restrictions coming into play. Further details on these license exceptions can be found here:

```
http://www.mysql.com/company/legal/licensing/faq.html
http://www.mysql.com/company/legal/licensing/foss-exception.html
```

Red Hat has long considered these license exceptions as not extensive enough. Therefore, the Linux distribution Red Hat Enterprise (RHEL) and Fedora Core for years contained the obsolete MySQL 3.23.*n* package. That has changed with Red Hat Enterprise 4 (February 2005) and Fedora Core 4 (April 2005). Both distributions contain MySQL 4.1, which at this time is the most stable version of MySQL.

MySQL Version Names

Since MySQL 4.0, the free (in the sense of GPL) and commercial versions have different names. Here they are:

Name	License	Functionality
MySQL Standard Community Edition	GPL	All default functions that can be considered stable (including InnoDB)
MySQL Max Community Edition	GPL	Same as MySQL Standard, but with additional functions and table drivers that have not reached full maturity
MySQL Classic	commercial	Like MySQL Standard, but without InnoDB
MySQL Pro	commercial	Like MySQL Standard, but with InnoDB (thus with transactions)
MySQL Pro Certified Server	commercial	Like MySQL Pro, but usable only in the context of the program MySQL Network and optimized for maximum stability and security

For ordinary GPL applications, the use of the Standard version is recommended. The additional functions in the Max version are for use only in special applications. Currently (version 5.0), the Standard and Max versions differ in the support of BDB tables and the SSL encryption of client/server connections. These functions will be incorporated into the Standard and commercial versions only when they are considered sufficiently stable. You can determine which functions the running version of MySQL supports with the SQL command *SHOW VARIABLES*. In the following code you can see the results of MySQL Standard 5.0.2.

```
mysql> SHOW VARIABLES LIKE 'have%';
```

Variable_name	Value
have_archive	NO
have_bdb	NO
have_compress	YES
have_crypt	YES
have_csv	NO
have_example_engine	NO
have_geometry	YES
have_innodb	YES
have_isam	NO
have_ndbcluster	NO
have_openssl	NO
have_query_cache	YES
have_raid	NO
have_rtree_keys	YES
have_symlink	YES

In the case of commercial applications, the decision between Classic and Pro depends simply on whether InnoDB is needed. (The license for the Pro version is more expensive.) The Classic and Pro versions cannot be simply downloaded at www.mysql.com, but are provided only after a license has been issued.

MySQL Pro Certified Server has been available only since the beginning of 2005, as part of the program MySQL Network. MySQL promises users of this program particularly stable and secure versions.

If you wish to know which server version is being run, then execute the following SQL command:

```
mysql> SHOW VARIABLES LIKE 'version';
```

Variable_name	Value
version	5.0.2-alpha-standard

This output shows that the Standard version 5.0.2 is running. There is no additional Max functionality and no license for commercial use.

■**Note** Do not confuse MySQL Max with MaxDB. The latter is the former SAP-DB database system that since 2004 has been maintained and sold by the MySQL firm. There are indeed similarities between the database systems MySQL and MaxDB, but there are considerable differences. This book is strictly about MySQL, not MaxDB.

Support Contracts

Regardless of whether you are using a commercial or GPL version of MySQL, you may take out a support contract with MySQL. You thereby simultaneously support the further development of MySQL.

■**Tip** Details on commercial MySQL licenses and paid support can be found at http://www.mysql.com/support/. Links to various companies that offer commercial MySQL support can be found at http://solutions.mysql.com.

Alternatives to MySQL

Of course, there are many alternatives to MySQL, particularly if you are prepared to pay (lots of) money for licenses and perhaps also for the requisite hardware. Among these are IBM DB2, Informix, Microsoft SQL Server, and Oracle.

If you are looking for a database in the open source realm, then PostgreSQL is currently perhaps the most interesting alternative. However, be warned: The discussion between advocates of MySQL and those of PostgreSQL usually resembles more a war of religions than what might be termed measured intellectual discourse. In any case, PostgreSQL (http://www.postgresql.org/) offers more functions than MySQL (even if MySQL is slowly catching up). At the same time, PostgreSQL is considered slower and less stable (even if in this regard the reputation of PostgreSQL has greatly improved).

For small database solutions (also in the sense of saving memory) you might consider SQLite (http://www.sqlite.org/). This is a tiny library (about 250 KB binary code) that is available for elementary database functions. SQLite is available free of charge even for commercial applications and is especially suited for stand-alone solutions (less for network applications). SQLite is moreover integrated into the current versions of PHP.

There are also several formerly commercial database systems that have been converted to open source. The best known of these is Firebird, formerly Interbase from Inprise/Borland (http://firebird.sourceforge.net/).

Finally, I refer you to the already mentioned database MaxDB, formerly SAP-DB (http://www.mysql.com/products/maxdb/). It is maintained and marketed by the firm MySQL but otherwise has little to do with the MySQL database system. MaxDB is a professional and comprehensive –database system that shares the drawbacks of large (commercial) database systems: complex installation, administration, and maintenance, and comparatively small user base and correspondingly small amount of documentation and help in the Internet.

Summary

MySQL is a very capable relational client/server database system. It is sufficiently secure and stable for many applications, and it offers an excellent cost/benefit ratio (not only because MySQL is free itself, but also because it makes comparatively modest demands on hardware). MySQL has thus developed into a quasi standard in the realm of Internet databases.

Above all, in the Linux world, MySQL is used increasingly by applications as the background database engine, whether it be managing logging data more efficiently than previously or managing e-mail, MP3 files, addresses, or comparable data. MySQL is poised to play a similar role to that of the Jet Engine in the Microsoft operating system (where in many respects, MySQL offers a meaningfully better technical basis). Thanks to the ODBC interface, MySQL is now being used in the Windows world for such tasks.

Apart from technical data, MySQL has the advantage over other open source database systems in that it is by far the most widely used such system. It follows that MySQL has been more thoroughly tested and documented than other database systems and that it is relatively easy to find developers with MySQL experience.

However, MySQL cannot (yet) compete in every respect with the big boys of the commercial database system world. You are not likely to choose MySQL if you require functions that MySQL does not yet support.

The decisive question is, then, Is MySQL good enough for my application? Not only millions of website developers, but also firms and organizations such as Associated Press, Citysearch, Cox Communications, Los Alamos National Labs (7 terabytes of data), Lycos, NASA, Sony, Suzuki, Wikipedia, and Yahoo! have answered this question in the affirmative. If you choose MySQL, you will be in good company.

CHAPTER 2

■ ■ ■

The Test Environment

In this chapter we discuss how to set up the test environment for MySQL on a local computer. Since MySQL usually doesn't run all by itself, but in combination with other programs, this chapter also discusses Apache, PHP, and Perl, as well as the configuration of these programs.

We consider installation under Windows and under Linux. The chapter includes some advanced topics, such as administration of the MySQL service under Windows and the compilation of a MySQL developer version under Linux.

Windows or Unix/Linux?

The question of under which operating system to run MySQL can easily lead to fisticuffs, so strongly are opinions held. But we shall remain civil in this section, and perhaps for the entire book. The fact is that MySQL, as well as Apache, PHP, Perl, and most of the other programs that are usually run in conjunction with MySQL, were developed originally under Unix/Linux and only later ported to Windows.

MySQL in Practice (Public Internet Server)

In practice, that is, on a publicly available server on the Internet, the above-mentioned programs are run predominately under Unix/Linux. For this reason alone—the greater deployment in the world at large—the programs running under Unix/Linux have been better and more extensively tested. Possible errors or security holes in the Unix/Linux version of MySQL are thus more likely to be discovered and repaired quickly.

A further argument for deployment under Unix/Linux is that the programs function more efficiently as a rule. This has less to do with the view that Windows is generally slower than Unix/Linux (I have no desire to discuss that issue here), but with the fact that the process and thread models of these operating systems are quite different from each other. Programs such as Apache and MySQL are first and foremost optimized for the programming model of Unix/Linux, not for that of Windows, and this by itself often gives a significant speed advantage to Unix/Linux.

Therefore, the development communities of the programs mentioned above are unanimously in favor of having their programs run under Unix/Linux, and not under Windows. You would do well to take this opinion to heart.

■**Note** When speaking of Windows, we generally mean Windows 2000/XP/2003. In principle, MySQL runs under Windows 9x/ME, but there it is impossible to provide reasonable security of the system against unauthorized access. In general, the tests in this book were carried out under Windows XP.

17

Development Environment

Things look somewhat different if you are currently only developing a database application. During the development you will use a test environment that is usually accessible only to you or your team. Thus you have no reason to expect problems in security or in efficiency due to large numbers of accesses to the system. Since there is good compatibility between the Windows and Unix/Linux versions, there is little to be said against, for example, developing a discussion group first under Windows and then porting the completed solution to the Linux server of your ISP.

If you have at least two computers in your test environment, you can, of course, install MySQL, Apache, etc., on one computer under Linux, and carry out the actual development work (database design, creation of script files, etc.), on the second computer under Windows (say, because your favorite editor runs under Windows).

To this extent, the entire discussion of Windows versus Unix/Linux doesn't amount to much, and for development you should use the operating system that you find more to your liking.

Nevertheless, there are also arguments against Windows for the development phase. One is that by developing the entire project under Unix/Linux you gain considerable experience that will be valuable later during the process of bringing the project on line on a Unix/Linux server (specifically in reference to issues of access rights and security).

Another argument deals with the deployment of system functions that under Unix/Linux usually are available in a form different from that offered under Windows. For example, under Unix/Linux one can simply send an e-mail by program code (such as in a PHP or Perl script). Under Windows there are no standard interfaces for such tasks.

Installation Under Windows

The following sections describe the separate installation of Apache 2, PHP 5, Perl 5.8, and MySQL 5.0. Separate installation has the advantage that you can choose the version for each component and have a better understanding of which programs are installed on your computer and how they are configured. This also simplifies management later and updating specific components.

■**Note** The installation is easier if you use a complete package that contains all the components. The best-known such packages are *The Saint WAMP* (TSW) and *XAMPP for Windows*:

```
http://sourceforge.net/projects/yawamp/
http://www.apachefriends.org/de/xampp-windows.html
```

The packages have two disadvantages: First, in addition to Apache, PHP, Perl, and MySQL, they contain countless additional components that you probably don't need. Second, as this book went to press there was no complete package with MySQL 5.0. Instead, you get the older, but more stable, versions MySQL 4.1 or 4.0.

Installing Apache 2.0

Deactivate IIS

If you are working on a Windows server version, you should first ensure that the Microsoft Internet Information Server (IIS for short) is not running. Installation of Apache in the standard setting (port 80) fails if IIS is running in parallel (for which there is seldom any reason).

To check on or deinstall IIS, execute SETTINGS | CONTROL PANEL | ADD OR REMOVE PROGRAMS | ADD/ REMOVE WINDOWS COMPONENTS. If necessary, deactivate the option IIS in WINDOWS COMPONENTS WIZARD, which will stop and deinstall the program.

Install Apache

Apache is available for Windows at `www.apache.org` (and various mirror sites). Download the `apache_2.n_xxx.msi` file onto your computer and launch the installation program in Windows Explorer with a double click. A dialog box appears for the basic configuration (see Figure 2-1). There you must enter the domain name (e.g., *sol*) and the server name (e.g., *uranus.sol*). This information will be needed if your computer runs as a single test computer. As a rule, the proper values are automatically entered in the dialog fields. If you are unsure what these names are on your computer, you can look at the dialog SETTINGS | CONTROL PANEL | SYSTEM | COMPUTER NAME. You must also specify the e-mail address of the web server administrator (you, that is) and whether the web server should use port 80.

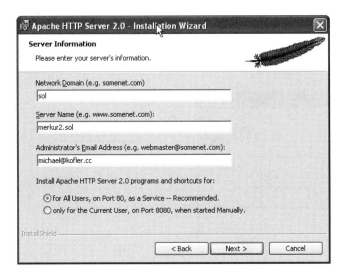

Figure 2-1. *Apache installation*

After installation, Apache will be automatically configured as a service under Windows NT/2000/XP and immediately launched. On the right side of the task bar there appears a small icon that shows the state of Apache (a green arrow when the program is running). You can use this icon to start and stop Apache.

Starting and Stopping Apache

You can start and stop Apache with the menu commands PROGRAMS | APACHE HTTP SERVER | CONTROL APACHE SERVER | START and | STOP. The command PROGRAMS | APACHE HTTP SERVER | CONFIGURE APACHE SERVER | EDIT HTTPD.CONF starts the editor notepad and shows there the Apache configuration.

As a first test to determine whether Apache is actually running, open in your web browser the page `http://localhost`. You should be able to see the default start page of the web browser. Then there should be two directory entries that are valid for a default installation: for the configuration file, `C:\Programs\Apache Group\Apache2\conf\httpd.conf`; for the web files, `C:\Programs\Apache Group\Apache2\htdocs`.

Installing MySQL 5.0

The MySQL installation file for MySQL 5.0 can be found as a ZIP archive at `http://dev.mysql.com/downloads/mysql/5.0.html`. The archive contains `setup.exe` as a single file. After it is launched, an installation assistant appears in which generally you can set only the installation type (SETUP TYPE) to TYPICAL.

After installation of the server in the directory `C:\Programs\MySQL\MySQL Server 5.0`, the installation program asks whether you wish to set up an account at `mysql.com`. You will generally skip this optional step with SKIP SIGN-UP.

The MySQL Configuration Assistant

Much more useful is the configuration assistant, which is automatically executed after installation (see Figure 2-2). If needed, you can later start this assistant anew with PROGRAMS | MYSQL | MYSQL SERVER 5.0 | MYSQL SERVER INSTANCE CONFIG WIZARD. The assistant fulfills two functions: it sets up the MySQL configuration file and secures the MySQL server with a password.

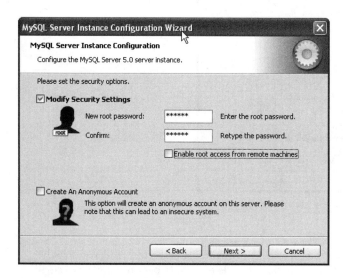

Figure 2-2. *The MySQL configuration assistant*

The following list describes the most important steps the assistant takes when you choose DETAILED CONFIGURATION. (You will never go wrong by selecting, in case of doubt, the default suggestions of the assistant.)

Server Type: Here you can choose among DEVELOPER, SERVER, and DEDICATED SERVER. The options influence how much of main memory the MySQL server attempts to reserve. The greater the portion, the faster the server will run, but the more strongly other programs will be affected. For web developers, DEVELOPER is the optimal setting. (If you carry out benchmark tests, you will get better results with large databases using SERVER or DEDICATED SERVER.)

Database Usage: The options MULTIFUNCTIONAL, TRANSACTIONAL, ONLY, and NON-TRANSACTIONAL ONLY determine for which table types the MySQL server will be configured (for experts: MyISAM, InnoDB, or both). The default setting is MULTIFUNCTIONAL, and you should choose that.

InnoDB Tablespace Setting: At this point you should specify where InnoDB database files should be stored (by default in the installation directory).

Concurrent Connections: This determines the number of database connections that generally can be open simultaneously. As long as MySQL is running on a development computer, the number will be somewhat small. Therefore, choose the option DECISION SUPPORT (20 connections). On the other hand, if the MySQL server is in full operation with a well-frequented website, the number of connections will be significantly higher (option ONLINE TRANSACTION PROCESSING).

Enable TCP/IP Networking: There are two possibilities under Windows for how the MySQL server communicates with applications: via *named pipes* or via the network protocol TCP/IP. The assistant recommends activating TCP/IP and to using port 3306. Here, too, you should follow the assistant's suggestion if there is no compelling reason to do otherwise.

Default Character Set: MySQL supports all possible character sets for storing text in a database. Here you set the default character set. It holds whenever you do not explicitly choose a different set for the database design (that is, this setting in no way restricts what you can do in the future). Since all examples in this book use the *latin1* character set, it is a good idea to choose this as the default.

Install as Windows Service: The MySQL server can be launched as a *.exe file or a Windows service. The second variant is more convenient and secure. Accept the default setting.

Security Options: At this, perhaps most important, point in the setup assistant you determine who will be allowed to make a connection to the MySQL server and whether a password will be required. The most secure setting, and the one that I recommend, is shown in Figure 2-2: the only user is *root*, which is protected by a password. The user *root* will be the database administrator and will be allowed to register only from the local computer (not from another computer in the network). Moreover, there are no anonymous accounts (connection allowed without a password).

Of course, you can set up other users later who can access MySQL or particular MySQL databases (more on this in Chapter 11).

To test whether your MySQL installation was successful, launch the MySQL command line interpreter mysql.exe using PROGRAMS | MYSQL | MYSQL SERVER 5.0 | MYSQL COMMAND LINE CLIENT. Then give the password that you used for the MySQL configuration. If all goes as it should, the MySQL input request appears in the input window. There you execute the command status. The result should look like that in Figure 2-3.

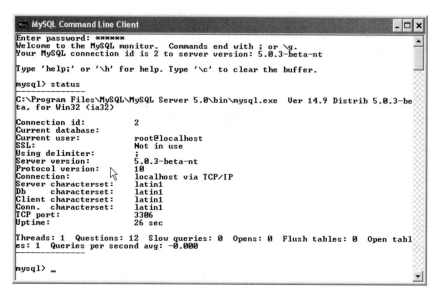

Figure 2-3. *Testing MySQL*

MySQL Service: Manual Setup, Removal, Starting, and Stopping

During installation, MySQL is set up as a Windows service, which is launched automatically when the computer is started. Normally, there is no reason to change this configuration. Should it be necessary, however, to do so, the following suggestions should be of help:

MySQL System Tray Monitor: Using START | PROGRAMS | MYSQL SYSTEM TRAY MONITOR, you launch a small program that appears as an icon in the right side of the Windows task bar (where the time is displayed). With the right mouse button you can start and stop the MySQL service.

MySQL Administrator: In the module Service Control of the MySQL administrator described in Chapter 5 you can set up, delete, start, and stop a service.

Windows System Control: With SETTINGS | CONTROL PANEL ADMINISTRATIVE TOOLS | SERVICES you find yourself in a dialog for managing all services running under Windows. There you can also start and stop services and perform numerous other functions (see Figure 2-4).

Commands: Finally, you can carry out these administrative tasks in an input request window. For installation, execute the following two commands. The `mysqld` command installs the service under the name *MySQL* and must be written all on one line:

```
> cd C:\Programs\MySQL\MySQL Server 5.0\bin
> mysqld –install MySQL
         –defaults-file="C:\Programs\MySQL\MySQL Server 5.0\my.ini"
```

The program is thereby installed as a Windows service, but not launched. In the future, the service will be automatically started when the computer is started and terminated when the computer is shut down. To start or stop the service manually, execute the following two commands:

```
> net start MySQL
> net stop MySQL
```

To deinstall the service, use the option –remove:

```
> mysqld –remove MySQL
```

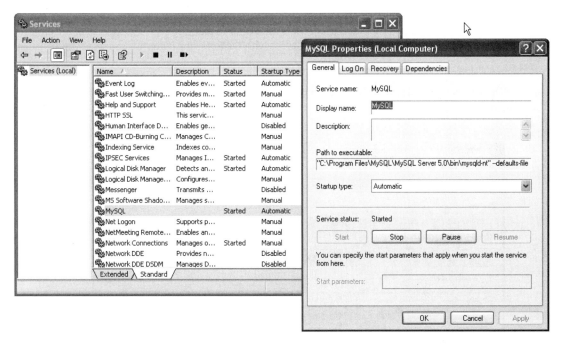

Figure 2-4. *Managing Windows services*

Installing PHP 5.0

On the website `http://www.php.net/downloads.php` you can find the latest version of PHP in two variants: as a ZIP archive and as an installation program. Since the installation program is geared toward the Internet Information Server, but in this book Apache is used as a web server, you should opt for the ZIP variant.

Installation comprises the following steps:

- Extract the contents of the archive into the directory of your choice. (For the following examples we assume that the installation directory is `C:\php5`).

- Insert the lines below given in boldface into the Apache configuration file `httpd.conf`. The best location within that file is in the other *LoadModule* instructions, of which there are generally quite a few:

  ```
  # Changes in C:\Programs\Apache Group\Apache2\conf\httpd.conf
  ...
  LoadModule php5_module "c:/php5/php5apache2.dll"
  AddType application/x-httpd-php .php
  PHPIniDir "C:/php5"
  ...
  ```

- Create a copy of `C:\php5\php.ini-recommended` with the new name `C:\php5\php.ini`.

- Restart Apache (command Programs | Apache HTTP Server | Control Apache Server | Restart). Restarting Apache is required whenever there is a change in `php.ini` or `httpd.conf`.

PHP is now installed as an extension of Apache and will be launched along with Apache. To test whether the installation was successful, use a text editor to place the file `phptest.php` in the directory `C:\Programs\Apache Group\Apache2\htdocs` with the following content:

```
<?php phpinfo(); ?>
```

Then open `http://localhost/phptest.php` with a web browser. You should see the status of PHP, as shown in Figure 2-5.

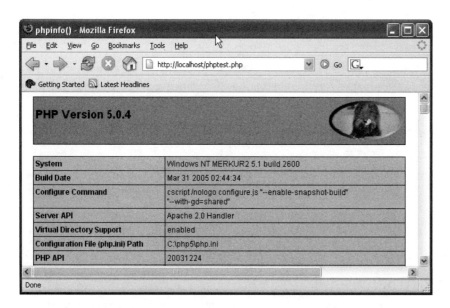

Figure 2-5. *The PHP test page*

MySQL Extensions for Configuring PHP

As a final step, PHP must be so configured that it can access the MySQL server. It is necessary that PHP be able to find two DLL files that are included with PHP. You must carry out the following steps:

- Copy the file `C:\php5\libmysql.dll` into the Windows directory, generally `C:\Windows` or `C:\Winnt`.

- Open the file with a text editor (e.g., Notepad) and change the following lines shown in boldface or insert them:

  ```
  ; changes in c:\php5\php.ini
  ...
  extension_dir = "c:/php5/ext"
  extension = php_mysql.dll
  extension = php_mysqli.dll
  ```

  To find the right lines, your best bet is to use EDIT|FIND. Note that the forward slash, not the usual backslash, is used as a separator. Before the lines `extension=...` there should be no semicolon; otherwise, the line will be considered a comment and ignored.

- For the changes to take effect, Apache must be restarted (command PROGRAMS | APACHE HTTP SERVER | CONTROL APACHE SERVER | RESTART).

Should problems arise, load the PHP test page (see Figure 2-5) once more. Check whether the file name in the line *Configuration Path (php.ini) File* (fifth line) is indeed `C:\php5\php.ini`. If that is not the case, copy your `php.ini` file to the location that specifies the test page. (The likely configuration error, from experience, is that PHP expects the configuration file to be in a different place. That is why your changes in `php.ini` were ignored.)

You can again check whether all is ok in the PHP test page. It now contains a description of the parameters of the interfaces *mysql* and *mysqli* (see Figure 2-6).

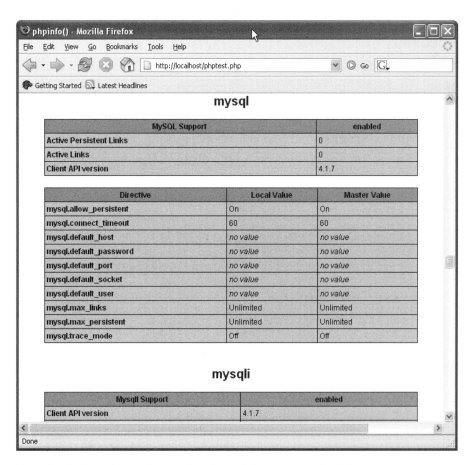

Figure 2-6. *Information on the mysql and mysqli interfaces on the PHP test page*

Installing Perl

The firm ActiveState offers the current version of Perl for Windows with the package ActivePerl. ActivePerl can be downloaded without cost as an MSI file from `www.activestate.com`. (You will also find on this website a host of commercial products related to Perl.) In Windows ME and Windows 2000 you begin the installation with a double click on the MSI file. In older versions of Windows you must first install the Windows installer. (A download link can be found at `www.activestate.com`, keyword *System Requirements*.)

Testing the Perl Installation

To test the Perl installation, create a test file with the name `test.pl` and the following content:

```
#!/usr/bin/perl -w
print "Hello world!\n";
print
Please hit Return to end the program!";
$wait_for_return = <STDIN>;
```

It should now be possible to start with a double click on the file. The program shows the text "Hello world!" in a command window, waits for a Return, and then ends. If a double click fails, open the input request window and try the following command:

```
C:\> perl C:\directory_with_my_perl_files\test.pl
```

MySQL Support for Perl Installation

Having installed Perl does not mean that you are done. Perl is not yet capable of communicating with MySQL. Perl must be extended through two supplementary modules:

DBI: *DBI* stands for *database interface*. The DBI module is a general interface for database programming.

DBD-MySQL: *DBD* stands for *database driver*. This module contains the MySQL-specific extensions of DBI.

The installation of both packages is done with the program `ppm` (Perl package manager), which is included with ActivePerl. The program can be launched in an input request window. It assumes a running Internet connection. The use of `ppm` is via the following lines (for ActivePerl 5.8.6):

```
C:> ppm
PPM - Programmer's Package Manager version 3.1.
Type 'help' to get started.
PPM> install dbi
Install 'dbi' version 1.46 in ActivePerl 5.8.6.811.
Downloaded 540637 bytes.
Extracting 73/73: blib/arch/auto/DBI/Driver_xst.h
Installing C:\Programs\Perl\site\lib\auto\DBI\dbd_xsh.h
Installing C:\Programs\Perl\site\lib\auto\DBI\DBI.bs
...
Successfully installed dbi version 1.46 in ActivePerl 5.8.6.811.
PPM> install DBD-Mysql
Install 'DBD-Mysql' version 2.9003 in ActivePerl 5.8.6.811.
Downloaded 178968 bytes.
Extracting 17/17: blib/arch/auto/DBD/mysql/mysql.lib
Installing C:\Programs\Perl\site\lib\auto\DBD\mysql\mysql.bs
Installing C:\Programs\Perl\site\lib\auto\DBD\mysql\mysql.dll
...
```

Unfortunately, DBD MySQL version 2.9003 is incompatible with the current version of MySQL. The version is based on an old version of the MySQL client library and can create a connection with MySQL version 4.1 or 5.0 only if the MySQL server is so configured that it uses the old and insecure authentication procedure (MySQL option `old-passwords`; see Chapter 11).

Fortunately, there is already a new version of the DBD MySQL module on the Internet. The following commands show how to install it:

```
ppm> remove DBD-Mysql
Remove 'DBD-Mysql' version 2.9003 from ActivePerl 5.8.6.811.
...
ppm> install http://theoryx5.uwinnipeg.ca/ppms/DBD-mysql.ppd
Install 'DBD-mysql' version 2.9005_3 in ActivePerl 5.8.6.811.
=====================
Downloaded 625824 bytes.
Extracting 37/37: blib
Installing C:\Programs\Perl\site\lib\auto\DBD\mysql\mysql.bs
Installing C:\Programs\Perl\site\lib\auto\DBD\mysql\mysql.dll
...
Successfully installed DBD-mysql version 2.9005_3 in ActivePerl 5.8.6.811.
```

■**Tips** If your Internet connection runs over an HTTP proxy, you must execute the following command before the install command. Of course, *myproxy.com:8080* must be replaced by the actual proxy address: `set http_proxy=http://myproxy.com:8080/`. If a firewall is installed on your computer, the program `perl.exe` must have the right to access the Internet. Make a corresponding rule as necessary.

You can determine the available packages with `search pattern`. Furthermore, `search mysql` finds, for example, all additional Perl packages whose names contain *mysql* (regardless of whether in the middle, beginning, or end).

DBD-MySQL assumes that the MySQL client library is installed on the computer. This library is located in the file `C:\Programs\MySQL\MySQL Server 5.0\bin\libmysql.dll` and is part of the MySQL installation. For Perl to be able to find the file, it must be copied into the Windows directory, or else the *PATH* environment variable must be extended to include the directory `C:\Programs\MySQL\MySQL Server 5.0\bin\` (see Chapter 4).

Precise instructions for testing the Perl environment and programming MySQL applications with Perl are given in Chapter 16.

Installation Under SUSE Linux 9.3

SUSE Linux 9.3 contains Apache 2, PHP 4.3 and PHP 5, Perl 5.8, and MySQL 4.1. In order to follow the examples of this book, you need PHP 5 and MySQL 5. The following two sections show how to install the packages Apache 2, PHP 5, and Perl 5.8, and then the current MySQL package, available from `dev.mysql.com`.

Installing Apache 2, PHP 5, and Perl

During installation, you must pay attention a bit, because SUSE installs PHP 4.3 and MySQL 4.1 by default. If you wish to follow the instructions given here, install, instead of the PHP 4.3 package, the PHP 5 variant. Ignore the MySQL package shipped with SUSE entirely. This will spare you having to deinstall packages later.

Selecting Apache Modules: To install, execute SYSTEM | YAST, start the module SOFTWARE | INSTALL SOFTWARE, set the filter to SELECTIONS, and choose the item SIMPLE WEBSERVER WITH APACHE2.

Deactivating PHP 4 Packages: Now change the filter to SEARCH and specify *php4* as the search pattern. Deactivate all packages shown.

Activate PHP 5 Packages: Give *php5* as the search pattern and activate all packages shown except for php5-devel.

Deactivate MySQL Packages: Give *mysql* as the search pattern and deactivate the packages mysql, mysql-client, and mysql-shared. (These are 4.1 packages. In the next section you will find instructions on installing MySQL 5.0.)

Activate the MySQL Driver for Perl: In the *mysql* search results you will find the package perl-DBD-mysql. You will need this package to access MySQL from Perl. (Perl itself is already installed.)

Resolve Package Dependencies: Click on CHECK DEPENDENCIES. YaST now shows a warning that the packages php5-mysql, php5-mysqli, and perl-DBD require the package mysql-shared. Select IGNORE THIS CONFLICT. (The conflict will be resolved later in the manual installation of MySQL 5.0.)

Display Summary: To check things, change the filter to SUMMARY. YaST shows which packages it will install (the boxes are checked) and whichit will not (symbol for "do not enter"). The result should look like Figure 2-7.

Package Installation: With ACCEPT, all selected packages are installed. YaST may first show a dialog in which it indicates additional packages that must be installed (e.g., Perl-DBI).

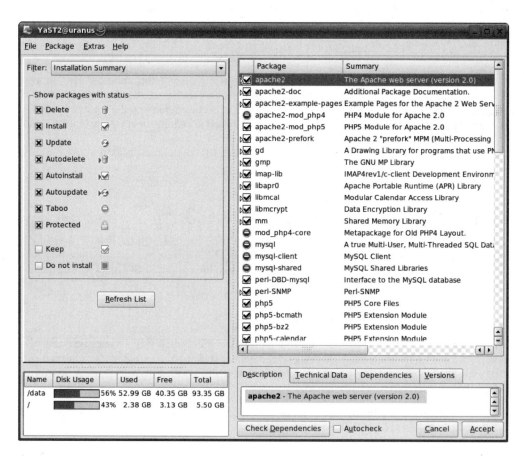

Figure 2-7. *Package installation in SUSE Linux with YaST*

The web server Apache is not launched by default. For that, you must execute the following command as *root*:

root# **/etc/init.d/apache2 start**

If you wish Apache to be started automatically in the future, execute in addition the command

root# **insserv apache2**

and then two directory specifications: configuration files, /etc/apache2/*; web files, /srv/www/htdocs.

Testing Apache and PHP

To test whether the server is actually running, open with your web browser the page http://localhost. You should see an Apache test page.

To check that PHP also is functioning, place, using a text editor, the file phptest.php in the directory /srv/www/htdocs with the following content:

```
<?php phpinfo(); ?>
```

Then open http://localhost/phptest.php with a web browser. You should see the PHP status page (see Figure 2-8).

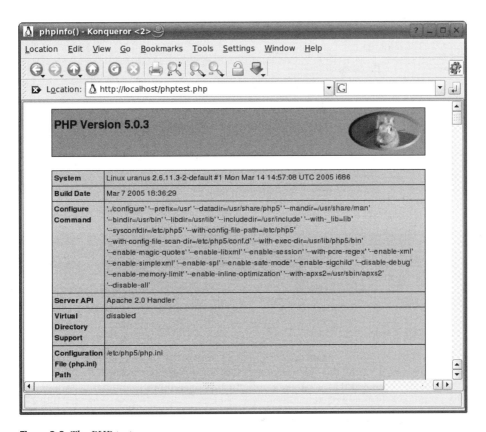

Figure 2-8. *The PHP test page*

Testing Perl

Hints for testing the Perl environment and programming MySQL applications in Perl are given in Chapter 16.

Installing MySQL 5.0

To install the MySQL server, download the current version from the following site in the form of RPM files: http://dev.mysql.com/downloads/mysql/5.0.html. (RPM is the usual format for packages under Linux.)

The packages listed in Table 2-1 are generally needed only by the MySQL server, MySQL client, and MySQL shared. To install, execute the following command, which here for reasons of space is broken by a backslash into three lines. After successful installation, you will be directed to set a *root* password for the MySQL server:

```
root# rpm -i MySQL-server-5.0.n-0.i386.rpm \
         MySQL-client-5.0.n-0.i386.rpm \
         MySQL-shared-5.0.n-0.i386.rpm
PLEASE REMEMBER TO SET A PASSWORD FOR THE MySQL root USER !
To do so, start the server, then issue the following commands:
/usr/bin/mysqladmin -u root password 'new-password'
/usr/bin/mysqladmin -u root -h uranus password 'new-password'
See the manual for more instructions.
```

Table 2-1. *RPM MySQL Package*

Package Name	Contents
MySQL-server-n.rpm	Contains the MySQL server.
MySQL-client-n.rpm	Contains client programs (mysql, mysqladmin, etc.).
MySQL-shared-n.rpm	Contains the shared libraries used by many programs to access MySQL.
MySQL-devel-n.rpm	Contains libraries and include files for program development in C.
MySQL-embedded-n.rpm	Contains a special version of the MySQL server that can be integrated into other programs (for C developers only).
MySQL-bench-n.rpm	Contains scripts with benchmark tests.
MySQL-Max-n.rpm	Contains the Max version of the MySQL server, which contains some supplementary table formats and experimental functions.

The MySQL server is launched at once after installation. If you wish the database server to be launched automatically in the future, execute this command:

```
root# insserv mysql
```

Securing the MySQL Server

After a new installation, anyone can log in as *root* without a password to MySQL and have unrestricted privileges to read, change, and delete all databases. For reasons of security it is absolutely necessary that you give a password for *root*. To do this, execute the following commands, where instead of *hostname* give the name of your computer:

```
root# mysqladmin -u root password 'secret'
root# mysqladmin -u root -h hostname password 'secret'
```

It can happen that you will obtain the error *Host 'hostname' is not allowed to connect to this MySQL server'*. If that happens, the host name was entered into the access database during installation without the domain name. To solve this problem, you must restart the program `mysql` and update the table *mysql.user* with an *UPDATE* command. Then you can change the second *root* password with `mysqladmin`. The following lines summarize the commands that must be executed. Of course, you must replace *uranus.sol* and *uranus* with the real name of your computer, once with and once without the domain name:

```
root# mysql -u root -p
Enter password: *******
mysql> USE mysql;
mysql> UPDATE user SET host="uranus.sol" WHERE host="uranus";
mysql> FLUSH PRIVILEGES;
mysql> exit
root# mysqladmin -u root -h uranus password 'secret'
```

Extensive background information on MySQL access management can be found in Chapter 11. The problem with incorrect host names in the MySQL access database has to do with the Linux network configuration and is described in Chapter 11.

Installation Under Red Hat Enterprise Linux 4

Red Hat Enterprise Linux 4 contains Apache 2, PHP 4.3, Perl 5.8, and MySQL 4.1. However, to follow the examples of this book, you need PHP 5 and MySQL 5. The following sections carry out a custom installation step by step.

- Install Apache 2 (included package)
- Install MySQL 5 (package from dev.mysql.com)
- Compile PHP 5
- Install Perl 5.8 (included package)

The installation instructions assume that none of the above programs, nor PHP 4.3 or MySQL 4.1, was installed. If any of them have been, then they should be deinstalled with `system-config-packages` or with `rpm -e`.

My installation was tested under Red Hat Enterprise Linux 4 ES. The information given should hold as well for other RHEL versions and, with some restrictions, for Fedora. (Fedora Core 4 contains PHP 5 packages, so you can save the trouble of compilation.)

Installing Apache 2

To install Apache 2, launch, using Applications | System Settings | Add/Remove Applications, the program `system-config-packages`. There activate the option Web-Server and then click on the link Details. In the detail dialog, deactivate the packages `php-ldap` and `php` (see Figure 2-9). Then start the installation with the button Update.

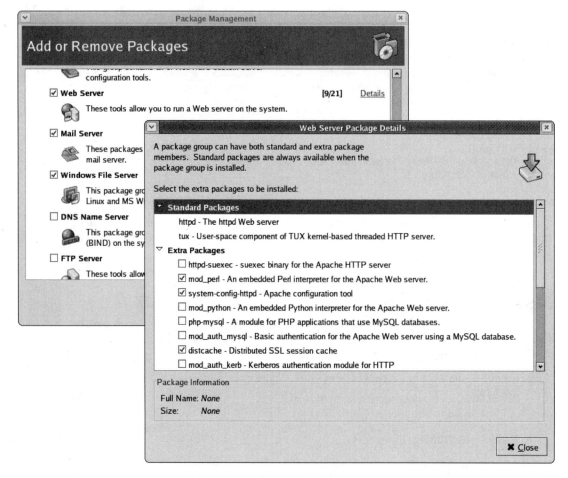

Figure 2-9. *Installation of Apache under Red Hat Enterprise Linux 4*

To start Apache, execute the following command:

```
root# /etc/init.d/httpd start
```

If you want Apache to be started each time the computer is turned on, then execute as well the following two commands:

```
root# chkconfig –add httpd
root# chkconfig –level 35 httpd on
```

To test whether the web server is actually running, open the page `http://localhost` with a web browser. You should see an Apache test page. Then there are two directory specifications: configuration files, `/etc/httpd/*`; web files `/var/www/html`.

Installing MySQL 5

The installation of the MySQL packages is done as under SUSE Linux. In brief, download the packages MySQL server, MySQL client, and MySQL shared from `dev.mysql.com` and install them with `rpm -i`:

```
root# rpm -i MySQL-server-5.0.n-0.i386.rpm \
            MySQL-client-5.0.n-0.i386.rpm \
            MySQL-shared-5.0.n-0.i386.rpm
```

Under Red Hat the MySQL server is installed in such a way that it is started automatically each time the computer is turned on. The insserv command given in the previous section is therefore unnecessary (and if it were, under Red Hat, it would be –addmysql).

Then execute the following commands to secure the MySQL user *root* with a password. Of course, give your computer name instead of *hostname*:

```
root# mysqladmin -u root password 'secret'
root# mysqladmin -u root -h hostname password 'secret'
```

MySQL 5.0.3 is incompatible with the SELinux default installations from RHEL 4. This has the consequence that many commands (e.g., *SHOW DATABASES*) do not work. It is unclear whether new versions of the MySQL server or new versions of the SELinux policy will solve this problem. Should that not be the case, you must deactivate SELinux for the MySQL server. To do this, execute as *root* the command system-config-securitylevel, switch into the dialog SELinux, search in SELinux Policy for the option SELinux Service Protection | Disable SELinux Protection for MySQLD Daemon, and activate this option. The MySQL server then must be restarted.

Compiling PHP 5

Installing the Development Tools

Before you begin compilation, you need various development tools (compiler, make, etc.). To install these programs, launch system-config-packages, activate the group, and install the programs contained therein.

In my test system, this seemingly trivial problem caused mammoth headaches: an update previously carried out with up2date was apparently in conflict with the development packages, and system-config-packages was incapable of resolving the package dependencies.

I eventually installed the necessary programs with an up2date command. The most current versions of the desired packages and all dependent packages were installed from the Internet. The command assumes that you have set up up2date and have access to a fast Internet connection. Depending on what packages are already installed in your system, it could happen that the following command should be extended to include other packages:

```
root# up2date gcc gcc.c++ make autoconf gettext binutils bison flex \
            libxml2 libxml2-devel libjpeg libjpeg-devel \
            libpng libpng-devel libpng10 libpng10-devel \
            gd gd-devel httpd-devel
```

In addition, for your MySQL installation you will need a suitable MySQL-devel package with the developer files. You can find the package at dev.mysql.com for download. Installation is carried out with rpm:

```
root# rpm -i MySQL-devel-5.0.n.i386.rpm
```

Downloading and Installing PHP 5 Source Code

The source code for PHP 5 can be found at the following site as a *.tar.bz2 archive:

```
http://www.php.net/downloads.php
```

The directory /usr/local/src will be used for all further work. To be able to work there as a regular user, as *root*, change the owner of this directory:

```
root# chown username.username/usr/local/src
```

Now unpack the PHP 5 source code in this directory:

```
user$ cd /usr/src/linux
user$ tar xjvf php-5.0.n.tar.bz2
user$ cd php-5.0.n
```

Compiling PHP 5

With ./configure you specify the options with which PHP is to be compiled. If you wish to use particular PHP extensions, you must specify additional options. The configure command given here suffices for the examples in this book. When you input the commands on a single line, the backslash should be omitted.

A couple of words on the option configure are in order: –prefix specifies where PHP 5 is to be installed; –with-apxs2 means that PHP 5 is to be compiled as an extension module for Apache 2. The directory that follows specifies the location for the Apache module. –with-libxml-dir specifies where the XML libraries are located. Analogously, –with-zlib-dir gives the path to the zlib library.

–with-mysql specifies that PHP is to be compiled with the traditional *mysql* interface (see Chapter 15). The path that follows points to the MySQL installation directory, which in the precompiled MySQL packages from dev.mysql.com is simply /usr.

–with-mysqli specifies that the new *mysqli* interface is to be integrated into PHP (see Chapter 15). The file that follows is part of the MySQL-devel package. This involves a script that gives information about the installed MySQL version and its installation locations.

The additional –with-xxx and –enable-xxx options activate various supplementary functions of PHP. An endless list with further options is given by the command ./configure –help. An example configure command follows:

```
user$ ./configure –prefix=/usr/local/php5 \
      –with-apxs2=/usr/local/apache2/bin/apxs \
      –with-libxml-dir=/usr/lib \
      –with-zlib –with-zlib-dir=/usr/lib \
      –with-mysql=/usr –with-mysqli=/usr/bin/mysql_config \
      –with-jpeg-dir=/usr –enable-exif \
      –with-gd –enable-soap –enable-sockets \
      –enable-force-cgi-redirect –enable-mbstring
```

If configure complains that certain programs or libraries are missing, you must install these with up2date and then execute configure again.

To compile, execute the command make. The process takes several minutes. (If you later execute ./configure again with different options, you must execute make clean before make. This deletes the results of previous compilations.)

```
user$ make
```

■**Tip** If a large number of *multiple-defined* errors for the library `libmysql` occur during compilation, then `./configure` has introduced an error in the `Makefile`. (This has happened frequently in my tests; it remains unclear why.)

The solution consists in opening the file `Makefile` in an editor before executing `make`. There, search for the line *EXTRA_LIBS* = ... In this line, you will find *-lmysqlclient* contained twice. Delete one occurrence, save the file, and execute `make` again.

Finally, the freshly compiled PHP module must be installed in such a way that Apache can find it. So `make install` must be executed by *root*:

```
root# make install
```

PHP 5 is thereby installed in the directory /usr/local/php5. The place for the configuration file php.ini is /usr/local/php5/lib/. By default, this file does not yet exist. That is, PHP 5 runs with the default settings (which will suffice for the time being). The pattern for *.ini files can be found in /usr/local/src/php-5.n.

Changing the Apache Configuration; Restarting Apache

The next step consists of altering the Apache configuration file /etc/httpd /conf/httpd.conf so that Apache uses the PHP 5 module. To do this, open the file in a text editor and add the line given below in boldface:

```
# changes in /usr/local/apache2/conf/httpd.conf
...
LoadModule php5_module modules/libphp5.so
AddType application/x-httpd-php .php
...
### Section 2: ...
```

The web server must be restarted before Apache can use the module:

```
root# /etc/init.d/httpd restart
```

To test whether PHP 5 is working, create the test file /var/www/html/phptest.php. This file must be readable from the Apache account *nobody* and have the following content:

```
<? phpinfo(); ?>
```

Now look at the page http://localhost/testphp.php with your web browser. The result should look like Figure 2-10.

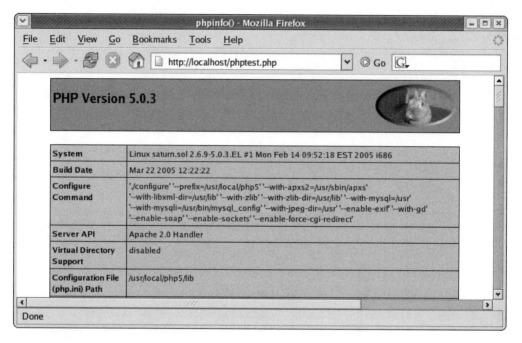

Figure 2-10. *PHP 5 under Red Hat Enterprise Linux 4*

Installing Perl 5.8

Perl 5.8 is installed under Red Hat Linux by default. What is missing are the modules `perl-DBI` and `perl-DBD-MySQL`, which allow Perl to communicate with MySQL. These packages are included, but they cannot be installed with the program `system-config-packages`, because MySQL 4.1 would also be installed. Therefore, manual installation with the command `rpm -i` is required. With Red Hat Enterprise ES 4 these two packages are on CD 2. Insert the disk and execute the following commands:

```
root# cd /mnt/cdrom/RedHat/RPMS
root# rpm -i perl-DBI-*.rpm
root# rpm -i perl-DBD-MySQL-*.rpm
```

Hints for testing the Perl environment and programming MySQL applications appear in Chapter 16.

Compiling the MySQL Developer Version (Linux)

This section is directed at MySQL pros who wish to compile the current MySQL developer version themselves. This not particularly difficult under Linux, but it is advisable to do this only under certain circumstances, and then only if you are unwilling to wait several months for the next version of MySQL. (The first test versions of MySQL 5.0 appeared every half year. So it is wearying to be working continually with the latest official version, while in the current developer version, countless errors have been corrected and new functions implemented.)

If you already have MySQL installed on your computer, you should make a backup of all your databases with phpMyAdmin or `mysqldump`. Then stop MySQL (`/etc/init.d/mysql stop`) and delete the existing MySQL installation.

Installing Bitkeeper

The source code of the MySQL developer version is not available on the Internet as a `tar` package. Instead, MySQL enables access to the source code through the version control system Bitkeeper. The first step is to download Bitkeeper from `http://www.bitmover.com/cgi-bin/download.cgi` and install it. A no-charge registration is required. To install Bitkeeper in the directory `/usr/local/bk`, execute the following commands:

```
root# chmod u+rx bk-<version>-x86-glibc23-linux.bin
root# ./bk-<version>-x86-glibc23-linux.bin /usr/local/bk
```

Downloading the MySQL Developer Version

The following commands show how to install the MySQL 5.0 developer version. The commands assume that the user *user* has write permission in `/usr /src`. The `export` command is necessary only if your web access is via a proxy server. In this case, you must specify the address and port number:

```
user$ cd /usr/src/
user$ export http_proxy="http://proxy.firma.de:8080/"
user$ bk clone bk://mysql.bkbits.net/mysql-5.0 mysql-5.0
```

The following two commands release the source code files for local use:

```
user$ cd /usr/src/mysql-5
user$ bk -r edit
```

At the first startup of bk, its license must be verified (press Q to terminate the display of the license text and then confirm the license with Y). Then bk will give extensive information about which files it has just copied, deleted, or synchronized.

Compiling MySQL

To compile MySQL with InnoDB, execute the following commands:

```
user$ aclocal; autoheader; autoconf; automake
user$ (cd innobase; aclocal; autoheader; autoconf; automake)
user$ ./configure
user$ make
root# make install
```

Setting Up the mysql Database for Managing Access Privileges

Before the MySQL server can be started for the first time, the database *mysql* must be set up for managing MySQL access privileges. The following lines assume that the database files are to be stored in `/usr/local/mysql` and that the MySQL server uses the account *mysql*. (If MySQL has already been run on your computer, you can continue to use its databases. In this case, skip the following two commands.)

```
root# ./scripts/mysql_install_db —ldata=/usr/local/mysql
root# chown -R mysql /usr/local/mysql
```

Configuration Files and Init-V Scripts

To start the MySQL server you need an Init-V script. In the MySQL source files you will find a suitable model in `support-files/mysql.server`. The file `/etc /my.cnf` is used to configure various MySQL parameters. Here, too, the `support-files` directory contains a model:

```
root# cp support-files/mysql.server  /etc/init.d/mysql
root# cp support-files/my-medium.cnf /etc/my.cnf
```

Now you must make some small changes in the two files, which are shown in boldface in the following lines of code. /etc/my.cnf governs which socket file client and server should be used for local communication. By default, the MySQL server uses /tmp/mysql.sock, while PHP is generally set to /var /lib/mysql/mysql.sock:

```
# Changes in /etc/my.cnf
...
[client]
socket = /var/lib/mysql/mysql.sock
...
[mysqld]
socket = /var/lib/mysql/mysql.sock
...
```

/etc/init.d/mysql is responsible for starting the MySQL server. There you specify where the MySQL binary files and where the MySQL database files are to be found. (If MySQL has already been run on your computer, you can continue to use its databases. In this case, set *datadir* so that it points to the previous database directory. As a rule, this is /var/lib/mys.)

```
# Changes in /etc/init.d/mysql
...
basedir=/usr/local
datadir=/usr/local/mysql
...
```

Starting the MySQL Server

To start the MySQL server, finally, execute the following command:

```
root# /etc/init.d/mysql start
```

If you wish the server to start automatically when the computer is booted up, execute the following two commands:

```
root# insserv mysql        (for SUSE)
root# chkconfig –add mysql  (for Red Hat, Fedora, Mandrakelinux, etc.)
```

Configuring Apache

Configuration Files

Almost all Apache settings are governed by the configuration file httpd.conf. This file's location depends on the operating system:

> **Windows:** Programs\Apache Group\Apache2\conf\httpd.conf
>
> **Red Hat Enterprise Linux:**/etc/httpd/conf/httpd.conf/etc/httpd/conf.d/*.conf
>
> **SUSE Linux:** /etc/apache2/httpd.conf/etc/apache2/*.conf/etc/apache2/conf.d/*.conf/etc/sysconfig/apache2

With Red Hat and SUSE, the configuration is not to be found in a single file. It is scattered among countless files in the directories given above. You should use grep as needed to search for a file in which you wish to make changes.

You need to take particular care with SUSE. There, some *.conf files are generated afresh at each start. For this reason, you should make configuration changes under SUSE either directly in /etc/sysconfig/apache2 or in a separate file, such as /etc/apache2/httpd.conf.local. To ensure that this file is looked at, you must add the file name to the variable APACHE_CONF_INCLUDE_FILES in the file /etc/sysconfig/apache2.

■**Caution** Configuration changes do not become effective until Apache has been restarted. Under Windows, you must use the forward slash as the separator in Apache configuration files, not the usual backslash.

Elementary Settings

There is insufficient space here to give too many details on the Apache configuration. In the following, then, only the most elementary settings from httpd.conf will be described.

ServerName: This setting gives the network name of the computer on which Apache is running. It is under this name that the web server is reachable by other computers on the network. (If this setting is absent, Apache attempts to discover the network name on its own.)

DocumentRoot: This setting gives the directory in which the web files (*.html, *.php, etc.) are located. Table 2-2 summarizes the default settings for various installations.

LoadModule: When Apache is compiled so that it can load modules at run time (which is generally the case), LoadModule instructions are necessary, which look something like this:

```
LoadModule php5_module modules/libphp5.so        # for Linux
LoadModule php5_module "c:/php5/php5apache2.dll" # for Windows
```

AddType: *AddType* instructions create the association between file identifiers and application type. Thanks to the following setting, Apache knows that *.php should be executed by the PHP interpreter:

```
AddType application/x-httpd-php .php
```

PHPIniDir: This setting is passed to the PHP interpreter and tells it from what location it should read the file php.ini. This option should make the configuration of PHP easier; it often fails for some quite trivial reason: PHP could not find the php.ini file or it evaluated obsolete versions of the file. PHPIniDir has been available only since Apache 2 and is evaluated only by the Windows version of Apache:

```
PHPIniDir "C:/php5"
```

AddDefaultCharset: This setting tells which character set the web files have.

<Directory "xxx">: This block, consisting of many lines, describes all the properties of a web directory. <Directory /> contains the default settings that hold for, among others, DocumentRoot. The <Directory> block ends with </Directory>. The following lines give an example:

```
<Directory /> or <Directory "directory ...">
  ...
  AllowOverride AuthConfig FileInfo
  Option Indexes
</Directory>
```

Within the `<Directory>` block, various options control what is allowed or forbidden in this directory and who has access to it. Here only two options will be presented:

AllowOverride: It is often desirable that Apache not evaluate the file `.htaccess` in web directories and apply the supplementary settings contained therein to the directory (see the next section). For this to work, you must specify with `AllowOverride` which changes are permissible. Possible settings are `None` (forbids all changes, often is the default), `All` (permits all changes), and a combination of `AuthConfig` (authentication), `FileInfo` (language and character set settings, error file), `Indexes`, `Limit` (access privileges), and `Options`.

Options Indexes: If the address `http://computername/directory/` is given in the browser, Apache returns automatically, depending on the configuration of `DirectoryIndex`, the page `index.html`, `index.php`, etc. (more on this later). If no `DirectoryIndex` files exist, then `Options Indexes` has the effect that Apache displays a table of contents. This is often useful during program development, but thereafter can represent a security risk. (In addition to `Indexes` there are many other keywords that can be set with `Options`.)

DirectoryIndex: With this option you can specify one or more files that Apache looks for when only a directory is given in the web browser. A usual setting is `index.html index.php main.php default.php`. Now if only the address `http://computername/directory/` is given in the browser, Apache searches this directory for the given files and returns the first valid file.

Default Directory for Web Files

Table 2-2 summarizes the directories in which web files (`*.html`, `*.php`, etc.) are stored by default. In this directory, or in subdirectories that you create, you can store your own PHP examples.

Note that Apache runs under a separate account under Linux (under Red Hat it is *apache*, under SUSE it is *wwwrun*). With all web files, access privileges should be set such that the user and also Apache can read them. To change access privileges use the Unix commands `chown` and `chmod`. For example, `chmod a+x *` has the effect that everyone can read all files.

Table 2-2. *Directory with Web Files*

Installation	DocumentRoot Location
Windows	`C:\Programs\Apache Group\Apache2\htdocs`
Red Hat / Fedora by default	`/var/www/html`
SUSE Linux by default	`/srv/www/htdocs`

Access Privileges for Individual Directories (.htaccess)

Once Apache is running, everyone on the network or with the Internet has access to all web pages that Apache can process. This is not always desirable, particularly on development computers. There are three options for restricting access to web pages:

Protection in httpd.conf: In `httpd.conf` you can set precisely from what addresses the web pages of a particular directory can be read. Space limitation forbids a description of these mechanisms.

Protection via a Firewall: If a firewall is running on the development computer, it can be so configured that Apache cannot be contacted from outside (that is, over the network). The web pages can then be viewed only from the local computer.

Password Protection of an Individual Directory: For such protection, place in the web directory to be protected a file with the name `.htaccess` and specify that this directory can be read only after authentication witha user name and password. Apache evaluates `.htaccess` and displays a login dialog to all surfers who wish to view files from this directory with their browsers.

In what follows, we will deal with the last of these variants. It is also useful for securing a directory that is publicly accessible over the Internet from unknown users. A typical example is the PHP program phpMyAdmin, which is used on countless web sites for administration of MySQL (see Chapter 6).

Password File

The first step in password protection is to create a password file. For security reasons, the password data are not stored in .htaccess, but in a separate file. This file can be located outside the publicly accessible web directories. In the following example the password file is named site.pwd.

The password file is generated with the Apache auxiliary program htpasswd. (If you are working under SUSE with Apache 2, the command is htpasswd2.) Choose the option -c (*create*), and specify the name of the password file and a user name. The program will ask you for the desired password, and then it generates the password file, in which the user name appears in plain text, the password in encrypted form.

```
> htpasswd -c site.pwd myname
New password: **********
Re-type new password: **********
Adding password for user myname
```

To add an additional combination of user name and password to a preexisting password file, execute htpasswd again, this time without the option -c:

```
> htpasswd site.pwd name2
New password: **********
Re-type new password: **********
Adding password for user name2
```

The resulting password file will look something like this:

```
myname:$apr1$gp1.....$qljDszVJOSCS.oBoPJItS/
name2:$apr1$A22.....$OVO1Nc1FcXgNsruT9c6Iq1
```

■**Tip** If you wish to execute htpasswd.exe under Windows, you have to open a command window (command prompt) and specify the complete path name inside quotation marks (usually "Programs\Apache Group\Apache\bin\htpasswd.exe").

If you want to create or enlarge the password file in a directory of an Internet service provider, then use ssh or ssh to access the computer of the ISP (in order to execute htpasswd there). Many ISPs make available other configuration aids.

The .htaccess File

When a file with the name .htaccess is located in a web directory, Apache evaluates all configuration settings in this file. The same syntax holds as in httpd.conf. However, only certain directory-specific settings can be made.

With the following .htaccess file, the content of a directory (including all subdirectories!) is protected:

```
AuthType Basic
AuthUserFile "c:/Programs/Apache Group/Apache2/htdocs/test/site.pwd"
AuthName "myrealm"
Require valid-user
```

AuthUserFile specifies the complete file name of the password file. AuthName denotes the extent (*realm*) for which access is valid. The idea is that you shouldn't have to log in every time you wish to access directories protected by .htaccess. Once you have logged in with a particular AuthName designation, this login is valid for all directories with this AuthName designation.

For .htaccess this means that you give the same AuthName character string for directories with a common login. Conversely, you can give differing domain names for different directories; then a new login is required for each directory.

Require valid-user means that every valid combination of user name and password is valid for login. Alternatively, you could specify here that a login is permitted only for specified users:

```
Require user myname name2 name3
```

Further details on user authentication and .htaccess configuration can be found, for example, on these web pages:

```
http://apache-server.com/tutorials/ATusing-htaccess.html
http://www.apacheweek.com/features/userauth
```

Caution .htaccess files are effective only if httpd.conf is permitted in the Apache configuration file. If the Apache default configuration contains the entry AllowOverride None for the affected directory or for the default directory /, then all .htaccess files are without any effect. If only individual options are specified in AllowOverride, but in .htaccess additional settings are changed, an error can even be triggered that makes it impossible to view certain files in the directory.

For .htaccess files to be considered, httpd.conf must contain the setting AllowOverride All or AllowOverride AuthConfig for the affected directory (that is, in the relevant <Directory> group).

Tip Under Windows it is impossible using Windows Explorer to create a file with the name .htaccess. Explorer believes that this name is invalid. Name the file htaccess.txt, and then use an input request window to rename the file with the command RENAME htaccess.txt .htaccess.

Windows users will perhaps wonder why the file name must begin with a period. This is the usual method under Unix/Linux to identify hidden files. Such files are not displayed by file managers by default.

Access to a Protected Directory

As soon as you attempt to read a file from a protected directory with a browser, the web browser presents a login dialog (see Figure 2-11).

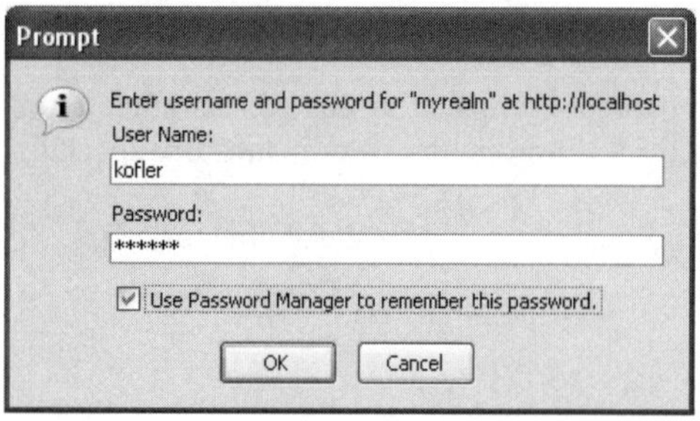

Figure 2-11. *Access to a web directory protected by* .htaccess

Configuring PHP

The settings and options of the PHP interpreter are governed by the file php.ini. Table 2-3 summarizes where this file is usually found.

Table 2-3. *Location of the PHP Configuration File*

Installation	Location of php.ini
Windows	C:\php5\php.ini
Linux self-compiled	/usr/local/php5/lib/php.ini
Red Hat / Fedora by default	/etc/php.ini
SUSE by default	/etc/php5/php.ini

Under Windows, the location of php.ini is usually set by PHPIniDir in the Apache configuration file httpd.conf (since Apache 2). If this setting is lacking, the PHP interpreter php.ini searches in the Windows directory.

■**Note** When the PHP interpreter php.ini cannot find this file or if it doesn't exist, it uses the default setting.

If you are uncertain whether or from where the PHP interpreter php.ini is reading, have a look at the PHP test page, which is created by the PHP function phpinfo() (see Figure 2-5).

The pattern for php.ini can be found under Windows in the PHP installation directory (e.g., C:\php5\) and under Linux after a self-installation in /usr/local/src/php-5.n/. As a starting point for your own settings, you are best off using the provided file php.ini-recommended.

Changes in php.ini become effective only after Apache is restarted.

Elementary Settings

There is insufficient space here to go into the countless options in php.ini. In what follows we shall therefore describe only the most important options, always giving you the settings used in this book.

display_errors = On: This setting has the effect that error alerts are displayed when there is an error in a PHP script. This is very useful during program development. It should be turned off for servers on the Internet, since error messages often give information about the code, which could lead to a breach in security. (If during the development of a PHP page you see a blank page in your web browser instead of a result, then the display_errors setting is almost always to blame.)

error_reporting = E_All: This setting results in all PHP errors and warnings being displayed.

magic_quotes_gpc = On: This setting has the effect that when data is transferred between web pages (Get/Post/Cookie), special characters such as ', ", \, and the zero byte are replaced by \', \", \\, and \0. Details on *Magic Quotes* can be found in Chapter 15. This setting was turned to *On* because currently (alas), the default setting is used by almost all Internet service providers, and in developing code it is useful to have the same settings as those of the ISP.

default_charset: This option should either not be set at all (which is the case in the default configuration) or for the examples of this chapter be set to *"iso-8859-1"*. *default_charset* governs whether the PHP interpreter should report in the transfer of HTML documents that the pages are coded according to a particular character set.

max_execution_time = 30: This option tells after how much time (in seconds) the execution of the PHP script should be aborted.

max_imput_time = 60: This option specifies how long PHP should wait for data (e.g., during file upload by a client to the PHP program).

file_uploads = On: This setting has the result that PHP can process file uploads.

upload_max_filesize = 2M: This option specifies how large a file can be in a file upload.

post_max_size = 8M: This option specifies the maximum size of a data set that can be sent to the PHP program via a (*POST*) form.

memory_limit = 8M: This options specifies how much memory a PHP script is allowed to take up.

PHP Extensions

PHP extensions enable the use of additional functions that are not integrated directly into PHP. Which functions are directly integrated into PHP and which are realized as extensions depends on how PHP is compiled.

- If you compile PHP yourself under Unix/Linux, you generally integrate desired extensions directly into the PHP interpreter (through suitable `./configure` options) and therefore do not need to bother with extensions in `php.ini`.

- In some Linux distributions (e.g., SUSE), PHP is delivered strongly modularized; that is, each extension can be installed individually as a package. Thus in this case as well you need not be concerned with `php.ini`; the package management system manages the work for you.

- Most likely, you will be dealing with the PHP extension mechanism for Windows. The PHP version for Windows contains hardly any supplementary functions. Instead, all possible extensions are provided in the form of extension libraries (`*.dll` files in the subdirectory ext).

If you wish to use extensions, the variable `extension_dir` must be set in `php.ini` in such a way that it specifies the directory in the PHP installation:

```
extension_dir = "c:\php5\ext\"
```

Furthermore, you must specify in `php.ini` the desired extensions via *extension* settings. The line for the OpenSSL module would look like this:

```
extension=php_openssl.dll
```

`php.ini` normally already contains a host of such *extension* instructions, to which a semicolon is prefixed. In `php.ini`, the semicolon indicates a comment. To use the extension, you must remove the semicolon. Under Unix/Linux, the file identifier for libraries is `.so` instead of `.dll`.

■**Note** Many PHP extensions access additional libraries. These must be installed in such a way that the PHP interpreter can find them. Under Windows, this means that such libraries must be copied into the Windows directory or the Windows system directory.

For example, the PHP extension DLL `php_mysql.dll` uses functions from `libmysql.dll`. This file is included with the current versions of PHP, but by default it is located in the PHP directory, where it will not be found by the PHP interpreter. Therefore, you must copy the file `libmysql.dll` into the Windows directory before you restart Apache. If you neglect this copying, the Apache restart will fail with an error message that a DLL cannot be loaded.

Configuring MySQL

There are many settings that can be made and changed via a configuration file. Table 2-4 summarizes the usual location of this configuration file.

Table 2-4. *Location of the MySQL Configuration File*

Installation	Name of the MySQL Configuration File
Recent Windows installations	`C:\Programs\MySQL\MySQL Server n.n\my.ini`
Old Windows installations	`C:\my.cnf` or `Windows\my.ini`
Linux	`/etc/my.cnf`

Basically, there are default setting for all MySQL options, so that it is possible to run MySQL without a configuration file or without changes to an existing file. Details on the syntax and countless available options in the configuration file can be found in Chapters 14 and 22.

Launching the MySQL Server

Changes in configuration files become effective only after a restart of the MySQL server:

Windows: Under Windows, the simplest way to restart the server is to execute MYSQL SYSTEM TRAY MONITOR. This is a small icon on the task bar (near the clock), in which you can execute the commands SHUTDOWN INSTANCE (end the server) and START INSTANCE.

If SYSTEM TRAY MONITOR does not run, launch the program in the menu START | PROGRAMS | MYSQL. If the program does run but is not shown in the task bar, the problem is usually the task bar setting. Click the task bar with the right mouse button, execute the command TASKBAR, and deactivate the option HIDE INACTIVE ICONS.

Linux: Under Unix/Linux everything is much easier. A brief command suffices. To restart, you use the relevant Init-V script, which you execute first with the parameter *stop* and then with the parameter *start*. Depending on the distribution, this script has the name `mysql` or `mysqld`.

```
root# /etc/init.d/mysql[d] restart
```

## CHAPTER 3

Introductory Example
(An Opinion Poll with PHP)

The best way of becoming familiar with a new database or development system is to work through a full-fledged example. Thus in this chapter our goal is to create a web site for the purpose of conducting an opinion poll.

To a certain extent this is a trivial example, and its results certainly could be accomplished without the use of MySQL. However, it brings into focus the interplay between MySQL and a script programming language (for this example we have used PHP). Moreover, our example casts light on the entire process of database design from first beginnings right up to the completed application.

Overview

Our opinion poll consists of two pages. The file vote.html contains a simple questionnaire with a single question: What is your favorite programming language for developing MySQL applications? The question is followed by a selection of choices for a response (see Figure 3-1). After one of the options is selected and OK is clicked, the result page results.php is displayed (see Figure 3-2).

Assumptions

You can try out this example on my web site (www.kofler.cc). However, from a pedagogical point of view it would be better for you to attempt to re-create this example for yourself. For this you will need a test environment consisting of Apache/MySQL/PHP that permits you the following:

- creation of a new MySQL database (that is, you need sufficient privileges to be able to execute *CREATE DATABASE*)

- moving files into a directory on the web server

- executing PHP script files

Information on setting up such a test environment on a local computer can be found in the previous chapter.

A complete understanding of our example requires some basic knowledge of databases. If you have never had much, if anything, to do with databases and as a consequence run into difficulties in understanding what is going on, please do not despair. Chapter 8 provides an introduction to relational database systems, while Chapter 9 explains how to use the database query language SQL.

In this example, the programming language PHP will be used. The code is rather straightforward; that is, you should have no difficulty in understanding it even you don't know a word of PHP. However, you should know in general how embedded script languages function in HTML. (The Active Server pages developed by Microsoft are based on the same idea.)

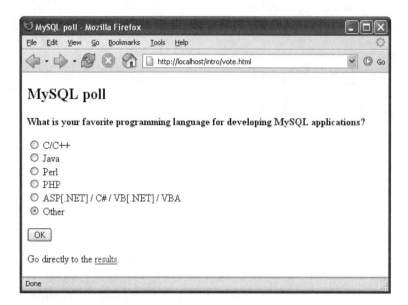

Figure 3-1. *The questionnaire*

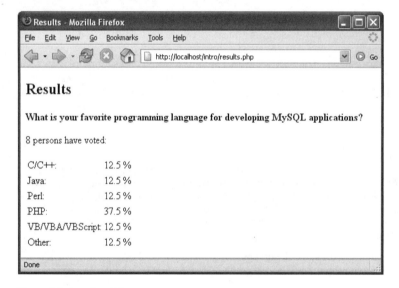

Figure 3-2. *Results of the survey*

Database Development

To save the results of our questionnaire with MySQL, you must first set up a database and then place a table in that database. (Every MySQL database consists of tables. A particular feature of this example is that only a single table is required. As a rule, when the requirements of the project are more complex, several linked tables will be used.)

Executing the `mysql` Command-Line Interpreter

Both operations—generating a database and creating a new table—require that you communicate with MySQL. Under Unix/Linux you execute the command `mysql`. Under Windows, execute the menu command PROGRAMS | MySQL | MySQL SERVER *N.N* | MySQL COMMAND LINE CLIENT.

■**Note** If `mysql` immediately terminates, possibly with an error message such as *Access denied for user xy*, then either access to MySQL is completely denied to user xy, or it is protected by a password. In either case you must invoke `mysql` with the options `-u name` and `-p`:

```
> mysql -u username -p
Enter password: xxx
```

Furthermore, `mysql` has dozens of other options. The most important of these are described in Chapter 4, while all of them are collected in Chapter 22. Background information on the MySQL security system (access protection, passwords, privileges) can be found in Chapter 11.

The distinction between MySQL and `mysql` is somewhat confusing: MySQL denotes the database server, which normally is launched automatically at system startup. The server runs continuously in the background. (This chapter assumes that the server is up and running.) The program name of the server is, depending on the operating system, `mysqld` (Unix/Linux) or `mysqld.exe`, `mysqld-nt.exe`, etc. (Windows).

In contrast to these, we have the command-line interpreters `mysql` and `mysql.exe`. These programs come into play when administration or maintenance are to be carried out interactively. The program `mysql` has the task of transmitting interactive commands to the server and displaying the results of these commands on the monitor.

Alternatives to `mysql`, such as the MySQL Administrator and the convenient HTML interface phpMyAdmin, will be introduced in Chapters 5 and 6.

In `mysql` you can now input commands that will be transmitted to the database server (see Figure 3-3). To test whether a connection can even be made, execute the command *STATUS*. The result should be the display of various pieces of status information about the database (such as the version number):

```
mysql> STATUS;
mysql Ver 14.7 Distrib 5.0.2, for Win95/Win98 (i32)
Connection id:          2
Current database:
Current user:           ODBC@localhost
SSL:                    Not in use
Using delimiter:        ;
Server version:         5.0.2-alpha
Protocol version:       10
Connection:             localhost via TCP/IP
Server characterset:    latin1
Db      characterset:   latin1
Client characterset:    latin1
Conn.   characterset:   latin1
TCP port:               3306
Uptime:                 12 days 1 hour 26 min 20 sec1

Threads: 2  Questions: 3099  Slow queries: 0  Opens: 6
Flush tables: 1 Open tables: 0  Queries per second avg: 0.003
```

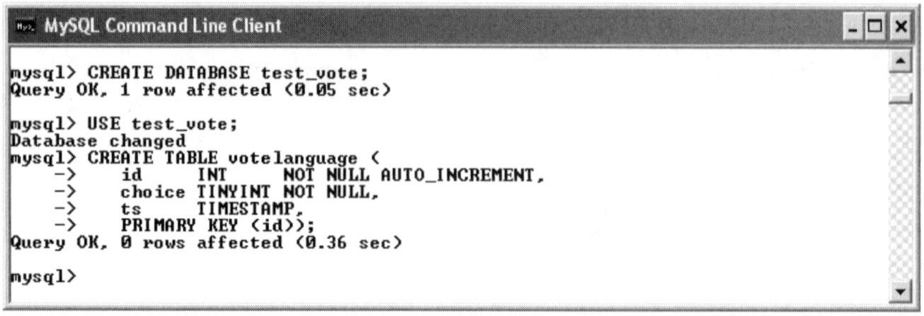

Figure 3-3. *The MySQL monitor*

If problems arise in starting up `mysql` or in executing `status`, the most probable cause is that the database server hasn't even been started or that access has been denied to you. More information on installation can be found in Chapter 2, while information on access and security can be found in Chapter 11.

Setting Up the Database

To set up the new database *test_vote*, in `mysql` execute the command *CREATE DATABASE*. Note that you must end the command with a semicolon. In the following two lines your input appears in boldface:

```
mysql> CREATE DATABASE test_vote;
Query OK, 1 row affected (0.09 sec)
```

The reply delivered by `mysql` may look a bit weird. The output `1 row affected` indicates that in the list of all databases, which internally, of course, is in the form of a MySQL table, one row was changed. What is important here is only that the *CREATE DATABASE* command was executed correctly.

The database name *test_vote* was not chosen quite arbitrarily. In the default setting of MySQL access privileges, every user is permitted to create databases on a local computer that begin with the word "test." In particular, when you are not the MySQL administrator (but rely on the help of a system administrator), a name of the form *test_xy* can save any number of emails or telephone calls.

The drawback of the name *test_xy* is that every user of the local computer can edit, or even delete, the database. This is no problem for this introductory example, but in the case of a real-life application you probably will want to give your database a bit more security. Necessary information on this can be found in Chapter 11.

Creating Tables

The database *test_vote* has been created, but it is not yet possible to store any information. For this you need tables. To create a new table within the database *test_vote*, use the command *CREATE TABLE*.

Before you execute this command, however, you must specify the database into which the table is to be placed. The requisite command for this is *USE*. It determines the default database to which further commands are to be applied. (MySQL is managing other databases besides the newly created database *test_vote*.)

```
mysql> USE test_vote;
Database changed
mysql> CREATE TABLE votelanguage (
    ->    id      INT     NOT NULL AUTO_INCREMENT,
    ->    choice  TINYINT NOT NULL,
    ->    ts      TIMESTAMP,
    ->    PRIMARY KEY (id));
Query OK, 0 rows affected (0.75 sec)
```

The *CREATE TABLE* command may seem a bit strange at first. But just go ahead and input the boldface commands listed above line for line. (You can terminate each command with Return. The semicolon indicates to mysql that the end of a command has been reached.)

If you should make a typing error during the input of a command, MySQL will usually inform you of this fact with an error message. You must now repeat the entire command. Using the cursor keys ↑ and ↓ you can recall and correct previously input lines.

If MySQL has accepted *CREATE TABLE* in spite of a typographical error (because the command, though semantically not what you had in mind, is nonetheless syntactically correct), you can delete the incorrectly defined table with *DROP TABLE votelanguage;*. That accomplished, you can repeat the command *CREATE TABLE*.

Instead of creating the table *votelanguage* via a *CREATE TABLE* command, you could, of course, use an administration tool such as MySQL Administrator or phpMyAdmin. This assumes, of course, that such a program is installed and that you have learned how to use it. The program mysql is not known for its ease of use, but it has the advantage of offering the best way of documenting the steps to be executed.

Now let us explain what is actually going on. With *CREATE TABLE* you have brought into being a table with three columns, *id*, *choice*, and *ts*. Once the table is filled with data (namely, the results of the survey), the content of the table can be displayed something like this:

id	choice	ts
1	4	20050114154618
2	5	20050114154944
3	4	20050114154953
4	3	20050114154954
5	3	20050114154957
6	6	20050114155012
7	3	20050114155021
8	1	20050114155027
...		

The interpretation of these data is that the first person to respond to the survey chose the programming language PHP, while the second chose VB, and the third selected PHP. The next respondents chose, in order, Perl, Other, Perl, and C. The column *id* thus contains a running identification number that identifies the lines (the data set). The column *choice* contains, in coded form, the selection made by the survey participant, where the numbers 1 through 6 correspond to the programming languages C, Java, Perl, PHP, VB, and Other. The column *ts* contains the time at which the query was executed. (For example, the first participant filled out vote.html on January 14, 2005, at 15:46:18.)

■Note Like any other specialized subject, the database world has its own argot. Database vocabulary includes the term *data record* for each line of the table above. Instead of *columns* (here id and choice) one often speaks of *fields*.

In order to generate a table with the two columns *id* and *choice*, the following command would suffice:

```
CREATE TABLE votelanguage (id INT, choice TINYINT, ts TIMESTAMP);
```

The result is that the column *id* is declared with the data type *INT*, and *choice* is declared to be of data type *TINYINT*. This means that in theory, 2^{31} individuals (2,147,483,648, that is) could participate in our survey before the range for *id* was exhausted. (If *id* were declared as type *UNSIGNED INT*, then the number of potential participants would be doubled.) In *choice*, on the other hand, there are 2^{16} different values available. (The data types *INT* and *TINYINT* are discussed in Chapter 8 together with the other MySQL data types.)

By this point, you may be wondering why I have plagued you with such a complicated command as *CREATE TABLE* when there is a much easier way to achieve the same result. The difference between the complicated and simple variants is the difference between good and bad database creation. (And you wouldn't want me to be leading you astray on our very first example, would you?)

The attribute *AUTO_INCREMENT* for the column *id* has the effect that with each new record the appropriate value for *id* is automatically inserted. Thus when the results of the survey are saved, only *choice* has to be specified, since the database takes care of *id* on its own. This attribute ensures a consistent numbering of the data records, which is important for efficient management of the table.

The attribute *NOT NULL* ensures that actual values must be placed in both columns. It is not permitted to store the data record *NULL* or (in the case of *choice*) not to insert any value at all. Thus this attribute prevents invalid data records from being stored. (Go ahead and try to force MySQL to accept such a data record. It will refuse and present you with an error message.)

PRIMARY KEY (id) has the effect that the column *id* is used to identify the data records. That is the reason that the column was provided for in the first place, but MySQL is not so clever as to be able to read your mind, and it requires that it be informed precisely as to what your wishes are. (In this case, *id* will from now on be called a *primary key*.) The definition of a primary key has a decisive influence on the speed with which data records can be accessed. That holds especially for linked tables—but let us not get ahead of ourselves. We shall stick for the moment with simple tables, always define a single primary key (and do so, if possible, for an *INT* field with the attributes *NOT NULL* and *AUTO_INCREMENT*).

Why Make It Complicated, When It Could Be So Much Easier?

Perhaps it has occurred to you that we have presented a rather convoluted solution to an easy problem. It could done in a much simpler fashion. All we need to do is to control six counters, such as in a table of the following form:

id	counter
1	2
2	0
3	7
4	9
5	2
6	1

Such a display would mean that two participants expressed a preference for the C language, none for Java, seven for Perl, nine for PHP, and so on. Each time a preference is registered, the corresponding counter is incremented by 1. The database would consist altogether of six lines; one wouldn't have to worry about performance; memory requirements would be essentially zero—nothing but advantages! And all of this is aside from the fact that the six counters could be effortlessly stored in a small text file. In short, MySQL is totally unnecessary for this survey.

All right, then, you are correct! However, such an attitude is helpful only as long as we are dealing with a simple application. What happens when you would like to offer each participant the opportunity to make a comment? What if you allow the participants to fill out the questionnaire only after a login (to rule out the possibility of multiple voting)? What if you wish to record the time and IP address for each participant (again to secure against attempts at manipulating the survey)?

In all these cases, you would have to store the responses in a table like the one that we have presented. (The table would have merely to be enlarged by a column or two. The structure of the program can remain essentially the same.) So, if the conception of this example seems a bit overly complicated at first glance, the reason is that we are keeping open the possibility, even in this first example, of a later extension.

The Questionnaire

As we have mentioned already in the introduction, our entire project consists of two web pages. The first page (vote.html) contains the questionnaire. This is pure HTML code (without PHP). The second page (results.php) carries out two tasks: evaluating the questionnaire and displaying the results.

The HTML code of the questionnaire is given here, so that the code for evaluation in the next section will be understandable. Most important are the attributes *name* and *value* of the elements of the questionnaire. All of the radio buttons have the name *vote*, while *value* contains values between 1 and 6. The OK button has the name *submitbutton*, and as *value* the character string *"OK"* is used.

```
<!DOCTYPE HTML PUBLIC "-//W3C//DTD HTML 4.0//EN">
<!- php/vote/vote.html ->
<html><head>
 <meta http-equiv="Content-Type"
       content="text/html; charset=iso-8859-1" />
  <title>MySQL-poll</title>
</head>
<body>
<h2>MySQL-poll</h2>

<p><b>What is your favorite
programming language for developing MySQL applications?</b></p>

<form method="POST" action="results.php">
  <p>    <input type="radio" name="vote" value="1" />C/C++
  <br /><input type="radio" name="vote" value="2" />Java
  <br /><input type="radio" name="vote" value="3" />Perl
  <br /><input type="radio" name="vote" value="4" />PHP
  <br /><input type="radio" name="vote" value="5" />
                    ASP[.NET] / C# / VB[.NET] / VBA
  <br /><input type="radio" name="vote" value="6" />
                    another language
  </p>
  <p><input type="submit" name="submitbutton" value="OK" /></p>
</form>
<p>Go directly to the <a href="results.php">result</a>.</p>
</body>
</html>
```

Questionnaire Evaluation and Displaying Results

One can call results.php either directly (for example, via a link) or using the data in the questionnaire. In one case, what is shown is only the current state of the questionnaire. In the other case, the data are also evaluated and stored in the database.

The `mysql` Interface Versus the `mysqli` Interface

The programming language PHP offers, starting with version 5, the interfaces *mysql* and *mysqli* as two alternatives for communication with MySQL.

- The *mysql* functions are already familiar from previous versions of PHP, and they work with almost all versions of MySQL. This example is based on the old *mysql* interface and therefore works as well with older versions of PHP and MySQL.

- The new *mysqli* interface, on the other hand, is object oriented and assumes at least PHP 5 and MySQL 4.1 (or newer versions). You will learn about the *mysqli* interface in Chapter 15.

Establishing a Connection to the Database

The opening lines of `results.php` consist of HTML code. Then comes the first task within the PHP code, which is to create a link to MySQL. For this purpose, the PHP function *mysql_connect* is used, to which three pieces of information are passed:

- user name
- password
- computer name (host name)

If you have installed MySQL on the local computer and have not yet secured it with a password, then you may simply pass empty character strings as parameters. The specification of the computer name is necessary only if the web server (that is, Apache) is running on a different computer from the one that is running MySQL.

The function `mysql_connect` returns an identification number that is stored in the variable *link*. In the present example, *link* is used only to identify possible problems in creating the link. In this case, an error message is displayed, and the PHP code is ended abruptly with *exit*. Otherwise, the active database is selected with *mysql_select_db*. (MySQL usually manages several databases, and the effect of *mysql_select_db* is that the following commands automatically refer to *test_vote*.)

Evaluating the Data and Storing It in the Database

The next task in `results.php` consists in evaluating the data in the questionnaire and storing them in the database. The data are passed to the elements *submitbutton* and *vote* of the global field *$_POST*. (Compare the *name* and *value* attributes in `vote.html`.) The auxiliary function *array_item* is used to read out this field.

If `results.php` was called via the questionnaire of `vote.html`, then the variable *submitbutton* contains the character string "OK". For the sake of security, a validation test is also carried out for the variable *vote*. (For example, a participant may have forgotten to select one of the choices.) If *vote* contains a valid value, then this value is stored in the database. The SQL command to accomplish this will look something like the following:

```
INSERT INTO votelanguage (choice) VALUES (3)
```

What *INSERT INTO* accomplishes is to insert a new data record (a new row) into the table *votelanguage*. The expression *(choice)* specifies all of the fields of the *data* record for which values should be passed by means of the command *VALUES (…)*. Since MySQL takes responsibility for the field *id* (attribute *AUTO_INCREMENT*; see above), in this example *choice* is the only field affected. Of course, instead of "3" the value of the variable *vote* will be placed, depending on which of the programming languages was selected in the questionnaire. The SQL command thus constructed is then passed along to MySQL with the PHP function *mysql_query*.

■**Tip** If you have never had dealings with SQL and thus are unfamiliar with the syntax of SQL commands, fear not. In Chapter 9 you will find an extensive introduction to SQL. The two commands used in this chapter, namely, *INSERT* and *SELECT*, are presumably more or less self-explanatory.

The columns *id* and *ts* of the *votelanguage* table are automatically filled in by MySQL: *id* with the unique running number, and *ts* with the current time.

Displaying the Survey Results

Regardless of whether the questionnaire has just been evaluated, the previous results of the survey must be able to be displayed. (If a new vote has been cast, it will be taken into account.)

First a check must be made as to whether the *votelanguage* table contains any data at all. (When the questionnaire is first placed on the Internet, no votes have yet been cast.) The required SQL query looks like this:

```
SELECT COUNT(choice) FROM votelanguage
```

The SQL command is again executed with *mysql_query*. What is new this time is that a link to the result of the query is stored in the variable *result*. The result of a *SELECT* command is, in general, a table. However, in the above example this table consists of merely a single row and a single column. (Furthermore, *result* contains only an ID number, which is used as a parameter in various other *mysql_xxx* functions. It is the task of PHP to take care of the actual management of the result.)

To evaluate the result, the function *mysql_result($result, 0, 0)* is used, by which the element in the table from the first row and first column is read. (With MySQL functions, counting begins with 0.)

Provided that the *votelanguage* table is not empty, a loop is executed to report the percentage of votes cast for each programming language. The requisite SQL queries look similar to the one above, only now the number of data records that contain a particular value of *choice* (for example, 3) is counted:

```
SELECT COUNT(choice) FROM votelanguage WHERE choice = 3
```

For evaluation, *mysql_result* is used. Then a bit of calculation is necessary to round the percentages to two decimal places.

Program Code (results.php)

```
<!DOCTYPE HTML PUBLIC "-//W3C//DTD HTML 4.0//EN">
<!- php/vote/results.php ->
<html><head>
<meta http-equiv="Content-Type"
      content="text/html; charset=iso-8859-1" />
<title>Survey Result</title>
</head><body>
<h2>Survey Result</h2>
<?php

  $mysqlhost="localhost";
  $mysqluser="root";
  $mysqlpasswd="";
  $mysqldbname="test_vote";
```

```php
// Create connection to the database
$link =
  @mysql_connect($mysqlhost, $mysqluser, $mysqlpasswd);
if ($link == FALSE) {
  echo "<p><b>Unfortunately, a connection to the
        database cannot be made. Therefore, the results cannot be
        displayed at this time. Please try again later.</b></p>
        </body></html>\n";
  exit();
}
mysql_select_db($mysqldbname);

// if questionnaire data are available:
// evaluate + store
function array_item($ar, $key) {
  if(array_key_exists($key, $ar)) return($ar[$key]);
  return('');  }

$submitbutton = array_item($_POST, 'submitbutton');
$vote = array_item($_POST, 'vote');

if($submitbutton=="OK") {
  if($vote>=1 && $vote<=6) {
    mysql_query(
      "INSERT INTO votelanguage (choice) VALUES ($vote)");
  }
  else {
    echo "<p> Not a valid selection. Please vote
          again. Back to
          <a href=\"vote.html\">questionnaire</a>.</p>
          </body></html>\n";
    exit();
  }
}

// display results
echo "<p><b> What is your favorite programming language
      for developing MySQL applications?</b></p>\n";

// Number of votes cast
$result  =
  mysql_query("SELECT COUNT(choice) FROM votelanguage");
$choice_count = mysql_result($result, 0, 0);

// Percentages for the individual voting  categories
if($choice_count == 0) {
  echo "<p>No one has voted yet.</p>\n";
}
else {
  echo "<p>$choice_count individuals have thus far taken part
        in this survey:</p>\n";
  $choicetext = array("", "C/C++", "Java", "Perl", "PHP",
                      "VB/VBA/VBScript", "Andere");
```

```
    print("<p><table>\n");
    for($i=1; $i<=6; $i++) {
      $result  = mysql_query(
        "SELECT COUNT(choice) FROM votelanguage " .
        "WHERE choice = $i");
      $choice[$i] = mysql_result($result, 0, 0);
      $percent = round($choice[$i]/$choice_count*10000)/100;
      print("<tr><td>$choicetext[$i]:</td>");
      print("<td>$percent %</td></tr>\n");
    }
    print("</table></p>\n");
  }
?>
</body>
</html>
```

The Resulting HTML Code

If you are relatively inexperienced with PHP, you might find it helpful to have a look at the resulting HTML code (that is, what the user finally sees in the browser, as depicted in Figure 3-2) as an aid to understanding the program presented above.

```
<!DOCTYPE HTML PUBLIC "-//W3C//DTD HTML 4.0//EN">
<!- results.php ->
<html><head>
<meta http-equiv="Content-Type"
      content="text/html; charset=iso-8859-1" />
<title>Survey Results</title>
</head><body>
<h2>Survey Results</h2>
<p><b>What is your favorite programming language
        for the development of MySQL applications?</b></p>
<p>17 people have thus far taken part
          in this survey:</p>
<p><table>
<tr><td>C/C++:</td><td>17.65 %</td></tr>
<tr><td>Java:</td><td>11.76 %</td></tr>
<tr><td>Perl:</td><td>17.65 %</td></tr>
<tr><td>PHP:</td><td>41.18 %</td></tr>
<tr><td>ASP[.NET] / C# / VB[.NET] / VBA:</td><td>11.76 %</td></tr>
<tr><td>Other:</td><td>0 %</td></tr>
</table></p>
</body></html>
```

Ideas for Improvements

Layout: It may have occurred to you that I have not paid much attention to the appearance of things in this example. Naturally, the results of the survey could be presented in a colorful bar graph. However, that has nothing to do with the subject of this book, namely, MySQL. Introductions to the attractive presentation of HTML documents, to the PHP programming of graphics libraries, and the like can be found in quantity in a number of books on HTML and PHP (and, of course, on the Internet).

Questionnaire and Results on a Single Page: It is certainly possible to execute all the elements of our survey—questionnaire, evaluation, and presentation of results—-with a single PHP script. However, as a rule, it is a good idea for the participants not to see the previous results before casting a vote.

Options: You could make the survey more interesting or more informative by offering additional opportunities for input. In our example, there could be a text field for the input of other programming languages or perhaps a text field for comments or for information about the professional background of the participants. However, you must consider that the more you ask, the more superfluous data you will collect. (If someone does not want to answer a required question, you may get a deliberately false response.)

Multiple Selection: In principle, you could construct the questionnaire in such a way that a participant could select more than one programming language. In the HTML form you would use check boxes instead of radio buttons. However, the necessary changes in the design of the database are somewhat more complicated. The table *votes* must now be able to store in each data record an arbitrary collection of programming languages. It would be easy, though inefficient, to reserve a separate column in the table for each programming language and then store the value 1 or 0 depending on whether or not the language was voted for. If you do not want the *votes* table to take up any more space in memory than necessary, then you could store a multiple selection as a combination of bits. For this purpose, MySQL offers the data type (*SET*). But this option would make the program code for the storage and evaluation of the survey results considerably more complicated.

Protection Against Manipulation: In most Internet surveys, the goal is not to obtain information but to promote interest, and thereby obtain a large number of accesses to one's web page. In such cases, there is not much point in protecting the survey against misuse. However, if you wish to provide such protection, you have a number of possibilities:

- You could place a "cookie" containing a random number on the participant's computer and store this same value in the database. In this way, an attempt to cast additional votes could be easily caught. (The disadvantage is that many Internet users are opposed to cookies and delete all cookies at startup or else prohibit their placement altogether.)

- You could require a login with e-mail address and password. Only those who have registered may vote. You store information in the database on who has already voted. (The disadvantage is that Internet users tend to have little patience for logins. Not many Internet users would give their e-mail address simply for the privilege of filling out your questionnaire.)

It is true, in general, that you cannot completely prevent such manipulation of a survey. That is, every system of security can be gotten around by someone who puts enough effort into the attempt.

▮Tip   You will find an extensive example that implements the ideas mentioned in this section in the book *PHP 5 & MySQL*, which I coauthored with Hernd Öggl (Addison-Wesley, 2005). Moreover, there are many complete PHP solutions for questionnaires available, both with and without MySQL support. Before you set about reinventing the wheel, you might want to take a look at some of the PHP sites on the Internet, for example the following: `http://phpsurveyor.sourceforge.net/`.

## PART 2

Administrative Tools and User Interfaces

CHAPTER 4

■■■

mysql, mysqladmin, and mysqldump

The end user should never see MySQL as a program. Instead, a convenient program or several web sites should be used to provide access to the database, assist in the input of new data, and execute backups.

For such tasks, you can use the commands mysql, mysqladmin, and mysqldump presented in this chapter or the user interfaces presented in the following chapters: MySQL Administrator, MySQL Query Browser, and phpMyAdmin. (On the Internet you will find countless additional administration programs, some of which are free, others commercial. In this book there is unfortunately insufficient space to describe these tools.)

The commands mysql, mysqladmin, and mysqldump are for use in text mode. They must be executed in an input or console window for Unix/Linux. There are neither menus nor other forms of assistance. What at first glance seems a drawback is in many circumstances an advantage: The commands can be employed over a network (e.g., in an ssh console). Furthermore, they are suitable for automating administrative tasks (script programming). Finally, the programs are so small that you can launch them in several windows to try out something quickly. To experienced MySQL users these programs are as necessary as a Swiss army knife is to a mountain climber.

■**Tip** In this chapter you will learn about the commands mysql, mysqladmin, and mysqldump only superficially. However, these commands offer many additional possibilities, as will be described elsewhere in the book. For example, you can import and export text files and make backups with all sorts of options. These application possibilities are demonstrated in Chapter 14. A reference to all options and functions follows in Chapter 22.

---

mysql

In the previous chapter you became acquainted with mysql as a simple command interpreter, with which you can execute SQL commands and view the resulting tables in text mode. This section gives some further tips for using mysql with MySQL.

Once again, just to be clear, mysql is a relatively small program that serves only to send commands to the MySQL server and display the results. mysql is therefore *not* the MySQL server, but a client program that communicates with the server.

Launching mysql

Unix/Linux: On Unix/Linux systems you simply specify `mysql` in a console window and press Return. Other command tools are also launched in this way (`mysqladmin`, `mysqldump`). The programs are normally installed in the directory `/usr/bin`, so that it is unnecessary to provide the name of the directory. See Figure 4-1.

Windows: `mysql` and some other command tools are stored in the directory `C:\Programs\`
`MySQL\MySQL Server n.n\bin`. This directory is normally not a part of the *PATH* system variable, which contains all directories with executable programs. There are the following possibilities for launching the programs:

- The easiest and most convenient method is to execute the command in PROGRAMS |
  MYSQL | MYSQL SERVER N.N. | MYSQL COMMAND LINE CLIENT. This starts `mysql` with the
  options `-u root -p`. After the launch, you must specify the *root* password. The menu
  command unfortunately does not allow you to start `mysql` with other options or to
  execute a command other than `mysql`.

- You can open an input request window (PROGRAMS | ACCESSORIES | COMMAND PROMPT)
  and there give the name of the program and the complete path:

  ```
  > C:\Programs\MySQL\MySQL Server n.n\bin\mysql.exe
  ```

- You can save some typing and use Explorer with Drag&Drop to copy the name into the
  window. Alternatively, you can first use CD to move into the directory `C:\Programs\`
  `MySQL\MySQL Server n.n\bin`.

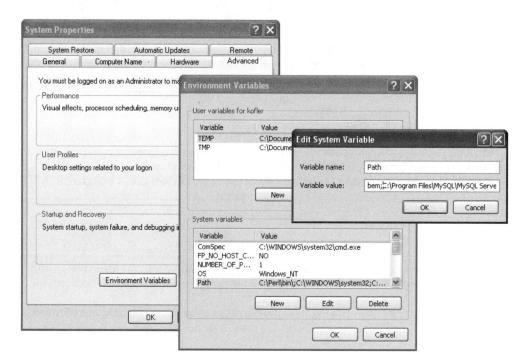

Figure 4-1. *Setting the Windows system variables*

- In the long run, it will prove most convenient to extend the system variable *PATH* to the MySQL tools. To do this execute START | SETTINGS | CONTROL PANEL | SYSTEM, click in the dialog sheet ADVANCED, select the system variable *PATH* with a double click, and add the MySQL `bin` directory (see Figure 4-1). All directories in *PATH* must be separated by semicolons.

From now on, in every command window (regardless of the current directory or drive), input of the MySQL command name is sufficient to execute it.

mysql Options

When you start `mysql` you can use various options. To get a connection to the server you generally need two options, namely, `-u name -p`. The following list describes these and a few additional options and also gives some background information. These options are not only for `mysql`, but also for `mysqladmin`, `mysqldump`, and most other command tools.

-u name or –user=name: This option specifies which MySQL user name you wish to use. Depending on how MySQL is configured, there can be many MySQL users (see also Chapter 11). If no users have yet been set up or if you have administrative tasks to perform, use the user name *root*. This user exists in every MySQL installation and is considered the system administrator.

If you omit the option `-u`, then under Unix/Linux the current login name will be used, while under Windows, it will be *ODBC*. A login is possible only if users with these names have been set up on the MySQL server.

-p: This option has the effect that when `mysql` is started, a password can be given. This option is absolutely required if MySQL users have passwords.

Alternatively, you can give the password when the command is given with `password="xxx"`. This is insecure, however, since the password appears in plain text in the process or task bar.

-h computername or –host=computername: `mysql` can also communicate with the MySQL server when it is running on another computer. For this you must specify the name or IP address of this computer with the option `-h`.

For this to function, some conditions must be satisfied: First, *computername* must be reachable over the network. You can check that independently with the command `ping computername`. Second, the TCP/IP port 3306 must be usable. If there is a firewall between your computer and the computer on which the MySQL server is running, it can happen that the firewall blocks communication over this port.

Third, the external MySQL server must be configured so that it permits connections from your local computer. This is not the default case! Extensive information on the correct configuration of access rights is given in Chapter 11.

–protocol=name: This option specifies which communication protocol you wish to use. It is seldom necessary to give this option, since `mysql` usually chooses the correct protocol by default.

If the program `mysql` and the MySQL server are running on different computers, then the only relevant protocol is `tcp` (that is, communication takes place over TCP/IP). `mysql` uses this protocol by default when the option `-h` is given.

On the other hand, if `mysql` is running on the same computer as the server, then, depending on the MySQL server configuration, there exist the alternatives `socket` (Unix/Linux) and `pipe` or `memory` (both Windows). Without the option `-h`, `mysql` uses by default under Windows the protocol `tcp`, while under Unix/Linux it uses `socket`.

-P n or –port=n: This option specifies which TCP/IP port number is to be used. This option is necessary only in exceptional cases, when the MySQL server does not use the default port 3306. This option has an effect only if communication is over TCP/IP.

–default-character-set=name: This option tells which character set will be used for communication between mysql and the MySQL server. This should be the same character set that is used by default in the input window (Windows) or the console window (Linux). Among the character sets supported by MySQL are *latin1* (ISO-8559-1), *latin2* (ISO-8559-2), *utf8* (Unicode), and *cp850* (the DOS character set for Western Europe).

databasename: As a final parameter, you can pass the name of a database to mysql (without options). This database then will be the default database for all future commands. You can change the default database at any time thereafter with the command *USE databasename*.

Example: With the following command you can create a connection to the MySQL server on the computer *uranus*. As default database, *mylibrary* is used, and as character set, Unicode (*utf8*):

```
> mysql -u root -p -h uranus –default-character-set=utf8 mylibrary
Password: ********
```

Using mysql Interactively

The program mysql is launched as usual with the options -u and -p. Now SQL commands can be input. The commands can extend over several lines and must be terminated with a semicolon. If you have not specified the desired default database at the start of mysql, then execute *USE databasename* as your first command:

```
> mysql -u root -p
Enter password: xxx
Welcome to the MySQL monitor.  Commands end with ; or \g.
Your MySQL connection id is 248 to server version: 5.0.2-alpha-standard
Type 'help;' or '\h' for help. Type '\c' to clear the buffer
mysql> USE mylibrary;
Database changed
 mysql> SELECT titelID, title FROM titles LIMIT 10;
+---------+----------------------------------------+
| titleID | title                                  |
+---------+----------------------------------------+
|      11 | A Guide to the SQL Standard            |
|      52 | A Programmer's Introduction to PHP 4.0 |
|      19 | Alltid den där Annette                 |
|      51 | Anklage Vatermord                      |
|      78 | Apache Webserver 2.0                   |
|       3 | Client/Server Survival Guide           |
|      63 | Comédia Infantil                       |
|      77 | CSS-Praxis                             |
|      86 | Dansläraren Återkomst                  |
|      80 | Darwin's Radio                         |
+---------+----------------------------------------+
10 rows in set (0.01 sec)
```

■Caution You can do a great deal of damage with `mysql`. For example, `DELETE FROM tablename` deletes all data records from the table *tablename* without so much as a "by your leave." And what is more, there is no way of undoing the damage. If you would like to avoid such fatal errors, you should use `mysql` with the option `--i-am-a-dummy`. Then `mysql` permits the commands *UPDATE* and *DELETE* only if they are protected with the keyword *WHERE* or *LIMIT*. There are some additional security limitations.

In addition to the SQL commands, you can use some commands offered by `mysql` (for example, *source filename*). These commands do not need to be terminated with a semicolon. As with SQL commands, these are case-insensitive. Each of the commands exists in a two-character short form, such as \h for *help*. In the short form the commands can also be given at the end of a line; the only place they must be written out in full is at the beginning of a new line. Table 4-1 gives only the most important commands. A list of all the commands can be found in Chapter 22.

Table 4-1. *The Most Important mysql Commands*

Abbreviation	Command	Interpretation
\c	clear	terminates input of command.
\h	help	displays a list of commands.
\q	exit or quit	ends `mysql`. Under Unix/Linux this also works with Ctrl+D.
\s	status	shows status information on the MySQL server.
\T [f]	tee [filename]	logs all input and output into the specified file.
\t	notee	ends tee. The logging can be resumed at any time with tee or \T. The file name does not have to be given again.
\u db	use database	makes the specified database the default.
\. fn	source filename	executes the SQL commands contained in the given file. The commands must be separated by semicolons.

Simplifying Input

Terminating Input: It often occurs, particularly with multiline commands, that you note an error in a line above the one that you are typing and as a result wish to terminate the entire input (so that you can start all over again). To accomplish this, regardless of the cursor position, simply input \c and press Return. Note, however, that \c does not have this effect within a character string enclosed in single or double quotation marks.

History Function: `mysql` remembers the last commands that were input (even after program termination!). These commands can be recalled with the cursor keys ↑ and ↓.

Terminating mysql

With *exit* or *quit* or *\q* or Ctrl+D (the last of these only under Unix/Linux) you can terminate `mysql`. Under Windows you can also simply close the command window.

Tips for Using mysql Under Unix/Linux

Scroll Region: Under Unix/Linux, mysql is usually executed in a shell window (see Figure 4-2). Every such program (xterm, console, gnome-terminal, etc.) offers the possibility of setting the number of lines that are kept in temporary storage. If you provide a large enough value, then you can use a scroll bar to examine previously input commands and copy them with the mouse to the clipboard.

```
[redhat@saturn ~]$ mysql -u root -p
Enter password:
Welcome to the MySQL monitor.  Commands end with ; or \g.
Your MySQL connection id is 1 to server version: 5.0.2-alpha-standard

Type 'help;' or '\h' for help. Type '\c' to clear the buffer.

mysql> SET names utf8;
Query OK, 0 rows affected (0.02 sec)

mysql> USE mylibrary;
Reading table information for completion of table and column names
You can turn off this feature to get a quicker startup with -A

Database changed
mysql> SELECT titleID, title FROM titles LIMIT 10;
+---------+-------------------------------------+
| titleID | title                               |
+---------+-------------------------------------+
|      11 | A Guide to the SQL Standard         |
|      52 | A Programmer's Introduction to PHP 4.0 |
|      19 | Alltid den där Annette              |
|      51 | Anklage Vatermord                   |
|      78 | Apache Webserver 2.0                |
|       3 | Client/Server Survival Guide        |
|      63 | Comédia Infantil                    |
|      77 | CSS-Praxis                          |
|      86 | Dansläraren Återkomst               |
|      80 | Darwins Radio                       |
+---------+-------------------------------------+
10 rows in set (0.00 sec)

mysql> 
```

Figure 4-2. *Use of the MySQL command interpreter under Linux in a console window*

Keyboard Shortcuts: Under most operating systems, mysql relies on the readline library. Therefore, the usual suspects in the lineup of Unix/Linux keyboard shortcuts are available for editing input (for example, Ctrl+K for deleting a line from the cursor location to the end, Ctrl+Y for restoring the most recently deleted text). Most of the keyboard shortcuts correspond to those under the editor Emacs.

Furthermore, names of tables and columns can be automatically completed with Tab, after the initial letters have been input.

Private Configuration File: Frequently used settings or options (such as user name and password) can be stored under Unix/Linux in a user-specific configuration file with the name ~/.my.cnf. Options related to all client tools are placed in the group [client], while those relating specifically to mysql go into the group [mysql]. The following lines provide an example. (Further details on creating configuration files can be found in Chapter 22.)

```
# Options for all MySQL tools
[client]
user=username
password=xxx
# Options for mysql
[mysql]
database=mydatabase
```

Since the file contains a password in plain text, it should be protected from prying eyes:

```
user$ chmod 600 ~/.my.cnf
```

Problems with Character Sets

With many current Linux distributions, the character set *utf8* is the default; otherwise, it is generally *latin1* (ISO-8559-1) or *latin9* (ISO-8559-15). If communication between mysql and the MySQL server does not take place in a single character set, then international special characters will get screwed up. The problem can be simply solved in one of two ways:

- The simplest approach is to start mysql as usual and then execute the SQL command *SET NAMES 'name'*, where *name* is the character set valid in the console. MySQL supports considerably fewer character sets than Unix/Linux, but in most cases, *latin1* or *utf8* will work. (MySQL does not know about the character set *latin9*. Use instead *latin1*. The only difference between the two character sets is the euro symbol.)

- The other variant consists in starting mysql with the option –default-character-set=name, where instead of name, again the desired character set is given.

Which character set is being used for communication between mysql and the MySQL server can be determined in mysql quite easily with the command *status*. The relevant lines are *Server* and *Conn. character set*.

Tips for Using mysql Under Windows

mysql is executed in an input window. (The window is sometimes called a command window or DOS window.) Many of the particulars of this program are configurable. You can access the configuration dialog by clicking on the title bar with the right mouse button (see Figure 4-3).

Color: In the command window are usually displayed white characters on a black background. That is not particularly easy on the eyes. If your eyes would prefer a white background and black characters, then consult the COLORS dialog sheet to change the setting.

Window Size: There is not much room in an 80 × 25 character display for representing the results of *SELECT*. The dialog sheet LAYOUT comes to your aid here, allowing you to change the window size.

Scroll Region: A larger window does nothing to increase the number of lines displayed. This setting can be changed by enlarging the SCREEN BUFFER SIZE in the dialog sheet LAYOUT. This sets the virtual window size. In the window, a segment of the virtual window is visible, and you can use the scroll bar to see previous commands and results.

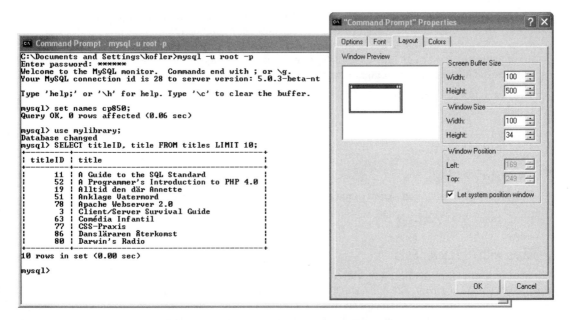

Figure 4-3. *Configuration of the MySQL command interpreter under Windows*

Clipboard: The command window offers the possibility of copying and pasting text to and from the clipboard. To copy, select a rectangular region with the mouse and simply press Return. To paste, click anywhere in the window with the right mouse button. For these shortcuts to function you must have activated the option QUICKEDIT MODE in the OPTIONS dialog sheet.

When you close the configuration dialog, you are asked whether the settings should hold only for the current window or whether they should be saved, with the result that the shortcut (link) to the input window will be changed. Choosing the second variant will ensure that in the future, the command window will have the properties described here.

Problems with Character Sets

The MySQL server generally uses the character set *latin1* or *utf8* by default. In the command window, however, what is used is the DOS-compatible character set *cp850*. For this reason, various special characters (such as äåèéöüß) are incorrectly displayed in the command window. What is worse, the DOS character set is also used in data records that are stored using an *INSERT* or *UPDATE* command in the command window. If you then look at those data records with another program (for example, with phpMyAdmin), the special characters are seen to be incorrect.

As usual, there is a variety of ways of solving the problem:

- The simplest solution is to start mysql as usual and then execute the SQL command *SET NAMES cp850*. This informs the MySQL server that the *cp850* character set is to be used for communication with mysql. The MySQL server will adapt all character strings as needed.

- You get the same result by starting `mysql` with the option `default-character-set=cp850`. You might, however, get the error message *Character set 'cp850' is not a compiled character set and is not specified in the … file.* That is, `mysql` has not found the file that describes the character set *cp850*. You can get around this by using the additional option `--character-sets-dir="C:/Programs/MySQL/MySQL Server 5.0/share/charsets"`, with the appropriate directory specification for your MySQL installation. This variant has the drawback of lots of typing.

- The third variant involves the typeface and character set of the input window.

  You have to change the typeface, because RASTER FONTS (the default) is incompatible with most character sets. Click on the window bar with the right mouse button, choose PROPERTIES, and set the typeface LUCIDA CONSOLE.

  Now you just have to set the proper character set *before* starting `mysql`. If the MySQL server uses *latin1* by default, then give the command `CHCP 65001` in the window to activate *Codepage 1252*. (A *Codepage* is the Windows expression for a character set. *Codepage 1252* corresponds primarily to the *Latin1* character set.) After these preparations, start `mysql`.

  If the MySQL server is so configured that the character set *utf8* is used, then execute `CHCP 65001`. (The Windows *Codepage 65001* corresponds to the Unicode character set *utf8*.)

Which character set is actually used for communication between `mysql` and the MySQL server can be determined with the command *status*. The relevant lines are *Server* and *Conn. characterset*.

Processing SQL Files with mysql

Up to now you have learned how to use `mysql` for interactive execution of SQL commands. However, you can also use `mysql` to process SQL commands that are located in a file. For this, start `mysql` as follows:

```
> mysql [options] databasename < file.sql
```

This will execute all SQL commands for the database *databasename* contained in `file.sql`. The file does not, of course, have to end in `.sql`. It is only the content that matters. In particular, all the commands must be separated by semicolons. (You can set a different delimiter in the file using the command *DELIMITER symbol*. This is necessary when the SQL file contains the command *CREATE FUNCTION, PROCEDURE*, or *TRIGGER*, since semicolons occur inside these commands.)

Reading In Database Backups

In practice, you will relatively often come across `*.sql` files containing a database backup done with `mysqldump`. To read in such files, you generally first create the new database with `mysqladmin`. The following two commands show how to proceed. (`mysqladmin` and `mysqldump` are introduced in the next section.)

```
> mysqladmin -u root -p create dbname
Password: *******
> mysql -u root -p dbname < backupfile.sql
Password: *******
```

■Tip Database backups made with a current version of mysqldump contain SQL commands for activation of the character set of the backup file. So you do not have to worry about the character set.

As for backups made with earlier versions of mysqldump or with another program (e.g., phpMyAdmin), this information can be absent. For a backup to be read in correctly, you must therefore use the option default-character-set=... when you start with the command mysql. If you don't know the character set that was used, try *latin1*. This character set was the default with MySQL 4.0 and was changed in relatively few installations:

```
> mysql -u root -p —default-character-set=latin1 name < backup.sql
```

Backups made with current versions of phpMyAdmin use the character set *utf8* by default.

---

mysqladmin

The program mysqladmin assists in various administrative tasks, for example, in creating and deleting databases and in changing passwords. The syntax is simple:

```
> mysqladmin [options] admincommand
```

The same options as for mysql are passed to mysqladmin for creating a connection to the server (-u, -p, -h, etc.). The *admincommand* that follows determines which task mysqladmin carries out. Here we will look at only three of the most important commands: *create* creates a new database; *drop* deletes a database; and *password* changes a password of the MySQL user designated via -u.

```
> mysqladmin -u root -p create newdatabase
Password: *******
> mysqladmin -u root -p drop testdatabase
Password: *******
Dropping the database is potentially a very bad thing to do.
Any data stored in the database will be destroyed.
Do you really want to drop the 'testdatabase' database [y/N] y
Database "'testdatabase'" dropped
> mysqladmin -u root -p password "new password"
Password: old password
```

mysqldump

The program mysqldump creates a backup of a database. The resulting backup file contains SQL commands for creating its tables and inserting the data. The syntax of mysqldump looks like this:

```
> mysqldump [options] dbname > backupfile.sql
```

The same options are passed to mysqldump as to mysql for creating a connection to the MySQL server (-u, -p, -h, etc.). In addition, you can control various details of the backup with additional options. For ordinary backups, however, that is usually unnecessary.

The resulting backup file is a text file. In current versions of mysqldump, the character set *utf8* is used by default. If you wish to use a different character set, you must specify this with default-character-set=....

CHAPTER 5

■■■■

MySQL Administrator and MySQL Query Browser

The programs MySQL Administrator and MySQL Query Browser are two relatively new MySQL user interfaces. As the name suggests, MySQL Administrator helps with administrative tasks. The MySQL Query Browser helps in assembling and trying out SQL commands.

Unlike other programs (like the program phpMyAdmin introduced in the next chapter), MySQL Administrator and MySQL Query Browser were developed directly by the firm MySQL AB. Thus these two programs have somewhat of an official character. They replace the old standbys WinMySQLadmin and MySQL ControlCenter from earlier versions of MySQL, neither of which will be developed further.

This chapter is based on version 1.0.19 of MySQL Administrator and version 1.1.5 of MySQL Query Browser, which became the current version in February 2005. Both versions were then considered stable (attribute *Generally Available*), though they continue to exhibit obvious problems and instabilities. In other words, the functionalities of the programs are promising, but crashes are a daily occurrence. Before you install the programs, you should certainly download the latest version of dev.mysql.com.

■**Tip** The programs MySQL Administrator and MySQL Query Browser simplify many administrative tasks and tests of SQL commands. Nevertheless, the use of these programs assumes that you are familiar with MySQL administration, database design, the security system, and the syntax of SQL. Relevant chapters for such fundamentals are Chapters 8 through 14. This chapter gives only a first taste of these topics without much on details or background.

Installation

Windows: The programs are available as a *.msi file (Microsoft Installer) under dev.mysql.com as a free download (GPL license). To install, open the file with a double click. Installation proceeds without difficulty and files are placed by default in the directory C:\Programs\MySQL. Then you can launch the program with START | PROGRAMS | MYSQL | *NAME*.

Linux (i386-Compatible RPM System): These programs are included with some current distributions of Linux and can be installed with the package management system of the distribution (e.g., YaST under SUSE).

If that is not the case, then precompiled RPM packages for i386-compatible processors are available at dev.mysql.com for download. To install them, download the *.rpm files and execute the command rpm -i packagename.rpm. Then you can execute the programs with the commands mysql-administrator and mysql-query-browser.

Linux (i386-Compatible Other Package System): For distributions with another package system (e.g., Debian), you will find precompiled `tar.gz` packages. Their installation is a bit more complicated. After download, unpack the archive into the directory `/usr/local`:

```
root# cd /usr/local
root# tar xzf mysql-query-browser-<version>-linux.tar.gz
root# tar xzf mysql-administrator-<version>-linux.tar.gz
```

Then change the variable *MYPATH* in the script files for launching the two programs:

```
...
# change in /usr/local/mysql-query-browser/bin/mysql-query-browser
...
MYPATH=/usr/local/mysql-query-browser/bin
# change in /usr/local/mysql-administrator/bin/mysql-administrator
...
MYPATH=/usr/local/mysql-administrator/bin
```

Finally, create two links so that every user of the system can easily launch the programs:

```
root# cd /usr/bin/X11
root# ln -s /usr/local/mysql-administrator/bin/mysql-administrator .
root# ln -s /usr/local/mysql-query-browser/bin/mysql-query-browser .
```

Unix/Linux/Mac OS X: If you are using a non-i386 system (e.g., PowerPC) or if you are using another Unix derivative, you must compile the program yourself. The source code together with installation instructions can be found at `dev.mysql.com`.

Stable versions for Mac OS X were not available as of February 2005, but they are being prepared. Friends of Apple will have to use other administrative tools for the time being.

Establishing a Connection

After launching the MySQL Administrator or the MySQL Query Browser, you must establish a connection to the MySQL server before you can use the programs (see Figure 5-1). This section treats both programs equally, since the mechanisms for making a connection are the same.

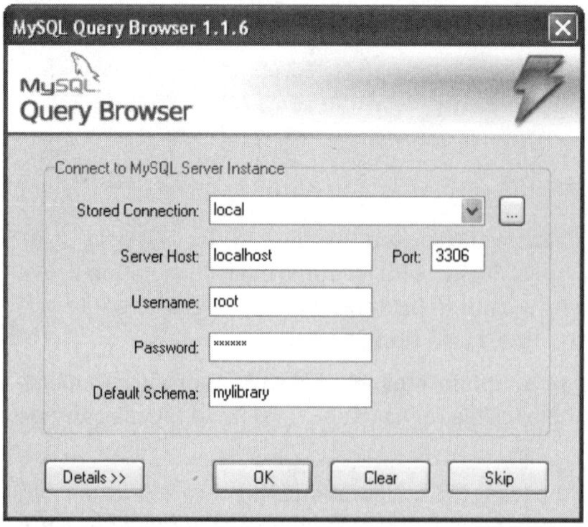

Figure 5-1. *Connection dialog for the MySQL Query Browser*

You need to provide the following information:

STORED CONNECTION: With the Windows version of MySQL Administrator you give the following connection parameters a name. Under this name you can call up the connection data at a later launch of the program and save having to input all the parameters anew. This field is then of particular practicality when you use the programs in combination with several MySQL servers.

With the Linux version it is somewhat more complicated to save the connection data. After you have given all additional parameters, you choose from a list box the entry SAVE THIS CONNECTION. Then a dialog appears in which you can give the connection a name.

SERVER HOST: Here you give the network name of the computer on which the MySQL server is executed. If it is a local computer, then specify *localhost*.

PORT: By default, the connection takes place via the TCP/IP protocol, where the MySQL default port 3306 is used. Another port number should be given only if your MySQL server is specially configured.

USERNAME AND PASSWORD: Here you give the MySQL user name (e.g., *root*) and the associated password. The password is not stored together with other connection data for reasons of security, and so it must be given each time.

There is an easier way. After the first connection is established, execute TOOLS | OPTIONS | GENERAL OPTIONS and activate the option STORE PASSWORDS. (This is, of course, a security risk, since someone could find the file in which the password is stored.)

DEFAULT SCHEMA (only with Query Browser): This input field specifies the name of the database for which you must execute SQL commands. The input is optional. If you leave the field empty, you can choose a database later with FILE | CHANGE DEFAULT SCHEMA.

DETAILS: Only in rare cases is it necessary to input optional connection parameters in this field. If the MySQL server is configured without TCP/IP for security reasons, give here, under Windows, the name of the *Named Pipe*, under Linux, the file name of the *Socket File*. (These terms will be explained in Chapter 11.)

Tip MySQL Administrator offers the possibility of launching the MySQL server from the local computer. To do so, press Ctrl in the connection dialog (see Figure 5-1). This will turn the OK button into a SKIP button, so that you can skip the connection dialog. (The connection dialog is useful only when the MySQL server is already running.) MySQL Administrator offers only a small fraction of the usual functionality.

MySQL Administrator

MySQL Administrator helps with management of a MySQL server (loading, determining the number of open connections, determining the status, etc.) as well as carrying out a number of management tasks. The program can be used for administration both on a local server and over a network.

Many functions of the program are available

- only for administration of local servers
- only for those with sufficient access privileges (*root*)
- only for those with sufficient operating system access privileges

For example, you can launch or halt a local MySQL server only if you are logged in as *root* (Unix/Linux) or system administrator (Windows).

The large number of functions of MySQL Administrator are dispersed among several modules. These modules are selected via a sidebar, and then make their functions available in one or more dialog sheets. These modules will be briefly introduced in the following sections.

Server Information

This module collects status information on connections to the MySQL server, its version, and the client library of MySQL Administrator (see Figure 5-2).

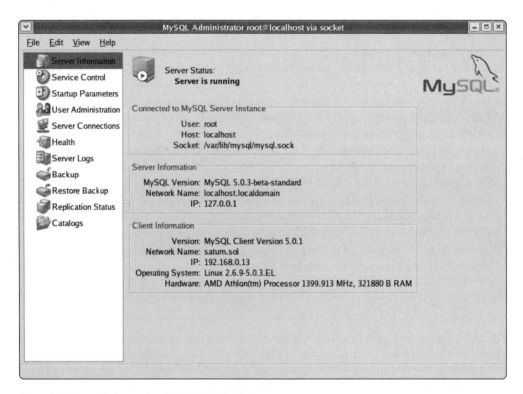

Figure 5-2. *Server information in MySQL Administrator*

Service Control

With this module you can start and stop the MySQL server. This works only for local MySQL servers (not for those running on another computer over a network) and only if MySQL Administrator was launched by someone with system administrator privileges. The Linux version of MySQL Administrator that I tested crashes during startup and shutdown of the MySQL server. The Windows version, on the other hand, works just fine.

In the Windows version of MySQL Administrator you can set a number of options in the dialog sheet CONFIGURE SERVICE. In the Linux version of MySQL Administrator this possibility is lacking. There you have to set the options in the dialog sheet STARTUP VARIABLES (see the next section).

Startup Variables

This module enables, in a number of dialog sheets (see Figure 5-3), a convenient changing of the MySQL configuration file, which usually is located at /etc/my.cnf (Unix/Linux) or C:\Programs\MySQL\ MySQL Server n.n\my.ini (Windows). The text file can contain countless options, of which the most important are described in Chapters 14 and 22. The options are evaluated by the MySQL server at startup. Changes to the file take effect only after a restart of the MySQL server.

If the file does not yet exist, it will be automatically created after a query. Each change to the file assumes that MySQL Administrator has write privileges to the file. If MySQL Administrator does not find the file, you will have to search for it yourself.

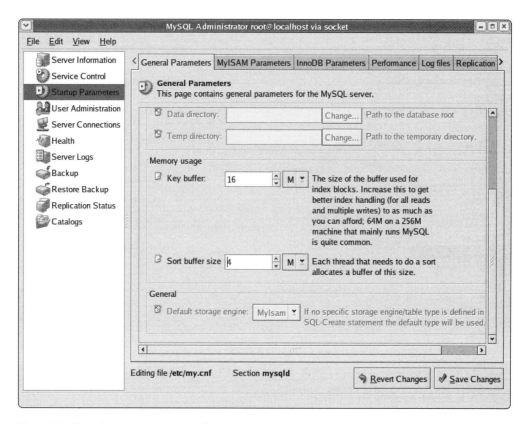

Figure 5-3. *Changing startup options of MySQL*

MySQL Administrator displays a small button before each option that tells whether the option is active (red X symbol). Inactive options are not stored in the configuration file. The MySQL server then uses internal default values for such options.

User Administration

This module helps in setting up new MySQL users and in changing the access privileges of existing users. This part of MySQL Administrator assumes that you understand the MySQL security system (see Chapter 11). The User Administration module differs in certain respects from comparable administration tools (e.g., phpMyAdmin), for which reason it is worthwhile going into some details of how it is used.

Changing a Password for Several User/Host Combinations

The MySQL access system makes it possible to grant a user different access rights depending on the location from which the user establishes a connection to the MySQL server. Therefore, MySQL Administrator shows a list of permitted host names for each user. In Figure 5-4 you see, for example, that the user *root* can establish a connection to the MySQL server from the computers *localhost*, *merkur1.sol*, and *192.168.80.1*.

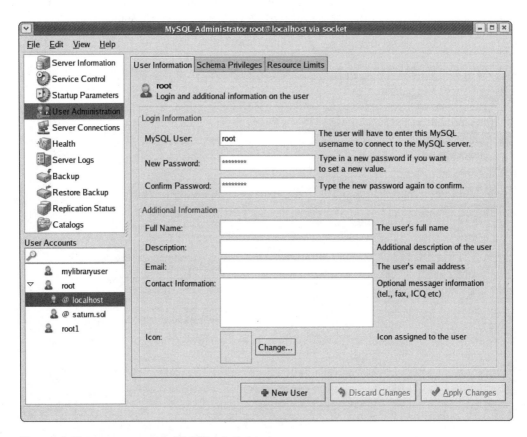

Figure 5-4. *User management in MySQL Administrator*

Basically, every combination of user name and host name can have its own password. In practice, however, it is usual to have a single password for each user, independent of the host names. MySQL Administrator makes it quite easy in such cases to change a user's password for all host names. You simply choose the user name, without host name, in the list USER ACCOUNTS (that is, without @*name*) and then change the password. This change is then valid for all host names.

Setting Up New Users

To set up a new user, click on the button NEW USER, specify a user name and password, and confirm the input with APPLY CHANGES. MySQL Administrator then creates a new user, where % is used as the host name. This allows the user to access MySQL from every location in the network. (The symbol %

is a wildcard for any host name. It is not directly visible in MySQL Administrator. Only a look at the table *mysql.user* shows what MySQL Administrator has done.)

Often, such free access is undesirable for security reasons. To limit access to certain computers, click with the right mouse button on the user name, execute ADD HOST, and provide the desired host name (e.g., *localhost*). The table *mysql.user* now contains two entries for the user name with the host names % and *localhost*. Then click on the user name again with the right mouse button and execute REMOVE HOST. This will delete the host name %.

Setting Privileges

MySQL distinguishes between global privileges (access rights), which hold for all databases, and object privileges, which hold for particular databases, tables, and columns. By default, MySQL Administrator shows object privileges only at the database level (dialog sheet SCHEMA PRIVILEGES). If you also wish to see global privileges as well as object privileges at the table and column level, you must set the corresponding options in the configuration dialog (TOOLS | OPTIONS | ADMINISTRATOR under Windows or FILE | PREFERENCES | ADMINISTRATOR under Linux).

To assign privileges to a user or take them away, first select the desired object in the relevant dialog sheet (e.g., a database). Then mark the desired privilege in the column AVAILABLE PRIVILEGES and push the arrow button in the column ASSIGNED PRIVILEGES (see Figure 5-5).

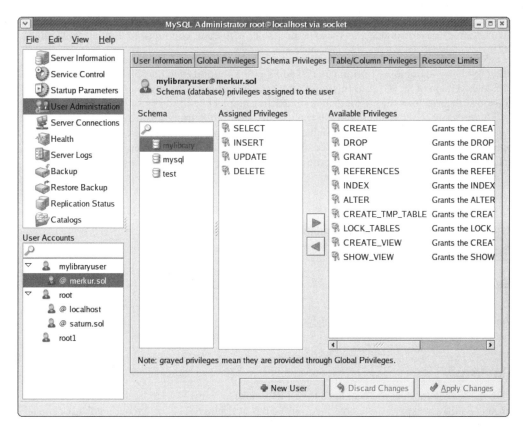

Figure 5-5. *Management of access privileges in MySQL Administrator*

Server Connections

This module consists of two dialog sheets:

- THREADS shows a list of all active MySQL threads (corresponds to the SQL command *SHOW PROCESSLIST*).

- USER CONNECTION contains a list of all currently active MySQL users together with their threads. These data as well come from *SHOW PRIVILEGES*, with the only difference being that the list is grouped by user name. One look will tell you which users have a large number of open connections.

Health

This module gives an overview in four dialog sheets of the use and load of the MySQL server.

- CONNECTION HEALTH shows in three charts the rate of the number of active connections, the amount of network traffic, and the number of SQL queries per second. The charts are of interest only when the MySQL server is heavily burdened. This is frequently the case in a production setting, but not on a development computer.

- MEMORY HEALTH shows the use of two important memory locations (*Query Cache* and *Key Buffer*).

- STATUS VARIABLES and SERVER VARIABLES use tables to manage countless additional status values.

Noteworthy in this module is that you can customize the graphical display with minimal effort. With the right mouse button you can add new graphs and even new dialog sheets. (The Windows version of MySQL Administrator offers considerably more convenience than the Linux version and also allows the customization of existing graphs.)

In the forms for custom graphs you can use all the variables from the dialog sheets STATUS VARIABLES and SERVER VARIABLES. The variable names must be placed in brackets. If you prefix the optional caret character (^), then instead of the absolute value of the variables, you get relative values since the previous refreshing of the graphs. For example, the formula for the *Query Cache Hitrate* looks like this:

```
(^[Qcache_hits] /
  (^[Qcache_hits] + ^[QCache_inserts] + ^[QCache_not_cached])) * 100
```

In this way, the relation between the number of cache hits and that of all cache inserts is calculated as a percentage (value between 0 and 100).

Server Logs

With this module you can conveniently read the logging data of the MySQL server. However, this functions only when the various logging functions have been activated. The relevant logging options can be changed in the dialog sheet LOG FILES of the module STARTUP PARAMETERS.

Backup

With the backup module you can, not surprisingly, make backups of your databases. The method of making a single backup is somewhat involved, so it is best suited for carrying out regular backups: First you have to create, using NEW PROJECT, a backup project. This project, which you give a name in the field PROJECT NAME, contains all the settings for the backup: which databases are to be backed up, which options hold for the backup, and when the backup should be regularly executed. (The last point is optional.)

Setting the Scope of the Backup

The backup project can encompass one or more databases. By default, all tables from the selected database are backed up. In the list box BACKUP CONTENT select individual tables (see Figure 5-6).

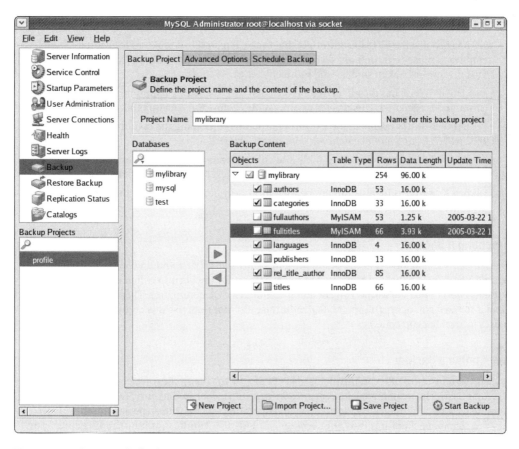

Figure 5-6. *Definition of a backup project*

Backup Options

In the dialog tab ADVANCED OPTIONS you can set the details of the backup. Here are some of the details:

> LOCK ALL TABLES has the effect that at the beginning of a backup all tables are blocked with the command *LOCK*. This makes possible a consistent backup of MyISAM tables. However, the entire database is locked during the backup. In addition, the start time of the backup depends on when the program receives a *LOCK* for all tables. (If the database is in use, first all *LOCK* operations must terminate.)

> SINGLE TRANSACTION has the effect that the entire backup is accomplished as a single large transaction. This ensures a consistent backup of InnoDB tables. However, such extensive transactions can have negative effects on the speed of database usage at the time of backup.

With a NORMAL BACKUP, each table is backed up individually. This is the most efficient method, but it has the disadvantage that changes in the database can be made during the backup. This can lead to inconsistencies among tables.

COMPLETE BACKUP has the effect that all tables of the selected databases are always backed up. The selection of individual tables in the dialog sheet BACKUP PROJECT is ignored in this case.

NO CREATEs results in the backup containing no *CREATE TABLES* commands.

NO EXTENDED INSERTs has the effect that for each record in a table, an individual *INSERT* command is used. (By default, several records are collected into a single *INSERT* command. This makes the backup smaller and more efficient.)

ADD DROP TABLE has the effect that before each *CREATE TABLE* command, a *DROP TABLE* command is executed. This deletes existing tables before the backup table is read in.

COMPLETE INSERTs results in the *INSERT* commands containing the column names (that is, *INSERT INTO tablename (colname1, colname2) VALUES …).*

ANSI QUOTES has the result that table and column names are set between ANSI-compatible quotation marks (*"name"*) instead of the MySQL-typical single quotes (*'name'*).

DISABLE KEYS results in table indices being temporarily deactivated when the data are read in. This saves some time with large tables.

Executing a Backup

To execute a backup, first save the project settings with SAVE PROJECT and then click on EXECUTE BACKUP NOW. You will then be requested to select a name for the file into which the backup is to be written. This is a text file with UTF8 encoding containing SQL commands. The backup file looks similar to the result of mysqldump. (MySQL Administrator does not use this command, however. It uses its own backup code.)

Automating a Backup

MySQL Administrator offers in the dialog sheet SCHEDULE the possibility of executing backups on a regular basis. The resulting backup files are written into a chosen directory. To this end, MySQL Administrator is automatically started up by the operating system with a special option.

For regular backups it is thus not necessary that MySQL Administrator be running constantly. Under Windows, it is the TASKPLANNER that deals with this (PROGRAMS I ACCESSORIES I SYSTEM TOOLS I SCHEDULED TASKS), while under Unix/Linux it is the cron system. However, in my tests, setting up regular backups has worked only with the Windows version of MySQL Administrator.

Restore

With this module you can read in previously backed up databases. In the dialog sheet RESTORE CONTENT you can specify after the selection of a backup file which table should be restored (by default all of them).

Normally, the tables will be read into the database that was used in the backup. However, sometimes it is desirable to read the tables into another database. If you wish to do this, in the Linux version of MySQL Administrator you give the name of the desired database in the field RESTORE SELECTED TABLES IN, while in the Windows version it is the field TARGET SCHEMA.

■**Caution** You should use this module only for backup files that you created with MySQL Administrator, not for backup files from other tools (phpMyAdmin, mysqldump, etc.). The RESTORE BACKUP module relies on the backup file following the conventions of MySQL Administrator. That is not always the case with other types of backups.

Replication Status

When the MySQL server is part of a replication system, this module shows the replication status. Background information on the topic of replication can be found in Chapter 14. In MySQL Administrator you can configure replication in the module STARTUP VARIABLES.

Catalogs

Behind the name *Catalogs* hides a module for managing databases and tables (Figure 5-7). With it you can get a quick look at existing databases, tables, indices, etc.

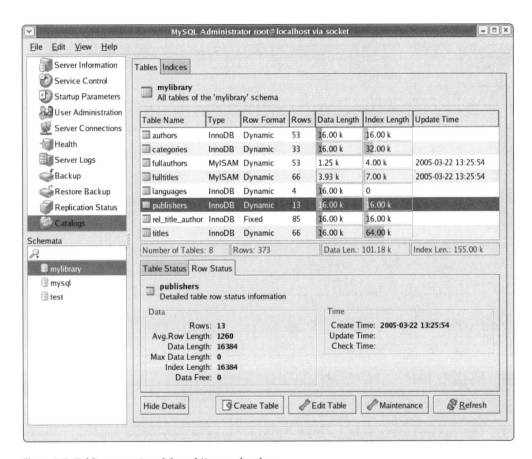

Figure 5-7. *Table properties of the* mylibrary *database*

This module was actually designed for creating new tables and modifying existing ones. In the version tested, however, these functionalities were difficult to use and also unstable. Until the situation changes, it is more efficient to type in the requisite *CREATE TABLE* and *ALTER TABLE* commands by hand or to use phpMyAdmin for database design.

MySQL Query Browser

The main task of the MySQL Query Browser is to help you in composing and testing SQL commands. Additionally, the program offers some auxiliary functions: you can insert data into tables, alter data in tables, test regular expressions (for the SQL operator *REGEX*), read MySQL help texts, etc.

Input and Execution of SQL Commands

To become familiar with the MySQL Query Browser, input a simple SQL command. SQL keywords are shown automatically in color. Execute the command with the EXECUTE button. The results are then displayed as a table (see Figure 5-8).

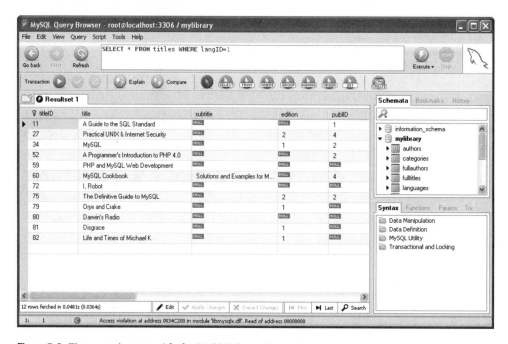

Figure 5-8. *First experiments with the MySQL Query Browser*

■Tip A few keyboard shortcuts make using the MySQL Query Browser more efficient and convenient:

Ctrl+Return executes the current SQL command (like EXECUTE).

Ctrl+Shift+Return executes the command, but shows the result in a new dialog sheet. This has the advantage that the results of previous commands remain available.

F11 changes the arrangement of the individual windows and enlarges the input region for SQL commands. This makes it easier to enter long SQL commands. If you press F11 again, the standard layout is restored.

F12 closes the individual windows except for the current result region. This makes it easier to read extensive results. Pressing F12 again restores the original window layout.

SQL commands with a mouse click: Using various arrow buttons you can assemble SQL commands with minimal typing effort. The following click sequences provide an example:

- Click on the button SELECT.
- Click on the columns *title*, *subtitle*, and *edition* of the *titles* table.
- Click on the button WHERE.
- Click on the column *langID* of the *titles* table.
- Input the *WHERE* condition =2 from the keyboard.
- Click on the button ORDER.
- Click on the column *title* of the *titles* table.

From these mouse clicks the MySQL Query Browser forms the following command, which you can now execute with EXECUTE:

```
SELECT t.title, t.subtitle, t.edition, t.catID FROM mylibrary.titles t
WHERE t.langID=2 ORDER BY t.title
```

Here *t* is an alias (abbreviation) for the table *mylibrary.titles*. This alias could also have been defined via *…FROM mylibrary.titles AS t …*. The MySQL Query Browser does not use the optional *AS*, which leaves some SQL pros perplexed. MySQL users familiar with SQL will prefer to type in SQL commands from the keyboard.

Exporting SELECT results: With FILE | EXPORT RESULTSET you can export the most recent result of *SELECT* commands in the formats CSV, HTML, XML, and Excel.

Comparing SELECT results: A special function of the MySQL Query Browser is that it can compare the results of two *SELECT* commands. To do this, first you must divide the result table with the context menu command SPLIT TAB VERTICALLY. Then execute an SQL command for each of the two domains. Both SQL commands must refer to the same column. Finally, execute QUERY | COMPARE RESULTSETS. The program marks records in white, green, and red depending on whether they are present in the second result, lacking in the second result, or additional records exist (see Figure 5-9).

BLOBs: The content of *BLOB* columns is not directly displayed. However, you can look at the data in a separate editor window or store them in a file.

Analyzing internal SQL execution: The button EXPLAIN gives internal information about the execution of the most recent SQL command. MySQL pros can thus find out which indices were used. The interpretation of the result is relatively difficult (see also Chapter 8).

Transactions: In addition to *SELECT* commands, you can also, of course, execute *UPDATE, INSERT, DELETE*, and other commands. In this case, the result table simply remains empty.

If you are working with InnoDB tables, you can also execute such commands as transactions with the buttons START/COMMIT/ROLLBACK TRANSACTION.

Using several result regions: With FILE | NEW QUERY TAB you open an additional SQL input field and result region. In this way you can test several SQL commands in parallel.

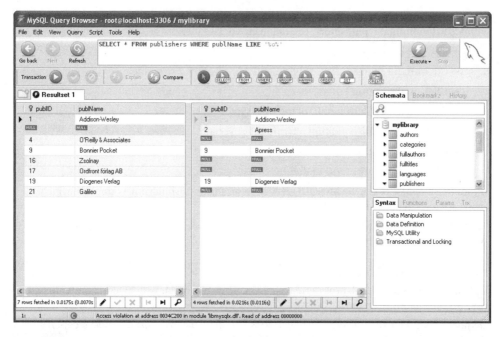

Figure 5-9. *Comparing SELECT results*

Changing Data in SELECT Results

With simple *SELECT* queries containing data from only one table (no *JOIN*s) and without *GROUP BY* or aggregation functions, the results can be changed. To do so, click on the EDIT button at the bottom of the table. This button is available only for results that can be changed.

To change a table field, you must activate it with a double click. You simply add new records to the end of the table. To delete a record (a row), execute DELETE ROWS with the right mouse button. Changes take effect only after you click the button APPLY CHANGES.

History and Bookmarks for SQL Commands

The MySQL Query Browser stores all executed SQL commands automatically in a so-called history list, which can be accessed via the sidebar at the right edge of the window (if the sidebar is wide enough). With Drag&Drop you can move the command into the input region and execute it with a double click.

You can give frequently used commands a name with Ctrl+B and store them in the bookmark list. This list is also found in the sidebar.

Executing Several Commands at Once (Scripts)

Open an SQL script input area with FILE | NEW SCRIPT TAB. There you can specify several SQL commands separated by semicolons. You can then execute these commands all at once (EXECUTE button) or step by step (SCRIPT menu).

These scripts represent several ordinary SQL commands, and not stored procedures (see the next section). The commands can be stored as a `*.sql` file using the FILE menu. The history and bookmark functions, however, are not available.

Stored Procedures

The MySQL Query Browser makes available a number of elementary functions for input of stored procedures. These functions will be considered in greater detail in Chapter 13. (Stored procedures are functions composed of several SQL commands that are controlled directly by the MySQL server. Stored procedures are thus a characteristic of the MySQL server, while scripts belong to the MySQL Query Browser.)

MySQL Help

The MySQL Query Browser can also be used for reading MySQL help (see Figure 5-10). The help texts are accessible via the lists SYNTAX and FUNCTIONS in the sidebar. These are extracts from the online documentation available at http://dev.mysql.com/doc/.

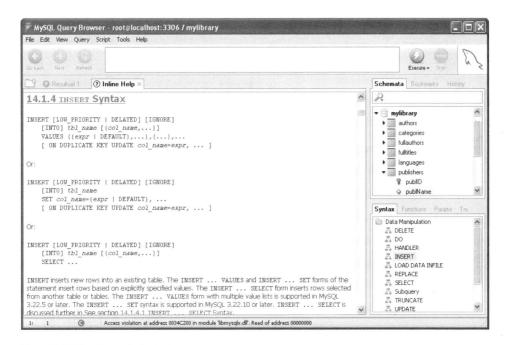

Figure 5-10. *Reading a help text*

CHAPTER 6

■■■

phpMyAdmin

The program phpMyAdmin is perhaps the best-beloved administrative tool for MySQL. You can create, modify, and delete databases and tables; insert, change, and delete data records; and import and export entire databases, among many other administrative tasks.

Which administrative functions are available in phpMyAdmin depends on the access privileges that phpMyAdmin has on the MySQL server. On your local test system, you will set up phpMyAdmin with *root* privileges; then you will be able to access all databases and carry out all administrative functions. On the other hand, with your Internet service provider (ISP) you will have phpMyAdmin access privileges only to your own databases.

phpMyAdmin comprises a number of PHP script files. The use of phpMyAdmin assumes that a web server (generally Apache) and PHP are installed. As with any PHP program, the following holds true for phpMyAdmin: Scripts are executed on the web server, but the resulting HTML pages can be accessed from any location. This shows the great advantage of phpMyAdmin: You can use the program for the administration of a MySQL server that is not running on the local computer but, for example, on that of your ISP. From the point of view of the ISP, phpMyAdmin is a local program and therefore has full access to the MySQL server.

The programs MySQL Administrator and MySQL Query Browser introduced in the previous chapter, in contrast, are suitable only for administration of an external MySQL server when database access is possible over a network. It is thus that your application generally fails: Most MySQL installations are so configured by the ISP for security reasons that only local database access is permitted (and not over the Internet).

This chapter describes the installation and configuration of phpMyAdmin 2.6.1 and the use of its most important functions. Please note that this version is still incompatible with MySQL 5.0. For this reason you cannot use or administer some new functions of MySQL 5, including views, stored procedures, and triggers. Another innovation of MySQL 4.1, namely, the management of geometric data (GIS functions) is not supported by phpMyAdmin. However, one can expect that there will be a new version of phpMyAdmin once MySQL 5.0.n becomes sufficiently widespread.

■**Tip** While phpMyAdmin simplifies interaction with the MySQL server, the assumption is that you understand the concepts of MySQL administration, database design, the security system, and the syntax of SQL. Fundamentals on these topics can be found in Chapters 8 through 14.

Installation and Configuration

This section assumes that Apache and PHP are already available on the computer on which php-MyAdmin is to be installed, and that PHP is able to communicate with MySQL (see Chapter 2).

Installing phpMyAdmin Files

You will find phpMyAdmin on the website http://www.phpmyadmin.net/ as a *.zip or *.tar.bz2 archive. All files in this archive must be copied into a subdirectory of the DocumentRoot directory of Apache. Depending on the operating system, this directory might be called Programs\Apache Group\ Apache2\htdocs, /var/www/html, or /srv/www/htdocs. The amount of space needed for phpMyAdmin after unpacking is about 8 MB.

> **Local Windows Computer:** Under Windows, use a ZIP file utility such as WinZip for unpacking the files, or with Windows XP use Windows Explorer (file manager). Then rename the new directory phpMyAdmin-version to a simpler name (in the following examples, simply phpmyadmin).

> **Local Linux Computer:** Under Linux, switch into the DocumentRoot directory and unpack the archive with tar:

> ```
> root# cd <documentroot directory >
> root# tar xjf phpMyAdmin-version.tar.bz2
> root# mv phpMyAdmin-version phpmyadmin
> ```

> phpMyAdmin is included with some Linux distributions. In such a case, you need only to install the relevant packages. Note, however, that the version provided may not be the most recent one.

> **Web Server with ISP:** Somewhat more complicated is installing phpMyAdmin on an external web server (assuming that phpMyAdmin is not already available there by default).

> > **ISP with Shell Login:** First load phpMyAdmin-version.tar.bz2 from phpmyadmin.net onto your local computer. Then transfer this file with an FTP client to the ISP. There, log in with ssh and execute the above three Linux-specific commands.

> > **ISP without Shell Login:** If you have ssh access to your account at the ISP, you must unpack phpMyAdmin on the local computer into an arbitrary directory. Then transfer the entire directory tree with an FTP client to the ISP. Since there are over five hundred files totaling about 8 MB, it will take awhile. Note that your FTP client should use binary (not text) mode.

Configuring phpMyAdmin

Before you can use phpMyAdmin, you must change some of the settings in the file config.inc.php in the phpMyAdmin installation directory. There are different variants that depend on how the password for MySQL access is specified. These variants are described in detail in the following two sections:

> **Password as plain text in config.inc.php (config authentication):** In the simplest case, you enter the MySQL user name and password directly into config.inc.php. This variant is recommended for a local test system or an individual ISP account.

> ***http*** and ***cookie*** **authentication:** With these two variants, the user must register in a login window before using phpMyAdmin. This has two immediate advantages: First, authentication is more secure, since the MySQL password does not have to be present in config.inc.php. Second, in this way, various users can register to administer their own databases. Thus these two methods are particularly recommended for ISPs that manage a number of accounts.

config Authentication

The lines of config.inc.php shown below show what is relevant for a minimal configuration. Normally, only the character strings shown in boldface have to be changed.

> **Address of phpMyAdmin:** *$cfg['PmaAbsoluteUri']* must contain the address under which php-MyAdmin is to be reached over the network. For the computer name, the actual computer in the network must be used (in my local test network it is *uranus.sol*). *localhost* is permissible only for a local installation that is not accessible over a network. Instead of *phpmyadmin*, the directory under which phpMyAdmin is reachable in your installation must be given (with case distinction and a slash at the end).

```
# changes in config.inc.php
...
# must contain the computer name and the phpMyAdmin installation directory:
$cfg['PmaAbsoluteUri'] = 'http://uranus.sol/phpmyadmin/';
...
```

> You can also attempt to leave *$cfg['PmaAbsoluteUri']* empty; in many cases, phpMyAdmin is able to determine the correct setting. However, phpMyAdmin will constantly give a warning. You can avoid this by setting the variable config.inc.php to *TRUE* in *$cfg['PmaAbsoluteUri_DisableWarning']*.

> **MySQL user name and password:** The following parameters specify how phpMyAdmin makes the connection to the MySQL server. Normally, you must give the password and can leave the other values as they are. If MySQL is not yet secured with a password, the password string must be left empty.

> If you are setting up config.inc.php for the phpMyAdmin installation at an ISP, then instead of *root*, you must give the MySQL user name that was given you by the ISP. You may have to give a computer name from the local network of your ISP instead of *localhost* (only if at your ISP the web server and the MySQL server are running on different computers).

```
$cfg['Servers'][$i]['host']      = 'localhost';  // MySQL computer name
...
$cfg['Servers'][$i]['auth_type'] = 'config';     // must be 'config'
$cfg['Servers'][$i]['user']      = 'root';       // MySQL user
$cfg['Servers'][$i]['password']  = 'xxx';        // MySQL password
...
```

> **Optional communication parameters:** If the MySQL server running under Unix or Linux is so configured that only local access over a socket file is possible (and not over TCP/IP), you must use the setting *socket* as *connect_type*. If phpMyAdmin does not find the socket file, then give its file name:

```
$cfg['Servers'][$i]['connect_type'] = 'socket'; // access over socket file
$cfg['Servers'][$i]['socket']       = '';       // socket file name
```

> If *localhost* is not given as the host name, the access takes place automatically over TCP/IP. You can now optionally specify the TCP/IP port over which the connection should be established.

■Note With RHEL 4, TCP/IP must be used, since Apache cannot access the MySQL socket file by default because of the SELinux configuration.

```
$cfg['Servers'][$i]['port']         = '3306'; // port number
$cfg['Servers'][$i]['connect_type'] = 'tcp';  // access over TCP/IP
```

mysql or mysqli interface: Since version 5, PHP supports two interfaces (modules) for communicating with MySQL: *mysql* and *mysqli*. Both variants will be presented in detail in Chapter 15. Keep in mind you should use the `mysqli` extension for MySQL 4.1 and newer. It is faster and more secure:

```
$cfg['Servers'][$i]['extension']     = 'mysqli'; // mysqli interface
```

Trying Out phpMyAdmin

Now you can test phpMyAdmin by typing the address `http://localhost/phpmyadmin/index.php` or `http://computername/phpmyadmin/index.php` in your web browser. On the start page of phpMyAdmin you can set the language and the layout of phpMyAdmin.

The start page should look something like Figure 6-1 (depending on the version of phpMyAdmin that you have installed and what access privileges phpMyAdmin has on the MySQL server). If all goes well, create a bookmark to this page to save having to type in the address in the future.

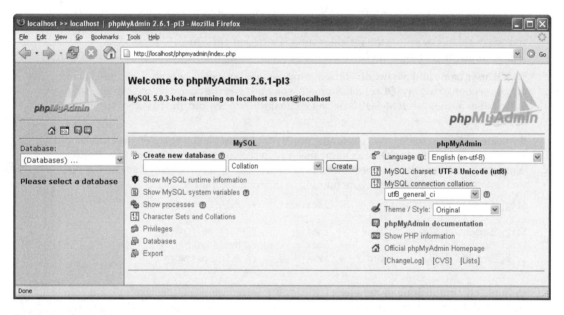

Figure 6-1. *phpMyAdmin start page*

If a warning is displayed on the phpMyAdmin start page that you are using a multibyte character set but the PHP extension *mbstring* is unavailable, you must activate this extension. In most Linux distributions it suffices to install the relevant package. Under Windows, the extension is already installed, but it must be explicitly activated. To do so, search in `php.ini` for the line *extension=php_mbstring.dll* and remove the prefixed semicolon. Then restart Apache, both under Unix/Linux and under Windows for the change to take effect.

Protecting the phpMyAdmin Directory

There is a security problem with the phpMyAdmin installation at your ISP: Not only you, but every web surfer who can guess the name of your phpMyAdmin directory can alter or delete your databases using phpMyAdmin.

You can prevent this by securing access to the phpMyAdmin directory with a password using an `.htaccess` file. Then everyone who wishes to use a browser to view a PHP file from the phpMyAdmin directory will have to log in and provide a password. (The login name and password are completely independent of the account login and from MySQL's internal access system. Details on the use of an `.htaccess` file can be found in Chapter 2.)

An additional security problem can result from the fact that the file `config.inc.php` contains your MySQL password in plain text. Sometimes, the computer of an ISP is configured in such a way that the web files can be accessed via FTP. In that case, the protection offered by `.htaccess` is insufficient. You must ensure that it is impossible to read `config.inc.php` with anonymous FTP.

Servicing Several MySQL Servers with phpMyAdmin

Host, user, and password entries for multiple MySQL servers are possible in `config.inc.php`. If you make such entries, then on the start page of MySQL there appears a listbox with the names of the computers whose MySQL servers can be managed. Selecting one of these names establishes a link to that server.

The variable *$cfg['ServerDefault']* determines the server that phpMyAdmin uses to establish a link at startup. If the variable is set to 0, then at startup phpMyAdmin initially sets no link, but merely presents a listbox with the selection of servers.

If you do not wish to have simply the computer name (array variable *host*) displayed in the listbox, then you can use *$cfg['Servers'][$i]['verbose']* to display a different character string.

Additional Configuration Options

In addition to the MySQL access data in `config.inc.php`, you can also set various options. The following list describes only the most important of these, together with their associated variables:

$cfg['Confirm'] = true/false: This variable specifies whether a confirmation query should be displayed before data are deleted (default: true).

$cfg['MaxRows'] = n: Specifies how many data records should be displayed per page as the result of a query (default is 30).

$cfg['ExecTimeLimit'] = n: Specifies how long the execution of the PHP code will be allowed to run (default is 300 seconds). The time is relevant primarily for time-intensive import/export commands.

$cfg['ShowBlob']=true/false: Specifies whether the contents of fields of type *xxxBLOB* are to be displayed (default: false).

$cfg['ProtectBinary'] = false/'blob'/'all': Specifies whether the contents of *BLOB* fields are to be write protected. By default (*'blob'*), *BLOB*s cannot be changed. The prohibition against change to any table content (regardless of data type) is effected by *'all'*, while *'false'* permits everything to be changed.

If you wish to change the width of the left column of the main window (by default, 200 pixels), open the file `themes/themename/layout.inc.php` and there change *$cfg['LeftWidth']*. In this column are displayed the listbox for database selection and the list of tables in the current database. Here `themename` gives the name of the layout (e.g., `original` or `darkblue_orange`).

http and Cookie Authentication

The configuration described in the previous section with *$cfg['Servers'][$i]['auth_type'] = 'config'* is simple, but it is inflexible if various users wish to manage their own databases, and insecure because user names and passwords appear in plain text in `config.inc.php`. If you wish to allow many users uniform access to phpMyAdmin, you should consider the two configuration variants described here.

Assumptions

- This section assumes that you are using at least phpMyAdmin 2.6.1 and MySQL 4.1.2. With older versions of the two programs, *http* and *cookie* authentication function only if you first set up an additional MySQL user that is able to read the tables *mysql.user*, *mysql.db*, and *mysql.tables_priv*. This user must be registered in `config.inc.php` together with a password (parameters *controluser* and *controlpasswd*). The precise process is described in the phpMyAdmin help file `Documentation.html` under *Using authentication modes*).

- *http* authentication assumes that the PHP interpreter is executed as an Apache module (and not as a CGI program). That is the case in current versions of PHP.

- For *http* authentication to function, the phpMyAdmin directory may not be protected via `.htaccess`. (If that is the case, then *http* authentication and that for `.htaccess` come into conflict.)

- *cookie* authentication is designed for the case in which *http* authentication is not possible (for example, when the Microsoft Internet Information Server (IIS) is used as the web server). This form of authentication assumes that the user permits cookies from phpMyAdmin.

http Authentication

To get phpMyAdmin to use *http* authentication, execute the boldface changes below in `config.inc.php`:

```
# in config.inc.php
$cfg['Servers'][$i]['controluser']  = '';       // empty since phpMyAdmin
$cfg['Servers'][$i]['controlpass']  = '';       //  version 2.6.1
$cfg['Servers'][$i]['auth_type']    = 'http';   // http authentication
$cfg['Servers'][$i]['user']         = '';       // empty!
$cfg['Servers'][$i]['password']     = '';       // empty!
```

All other settings in `config.inc.php` are as described in the previous section (thus the parameters *host, connect_type, port, extension,* etc.). Whenever you now wish to use phpMyAdmin, a web browser dialog appears (see Figure 6-2) in which you must input a MySQL user name and associated password. For further work in phpMyAdmin you then have the privileges of a MySQL user.

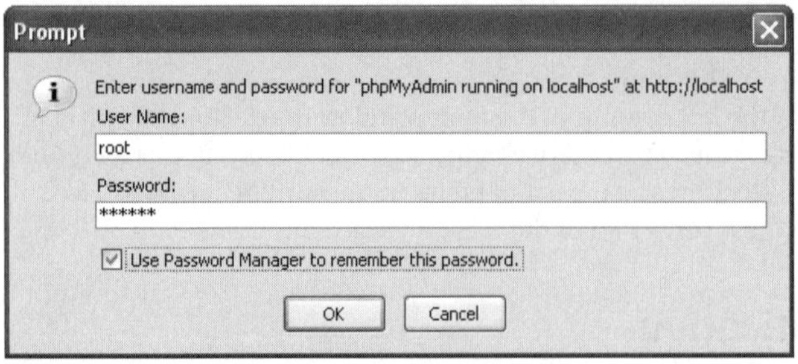

Figure 6-2. *Login dialog for http authentication*

The *http* authentication is more secure than the direct entry of a user name and password in `config.inc.php`. Note, however, that the login data in the *http* protocol are transmitted from the browser to the web server in plain text. You can attain greater security if your web server also supports the *https* protocol. In this case, the login data are encrypted before being transmitted.

■**Note** If an error occurs with phpMyAdmin 2.6.1 at login, an empty page will appear in the web browser. There is no way to repeat the login. You will have to close the web browser and restart it. It is also impossible to log out and then log in again. In this case as well you must restart the web browser.

---

cookie Authentication

For *cookie* authentication you must change the *auth_type* line in `config.inc.php`. Moreover, you must provide a character string for the parameter *blowfish_secret*. This string is used to encrypt the login data (user name and password) before they are stored as cookies on the local computer.

```
# in config.inc.php
$cfg['blowfish_secret']               = 'xxxxxx';
...
$cfg['Servers'][$i]['controluser']    = '';          // empty since pma
$cfg['Servers'][$i]['controlpass']    = 'xxx';       // version 2.6.1
$cfg['Servers'][$i]['auth_type']      = 'cookie';    // cookie authentication
$cfg['Servers'][$i]['user']           = '';          // empty!
$cfg['Servers'][$i]['password']       = '';          // empty!
```

The login input fields are displayed only within the phpMyAdmin start page (see Figure 6-3).

Figure 6-3. *Login dialog for cookie authentication*

User Management, Securing MySQL

MySQL employs a rather complex system for managing access privileges. The basic idea is that every user and every program that wishes to use MySQL must have an account. The account data consist of three pieces of information: a user name, a password, and the name of the client computer. (Here the client is the program that wishes to communicate with the MySQL server.) This section shows how you can register new phpMyAdmin users, change access privileges, and protect MySQL. Further details and basic information on user management can be found in Chapter 11.

Note Changes in the MySQL user management can be carried out only from a MySQL local installation if php-MyAdmin is running with *root* privileges. The MySQL installation of your ISP prevents other users from using this account. (If that is not the case, you should immediately seek another ISP.) Your MySQL account at your ISP does not allow you to change MySQL access privileges.

Securing MySQL

For a MySQL installation to be considered secure, it must satisfy the following conditions:

- There is no user without a password.

- There is no user without a user name. (If the *User* column has empty entries, then anyone can log in!)

- There is no user whose *Host* column contains % (which here indicates that the user can log in from anywhere in the network or the Internet).

- There are as few users as possible (in the ideal case only *root*) who have unrestricted access (all privilege columns contain Y). In managing access privileges in phpMyAdmin you can recognize unrestricted access privileges in that the column GLOBAL PRIVILEGES contains the value ALL PRIVILEGES.

After installation under Linux, MySQL recognizes four combinations of user and host names (see Table 6-1). None of these combinations is secured by a password. That is, all four violate the above-mentioned security rules.

Table 6-1. *Data Types for* bind_param

User Name (User)	Host Name (Host)	Access Privileges
root	*localhost*	unrestricted
root	*computer name*	unrestricted
empty (arbitrary name)	*localhost*	greatly restricted
empty (arbitrary name)	*computer name*	greatly restricted

For the sake of security, the two entries without user names should be deleted, and both *root* entries should be password protected. Of help here is phpMyAdmin's privilege management (see Figure 6-4). To navigate to this page, click in the phpMyAdmin start page on the link PRIVILEGES.

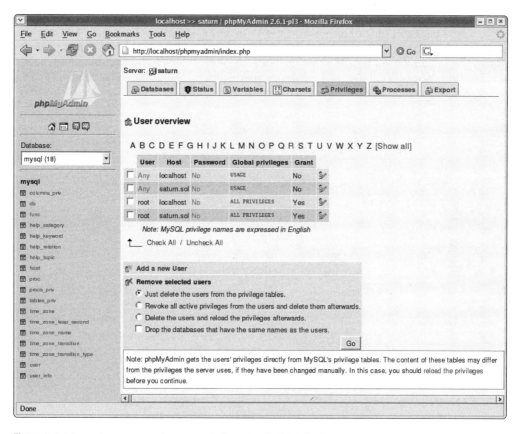

Figure 6-4. *Managing users and access privileges in phpMyAdmin*

Deleting insecure entries: To do this, check the affected users in the user overview (in Figure 6-4, this includes the two users "Any") and then click OK to delete these users.

Securing entries with a password: With a click on the EDIT symbol in the last column of a given user you reach a new page that summarizes all the access privileges of the selected user. This page offers, among other things, the possibility of giving a new password. To reduce the chance of a typo, you have to enter it twice.

■**Note** After the password for *root* for *localhost* has been changed, phpMyAdmin will display the error message *access denied* the next time a page is changed. To get phpMyAdmin to work again you have either to enter the new password in config.inc.php (*config* authentication) or log in again (*http* and *cookie* authentication).

Creating New Users

For the sake of security, the user *root* should be used only for administrative purposes. If you wish to develop a new MySQL application, you should create a new MySQL user that has exactly the privileges that are required for the application. As a rule, it suffices for this user to be able to read and alter a particular database.

Adding a user: To add a new user, click on the phpMyAdmin start page on PRIVILEGES, and on the PRIVILEGES page click on the link ADD A NEW USER. On the following page (see Figure 6-5), type in the new name in the field USER NAME. In the field HOST, you normally choose the entry LOCAL. Then phpMyAdmin adds the text LOCALHOST automatically to the next column. This means that the new user can contact MySQL only from the local computer, which for PHP applications is generally sufficient. Finally, you must give the password twice (which should differ as much as possible from the *root* password!).

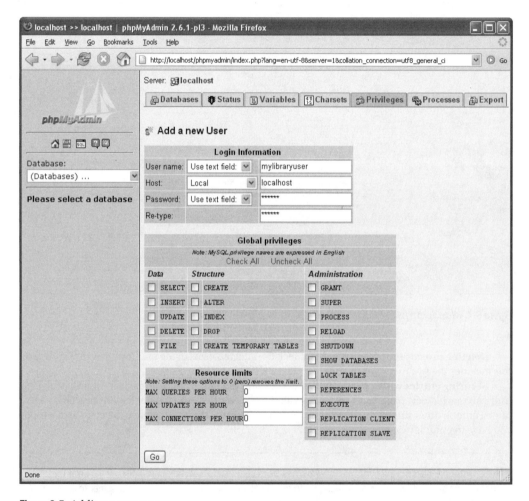

Figure 6-5. *Adding a new user*

Leave all the global privileges empty! (Only in the next step will the user obtain privileges for access to a particular database. Global privileges are unnecessary.)

Adding database-specific privileges: The OK button in the previous dialog leads to a new page, in which you can set the access details. At DATABASE-SPECIFIC PRIVILEGES you select, in the listbox, the database to which the user should have access (see Figure 6-6). This database must already exist for it to appear. If it does not yet exist, you can type the name in the text field.

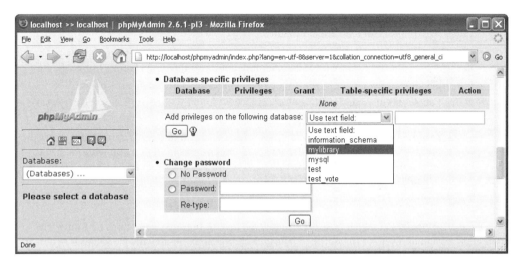

Figure 6-6. *Selecting a database for the new user*

The selection of a database in the list box leads at once to another page, on which you specify the privileges that the user is to have for the given database (see Figure 6-7). Here are a few words about the meaning of these privileges:

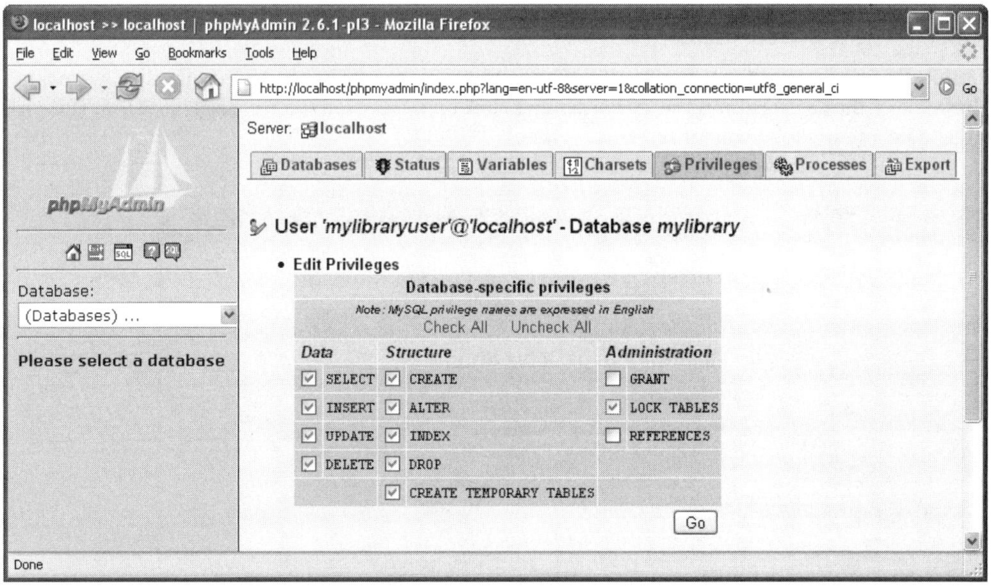

Figure 6-7. *Setting database-specific privileges*

- *SELECT, INSERT, UPDATE*, and *DELETE* are always necessary so that the user (and the associated PHP pages) can read and edit tables.

- *CREATE, ALTER, INDEX, DROP*, and *CREATE TEMPORARY TABLES* permit the user to change the structure of the database (the schema). It depends on the type of application whether this is necessary.

- *GRANT* allows the user to pass his or her privileges along to other users. For security's sake, this privilege should not be granted.

- *LOCK TABLES* allows the user to lock tables using the command *LOCK*. This is necessary in rare cases so that several linked SQL commands can be executed as a unit without other users being able to alter the underlying data. A better alternative to *LOCK TABLES* is the use of InnoDB tables and transactions.

- *REFERENCES* is currently neither documented nor implemented.

Table-specific rights make it possible to allow the user to perform operations on individual tables that are not allowed for the entire database. A change in table-specific privileges is necessary only in rare special cases and will not be described here.

Creating and Editing Databases

This section assumes that you understand the fundamentals of database design and in particular, MySQL tables and data types. This information can be obtained in Chapter 8. There the *mylibrary* database, which is used as an example in this section, is described in detail.

Creating a Database

Nothing is simpler than creating a new database. In the start page of phpMyAdmin, simply type in the name of the database and the sort order and click on the button CREATE. See Figure 6-8. The sort order determines the character set.

Figure 6-8. *Creating a new database*

The most important character sets for the United States and Western Europe are *latin1* (with the sort orders *general, german1, german2, danish, spanish,* and *swedish)* and *utf8* (Unicode, with a variety of sort orders).

The new database is empty; that is, it does not yet contain any tables. The next step is to create one or more tables (see Figure 6-9). To do this, first select the desired database in the database list-box to arrive at the STRUCTURE page of the database. (After creating a new database you are sent to this page automatically.)

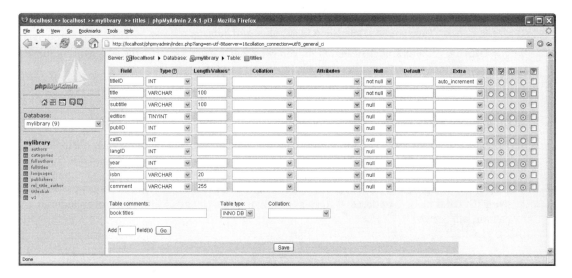

Figure 6-9. *Creating new tables*

In the first step, you give the name of a table as well as the desired number of columns (fields). When in doubt, it is better to specify too many than too few. Simply leave the excess columns empty.

Now phpMyAdmin displays an enormous input form. Here you provide the following data for each column (field) of the table:

FIELD: Name of the column.

TYPE: Data type, e.g., *INT* or *VARCHAR*.

LENGTH: This field is optional for most data types. Only with *VARCHAR* columns must you specify the maximum number of characters (up to 255).

COLLATION: This field determines the desired character set and the sort order (only when these settings differ from the default settings).

ATTRIBUTES: This field is normally left empty. With integer numeric types you can set UNSIGNED if you wish to limit to nonnegative values.

NULL: This field specifies whether the column is allowed to contain *NULL* values.

DEFAULT: Here you can specify the default values for the column that will be stored if another value is not specifically input when a data record is added (optional).

EXTRA: The only option that you can select here is AUTO_INCREMENT. This normally makes sense only for the primary key field.

INDEX OPTIONS: The five options that follow determine whether a primary index, a regular index, a UNIQUE index, no index at all, or a full-text index should be created.

Below the column definition block you can place a comment, which usually contains information about the table's content. Furthermore, you should select here the table type (MyISAM or InnoDB). The field for sorting is relevant only if the default sort order of the table is to vary from that of the database. You terminate the design process with SAVE.

Editing Existing Tables

To make changes to a table, first select the desired database in phpMyAdmin and then the table. The options for processing the table are given in a number of views:

STRUCTURE: Here you can delete or add columns and indexes.

OPERATIONS: Here, among other things, you can rename a table, change the table type, or move or copy the table into another database.

EMPTY: Here you can delete all the records from the table. The table itself is not thereby deleted.

Creating an Index Across Several Columns

To create a new index for a column, simply click the mouse on the relevant index symbol in the STRUCTURE view for the table. However, if you wish to insert an index across more than one column, you must specify the number of columns in the STRUCTURE view, in the Indexes area, and then click OK. On the next page you can select the desired columns and the index type (see Figure 6-10). Specifying the index name is optional. If you leave the name blank, generally the name of an indexed column will be used.

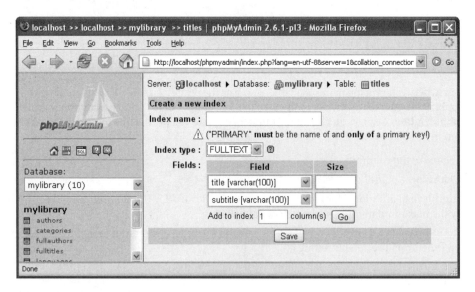

Figure 6-10. *Creating a full-text index across two columns*

Setting Foreign Key Rules

If you are using InnoDB tables, you can maintain the relationships between the tables using integrity rules (*foreign key* rules; see Chapter 8). To do so, first select a table that contains one or more foreign keys (that is, fields that refer to other tables) and then click on the link RELATION VIEW.

On the following page you can now specify, for each foreign key, to which primary key of another table it refers (see Figure 6-11). For example, the field *titles.catID* refers to the field *categories.catID*. If you define a *foreign key* rule for this, then it will be impossible for *titles* to refer to a nonexistent entry in *categories*.

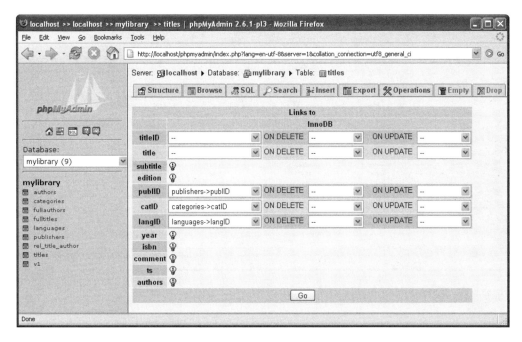

Figure 6-11. *Setting foreign key rules*

With the fields *ON DELETE* and *ON UPDATE* you can define how MySQL should behave with *DELETE* and *UPDATE* commands that would violate the integrity rules. The default behavior is simply to trigger an error and not execute the command. In many cases, however, it can be a good idea to delete all affected records (*CASCADE*) or to set the affected foreign fields to *NULL* (*SET NULL*). If you wish to do one of these things, you must select the corresponding option.

Documenting the Database Structure

If you have completed the definition of a new database, you may wish to document your results, and phpMyAdmin can assist you: Click in the left column on the database name and then on the link DATA DICTIONARY. This takes you to a page in which phpMyAdmin shows the most important properties of all the tables (see Figure 6-12).

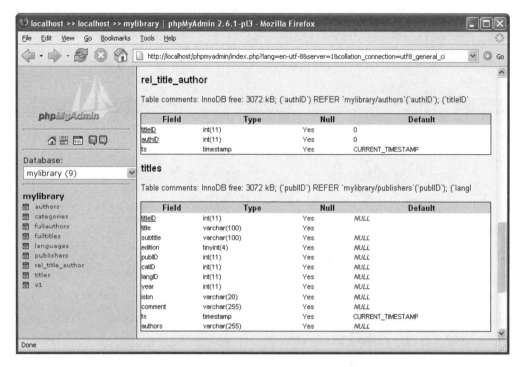

Figure 6-12. *Overview of the mylibrary database structure*

■**Tip** phpMyAdmin is able to draw a graphical relational diagram and export it as a PDF file. However, to have this functionality available, you must first generate some auxiliary tables and configure phpMyAdmin in such a way that it can access these tables. This will be discussed in detail later in the chapter.

Viewing, Inserting, and Editing Data

Once a database contains some date, you can effortlessly browse through tables with the help of phpMyAdmin. To do so, select the desired table and choose the view BROWSE. phpMyAdmin now displays the first 30 records. If you click on the column titles, phpMyAdmin sorts the list accordingly (see Figure 6-13). With the buttons <<, <, >, and >> you can move to the first, previous, next, and last pages. Fields with extensive text are automatically shortened if you click on the T symbol (in the upper left corner of the table).

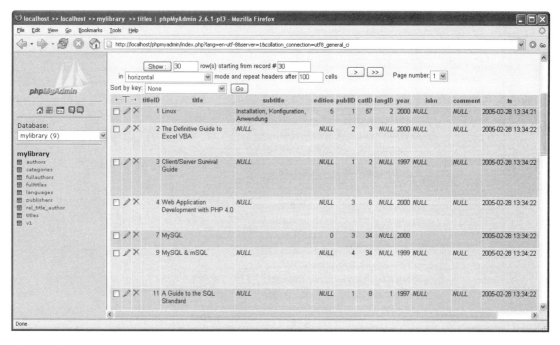

Figure 6-13. *Examining the content of a table*

Starting with this view, you can now delete individual data records (x button) or edit them (EDIT button). You can also first check several records and then edit or delete them as a group.

The view INSERT allows for the input of exactly two new records (see Figure 6-14). Note that for columns with the *AUTO_INCREMENT* attribute (typically ID columns or primary keys) and with *TIMESTAMP* columns you normally should not provide a value. MySQL supplies a suitable value automatically.

The selection list FUNCTION in the input form makes it possible to apply an SQL function to the following input character string. For example, you can store *PASSWORD('abc')* instead of simply *'abc'* in a column that contains encrypted passwords.

■Tip The input of large numbers of records using phpMyAdmin is rather cumbersome. In practice, however, it is seldom necessary. Normally, it is the task of your PHP program to store data in the database. Nevertheless, if you wish to enter some test data records quickly, it is best to compose them in a text editor or table calculation program, store them as a text file, and then import the file, as discussed later in this chapter.

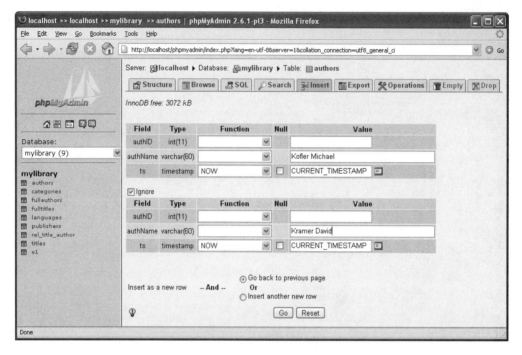

Figure 6-14. *Inputting a new record*

Executing SQL Commands

After selecting a database or table, you can input an SQL command in the SQL view and then execute it. If this is a *SELECT* command, the results are displayed as in Figure 6-13.

Of particular practicality is the possibility of inputting SQL commands in a separate window (see Figure 6-15). To open this window, click in phpMyAdmin in the left column on the SQL button (above the list of databases). This window offers the most convenient way of inserting columns into the current table in the edit region.

You can also input and execute several SQL commands at once. In this case, the commands must be separated by semicolons.

■Note If you have set up a database for phpMyAdmin to support various auxiliary functions, as discussed later in the chapter, phpMyAdmin keeps track of the executed SQL commands. In the view SQL-HISTORY you can conveniently access the most recently executed commands.

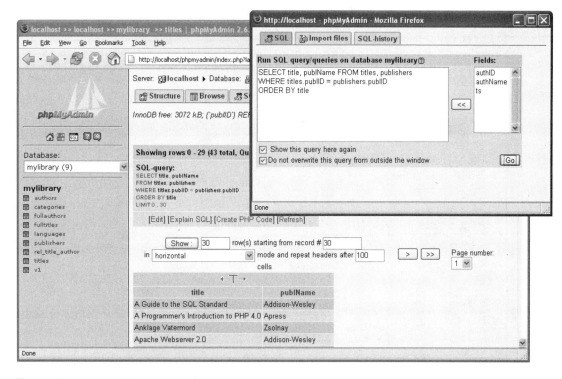

Figure 6-15. *Executing SQL commands*

Import and Export

There are several options offered by phpMyAdmin for importing and exporting tables or entire databases. This section summarizes these possibilities.

■**Note** The import and export of large databases and tables is problematic, since the maximum run time of a PHP script is limited. You can attempt to increase this time in `config.inc.php` (*$cfg['ExecTimeLimit'] = n*). However, if PHP is securely configured, this setting is ignored. The only thing to do is to make a change to *max_execution_time* in the PHP configuration file `php.ini`. Another consideration is that PHP is limited in the size of upload files (setting *upload_max_filesize = 2M* in `php.ini`).

If PHP is executed on your ISP's computer, you have no control over the file `php.ini`. (You could, of course, ask your ISP to change some variables, but you are not likely to receive a positive response.) So you should try to break up your imports and exports into small portions (e.g., store each table individually instead of the entire database all at once).

Another alternative is to execute the database exportation with the command `mysqldump` and importation with `mysql`.

Database Backup (SQL File)

To save an entire database that can later be completely restored (even on another computer), select the desired database, switch into the view EXPORT, and select there the option SQL (see Figure 6-16). Then select all the tables and change options as required. As a rule, you will not go wrong by sticking with the default settings.

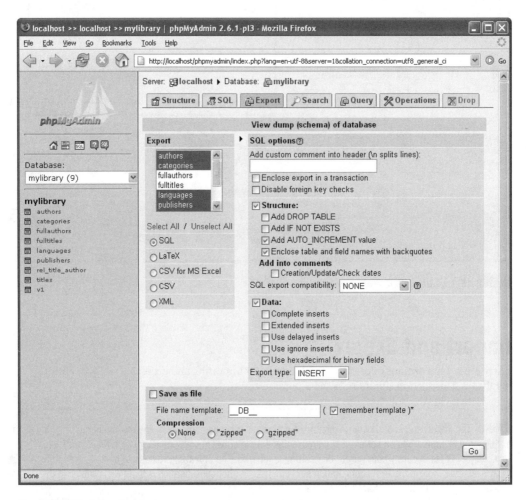

Figure 6-16. *Database backup*

When you click OK, phpMyAdmin creates a new page with countless *CREATE TABLE* and *INSERT* commands. You can now select these commands, copy them into a text editor, and save them. Even simpler is to click on the option SAVE as file. Then phpMyAdmin transfers the data to your web browser, which displays a SAVE dialog that allows you to save the transferred data to a local *.sql file. (Optionally, you can execute the upload in compressed form. Then the SQL commands are stored in a *.gz or *.zip file.)

Here is a brief explanation of the most important export options:

Disable foreign key checks: If you are exporting InnoDB tables with foreign key rules, you should activate this option. Then phpMyAdmin adds *SET FOREIGN_KEY_CHECKS=0* to the beginning of the SQL file and *SET FOREIGN_KEY_CHECKS=1* at the end. This deactivates checking the integration rules during a later importation. This not only speeds up the importation; it also prevents errors if the tables are not created in the correct order.

Structure options: These options control the construction of the *CREATE TABLE* commands. For example, you can insert the command *DROP TABLE* before *CREATE TABLE* to delete a like-named preexisting table.

Data options: These options control the formation of *INSERT* commands. COMPLETE INSERTS means that at each *INSERT* command, all column names are given, which as a rule is superfluous.

EXTENDED INSERTS means that several records can be inserted with a single *INSERT* command. That is more efficient, but it can result in commands that are so long that they cannot be processed at a later importation (error message *got a packet bigger than 'max_allowed_packet' bytes*).

In the listbox EXPORT TYPE you can select the commands *UPDATE* or *REPLACE* instead of *INSERT*. (This makes sense if you merely wish to update existing data.)

Please note that the resulting SQL file is a UTF8 (Unicode) file.

Exporting Tables (CSV Text File)

CSV stands for *comma-separated value*. CSV files are simply text files whose entries are separated by commas or optionally another symbol. Most spreadsheet programs are capable of importing such files without problems. As a rule, it is a good idea to export only one table per CSV file, and not all tables of a database at once.

There is a problem with character sets. In the default setting, phpMyAdmin 2.6 offers no possibility of setting the character set of a CSV file. Instead, phpMyAdmin creates Unicode files (UTF8), which causes importation problems under Excel. Fortunately, the solution is easy. Simply change a variable in config.inc.php:

```
# in config.inc.php
$cfg['AllowAnywhereRecoding'] = TRUE;
```

From now on, a listbox appears at the end of the export dialog in which you can select the desired text code.

Importing a Database or Tables (SQL File)

When a database or table is exported in the form of SQL commands (either with the export function just described or with the command mysqldump), you use the SQL view for importing. The following points summarize how to import a database from a *.sql file:

Create a database: On the phpMyAdmin start page, create a new, initially empty, database.

Select an SQL file: The new database is automatically active. Change into the SQL view (see Figure 6-17) and select with Browse the local *.sql file with the *CREATE TABLE* and *INSERT* commands. (The commands must be separated with semicolons.)

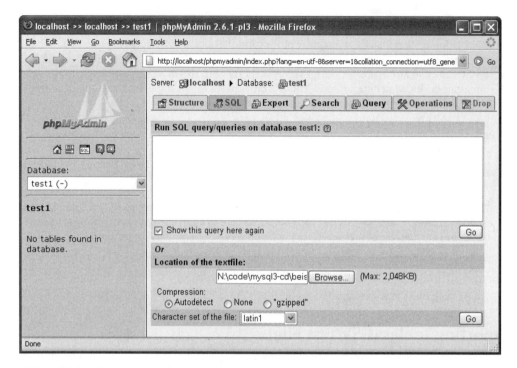

Figure 6-17. *Database importation from an SQL file*

Select the character set: By default, phpMyAdmin assumes that it is dealing with a *.sql file with the *utf8* character set. If that is not the case, set the desired character set. (The *.sql files containing the example databases for this book use the *latin1* character set.)

Begin the importation: With OK, the file is read from the local file system, transferred via the Internet to phpMyAdmin, and there evaluated.

Inserting Table Data (Text File)

The content of individual tables can be imported from a text file by phpMyAdmin. The table must already exist with the proper number of columns and the correct data types. To import the data, first activate the STRUCTURE view of the table and click on INSERT DATA FROM A TEXTFILE INTO TABLE. The link, which is easy to overlook, is located at the end of the page.

On the following page, select the file to be imported and specify how the files are to be separated, how the individual fields are labeled, etc. With the settings in Figure 6-18, the importation of a typical CSV file succeeds, whose lines look like this:

```
"1";"Linux";"Installation, Konfiguration, Anwendung";"5";"1";"57";
  "2";"2000";NULL;NULL
"2";"The Definitive Guide to Excel VBA";NULL;NULL;"2";"3";
  NULL;"2000";NULL;NULL
```

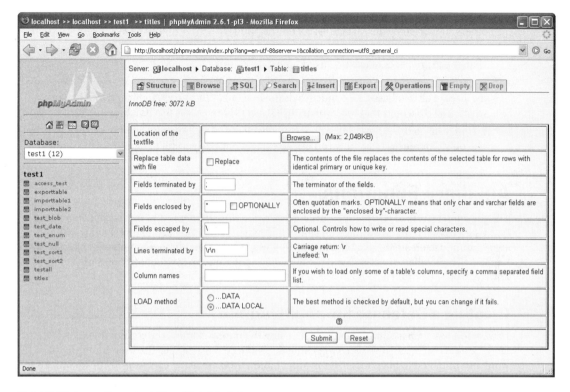

Figure 6-18. *Importing a text file with table data*

Character set problems: phpMyAdmin 2.6 does not allow you to set the character set for importation. For it to succeed, the text file must have the same character set as holds for the MySQL server and the connection to the server. You can determine this character set by looking at the contents of the MySQL variables *character_set_server* and *character_set_connection*. To do so, click in the phpMyAdmin start page on the link SHOW MYSQL SYSTEM VARIABLES.

Server Administration

The dialog sheet OPERATIONS in the DATABASE and TABLE views contains commands for renaming and copying databases and tables and transferring tables to another database.

If you click on the HOME symbol at the top of the phpMyAdmin window, you find yourself at the phpMyAdmin start page. If you have sufficient phpMyAdmin login privileges, this page contains links for carrying out various administrative tasks:

SHOW MYSQL RUNTIME INFORMATION displays the status of the MySQL server (corresponds to *SHOW STATUS*).

SHOW MYSQL SYSTEM VARIABLES displays the content of the MySQL variables (corresponds to *SHOW VARIABLES*).

SHOW PROCESSES displays the current process list (corresponds to *SHOW PROCESSLIST*). If you have sufficient privileges, you can also terminate a process.

Character Sets and Collations leads to a page with a summary of all character sets and sort orders supported by the MySQL server (corresponds to *SHOW COLLATION*).

Privileges leads to a page that lists all MySQL users. From this page you can add new users, change the privileges of existing users, and delete users.

Databases leads to a list of all databases. With Activate Database Statistics you can determine the sizes of all databases. Also practical is the link Check Privileges, indicated by a padlock, which leads to a page that tells which MySQL users have access to a database.

Export leads to the export dialog that was considered in the previous section (see Figure 6-16). The only difference is that now you can select and back up several databases at the same time.

Auxiliary Functions

The common feature of all the functions considered in this chapter is that first, several tables must be created in which phpMyAdmin can store information. Therefore, this section begins with the steps required to create these tables. In what follows, you will learn about other ways that this can happen. (The auxiliary functions and the following configuration instructions are geared to the advanced phpMyAdmin user.)

Creating a Database for phpMyAdmin

In what follows, I am assuming that you are using the phpMyAdmin *config* authentication (*$cfg['Servers'][$i]['auth_type'] = 'config'*), that is, that in config.inc.php the user name and password are contained in plain text. On the other hand, if you are using *cookie* or *http* authentication, the optimal way of proceeding is a bit different. (Tips in that direction can be found in the unfortunately difficult to read phpMyAdmin documentation.)

Creating the database *phpmyadmin*: Ideally, you will place all auxiliary tables for phpMyAdmin in a single database, which you will name *phpmyadmin*. So create a new, empty database with this name. (If you do not have the privileges to create new databases, you can place the phpMyAdmin auxiliary tables in the next step in any existing database.)

Creating auxiliary tables: Open the file scripts/create_tables_mysql_4_1_2+.sql from the phpMyAdmin installation directory into a text editor. If you are using a version of MySQL older than 4.1.2, you must use create_tables.sql.

In the editor, copy all the *CREATE TABLE* commands and execute them in SQL view in the new SQL database. You thereby create the phpMyAdmin tables *pma_bookmark*, *pma_column_info*, *pma_history*, *pma_pdf_pages*, *pma_relation*, *pma_table_coords*, and *pma_table_info*. (But do not execute the commands *DROP DATABASE*, *CREATE DATABASE*, *USE*, and *GRANT* also contained in the *.sql file.)

Adapting config.inc.php: Now you must adapt config.inc.php. At issue are the following two lines, which set the user name and password for access to the database with the phpMyAdmin auxiliary table. Here you enter the same user and the same password as in the phpMyAdmin basic configuration:

```
// in config.inc.php
$cfg['Servers'][$i]['controluser'] = 'root';      // MySQL user name
$cfg['Servers'][$i]['controlpass'] = 'xxx';
```

If you have created the phpMyAdmin auxiliary tables not in their own database *phpmyadmin* but in some other database, you must replace *phpmyadmin* in the following line with the database name:

```
$cfg['Servers'][$i]['pmadb']      = 'phpmyadmin'; // DB name
```

SQL Bookmarks and History

If you frequently execute SQL commands in phpMyAdmin, it is burdensome to have to repeatedly input them. But phpMyAdmin can store these commands in a separate table. You simply need to make a small change in the file `config.inc.php`, in which you indicate in what table phpMyAdmin should store the SQL commands or the sequence of most recently executed commands:

```
# in config.inc.php
$cfg['Servers'][$i]['bookmarktable'] = 'pma_bookmark';
$cfg['Servers'][$i]['history']       = 'pma_history';
```

From now on, you can store all SQL commands that you process in the SQL window provided by phpMyAdmin under an arbitrary name (*bookmark*). In the dialog sheet SQL-HISTORY you can execute or edit again all sorts of stored entries (see Figure 6-19). The history shows only stored SQL commands that were used with SUBMIT or VIEW ONLY.

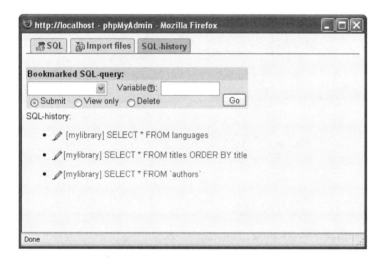

Figure 6-19. *SQL bookmarks and history*

Saving Information on Relations

By itself, phpMyAdmin is incapable of determining through which fields tables are linked (not even if integrity rules were defined for InnoDB tables). However, you can specify this information yourself, which simplifies editing tables in the future. You need to make a small change in `config.inc.php`:

```
# in config.inc.php
$cfg['Servers'][$i]['relation']   = 'pma_relation';
$cfg['Servers'][$i]['table_info'] = 'pma_table_info';
```

Now from the STRUCTURE sheet of each table, via the link RELATION VIEW, you enter a dialog in which you can specify, for each foreign key field, which field of another table it refers to. (With InnoDB tables with *foreign key* rules you can skip this step.) Moreover, you can specify which columns of the current table should be shown with references.

This is most easily understood with the help of an example: The fields *publID*, *catID*, and *langID* of the table *titles* from the sample database *mylibrary* refer to the tables *publishers*, *categories*, and *languages*. This information was given in Figure 6-20 in the section LINKS TO. If another table refers to the *titles* table, then instead of the *titleID* number, the book title (CHOOSE FIELD TO DISPLAY) should be displayed.

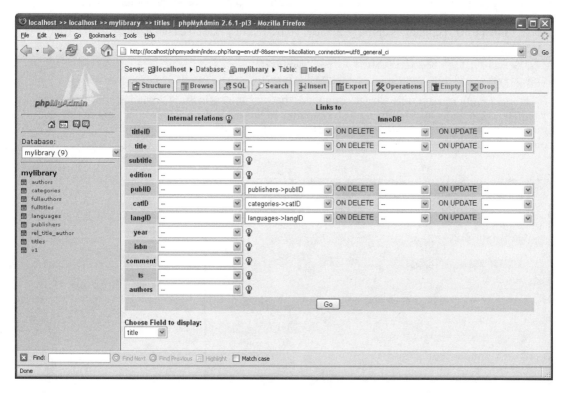

Figure 6-20. *References from the table titles to other tables in the database mylibrary*

The input of such additional information for all tables is, to be sure, a bit tedious. In the following, the processing of this database with phpMyAdmin will be much simpler.

- When you look at the contents of a table, foreign key fields are executed as links. When you click on a link, the corresponding record of the linked table will be displayed.

- When you change a record in a table or insert a new one, you do not have to give an ID number in the foreign key field. Instead, listboxes are displayed that offer a convenient selection of linked fields (see Figure 6-21). The listbox contains each entry twice: once ordered by the ID field and a second time ordered by the field to be displayed.

- The link DATA DICTIONARY in the STRUCTURE sheet of the TABLE view provides detailed information about the structure of a database and is well designed for printing (as documentation on the database).

- Finally, you can create a PDF file for documenting the table structure that contains all the relevant information.

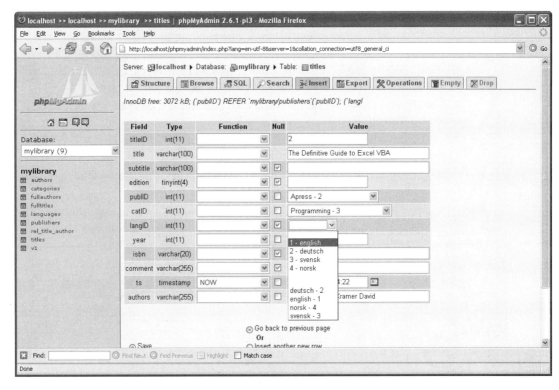

Figure 6-21. *Listboxes simplify input and editing of foreign key fields.*

Creating a PDF Relational Diagram

You can also use phpMyAdmin to draw a diagram that shows the relationships among the tables of a database. The procedure is a bit cumbersome, however, and the result hardly justifies the effort. You first need to make a small change in config.inc.php:

```
# in config.inc.php
$cfg['Servers'][$i]['table_coords']  = 'pma_table_coords';
$cfg['Servers'][$i]['pdf_pages']     = 'pma_pdf_pages';
```

The creation of a PDF document now proceeds in several steps:

- The process begins in the STRUCTURE sheet of the DATABASE view with the link EDIT PDF PAGES.

- Now you must give the PDF to be created a name and select the document for editing.

- You must select all the tables to be documented. (For some reason, each table must be selected separately.)

- For the STRUCTURE view in which the links among the tables are to be displayed, you must specify for each table the start coordinates within the page. The coordinate range for an A4 page is from 0 (left) to 750 (right) for the X coordinate, and from 0 (above) to 600 (below) for the Y coordinate.

  With a modern web browser you can move the tables directly to the screen with drag&drop (button TOGGLE SCRATCHBOARD).

- The remaining options specify how the PDF document should be formatted:

  SHOW GRID produces a background of lattice lines and coordinate axes. This is helpful in the layout phase.

  SHOW COLOR relates to the color of the connecting lines between the tables. (The output of colored lines on a black-and-white printer generally doesn't look very good.)

  SHOW DIMENSION OF TABLES shows the size of each table in the coordinate system of the PDF document. This option is useful only during layout.

  DISPLAY ALL TABLES WITH SAME WIDTH relates to the width of the tables in the PDF document. A uniform width can be easier to read in some circumstances.

  DATA DICTIONARY specifies whether a detailed description of the properties of all the tables should be integrated into the PDF document (one page per table).

With OK the PDF document is created and sent to the web browser. Depending on the browser settings, you can display the document at once with Adobe Acrobat or you may have to store it in a local file first. Such a diagram is shown in Figure 6-22.

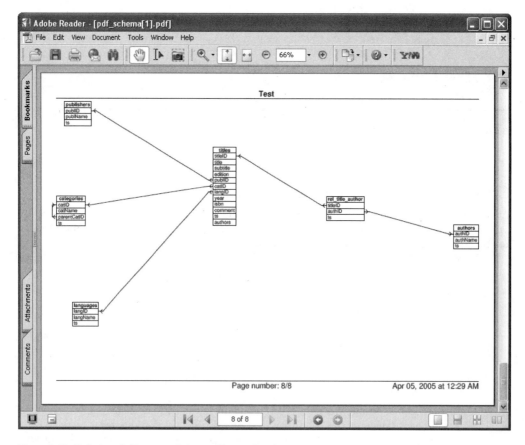

Figure 6-22. *Relational diagram of the mylibrary database*

Transformations (Alternative Representation of Column Contents)

phpMyAdmin can transform the contents of individual columns based on specified rules. This leads to some new possibilities for displaying tables:

Inline images: With *BLOB* columns with images (JPEG/PNG), the images can be displayed directly in the TABLE view. Figure 6-23 shows a table whose *thumbnail* column contains JPEG images. For this column the MIME type *image/jpeg* and the transformation rule *image/jpeg inline* were set.

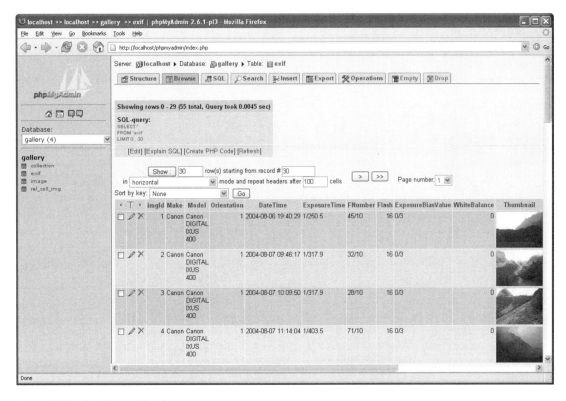

Figure 6-23. *Table view with inline images*

Links: With text columns containing web links or file names, links to the web site or file can be built into the TABLE view.

A small change needs to be made in `config.inc.php` so that phpMyAdmin knows in which table to store the transformation rules:

```
# in config.inc.php
$cfg['Servers'][$i]['column_info'] = 'pma_column_info';
```

If you now wish to change the properties of a column, phpMyAdmin offers three new input fields:

MIME/TYPE: In this listbox you can select the data type of the column (e.g., *image/jpeg* or *text/plain*). The list entry *auto-detect* does not work, unfortunately.

TRANSFORMATION OPTIONS: Here you can specify additional transformation options. For example, you can give a prefix to the address with *text/plain link* as the first option.

ISBN: In the *titles* table of *mylibrary* there is an *ISBN* field. If you specify for this field the MIME type *text/plain*, the transformation *text/plain link*, and the option *'http://www.amazon.com/exec/obidos/ASIN/'*, then phpMyAdmin creates suitable links to amazon.com from the ISBN.

∎∎∎

## CHAPTER 7

Microsoft Office, OpenOffice/StarOffice

In practice, it often happens that a Microsoft Office program will wish to access a database, for example, to evaluate data with pivot tables, represent data in charts, or insert data in a mail-merge document. This chapter describes how to create a connection between any of Microsoft Office, Sun StarOffice, and OpenOffice and the MySQL server. There are two possibilities:

- ODBC (*Open Database Connectivity*) is a popular mechanism, above all under Windows, for integrated access to a variety of database systems. The only assumption is a so-called ODBC driver for the database system, which creates an interface between the ODBC system and the database. The freely available Connector/ODBC at `http://dev.mysql.com` performs this task.

- JDBC (*Java Database Connectivity*) is the Java counterpart to ODBC. Under Unix/Linux JDBC in combination with the MySQL driver Connector/J represents the simplest way of accessing the MySQL server from StarOffice and OpenOffice. (There is also an ODBC implementation for Unix/Linux, but it is not available by default in many systems.)

Installing Connector/ODBC

Connector/ODBC 3.51 (formerly MyODBC) is the ODBC driver for MySQL. The driver supports the functions defined in ODBC version 3.5.1 (according to the on-line handbook, *Complete Core API and Level 2 Features*). For installation you should obtain Connector/ODBC from the MySQL web server. Most recently, Connector/ODBC was to be found at the following address: `http://dev.mysql.com/downloads/connector/odbc/3.51.html`.

Installation is quite easy. The two DLL files `myodbc3.dll` and `myodbc3S.sll` are copied into the `Windows\System32` directory and registered. The library `libmysql.dll`, which is used by other MySQL applications, is not required for Connector/ODBC and is therefore not installed.

You can convince yourself that installation was successful by looking at the ODBC driver window (see Figure 7-1). You reach this dialog with Settings | Control Panel | Administrative Tools | Data Sources.

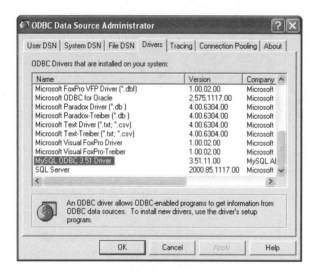

Figure 7-1. *List of ODBC drivers*

■Note ODBC is also used under Unix. Thus there exists Connector/ODBC for Unix as well. However, in this book we will consider only the Windows application of Connector/ODBC.

Setting Up ODBC Data Sources

Since the repeated setting of database connection parameters (user name, password, etc.) becomes tedious after a while, ODBC provides for the definition of so-called data sources. Once such a data source has been set up, for establishing a connection one needs only the selection of the data source name (DSN).

Many programs with an ODBC interface consider DSNs merely a convenient option for creating a connection. With other programs, such as Access and Excel, however, DSNs are the only way to an ODBC connection. That is, you must set up such a data source before you can create an ODBC connection to a MySQL server.

DSNs are usually set up in the ODBC administrator dialog. (Many Windows programs themselves provide dialogs for this purpose, but they are no improvement.) You launch the ODBC administrator dialog in the system control, under Windows, for example, with START | SETTINGS | CONTROL PANEL | ADMINISTRATIVE TOOLS | DATA SOURCES (ODBC). There you have the choice among three DSN types: user, system, and file DSNs.

User DSNs: These are available only to the user who has defined the DSN.

System DSNs: These DSNs are available to all users of the computer. With both user and system DSNs the settings are managed internally by ODBC.

File DSNs: Here we are dealing with individual files with the identifier *.dsn, in which all setting data are stored in text format. These files are usually stored in the directory Program Files\Common Files\ODBC\Data Sources. File DSNs are more transparent to some extent, because it is clear what information is stored where.

If you wish to access more than one MySQL database, you must make use of the corresponding number of DSNs.

The definition of a new DSN begins with clicking on the Add button in the User DSN or System DSN dialog sheet. There appears a dialog in which you can choose from among various ODBC drivers. The correct choice in our case is, of course, MySQL. A double click now leads into a further dialog (see Figure 7-2) in which you must make the following settings:

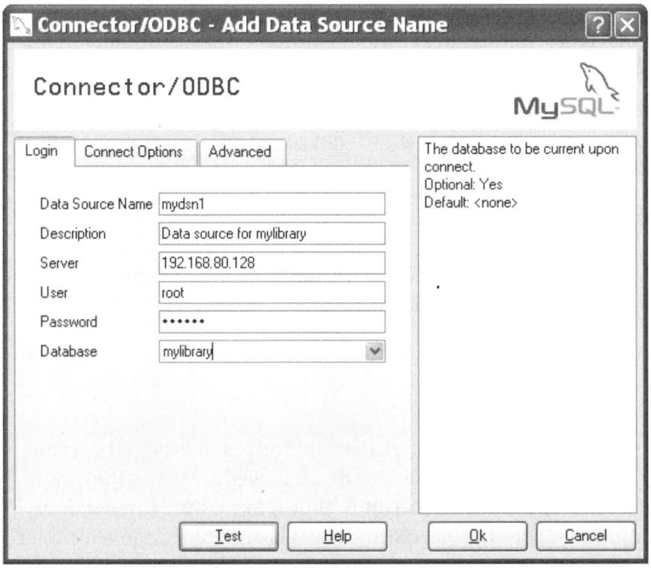

Figure 7-2. *Connector/ODBC basic setting*

Data Source Name: Here is where you specify the name of the DSN (that is, under what name the data source can be addressed by ODBC programs). Select a name that is connected to the database name and the use to which the DSN is to be put.

Server: Here you give the name or IP address of the computer on which MySQL (i.e., the server) is running. If it is the local computer, then give *localhost*.

User and **Password:** The access system described in Chapter 11 holds for Connector/ODBC, as it does for all other MySQL programs. (If you are unable to achieve a Connector/ODBC connection, then inadequate access privileges is the most likely cause of the difficulty.)

In the fields *User* and *Password* you can input the user name and password for access to the database. However, whether you should actually do this is another question entirely. First, you provide access to the database to anyone who can use the DSN. Second, the password is not encrypted and can therefore easily be discovered.

To circumvent this security risk, you can leave both fields empty. Then every time you or someone else wishes to use this DSN to obtain a connection to MySQL, the dialog pictured in Figure 7-2 appears. While this is very practical, in that the name and password can be input, it is very confusing for the average user. It is not clear that a user name and password are indeed to be entered, and it is possible that some poor user will stumble around in the other input fields of this dialog, which can lead to errors that will be difficult to unravel.

Database: Here you specify the name of the MySQL database (e.g., *mylibrary*, if you wish to access the most frequently mentioned database in this book).

Connect Options: In the PORT input field of this tab the IP port can be specified if the default port 3306 is not to be used. In most cases, this field remains empty. Also, additional input fields in the dialog sheet CONNECT OPTIONS are normally left empty.

If MySQL is running on a computer other than the one on which Connector/ODBC is running and there is a firewall between the two computers, then port 3306 must be opened. Otherwise, no communication between MySQL and Connector/ODBC will be possible.

Advanced: In this tab you can set a large number of additional options. These options will be described in detail in Chapter 19 in connection with ADO programming.

For now, what is important is that you activate the two options DON'T OPTIMIZE COLUMN WIDTH and RETURN MATCHING ROWS. These options are necessary so that Microsoft Access and Excel communicate correctly with MySQL.

With the button TEST you can quickly check whether a connection to the MySQL server succeeds with the current settings.

If you later change the settings of a DSN, simply open the ODBC administration dialog. A double click on the DSN (or the button CONFIGURE) leads again to the dialog shown in Figure 7-2.

Microsoft Access

Access and MySQL are two programs that are fundamentally different from each other. Access has a very well developed user interface, which simplifies the design of databases as well as the development of database programs. Unfortunately, Access can be quite slow if more than three or four users wish to access the database simultaneously. Furthermore, Access is quite unsuitable for Internet applications.

In comparison, MySQL is incomparably more efficient and secure in multiuser operation. However, while there exists a variety of user interfaces to MySQL, at present, none of these offers the convenience of Access.

Taking all of this into consideration, it seems a good idea to try to combine the best of both worlds. Even though there are many limitations, the potential applications of Access in combination with MySQL are quite numerous:

- Access tables can be exported to MySQL and there edited further.

- MySQL tables can be imported to Access or a link to the tables can be created and the data further edited.

- Data from Access and MySQL databases can be combined.

- You can develop the design of a new database in Access and then export the entire database to MySQL.

- You can use Access as an interface for changing the contents of MySQL tables.

- You can develop complex queries in Access and then place the SQL code in your scripts.

- You can create and print database reports.

- You can develop VBA code in Access for automatically processing data from MySQL databases in Access.

- You can create diagrams of database structures.

Note This section assumes that you are familiar with Access. An introduction to Access would be beyond the scope of this book. All procedures described in this section were tested with Access 2000.

Problems

Don't let your hopes soar too high. Access was never conceived as an interface to MySQL and will never become one. Thus it is not surprising that a number of difficulties exist when integrating the two:

- There are several data types that are available either only in Access or only in MySQL. In import/export such data types can create trouble. For example, MySQL *ENUM*s and *SET*s are turned into simple text fields upon importation. There are also problems to be had with single-precision *FLOAT*s. In general, you should use *DOUBLE* floating-point numbers if you plan on working with Access.

  You should generally count on having to change various attributes of a MySQL table as a result of importing it into Access and later exporting it back to MySQL.

- MySQL presently offers a way of creating links between tables only for the InnoDB format. Relations (including rules for ensuring referential integrity) that are easily constructed in Access are lost upon exportation to MySQL.

- The SQL dialect of MySQL and that of Access are not quite identical. Thus it can happen that SQL queries developed in Access will function in MySQL only after some minor adjustments.

Assumptions

- If you wish to change data from linked MySQL tables in Access, the option *Return Matching Rows* must be set in the definition of the ODBC data source (DSN). If you are working with Access 2.0, you will also need the option *Simulate ODBC 1.0*.

- All linked MySQL tables must be equipped with a *TIMESTAMP* field so that data can be altered. (You don't need to concern yourself with the care and feeding of this field, since both MySQL and Access automatically store the time of the last change. Access requires this information to distinguish altered data from unaltered data.)

- All MySQL tables must be equipped with a primary index (usually an *INT* field with the property *AUTO_INCREMENT*).

- A significant source of problems is the existence of incompatible data types:

  - MySQL tables use *DOUBLE* instead of *FLOAT* and *DATETIME* instead of *DATE*.

  - Avoid *BIGINT, SET*, and *ENUM*.

  - Access has occasional problems with *BLOB*s and believes that it is dealing with OLE objects.

▪Tip If you are working in Access with linked tables and if after an alteration in a data record you see *#deleted* displayed, then one of the above conditions has not been satisfied.

  If you develop queries in Access and then wish to use the SQL code in MySQL, you will frequently find yourself in a compatibility quagmire. (The SQL dialect of Access is different from that in MySQL.) Here is how you can solve this problem: Work with linked tables, and in Access execute the following command (while the window for query formulation is open): Query | SQL Specific | Pass-Through. You thereby let Access know in no uncertain terms that the program should hold more rigorously to SQL standards.

Importing and Exporting Tables

Imported Tables Versus Linked Tables

If you wish to process MySQL data in Access, then you have two possibilities: You can first import the table(s) into Access and then do the processing, or else you can merely create a link between Access and the MySQL tables.

- With linked tables you can insert or alter data, although the table will then be managed by MySQL. Here Access serves simply as the interface. A change in the table's properties (insertion or deletion of a column, for example) is not possible with linked tables. The principal advantages are that the creation of links proceeds very quickly (independent of the size of the tables) and the data remain with MySQL.

- There are no restrictions on imported tables as they pertain to changes in the table design. Since the tables are now stored in an Access database file, you can carry out all the operations provided by Access. However, there can be problems if you later attempt to return the table(s) to MySQL, since not all of the Access data types can be transformed to MySQL data types without further ado.

Importing MySQL Tables into Access

The first step is either to open an existing Access database or to create a new (empty) database. Then you execute FILE | GET EXTERNAL DATA | IMPORT and in the file selection dialog you choose ODBC as the file type. As if by magic, the dialog SELECT DATASOURCE appears. In the dialog sheet MACHINE DATA SOURCES, all the user and system DSNs are enumerated. Select the DSN of your choice. As a rule, there will now appear the dialog shown in Figure 7-2, in which you have merely to provide the user name and password.

  If the connection to MySQL can be established, then the next dialog (see Figure 7-3) shows a list of all tables in the database specified by the DSN. There you can mark several tables at once (mouse button+Ctrl). The importation is initiated by clicking OK, which can take a bit of time if the tables are large. (Access creates a local copy of the tables and stores them in an Access database file.)

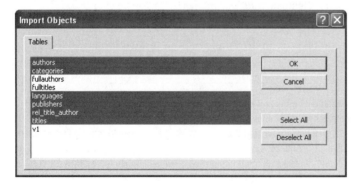

Figure 7-3. *Selection of tables to be imported into Access*

  Note that on being imported, many column attributes (e.g., *AUTO_INCREMENT*) are lost, and that the forms of indexes are frequently changed (so that a MySQL *UNIQUE* index in Access becomes an index that allows duplicates).

Creating Links to MySQL Tables

The way to create a database link is the same as with the importation of a MySQL table. The only difference is that this time, you begin with the Access menu command File | Get External Data | Import | Link Tables.

Caution If you change the properties of a table in MySQL (for example, if you add a new column), then you must update the connection to this table in Access. To do this, execute Tools | Database Utilities | Linked Table Manager and select the table to be updated.

Exporting Access Tables to MySQL

If you have imported a table from MySQL to Access and then changed it, or if you have developed an entire database in Access and then wish to transport it to MySQL, then you have to go in the opposite direction.

To do this, you mark the table in the Access database window, execute the command File | Export, and choose the file type ODBC. In the Export dialog you can specify the name of the table under MySQL. (As a rule, you can use the name being used under Access by clicking OK.)

In principle, exportation functions acceptably well, but usually there is some additional manual work required. The following list gives some of the basic problems with exportation:

- All indexes defined in Access are lost (including the primary index).

- The Access column property *Required* is not translated into the MySQL attribute *NOT NULL*.

- The Access column property *Autonumber* is not translated into the MySQL attribute *AUTO_INCREMENT*.

- The translation of data types is not always optimal. For example, *Currency* is translated to *DOUBLE* (MySQL). Here *DECIMAL* would be preferable. In general, you should check your MySQL tables carefully for such losses in translation.

Unfortunately, there is no possibility in Access to export several tables simultaneously. Thus if you wish to export an entire database, you must repeat the steps outlined above for each table.

Converter: Access ➤ MySQL (exportsql.txt)

Due to the problems enumerated in the previous section that arise in the export of individual tables from Access to MySQL, Pedro Freire has programmed a converter that writes an entire Access database to a file *.sql, which then can be input with mysql. The quality of this converter is considerably better than ODBC Export, which is integrated into Access. This free program, exportSQL.txt, can be obtained at the following address: http://www.cynergi.net/exportsql.

The method for exporting is documented in the program code. Here is a summary:

- Load the database to be exported into Access.

- With Alt+F11 switch into the VBA editor, there insert a new module (Insert | Module), and copy the entire file exportsql.txt into the module (see the link above). You can work in the VBA editor only if you are working with an Access 2000 database. If the database was created with an earlier version of Access, then you must open a new module in the database window and insert the code into this module.

- Change the export options in the program code. This involves a block of constants (*Private Const name =...*) that control certain parameters of the exportation process. As a rule, you will have to change only the two constants *ADD_SQL_FILE* and *DEL_SQL_FILE*, which specify the names of the file into which the export files are to be written.

- Begin exporting with F5. (In the macro dialog you must select the procedure *exportSQL.*)

- During the exportation process you may see displayed some warning messages relating to incompatibilities between Access and MySQL data types, which you must approve by clicking OK. The warnings will appear as well in the resulting files. (The affected lines begin with *#Warning.*)

- In MySQL generate an empty new database (with *CREATE DATABASE*).

- Execute the SQL command specified in esql_add.txt. You can best accomplish this with mysql:

```
> mysql -u root -p databasename < C:\tmp\esql_add.txt
Enter password: xxxxx
```

If errors occur, you may have to alter esql_add.txt in a text editor. In some situations some small changes in the program code of the converter may be necessary. Before making a new attempt, you must delete any existing data. For this, the second file esql_del.txt will be of help:

```
> mysql -u root -p databasename < C:\tmp\esql_del.txt
Enter password: xxxxx
```

Problems

- Access permits a number of special characters in table and column names that MySQL does not allow. The following changes in the program code (indicated in boldface) will permit exportSQL.txt to replace these characters automatically with an underscore (_):

```
Private Function conv_name(strname As String) As String
  ...
  Select Case Mid$(str, I, 1)
    Case " ", Chr$(9), Chr$(10), Chr$(13), "-", ")", "("
  ...
```

- In those countries where floating-point numbers are formatted with a comma for the decimal point (MySQL doesn't support this format), the following remedy is available:

```
Sub exportSQL()
  ...
  Select Case crs.Fields(cfieldix).Type
  ...
  Case Else
    sqlcode = sqlcode & conv_str(str(crs.Fields(cfieldix).Value))
```

- *PRIMARY KEY* columns must have the attribute *NOT NULL* in MySQL. However, exportsql.txt does not guarantee this condition, and that can lead to problems. The solution is to edit the column definitions of the export file esql_add.txt in a text editor.

Other Converters Between MySQL and Access

In addition to exportsql.txt, there are many other converters between MySQL and Access (in both directions) that I have not tested in detail, such as importsql and MyAccess. Many of these tools are freely available, while others are commercial programs. An overview of such programs is available at http://solutions.mysql.com/.

Microsoft Excel

Excel is of interest to users of MySQL primarily as a data analysis tool. Thanks to Connector/ODBC, you can import MySQL data into an Excel worksheet and there perform analyses, create graphics, and so on. In Figure 7-4 you can see, as an example, a pivot table that for the *mylibrary* database tells which publisher has published how many books in a given category. (Because of the relatively small number of data records the result is, of course, not very informative. But if *mylibrary* contained a large number of books, then this table would allow you to determine easily which publishers specialize in which subjects.)

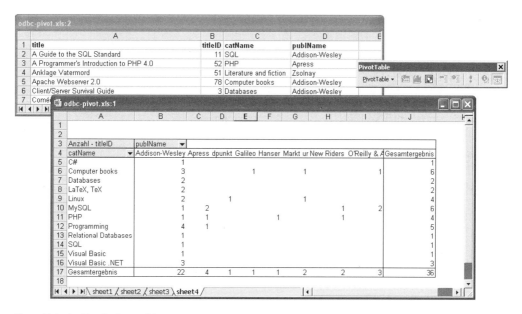

Figure 7-4. *An Excel pivot table*

Importing Data with MS Query

Whether you wish to insert MySQL data directly into an Excel worksheet (command DATA | GET EXTERNAL DATA | NEW DATABASE QUERY) or to create a pivot table or chart based on external data, Excel will launch the auxiliary program MS Query. This program functions as the interface between Excel and an external database, and it assists in the setting of import and query parameters.

In this program you select the DSN in the dialog CHOOSE DATA SOURCE. At that point, the QUERY WIZARD appears, which assists in the creation of a database query. In the first step you select the required tables or table fields (see Figure 7-5). In the next two steps you can specify the filter criteria (corresponding to *WHERE* conditions) and the sort order.

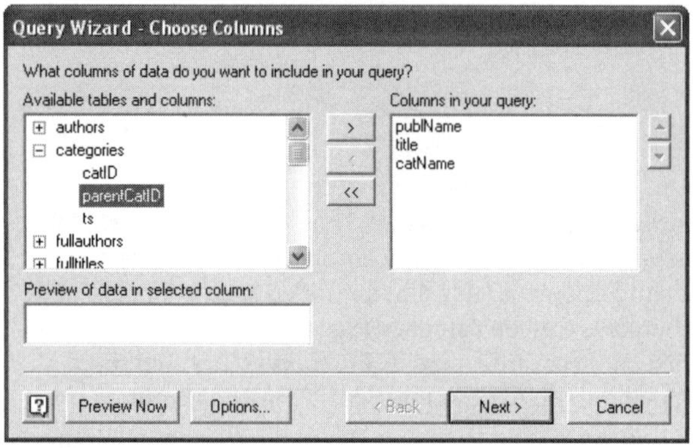

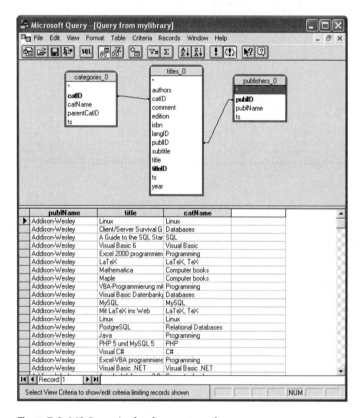

Figure 7-5. *Selection of a column in MS Query*

If these specifications suffice for executing the query, you can terminate MS Query with FINISH. However, it is usually preferable first to click on the option VIEW DATA OR EDIT QUERY. In this case, the query is displayed by MS Query in development mode, where it can be optimized (see Figure 7-6). In particular, any relations between the tables that MS Query has not recognized on its own can be established. To accomplish this you simply *Drag&Drop* the ID fields from one table to the other. A dialog appears in which you can set the relational properties.

Figure 7-6. *MS Query in development mode*

■**Tip** Excel frequently has difficulties with the importation of information about data. You can solve some of these problems with the help of the SQL function CONCAT. To format a column with this function, open the dialog EDIT COLUMN in MS Query with a double click on the column in question. In the input field FIELD you set the expression present there in *CONCAT(...)*. For example, from *table.birthdate* you would produce *CONCAT(table.birthdate)*.

Connector/J Installation

OpenOffice and StarOffice can access MySQL databases either via ODBC or JDBC. If you wish to work under Windows with ODBC, then you must, as described at the beginning of this chapter, install Connector/ODBC and set up a data source. Under Unix/Linux, however, JDBC is generally the better option, since JDBC is much easier to set up under these operating systems.

JDBC (*Java database connectivity*) is part of the Java system. This section assumes that a Java runtime environment is installed on your computer, e.g., the J2SE Runtime Environment 5.0 from Sun. This runtime environment is necessary for executing Java programs. (OpenOffice and StarOffice are not pure Java programs, but they use certain Java functions.) If you need to obtain a runtime environment for your operating system, you can download one from (search for *JRE*) http://java.sun.com/j2se/1.5.0/download.jsp.

Connector/J

JDBC does not contain a driver for MySQL. This task is handled by Connector/J, available (free of charge, GPL license) from http://dev.mysql.com. For this book the stable version 3.1.7 was tested. (The new version 3.2.*n* was still in alpha phase as of March 2005.)

At http://dev.mysql.com/ you can find Connector/J in various versions as a tar.gz archive for Unix/Linux or as a ZIP file for Windows. Both archives contain exactly the same files: Java is platform-independent.

■**Note** Connector/J is included as a package with many Linux distributions and is easily installed with the appropriate package management program.

Installation

Installation is quite easy: Unpack the archive into the directory of your choice and copy the file mysql-connector-java-n.n.n-bin.jar into the directory lib/ext of your Java installation. This *.jar file contains the entire driver. All the other files of the Connector/J package contain the source code, documentation, etc., many things that you don't need for running the driver. (Under Unix/Linux you need *root* privileges to copy the *.jar file.)

There now remains the question of where Java is installed on your computer. Here are two typical paths: under Windows, C:\Programs\Java\jre1.5.0_01\lib\ext; under Linux, /usr/lib/jvm/jre-1.4.2-sun/lib/ext. If you are using OpenOffice 2.0, you can determine the location of the Java installation with OPTIONS | OPENOFFICE.ORG | JAVA (see Figure 7-7).

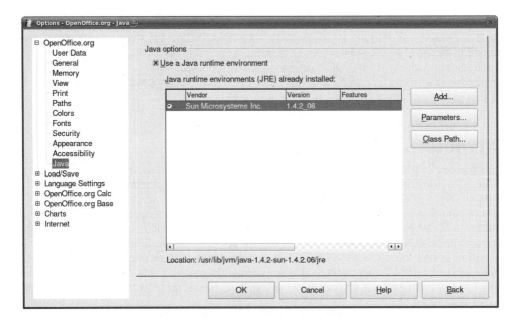

Figure 7-7. *Determining the Java installation path with OpenOffice*

Note that OpenOffice must be restarted before it will recognize the newly installed Connector/J. This includes the Quickstart program in the task bar.

OpenOffice/StarOffice Base

A significant innovation in OpenOffice 2.0 and StarOffice 8.0 is the database component Base. It makes possible the generation of custom databases and simplifies management and use of external databases. This section describes the basic functions of Base for accessing MySQL databases. (The previous versions OpenOffice 1.1 and StarOffice 7.0 also had database functions, but they were less conveniently hidden in the data view. The next section, on OpenOffice/StarOffice Calc, goes into this data view.)

Creating a Connection to a MySQL Database

To open a new database project, execute FILE | NEW | DATABASE and select the option CONNECT TO AN EXISTING DATABASE and the database type MYSQL. In the next step you have the choice between ODBC and JDBC. If you wish to use Connector/J, as described in the previous section, choose JDBC.

In the third step you can check with the button TEST CLASS (see Figure 7-8) whether the installation of Connector/J was successful. If that is the case, provide the name of the database and the computer name of the MySQL server (usually *localhost*).

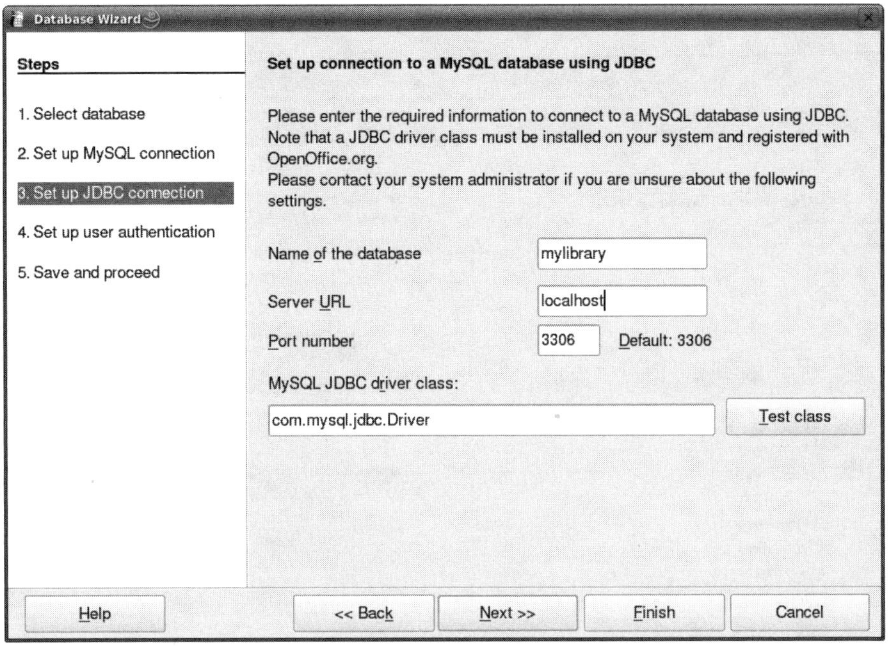

Figure 7-8. *Creating a connection to a MySQL database*

In step four you need to give the MySQL user name. If this user is secured with a password (which is generally the case), then activate the option PASSWORD REQUIRED. Now you can check with the button TEST CONNECTION whether all went well. You will be asked for the password.

Before ending the DATABASE WIZARD you need to give a file name. In the Base file, first only the connection parameters are stored, then later queries, forms, and reports. The actual data remain on the MySQL server. The Base file thus contains not the content of the database, but simply objects that enable access to and management of the database. For this reason, the Base file is generally quite small.

Now the database component Base appears. This gives, in basic view, an overview of four modules: TABLES, QUERIES, FORMS, and REPORTS (see Figure 7-9). At first, the existing tables in the MySQL database are available. Queries and other database objects have to be created. A preview of the currently selected table can be obtained by setting the listbox at the lower right in the window to DOCUMENT.

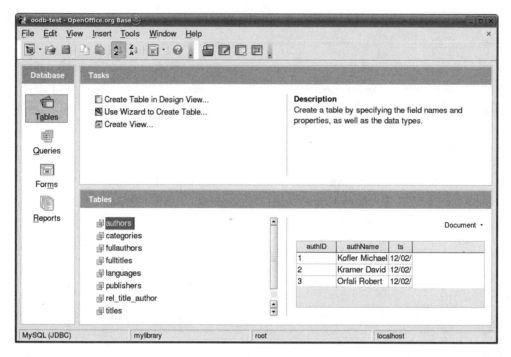

Figure 7-9. *The OpenOffice/StarOffice database component Base*

Tables

The module TABLES displays a list of all existing tables and views. You now have various options, which are briefly described here:

Open a table: A double click on the table name opens the table view. You can browse through the table, and add, change, and delete records (see Figure 7-10). You can also copy or move via drag&drop rows that you have selected with Ctrl or Shift into other OpenOffice/StarOffice components.

Create a new table: You can create new tables either with a simple table editor (OpenOffice calls this the DESIGN VIEW) or with a wizard. The wizard offers a number of predefined table layouts and can save you time if one of the model tables suits your requirements.

Change the table layout: The context menu EDIT leads into the DESIGN VIEW of an existing table. There you can add, edit, or delete columns; define or delete indexes; etc. Note, however, that not all functions offered by MySQL are available. Since Base is also compatible with other database systems, the editing possibilities are reduced to the lowest common denominator.

Copy data to the clipboard: The context menu command COPY copies all records of the current table to the clipboard. You can then insert the data into other OpenOffice/StarOffice components or into other text editors (format RTF or HTML).

Create a new view: This point leads to the query editor described later, in which you can create an SQL query. On the basis of this query a new view is created and stored in the database (see also Chapter 8).

Delete tables or views: You can also delete database objects via the context menu.

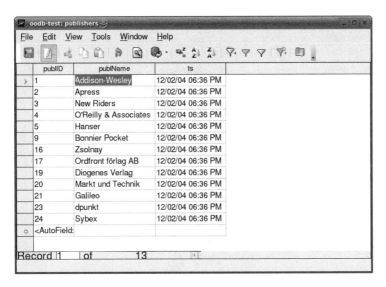

Figure 7-10. *Viewing and editing a table with Base*

■**Caution** All operations change the MySQL database directly, not just some local copy of the data. If you delete a table in Base, it is irretrievably lost.

Queries

The module QUERIES is the most interesting part of Base. Here you can formulate queries simply and conveniently. This is particularly helpful to SQL beginners. You can create queries either in DESIGN view, with a wizard, or in SQL view. The wizard, however, is useful only for queries that process data in only one table. In SQL view you must input the SQL code directly, which you can do just as well without Base. Therefore, we will concentrate on the query editor in DESIGN view, which looks much like the program MS Query introduced earlier in this chapter.

In the query design window you add with a double click all the tables whose data you wish to edit. The next step is to link fields between the tables using drag&drop. For example, in Figure 7-11, the *publishers* and *titles* tables are linked by the *publID* field. For Base to execute this link, move the *publID* field from the *publishers* table to the *publID* field of the *titles* table. (You can also use the reverse order, from *titles* to *publishers*.)

By default, Base creates so-called *INNER JOINS*. This means that in linking, only those fields that appear in both tables are considered. If *NULL* fields are to be allowed in one table, then you need a *LEFT* or *RIGHT JOIN*. The relational properties can be set by double clicking on the linking line. (More on the *JOIN* variants appears in Chapter 9.)

■**Tip** For Base to be able to generate the correct SQL code for MySQL for links among several tables, you must deactivate the option Use the SYNTAX {OJ} FOR OUTER JOINS in EDIT | DATABASE | ADVANCED SETTINGS.

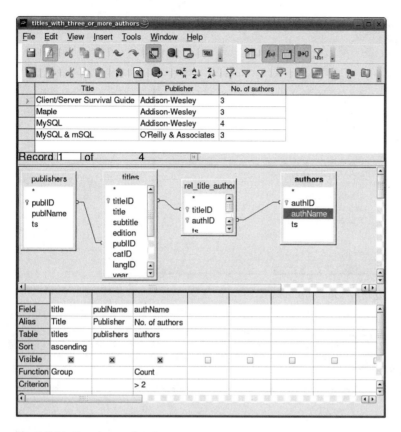

Figure 7-11. *Creating and testing a query*

After these preparations, you simply need to select the desired result columns with a double click, provide a label (row ALIAS), and if necessary set the sort order and grouping and aggregate functions. In the query shown in Figure 7-11, the result is grouped by title. For every such group, the number of authors is calculated. In the result, only titles with more than two authors will be displayed.

A click on the button EXECUTE QUERY returns the result of the query. If you wish to know what the SQL code of your query looks like, you can toggle between design and SQL modes with the DESIGN VIEW button.

Forms, Reports, and Additional Functions

The modules FORMS and REPORTS and the TOOLS menu lead to additional Base functions, which will be described here only briefly. The problem is that these functions are not fully developed and are useful at best only in very simple situations.

In the FORMS module, you can create input and editing forms (see Figure 7-12). Such forms make input and searching for data easier than via direct processing of tables. Base offers two ways of creating forms: via DESIGN view or a wizard. As a Base novice you will be better off with the wizard; using design view requires extensive experience in trying things out, and even then, it remains complex to work with. (Tip: Via VIEW | TOOLBARS you can activate the DATABASE toolbars. They contain the elements you need for creating forms.)

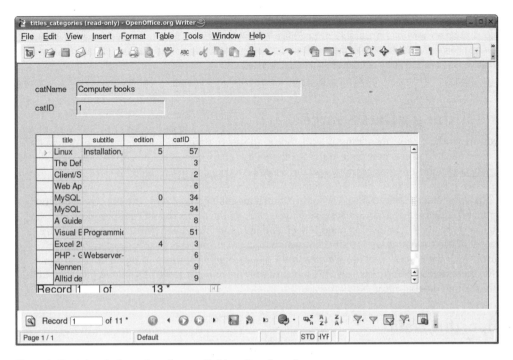

Figure 7-12. *A simple form that shows all titles of a selected category*

The module REPORTS makes it possible to define a database report with the help of a wizard. Reports allow for pretty-printing of a table, view, or query. Unfortunately, the REPORTS module does not come close to offering the functionality of Microsoft Access, neither in creating the report nor in its structure. Reports can process data in only a single database object. If you wish to print linked data from several tables, you must first create a suitable query. Changing a report after it has been created is well-nigh impossible. The context menu EDIT opens the report as a Writer document, but there you can carry out only very elementary changes in the layout (e.g., text size). A more extensive editing fails because the internal structure of the report is inaccessible via menu commands or tool-bars.

TOOLS | RELATIONSHIPS should lead to an editor in which you can set links between tables of a database that Base doesn't recognize. With MySQL databases, however, this command leads to an error, *The database does not support relations!* which of course is completely false: MySQL is a relational database.

TOOLS | USER ADMINISTRATION displays a dialog for MySQL user administration. The information contained in this dialog is mostly incorrect. In my experience, this dialog causes more problems than it solves. Avoid it! (You are better off using phpMyAdmin for user administration.)

OpenOffice/StarOffice Data Source View

Independently of the Base components described in the previous sections, all other OpenOffice/StarOffice components offer a so-called DATA SOURCE view. This view can be toggled on and off with F4 or VIEW | DATA SOURCES, and it helps in entering data from external databases into Calc, Writer, etc.

■**Tip** DATA SOURCE view is also available in OpenOffice 1.1 and StarOffice 7. It offers functions for administering tables and queries similar to those of the new Base components. However, these functions are hidden behind an unintuitive interface and some of them are not well developed.

Establishing a Data Source

If you are working with OpenOffice 2/StarOffice 8, all known Base data sources are displayed in DATA SOURCE view. To define a new data source, execute FILE | NEW | DATABASE. You can change the assignment between the data source name and the Base files as needed in the dialog TOOLS | OPTIONS | BASE | DATABASES.

In OpenOffice 1.1/StarOffice 7, you can launch an analogous wizard with the context menu command ADMINISTRATE DATA SOURCES. There you click on the button NEW DATA SOURCE, choose the database type MySQL in the first dialog sheet, and in the second sheet, the option CONNECTOR/J. The rest of the configuration is more complex than in Base: you have to specify so-called data source URLs with *localhost:3306/dbname*. If the MySQL server is not running on the local computer, then instead of *localhost*, give the name of the computer. Instead of *dbname*, give the name of the desired database (e.g., *mylibrary*).

Importing Data

In DATABASE view you can select a table or a query and execute it with a double click. Now you can insert an entire table or a set of lines selected with Ctrl or Shift into a table calculation sheet or text document. See Figure 7-13.

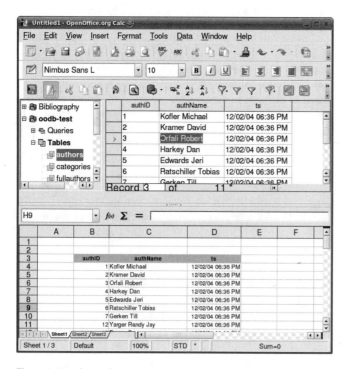

Figure 7-13. *Above, the* DATA SOURCE *view; below, a Calc table sheet*

## PART 3

Fundamentals

CHAPTER 8

■■■

Database Design

The first stage in any database application is the design of the database. The design will have a great influence on the efficiency of the application, the degree of simplicity or difficulty in programming and maintenance, and the flexibility in making changes in the design. Errors that occur in the design phase will come home to roost in the heartache of future efforts at correction. But don't expect any easy recipe! Database design has a great deal to do with experience, and in a single chapter one can do no more than present some pointers to get you started.

This chapter discusses the fundamentals of relational databases, summarizes the different data and table types available under MySQL, and demonstrates, using the *mylibrary* database, the application of normalization rules. (The *mylibrary* database is used to manage a collection of books, and authors and publishers will be used in many of the examples in the book.) Additional topics are the correct use of indexes and integrity rules (foreign key constraints).

■**Tip** This chapter serves as the basis for database design, but it does not explain how to create a new database and its associated tables. There are two ways of doing this:

The easiest is to use an interface such as MySQL Administrator or phpMyAdmin (see Chapters 5 and 6). This allows you to define the properties of new tables with a few clicks of the mouse.

The other possibility is to create databases and tables with SQL commands (e.g., *CREATE TABLE name...*; see Chapter 9). To be sure, the formulation of such commands is relatively tedious, but the advantage is that such commands can also be executed in a PHP script, which can be useful if you want to create temporary tables.

Further Reading

There are countless books that deal exclusively, independently of any specific database system, with database design and SQL. Needless to say, there is a variety of opinion as to which of these books are the good ones. Therefore, consider the following recommendations as my personal hit list:

Joe Celko: *SQL for Smarties*, Morgan Kaufmann Publishers, 1999. (This is not a book for SQL beginners. Many examples are currently not realizable in MySQL, because MySQL is not sufficiently compatible with ANSI-SQL/92. Nonetheless, it is a terrific example-oriented book on SQL.)

Judith S. Bowman et al.: *The Practical SQL Handbook*, Addison-Wesley, 2001.

Michael J. Hernandez: *Database Design for Mere Mortals*, Addison-Wesley, 2003. (The first half is somewhat long-winded, but the second half is excellent and very clearly written.)

Another book that is frequently recommended, but with which I am not familiar, is Peter Gulutzan and Trudy Pelzer's *SQL-99 Complete, Really*, R&D Books, 1999.

If you are not quite ready to shell out your hard-earned cash for yet another book and you are interested for now in database design only, you may find the compact introduction on the design of relational databases by Fernando Lozano adequate to your needs. See http://www.edm2.com/ 0612/msql7.html.

Table Types

A peculiarity of MySQL is that when you create a new table, you can specify its type. MySQL supports a number of table types, distinguished by a variety of properties. The three most important types are MyISAM, InnoDB, and HEAP.

If you do not specify the type when you create a table, then the MySQL server decides for you, based on its configuration, either for MyISAM or InnoDB. The default type is set with the option default-table-type in the MySQL configuration file.

This section provides a brief look at the different table types recognized by MySQL as well as some of their properties and when the use of one type or another is appropriate.

MyISAM Tables

The MyISAM table type is mature, stable, and simple to manage. If you have no particular reason to choose another type, then you should use this type. Internally, there are two variants of this table type, and the MySQL server chooses the appropriate type on its own:

MyISAM Static: These tables are used when all columns of the table have fixed, predetermined size. Access in such tables is particularly efficient. This is true even if the table is frequently changed (that is, when there are many *INSERT*, *UPDATE*, and *DELETE* commands). Moreover, data security is quite high, since in the case of corrupted files or other problems, it is relatively easy to extract records.

MyISAM Dynamic: If in the declaration of a table there is also only a single *VARCHAR*, *xxxTEXT*, or *xxxBLOB* field, then MySQL automatically selects this table type. The significant advantage over the static MyISAM variant is that the space requirement is usually significantly less: Character strings and binary objects require space commensurate with their actual size (plus a few bytes overhead).

However, it is a fact that data records are not all the same size. If records are later altered, then their location within the database file may have to change. In the old place there appears a hole in the database file. Moreover, it is possible that the fields of a record are not all stored within a contiguous block within the database file, but in various locations. All of this results in increasingly longer access times as the edited table becomes more and more fragmented, unless an *OPTIMIZE TABLE* or an optimization program is executed every now and then (myisamchk; see Chapter 14).

MyISAM Compressed: Both dynamic and static MyISAM tables can be compressed with the auxiliary program myisamchk. This usually results in a shrinkage of the storage requirement for the table to less than one-half the original amount (depending on the contents of the table). To be sure, thereafter, every data record must be decompressed when it is read, but it is still possible under some conditions that access to the table is nevertheless faster, particularly with a combination of a slow hard drive and fast processor.

The decisive drawback of compressed MyISAM tables is that they cannot be changed (that is, they are read-only tables).

InnoDB Tables

In addition to the MyISAM format, MySQL supports a second table format, namely InnoDB. This is a modern alternative to MyISAM, which above all offers the following additional functions:

Transactions: Database operations in InnoDB tables can be executed as transactions. This allows you to execute several logically connected SQL commands as a single entity. If an error occurs during execution, then all of the commands (not only the one during which the error occurred) are nullified. In addition, transactions offer other advantages that improve the security of database applications.

Transactions can be executed in all four isolation levels of the ANSI-SQL/92 standard (*READ UNCOMMITTED, READ COMMITTED, REPEATABLE READ, SERIALIZABLE*; see also Chapter 10).

Row Level Locking: In implementing transactions, the InnoDB table driver uses internal *row level locking*. This means that during a transaction, the entire table does not have to be blocked for access by other users (which is the case for a MyISAM table during a *LOCK TABLE* command), but only the data records are actually affected. If many users are simultaneously making changes on a large table, row level locking can bring about an enormous advantage in efficiency.

The InnoDB table driver automatically recognizes *deadlocks* (that is, the condition in which two processes mutually block each other) and in such a case, terminates one of the two processes automatically.

Foreign Key Constraints: When you define relations between your tables, the InnoDB table driver automatically ensures that the referential integrity of the table is preserved after *DELETE* commands. Thus it is impossible, for example, for a record in table A to refer to a no longer existing table B. (In database lingo this function is called a *foreign key constraint.*)

Crash Recovery: After a crash, InnoDB tables are automatically and very quickly returned to a consistent state (provided that the file system of the computer was not damaged). I have not tested this functionality.

The InnoDB table driver has been an integral component of MySQL since version 3.23.34. The development of the table driver and its commercial support come from the independent company Innobase (see `http://www.innodb.com`).

Limitations and Drawbacks

If InnoDB tables had only advantages and no drawbacks, one could dump MyISAM tables in the garbage and be done with it. But that is not the case, as the following list reveals:

Tablespace Administration: While with the MyISAM table driver, each table is stored in its own file, which grows or shrinks as required, the InnoDB table driver stores all data and indexes in a *tablespace*, comprising one or more files, that forms a sort of virtual file system. These files cannot later be made smaller. Nor is it possible to stop the MySQL server and then copy a table by simply copying its file. Therefore, in the administration of InnoDB tables, the command `mysqldump` must be employed more frequently than with MyISAM tables.

Record Size: A data record can occupy at most 8000 bytes. This limit does not hold for *TEXT* and *BLOB* columns, of which only the first 512 bytes are stored in the database proper. Data in such columns beyond this size are stored in separate pages of the master space.

Storage Requirement: The storage requirements for InnoDB tables are much greater than those for equivalent MyISAM tables (up to twice as big).

Full-Text Index: For InnoDB tables one cannot use a full-text index.

GIS Data: Geometric data cannot be stored in InnoDB tables.

COUNT Problem: On account of open transactions, it is relatively difficult for the InnoDB table driver to determine the number of records in a table. Therefore, executing a *SELECT COUNT(*) FROM TABLE* is much slower than with MyISAM tables. This limitation should be eliminated soon.

Table Locking: InnoDB uses its own locking algorithms in executing transactions. Therefore, you should avoid *LOCK TABLE ... READ/WRITE*. Instead, you should use *SELECT ... IN SHARE MODE* or *SELECT ... FOR UPDATE*. These commands have the additional advantage that they block only individual records and not the entire table. For future versions of MySQL, the InnoDB-specific commands *LOCK TABLE ... IN SHARE MODE* and *LOCK TABLE ... IN EXCLUSIVE MODE* are planned.

mysql Tables: The *mysql* tables for managing MySQL access privileges cannot be transformed into InnoDB tables. They must remain in MyISAM format.

License Costs: Adding InnoDB support to a commercial MySQL license doubles the cost. (This is relevant only if you are developing a commercial product. With open source programs, *Indoor* projects, and normal websites, the free MySQL version suffices. See also Chapter 1.)

■**Tip** Further details on the limitations of InnoDB tables in relation to MyISAM tables can be found at the following address: `http://dev.mysql.com/doc/mysql/en/innodb-restrictions.html`.

MyISAM or InnoDB?

You can specify individually for each table in your database which table driver is to be used. That is, it is permitted within a single database to use both MyISAM and InnoDB tables. This allows you to choose the optimal table driver for each table, depending on its content and the application that will be accessing it.

MyISAM tables are to be recommended whenever you want to manage tables in the most space- and time-efficient way possible. InnoDB tables, on the other hand, take precedence when your application makes use of transactions, requires greater security, or is to be accessed by many users simultaneously for making changes.

There is no generally valid answer to the question of which table type offers faster response. In principle, since transactions take time and InnoDB tables take up more space on the hard drive, MyISAM should have the advantage. But with InnoDB tables you can avoid the use of *LOCK TABLE* commands, which offers an advantage to InnoDB, which is better optimized for certain applications.

Furthermore, the speed of an application depends heavily on hardware (particularly the amount of RAM), the settings in the MySQL configuration file, and other factors. Therefore, I can provide here only the following advice: In speed-critical applications, perform your own tests on both types of tables.

HEAP Tables

HEAP tables exist only in RAM (not on the hard drive). They use a *hash index*, which results in particularly fast access to individual data records. HEAP tables are often used as temporary tables. See the next section for more about this topic.

In comparison to normal tables, HEAP tables present a large number of functional restrictions, of which we mention here only the most important: No *xxxTEXT* or *xxxBLOB* data types can be used. Records can be searched only with = or <=> (and not with <, >, <=, or >=). *AUTO_INCREMENT* is not supported. Indexes can be set up only for *NOT NULL* columns.

HEAP tables should be used whenever relatively small data sets are to be managed with maximal speed. Since HEAP tables are stored exclusively in RAM, they disappear as soon as MySQL is terminated. The maximum size of a HEAP table is determined in the MySQL configuration file by the parameter `max_heap_table_size`.

Temporary Tables

With all of the table types listed above there exists the possibility of creating a table on a temporary basis. Such tables are automatically deleted as soon as the link with MySQL is terminated. Furthermore, temporary tables are invisible to other MySQL links (so that it is possible for two users to employ temporary tables with the same name without running into trouble).

Temporary tables are not a separate table type unto themselves, but rather a variant of the types that we have been describing. Temporary tables are often created automatically by MySQL in order to assist in the execution of *SELECT* queries.

Temporary tables are not stored in the same directory as the other MySQL tables, but in a special temporary directory (under Windows it is usually called `C:\Windows\Temp`, while under Unix it is generally `/tmp` or `/var/tmp` or `/usr/tmp`). The directory can be set at MySQL startup.

Other Table Types

MySQL recognizes a variety of other table types, of which those listed here are the most important variants. Note that these table types are available only in the Max version or self-compiled version of MySQL. You can determine which table types your MySQL version supports with the command *SHOW ENGINES*.

BDB Tables: BDB tables were historically the first transactions-capable MySQL table type. Now that the InnoDB table driver has matured, there is not much reason to use BDB tables.

Compressed Tables (type ARCHIVE, since MySQL 4.1): This table type is designed for the archiving and logging of large data sets. The advantage of this table type is that the records are immediately compressed when they are stored.

However, *ARCHIVE* tables make sense only if the records are not to be altered. (*INSERT* is permitted, but *UPDATE* and *DELETE* are not allowed.)

ARCHIVE tables cannot be indexed. For each *SELECT* command, therefore, all records must be read! So use this table type only if you expect to access the data relatively rarely.

Tables in Text Format (type CSV, since MySQL 4.1): Records from CSV tables are saved as text files with comma-separated values. For example, *"123","I am a character string"*. CSV tables cannot be indexed.

NDB Tables (MySQL Cluster, since MySQL 4.1): The NDB table type belongs with the MySQL cluster functions, which are integrated into the MySQL Max version. (NDB stands for *network database*.) This table type is transactions-capable and is most suitable for databases that are distributed among a large number of computers. However, the use of this table type requires that first a number of MySQL Max installations be specially configured for cluster operation. Detailed information can be found at `http://dev.mysql.com/doc/mysql/en/ndbcluster.html`.

External Tables (type FEDERATED, since MySQL 5.0): This table type enables access to tables in an external database. The database system can be located, for example, on another computer in the local network. At present, the external database must be a MySQL database, though perhaps in the future, MySQL will allow connection with other database systems.

There are some restrictions in accessing *FEDERATED* tables: Neither transactions nor query optimization with Query Cache are possible. The structure of external tables cannot be changed (though the records can be). In other words, *ALTER TABLE* is not permitted, while *INSERT*, *UPDATE*, and *DELETE* are.

Further information on all the MySQL table types can be found as a separate chapter in the MySQL documentation at `http://dev.mysql.com/doc/mysql/en/storage-engines.html`.

Table Files

You can specify the location for database files at MySQL startup. (Under Unix/Linux `/var/lib/mysql` is frequently used, while under Windows it is usually `C:\Programs\MySQL\MySQL Server n.n\data`.) All further specifications are relative to this directory.

A description of each table is saved in a `*.frm` file. The `*.frm` files are located in directories whose names correspond to the name of the database: `data/dbname/tablename.frm`. This file contains the table schema (data types of the columns, etc.).

Beginning with MySQL 4.1, an additional file, `db.opt`, is stored in the database directory, which relates to the entire database: `data/dbname/db.opt`. This file contains the database settings.

For each MyISAM table, two additional files are created: `data/dbname/tablename.MYD`, with MyISAM table data, and `data/dbname/tablename.MYI`, with MyISAM indexes (all indexes of the table).

InnoDB tables are stored in individual files for each table or else collectively, in the so-called *tablespace* (depending on whether `innodb_file_per_table` is specified in the MySQL configuration file). The location and name of the tablespace are also governed by configuration settings. In current MySQL installations, the default is `data/dbname/tablename.ibd` for InnoDB table data (data and indexes), and `data/ibdata1, -2, -3` for the tablespace and undo logs, and `data/ib_logfile0, -1, -2` for InnoDB logging data.

If triggers are defined for the tables (see Chapter 13), then their code is currently stored in a file `data/dbname/tablename.TRG`, though it is possible that this will change in future versions of MySQL.

MySQL Data Types

Every table is composed of a number of columns. For each column, the desired data type may be specified. This section provides an overview of the data types available in MySQL.

Integers (xxxINT)

With the *INT* data type, both positive and negative numbers are generally allowed. With the attribute *UNSIGNED*, the range can be restricted to the positive integers. But note that then subtraction returns *UNSIGNED* integers, which can lead to deceptive and confusing results.

With *TINYINT*, numbers between -128 and +127 are allowed. With the attribute *UNSIGNED*, the range is 0 to 255. If one attempts to store a value above or below the given range, MySQL simply replaces the input with the largest or, respectively, smallest permissible value. See Table 8-1.

Table 8-1. *Data Types for Integers*

MySQL Data Type	Meaning
TINYINT(m)	8-bit integer (1 byte, -128 to +127); the optional value *m* gives the desired column width in *SELECT* results (*Maximum Display Width*), but has no influence on the permitted range of numbers.
SMALLINT(m)	16-bit integer (2 bytes, -32,768 to + 32,767)
MEDIUMINT(m)	24-bit integer (3 bytes, -8,388,608 to +8,388,607)
INT(m), INTEGER(m)	32-bit integer (4 bytes, -2.147,483,648 to +2,147,483,647)
BIGINT(m)	64-bit integer (8 bytes, $\pm 9.22 * 10^{18}$)
SERIAL	Synonym for *BIGINT AUTO_INCREMENT NOT NULL PRIMARY KEY*

Optionally, in the definition of an integer field, the desired column width (number of digits) can be specified, such as, for example, *INT(4)*. This parameter is called *M* (for *Maximum Display Size*) in the literature. It assists MySQL as well as various user interfaces in presenting query results in a readable format.

■**Note** Note that with the *INT* data types, the *M* restricts neither the allowable range of numbers nor the possible number of digits. In spite of setting *INT(4)*, for example, you can still store numbers greater than 9999. However, in certain rare cases (such as in complex queries for the evaluation of which MySQL constructs a temporary table), the numerical values in the temporary tables can be truncated, with incorrect results as a consequence.

AUTO_INCREMENT Integers

With the optional attribute *AUTO_INCREMENT* you can achieve for integers that MySQL automatically inserts a number that is 1 larger than the currently largest value in the column when a new record is created for the field in question. *AUTO_INCREMENT* is generally used in the definition of fields that are to serve as the primary key for a table.

The following rules hold for *AUTO_INCREMENT*:

- This attribute is permitted only when one of the attributes *NOT NULL, PRIMARY KEY*, or *UNIQUE* is used as well.

- It is not permitted for a table to possess more than one *AUTO_INCREMENT* column.

- The automatic generation of an ID value functions only when in inserting a new data record with *INSERT*, a specific value or *NULL* is not specified. However, it is possible to generate a new data record with a specific ID value, provided that the value in question is not already in use.

- If you want to find out the *AUTO_INCREMENT* value that a newly inserted data record has received, after executing the *INSERT* command (but within the same connection or transaction), execute the command *SELECT LAST_INSERT_ID()*.

- If the *AUTO_INCREMENT* counter reaches its maximal value, based on the selected integer format, it will not be increased further. No more insert operations are possible. With tables that experience many *INSERT* and *DELETE* commands, it can happen that the 32-bit *INT* range will become used up, even though there are many fewer than two billion records in the table. In such a case, use a *BIGINT* column.

Binary Data (BIT and BOOL)

The keyword *BOOL* in MySQL is a synonym for *TINYINT*. This was also true prior to version 5.0.2 for *BIT*. Beginning with version 5.0.3, *BIT* is an independent data type for storing binary values with up to 64 bits.

Floating-Point Numbers (FLOAT and DOUBLE)

Since version 3.23 of MySQL, the types *FLOAT* and *DOUBLE* correspond to the IEEE numerical types for single and double precision that are available in many programming languages.

Optionally, the number of digits in *FLOAT* and *DOUBLE* values can be set with the two parameters m and d. In that case, m specifies the number of digits before the decimal point, while d gives the number of places after the decimal point. The floating-point data types are summarized in Table 8-2.

Table 8-2. *Data Types for Floating-Point Numbers*

Data Type	Meaning
FLOAT(m, d)	Floating-point number, 8-place accuracy (4 byte); the optional values m and d give the desired number of places before and after the decimal point in *SELECT* results; these values have no influence on the actual way the numbers are stored.
DOUBLE(m, d)	Floating-point number, 16-place accuracy (8 byte).
REAL(m, d)	Synonym for *DOUBLE*.

The parameter m does no more than assist in the formatting of numbers; it does not limit the permissible range of numbers. On the other hand, d has the effect of rounding numbers when they are stored. For example, if you attempt to save the number 123456.789877 in a field with the attribute *DOUBLE(6,3)*, the number stored will, in fact, be 123456.790.

■**Note** MySQL expects floating-point numbers in international notation, that is, with a decimal point, and not a comma (which is used in a number of European countries). Results of queries are always returned in this notation, and very large or very small values are expressed in scientific notation (e.g., 1.2345678901279e+017).

If you have your heart set on formatting floating-point numbers differently, you will have either to employ the function *FORMAT* in your SQL queries (though this function is of use only in the thousands groupings) or to carry out your formatting in the client programming language (that is, in PHP, Perl, etc.).

Fixed-Point Numbers (DECIMAL)

The integer type *DECIMAL* is recommended when rounding errors caused by the internal representation of numbers as *FLOAT* or *DOUBLE* are unacceptable, perhaps with currency values. Since the numbers are stored as character strings, the storage requirement is much greater. At the same time, the possible range of values is smaller, since exponential notation is ruled out. The fixed-point data types are summarized in Table 8-3.

Table 8-3. *Data Types for Fixed-Point Numbers*

Data Type	Meaning
DECIMAL(p, s)	Fixed-point number, saved as a character string; arbitrary number of digits (1 byte per digit + 2 bytes overhead)
NUMERIC, DEC	Synonym for *DECIMAL*

The two parameters *p* and *s* specify the total number of digits (*precision*) and, respectively, the number of digits after the decimal point (*scale*). The range in the case of *DECIMAL(6,3)* is from 9999.999 to -999.999. This bizarre range results from the apparent fact that six places are reserved for the number plus an additional place for the minus sign. When the number is positive, the place for the minus sign can be commandeered to store another digit. If *p* and *s* are not specified, then MySQL automatically uses (10, 0), with the result that positive integers with eleven digits and negative integers with ten digits can be stored.

Date and Time (DATE, TIME, DATETIME, TIMESTAMP)

Table 8-4 summarizes the data types for storing time values.

Table 8-4. *Data Types for Date and Time*

MySQL Keyword	Meaning
DATE	Date in the form '2003-12-31', range 1000-01-01 to 9999-12-31 (3 bytes)
TIME	Time in the form '23:59:59', range ±838:59:59 (3 bytes)
DATETIME	Combination of *DATE* and *TIME* in the form '2003-12-31 23:59:59' (8 bytes)
YEAR	Year 1900–2155 (1 byte)

Data Validation

In older versions of MySQL, the *DATE* and *DATETIME* data types did only a limited amount of type checking. Values between 0 and 12 for months, and between 0 and 31 for days, were generally allowed. However, it is the responsibility of the client program to provide correct data. (For example, 0 is a permissible value for a month or day, in order to provide the possibility of storing incomplete or unknown data.)

Beginning with MySQL 5.0.2 there is a more thorough validation, so that only valid data can be stored. Still allowed are the month and day values 0, as well as the date 0000-00-00.

Validation can be controlled through the MySQL system variable *sql_mode* (see also Chapter 14). Table 8-5 summarizes the *sql_mode* values that are relevant for time validation.

Table 8-5. *sql_mode Settings*

Setting	Meaning
ALLOW_INVALID_DATES	Obviously incorrect dates (e.g., 2005-02-31) are accepted.
NO_ZERO_DATE	0000-00-00 will no longer be accepted as a valid date.
NO_ZERO_IN_DATE	0 will not be accepted as a valid month or day.

Peculiarities of TIMESTAMP

Among the data types for date and time, *TIMESTAMP* plays a particular role. Fields of this type are automatically updated whenever the record is altered, thereby reflecting the time of the last change. Fields of type *TIMESTAMP* are therefore usually employed only for internal management, not for the storage of "real" data, though such is possible.

Many database operations with particular client libraries (such as with Connector/ODBC) work correctly only if every table in the database has a *TIMESTAMP* column. The time of the last change is often needed for internal administration of the data.

For the automatic *TIMESTAMP* updating to function properly, the column involved must have either no explicit value assigned or else *NULL*. In either case, MySQL itself inserts the current time.

If there is more than one *TIMESTAMP* column in a table, then the first column is updated for which a constant time value is not explicitly defined (*DEFAULT 0*).

Since MySQL 4.1.3 it has been possible to control the behavior of *TIMESTAMP* columns more precisely through two attributes. Possible combinations of attributes are shown in Table 8-6.

Table 8-6. *TIMESTAMP Variants*

Setting	Meaning
TIMESTAMP DEFAULT CURRENT_TIMESTAMP ON UPDATE CURRENT_TIMESTAMP	The column is automatically updated both when a new record is created and for each change in a record.
TIMESTAMP	As above, but with less typing.
TIMESTAMP DEFAULT CURRENT_TIMESTAMP	The column is initialized when a new record is created, but is left unchanged thereafter.
TIMESTAMP ON UPDATE CURRENT_TIMESTAMP	The column is initialized to zero when it is created. The current time is stored only on subsequent changes.
TIMESTAMP DEFAULT 'yyyy-mm-dd hh:mm:ss' ON UPDATE CURRENT_TIMESTAMP	The column is initialized on creation to the given time; the current time is stored only when changes are subsequently made.

■**Caution** Do not use a *TIMESTAMP* column if you wish to store the date and time yourself. For that, one has the data type *DATETIME*.

If you wish to deviate from the default behavior and not have the *TIMESTAMP* column change when a record is changed, then you must specify the date and time explicitly:

```
UPDATE tablename SET col='new value, ts=ts;
```

MySQL versions through 4.0 formatted *TIMESTAMP* values in the form *YYYYMMDDHHMMSS* (instead of *YYYY-MM-DD HH:MM:SS*). This can lead to eventual incompatibilities when data are later processed. Add a zero if you prefer the old format (that is, *SELECT ts+0 FROM table*).

Microseconds: In future versions of MySQL it is possible that TIMESTAMP columns will also store microseconds. The syntax for such times has already been set (*2005-31-12 23:59:59.nnnnnn*), and there exist various *MICROSECOND* functions for processing such data. However, actually storing the data is not yet possible (this includes MySQL 5.0.2).

Functions for Processing and Formatting Dates and Times

MySQL returns dates in the form 2005-12-31. However, with *INSERT* and *UPDATE* it manages to deal with other formats, provided that the order year/month/day is adhered to and the values are numeric. If the year is given as a two-digit number, then the following interpretation is made: 70–99 becomes 1970–1999, while 00–69 becomes 2000–2069.

If query results are to be specially formatted, there are several MySQL functions available for processing date and time values. The most flexible of these is *DATE_FORMAT*, whose application is demonstrated in the following example:

```
SELECT DATE_FORMAT(birthdate, '%Y %M %e') FROM students
1977 September 3
1981 October 25
...
```

■Tip *DATE_FORMAT*, as well as many other MySQL functions for processing dates and times, are introduced in Chapter 10. There you will also learn how to convert times among different time zones. A reference for all time and date functions is in Chapter 21.

Character Strings (CHAR, VARCHAR, xxxTEXT)

Table 8-7 summarizes the data types for storing character strings.

Table 8-7. *Data Types for Character Strings*

MySQL Keyword	Meaning
CHAR(n)	character string with specified length, maximum 255 characters
VARCHAR(n)	character string with variable length, maximum 255 characters (MySQL through 4.1: $n<256$; MySQL from 5.0.3: $n<65,535$)
TINYTEXT	character string with variable length, maximum 255 bytes *TEXT* character string with variable length, maximum 2^{16}-1 characters
MEDIUMTEXT	character string with variable length, maximum 2^{24}-1 characters
LONGTEXT	character string with variable length, maximum 2^{32}-1 characters

With *CHAR*, the length of a character string is strictly specified. For example, *CHAR(20)* demands 20 bytes in each record, regardless of the length of the character string actually stored. (Blank characters at the beginning of a character string are eliminated before storage. Short character strings are extended with blanks. These blank characters are automatically deleted when the data are read out, with the result that it is impossible to store a character string that actually has blank characters at the end.)

In contrast, the length of a character string of type *VARCHAR* or one of the four *TEXT* types is variable. The storage requirement depends on the actual length of the character string.

Although *VARCHAR* and *TINYTEXT*, both of which can accept a character string up to a length of 65,535 characters, at first glance seem equivalent, there are, in fact, several features that distinguish one from the other: The maximum number of characters in *VARCHAR* columns must be specified (in the range 0 to 65,535) when the table is declared. Character strings that are too long will be unceremoniously, without warning, truncated when they are stored. In contrast, with *xxxTEXT* columns one cannot specify a maximal length. (The only limit is the maximal length of the particular text type.)

■Caution When it creates a new table, MySQL frequently changes the column definition into a form that is more efficient for MySQL (see also Chapter 9). These automatic changes are described in the MySQL documentation as *silent column changes*. They affect both *CHAR* and *VARCHAR* columns:

VARCHAR(n) with $n<4$ is always changed into *CHAR(n)*.

CHAR(n) with $n>3$ is changed into *VARCHAR(n)* if there are additional *VARCHAR*, *TEXT*, or *BLOB* columns in the table. If the table contains only columns with constant length, then *CHAR(n)* remains unchanged.

New Aspects of VARCHAR: In MySQL 5.0 there are two significant innovations for the data type *VARCHAR*. (In the tested version 5.0.3, the new *VARCHAR* implementation was available only for MyISAM tables, and not for InnoDB tables.)

- The maximal column size for MyISAM tables is now 65,535 bytes (it was previously 255 bytes). The maximum number of characters depends on the character set, since many character sets require more than 1 byte per character.

- Spaces at the beginning and end of *VARCHAR* values are now stored in the table. Thus *INSERT INTO table (varcharcolumn) VALUES (' abc ')* actually stores ' abc ' in the column, that is, a space, the characters *a*, *b*, and *c*, and finally another space character. (Previously, MySQL deleted spaces at the end of *VARCHAR* values, which was in violation of the ANSI standard.)

Binary Attribute: Columns of type *CHAR* and *VARCHAR* can optionally be given the attribute *BINARY*. They then behave essentially like *BLOB* columns (see below). The attribute *BINARY* can also be useful when you store text: What you achieve is that in sorting, it is exclusively the binary code of the characters that is considered (and not a particular sorting table). Thus case distinction is made, which otherwise would not be the case. This makes the internal management of binary character strings simpler and therefore faster than is the case with garden-variety character strings.

Character Set Fundamentals

With all text columns you can use the additional attributes *CHARACTER SET charactersetname COLLATE sortorder* to specify the desired character set and sort order. Character sets determine what code is used to represent the various characters. Most character sets agree on the 128 English ASCII characters (e.g., code 65 for the letter A). More problematic is the representation of international characters.

Latin Character Sets: In the past, each linguistic region developed various one-byte character sets, of which the *Latin* character sets have achieved the most widespread use: *Latin1*, alias ISO-8859-1, contains all characters usual in Western Europe (äöüßáàå etc.). *Latin2*, alias ISO-8859-2, contains characters from Central and East European languages. *Latin0*, alias Latin9, alias ISO-8859-15, is the same as Latin 1, but with the euro symbol included.

The problem with these character sets is obvious: None of these character sets contains all the characters of all the European languages, so there is no Latin character set for all of Europe.

Unicode Variants: To solve this problem, the 2-byte Unicode character set was developed. With 65,535 possible characters, it covers not only all of Europe, but most of the Asian languages as well.

However, Unicode determines only which code is associated with which character, not how the codes are internally stored. For this there are several variants, of which UCS-2 (universal character set) and UTF-8 (Unicode transfer format) are the most important.

- UCS-2, alias UTF-16, represents what is apparently the simplest solution, to represent each character by 2 bytes (thus 16 bits). This format is called UTF-16 or UCS-2. Almost all operating system functions of Microsoft Windows use this representation.

  However, this representation has two drawbacks: First, the storage requirement for characters is automatically doubled, even in those cases in which only European or even only the English ASCII characters are to be stored. Second, the byte code 0 appears in many places in Unicode character strings. Thus in texts with English ASCII characters, every second byte is zero. Many C programs, email servers, and the like assume that a zero byte signals the end of a character string.

- UFT-8 is the most popular alternative to UTF-16. In this case, all the ASCII characters (7 bit) are represented as before by a single byte whose first bit is 0. All other Unicode characters are represented by strings of 2 to 4 bytes.

  The clear disadvantage of this format is that there is no obvious relationship between the number of bytes and the number of characters in a document. Because of its greater compatibility to existing programs and a number of other advantages, UTF-8 has established itself as the standard under Unix/Linux and most other components important for Web development. When Unicode is mentioned in this book, it will always mean the UTF-8 format.

Despite the clear advantages of Unicode, in any of its formats, there are two reasons not to jump on the bandwagon immediately: First, the Unicode character set is incompatible with the well-known 1-byte character sets. Second, Unicode support for components used in Web development are anything but perfect. (The weakest link in the chain is PHP, and the situation will likely not improve before version 5.2.)

MySQL Character Set Support

Through version 4.0 of MySQL, the character set and sort order for all text fields were specified by the MySQL server. The *Latin1* character set was the default, together with the Swedish sort order. Another character set and sort order could be specified in the MySQL configuration file, but this setting then held for all databases. Furthermore, any change required restarting the database server and re-creation of all indexes. Unicode was not supported at all.

Beginning with MySQL 4.1, the situation has greatly improved: Now the character set and sort order can be specified individually for every column. At the same time, the selection of character sets and sort orders is larger than ever, including Unicode UTF-8 and UCS-2.

A long list of all the character sets as well as the associated possible sort orders can be displayed with the SQL command *SHOW COLLATION*, and the result is displayed here in abbreviated form. (Note that character sets and sort orders cannot be randomly mixed. Each character set offers a particular selection of sort orders. The default sort order for each character set is indicated by *Yes* in the column *Default*.)

```
SHOW COLLATION
```

Collation	Charset	Id	Default	Compiled	Sortlen
ascii_bin	ascii	65			0
ascii_general_ci	ascii	11	Yes		0
binary	binary	63	Yes	Yes	1
latin1_bin	latin1	47		Yes	1
latin1_danish_ci	latin1	15			0
latin1_general_ci	latin1	48			0
latin1_general_cs	latin1	49			0
latin1_german1_ci	latin1	5			0
latin1_german2_ci	latin1	31		Yes	2
latin1_spanish_ci	latin1	94			0
latin1_swedish_ci	latin1	8	Yes	Yes	1
latin2_bin	latin2	77			0
latin2_croatian_ci	latin2	27			0
latin2_general_ci	latin2	9	Yes		0
latin2_hungarian_ci	latin2	21			0
latin5_bin	latin5	78			0
latin5_turkish_ci	latin5	30	Yes		0
latin7_bin	latin7	79			0
latin7_estonian_cs	latin7	20			0
latin7_general_ci	latin7	41	Yes		0

```
latin7_general_cs     latin7    42                          0
utf8_bin              utf8      83          Yes             1
utf8_czech_ci         utf8      202         Yes             8
utf8_danish_ci        utf8      203         Yes             8
utf8_estonian_ci      utf8      198         Yes             8
utf8_general_ci       utf8      33    Yes   Yes             1
utf8_icelandic_ci     utf8      193         Yes             8
utf8_latvian_ci       utf8      194         Yes             8
utf8_lithuanian_ci    utf8      204         Yes             8
utf8_persian_ci       utf8      208         Yes             8
utf8_polish_ci        utf8      197         Yes             8
utf8_roman_ci         utf8      207         Yes             8
utf8_romanian_ci      utf8      195         Yes             8
utf8_slovak_ci        utf8      205         Yes             8
utf8_slovenian_ci     utf8      196         Yes             8
utf8_spanish2_ci      utf8      206         Yes             8
utf8_spanish_ci       utf8      199         Yes             8
utf8_swedish_ci       utf8      200         Yes             8
utf8_turkish_ci       utf8      201         Yes             8
utf8_unicode_ci       utf8      192         Yes             8
...
```

Table 8-8 gives additional information about the most important combinations of character set and sort order.

Table 8-8. *The Most Important Character Sets and Sort Orders*

Character Set	Sort Order	Meaning
latin1	*latin1_swedish_ci*	Swedish sort order, valid in MySQL by default for *latin1* columns; *ci* stands for case-insensitive.
latin1	*latin1_general_ci*	General sort order, suitable for many Western European languages without taking country-specific issues into account.
latin1	*latin1_general_cs*	As above, but case-sensitive: uppercase letters are sorted before lowercase letters.
latin1	*latin1_german1_ci*	German sort order according to the DIN-1 standard (ä=a, ö=o, ü=u, ß=s).
latin1	*latin1_german2_ci*	German sort order according to the DIN-2 standard (telephone directory rules, thus ä = ae, ö = oe, ü = ue, ß = ss).
utf8	*utf8_general_ci*	General sort order, suitable for many Western European languages without taking country-specific issues into account; is the default in MySQL for *utf8* columns.

If you do not specify a character set and sort order for a column, then the default character set for the table, the database, or the MySQL server is used, depending on the level at which the default settings are defined.

Which character set is optimal for your database depends, of course, on the application. If there will be no need to use characters outside of the Western European languages, then you can stick with *latin1*. This character set generally poses no problems for further data processing.

> ■**Tip** There is much more in this book on the subject of character sets and sort orders. See the topics SQL syntax, SQL commands, MySQL variables, and MySQL configuration. Furthermore, all the chapters on programming discuss issues surrounding the processing of Unicode character strings. Look in the index under *Unicode*.

Binary Data (xxxBLOB and BIT)

For the storage of binary data there are four *BLOB* data types at your service, all of which display almost the same properties as the *TEXT* data types. (Recall that "BLOB" is an acronym for "binary large object.") The only difference is that text data are usually compared and sorted in text mode (case-insensitive), while binary data are sorted and compared according to their binary codes.

There is considerable disagreement as to whether large binary objects should even be stored in a database. The alternative would be to store the data (images, for example) in external files and provide links to these files in the database.

The advantage to using BLOBs is the resulting integration into the database (more security, simpler backups, unified access to all data). The drawback is the usually significant slowdown. It is particularly disadvantageous that large and small data elements—strings, integers, etc.—on the one hand and BLOBs and long texts on the other must be stored all mixed together in a table file. The result is a slowdown in access to all of the data records.

Note as well that BLOBs in general can be read only as a whole. That is, it is impossible to read, say, the last 100 kilobytes of an 800-kilobyte BLOB. The entire BLOB must be transmitted.

Table 8-9 summarizes the data types for binary data.

Table 8-9. *Data Types for Binary Data*

MySQL Keyword	Meaning
BIT(n)	Bit data, where *n* is the number of bits (up to 64)
TINYBLOB	Binary data with variable length, maximum 255 bytes
BLOB	Binary data with variable length, maximum 2^{16}-1 bytes
MEDIUMBLOB	Binary data with variable length, maximum 2^{24}-1 bytes
LONGBLOB	Binary data with variable length, maximum 2^{32}-1 bytes

BIT Data

New since MySQL 5.0.3 is the possibility of defining columns of width up to 64 bits. To be sure, the data type *BIT* existed previously, but in earlier versions of MySQL, *BIT* was a synonym for *TINYINT(1)*.

There is a new syntax *b'0101'* for writing bit values. *SELECT* queries return binary values for *BIT* columns. However, the tested client programs were incapable of displaying these values correctly. If necessary, use *SELECT bitcolumn+0* to convert binary values to integers, and use *SELECT BIN(bitcolumn+0)* to display these integers in binary notation.

If you insert numbers into *BIT* columns causing underflow or overflow, all the bits will be set to 1. If, for example, you were to insert the numbers -1, 0, 1, 7, 8 into a *BIT(3)* column, the following binary values will be stored: *b'111'*, *b'000'*, *b'001'*, *b'111'*, *b'111'*.

Other Data Types

The two data types *ENUM* and *SET* are a peculiarity of MySQL. They enable a particularly efficient management of character set enumerations and combinations for the MySQL server.

With *ENUM* you can manage a list of up to 65,535 character strings assigned consecutive numbers. Then one of these strings can be selected in a field.

SET follows a similar idea, but here arbitrary combinations are possible. Internally, the strings are associated with powers of 2 (1, 2, 4, 8, etc.), so that a bitwise combination is possible. Accordingly, the memory requirement is greater than with *ENUM*s (1 bit per string). At most 64 strings can be thus combined. (The memory requirement is then 8 bytes.)

These data types have some drawbacks, however. First, managing them with PHP is relatively complex (for example, if you wish to determine the strings available in an *ENUM* field). Second, most other database systems know nothing about *ENUM* and *SET*, which could complicate a future transition to another database system. Therefore, it is often better to use additional linked tables in place of *ENUM*s and *SET*s.

Table 8-10 summarizes the additional data types.

Table 8-10. *Additional Data Types*

MySQL Keyword	Meaning
ENUM	Enumeration of up to 65,535 strings (1 or 2 bytes; see Chapter 10)
SET	Combination of up to 255 strings (1 to 8 bytes; see Chapter 10)
GEOMETRY, POINT, etc.	Geometric object (since MySQL 4.1; see Chapter 12)

Options and Attributes

A variety of options and additional attributes can be specified when a column is created. Table 8-11 lists the most important options. Note that many attributes are suitable only for particular data types.

Table 8-11. *Important Column Attributes and Options*

MySQL Keyword	Meaning
NULL	The column may contain *NULL* values. (This setting holds by default.)
NOT NULL	The value *NULL* is not permitted.
DEFAULT xxx	The default value *xxx* will be used if no other value is specified on input.
DEFAULT CURRENT_TIMESTAMP	For *TIMESTAMP* columns, the current time is stored when new records are input.
ON UPDATE CURRENT_TIMESTAMP	For *TIMESTAMP* columns, the current time is stored when changes are made (*UPDATE*).
PRIMARY KEY	Defines the column as a primary key.
AUTO_INCREMENT	A sequential number is automatically input. *AUTO_INCREMENT* can be used only for a column with integer values. Moreover, the options *NOT NULL* and *PRIMARY KEY* must be given. (Instead of *PRIMARY KEY*, the column can be given a *UNIQUE* index.)
UNSIGNED	Integers are stored without a sign. Warning: calculations are then also made without a sign.
CHARACTER SET name [COLLATE sort]	For strings, specifies the character set and optionally the desired sort order.

Unfortunately, MySQL does not allow a function to be given as default value. It is also impossible, for example, to specify *DEFAULT RAND()* if you wish to have a random number automatically stored in a column. It is also impossible to define validation rules for columns (so that, for example, only values between 0 and 100 can be stored).

Tips and Tricks on Database Design

Rules for Good Database Design

- Tables should not contain redundant (repetitive) data. (If you are repeatedly entering the same numbers or strings in a table, something is wrong.)

- Tables should not have columns like *order1*, *order2*, *order3*. Even if you allow for 10 such columns, the day will come when a customer orders 11 articles.

- The storage requirements for all your tables should be as small as possible.

- Frequently required database queries should be able to be executed simply and efficiently. (One usually notices a violation of this rule only when the database contains not a couple of test records, but thousands or even millions. At that point, a change in the design may no longer be possible.)

These rules have the same import as the normalization rules presented in the next section, but these here are often easier to follow.

Tips for Naming

- MySQL is case-sensitive in regard to database and table names, but not so with column names. It is thus important, at least with your databases and tables, to arrive at a uniform system for using upper- and lowercase letters. (In the example databases in this book, only lowercase letters are generally used for naming databases and tables.)

- Names of databases, tables, and columns can be at most 64 characters long.

- Avoid special characters (e.g., üàû) in names. MySQL allows all alphanumeric characters, but different operating systems and Linux distributions use different default character sets, and changing a system could lead to problems.

- Choose clear field and table names. Take care in naming fields that they describe the content accurately. Thus *authName* is better than *name*.

- A uniform naming system for fields can save many careless errors. Whether you prefer *author_name* or *authName* is irrelevant, as long as you are consistent.

- Similarly, you should consider how you want to deal with singular and plural. In my tables, I have tried to use plural exclusively. There is no rule as to what is correct, but it is confusing if half your tables use singular, the other half plural.

Tips on the Design Process

It is no easy matter to distribute a collection of data efficiently and intelligently among several tables. Novices in the area of database design should take the following suggestions to heart:

- Begin with a relatively small number of test data, and attempt to enter them in one or more tables. (The scope of the test data should not, however, be so small that obvious design problems go undetected. But it should not be so large that the time taken up in design is too great.)

- Perform your first experiments not with real MySQL tables, but instead, with some worksheets in a table calculation program such as Excel or OpenOffice Calc. (Figure 8-1 gives a preview of the next section.) This allows you to work in a far less complex environment. At this point, you should be focusing on the distribution of data among the tables and their columns, not on database-specific details such as column format and indexes.

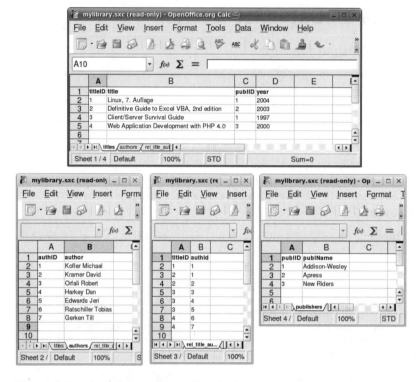

Figure 8-1. *Database design with a table calculation program*

Normalization Rules

Why is it that authors of books think about nothing (well, almost nothing) but books? The author begs the indulgence of his readers in that the example in this section deals with books. The goal of the section is to create a small database in which data about books can be stored: book title, publisher, author(s), publication date, and so on. These data can of course, be stored without a database, in a simple list in text format, for example, as appears in the Bibliography at the end of this book:

Michael Kofler: *Linux*, 7th edition. Addison-Wesley 2004.

Michael Kofler, David Kramer: *Definitive Guide to Excel VBA*, Second Edition. Apress 2003.

Robert Orfali, Dan Harkey, Jeri Edwards: *Client/Server Survival Guide*. Addison-Wesley 1997.

Tobias Ratschiller, Till Gerken: *Web Application Development with PHP 4.0*. New Riders 2000.

This is a nice and convenient list, containing all necessary information. Why bother with all the effort to transform this text (which perhaps exists as a document composed with some word-processing program) into a database?

Needless to say, the reasons are legion. Our list can be easily searched, but it is impossible to organize it in a different way, for example, to create a list of all books by author *x* or to create a new list ordered not by author, but by title.

The resulting database *mylibrary* will be improved step by step in the course of this chapter. The finished database is available for download at the Apress website. In addition, the *mylibrary* database is the basis for countless examples in this book.

A First Attempt

Just think: Nothing is easier than to turn our list into a database table. (To save space we are going to abbreviate the book titles and names of authors.)

Table 8-12 immediately shows itself to be riddled with problems. A first glance reveals that limiting the number of authors to three was an arbitrary decision. What do you do with a book that has four or five authors? Do we just keep adding columns, up to *authorN*, painfully aware that those columns will be empty for most entries?

Table 8-12. *Library Database: First Attempt*

title	publName	year	authName1	authName2	authName3
Linux	Addison-Wesley	2004	Kofler M		
Definitive Guide ...	Apress	2003	Kofler M	Kramer D	
Client/Server ...	Addison-Wesley	1997	Orfali R	Harkey D	Edwards E.
Web Application ...	New Riders	2000	Ratschiller T	Gerken T	

The First Normal Form

Database theorists have found, I am happy to report, a solution to such problems. Simply apply to your database, one after the other, the rules for the three *normal forms*. The rules for the first normal form are as follows (though for the benefit of the reader, they have been translated from the language of database theorists into what we might frivolously call "linguistic normal form," or, more simply, plain English):

- Columns with similar content must be eliminated.
- A table must be created for each group of associated data.
- Each data record must be identifiable by means of a *primary key*.

In our example, the first rule is clearly applicable to the *authorN* columns.

The second rule seems not to be applicable here, since in our example we are dealing exclusively with data that pertain specifically to the books in the database. Thus a single table would seem to suffice. (We will see, however, that this is not, in fact, the case.)

The third rule signifies in practice that a running index must be used that uniquely identifies each row of the table. (It is not strictly necessary that an integer be used as primary key. Formally, only the uniqueness is required. For reasons of efficiency the primary key should be as small as possible, and thus an integer is generally more suitable than a character string of variable length.)

A reconfiguration of our table after application of the first and third rules might look like that depicted in Table 8-13.

Table 8-13. *Library Database: First Normal Form*

titleID	title	publName	year	authName
1	Linux	Addison-Wesley	2004	Kofler M.
2	Definitive Guide ...	Apress	2003	Kofler M.
3	Definitive Guide ...	Apress	2003	Kramer D.
4	Client/Server ...	Addison-Wesley	1997	Orfali R.
5	Client/Server ...	Addison-Wesley	1997	Harkey D.
6	Client/Server ...	Addison-Wesley	1997	Edwards E.
7	Web Application ...	New Riders	2000	Ratschiller T.
8	Web Application ...	New Riders	2000	Gerken T.

Clearly, the problem of multiple columns for multiple authors has been eliminated. Regardless of the number of authors, they can all be stored in our table. Of course, there is no free luncheon, and the price of a meal here is rather high: The contents of the columns *title*, *publName*, and *year* are repeated for each author. There must be a better way!

Second Normal Form

Here are the rules for the second normal form:

- Whenever the contents of columns repeat themselves, this means that the table must be divided into several subtables.

- These tables must be linked by *foreign keys*.

If you are new to the lingo of the database world, then the term *foreign key* probably seems a bit, well, foreign. A better word in everyday English would probably be *cross reference*, since a foreign key refers to a line in a different (hence foreign) table. For programmers, the word *pointer* would perhaps be more to the point, while in Internet jargon the term *link* would be appropriate.

In Table 8-13, we see that data are repeated in practically every column. The culprit of this redundancy is clearly the author column. Our first attempt to give the authors their very own table can be seen in Tables 8-14 and 8-15.

Table 8-14. *titles Table: Second Normal Form*

titleID	title	publName	year
1	Linux	Addison-Wesley	2004
2	Definitive Guide	Apress	2003
3	Client/Server	Addison-Wesley	1997
4	Web Application	New Riders	2000

Table 8-15. *authors Table: Second Normal Form*

authID	titleID	authName
1	1	Kofler M.
2	2	Kofler M.
3	2	Kramer D.
4	3	Orfali R.
5	3	Harkey D.
6	3	Edwards E.
7	4	Ratschiller T.
8	4	Gerken T.

In the *authors* table, the first column, with its running *authID* values, provides the primary key. The second column takes over the task of the foreign key. It points, or refers, to rows of the *titles* table. For example, row 7 of the *authors* table indicates that *Ratschiller, T.* is an author of the book with ID *titleID=4*, that is, the book *Web Application* ....

Second Normal Form, Second Attempt

Our result could hardly be called optimal. In the *authors* table, the name *Kofler, M.* appears twice. As the number of books in this database increases, the amount of such redundancy will increase as well, whenever an author has worked on more than one book.

The only solution is to split the *authors* table again and live without the *titleID* column. The information as to which book belongs to which author must be specified in yet a third table. These three tables are shown in Tables 8-16 through 8-18.

Table 8-16. *titles Table: Second Normal Form*

titleID	title	publName	year
1	Linux	Addison-Wesley	2004
2	Definitive Guide	Apress	2003
3	Client/Server	Addison-Wesley	1997
4	Web Application	New Riders	2000

Table 8-17. *authors Table: Second Normal Form*

authID	authName
1	Kofler M.
2	Kramer D.
3	Orfali R.
4	Harkey D.
5	Edwards E.
6	Ratschiller T.
7	Gerken T.

Table 8-18. *rel_title_author Table: Second Normal Form*

titleID	authID
1	1
2	1
2	2
3	3
3	4
3	5
4	6
4	7

This is certainly the most difficult and abstract step, probably because a table of the form *rel_title_author* has no real-world content. Such a table would be completely unsuited for unautomated management. But once a computer has been provided with a suitable program, such as MySQL, it has no trouble at all processing such data. Suppose you would like to obtain a list of all authors of the book *Client/Server* …. MySQL would first look in the *titles* table to find out what *titleID* number is associated with this book. Then it would search in the *rel_title_author* table for data records containing this number. The associated *authID* numbers then lead to the names of the authors.

■**Note** It may have occurred to you to ask why in the *rel_title_author* table there is no *ID* column, say, *rel_title_author_ID*. Usually, such a column is omitted, since the combination of *titleID* and *authID* is already an optimal primary key. (Relational database systems permit such primary keys, those made up of several columns.)

Third Normal Form

The third normal form has a single rule, and here it is:

- Columns that are not directly related to the primary key must be eliminated (that is, transplanted into a table of their own).

In the example under consideration, the column *publisher* appears in the *titles* table. The set of publishers and the set of book titles are independent of one another and therefore should be separated. Of course, it should be noted that each title must be related to the information as to the publisher of that title, but it is not necessary that the entire name of the publisher be given. A foreign key (that is, a reference, a pointer, a link) suffices. See Tables 8-19 and 8-20.

Table 8-19. *titles Table: Third Normal Form*

titleID	title	publID	year
1	Linux	1	2001
2	Definitive Guide	2	2003
3	Client/Server	1	1997
4	Web Application	3	2000

Table 8-20. *publishers Table: Third Normal Form*

publID	publName
1	Addison-Wesley
2	Apress
3	New Riders

The *authors* and *rel_title_author* tables remain the same in the third normal form. The completed book database now consists of four tables.

If we had paid closer attention to the rules for the first normal form (associated data belong together in a table), we could, of course, have saved some of our intermediate attempts. But that would have diminished the pedagogical value of our example. In fact, in practice, it often occurs that only when test data are inserted and redundancies are noticed does it become clear how the tables need to be subdivided.

■**Tip** The *mylibrary* database is somewhat more complex than the previous sections would indicate. The *titles* table contains some additional fields, for example, for storing a subtitle or a comment. An additional *languages* table contains a list of all languages in which the books are written. The *langID* field of the *titles* table contains the language for each title. Finally, the *categories* table contains a hierarchical list of all book categories (e.g., *Computer books*). The *catID* field of the *titles* table supplies the category for each title.

The structure of the *categories* table is handled in the next section. A summary of all the database properties can be found at the end of the chapter.

Normalization Theory

More Theory …

The three normal forms for relational databases were first formulated by the researcher E. F. Codd. They continue to form the basis for a branch of research that is concerned with the formal description of mathematical sets in general and of relational databases in particular.

Depending on what you read, you may come across three additional normal forms, which, however, are of much less significance in practice. The normal forms and their rules are described much more precisely than we have done. However, such descriptions are so teeming with such exotica as *entities*, *attributes*, and their ilk that the connection with relational databases can easily be lost.

If you are interested in further details on this topic, then you are encouraged to look into a good book on the subject of database design (see also the suggestions at the beginning of this chapter).

Less Theory …

I have attempted to present the first three normal forms in as simple and example-oriented a way as possible, but perhaps even that was too theoretical. Actually, the normal forms are not necessarily helpful to database beginners, since the correct interpretation of the rules is often difficult. Here are some rules that will perhaps make those first steps less shaky:

- Give yourself sufficient time to develop the database. (If at a later date you have to alter the database design, when the database is already stuffed with real data and there is already client code in existence, changes will take a great deal of time and effort.)

- Avoid giving columns names with numbers, such as *name1*, *name2*, or *object1*, *object2*. There is almost certainly a better solution involving an additional table.

- Immediately supply your database with some test data. Attempt to include as many special cases as possible. If you encounter redundancies, that is, columns in which the same content appears several times, this is usually a hint that you should break your table into two (or more) new tables.

- Try to understand the ideas of relations (more on this later in the chapter).

- A good database design cannot be obtained unless you have had some experience with SQL (see also the following two chapters). Only when you know and understand the range of SQL queries can you judge the consequences of the various ways of organizing your data.

- Orient yourself using an example database (from this book or from another book on databases).

■Tip A good example of normalizing a database can be found at `http://www.phpbuilder.com/columns/barry20000731.php3`.

Normal Forms: Pro and Con

Normal forms are a means to an end, nothing more and nothing less. Normal forms should be a help in the design of databases, but they cannot replace human reasoning. Furthermore, it is not always a good idea to follow the normal form thoughtlessly, that is, to eliminate every redundancy.

Con: The input of new data, say, in a form on a web page, becomes more and more complex as the number of tables among which the data are distributed increases. This is true as much for the end user (who is led from one page to another) as for the programmer.

Furthermore, for efficiency in queries, it is sometimes advantageous to allow for a bit of redundancy. Bringing together data from several tables is usually slower than reading data from a single table. This is true especially for databases that do not change much but that are frequently given complex queries to respond to. (In a special area of databases, the *data warehouses*, redundancy is often deliberately planned for in order to obtain better response times. The purpose of data warehouses is the analysis of complex data according to various criteria. However, MySQL is not a reasonable choice of database system for such tasks anyhow, and therefore, we shall not go more deeply into the particular features of this special application area.)

Pro: Redundancy is generally a waste of storage space. You may hold the opinion that in the era of 400-gigabyte hard drives this is not an issue, but a large database will inevitably become a slow database (at the latest, when the database size exceeds the amount of RAM).

As a rule, databases in normal form offer more flexible query options. (Unfortunately, one usually notices this only when a new form of data query or grouping is required, which often occurs months after the database has become operational.)

Managing Hierarchies

In the *mylibrary* database, the table *categories* helps to order the books into various categories (textbooks, children's books, etc.). What is important here is that the categories can be ordered hierarchically. From the point of view of database design, this is simple: The field *parentID* simply refers, for each category, to the parent category. (For the root category *All books, parentID* contains the value *NULL*. This special case must always be taken into account in management and evaluation of the *categories* table.) Table 8-21 shows the hierarchy, and Table 8-22 shows how this hierarchy can be represented in a database table.

Table 8-21. *Example Data for the categories Table*

All books
Children's books
Computer books
Databases
Object-oriented databases
Relational databases
SQL
Programming
Perl
PHP
Literature and fiction

Table 8-22. *Database Representation of the Hierarchy of Table 8-20*

catID	CatName	parentCatID
1	Computer books	11
2	Databases	1
3	Programming	1
4	Relational databases	2
5	Object-oriented databases	2

catID	CatName	parentCatID
6	PHP	3
7	Perl	3
8	SQL	2
9	Children's books	11
10	Literature and fiction	11
11	All books	*NULL*

Hierarchy Problems

Although the representation of such hierarchies looks simple and elegant at first glance, they cause many problems as well. For example, it is impossible with simple *SELECT* queries to determine all subcategories or supercategories. Therefore, generally a number of queries have to be executed in the client program to construct the hierarchy. The necessary programming techniques are described in Chapter 15 for the programming language PHP. You can also use stored procedures for evaluating hierarchies (see Chapter 13).

■**Tip** In point of fact, this chapter is supposed to be dealing with database design and not with SQL, but these two topics cannot be cleanly separated. There is no point in creating a super database design if the capabilities of SQL do not suffice to extract the desired data from the database's tables.

If you have no experience with SQL, you should dip into the following chapter a bit. Consider the following instructions as a sort of "advanced database design."

Almost all problems with hierarchies have to do with the fact that SQL does not permit recursive queries:

- With individual queries it is impossible to find all categories lying above a given category in the hierarchy.

  Example: The root category is called *Relational databases* (*parentCatID=2*). You would like to create a list that contains *Computer books* ➤ *Databases* ➤ *Relational databases*.

  With *SELECT * FROM categories WHERE catID=2*, you indeed find *Databases*, but not *Computer books*, which lies two places up the hierarchy. For that, you must execute an additional query *SELECT * FROM categories WHERE catID=1*. Of course, this can be accomplished in a loop in the programming language of your choice (Perl, PHP, etc.), but not with a single SQL instruction.

- It is just as difficult to represent the entire table in hierarchical form (as a tree). Again, you must execute a number of queries.

- It is not possible without extra effort to search for all books in a higher category.

  Example: You would like to find all books in the category *Computer books*.

  With *SELECT * FROM titles WHERE catID=1* you find only those titles directly linked to the category *Computer books*, but not the titles in the categories *Databases*, *Relational databases*, *Object-oriented databases*, etc. The query must be the following: *SELECT * FROM titles WHERE catID IN (1, 2 …)*, where *1, 2 …* are the ID numbers of the subordinate categories. The actual problem is to determine these numbers.

- In the relatively simple representation that we have chosen, it is not possible to associate the same subcategory with two or more higher-ranking categories.

  Example: The programming language *SQL* is linked in the above hierarchy to the higher-ranking category *Databases*. It would be just as logical to have a link to *Programming*. Therefore, it would be optimal to have *SQL* appear as a subcategory of both *Databases* and *Programming*.

- There is the danger of circular references. Such references can, of course, appear only as a result of input error, but where there are human beings who input data (or who write programs), there are certain to be errors. If a circular reference is created, most database programs will find themselves in an infinite loop. The resolution of such problems can be difficult.

None of these problems is insuperable. However, hierarchies often lead to situations in which answering a relatively simple question involves executing a whole series of SQL queries, and that is a slow process. Many problems can be avoided by doing without genuine hierarchies (for example, by allowing at most a two-stage hierarchy) or if supplementary information for a simpler resolution of hierarchies is provided in additional columns or tables (see the following section).

Building the Hierarchy Tree

If you have taken to heart the section on normalization of databases, then you know that redundancy is bad. It leads to unnecessary usage of storage space, management issues when changes are made, etc.

Yet there are cases in which redundancy is quite consciously sought in order to increase the efficiency of an application.

The following lines should make clear that database design is a multifaceted subject. There are usually several ways that lead to the same goal, and each of these paths is, in fact, a compromise of one sort or another. Which compromise is best depends largely on the uses to which the database will be put: What types of queries will occur most frequently? Will data be frequently changed?

The necessity will continually arise to display the *categories* table in hierarchical representation similar to that of Table 8-21. As we have already mentioned, such processing of the data is connected either with countless SQL queries or complex client-side code.

A possible solution is provided by the two additional columns *hierNr* and *hierIndent*. The first of these gives the row number in which the record would be located in a hierarchical representation. (The assumption is that data records are sorted alphabetically by *catName* within a level of the hierarchy.) The second of these two columns determines the level of indentation. In Table 8-23 are displayed for both of these columns the values corresponding to the representation in Table 8-21.

Table 8-23. *categories Table with the hierNr Column*

catID	CatName	parentCatID	HierNr	hierIndent
1	Computer books	11	2	1
2	Databases	1	3	2
3	Programming	1	7	2
4	Relational databases	2	5	3
5	Object-oriented databases	2	4	3
6	PHP	3	9	3
7	Perl	3	8	3
8	SQL	2	6	3

catID	CatName	parentCatID	HierNr	hierIndent
9	Children's books	11	1	1
10	Literature and fiction	11	10	1
11	All books	NULL	0	0

A simple query in mysql proves that this arrangement makes sense. Here are a few remarks on the SQL functions used: *CONCAT* joins two character strings. *SPACE* generates the specified number of blank characters. *AS* gives the entire expression the new Alias name *category*.

```
SELECT CONCAT(SPACE(hierIndent*2), catName) AS category,
  hierNr, hierIndent
FROM categories ORDER BY hierNr
category                    hierNr   hierIndent
All books                      0        0
  Children's books             1        1
  Computer books               2        1
    Databases                  3        2
      Object-oriented databases 4       3
      Relational databases     5        3
      SQL                      6        3
    Programming                7        2
      Perl                     8        3
      PHP                      9        3
  Literature and fiction      10        1
```

You may now ask how the numerical values *hierIndent* and *hierNr* actually come into existence. The following example-oriented instructions show how a new data record (the computer book category *Operating systems*) is inserted into the table:

1. The data of the higher-ranking initial record (that is, *Computer books*) are known: *catID=1, parentCatID=11, hierNr=1, hierIndent=1*.

2a. Now we search within the *Computer books* group for the first record that lies in the hierarchy immediately after the record to be newly inserted (here, this is *Programming*). All that is of interest in this record is *hierNr*.

Here is a brief explanation of the SQL command:

WHERE parentCat_ID=1 finds all records that are immediately below *Computer books* in the hierarchy (that is, *Databases* and *Programming*).

catName>'Operating Systems' restricts the list to those records that occur after the new record *Operating Systems*.

ORDER BY catname sorts the records that are found.

LIMIT 1 reduces the result to the first record.

```
SELECT hierNr FROM categories
WHERE parentCatID=1 AND catName>'Operating Systems'
ORDER BY catName
LIMIT 1
```

The query just given returns the result *hierNr=7*. It is thereby clear that the new data record should receive this hierarchy number. First, however, all existing records with *hierNr>=7* should have their values of *hierNr* increased by 1.

2b. It can also happen that the query returns no result, namely, when there are no entries in the higher-ranking category or when all entries come before the new one in alphabetic order. (This would be the case if you wished to insert the new computer book category *Software engineering*.)

In that case, you must search for the next record whose *hierNr* is larger than *hierNr* for the initial record and whose *hierIndent* is less than or equal to *hierIndent* of the initial record. (In this way, the beginning of the next equal- or higher-ranking group in the hierarchy is sought.)

```
SELECT hierNr FROM categories
WHERE hierNr>1 AND hierIndent<=1
ORDER BY hierNr LIMIT 1
```

This query returns the result 10 (that is, *hierNr* for the record *Literature and fiction*). The new record will get this hierarchy number. All existing records with *hierNr>=10* must have their *hierNr* increased by 1.

2c. If this query also returns no result, then the new record must be inserted at the end of the hierarchy list. The current largest *hierNr* value can easily be determined:

```
SELECT MAX(hiernr) FROM categories
```

3. To increase the *hierNr* of the existing records, the following command is executed (for case 2a):

```
UPDATE categories SET hierNr=hierNr+1 WHERE hiernr>=7
```

4. Now the new record can be inserted. For *parentCatID*, the initial record *catID* will be used. Above, *hierNr=7* was determined. Here *hierIndent* must be larger by 1 than was the case with the initial record:

```
INSERT INTO categories (catName, parentCatID, hierNr, hierIndent)
VALUES ('Operating systems', 1, 7, 2)
```

The new columns in *categories* simplify many read operations. But the insert operations are still complex. It is more complicated to alter the hierarchy after the fact. Imagine that you wish to change the name of one of the categories in such a way as to change its place in the alphabetical order. This would affect not only the record itself, but many other records as well. For large sections of the table it will be necessary to determine *hierNr*. You see, therefore, that redundancy is bad.

In summary, you will have to decide whether it is more important to optimize read operations or write operations. For this book I have left *categories* without the two additional columns *hierNr* and *hierIndent*. First of all, this has pedagogical justification: In Chapters 13 (on stored procedures) and 15 (PHP) I can demonstrate various programming techniques for processing hierarchical data with maximum efficiency. Furthermore, I have the impression that the advantages of the simpler database design would win out in the case of a real application. Even managing the huge book database at amazon.com, a few thousand categories would suffice. One can expect serious problems of efficiency as a rule only with much larger tables.

Searching for Lower-Ranked Categories in the categories Table

Suppose you want to search for all *Databases* titles in the *titles* table. Then it would not suffice to search for all titles with *catId=2*, since you also want to see all the titles relating to *Relational databases*, *Object-oriented databases*, and *SQL* (that is, the titles with *catID* equal to 4, 5, and 8). The totality of all these categories will be described in the following search category group.

There are two problems to be solved: First, you must determine the list of the *catID* values for the search category group. For this a series of *SELECT* queries is needed, and we shall not go into that further here. Then you must determine from the *titles* table those records whose *catID* numbers agree with the values just found.

Thus in principle, the title search can be carried out, but the path is thorny, with the necessity of several SQL queries and client-side code.

The other solution consists in introducing a new (redundant) table, in which are stored all records lying above each of the *categories* records. This table could be called *rel_cat_parent*, and it would consist of two columns: *catID* and *parentID* (see Table 8-24). We see, then, for example, that the category *Relational databases* (*catID=4*) lies under the categories *All books, Computer books,* and *Databases* (*parentID=11, 1, 2*).

Table 8-24. *Some Entries in the Table rel_cat_parent*

catID	parentID
1	11
2	1
2	11
3	1
3	11
4	1
4	2
4	11
	..

The significant drawback of the *rel_cat_parent* table is that it must be synchronized with every change in the *categories* table. But that is relatively easy to take care of.

In exchange for that effort, now the question of all categories ranked below *Databases* is easily answered:

```
SELECT catID FROM rel_cat_parent
WHERE parentID=2
```

If you would like to determine all book titles that belong to the category *Databases* or its sub-categories, the requisite query looks like the following. The key word *DISTINCT* is necessary here, since otherwise, the query would return many titles with multiplicity:

```
SELECT DISTINCT titles.title FROM titles, rel_cat_parent
WHERE (rel_cat_parent.parentID = 2 OR titles.catID = 2)
      AND titles.catID = rel_cat_parent.catID
```

We are once more caught on the horns of the efficiency versus normalization dilemma: The entire table *rel_cat_parent* contains nothing but data that can be determined directly from *categories*. In the concrete realization of the *mylibrary* database, I decided to do without *rel_cat_parent*.

Searching for Higher-Ranked Categories in the categories Table

Here we confront the converse question to that posed in the last section: What are the higher-ranking categories above an initial, given category? If the initial category is *Perl* (*catID=7*), then the higher-ranking categories are first *Programming*, then *Computer books*, and finally, *All books*.

When there is a table *rel_cat_parent* like that described above, then our question can be answered by a simple query:

```
SELECT CONCAT(SPACE(hierIndent*2), catName) AS category
FROM categories, rel_cat_parent
WHERE rel_cat_parent.catID = 7
  AND categories.catID = rel_cat_parent.parentID
ORDER BY hierNr
```

category

```
All books
  Computer books
    Programming
```

On the other hand, if *rel_cat_parent* is not available, then a series of *SELECT* instructions must be executed in a loop *categories.parentCatID* until this contains the value *NULL*.

Relations

If you want to transform a database into normal form, you have to link a number of tables. These links are called *relations* in database-speak. At bottom, there are three possible relations between two tables:

1:1. In a one-to-one relation between two tables, each data record of the first table corresponds to precisely one data record of the second table and vice versa. Such relations are rare, since in such a case the information in both tables could as easily be stored in a single table.

1:*n*. In a one-to-many relation, a single record in the first table can correspond to several records in the second table (for example, a vendor can be associated with many orders). The converse may be impossible: A single order cannot, say, be filled by many vendors. Occasionally, one hears of an *n*-to-1 relation, but this is merely a 1-to-*n* relation from the opposite point of view.

n:m. Here a data record in the first table can be linked to several records in the second table, and vice versa. (For example, several articles can be included in a single order, while the same article may be included in several different orders. Another example is books and their authors. Several authors may have written a single book, while one author may have written several books.)

1:1 Relations

A one-to-one relation typically comes into being when a table is divided into two tables that use the same primary key. This situation is most easily grasped with the aid of an example. A table containing a corporation's personnel records contains a great deal of information: name, department, date of birth, date of employment, and so on. This table could be split into two tables, called, say, *personnel* and *personnel_extra*, where *personnel* contains the frequently queried and generally accessible data, while *personnel_extra* contains additional, less used, and more private data.

There are two possible reasons for such a division. One is the security aspect: It is simple to protect the table *personnel_extra* from general access. (For MySQL, this argument is less important, since access privileges can in any case be set separately for each column of a table. Since MySQL 5.0, the security problem can also be solved with *Views*.)

The other reason is that of speed. If a table contains many columns, of which only a few are required by most queries, it is more efficient to keep the frequently used columns in a single table. (In the ideal situation, the first table would contain exclusively columns of a given size. Such tables are more efficient to manage than tables whose columns are of variable size. An overview of the types of tables supported by MySQL can be found in the first section of this chapter.)

The significant disadvantage of such a separation of tables is the added overhead of ensuring that the tables remain synchronized.

1:*n* Relations

One-to-many relations come into play whenever a particular field of a data record in a detail table can refer to various columns of another table (the master table).

The linkage takes place via key fields. The columns of the master table are identified by a primary key. The detail table contains a foreign key field, whose contents refer to the master table. Here are a few examples:

The *mylibrary* database: Here there is a one-to-many relation between the *titles* and *publishers* tables. The table *publishers* is the master table with the primary key *publishers.publID*.

Each publisher (1) can publish several books (*n*).

The *mylibrary* database contains two additional 1-to-*n* relations: between *titles* and *languages* (field *langID*) and between *titles* and *categories* (field *catID*).

A business application containing tables with orders: A detail table contains data on all processed orders. In this table, a foreign key field refers to the master table, with its list of all customers.

Each customer (1) can execute many orders (*n*).

Discussion groups containing tables with messages: A detail table contains data on every contribution to a discussion group in place on the website (title, text, date, author, group, etc.). Two possible master tables are a group table with a list of all discussion groups, and an author table with a list of all members of the website who are allowed to make contributions to a discussion.

Each author (1) can contribute to arbitrarily many discussions (*n*). Each discussion group (1) can contain arbitrarily many contributions (*n*).

A database containing tables of music CDs: A detail table contains data on every CD in the collection (title, performer, number of disks, etc.). Two possible master tables are a table containing a list of performers occurring in the database, and a recording label table with a list of recording companies.

Each performer (1) can appear on arbitrarily many CDs (*n*). Each label (1) can market arbitrarily many CDs (*n*).

■Note Often during the creation of a database, one attempts to give the same name to fields of two tables that will later be linked by a relation. This contributes to clarity, but is not required.

It is also possible for the primary and foreign keys to be located in the same table. Then a data record in such a table can refer to another record in the same table. This is useful if a hierarchy is to be represented. Here are a few examples:

The *mylibrary* database: Each category in the *categories* table refers via the field *parentID* to a subcategory (or to *NULL*).

A table of personnel: In this table, each employee record (except for that of the top banana) refers to a field containing that individual's immediate supervisor.

Discussion groups, a table with messages: In these tables, each message refers to a field containing the next-higher message in the hierarchy (that is, the one to which the current message is responding).

A music database, containing tables with different types of music: Each style field refers to a field with the name of the genre of which the current style is a subset (for example, bebop within the category jazz, or string quartet within the category of chamber music).

n:m Relations

For *n:m* relations, it is necessary to add an auxiliary table to the two original tables so that the *n:m* relation can be reduced to two 1:*n* relations. Here are some examples:

> **The *mylibrary database:*** Here we have an *n:m* relation between book titles and authors. The relation is established by means of the *rel_title_author* table.
>
> A possible extension of this table could be an additional field that determines the order of authors (if it is not to be simply in alphabetical order).
>
> **Business application, a table with orders:** To establish a relation between an order and the articles included in the order, the auxiliary table specifies how many of article *x* are included in order *y*.
>
> This table could then consist of the columns *articleID*, *orderID*, *quantity*, and perhaps also *price*. To be sure, the price is contained in the articles table, but it could change over time, with the price at the time of purchase different from the current price. In this case, the orders table would contain the price that was valid at the time of the order.
>
> **College administration, list of exams:** To keep track of which student has passed which exam and when and with what grade, it is necessary to have a table that stands between the table of students and the table of exams.

Primary and Foreign Keys

Relations depend intimately on primary and foreign keys. This section provides a comprehensive explanation of these two topics and their application. Alas, we cannot entirely avoid a bit of a detour into referring to various SQL commands which are not formally introduced until the end of this chapter and the chapter following.

Primary Key

The job of the primary key is to locate, as fast as possible, a particular data record in a table (for example, to locate the record with *id=314159* from a table of a million records). This operation must be carried out whenever data from several tables are assembled—in short, very often indeed.

With most database systems, including MySQL, it is also permitted to have primary keys that are formed from several fields of a table. Whether it is a single field or several that serve as primary key, the following properties should be satisfied:

- The primary key must be unique. It is not permitted that two records have the same content in their primary key field.

- The primary key should be compact, and there are two reasons for this:

  First, for the primary key it is necessary to maintain an index (the primary index) to maximize the speed of search (e.g., for *id=314159*). The more compact the primary field key, the more efficient the management of this index. Therefore, an integer is more suitable than a character string of variable length for use as a primary key field.

  Second, the content of the primary key field is used as a foreign key in other tables, and there, as well, it is efficient to have the foreign key as compact as possible. (Relations between tables are established not least to avoid wasted space on account of redundancies. This makes sense only if the use of key fields doesn't take up even more space.)

With most database systems it has become standard practice to use a 32- or 64-bit integer as primary key field, generated automatically in sequence (1, 2, 3, …) by the database system. Thus neither the programmer nor the user need be concerned how a new and unique primary key value is to be found for each new record.

In MySQL such fields are declared as follows:

```
CREATE TABLE publishers
  (publID INT NOT NULL AUTO_INCREMENT,
   othercolumns ...,
   PRIMARY KEY (publID))
```

If we translate from SQL into English, what we have is this: The field *publID* is not permitted to contain *NULL*. Its contents are generated by the database (unless another value is explicitly inserted there). The field functions as a primary key; that is, MySQL creates an index to enable rapid search. It is thereby ensured that the *publID* value is unique when new records are input.

For tables in which one expects to make many new entries or changes, one should usually use *BIGINT* (64-bit integer) instead of *INT* (32 bits).

■**Note** The name of the primary key field plays no role. In this book we usually use *id* or *tablenameID*. Often, you will see combinations with *no* or *nr* (for "number") as, for example, in *customerNr*.

Foreign Keys

The task of the foreign key field is to refer to a record in the detail table. However, this reference comes into being only when a database query is formulated, for example, in the following form:

```
SELECT titles.title, publishers.publName FROM titles, publishers
WHERE titles.publID = publishers.publID
ORDER BY title
```

With this, an alphabetical list of all book titles is generated, in which the second column gives the publisher of the book. The result would look something like this:

title	*publName*
Client/Server ...	Addison-Wesley
Definitive Guide ...	Apress
Linux	Addison-Wesley
Web Application ...	New Riders

Decisive here is the clause *WHERE titles.publID = publishers.publID*. It is here that the link between the tables is created. Chapter 9 discusses some other ways of linking two tables with queries.

In the declaration of a table the foreign key plays no particular role. For MySQL, a foreign key field is just another ordinary table field. There are no particular key words that must be employed. In particular, no index is necessary (there is practically never a search to find the contents of the foreign key). Of course, you would not be permitted to supply the attribute *AUTO_INCREMENT*. After all, you want to specify yourself the record to which the field refers. You need to take care, though, that the foreign key field is of the same data type as the type of the primary key field. Otherwise, the evaluation of the *WHERE* condition can be very slow.

```
CREATE TABLE titles
  (othercolumns ...,
   publisherID INT NOT NULL)
```

Whether you specify the attribute *NOT NULL* depends on the context. In most cases, *NOT NULL* is to be recommended in order to avoid at the outset the occurrence of incomplete data. However, if you wish to allow, for example, that in the book database a book could be entered that had no publisher, then you should do without *NOT NULL*.

Referential Integrity (Foreign Key Constraints)

If you delete the author *Kofler* from the *authors* table in the *mylibrary* database, you will encounter problems in many SQL queries that access the books *Linux* and *Definitive Guide*. The *authID* number 1 specified in the *rel_title_author* table no longer exists in the *authors* table. In database language, one would put it like this: The referential integrity of the database has been damaged.

As a database developer, it is your responsibility to see that such events cannot happen. Therefore, before deleting a data record you must always check whether there exists a reference to the record in question in another table.

Since one cannot always rely on programmers, many databases have rules for maintaining referential integrity. So-called *foreign key constraints* (integrity rules) test at every change in the database whether any cross references between tables are affected. Depending on the declaration of the foreign key, there are then two possible consequences: Either the operation will simply not be executed (error message), or all affected records in dependent tables are deleted as well. Which modus operandi is to be preferred depends on the data themselves.

MySQL also offers such a control mechanism, though at the present only for InnoDB tables. The following lines show a fragment of SQL code for declaring a foreign key with integrity rules. (SQL commands for creating and editing tables are discussed in Chapter 9.)

```
CREATE TABLE titles
  (column1, column2, ...,
   publID INT,
   FOREIGN KEY (publID) REFERENCES publishers (publisherID)
```

This means that *titles.publID* is a foreign key that refers to the primary key *publishers.publID*. With options such as *ON DELETE*, *RESTRICT*, and *ON DELETE CASCADE*, one may further specify how the database system is to respond to potential damage to its referential integrity.

```
CREATE TABLE titles
  (column1, column2, ...,
   publID INT,
   FOREIGN KEY (publisherID) REFERENCES publishers (publID)
  )
```

This means that *titles.publID* is a foreign key that refers to the primary key *publishers.publID*. The integrity rule has the following effects on the two tables:

- In *titles*, you cannot insert a title with a *publID* number that does not exist in the *publishers* table. (Nor can you change the value of *publID* in *titles* for an existing title if there is no corresponding *publishers* data record.)

- You cannot delete a publisher from *publishers* that is referred to by the *titles* table. (Here as well the restriction on *UPDATE* commands is in effect.)

This has consequences for the order of operations: If you wish to store a new title for a new publisher, you must first enter the publisher and then the title. If you wish to delete a publisher and a title, you must first delete the title and then the publisher. (The latter operation is possible only if there are no additional titles from the publisher in question in the *titles* table.)

Syntax

The general syntax for defining a foreign key constraint for a foreign key field *table1.column1* looks as follows:

```
FOREIGN KEY [name] (column1) REFERENCES table2 (column2)
  [ON DELETE {CASCADE | SET NULL | NO ACTION | RESTRICT}]
  [ON UPDATE {CASCADE | SET NULL | NO ACTION | RESTRICT}]
```

The foreign key constraint can be named with *name*. The foreign key is *table1.column1* for which the constraint is defined. The field of the second table to which the constraint refers is *table2.column2*. (In many cases, *column2* is the primary key of *table2*. This is not requisite, but *column2* must be equipped with an index.)

One may also have foreign key constraints in which *table1* and *table2* are the same table. This makes sense when a table possesses references to itself. This is the case, for example, with the *categories* table in *mylibrary*, where *parentCatID* refers to *CatID*, thus creating a hierarchical relationship among the categories.

Actions When Integrity Is Damaged

The optional clause *ON DELETE* determines how the table driver should behave if a record that is referred to by *table1* is deleted from *table2*. There are four possibilities:

RESTRICT is the default behavior. The *DELETE* command causes an error, and the record is not deleted. (An error does not necessarily mean the termination of a running transaction. The command is simply not executed. The transaction must, as usual, be terminated with a *COMMIT* or *ROLLBACK*.)

SET NULL has the effect that the record from *table2* is allowed to be deleted. In *table1*, all records that refer to the deleted record will have *column1* set to *NULL*. This rule assumes that *NULL* is a permitted value for *table1.column1*.

For the *titles/publisher* example, this means that if you remove publisher *x* from *publishers*, then all records in *titles* that were published by this publisher will have their *publID* set to *NULL*.

CASCADE has the effect that the record from *table2* is allowed to be deleted. At the same time, however, all records from *table1* that refer to that record will be deleted.

For the *titles/publishers* example, this means that if you delete publisher *x* from the *publishers* table, then all records in *titles* that were published by publisher *x* will be deleted from *titles*.

NO ACTION has the effect that the loss of referential integrity is tolerated. This action seldom makes sense, since it is easier simply not to use a foreign key constraint.

These four actions can also be specified analogously for *ON UPDATE* (where by default, *RESTRICT* again holds). The *UPDATE* rules come into effect if in *table2*, the key field of an existing record is altered. In such a case, the effect of *RESTRICT*, *SET NULL*, and *NO ACTION* is the same as with *ON DELETE*.

On the other hand, the effect of *CASCADE* is a bit different: A change in the key field in *table2* is now also carried out in the foreign key field in *table1*. For the *titles/publishers* example, this means that if you change the *publID* field for publisher *x* in *publishers*, then the *publID* field will be updated for all affected records in *titles*.

■**Note** Integrity rules do not prevent you from deleting an entire table. For example, you can execute *DROP TABLE publishers*, even if this means damaging the referential integrity.

Conditions for Setting Up Integrity Rules

Foreign key constraints can be used only if a set of preconditions is satisfied. If such conditions have not been satisfied, then the result is an error message, generally *Error 1005: Can't create table xxx (errno: 150)*, and the constraint is not stored. (The cause of the error can be quite trivial, such as a typo in the name of a column.)

- Each of *table1.column1* and *table2.column2* must be equipped with at least an ordinary index. This index is not created by *FOREIGN KEY*, and must therefore be explicitly provided for in *CREATE TABLE* or after the fact with *ALTER TABLE*.

  table2.column2 is often the primary key field of *table2*, but that is not necessary.

  If you use keys across several fields (*INDEX(columnA, columnB)*), then the key field from the foreign key constraint must appear first. Otherwise, an additional separate index for the field must be created.

- The data types of *table1.column1* and *table2.column2* must agree to the extent that a direct comparison is possible without transformation of data types. Most efficient is if both fields are declared with *INT* or *BIGINT*. Both columns must be of the same sign type (*SIGNED* or *UNSIGNED*).

- If the optional rule *ON DELETE/UPDATE SET NULL* is defined, then the value *NULL* must be permitted in *table1.column1*.

- The foreign key constraint must be satisfied from the start: If the tables are already filled with data, it can happen that individual records do not conform to the integrity rules. In this case, an *ALTER TABLE* command results in error 1216 (*A foreign key constraint fails*). The records must be corrected before the constraint can be set up.

■**Tip** If an error occurs in setting up a foreign key constraint, you can obtain more precise information about the cause of the error with *SHOW INNODB STATUS*.

Finding Unsatisfied Integrity Rules

The obvious question upon receipt of error 1216 is, "How can the error-ridden records be found?" A simple sub*SELECT* command returns all records in the *titles* table for which *titles.publID* contains a value for which there is no corresponding value in *publishers.publID*:

```
SELECT titleID, publID FROM titles
WHERE publID NOT IN (SELECT publID FROM publishers)
```

titleID	publID	publishers.publID
66	99	NULL

The title with *titleID=66* thus refers to a publisher with *publID=99* in the *publishers* table, but there is no such ID number in that table. Now you must either insert the missing publisher or delete the title with ID equal to 66. (In the *titles* table you could also change erroneous *publID*s to *NULL*, though in practice, that is often not allowed in linked tables.)

Deleting Foreign Key Constraints

To delete a foreign key constraint, execute *ALTER TABLE*:

```
ALTER TABLE tablename DROP FOREIGN KEY foreign_key_id
```

You can determine the *foreign_key_id* of the index to be deleted with *SHOW CREATE TABLE*. Note that deleting foreign key constraints can cause problems if you are using replication at the same time. The reason is that the foreign key index can have a different name in the duplicated database from that in the original database.

Temporarily Deactivating Integrity Checks

With *SET foreign_key_checks=0* you can turn off the automatic checking of integrity rules. This can make sense, for example, to speed up the reading in of large backup tables. *SET foreign_key_checks=1* reactivates the rules. While the rules are deactivated, changes in the database will not be checked. If integrity rules have been violated, the errors incurred will not be automatically recognized.

Foreign Key Constraints for the mylibrary Database

The *mylibrary* database consists exclusively of InnoDB tables. All the relations among the tables are secured with integrity rules, as shown in Table 8-25.

Table 8-25. *Foreign Keys and Referenced Keys in the mylibrary Database*

Foreign Key	Referenced Key
titles.publID	*publishers.publID*
titles.langID	*languages.langID*
titles.catID	*categories.catID*
categories.parentCatID	*categories.catID*
rel_title_author.titleID	*titles.titleID*
rel_title_author.authID	*authors.authID*

Indexes

If you are searching for a particular record in a table or would like to create a series of data records for an ordered table, MySQL must load *all* the records of the table. The following lines show some of the relevant *SELECT* commands (details to follow in the next chapter):

```
SELECT column1, column2 ... FROM table WHERE column3=12345
SELECT column1, column2 ... FROM table ORDER BY column3
SELECT column1, column2 ... FROM table WHERE column3 LIKE 'Smith%'
SELECT column1, column2 ... FROM table WHERE column3 > 2000
```

With large tables, performance will suffer under such everyday queries. Fortunately, there is a simple solution to cure our table's performance anxiety: Simply use an index for the affected column (in the example above, for *column3*).

An index is a special file or, in the case of InnoDB, a part of the tablespace, containing references to all the records of a table. (Thus a database index functions like the index in this book. The index saves you the trouble of reading the entire book from one end to the other if you simply want to find out where a particular topic is covered.)

■**Caution** Indexes are not a panacea! They speed up access to data, but they slow down each alteration in the database. Every time a data record in changed, the index must be updated. This drawback can be ameliorated to some extent with various SQL commands by means of the option *DELAY_KEY_WRITE*. The effect of this option is that the index is not updated with each new or changed record, but only now and then. *DELAY_KEY_WRITE* is useful, for example, when many new records are to be inserted in a table as quickly as possible.

A further apparent disadvantage of indexes is that they take up additional space on the hard drive. Therefore, use indexes only for those columns that will often be searched and sorted. Indexes remain largely useless when the column contains many identical entries. (In such cases, you might ask yourself whether the normalization of the database has been optimally carried out.)

In principle, an index can be created for each field of a table, up to a maximum of sixteen indexes per table. (MySQL also permits indexes for several fields simultaneously. That makes sense if sorting is frequently carried out according to a combination of fields, as in *WHERE country='Austria' AND city='Graz'*).

Indexes for InnoDB Tables

Indexes are more important for InnoDB tables than for MyISAM tables. In the former, indexes are used not only for searching for records, but also for *row level locking*. This means that during a transaction, individual records are barred from access by other users. This affects, among others, the commands *SELECT ... LOCK IN SHARE MODE, SELECT ... FOR UPDATE*, and *INSERT, UPDATE*, and *DELETE*. (There is more on transactions in Chapter 10.)

The internal labeling of locked records takes place, for the sake of efficiency, not in the actual tables, but in the index. This works, of course, only if a suitable index is available.

Limitations

- MySQL cannot use indexes where inequality operators are used (*WHERE column != ...*).

- Likewise, indexes cannot be used for comparisons where the contents of the column are processed by a function (*WHERE DAY(column)= ...*).

- With *JOIN* operations (that is, in uniting data from various tables), indexes are of use only when primary and foreign keys refer to the same data type.

- If the comparison operators *LIKE* and *REGEXP* are used, an index is of use only when there is no wild card at the beginning of the search pattern. With *LIKE 'abc%'* an index is of use, but with *LIKE '%abc'*, it is not.

- Indexes are used with *ORDER BY* operations only if the records do not have to be previously selected by other criteria. (Unfortunately, an index rarely helps to speed up *ORDER BY* with queries in which the records are taken from several tables.)

- Indexes are ineffectual if a column contains the same value over and over. It is therefore not advisable to index a column with 0/1 or Y/N values.

Ordinary Indexes, Unique Indexes, Primary Indexes

Ordinary Index

The only task of an ordinary index (definition via the keyword *KEY* or *INDEX*) is to speed up access to data. You should therefore index columns that you frequently use in conditions (*WHERE column=...*) or for sorting (*ORDER BY column*). If possible, index columns with compact data (e.g., integers).

Unique Index

With an ordinary index it is allowed for several data records in the indexed field to refer to the same value. (In a table of personnel, for example, the same name can appear twice, even though it refers to two distinct individuals.)

When it is clear from context that a column contains unique values, you should then define an index with the key word *UNIQUE*. This has two consequences. One is that MySQL has an easier time managing the index; that is, the index is more efficient. The other is that MySQL ensures that no new record is added if there is already another record that refers to the same value in the indexed field. (Often, a *UNIQUE* index is defined for this reason alone, that is, not for access optimization, but to avoid duplication.)

Primary Index

For primary key fields, mentioned repeatedly in the previous section, a primary index must be defined. This involves a *UNIQUE* index that is distinguished only in that it has the name *PRIMARY*.

Foreign Key Index

Even if you define an integrity rule for a foreign key field (see the previous section), MySQL defines an internal index. This index serves to maintain the foreign key constraint as efficiently as possible.

Combined Indexes

An index can cover several columns, as in *INDEX(columnA, columnB)*. A peculiarity of such indexes is that MySQL can selectively use such an index. Thus when a query requires an index for *columnA* only, the combined index for *INDEX(columnA, columnB)* can be used. This holds, however, only for partial indexes at the beginning of the series. For instance, *INDEX(A, B, C)* can be used as index for *A* or *(A, B)*, but not as index for *B* or *C* or *(B, C)*.

Limits on the Index Length

In the definition of an index for *CHAR* and *VARCHAR* columns you can limit an index to a particular number of characters (which must be smaller than the maximum number of characters allowed in this field). The consequence is that the resulting index file is smaller and its evaluation quicker than otherwise. In most applications, that is, with character strings representing names, perhaps ten to fifteen characters altogether suffice to reduce the search set to a few data records.

With *BLOB* and *TEXT* columns you must institute this restriction, where MySQL permits a maximal index length of 255 characters.

Full-Text Index

An ordinary index for text fields helps only in the search for character strings that stand at the beginning of the field (that is, whose initial letters are known). On the other hand, if you store texts in fields that consist of several, or possibly very many, words, an ordinary index is useless. The search must be formulated in the form *LIKE '%word%'*, which for MySQL is rather complex and with large data sets leads to long response times.

In such cases it helps to use a full-text index. With this type of index, MySQL creates a list of all words that appear in the text. A full-text index can be created during the database design or afterwards:

```
ALTER TABLE tablename ADD FULLTEXT(column1, column2)
```

In *SELECT* queries, one can now search for records that contain one or more words. This is the query syntax:

```
SELECT * FROM tablename
WHERE MATCH(column1, column2) AGAINST('word1', 'word2', 'word3')
```

Then all records will be found for which the words *word1*, *word2*, and *word3* appear in the columns *column1* and *column2*.

Note The InnoDB table driver does not support full-text indexes.

An extensive description of the SQL syntax for full-text search, together with a host of application examples, can be found in Chapter 10.

Query and Index Optimization

Realistic performance estimates can be made only when the database has been filled with a sufficient quantity of test data. A test database with several hundred data records will usually be located entirely in RAM after the first query, and all queries will be answered quickly with or without an index. Things become interesting when tables contain well over 1000 records and when the entire size of the database is larger than the total RAM of the MySQL server.

In making the decision as to which columns should be provided with indexes, one may sometimes obtain some assistance from the command *EXPLAIN SELECT*. This is simply an ordinary *SELECT* command prefixed with the key word *EXPLAIN*. Instead of *SELECT* being simply executed, MySQL places information in a table as to how the query was executed and which indexes (to the extent that they exist) came into play.

Here are some pointers for interpreting the table created by *EXPLAIN*. In the first column appear the names of the tables in the order in which they were read from the database. The column *type* specifies how the table is linked to the other tables (*JOIN*). This functions most efficiently (i.e., quickly) with the type *system*, while more costly are the types *const, eq_ref, ref, range, index*, and *ALL*. (*ALL* means that for each record in the next-higher table in the hierarchy, all records of this table must be read. That can usually be prevented with an index.

The column *possible_keys* specifies which indexes MySQL can access in the search for data records. The column *key* specifies which index MySQL has actually chosen. The length of the index in bytes is given by *key_len*. For example, with an index for an *INTEGER* column, the number of bytes is 4. Information on how many parts of a multipart index are used is also given by *key_len*. As a rule, the smaller *key_len* is the better (that is, the faster).

The column *ref* specifies the column of a second table with which the linkage was made, while *rows* contains an estimate of how many records MySQL expects to read in order to execute the entire query. The product of all the numbers in the *rows* column allows one to draw a conclusion as to how many combinations arise from the query.

Finally, the column *extra* provides additional information on the *JOIN* operation, for example, *using temporary* when MySQL must create a temporary table in executing a query.

Tip Though the information proffered by *EXPLAIN* is often useful, the interpretation requires a certain amount of MySQL and database experience. You will find further information in the MySQL documentation: http://dev.mysql.com/doc/mysql/en/query-speed.html and http://dev.mysql.com/doc/mysql/en/explain.html.

A quite readable presentation on MySQL speed optimization can be found in the OpenOffice format: http://dev.mysql.com/tech-resources/presentations/ and http://dev.mysql.com/Downloads/Presentations/OSCON-2004.sxi.

Example 1

This query produces an unordered list of all books with all their authors. All *ID* columns are equipped with primary indexes.

```
USE mylibrary
EXPLAIN SELECT * FROM titles, rel_title_author, authors
  WHERE rel_title_author.authID =  authors.authID
  AND   rel_title_author.titleID = titles.titleID
```

table	type	key	key_len	ref	rows	Extra
titles	ALL	authName	60	NULL	53	Using index
rel_title_author	ref	authID	4	authors.authID	1	Using index
authors	eq_ref	PRIMARY	4	rel_title_author.titleID	1	

This *EXPLAIN* result means that first all records from the *titles* table are read, with the index *authName* being used. (This was not actually necessary, since the *SELECT* command does not require the sorting of results.) Then with the help of the *authID* index of *rel_title_author* and the primary index of *authors*, the links to the two other tables are made. The tables are thus optimally indexed, and for each part of the query there are indexes available.

To save space, some of the columns of the *EXPLAIN* result were removed, including *possible_keys*. This column contains a list of all indexes that were used for the corresponding part of the query. The column *key* tells which of these indexes MySQL chose.

Example 2

Here the query produces a list of all books (together with their authors) that have been published by a particular publisher. The list is ordered by book title. Again, all *ID* columns are equipped with indexes. Furthermore, in the *titles* table, *title* and *publID* are indexed:

```
EXPLAIN SELECT title, authName
FROM titles, rel_title_author, authors
WHERE titles.publID=2
  AND titles.titleID = rel_title_author.titleID
  AND authors.authID = rel_title_author.authID
ORDER BY title
```

table	type	key	key_len	ref	rows	Extra
titles	ref	publIDIndex	5	const	4	Using where; Using filesort
rel_title_author	ref	PRIMARY	4	titles.titleID	2	Using index
authors	eq_ref	PRIMARY	4	rel_title_author.authID	1	

The interpretation is this: The tables are optimally indexed; that is, for each part of the query there are indexes available. It is interesting that the title list (*ORDER BY title*) is apparently sorted externally, although there is an index for the *title* column as well. The reason for this is perhaps that the *title* records are first selected in accordance with the condition *publID=2*, and the *title* index can then no longer be applied.

Example 3

This example uses the same *SELECT* query as does Example 2, but it assumes that *titles.publID* does not have an index. The result is that now all 53 records of the *titles* table must be read. The index *authName* is indeed used, but it is of no help in speeding up the query. *Using temporary* means that a temporary table holding intermediate results was created.

table	type	key	key_len	ref	rows	Extra
titles	index	authName	60	NULL	53	Using index; Using temporary; Using filesort
rel_title_author	ref	PRIMARY	4	titles.titleID	4	Using index
authors	eq_ref	PRIMARY	4	rel_title_author.authID	4	Using where

Views

Views make it possible to define a special representation of one or more tables. A view behaves much like a table. That is, you can query data with *SELECT* queries and (depending on the definition of the view) alter data with *INSERT, UPDATE*, and *DELETE*.

Views have been available since MySQL 5.0. This section assumes that you are familiar with *SELECT* commands (see the following chapter) and that you understand MySQL access privileges (see Chapter 11). Note that phpMyAdmin 2.6, the version current at the time of writing, still cannot deal with views.

There are two basic reasons for using views:

Security: It can happen that you wish to prevent certain users of a database from having full access to a table. A typical example is a personnel table in a business setting, in which data on all employees are stored. You would like all users to have access to certain data (names and telephone numbers) but not to others (birth date and salary).

The solution is a view that contains the columns accessible by everyone. You have to set the MySQL access privileges in such a way that the user is allowed to access the view, but not the underlying table.

Convenience: In many applications, the same queries must be executed repeatedly to collect data from one or more tables according to certain requirements. Instead of forcing every user or programmer to formulate repeatedly the same complex *SELECT* commands, you, as the database administrator, can define a view.

The Definition of a View

Views act like virtual tables containing the result of a *SELECT* query. So it is no surprise that the definition is based on a *SELECT* command. The following two examples define two views for the *mylibrary* database and show five records for each of these views.

```
CREATE VIEW v1 AS
  SELECT titleID, title, subtitle FROM titles
  ORDER BY title, subtitle
SELECT * FROM v1 LIMIT 5
```

titleID	title	subtitle
11	A Guide to the SQL Standard	NULL
52	A Programmer's Introduction ...	NULL
19	Alltid den där Annette	NULL
51	Anklage Vatermord	Der Fall Philipp Halsmann
78	Apache Webserver 2.0	Installation, ...

```
CREATE VIEW v2 AS
  SELECT title, publname, catname FROM titles, publishers, categories
  WHERE titles.publid=publishers.publid
  AND titles.catID = categories.catID
  AND langID=2
SELECT * FROM v2 ORDER BY title LIMIT 5
```

title	publname	catname
Anklage Vatermord	Zsolnay	Literature and fiction
Apache Webserver 2.0	Addison-Wesley	Computer books
CSS-Praxis	Galileo	Computer books
Ein perfekter Freund	Diogenes Verlag	Literature and fiction
Excel 2000 programmieren	Addison-Wesley	Programming

To execute *CREATE VIEW* you must have the *Create View* privilege. What privileges are and how they are managed will be discussed in Chapter 11.

Changing View Records

Whether the commands *INSERT*, *UPDATE*, and *DELETE* can be used with a view (that is, whether the view is *updatable*) depends on the underlying *SELECT* command. For changeable views, the following rules hold:

- The *SELECT* command may not contain *GROUP BY*, *DISTINCT*, *LIMIT*, *UNION*, or *HAVING*.

- Views that process data from more than one table are almost always unchangeable.

- The view should contain all columns for which primary or unique indexes or foreign key constraints have been defined. If such columns are missing from the view, the MySQL option updatable_views_with_limit decides whether changes should be made with a warning (current default setting 1) or should trigger an error (setting 0).

View Options

The complete syntax of the *CREATE VIEW* command looks like this:

```
CREATE [OR REPLACE] [ALGORITHM = UNDEFINED | MERGE | TEMPTABLE]
VIEW name [(columnlist)] AS select command
[WITH [CASCADED | LOCAL] CHECK OPTION]
```

The following points provide a brief explanation of the various options:

- *OR REPLACE* means that an existing view should be replaced by the new view without an error message.

- *ALGORITHM* tells how the view is represented internally. This option was, alas, undocumented as this section was written. By default, MySQL always uses *UNDEFINED* (can be determined via *SHOW CREATE TABLE viewname*).

- *WITH CHECK OPTION* means that changes to view records are allowed only if the *WHERE* conditions of the *SELECT* command are satisfied. *WITH CHECK OPTION* is relevant, of course, only if the view is changeable.

The variant *WITH LOCAL CHECK OPTION* affects views that themselves are derived from other views (which is allowed!). *LOCAL* means that only the *WHERE* conditions of the *CREATE VIEW* command are considered, and not the *WHERE* conditions of the subordinate views.

The exact opposite effect is achieved by *CASCADED CHECK OPTION*: The *WHERE* conditions of all subordinate views are considered. If you specify neither *CASCADED* nor *LOCAL*, then the default *CASCADED* holds.

Viewing View Definitions

Just as you can determine with *SHOW CREATE TABLE name* the SQL code of the command for creating a table, *SHOW CREATE VIEW name* is possible for views. You must have the *Create View* privilege in order to be able to execute *CREATE VIEW*.

SHOW CREATE VIEW v1

```
CREATE ALGORITHM=UNDEFINED VIEW `mylibrary`.`v1` AS
  SELECT `mylibrary`.`titles`.`titleID`,
         `mylibrary`.`titles`.`title`,
         `mylibrary`.`titles`.`subtitle`
  FROM `mylibrary`.`titles`
  ORDER BY `mylibrary`.`titles`.`title`,
           `mylibrary`.`titles`.`subtitle`
```

Deleting Views

SHOW TABLES returns a list of all tables and views. To delete views, though, you cannot use *DROP TABLE*. Instead, you must use the command *DROP VIEW viewname*.

Example Database mylibrary (Library Management)

In the course of this chapter I have presented several aspects of database design in reference to the *mylibrary* database. This has caused the description of the *mylibrary* database to have been so extended that you may have lost an overview of the tables, fields, and indexes that this database comprises, the data types used, and so on. Therefore, this section offers a summary of all the properties of the *mylibrary* database. The totality of these properties is usually called a *database schema*.

Figure 8-2 presents a graphical summary of the schema. The figure shows neither the data types of the columns nor all the indexes, but nevertheless, one sees clearly which columns are used as primary indexes and how the tables are related one to the other. (Like all the schema figures in this book, this one was created with the query designer in OpenOffice.)

■**Note** A `*.sql` file with the complete definition of the *mylibary* database containing test data records can be found in the companion files to this book. To read in this file, use phpMyAdmin to create an empty database with *Latin1* as the default character set, then change to the page *SQL*, and load the `*.sql` file. Alternatively, you can create the database with the following two commands:

```
> mysqladmin -u root -p create mylibrary
> mysql -u root -p mylibrary < mylibrary.sql
```

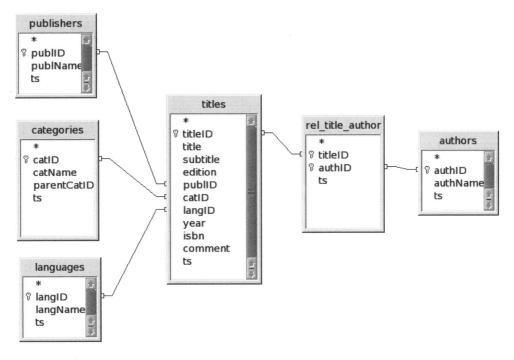

Figure 8-2. *The schema of the mylibrary database*

Properties of the Database

For the database *mylibrary* and all the text fields contained therein, the default character set is *latin1* and the sort order is *latin1_german1_ci*.

Properties of the Tables

All the tables are InnoDB tables. Tables 8-26 through 8-31 specify for each *mylibrary* table all fields, data types, attributes, and indexes. The meaning of most of the columns does not require additional explication. Worthy of note and as yet unexplained is the *ts* column that appears in each table. In this column the time of the last change is automatically logged. This column is necessary so that the database can be used by ODBC/ADO programs.

Table 8-26. *Properties of the authors Table*

Field	Data Type	Attribute	Index, Foreign Key Constraints
authID	*INT*	*NOT NULL AUTO_INCREMENT*	*PRIMARY KEY*
authName	*VARCHAR(60)*		*KEY*
ts	*TIMESTAMP*		

Table 8-27. *Properties of the categories Table*

Field	Data Type	Attribute	Index, Foreign Key Constraints
catID	INT	NOT NULL AUTO_INCREMENT	PRIMARY KEY
catName	VARCHAR(60)	NOT NULL	KEY
parentCatID	INT		KEY, FOREIGN KEY categories.catID
ts	TIMESTAMP		

Table 8-28. *Properties of the languages Table*

Field	Data Type	Attribute	Index, Foreign Key Constraints
langID	INT	NOT NULL AUTO_INCREMENT	PRIMARY KEY
langName	VARCHAR(60)	NOT NULL	KEY
ts	TIMESTAMP		

Table 8-29. *Properties of the publishers Table*

Field	Data Type	Attribute	Index, Foreign Key Constraints
publID	INT	NOT NULL AUTO_INCREMENT	PRIMARY KEY
publName	VARCHAR(60)	NOT NULL	KEY
ts	TIMESTAMP		

Table 8-30. *Properties of the rel_title_author Table*

Field	Data Type	Attribute	Index, Foreign Key Constraints
authID	INT	NOT NULL	PRIMARY KEY, FOREIGN KEY authors.authID
titleID	INT	NOT NULL	PRIMARY KEY, KEY, FOREIGN KEY titles.titleID
ts	TIMESTAMP		

Table 8-31. *Properties of the titles Table*

Field	Data Type	Attribute	Index, Foreign Key Constraints
titleID	INT	NOT NULL AUTO_INCREMENT	PRIMARY KEY
title	VARCHAR(100)	NOT NULL	KEY
subtitle	VARCHAR(100)		
edition	TINYINT		
publID	INT		KEY, FOREIGN KEY publishers.publID

Field	Data Type	Attribute	Index, Foreign Key Constraints
catID	INT		KEY, FOREIGN KEY categories.catID
langID	INT		KEY, FOREIGN KEY languages.langID
year	INT		
isbn	VARCHAR(20)		
comment	VARCHAR(255)		
ts	TIMESTAMP		

Example Database myforum (Discussion Group)

Most of the examples in this book use the *mylibrary* database, which we have been talking about throughout this chapter. Since all SQL concepts cannot be revealed by a single database, and particularly such a small one as *mylibrary*, two additional databases will be presented in this and the next sections: *myforum* and *exceptions*.

The first of these is a database for a real PHP application, whose code is not discussed in the book due to lack of space. What is at issue here is rather the design (schema) of the database. The database contains more than one thousand records and thus forms a good basis for trying out full-text search with MySQL (see Chapter 10).

There is no application behind the database *exceptions*. This database serves exclusively for experimenting with unusual MySQL data types and testing various sort orders.

The Discussion Group Database myforum

Among the best-loved MySQL applications are guest books, discussion groups, and other websites that offer users the possibility of creating a text and thereby adding their own voices to the website. The database *myforum* shows how a database can serve as the basis for a discussion group. The database consists of three tables:

- *forums* contains a list of the names of all discussion groups. Furthermore, each group can be assigned a particular language (English or German).

- *users* contains a list of all users registered in the database who are permitted to contribute to discussions. For each registered user, a login name, password, and email address are stored. The column *authent* contains a random character string that is sent to a new user by email at the time of registration. The account is activated only after the user clicks on the link contained in the email (column *active*) and supplies the random number.

- *messages* contains all the stored contributions. These consist of a *Subject* row, the actual text, *forumID*, *userID*, and additional management information. This table is the most interesting of the three from the standpoint of database design, and it will be considered further in this section.

MyISAM tables are used for this database, since at present only this format supports full-text search. All columns with strings use the *Latin1* character set and the sort order *latin1_german1_ci*. The schema for the database is summarized in Figure 8-3.

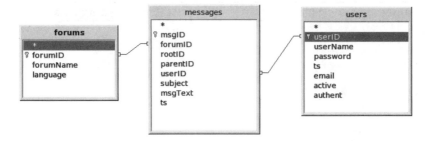

Figure 8-3. *The myforum database schema*

The *myforum* database, which is included in the files accompanying this book, contains more than 3,000 forum contributions from the website www.kofler.cc. (For this book, the authors' names have been concealed.) This database is well suited for trying out various aspects of full-text search (see also Chapter 10).

■Note The *messages* table is a good demonstration that a full-text index can occupy a considerable amount of space. In the test database, *messages* contains about 3000 messages with about 1.5 million characters altogether. For storing the *messages* data about 1.7 megabytes are required. The storage requirement for the full-text index is another 1.4 megabytes, which practically doubles the requirement for the entire table!

Hierarchies Among Messages

As we have already seen in the case of the *mylibrary* database, there is a battle in *myforum* in dealing with hierarchies. A significant feature of discussion groups is that the discussion thread is represented in a hierarchical list. The hierarchy is the result of the fact that each contribution can elicit a response. A discussion among the five participants Antony, Banquo, Coriolanus, Duncan, and Edmund (*A, B, C, D,* and *E* for short) might look like that depicted in Table 8-32.

Table 8-32. *Discussion Threads*

Sample Messages
A: How do I sort with MySQL Tables? (17.1.2005 12:00)
B: first answer (17.1.2005 18:30)
A: thanks! (17.1.2005 19:45)
C: better suggestion (19.1.2005 10:30)
D: second answer (18.1.2005 3:45)
A: I don't understand that (18.1.2005 9:45)
D: the same explanation, but with more detail (18.1.2005 22:05)
E: third answer (18.1.2005 19:00)

Here as illustration a description of the content is added to the title line (*subject*) of each contribution. In reality, the title line usually contains just the thread title.

A representation in database format might look like that shown in Table 8-33. It is assumed here that the five participants *A* through *E* have *userID* numbers 201 through 205. The messages of the thread have *msgID* numbers that begin with 301. (In practice, it is natural to expect that a thread will not exhibit sequential *msgID* numbers. More likely, other threads will break into the sequence.) The table is sorted chronologically (that is, in the order in which the messages were posted).

Table 8-33. *The messages Table with the Data Records of a Discussion Thread*

msgID	forumID	rootID	parentID	userID	subject	ts
301	3	301	NULL	201	How do I…	2005-01-17 12:00
302	3	301	301	202	first answer	2005-01-17 18:30
303	3	301	302	201	thanks!	2005-01-17 19:45
304	3	301	301	204	second answer	2005-01-18 3:45
305	3	301	304	201	I don't understand…	2005-01-18 9:45
306	3	301	301	205	third answer	2005-01-18 19:00
307	3	301	304	204	the same…	2005-01-18 22:05
308	3	301	302	203	better suggestion	2005-01-19 10:30

The hierarchy is expressed via the column *parentID*, which refers to the message up one level in the hierarchy. If *parentID* has the value *NULL*, then the contribution is one that began a new thread.

The column *rootID* refers to the first message of a thread. This column may not contain *NULL*. For the first message of a thread, one has *msgID=rootID*. The latter column actually contains redundant information, since one can determine via *parentID* the start message for any message. However, *rootID* simplifies this task and greatly increases the efficiency of the entire forum (for example, in determining the number of messages in a thread or assembling all the messages of a thread with a simple *SELECT* query).

Example Database Exceptions (Special Cases)

When you begin to develop an application with a new database, programming language, or API that is unfamiliar to you it is often practical to implement a simple test database for quickly testing various special cases. For the work on this book, as well as for testing various APIs and various import and export tests, the database *exceptions* was used. Among the tables of this database are the following:

- Columns with most data types supported by MySQL, including *xxxTEXT*, *xxxBLOB*, *SET*, and *ENUM*
- *NULL* values
- Texts and BLOBs with all possible special characters
- All 255 text characters (code 1 to 255)

The following paragraphs provide an overview of the tables and their contents. The column names indicate the data type (thus the column *a_blob* has data type *BLOB*). The *id* column is an *AUTO_INCREMENT* column (type *INT*). In all the columns except the *id* column the value *NULL* is allowed.

The Table testall

This table contains columns with the most important MySQL data types (though not all types).

Columns: *id, a_char, a_text, a_blob, a_date, a_time, a_timestamp, a_float, a_decimal, a_enum, a_set*

The Table text_text

With this table you can test the use of text.

Columns: *id, a_varchar (maximum 100 characters), a_text, a_tinytext, a_longtext*

The Table test_blob

With the *test_blob* table you can test the use of binary data (import, export, reading and storing a client program, etc.).

Columns: *id, a_blob*

Content: A record (*id=1*) with a 512-byte binary block. The binary data represent byte for byte the codes 0, 1, 2, …, 255, 0, 1, …, 255

The Table test_date

With this table you can test the use of dates and times.

Columns: id, a_date, a_time, a_datetime, a_timestamp

Content: A data record (*id=1*) with the values *2005-12-31, 23:59:59* and again *2005-12-31, 23:59:59*

The Table test_enum

With this table you can test the use of *SET* and *ENUM*.

Columns: *id, a_enum*, and *a_set* (with the character strings 'a', 'b', 'c', 'd', 'e')

Content:

```
id  a_enum   a_set
1   a        a
2   e        b,c,d
3
4   NULL     NULL
```

The Table test_null

With this table you can test whether *NULL* (first record) can be distinguished from an empty character string (second record).

Columns: *id, a_text*

Content:

```
id  a_text
1   NULL
2
3   'a text'
```

The Table test_sort1

With this table you can test various sort orders (*ORDER BY*) for the *Latin1* and *UTF-8* (Unicode) character sets. The table consists of three columns: *id* contains sequential numbers from 33 to 126 and from 161 to 255; *latin1char* contains the *Latin1* characters for the code in *id*; *utf8char* contains the associated Unicode characters. The two *CHAR* columns were deliberately not given an index.

Content:

```
id    latin1char   ut8char
...
65    'A'          'A'
66    'B'          'B'
...
```

The Table test_sort2

This table also serves for testing sort orders. It contains again three columns, *id, latin1text*, and *utf8text* (data type *VARCHAR(100)* for both character sets *Latin1* and *UTF8*). This time, the text columns contain entire words, namely *abc, Abc, ABC, Bar, Bär, Bären, Barenboim, bärtig*, and *Ärger*. In the next chapter you will find examples using the tables *test_sort1* and *test_sort2*.

The Tables importtable1, importtable2, exporttable

These three tables contain test data for importation and exportation of text files. A description of the tables as well as numerous possibilities for import and export by MySQL can be found in Chapter 14.

CHAPTER 9

■■■

An Introduction to SQL

This chapter provides an introduction to the database language *Structured Query Language*, or SQL for short. This language is used primarily to formulate instructions to a database system, including queries and commands to change or delete database objects. The most important of these commands are *SELECT*, *INSERT*, *UPDATE*, and *DELETE*, and these are the main attractions in this chapter, which aims to instruct in large part by presenting many examples.

The following chapter, as a sort of continuation of the present one, provides a selection of recipes for solving everyday SQL problems, such as dealing with character strings and with dates and times, and formulating sub*SELECT* instructions (that is, *SELECT* commands whose results depend on another *SELECT* command), using transactions, and full-text search.

Introduction

All of the examples presented in this chapter are based on the example databases presented in the previous chapter. If you wish to try out these databases for yourself, then you must download them to your own test environment. (All the source code is available at www.apress.com, in the Downloads section.) Which database is involved in a particular example will be clear from the line *USE databasename* that appears at the beginning of the example or the beginning of the section in question.

The best way of testing simple SQL commands is to use the MySQL command interpreter mysql. This program can be launched under Unix/Linux with the command mysql, while under Windows, you use PROGRAMS | MYSQL | MYSQL SERVER *N.N* | MYSQL COMMAND CLIENT. (Please note that you must terminate mysql commands with a semicolon. We shall not indicate the semicolon in this chapter, because it is not required by other client programs. That is, it is not part of the MySQL syntax. Additional information on mysql can be found in Chapter 4.)

When you get to the point of editing multiline SQL commands, you will find that the level of comfort and convenience afforded by mysql goes into a steep decline. A better alternative is to use one of the numerous MySQL interfaces (such as the MySQL Query Browser or phpMyAdmin). Such programs have the advantage that the results of a query are displayed in a reader-friendly tabular format.

■**Note** In this book we generally write SQL commands and key words in uppercase letters, reserving lowercase for the names of databases, tables, and columns. Sometimes, we use a mixed format (e.g., *columnName*). MySQL is largely case-insensitive. The exception is in the names of databases and tables, where case distinction is made. With names for such objects you must hew to the straight and narrow path of exactitude with regard to case. Details on MySQL naming rules can be found in Chapter 21.

DML, DDL, and DCL

SQL commands can be divided into three groups:

- **Data Manipulation Language (DML):** *SELECT, INSERT, UPDATE,* and *DELETE,* and several additional commands serve to read from the tables of a database and to store and update them. These commands form the centerpiece of this and the next chapter.

- **Data Definition Language (DDL):** With *CREATE TABLE, ALTER TABLE,* and their ilk the design (schema) of a database can be changed. Some such commands are presented at the end of this chapter.

- **Data Control Language (DCL):** *GRANT, REVOKE,* and several additional SQL commands help in setting the security mechanisms of MySQL. They will be presented in Chapter 11.

In Chapter 21 you will find an alphabetical reference to all SQL commands.

Simple Queries (SELECT)

Here is a simple database query: *SELECT * FROM tablename.* This query returns all data records of the table specified. The asterisk indicates that the query is to encompass all the columns of the table. (See Figure 9-1.)

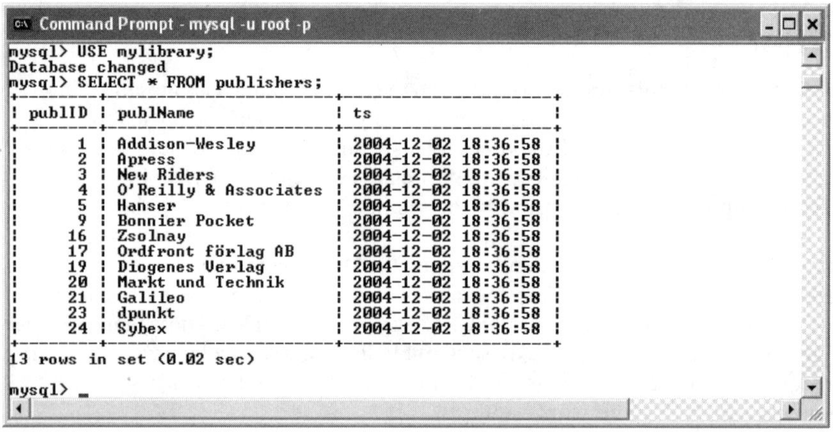

Figure 9-1. *First SQL experiments in the MySQL monitor* mysql

```
Use mylibrary
SELECT * FROM publishers
publID  publName
     1  Addison-Wesley
     2  Apress
     3  New Riders
     4  O'Reilly & Associates
     5  Hanser
```

■**Note** *SELECT* can be used without reference to a database or to tables, for example, in the form *SELECT 2*3*, in which case *SELECT* returns its result in the form of a small table (one column, one row). This is used relatively often to determine the content of MySQL variables or functions (as in, say, *SELECT NOW()*, to determine the current time).

Determining the Number of Data Records (Lines)

Perhaps you do not have a craving to view your data records in gruesome detail, but would like merely to determine how many records there are in one of your tables. For that, you can use the following query:

```
SELECT COUNT(publID) FROM publishers
```

*COUNT(publID)*___
$$\overline{5}$$

In this query you could specify, instead of *publID*, any column of the table (or * for all columns). In any case, MySQL optimizes the query and returns only the *number* of records, without actually reading them.

Determining the Number of Distinct Data Records (DISTINCT)

If the same values can appear multiple times in a column of a table and you wish to determine the number of distinct values, you must use the key word *DISTINCT*. For example, if you wish to know the number of publishers represented in the *titles* table, the query should look like this:

```
SELECT COUNT(DISTINCT publID) FROM titles
```

*COUNT(DISTINCT publID)*___
$$\overline{11}$$

It is not necessary that the result be identical to that of the previous query. It could happen that the *publishers* table contains names of publishers that have not published any titles.

The next example using *DISTINCT* shows that it is possible to carry out simple calculations in SQL commands. This command computes the average number of authors per book. To this end, *COUNT(*)* returns the number of entries in the table *rel_title_author*. (This table creates the relation between books and authors.) *COUNT(DISTINCT titleID)* returns the number of different titles in this table:

```
SELECT COUNT (*) / COUNT(DISTINCT titleID) FROM rel_title_author
```

*COUNT(*) / COUNT(DISTINCT titleID)*___
$$\overline{1.27}$$

Column Restriction

Often, you are not interested in all the columns of a table. In such a case you must specify the columns explicitly (instead of using the asterisk).

```
SELECT publName FROM publishers
```

publName_____
Addison-Wesley
Apress
New Riders
O'Reilly & Associates
Hanser

■Tip If a query is going to return a large number of data records, you should get accustomed to the idea of specifying explicitly only those columns of interest (instead of taking the lazy person's route of simply typing an asterisk). The reason is that MySQL (unnecessary data extraction), the client program (memory usage), and the network (unnecessary data transfer) work significantly more efficiently if the data set to be processed is limited to the absolute minimum.

Limiting the Number of Resulting Records (LIMIT)

You can limit not only the number of columns in a query result, but also the number of data records. Imagine that your *titles* table contains the names of 100,000 books, but you would like to access only the first ten of these (for example, to display in an HTML document). To query the remaining 99,990 records would be a gross squandering of CPU time, memory, and network capacity. To avoid such a scenario, you can limit the number of records returned with *LIMIT n*. The following command returns two records from the *titles* table:

```
USE mylibrary
SELECT title FROM titles LIMIT 2
```

title_____
Client/Server Survival Guide
Definitive Guide to Excel VBA

To return the next two records, execute a new query, but this time with *LIMIT offset, n*. Here *offset* specifies the number of the record at which access to the table is to begin. (Warning: The enumeration of data records begins with 0. An *offset* of *n* skips the first *n* records and, since counting begins with 0, starts processing at record number *n*.)

```
SELECT title FROM titles LIMIT 2, 2
```

title_____
Linux
Web Application Development with PHP 4.0

Determining the Number of Records Suppressed by LIMIT (SQL_CALC_FOUND_ROWS, FOUND_ROWS)

When you execute a *SELECT* query with *LIMIT*, you obtain only a partial result. Particularly in the page-by-page display of data, it would often be helpful to know exactly how many records are available altogether.

Beginning with MySQL 4.0, you can use in a *SELECT* query the additional option *SQL_CALC_FOUND_ROWS*. Then, in a second query you can evaluate the SQL function *FOUND_ROWS()*, which tells how many records the query would have returned without *LIMIT*.

The following query returns the three alphabetically first titles from the *titles* table. Then, with *FOUND_ROWS* it is determined how many records are available altogether:

```
SELECT SQL_CALC_FOUND_ROWS title FROM titles ORDER BY title LIMIT 3
```

*title*_____
```
A Guide to the SQL Standard
Alltid den där Annette
Client/Server Survival Guide
```

```
SELECT FOUND_ROWS()
```

FOUND_ROWS()_____
```
         26
```

The use of *CALC_FOUND_ROWS* and *FOUND_ROWS* is especially useful in complex queries in which a separate *SELECT* query for determining the number of records would be time intensive. Note, however, that the option *CALC_FOUND_ROWS* prevents certain kinds of optimization that MySQL carries out in *LIMIT* queries. Therefore, use *CALC_FOUND_ROWS* only when you then really wish to evaluate *FOUND_ROWS*.

Sorting Records (ORDER BY)

SELECT returns its results in no particular order. If you would like your list of results ordered, then you must request this explicitly via *ORDER BY column*. The following command returns an alphabetically ordered list of the authors in the *mylibrary* database.

```
SELECT authName FROM authors ORDER BY authName
```

*authName*_____
```
Bitsch Gerhard
Darween Hugh
Date Chris
DuBois Paul
Edwards E.
Garfinkel Simon
Gerken Till
Harkey D.
Holz Helmut
...
```

If you would like the reverse order, then you must add the key word *DESC* (for *descending*) to *ORDER BY*, as in, for example, *ORDER BY authName DESC*. The order of the results depends on the sort order that was specified for the relevant column when the table was defined.

■**Note** In point of fact, the sequence of *SELECT* results, even without *ORDER BY*, is not random, but it depends rather on the order in which the records are stored in the table. However, you probably have no influence on this order. Therefore, do not expect that *SELECT* results will have a particular order. In the case of new tables, query results usually are returned ordered by increasing *id* number (if *id* is an *AUTO_INCREMENT* field). But as soon as records are altered or deleted, the ordering is ruined. Do not rely on it!

You will learn in Chapter 10 how to select records in a truly random fashion.

Choosing the Sort Order

In sorting character strings, the sort order that was set for the relevant column is used. If no sort order has been defined for the column, then the sort order of the table is used. If there is no default setting here as well, then the sort order for the database is used. If no sort order has been defined for the database, then MySQL uses the default sort order that is valid for the character set for the column. (The default sort order for a given character string can be determined with the SQL command *SHOW CHARACTER SET*.)

If you wish to use a different sort order, you can specify it with *COLLATE*. However, the only sort orders that are allowed are those that are provided for the column's character set (see *SHOW COLLATION*). Note that then any index that is present cannot be used. In other words, using a different sort order with a large table is slow and inefficient!

```
SELECT authName FROM authors
ORDER BY authName COLLATE latin1_german2_ci
```

You can also change the sort order of a column after the fact. The index is then automatically updated:

```
ALTER TABLE authors MODIFY authName VARCHAR(60)
CHARACTER SET latin1 COLLATE latin1_german2_ci
```

If the desired sort order for the column's character set does not exist, you can use *CONVERT* to change the data to be sorted into another character set. It should be clear to you, however, that with large tables this is a very time-intensive process. In the following example, the author names are converted from *latin1* to *utf8* and then sorted in Polish order:

```
SELECT authName FROM authors
ORDER BY CONVERT(authName USING utf8) COLLATE utf8_polish_ci
```

Trying Out Different Sort Orders

You can use the tables *test_sort1* and *test_sort2* from the example database *exceptions* to try out at your leisure the sort orders supported by MySQL. The following commands provide some examples. You can determine the list of available sort orders with *SHOW COLLATION*. To save space, the *SELECT* results are not given in tabular format. Unrepresentable characters have been deleted.

The results of the first four commands differ in the order of international symbols and some special characters:

```
USE exceptions
```

```
SELECT latin1char FROM test_sort1
ORDER BY latin1char COLLATE latin1_general_ci
```

```
! " # $ % & ' ( ) * + , - . / 0 1 2 3 4 5 6 7 8 9 : ; < = > ? @ A a
À à á Á Â â Ã ã Ä ä Å å Æ æ b B c C ç Ç d D ? ð E e È è É é   ê Ë ë F
f g G h H I i ì Ì Í í î Î ï Ï j J K k L l m M n N ñ Ñ O o ò Ò ó Ó Ô ô
Õ õ Ö ö ø Ø P p Q q r R S s ß T t u U Ù ù ú Ú û Û Ü ü V v W w x X y Y
? ? ÿ Z z ? ? [ \ ] ...
```

```
SELECT latin1char FROM test_sort1
ORDER BY latin1char COLLATE latin1_german1_ci
```

```
! " # $ % & ' ( ) * + , - . / 0 1 2 3 4 5 6 7 8 9 : ; < = > ? @ Æ a
à á â ä å Å Ä Ã A ã À Á Â æ b B c C ç Ç d D é É Ë   e E È ê è ë f F G
g h H Í ï Ì I i ì í î Î Ï J j K k L l m M ñ Ñ n N ó Õ Ö Ø Ó Ò O Ô ò o
ø ö õ ô P p Q q r R S ß s t T ù ú u û ü U Ù Ú Ü Û V v w W x X y Y ? ?
z Z [ \ ] ^ _ ` { | } ...
```

```
SELECT latin1char FROM test_sort1
ORDER BY latin1char COLLATE latin1_swedish_ci
```

```
! " # $ % & ' ( ) * + , - . / 0 1 2 3 4 5 6 7 8 9 : ; < = > ? @ â á
à a Ã Â Á À ã A b B ç c Ç C D d ∂ ? e è Ë   É È é ê ë E f F G g h H Ï
i Ì í Í ï î ì Î I J j K k L l m M ñ Ñ n N ó Ô Ó Õ O ò o Ò õ ô P p Q q
r R S s T t u Ù û Ú Û U ù ú V v W w x X Y Ü ? y ü ? z Z å Å [ Æ æ Ä \
ä ö ] Ö ^ _ ` { | } ...
```

```
SELECT utf8char FROM test_sort1
ORDER BY utf8char COLLATE utf8_general_ci
```

```
! " # $ % & ' ` ( ) * + , - . / 0 1 2 3 4 5 6 7 8 9 : ; < = > ? @ a à
á â ä å Å Ä Ã A ã À Á Â b B c C ç Ç d D ë é E è Ë   É è é Ê E ê F f G g H
h I Ï Í Ì I Î î i í ì ï j J K k L l M m M ñ Ñ n N Ó o Ò O o ô Ô Õ Ö ö ó
P p Q q R r S s T t u ü Ù û ú ù Ú U Ü Û v V W w x X y ? ÿ Y ? z Z [ \
] ^ _ ` { | } ...
```

In the following examples as well you will have to look closely to detect the differences. For example, in the second example (German sort order according to the DIN-1 standard), *Bar* comes before *Bär*, while in the third example, (German DIN-2 standard), *Bär = Baer* comes before Bar. In the Swedish sort order the characters Ä, Å, and Ö come after all the other letters of the alphabet, and so *Ärger* appears at the end of the list. The last example shows that the Unicode sort order *utf8_general_ci* corresponds exactly to German DIN-1, at least for the words given here:

```
SELECT latin1text FROM test_sort2
ORDER BY latin1text COLLATE latin1_general_ci
```

```
abc Abc ABC Ärger Bar Barenboim Bär Bären bärtig
```

```
SELECT latin1text FROM test_sort2
ORDER BY latin1text COLLATE latin1_german1_ci
```

```
abc Abc ABC Ärger Bar Bär Bären Barenboim bärtig
```

```
SELECT latin1text FROM test_sort2
ORDER BY latin1text COLLATE latin1_german2_ci
```

```
abc Abc ABC Ärger Bär Bären bärtig Bar Barenboim
```

```
SELECT latin1text FROM test_sort2
ORDER BY latin1text COLLATE latin1_swedish_ci
```

```
abc Abc ABC Bar Barenboim Bär Bären bärtig Ärger
```

```
SELECT utf8text FROM test_sort2
ORDER BY utf8text COLLATE utf8_general_ci
```

```
abc Abc ABC Ärger Bar Bär Bären Barenboim bärtig
```

Selecting Data Records (WHERE, HAVING)

Often, it is not all of the records in a table that are of interest, but only those that satisfy one or more conditions. Such conditionals are introduced with *WHERE*. In our first example, we wish to display the names of only those authors whose surname starts with one of the letters L through Z:

```
SELECT authName FROM authors WHERE  authName>='M'
```

*authName*_____
Orfali R.
Pohl Peter
Ratschiller Tobias
Reese G.
...

In our second example, we employ the operator *LIKE* to compare character strings. The query determines all authors whose names contain the sequence of letters *er*. With the operator *LIKE*, the character % serves as a placeholder for an arbitrary character string.

```
SELECT authName FROM authors WHERE  authName  LIKE '%er%'
```

*authName*_____
Bitsch Gerhard
Gerken Till
Kofler Michael
Kramer David
Pohl Peter
Ratschiller Tobias
Schmitt Bernd
Yarger R.J.

■**Caution** Comparisons with *LIKE* can be very slow when they are applied to large tables. All the data records must be read and analyzed. It is impossible to use indexes to optimize such queries. A frequently used alternative to *LIKE* is the employment of a full-text index; see Chapter 10.

Comparisons with a large number of values can be carried out easily with *IN*:

```
SELECT authID, authName FROM authors
WHERE authID IN (2, 7, 12)
```

authID *authName*_____
  2   Kramer David
  7   Gerken Till
 12   Yarger R.J.

Instead of formulating conditionals with *WHERE*, you could instead use *HAVING*. The *WHERE* conditionals are executed first, while *HAVING* conditionals are used only on intermediate results (returned by *WHERE*). The advantage of *HAVING* is that the conditions can also be applied to calculated fields (for example, to *SUM(columnXy)* in a *GROUP BY* query). An example appears in the section after next.

HAVING conditionals are less easily optimized for MySQL than *WHERE* conditionals, and they should be avoided if an equivalent *WHERE* is possible.

■**Note** Please note that the conditional *colname = NULL* is not permitted. If you are searching for records that contain *NULL*, you must work with *ISNULL(colname)*.

Linking Data from Several Tables

Up to now, all of our examples with *SELECT* have been applied to the search for records from a single table. However, with relational databases we are usually dealing with a number of related tables. Therefore, we are usually interested in applying a *SELECT* command to combine data from several tables. For this we will use the *JOIN* syntax.

JOINs Across Two Tables

A first attempt to create a list of all book titles (column *title*) together with their publishers (column *publName*) from the tables *titles* and *publishers* is a colossal failure:

```
USE mylibrary
SELECT title, publName FROM titles, publishers
```

title	publName
Client/Server Survival Guide	Addison-Wesley
Definitive Guide to Excel VBA	Addison-Wesley
Linux	Addison-Wesley
Web Application Development with PHP 4.0	Addison-Wesley
Client/Server Survival Guide	Apress
Definitive Guide to Excel VBA	Apress
Linux	Apress
Web Application Development with PHP 4.0	Apress
Client/Server Survival Guide	New Riders
Definitive Guide to Excel VBA	New Riders
Linux	New Riders
Web Application Development with PHP 4.0	New Riders
...	

MySQL returns a list of all possible combinations of titles and publishers. In our relatively small database we can pick ourselves up from this minicatastrophe without too much damage. But imagine a database with 10,000 titles and 500 publishers, resulting in 5,000,000 combinations.

If queries spanning several tables are to return sensible results, precise information must be given as to how the data from the different tables are to be joined together. One possibility for formulating this connection is offered by *WHERE*. Since the linking field *publID* occurs in both tables, we must use the form *table.column* to indicate precisely which field is meant.

```
SELECT title, publName FROM titles, publishers
WHERE titles.publID = publishers.publID
```

title	publName
Linux, 5th ed.	Addison-Wesley
Definitive Guide to Excel VBA	Apress
Client/Server Survival Guide	Addison-Wesley
Web Application Development with PHP 4.0	New Riders
MySQL	New Riders
MySQL & mSQL	O'Reilly \& Associates
...	

There are quite a few additional ways of arriving at the same result. One variant consists in creating the table list with *LEFT JOIN* and then forming the linking connection with *ON*:

```
SELECT title, publName
 FROM titles LEFT JOIN publishers
  ON titles.publID = publishers.publID
```

Another variant makes use of the key word *USING*, in which the common linking field is specified. However, this variant assumes that the linking field (in this case *publID*) has the same name in both tables. That is, of course, not always the case:

```
SELECT title, publName
  FROM titles LEFT JOIN publishers
    USING (publID)
```

JOINs Across Three or More Tables

Things become a bit more confusing when the query must examine data from more than two tables. The following query returns a list of all book titles with all their authors. (Books with several authors occur in this list with multiplicity.) The relation between the tables *titles* and *authors* is created in the third table *rel_title_author*. The condition for the resulting data records is that *titleID* agree in the tables *titles* and *rel_title_author* and simultaneously *authID* in the tables *authors* and *rel_title_author*.

```
SELECT title, authName
  FROM titles, rel_title_author, authors
  WHERE titles.titleID = rel_title_author.titleID
    AND authors.authID = rel_title_author.authID
ORDER BY title
```

title	*authName*
A Guide to the SQL Standard	Date Chris
A Guide to the SQL Standard	Darween Hugh
Alltid den där Annette	Pohl Peter
Client/Server Survival Guide	Orfali R.
Client/Server Survival Guide	Harkey D.
Client/Server Survival Guide	Edwards E.
Definitive Guide to Excel VBA	Kofler Michael
Definitive Guide to Excel VBA	Kramer David
Excel 2000 programmieren	Kofler Michael
Jag saknar dig, jag saknar dig	Pohl Peter
LaTeX	Kopka Helmut
Linux für Internet und Intranet	Holz Helmut
Linux für Internet und Intranet	Schmitt Bernd
Linux für Internet und Intranet	Tikart Andreas
Linux, 5th ed.	Kofler Michael
Maple	Kofler Michael
Maple	Komma Michael
Maple	Bitsch Gerhard
...	

Our next example is somewhat more complex: Here we generate a list of publishers and their authors. (Thus the query determines which authors write for which publishers.) The connection between publishers and authors is made via the tables *titles* and *rel_title_author*, so that altogether, four tables are brought into play.

The SQL key word *DISTINCT* has the effect that equivalent data records are output only once. Since there are authors in the *mylibrary* database who have written several books (for the same publisher), the simple joining of these tables would result in many combinations in which an author and publisher combination occurred with multiplicity.

```
SELECT DISTINCT publName, authName
  FROM publishers, titles, rel_title_author, authors
 WHERE titles.titleID = rel_title_author.titleID
   AND authors.authID = rel_title_author.authID
   AND publishers.publID = titles.publID
ORDER BY publName, authName
```

publName	*authName*
Addison-Wesley	Bitsch Gerhard
Addison-Wesley	Darween Hugh
Addison-Wesley	Date Chris
Addison-Wesley	Edwards E.
Addison-Wesley	Harkey D.
...	
Apress	Kofler Michael
Apress	Kramer David
New Riders	DuBois Paul
New Riders	Gerken Till
New Riders	Ratschiller Tobias
...	

Syntax Variants

If you read about the details of *FROM* under the description of the *SELECT* syntax in the MySQL documentation, you may find your head spinning from the large number of (almost) identical variants. Tables 9-1 and 9-2 provide a brief overview.

Table 9-1. *Unconditional JOIN (Combination of All Possibilities; Seldom Useful)*

	Syntax Variant
(1)	*FROM table1, table2*
(2)	*FROM table1 JOIN table2*
(3)	*FROM table1 CROSS JOIN table2*
(4)	*FROM table1 INNER JOIN table2*
(5)	*FROM table1 STRAIGHT_JOIN table2*

Table 9-2. *Conditional JOIN*

	Syntax Variant
(6)	*FROM table1, table2 WHERE table1.xyID = table2.xyID*
(7)	*FROM table1 LEFT [OUTER] JOIN table2 ON table1.xyID = table2.xyID*
(8)	*FROM table1 LEFT [OUTER] JOIN table2 USING (xyID)*
(9)	*FROM table1 NATURAL [LEFT [OUTER]] JOIN table2*
(10)	*FROM table2 RIGHT [OUTER] JOIN table1 ON table1.xyID = table2.xyID*
(11)	*FROM table2 RIGHT [OUTER] JOIN table1 USING (xyID)*

In (1) through (4) in Table 9-1, MySQL tries on its own to find an optimal sequence for access to the data. Variant (5) is distinguished from the other four in that there, the order of data extraction from the tables is not optimized by MySQL. With (6), in joining the two tables, only those fields are considered that are identical.

With (7) and (9), for every record of the first (left) table a result record is generated, even when the linked field contains *NULL*. For example, if the *titles* table is used for *table1*, and the *publishers* table for *table2*, then *LEFT JOIN* will return even those titles for which no publisher name has been stored. (The key word *OUTER* is optional and has no effect on the function.)

Variants (10) and (11) correspond to (7) and (8). Note, however, that *table1* and *table2* have been interchanged. The MySQL documentation recommends not using *RIGHT JOIN* for improved compatibility with other databases, but instead using *LEFT JOIN* (with exchanged order of tables).

The *USING* variants assume that the *ID* fields in both tables have the same name. In the case of *NATURAL*, like-named fields in both tables are automatically used for joining. Therefore, except for the *ID* field, there can be no other like-named fields.

■**Caution**   Please note that with *LEFT JOIN* the order of the tables is significant.

- *titles LEFT JOIN publishers* returns titles that have no publisher, but no publishers that have not published a single title.

- *publishers LEFT JOIN titles* returns, contrariwise, publishers that have yet to publish a title, but no titles that do not have an associated publisher.

In contrast to many other SQL dialects, MySQL recognizes no *FULL JOIN*, which would return all such combinations. Such a function will likely exist beginning with MySQL 5.1.

Uniting Query Results

Starting with MySQL 4.0, with *UNION* you can unite two or more *SELECT* queries. You thereby obtain a table of results in which the results of the individual queries are arranged one after another:

```
SELECT command UNION [ALL] SELECT command ...
```

The following example shows how the results of two *SELECT* commands on the same table are united. (Of course, the queries could also be with regard to separate tables, but then you would have to be sure that the tables had the same number of columns. Furthermore, the columns should exhibit the same data type. If that is not the case, then MySQL attempts to fit the data to the data type of the first *SELECT* command.)

```
USE mylibrary
SELECT * FROM authors WHERE authName  LIKE 'b%'
UNION
SELECT * FROM authors WHERE authName LIKE 'g%'
```

authID	authName
22	Bitsch Gerhard
26	Garfinkel Simon
7	Gerken Till

Normally, duplicate records are automatically eliminated from the result. Only when you use *UNION ALL* does the result contain the duplicates.

You can also place the individual *SELECT* terms in parentheses. Then, for each part of the query, as well as for the complete result, you can use *LIMIT* and *ORDER* as you wish. The following query first selects at most ten records from the tables *tbl1* and *tbl2* and unites them. From these (at most twenty) records, only the five most recent are displayed:

```
(SELECT * FROM tbl1 ORDER BY colA LIMIT 10)
UNION
(SELECT * FROM tbl2 ORDER BY colA LIMIT 10)
ORDER BY colTimestamp LIMIT 5
```

■Note At present, *UNION* is the only set operator in MySQL. The key words *MINUS* and *INTERSECT*, available in many other database systems, are not available in MySQL.

Grouped Queries, Aggregate Functions

The data records for our books, stored in the *mylibrary* database, are assigned to various categories. If you require information as to which categories contain which books, then you will find the following query helpful. (Warning: Books that have not been assigned to a category will not appear at all. If you wish to see all books, then you must execute *FROM titles LEFT JOIN categories ON titles.catID = categories.catID.*)

```
USE mylibrary
SELECT catName, title FROM titles, categories
WHERE titles.catID = categories.catID
ORDER BY catName, title
```

catName	title
Children's books	Alltid den där Annette
Children's books	Jag saknar dig, jag saknar dig
Computer books	LaTeX
Computer books	Linux, 5th ed.
Computer books	Maple
Databases	Client/Server Survival Guide
Databases	Visual Basic Datenbankprogrammierung
Programming	Definitive Guide to Excel VBA
Programming	Visual Basic
SQL	A Guide to the SQL Standard

Aggregate Functions

If you wish to determine only how many books there are in each category, you can put the fingers of both hands to work and begin counting in the list just produced: two children's books, three computer books not more precisely categorized, two books on databases, and so on.

It has probably crossed your mind that there may be a more automated way of doing this: *GROUP BY name* creates in the resulting list a group for each member of the specified column. With *GROUP BY catName* in the above query a single row is made out of the two entries with *catName='Children's books'*. Which title is shown depends on the sort order, if any.

We see that with *GROUP BY* alone we do not accomplish much (unless we merely wanted to generate a list of all the categories, but there are easier ways of accomplishing that). However, in connection with *GROUP BY*, SQL supports aggregate functions. This means that in the column list at the beginning of a *SELECT* you can use functions like *COUNT, SUM, MIN,* and *MAX.* It is when these functions are brought into play that *GROUP BY* finally becomes a useful tool, as is demonstrated by the following example: We shall count (*COUNT*) how many entries are associated with each category.

New here is also the use of the key word *AS*, whereby the second column in the query is given the name *nrOfItems.* Without *AS*, the column would have the name *'COUNT(itemID)'*, which not only would be a bit confusing, but would increase the amount of typing each time the column was referenced (e.g., in *ORDER BY*).

```
SELECT catName, COUNT(title) AS nrOfItems
FROM titles, categories
WHERE titles.catID = categories.catID
GROUP BY catname
ORDER BY catname
```

catName	nrOfItems
Children's books	2
Computer books	3
Databases	2
Programming	2
SQL	1

If you would like a list of *all* categories, even those for which at present there are no books, then you must make the connection between the two tables with *LEFT JOIN* (as described in the previous section). This time, the resulting list will be sorted so that the categories with the most books are displayed first.

```
SELECT catName, COUNT(title) AS nrOfItems
FROM categories LEFT JOIN titles ON titles.catid = categories.catid
GROUP BY catname
ORDER BY nrOfItems DESC
```

catName	nrOfItems
Computer books	5
MySQL	4
Programming	3
Children's books	3
PHP	2
Databases	2
Literature and fiction	2
LaTeX, TeX	1
SQL	1
Object-oriented databases	0
All books	0
Relational Databases	0
Perl	0

■Tip The SQL function *IF* can be placed within an aggregate function, for example, to enable the consideration of only those values that satisfy a certain condition when you are using *COUNT* or *SUM*. Application examples can be found in the next chapter.

GROUP_CONCAT: Aggregate Functions

The aggregate function *GROUP_CONCAT* has been available since MySQL 4.1. It makes it possible to group together character strings. This function offers many fascinating application possibilities, as shown by the following example, which returns a table of all book titles that have more than one author, together with a character string with the authors arrayed in alphabetical order.

The simplest way to proceed is to pass only the column name to the function *GROUP_CONCAT*. MySQL then arranges the strings into a group in some arbitrary order, separated by commas. With *ORDER_BY* you can then sort the strings, while *SEPARATOR* provides the desired separator character:

```
SELECT title,
       GROUP_CONCAT(authname ORDER BY authname SEPARATOR ', ')
         AS authors,
       COUNT(authors.authID) AS cnt
FROM authors, titles, rel_title_author
WHERE authors.authID = rel_title_author.authID
AND   titles.titleID = rel_title_author.titleID
GROUP BY titles.titleID
HAVING cnt>1
ORDER BY title
```

title	authors	cnt
A Guide to the SQL Standard	Darween Hugh, Date Chris	2
Client/Server Survival Guide	Edwards Jeri, Harkey Dan, ...	3
Linux für Internet und Intranet	Holz Helmut, Schmitt Bernd, ...	3
Maple	Bitsch Gerhard, Kofler Michael, ...	3
Mit LaTeX ins Web	Goosens Michael, Rahtz Sebastian	2
MySQL	Kofler Michael, Kramer David	2
MySQL & mSQL	King Tim, Reese Georg, Yarger ...	3
PHP 5 und MySQL 5	Kofler Michael, Öggl Bernd	2
PHP and MySQL Web Development	Thomson Laura, Wellington Luke	2
The Definitive Guide to ...	Kofler Michael, Kramer David	2
The Definitive Guide to ...	Kofler Michael, Kramer David	2
Visual C#	Frank Eller, Kofler Michael	2
Web Application Development ...	Gerken Till, Ratschiller Tobias	2

GROUP BY for Several Columns

GROUP BY can also be used for several columns. The following query provides information about the numbers of book titles in various languages and the categories in which they appear. Note that with this query, all titles are lost that are not assigned a language or category:

```
SELECT, langName, catName, COUNT(*)
FROM titles, languages, categories
WHERE titles.catID = categories.catID
  AND titles.langID = languages.langID
GROUP BY langName, catName
```

langName	catName	COUNT(*)
deutsch	C#	1
deutsch	Children's books	1
deutsch	Computer books	5
deutsch	Databases	1
deutsch	LaTeX, TeX	2
deutsch	Linux	4
deutsch	Literature and fiction	7
deutsch	MySQL	1
deutsch	PHP	3
deutsch	Programming	4
deutsch	Relational Databases	1
deutsch	Visual Basic	1
deutsch	Visual Basic .NET	3
english	Computer books	1
english	Literature and fiction	2
english	MySQL	3
english	PHP	2

```
english   Science Fiction               3
english   SQL                           1
norsk     Literature and fiction        1
svensk    Children's books              2
svensk    Literature and fiction        9
```

GROUP BY WITH ROLLUP

Since MySQL 4.1, the key words *WITH ROLLUP* can be appended to *GROUP BY* column. If *GROUP BY* groups only a single column, then *WITH ROLLUP* simply has the effect that an additional sum row is added, with the group name *NULL* being used:

```
SELECT langName, COUNT(*)
FROM titles, languages
WHERE titles.langID = languages.langID
GROUP BY langName WITH ROLLUP
```

langName	COUNT(*)
deutsch	34
english	12
norsk	1
svensk	11
NULL	58

Of greater interest is the effect of *ROLLUP* on several columns. In this case, *GROUP BY* returns a final sum for the first column and supplementary partial sums for the second column. (The sum rows in the following are shown in boldface.)

```
SELECT langName, catName, COUNT(*)
FROM titles, languages, categories
WHERE titles.catID = categories.catID
  AND titles.langID = languages.langID
GROUP BY langName, catName WITH ROLLUP
```

langName	catName	COUNT(*)
deutsch	C#	1
deutsch	Children's books	1
deutsch	Computer books	5
deutsch	Databases	1
deutsch	LaTeX, TeX	2
deutsch	Linux	4
deutsch	Literature and fiction	7
deutsch	MySQL	1
deutsch	PHP	3
deutsch	Programming	4
deutsch	Relational Databases	1
deutsch	Visual Basic	1
deutsch	Visual Basic .NET	3
deutsch	**NULL**	34
english	Computer books	1
english	Literature and fiction	2
english	MySQL	3
english	PHP	2
english	Sience Fiction	3
english	SQL	1
english	**NULL**	12
norsk	Literature and fiction	1
norsk	**NULL**	1
svensk	Children's books	2

svensk	Literature and fiction	9
svensk	**NULL**	11
NULL	**NULL**	58

Altering Data (INSERT, UPDATE, and DELETE)

Executing a Backup

Before you start playing around with your database, you should consider backing up individual tables or perhaps the whole database, so that after you make a mess of things, you can restore the database to its original pristine condition. You have the choice of executing a backup with mysqldump (see Chapter 4) or directly with SQL commands. This section discusses one way of proceeding.

Tip MySQL novices frequently change or delete more records than intended in applying *UPDATE* and *DELETE* commands, by applying them to the entire table. If you launch `mysql` with the option `--i-am-a-dummy`, then the risk of accidental damage is reduced considerably: `mysql` refuses to execute *UPDATE* and *DELETE* commands without a *WHERE*.

Creating Copies of a Table

The following instruction creates a new table with the name *newtable* and copies all the data records of *table* into the new table. The column definitions of the new table are identical to those of the old one, but there are some occasional differences. For example, the attribute *AUTO_INCREMENT* is lost. Moreover, in the new table, no indexes are created:

```
CREATE TABLE newtable SELECT * FROM table
```

Restoring Tables

With the given commands, first all data records of the original table *table* are deleted. Then the records that were saved into *newtable* are copied back into *table*. (The original *AUTO_INCREMENT* values remain untouched during the copying back and forth.)

```
DELETE FROM table
INSERT INTO table SELECT * FROM newtable
```

If you no longer require the backup data, you can simply delete *newtable*:

```
DROP TABLE newtable
```

Making a Backup of an Entire Database

With the program `mysqldump` (under Windows it is `mysqldump.exe`) you can create a backup file (in text format) of a complete database. Note, please, that you cannot execute `mysqldump` from within `mysql`, but rather, you must launch it as a freestanding program in a shell or command window.

```
user$ mysqldump -u loginame -p dbname > backupfile
Enter password: xxxx
```

Restoring a Database

There is no counterpart to `mysqldump` for reading in a saved database. Instead, you will have to rely on the command `mysql`, where you give the backup file as input source. The database *dbname* must already exist.

```
user$ mysql -u loginname -p dbname < backupfile
Enter password: xxxx
```

Of course, you can also recreate the database in interactive mode:

```
user$ mysql -u root -p
Enter password: xxxx
mysql> CREATE DATABASE dbname; -- if dbname does not yet exist
mysql> USE dbname;
mysql> SOURCE backupfile;
```

Inserting Data Records (INSERT)

With *INSERT* you can add a new record to a table. After the name of the table there must appear first a list of the column names and then a list with the values to be inserted. (Columns with a default value, columns that can be *NULL*, and *AUTO_INCREMENT* columns do not have to be specified.)

In the following example, a new data record is saved in the table *titles* in the *mylibrary* database. Only two columns (*title* and *year*) will be specified. All remaining columns are taken care of by MySQL: A new *AUTO_INCREMENT* value is placed in *titleID*, and in the other columns, the requisite default value or *NULL*. (This process is allowed only because when the *titles* table was created, a default value was specifically provided for, and *NULL* was specified as a permissible value.)

```
USE mylibrary
INSERT INTO titles (title, year)
VALUES ('MySQL', 2005)
```

One may do without naming the columns if values for all columns (including default and *AUTO_INCREMENT* columns) are given and the order of the columns is followed exactly. In the case of titles, there are quite a few columns: *titleID, title, subtitle, edition, publID, catID, langID, year, isbn, comment,* and *ts.*

In the following command, for some columns the value *NULL* is given. In most cases MySQL then actually stores the value *NULL*. However, in the *titles* table there are two exceptions: MySQL automatically generates for the *titleID* column a new *ID* number (on account of the *AUTO_INCREMENT* attribute) and stores in *ts* the current date and time (since we are dealing with a *TIMESTAMP* column).

```
INSERT INTO titles
VALUES (NULL, 'deleteme', '', 1, NULL, NULL, NULL, 2005, NULL, NULL, NULL)
```

Another syntax variant enables several new records to be inserted with a single command:

```
INSERT INTO table (columnA, columnB, columnC)
VALUES ('a', 1, 2), ('b', 12, 13), ('c', 22, 33), ...
```

INSERT with Related Tables

If you are dealing with related tables, then normally, insertion of records is not accomplished with a single *INSERT* command. For example, to store a book record in the *mylibrary* database, new records must be stored in at least the tables *titles* and *rel_title_author*. If the new book was written by an author or authors whose names have not yet been stored in the database, or if it was published by a publisher that is currently unknown to the database, then new data records will also have to be added to the tables *publishers* and *authors*.

However, now we have the problem that not all the data for the *INSERT* command are known at the outset. To store a book published by a new publisher, the *publID* of the publisher must be given in the *titles* table. This is an *AUTO_INCREMENT* value, which is generated by MySQL only when the new publisher is stored in the database.

There must, then, be a way to access the last-generated *AUTO_INCREMENT* value. And indeed there is. The function for this is *LAST_INSERT_ID()*, which returns the *AUTO_INCREMENT* value of the last *INSERT* command. This function has effect only within the current connection. That is, *AUTO_INCREMENT* values that may have arisen through the *INSERT* commands of other database users are ignored.

The following lines show how a book with a good deal of new information (three new authors, a new publisher) is stored. The book in question is the following: Randy Yarger, George Reese, Tim King, *MySQL & mSQL*, O'Reilly 1999.

```
INSERT INTO publishers (publName) VALUES ('O\'Reilly & Associates')
SELECT LAST_INSERT_ID()
            4   <--- publID for the publishes
INSERT INTO authors (authName) VALUES ('Yarger R.')
SELECT LAST_INSERT_ID()
            12   <--- authID for the first author
INSERT INTO authors (author) VALUES ('Reese G.')
SELECT LAST_INSERT_ID()
            13   <--- authID for the second author
INSERT INTO authors (author) VALUES ('King T.')
SELECT LAST_INSERT_ID()
            14   <--- authID for the third author
INSERT INTO titles (title, publID, year)
    VALUES ('MySQL & mSQL', 4, 1999)
SELECT LAST_INSERT_ID()
            9  <--- titleID for the book
INSERT INTO rel_title_author
VALUES (9, 12), (9, 13), (9,14)
```

Of course, you will put in these values manually only for trying things out. In practice, you will not, of course, input these commands manually. In practice, the user interface of a PHP or Perl or Java program will take care of evaluation and reevaluation of the *ID* values. The program will also ensure that authors and publishers who already appear in the database are not stored again by mistake. (For the programming language PHP, such a program is introduced in Chapter 15.)

Altering Data Records (UPDATE)

With *UPDATE* you can change individual fields of an existing database. The usual syntax of this command is the following:

```
UPDATE tablename
SET column1=value1, column2=value2, ...
WHERE columnID=n
```

Thus individual fields of a record specified by its *ID* value are changed. In the following example we change the title of the Linux book (*titleID=1*):

```
USE mylibrary
UPDATE titles SET title='Linux, 6th ed.'  WHERE titleID=1
```

If *UPDATE* is used without *WHERE*, then the change is instituted for all data records (beware!). The following command, for example, would change the publication date of all books to the year 2005:

```
UPDATE titles SET year=2005
```

With certain restrictions, calculations are permissible in *UPDATE* commands. Let us suppose that the price of the book was stored in the *titles* table. Then it would be easy to increase all prices by five percent:

```
UPDATE title SET price=price*1.05
```

Editing Data Records in Sorted Lists (UPDATE with ORDER BY and LIMIT)

If you want to change the first or last *n* data records, with the *UPDATE* command you can also specify *ORDER BY* and *LIMIT* (since MySQL 4.0). The following command sets the field *mydata* to zero for the first ten data records (in alphabetical order) of the table *tablename*:

```
UPDATE tablename SET mydata=0 ORDER BY name LIMIT 10
```

Updating with Linked Tables

You can process the data from several tables using *UPDATE* commands (since MySQL 4.0). The following example changes the column *columnA* of *table1*, where the new data come from *table2.columnB*. The link between the two fields is established via the common *ID* field *table1ID* (a genuine example of a multitable *UPDATE* command is given in Chapter 10):

```
UPDATE table1, table1
SET table1.columnA = table.columnB
WHERE table1.table1ID = table2.table1ID
```

Deleting Data Records (DELETE)

There can be little doubt that the syntactically simplest command of this section is *DELETE*. All records selected with *WHERE* are simply deleted. Here it is not required to specify the columns (indeed, it is not possible), since in any case, the entire data record is made to disappear without a trace. The following instruction deletes a single record from the *titles* table:

```
USE mylibrary
DELETE FROM titles WHERE titleID=8
```

■Caution   If *DELETE* is executed without a *WHERE* condition, then all the records of the table will be deleted. There is no "undo" possibility. The table itself with its definition of columns, indexes, etc. remains intact. If you wish to delete the table itself, then you must execute the command *DROP TABLE*.

Deleting Records from Linked Tables

In MySQL 3.23, the *DELETE* command can be used with reference to only a single table. Since MySQL 4.0, the following syntax is allowed:

```
DELETE t1, t2 FROM t1, t2, t3 WHERE condition1 AND condition2 ...
```

With this, all data records from tables *t1* and *t2* that satisfy the specified conditions are deleted. The conditions may contain arbitrary connections among the tables *t1*, *t2*, and *t3*. (To formulate it more generally, *DELETE* deletes records from only those tables that are given before *FROM*. In the conditions, records can be used from all tables that appear after *FROM*.)

The following example deletes from the *titles* table all book titles of the author *Kofler Michael*. To find the titles to be deleted, a link is created among the three tables *titles*, *rel_title_author*, and *authors*:

```
USE mylibrary

DELETE titles FROM titles, rel_title_author, authors
WHERE titles.titleID=rel_title_author.titleID
  AND authors.authID=rel_title_author.authID
  AND authors.authName='Kofler Michael'
```

The following variant of the command given above deletes not only the titles, but *Kofler Michael* from the *authors* table, as well as all records from *rel_title_author* that create the link between the author *Kofler Michael* and his books (the difference here is that now all three tables are listed before *FROM*):

```
DELETE titles, rel_title_author, authors
  FROM titles, rel_title_author, authors
WHERE titles.titleID=rel_title_author.titleID
  AND authors.authID=rel_title_author.authID
  AND authors.authName='Kofler Michael'
```

The linkage between the tables can also be made via *JOIN* operators.

■**Caution** The two commands just presented are syntactically correct, to be sure, but they lead to the following error: *a foreign key constraint fails*. The reason is that there are two *Foreign Key* rules for the table *rel_title_author*. One of them says that a title still in use in *rel_title_author* cannot be deleted from *titles*. The second rule says that no author can be deleted from *authors* if it is being pointed to by *rel_title_author*. Therefore, you must first delete the relevant entry from *rel_title_author*, which alas requires the use of several separate *DELETE* commands.

There are several ways of getting around this difficulty: You can temporarily turn off the checking of *Foreign Key* rules via *SET foreign_key_checks=0*, and after the *DELETE* command reactivate it by *SET foreign_key_checks=1*. (*SET* is an independent SQL command.)

You can formulate the *Foreign Key* rules with *ON DELETE CASCADE*. Then even dependent data records from other tables are automatically deleted.

The third alternative consists in completely eschewing *Foreign Key* rules or else using MyISAM tables (which do not support data integrity rules).

Deleting Data Records from Sorted Lists (DELETE with ORDER BY and LIMIT)

ORDER BY can also be used in *DELETE* commands (since MySQL 4.0). This makes it possible, in combination with *LIMIT*, to delete the first or last *n* elements of a table. In doing so, one may use an arbitrary sort criterion. The following command deletes the most recently entered or changed author from the *authors* table (the column *ts* contains the time of the last change):

```
DELETE FROM authors ORDER BY ts DESC LIMIT 1
```

Creating New Tables, Databases, and Indexes

Normally, you will use the MySQL Administrator, phpMyAdmin, or another administration tool to create or alter databases or tables. This spares you from the error-prone formulation of *CREATE* and *ALTER* commands.

Sometimes, it can be useful to execute a change directly in the `mysql` command interpreter. Furthermore, it occasionally happens that you have to alter databases or tables in a client program (for instance, in a PHP script). For such cases you need to know the syntax of the *CREATE* and *ALTER* commands. In what follows, only the most important syntax variants will be described. A reference to the most important options for *ALTER* and *CREATE* is contained in Chapter 21.

■**Note** Regardless of the tool that you choose to work with, before you begin, the question of access rights must be clarified. If MySQL is securely configured and you do not happen to be the MySQL administrator, then you are not permitted to create a new database at all. The topics of access rights and security are discussed in Chapter 11.

With existing databases or tables, you can use *SHOW CREATE DATABASE name* or *SHOW CREATE TABLE name* in SQL code to create the database or table anew.

Creating a Database (CREATE DATABASE)

Before you can set up any tables, you must first create a database. This creates an empty directory on the hard drive. To create a database named *mylibrary*, use the command

```
CREATE DATABASE mylibrary
```

Optionally, you can specify a default character set and sort order:

```
CREATE DATABASE mylibrary
DEFAULT CHARACTER SET latin1 COLLATE latin1_general_ci
```

The following *USE* command makes the new database the default database for all future SQL commands:

```
USE mylibrary
```

Creating Tables (CREATE TABLE)

New tables are created with the command *CREATE TABLE*. The syntax for this command, somewhat simplified, looks like this:

```
CREATE [TEMPORARY] TABLE [IF NOT EXISTS] tblname (
   colname1 coltype coloptions reference,
   colname2 coltype coloptions reference...
   [ , index1, index2 ...]   )
[ ENGINE = MyISAM|InnoDB|HEAP ]
[ DEFAULT CHARSET = csname [ COLLATE = colname ]]
```

The main part of the command describes the columns of the table (name, data type, attributes) as well as the indexes (index name, indexed columns in parentheses, e.g., publIDIndex (publID)). The syntax will become clearer when we look at an example. The following command generates the *titles* table:

```
CREATE TABLE titles (
   titleID   INT          NOT NULL AUTO_INCREMENT,
   title     VARCHAR(100) NOT NULL,
   subtitle  VARCHAR(100),
   edition   TINYINT,
   publID    INT,
   catID     INT,
   langID    INT,
   year      INT,
   isbn      VARCHAR(20),
   comment   VARCHAR(255),
   ts        b,
   PRIMARY KEY     (titleID),
   KEY publIdIndex (publID),
   KEY langID      (langID),
```

```
  KEY catID        (catID),
  KEY title        (title),
  CONSTRAINT titles_ibfk_1 FOREIGN KEY (publID)
    REFERENCES publishers (publID),
  CONSTRAINT titles_ibfk_2 FOREIGN KEY (langID)
    REFERENCES languages (langID),
  CONSTRAINT titles_ibfk_3 FOREIGN KEY (catID)
    REFERENCES categories (catID) )
ENGINE = InnoDB
DEFAULT CHARSET = latin1 COLLATE = latin1_german1_ci
```

The formulation of the *Foreign Key* rules (*CONSTRAINT …*) assumes that the tables *categories*, *languages*, and *publishers* already exist. If that is not the case, you can add the integrity rules later using *ALTER TABLE*.

Creating New Tables with SELECT Results

You can store the result of a query directly in a new table. (In practice, this path is sometimes followed in order to store the results of a complex query temporarily.) To do this, you simply specify the name of a new table with *CREATE TABLE* and insert an ordinary *SELECT* command at the end of the instruction. The following instruction copies all titles with *catID=1* (category *Computer books*) into the new table *computerbooks*:

```
USE mylibrary
```

```
CREATE TABLE computerbooks
SELECT * FROM titles WHERE catID=1
```

From then on, the new table is available. With *SELECT* you can convince yourself that indeed the desired data are in the table:

```
SELECT title FROM computerbooks
```

title
```
Linux, 5th ed.
LaTeX
Mathematica
Maple
Practical UNIX & Internet security
```

When the time comes that you no longer have any need of the table *computerbooks*, you can easily delete it:

```
DROP TABLE computerbooks
```

MySQL determines the column properties of the new table corresponding to the results of the *SELECT* command. It can transpire that the old and new tables will differ in some details.

Creating Indexes (CREATE INDEX)

Indexes can be created either in the *CREATE TABLE* command, or later using *CREATE INDEX* or *ALTER TABLE*. The syntax for describing the index is the same in all three cases. The following three commands show three variants for providing the *title* column of the *title* table with an index. The index received the name *idxtitle*. (Of course, only one of the three commands can be executed. If you try a second command, MySQL will inform you that an index already exists.)

```
CREATE TABLE titles (
  titleID ..., title ..., publID ..., year ...,
  PRIMARY KEY \dots,
  INDEX idxtitle (title))
CREATE INDEX idxtitle ON title (title)
ALTER TABLE titles ADD INDEX idxtitle (title)
```

SHOW INDEX FROM tablename produces a list of all defined indexes. Existing indexes can be eliminated with *DROP INDEX indexname ON tablename*.

If you wish to reduce the number of significant characters per index in the index to the first 16 characters, the syntax looks like this:

```
ALTER TABLE titles ADD INDEX idxtitle (title(16))
```

Changing the Table Design (ALTER TABLE)

With *ALTER TABLE* you can change various details of a table such as adding or deleting columns, changing properties of columns (such as data type), and defining or deleting indexes. The following example shows how you can increase the maximum number of characters in the *title* column of the *titles* table to 150:

```
ALTER TABLE titles CHANGE title title VARCHAR(150) NOT NULL
```

Perhaps somewhat confusing in the *ALTER TABLE* command is the twofold naming of *title*. The first occurrence refers to the current name of the column, while the second is the new (but here unchanged) name of the column.

Here are the most important syntax variants of *ALTER TABLE*:

Add a Column

```
ALTER TABLE tblname ADD newcolname coltype coloptions
  [FIRST | AFTER existingcolumn]
```

Alter a Column

```
ALTER TABLE tblname CHANGE oldcolname newcolname coltype coloptions
```

Delete a Column

```
ALTER TABLE tblname DROP colname
```

Add an Index

```
ALTER TABLE tblname ADD PRIMARY KEY         (indexcols ...)
ALTER TABLE tblname ADD INDEX    [indexname] (indexcols ...)
ALTER TABLE tblname ADD UNIQUE   [indexname] (indexcols ...)
ALTER TABLE tblname ADD FULLTEXT [indexname] (indexcols ...)
```

Add Foreign Key Rules

```
ALTER TABLE tblname ADD FOREIGN KEY [idxname]
  (column1) REFERENCES table2 (column2)
```

Delete an Index

```
ALTER TABLE tblname DROP PRIMARY KEY
ALTER TABLE tblname DROP INDEX indexname
ALTER TABLE tblname DROP FOREIGN KEY indexname
```

Change the Character Set of All Text Columns

```
ALTER TABLE tblname CONVERT TO CHARACTER SET charsetname
```

Change the Type of the Table (MyISAM, InnoDB)

```
ALTER TABLE tblname ENGINE typename
```

The attempt to change from MyISAM to InnoDB fails if the MyISAM table contains a full-text index or geometric data. (These functions are not supported by InnoDB.)

If you wish to change the type of large number of tables, then under Unix/Linux, the use of the script `mysql_convert_table_format` is to be recommended. If you do not specify any table names, all tables of the database will be converted:

```
root# mysql_convert_table_format [opt] --type=InnoDB dbname [tblname]
```

■**Caution** Do not change the table type of the tables of the *mysql* database! These tables, which contain management information internal to MySQL (user and access privileges), should as a matter of principle be left in MyISAM format.

Deleting Databases and Tables (DROP)

The following two commands delete a table or an entire database. It cannot be undone:

```
DROP TABLE tblname
DROP DATABASE dbname
```

Automatic Table Design Changes (Silent Column Changes)

When you create (*CREATE TABLE*) or change (*ALTER TABLE*) a table, MySQL will under certain conditions automatically make changes to the table design. The reason is either that the table will thereby become more efficient or that your design wishes cannot be carried out by MySQL.

For those migrating from other database systems, such highhandedness can be an annoyance. You should therefore always convince yourself, using *SHOW CREATE TABLE* that the table design is what you think it is. The following example shows that MySQL makes a *VARCHAR(20)* column out of a *CHAR(20)* column and gives the two columns the attribute *DEFAULT NULL*.

```
CREATE TABLE test1 (col1 VARCHAR(20), col2 CHAR(20))
SHOW CREATE TABLE test1
  CREATE TABLE `test1` (
    `col1` varchar(20) default NULL,
    `col2` varchar(20) default NULL
  ) ENGINE=MyISAM DEFAULT CHARSET=latin1
```

The following list shows the most important design changes that MySQL carries out:

- *VARCHAR(n)* columns with *n* < 4 are transformed into *CHAR(n)* columns.

- *CHAR(n)* columns with *n* > 3 are transformed into *VARCHAR(n)* columns if there exist in the table additional *VARCHAR, TEXT,* or *BLOB* columns. However, if the table consists exclusively of columns of constant length, then *CHAR(n)* remains unchanged.

- In the case of *TIMESTAMP* columns, the attributes *NULL* and *NOT NULL* are not eliminated. The reason is that MySQL is incapable of storing the value *NULL* in *TIMESTAMP*. The assignment *NULL* has the effect that the current time or the value 0000-00-00 00:00:00 is stored.

- With *PRIMARY KEY* columns, the attribute *NOT NULL* is added if you do not do so yourself.

- If you do not specify a default value for a column, then MySQL defines a suitable value (*NULL*, 0, or an empty character string).

Further information on such peculiarities, which the MySQL documentation calls *silent column changes,* can be found at `http://dev.mysql.com/doc/mysql/en/silent-column-changes.html`. Retrieving Metadata About Databases and Tables Administration tools must be able to determine the databases that MySQL is managing, the tables contained within these databases, the properties of the columns of these tables, and so on. Even in everyday dealings with MySQL, it is often useful to retrieve a quick overview of the indexes in a table. Such information, not about the content of your tables but about the tables' properties, is called *metadata.*

The SHOW Command

The traditional way of retrieving metadata is to execute *SHOW* commands. For example, *SHOW DATABASES* returns a list of all databases to which the current user has access. *SHOW TABLES* returns a list of the tables in the current database, *SHOW COLUMNS* information about the columns of a table, and so on.

Table 9-3 collects these commands that return metadata about databases and tables. Most of them allow you to limit the results with the option *LIKE pattern.* For example, *SHOW DATABASES LIKE 'test%'* returns all databases whose name begins with *test.* Here is an example of a *SHOW* command:

```
SHOW COLUMNS FROM mylibrary.titles
```

Field	Type	Null	Key	Default	Extra
titleID	int(11)		PRI	NULL	auto_increment
title	varchar(100)		MUL		
subtitle	varchar(100)	YES		NULL	
edition	tinyint(4)	YES		NULL	
publID	int(11)	YES	MUL	NULL	
catID	int(11)	YES	MUL	NULL	
langID	int(11)	YES	MUL	NULL	
year	int(11)	YES		NULL	
isbn	varchar(20)	YES		NULL	
comment	varchar(255)	YES		NULL	
ts	timestamp	YES		CURRENT_TIMESTAMP	

The precise syntax of these commands can be found in Chapter 21. Some additional *SHOW* commands for retrieving additional data are also described there. For example, *SHOW COLLATIONS* returns all sort orders supported by MySQL, while *SHOW WARNINGS* returns all warnings returned by the most recently executed command.

Table 9-3. *SHOW Commands*

Command	Function
SHOW DATABASES	Returns a list of all databases
SHOW TABLES FROM dbname	Returns a list of all tables in *dbname*
SHOW [FULL] COLUMNS FROM tablename	Returns detailed information about all columns of the table *tablename*
SHOW INDEX FROM tablename	Returns information about all indexes of the table

INFORMATION_SCHEMA Tables

The *SHOW* commands work properly. However, they do not conform to the SQL:2003 standard and are furthermore inconsistent: For each type of query, the powerful *SELECT* command can be used, only not for determining data that underlie the database system itself.

MySQL 5.0 comes to the rescue with *INFORMATION_SCHEMA* tables. Using *SELECT* commands, you can retrieve specific metadata from these tables about databases, tables, columns, and so on. The great advantage vis-à-vis *SHOW* commands is that the whole panoply of syntax variants of *SELECT* is available. Furthermore, *INFORMATION_SCHEMA* tables return considerably more information than do *SHOW* commands. The following command offers an example:

```
SELECT column_name, ordinal_position, column_default,
  data_type, collation_name
FROM information_schema.columns
WHERE table_schema="mylibrary" AND table_name="titles"
```

column_name	ordinal_position	is_nullable	data_type	collation_name
titleID	1		int	NULL
title	2		varchar	latin1_german1_ci
subtitle	3	YES	varchar	latin1_german1_ci
edition	4	YES	tinyint	NULL
publID	5	YES	int	NULL
catID	6	YES	int	NULL
langID	7	YES	int	NULL
year	8	YES	int	NULL
isbn	9	YES	varchar	latin1_german1_ci
comment	10	YES	varchar	latin1_german1_ci
ts	11	YES	timestamp	NULL

Table 9-4 collects the content of these tables. Here *information_schema* is a virtual database, one that does not actually exist as a file. Therefore, neither *SHOW DATABASES* nor *SELECT * FROM information_schema.schemata* works with this database, nor does *USE information_schema* work either.

The *information_schema* tables cannot be changed (*INSERT, UPDATE*, etc. are not allowed). In accessing these tables and columns, there is no case distinction. A list of all available tables can be determined with *SHOW TABLES FROM information_schema*, and the available columns with *SHOW COLUMNS FROM information_schema.tablename*. So you can see that *SHOW* still has its uses.

The names of the tables and columns are in conformity with the SQL:2003 standard. However, there are some tables and columns provided for in the standard that MySQL does not yet implement. In return, however, there are some additional columns with MySQL-specific information, for example, for the table type (Engine = MyISAM, InnoDB, etc.).

Table 9-4. *information_schema Tables*

Table	Content
information_schema.schemata	Contains data on all available databases.
.tables	Describes the properties of all tables.
.columns	Describes the properties of all table columns.
.statistics	Contains statistical information on the table indexes.
.views	Describes the properties of all views.
.table_constraints	Lists the *PRIMARY, UNIQUE,* and *FOREIGN KEY* indexes of all tables.
.key_column_usage	Also lists all indexes, but contains even more detail than *table_constraints.*
.referential_constraints	Describes all *FOREIGN KEY* rules (not yet implemented).
	User Management and Privileges
.user_privileges	Contains a list of every MySQL user. The data come from the table *mysql.user.*
.schema_privileges	Describes database-specific privileges (table *mysql.db*).
.table_privileges	Describes table-specific privileges (table *mysql.tables_priv*).
.column_privileges	Describes access privileges to individual columns (table *mysql.columns_priv*).
	Character Sets and Sort Orders
.character_sets	Contains all available character sets.
.collations	Contains all available sort orders.
.collation_character_set_applicability	Specifies which sort orders are stuitable for which character sets.
	Stored Procedures and Trigger
.routines	Contains information about all stored procedures (corresponds to the content of the table *mysql.proc*).
.parameters	Describes the parameters of stored procedures (not yet implemented).
.triggers	Contains data on all triggers (not yet implemented).

For the *information_schema* tables, the usual MySQL access privileges do not apply. Every user who wishes to register with the MySQL server can execute *SELECT* commands for all *information_schema* tables.

## CHAPTER 10

SQL Recipes

This chapter contains a collection of small SQL examples that go somewhat beyond the elementary level of the other examples in this chapter. The goal is to give you an idea of some of the possibilities that the world of SQL opens to you and to provide recipes for solving frequently occurring problems.

Most of these examples are based on the example databases introduced in Chapter 8, and so you can easily try these commands out yourself. However, we will also introduce some techniques based on imaginary databases and tables.

Character Strings

MySQL recognizes a large number of functions that allow for the processing of character strings in queries. The following examples introduce several of these functions. A reference for MySQL functions for processing character strings can be found in Chapter 21.

Basic Functions

Concatenating Character Strings

CONCAT(s1, s2, …) concatenates the given character strings into a single string. This function is useful for joining together several columns (for example, when you have stored first and last names in different columns and now wish to put them together):

```
SELECT CONCAT(firstname, ' ', lastname) FROM addresses
```

Extracting Parts of Character Strings

SUBSTRING(s, pos, n) returns *n* characters of the character string *s* starting at position *pos*. (The first character is addressed at position *pos=1*, not at *pos=0*.) The following command returns the first ten characters of all book titles from the *mylibrary* database:

```
USE mylibrary
SELECT SUBSTR(title, 1, 10) FROM titles
```

Those familiar with the syntax of the Basic programming language can use *LEFT, RIGHT,* and *MID* instead of *SUBSTR* to read strings conveniently from the beginning or from the end. We will offer an example of this later.

Determining the Length of a Character String

CHAR_LENGTH(s) returns the number of characters in a character string, and *LENGTH* the number of bytes required to store the string. In the case of *latin1* strings, both values are always the same.

But if you use Unicode or another multibyte character set, then more than one byte per character is frequently necessary.

Shortening Strings to a Particular Length

The function *IF(a, b, c)* evaluates expression *a*. If the result is (*TRUE*), the function returns *b*; otherwise, *c*. The goal of the following example is to shorten book titles to the form "beginning of title, … end of title," so that the entire length of the resulting character string is at most thirty characters. Titles with thirty characters or fewer are unchanged:

```
SELECT IF(CHAR_LENGTH(title)>30,
        CONCAT(LEFT(title, 20), ' ... ', RIGHT(title, 5)),
        title)
FROM titles AS shorttitle
```

*shorttitle*_____
```
Linux für Internet u ... ranet
Mathematica
Practical UNIX & Int ... urity
Visual Basic Datenba ... erung
...
```

Storing Altered Character Strings

Of course, you can also use character string functions to alter MySQL tables. The following command replaces the character "with the character 'in the column *mycolumn* of the table *mytable*. The function *REPLACE* is used for this purpose:

```
UPDATE mytable SET mycolumn = REPLACE(mycolumn, '"', '\'')
```

The next command searches for the blank character. If this character is found, then presumably the string is composed of several parts (words). The *UPDATE* command shortens this string to the first word. New here is the function *LOCATE*, which returns the position of the search pattern within a character string:

```
UPDATE mytable
SET mycolumn = LEFT(mycolumn, LOCATE(" ", mycolumn )-1)
WHERE LOCATE(" ", mycolumn) > 1
```

Changing the Character Set

With the function *CONVERT(x USING charset)* you can change the character set of a string. The following command returns its results in Unicode (the example databases for this book use *latin1* character strings). Note that in general, changing the character set has no effect, since the change occurs only in the MySQL server. The server passes its results to the client, and in this passage, all character strings are adapted to the client's character set:

```
SELECT CONVERT(title USING utf8) FROM titles
```

That *CONVERT* actually works can be seen by transforming the character string into hexadecimal representation:

```
SELECT HEX(CONVERT('äöü' USING latin1))
  E4F6FC
SELECT HEX(CONVERT('äöü' USING utf8))
  C3A4C3B6C3BC
```

You can also use the *CONVERT* function to copy data from one column of a table into another and thereby change the character set. The following commands add a new column, *title_utf8*, to the *titles* table and copy into it the book titles in Unicode format:

```
ALTER TABLE titles ADD title_utf8 VARCHAR(100) CHARSET utf8
UPDATE titles SET title_utf8 = CONVERT(title USING utf8)
```

As a check, you can determine how many bytes are necessary for storing the title. Titles with special characters require more bytes in *utf8* format than in the original *latin1* column:

```
SELECT title,
       LENGTH(title)       AS latin1length,
       LENGTH(titles_utf8) AS utf8length FROM titlescopy
HAVING latin1length!=utf8length ORDER BY title
```

title	latin1length	utf8length
Alltid den där Annette	22	23
Comédia Infantil	16	17
Dansläraren Återkomst	21	23
Das Haus meiner Väter	21	22
Gengångare	10	11
Kärleken	8	9
Linux für Internet und Intranet	31	32
Linux im Büro	13	14
Nicht alle Eisbären halten Winterschlaf	39	40
PHP - Grundlagen und Lösungen	29	30

Specifying the Character Set of a Character String (Cast Operator)

When character strings in an SQL command appear in an encoding that differs from the default character set of the client (see the following section), then such strings must be prefixed with a cast operator that specifies the character string. Such operators consist of the name of the character set preceded by the underscore character, for example, _utf8 or _latin1:

```
INSERT INTO titles (title) VALUES( _utf8 'title in UTF-8 encoding)
```

Setting the Client Character Set

What good is it if the MySQL server can operate with all sorts of character sets, but the client (that is, for example, your PHP program or the command line interpreter) assumes a single particular character set? The MySQL client libraries thus automatically translate all character strings from the client's character set into the character set of the server (and vice versa). In the given character set, characters that cannot be represented are replaced with a question mark.

Which aspects of the relation between client and server are used with which character sets is governed by several MySQL system variables, which are listed in Table 10-1.

Table 10-1. *MySQL Character Set Variables*

Variable	Interpretation
@@*character_set_client*	Client's character set
@@*character_set_server*	Server's default character set
@@*character_set_connection*	Character set for the connection between client and server
@@*character_set_results*	Character set for *SELECT* results
@@*character_set_database*	Default character set for the database

The client does not always guess correctly the character set in which you wish to process your data. The simplest thing to do is to check the state of the variables with the following command:

```
SHOW VARIABLES LIKE 'character_set\_%'
```

Variable_name	Value
character_set_client	latin1
character_set_connection	latin1
character_set_database	latin1
character_set_results	latin1
character_set_server	latin1
character_set_system	utf8

With some client programs you can specify the desired character set right at the start or when the connection is established, for example, in the program mysql or mysqldump using the option --default-character-set=utf8. Otherwise, you must set the variables shown above in your client program yourself. For example, if you wish to process UTF-8 data, the command looks like this:

```
SET @@session.character_set_client     = 'utf8'
SET @@session.character_set_results    = 'utf8'
SET @@character_set_connection         = 'utf8'
```

Instead of the three *SET* commands, you can simply execute the command *SET NAMES 'utf8'*; it resets all three variables. As an alternative, the command *SET CHARACTER SET 'utf8'* is available. It assigns *utf8* to *character_set_client* and *character_set_results* and provides *character_set_connection* the value of *character_set_database*, which is sufficient in most cases.

After these preparations you should be able to execute SQL commands with UTF-8 character strings and retrieve *SELECT* results in UTF-8 format.

Pattern Matching

Pattern Matching with LIKE

The operator *LIKE* is suited for simple pattern matching. It supports two wild cards: _ for a single arbitrary character, and % for an arbitrary number (including 0) of characters. As with ordinary string comparison, *LIKE* does not distinguish between uppercase and lowercase. Here is an example:

```
SELECT 'MySQL' LIKE '%sql'
     1
```

The following *SELECT* command returns all book titles that contain the character string "SQL":

```
USE mylibrary
SELECT title FROM titles WHERE title LIKE '%SQL%'
```

If the character _ or % is itself to be used in the pattern to be matched, then it must be preceded by a backslash, as in *'50%' LIKE '%\%'*, which returns 1. If you wish to use a character other than the backslash as the escape character, then you may specify such a character with *ESCAPE: '50%' LIKE '%&%' ESCAPE '&'*, which also returns 1.

■**Note** Please note that doing pattern matching in large tables is very slow. This holds for *LIKE*, and even more so for *REGEXP*. In many cases it makes more sense to do a full-text search instead of pattern matching.

Pattern Matching with REGEXP

The command *REGEXP* offers many more possibilities for formulating a pattern, as does the equivalent command *RLIKE*. As with *LIKE*, case distinction is not made. Here we give a few syntactic examples. A table with the most important elements of *REGEXP* pattern matching appears in Chapter 21.

In the simplest case, *expr REGEXP pattern* tests whether the character string *pattern* is contained in *expr*:

```
SELECT 'abcabc' REGEXP 'abc',    'abcabc' REGEXP 'cb'
      1, 0
```

The search pattern does not have to describe the entire character string, but only a part. If you wish to encompass the entire character string, you must use ^ and $ in the search:

```
SELECT 'abc' REGEXP '^abc$', 'abcabc' REGEXP '^abc$'
      1, 0
```

Square brackets indicate a selection from among several characters, where a hyphen is used to indicate a range of characters; for example, a-c indicates the inclusive range from a to c. The operator + indicates that at least one of the characters must appear at least once in the search expression:

```
SELECT 'cde' REGEXP '[a-c]+', 'efg' REGEXP '[a-c]+'
      1, 0
```

Parentheses indicate an entire character string, and curly braces indicate how many times the character string must appear in succession:

```
SELECT 'xabcabcz' REGEXP '(abc){2}', 'xabcyabcz' REGEXP '(abc){2}'
      1, 0
```

Note that *REGEXP* is successful when the search pattern is found at any location within the character string.

■**Tip** A large number of additional examples can be found in the appendix to the MySQL documentation: http://dev.mysql.com/doc/mysql/en/regexp.html.

Binary Character String Comparison

Character strings are generally compared without regard to case sensitivity. That is, 'a'='A' returns 1 as a result. If you wish to execute a binary search, you must write *BINARY* in front of one of the operands. *BINARY* is a "cast" operator. That is, it changes the data type of an operand (thus changes a number or character string into a binary object). *BINARY* can be used for ordinary string comparison and also for pattern matching with *LIKE* and *REGEXP*:

```
SELECT 'a'='A', BINARY 'a' = 'A', 'a' = BINARY 'A'
      1, 0, 0
SELECT 'abcabc' REGEXP 'ABC', 'abcabc' REGEXP BINARY 'ABC'
      1, 0
```

Date and Time

Most of the examples of this section assume that *mytable* has a column *ts* with time values (data type *DATETIME* or *TIMESTAMP*).

Syntax for Date and Time

Basically, dates and times in SQL commands must be given as character strings, using a syntax that the MySQL server understands. The following three queries are equivalent, and work for both *DATETIME* and *TIMESTAMP* columns:

```
SELECT COUNT(*) FROM mytable
WHERE ts BETWEEN '2004-05-16 08:34:07' AND '2005-02-11 00:15:44'
SELECT COUNT(*) FROM mytable
WHERE ts BETWEEN '2004/05/16 08:34:07' AND '2005/02/11 00:15:44'
SELECT COUNT(*) FROM mytable
WHERE ts BETWEEN '20040516083407' AND '20050211001544'
```

Note that *BETWEEN a AND b* means that the start and end times are included (that is, *d>=a AND d<=b*).

Determining the Number of Records by Day, Month, and Year

It happens quite often that you want to know how many records there are for a particular day or month. Of course, you can execute a number of queries with *BETWEEN start AND end*. But it is much simpler to format the data field with various functions and determine the number using *GROUP BY* and *COUNT*.

Our first example returns the number of votes by month for the year 2005 for the database *bigvote*. Month and year are determined by the MySQL functions *MONTH* and *YEAR* (the database *bigvote* has the same structure as *test_vote* from Chapter 3, but it contains about 5,000 entries):

```
USE bigvote
SELECT COUNT(*), MONTH(ts) AS m
FROM votelanguage
WHERE YEAR(ts)=2002
GROUP BY m
```

COUNT(*)	m
152	1
227	2
...	...
58	12

If you want all results (not just for one year), then the expression for the grouping must contain both the year and the month. For this, you should use the *DATE_FORMAT* function (whose syntax is described in Chapter 21):

```
SELECT COUNT(*), DATE_FORMAT(ts, '%Y-%m') AS m_y
FROM votelanguage
GROUP by m_y
```

count(*)	m_y
214	2002-05
111	2002-06
226	2002-07
...	....
73	2006-01

Formatting Dates and Times

DATE_FORMAT(date, format) and *TIME_FORMAT* assist in the representation of dates and times in formats other than the MySQL default format. Three examples illustrate the syntax:

```
SELECT DATE_FORMAT('2005-12-31', '%M %d %Y')
   December 31 2005
SELECT DATE_FORMAT('2005-12-31', '%D of %M')
   31st of December
SELECT TIME_FORMAT('02:17', '%H')
   02
```

Names of weekdays, months, and so on are always given in English, regardless of the language in which MySQL is executed (*language* option). A list of all formatting codes of both functions is provided in Chapter 21.

Calculating with Date and Time

For calculations with date and time, you can generally not use the operators +, -, etc., but rather must use special SQL functions. The following list names the most important such functions. A complete reference is given in Chapter 21:

- ***ADDDATE, DATE_ADD:*** These two equivalent functions add a time interval to a date (*DATETIME* or *TIMESTAMP*) (e.g., 3 days or 7 minutes).

- *ADDDATE('2005-12-31 6:00', INTERVAL 3 MINUTE)* returns *2005-31-12 6:03*.

- If you wish to add an arbitrary *TIME* interval, then specify the interval as *HOUR_SECOND* or use the function *ADDTIME*.

- *ADDDATE('2005-12-31 6:00', INTERVAL '3:15:22' HOUR_SECOND)* returns *2005-31-12 9:15:22*.

- ***SUBDATE, DATE_SUB:*** As above, but now the time interval is subtracted.

- ***ADDTIME* (since MySQL 4.1):** Adds a date to a date or a time to a time. In contrast to *ADDDATE*, the first parameter may now be of data type *TIME*. In the second parameter, the involved interval specification is absent.

- *ADDTIME('2005-12-31 6:00', '3:15:22')* returns *2005-31-12 9:15:22*.

- ***SUBTIME* (since MySQL 4.1):** As above, but now a time is subtracted.

- ***DATEDIFF* (since MySQL 4.1):** Returns the number of days between two dates. The time portions of the dates are ignored in the calculation.

- *DATEDIFF('2005-12-31', '2005-12-28')* returns *3*.

- *DATEDIFF('2005-12-31 00:00:00', '2005-12-28 23:59:59')* also returns *3*.

- ***TIMEDIFF* (since MySQL 4.1):** Returns the time difference between two times (*TIME*) or between two dates (*DATETIME* or *TIMESTAMP*). However, the function cannot be used to subtract a time from a date.

- *TIMEDIFF('2005-12-31 12:30', '2005-12-30 19:45')* returns *16:45:00*.

- **Conversion functions:** MySQL offers countless functions for extracting parts of time data or for calculating the time between various intervals: *HOUR, MINUTE, SECOND, TIME_TO_SEC, SEC_TO_TIME, DAYOFYEAR, LAST_DAY, MONTH, WEEK, STR_TO_DATE, UNIX_TIMESTAMP, FROM_UNIXNAME, UTC_DATE, UTC_TIME*, etc.

■**Tip** Since MySQL 4.1, many MySQL time functions are able to work with microseconds. However, since there is no MySQL data type that can store microseconds, these functions are at present rather worthless. Further information on this topic can be found at http://dev.mysql.com/tech-resources/articles/4.1/time.html.

Some Examples

The table *workingtimes* will serve as the basis for the following examples, in which you can store, for example, your hours spent at work:

```
USE test

CREATE TABLE workingtimes (
  id INT AUTO_INCREMENT,
  begintime DATETIME,
  endtime DATETIME,
  PRIMARY KEY (id))

INSERT INTO workingtimes (begintime, endtime) VALUES
  ('2005-03-27 7:15', '2005-03-27 18:00'),
  ('2005-03-28 8:00', '2005-03-28 18:00'),
  ('2005-03-29 7:30', '2005-03-29 16:50'),
  ('2005-03-30 7:00', '2005-03-30 17:15')
```

The first attempt to calculate the working time for each workday fails miserably. The reason is that MySQL interprets the character strings for the subtraction *endtime - begintime* with time values simply as integers, for example, *'2005-03-27 7:15:00'* as *20050327071500*. MySQL can subtract these numbers, of course, but the result is pure nonsense, since time is not recorded in the decimal system, but rather with seconds and minutes in the range 0 to 59 instead of 0 to 99:

```
SELECT DATE_FORMAT(begintime, '%Y-%m-%d') AS dt,
       endtime - begintime AS s
FROM workingtimes
```

dt	s
2005-03-27	108500
2005-03-28	100000
2005-03-29	92000
2005-03-30	101500

The simplest path to the desired result is to use the function *TIMEDIFF*:

```
SELECT DATE_FORMAT(begintime, '%Y-%m-%d') AS dt,
       TIMEDIFF(endtime, begintime) AS s
FROM workingtimes
```

dt	t
2005-03-27	10:45:00
2005-03-28	10:00:00
2005-03-29	09:20:00
2005-03-30	10:15:00

An attempt to simply add these times with *SUM* again fails. MySQL attempts to interpret results like 10:45:00 as ordinary numbers:

```
SELECT SUM(TIMEDIFF(endtime, begintime)) AS sumtime
FROM workingtimes
```

sumtimes
39

To obtain the correct result, you must transform the time differences into seconds using *TIME_TO_SEC*, add them, and then convert them back into usual time representations with *SEC_TO_TIME*, which returns even time intervals of more than 24 hours in the format *hhhhh:mm:ss*. That is, days are not counted:

```
SELECT SEC_TO_TIME(SUM(TIME_TO_SEC(TIMEDIFF(endtime, begintime))))
        AS sumtime
FROM workingtimes
```

sumtime
___
40:20:00

The following query returns the number of workdays with ten or more hours:

```
SELECT COUNT(*) FROM workingtimes
WHERE endtime >= ADDTIME(begintime, '10:00')
```

COUNT(*)
___
3

Unix Timestamps

In Unix, time is reckoned from January 1, 1970. Since then, every second has been counted. The resulting integer is called a Unix timestamp. Timestamps are of interest to MySQL users for two reasons: First, they are useful in carrying out calculations (since simple addition and subtraction yield correct results); second, programming languages like PHP and Perl offer many functions that take timestamps as parameters or return them as results.

■**Caution** Unix timestamps should not be confused with the MySQL *TIMESTAMP*. MySQL uses a format similar to that of Unix for internal storage. However, in the execution of SQL commands, MySQL *TIMESTAMP*s are transformed into character strings of the form '2005-12-31 23:59:59'.

Unix timestamps are stored, for historical reasons, as signed 32-bit integers. Therefore, an overflow will occur in the year 2038. Thus for the time period between 1970 and 2038, timestamps are very practical objects: compact and simple to work with. But what then? First of all, there is a bit in reserve if the timestamp is viewed as an unsigned integer. Under this assumption, the overflow will not occur until the beginning of the twenty-second century. Moreover, it is anticipated that Unix/Linux will move to a 64-bit timestamp in the coming years. It is thus highly unlikely that the "year-2000" problem will recur in the year 2038.

Transformation Functions

With the MySQL functions *FROM_UNIXTIME* and *UNIX_TIMESTAMP* you can carry out transformations between MySQL dates (*DATE, DATETIME,* and *TIMESTAMP*) and Unix timestamps:

```
SELECT NOW(), UNIX_TIMESTAMP(NOW())
  2004-12-20 11:19:53          1103537993
SELECT FROM_UNIXTIME(1103600000)
  2004-12-21 04:33:20
```

Application Example

The following command uses the table *workingtimes* from the previous section. To calculate the working time, the time values will be transformed in Unix timestamps using *UNIX_TIMESTAMP*:

```
SELECT DATE_FORMAT(begintime, '%Y-%m-%d') AS dt,
UNIX_TIMESTAMP(endtime) - UNIX_TIMESTAMP(begintime) AS s
FROM workingtimes
```

dt	s
2005-03-27	38700
2005-03-28	36000
2005-03-29	33600
2005-03-30	36900

To make these values, which are in seconds, more understandable, you can use the function *SEC_TO_TIME*:

```
SELECT DATE_FORMAT(begintime, '%Y-%m-%d') AS dt,
SEC_TO_TIME(UNIX_TIMESTAMP(endtime) - UNIX_TIMESTAMP(begintime)) AS t
FROM workingtimes
```

dt	t
2005-03-27	10:45:00
2005-03-28	10:00:00
2005-03-29	09:20:00
2005-03-30	10:15:00

You can even return the total working time, using *SUM*. For example, here is the result for all the days in March 2005:

```
SELECT SEC_TO_TIME(SUM(UNIX_TIMESTAMP(endtime) -
                       UNIX_TIMESTAMP(begintime))) AS sumtime
FROM workingtimes
WHERE begintime>='2005-03-01 00:00:00' AND
      begintime<='2005-03-31 23:59:59'
```

sumtime
40:20:00

Avoiding Changes to TIMESTAMP

If you have a table with a *TIMESTAMP* column and execute an *UPDATE* on that table, then the content of the *TIMESTAMP* columns changes as well. (After all, the purpose of a *TIMESTAMP* column is to log the time of creation and the most recent change.)

It can happen, however, that in correcting a record you wish to avoid changing the *TIMESTAMP* value. For this, you can deal with the *TIMESTAMP* column explicitly with *SET*, returning the column to its previous value. The following example assumes that the *TIMESTAMP* column has the name *ts*:

```
UPDATE table SET data='new text', ts=ts WHERE id=123
```

When a large number of changes are in play, it is safer first to create a new column *oldts* of the previous *TIMESTAMP* values and copy all the *TIMESTAMP* values into it:

```
ALTER TABLE table ADD oldts DATETIME
UPDATE table SET ts=ts, oldts=ts
```

Now you can carry out all the changes you want without worrying about the *ts* column. When you are done, you simply restore the *ts* column to its original condition and delete the *oldts* column:

```
UPDATE table SET ts=oldts
ALTER TABLE table DROP oldts
```

Time Zones

As a rule, MySQL users do not need to be concerned about time zones, since the interchange of dates and times functions automatically within the local time zone with most SQL functions. Internally, MySQL stores *TIMESTAMP*s in *Coordinated Universal Time* (UTC) format. In SQL commands, however, *TIMESTAMP*s are automatically translated into local time.

This section goes in some detail into the subject of time-zone management by MySQL. Here you will find extensive information, such as how you can set the time zone yourself and which functions are thereby affected.

Server and Client Time Zones

Through MySQL 4.0, only the time zone of the server was configurable. Since version 4.1, MySQL distinguishes two time zones.

Server Time Zone (System Variable *global.time_zone*)

To the extent that the MySQL server is not otherwise explicitly configured, it acquires at startup the time zone of the computer on which it is running. You can determine the currently valid time zone with *SELECT @@global.time_zone*. The result is usually *SYSTEM*, which in and of itself is not particularly informative:

```
SELECT @@global.time_zone
  SYSTEM
```

Fortunately, you can determine the computer's time zone with *SHOW_VARIABLES* (system variable *system_time_zone*; this variable cannot be read with *SELECT*). In the following example, the MySQL server is running in the Central European (CET) time zone, which encompasses many of the capitals of "Old Europe," such as Paris, Vienna, and Berlin:

```
SHOW VARIABLES LIKE 'system_time_zone'
  CET
```

It is easier to calculate the difference in time between *NOW* and *UTC_TIMESTAMP*:

```
SELECT TIMEDIFF(NOW(), UTC_TIMESTAMP)
  01:00:00
```

MySQL users who have *SUPER* privileges can change the time zone of the MySQL server on the fly with *SET GLOBAL time_zone = ...* However, this works only if no binary logging and no replication are engaged. If that is the case, you must change `default-time-zone` in `my.cnf/my.ini` (see Chapter 22) and then restart the MySQL server.

Client Time Zone (System Variable *session.time_zone*)

By default, the client takes its time zone from that of the server. This makes sense, in general, because server and client usually are running in the same time zone.

However, it is possible to set the client time zone with *SET time_zone = ...* (now without the keyword *GLOBAL!*). You can determine the current state with *SELECT @@session.time_zone*.

Setting the Client Time Zone

MySQL is often used as a web database. In this case, the MySQL server and the web server run either on the same computer or on two different computers in the same network, in any case, in the same time zone. Even if the users are distributed throughout the world, the connection to the MySQL server launches a PHP or Java program that runs on the web server and thereby in the same time zone as the MySQL server. Time-zone management has no effect.

However, if you are programming a web application, you could certainly make use of MySQL's ability to manage time zones: You can give your web users the option of setting their own time zone. With this information it is a simple matter to set *time_zone* accordingly after the connection is made to the MySQL server. A single SQL command suffices for the web user to see date and time values in the local time zone.

The following example assumes that the server is running in the CET time zone (Central Europe). The SQL function *NOW()* returns the CET time. After adjusting *time_zone* to GMT-8, *NOW()* returns the local time of Los Angeles, Seattle, Vancouver, and their longitudinal brethren:

```
SELECT NOW()
  2005-12-07 16:29:54
SET time_zone='-8:00'
SELECT NOW()
  2005-12-07 07:29:57
```

With *SET* only *session.time_zone* is changed, not *global.time_zone*. The setting is valid only until the connection to the MySQL server is ended.

Specifying the Time Zone

Windows: If the MySQL server is running under Windows, time zones must be given with respect to *Coordinated Universal Time* (UTC), for example, '+1:00' for Berlin, '0:00' for London, '-5:00' for New York.

Linux: If the MySQL server is running under Unix/Linux and has been properly configured (see Chapter 14), then one may use the operating system's time-zone names, such as *Europe/Berlin* or *CET* for Berlin, *Europe/London* or *Greenwich* or *GMT* for London, and *America/New_York* for New York.

Automatic Calculation of the Time Zone

Table 10-2 shows which data and functions are affected by time-zone settings.

Table 10-2. *Adjusting the Time Zone*

Function	Automatic Time-Zone Adjustment	No Time-Zone Adjustment
Storing dates/times	*TIMESTAMP* columns	*DATE, TIME*, and *DATETIME* columns
Determine current time	*NOW(), CURDATE(), CURTIME(), CURRENT_xxx(), LOCALTIMExxx(), SYSDATE()*	*UNIX_TIMESTAMP(), UTC_DATE(), UTC_TIME(), UTC_TIMESTAMP()*
Conversion between Unix timestamps and *DATETIME*	*UNIX_TIMESTAMP(datetime), FROM_UNIXTIME(timestamp)*	
Calculation and formatting of dates and times		All other date and time functions, such as *ADDDATE, SUBDATE, HOUR, MINUTE, DATE_FORMAT, TIME_FORMAT, CONVERT_TZ*

Manual Time-Zone Conversion

Independently of which time zones are valid for client and server, you can convert between time zones using *CONVERT_TZ*. This function expects in its first parameter a time value (date plus time; a time alone will not suffice), in the second parameter the time zone of the first parameter, and in the third parameter the time zone into which the time is to be converted.

In the following example, a time in Berlin is converted to the time in New York. When it is 12 noon in Berlin, it is 6 a.m. in New York:

```
SELECT CONVERT_TZ('2005-12-31 12:00', 'Europe/Berlin', 'America/New_York')
  2005-12-31 06:00:00
```

ENUMs and SETs

The data types *ENUM* and *SET* introduced in Chapter 8 offer a particularly efficient way of storing a single character string from among *n* given character strings (1 out of *n*, with *n* < 65,536) or any combination of *n* given strings (*m* out of *n*, with *n* < 256). This section offers some tips for operating with *ENUM* and *SET* columns.

ENUM

With *ENUM* you can manage a list of up to 65,535 character strings. Each string is given a number in sequence, and these are stored by MySQL in the *ENUM* column instead of the string itself. This saves on space and speeds up processing. Note that in each field of an *ENUM* column you can save only a single string, that is, a single number associated with that string. Saving multiple strings in such a field is impossible. (If you want to store a combination of several predefined strings, you can use a *SET* column.)

In queries involving comparison of character strings there is no case distinction. In addition to the predefined character strings, an empty character string can also be stored in a field (as well as *NULL*, unless this has been excluded via *NOT NULL*).

Such a field is then handled like any other character string field. The following commands show how a table with an *ENUM* enumeration is generated and used. In the field *color* of the table *testenum*, one of five predefined colors can be stored:

```
CREATE TABLE testenum
  (color ENUM ('red', 'green', 'blue', 'black', 'white'))
INSERT testenum VALUES ('red')
SELECT * FROM testenum WHERE color='red'
```

SET

SET uses a similar idea, though here arbitrary combinations are possible. Internally, the character strings are ordered by powers of 2 (1, 2, 4, 8, etc.), so that a bitwise combination is possible. The storage requirement is correspondingly larger (one bit per character string). At most 64 character strings can be combined (in which case the storage requirement is 8 bytes).

For a combination of several character strings to be stored in one field, these must be given separated by commas (and with no blank characters between strings). The order of the strings is irrelevant and is not considered. In query results, combinations are always specified in the order in which the set was defined:

```
CREATE TABLE testset
  (fontattr SET ('bold', 'italic', 'underlined'))
INSERT testset VALUES ('bold,italic')
```

In queries using the operator "=" an exact comparison is made of the entire combination. The result is that only those records are returned for which the combination corresponds exactly. Thus if in *testset* only the above-inserted record is stored with '*bold, italic*', then the following query returns no result:

```
SELECT * FROM testset WHERE fontattr='italic'
```

In order to locate records in which an attribute has been set (regardless of its combination with other attributes), the MySQL function *FIND_IN_SET* can be used. This function returns the position of the sought character string within the set (in our example, 1 if *'bold'* is found, 2 for *'italic'*, etc.):

```
SELECT * FROM testset WHERE FIND_IN_SET('italic', fontattr)>0
```

ENUM and *SET* values are represented internally as integers, not as character strings. If you wish to determine the internally stored value via a query, simply use *SELECT x+0 FROM table*, where *x* is the column name of the *ENUM* or *SET* column. It is also permitted to store numeric values with *INSERT* and *UPDATE* commands.

If you would like to determine the list of all admissible character strings for an *ENUM* or *SET* field (in a client program, for example), you must summon *DESCRIBE tablename columnname* to your aid. This SQL command returns a table in which the field *columnname* is described. The column *Type* of this table contains the *ENUM* or *SET* definition.

■**Note** The contents of *ENUM* and *SET* fields are not alphabetically sorted, but are maintained in the order in which the character strings for selection were defined. The reason for this is that MySQL works internally with numeric values associated with the character strings. If you would like an alphabetic sorting, you must transform the string explicitly into a character string, for example, via *SELECT CONCAT(x) AS xstr ...ORDER BY xstr*.

Variables and Conditionals (IF, CASE)

This section shows how you can read and edit variables with SQL commands and how you can construct simple *IF* and *CASE* distinctions in queries.

■**Tip** A new feature of MySQL 5.0 is that now one can create functioning SQL programs in so-called stored procedures (SPs). The SQL dialect of MySQL has been extended to allow for programming of the kind done in ordinary programming languages. However, these language constructs can be used only in SPs, not in usual SQL commands. They will be explored in detail in Chapter 13.

Variables

MySQL offers the possibility of storing simple values (scalars, but not lists, as, for example, the results of a *SELECT* command) in variables. In normal applications, variables generally play a small role, yet they are an important element of SQL when used to call stored procedures (see Chapter 13).

There are three types of variables in MySQL:

Ordinary variables: Such variables are indicated by a prefixed @ sign. They lose their content at the close of the SQL connection.

System and server variables: Such variables contain states or attributes of the MySQL server. They are indicated by two prefixed @ signs (e.g., *@@binlog_cache_size*).

Many system variables exist in two forms, one specifically for the current connection (e.g., *@@session.wait_timeout*) and one globally for the MySQL server (e.g., *@@global.wait_timeout* containing the default value for this variable).

Local variables and parameters within stored procedures: These variables are declared locally within an SP and are valid only within the stored procedure. They are not indicated by a special sign, but they must have names that are distinguishable from names of tables and columns.

In this section we will be dealing primarily with ordinary variables. Variables in stored procedures will be considered in detail in Chapter 13, while system variables and server variables will be treated in Chapters 14 and 21. The syntax for assignment and use of variables is always the same.

Variable Assignment

As the following examples show, there are several ways of assigning values to variables. Note that *SET* uses the assignment operator =, while *SELECT* users :=. The last variant, the assignment of several columns to several variables, has been permissible only since MySQL 5.0, and then only if the *SELECT* command returns precisely one data record. You must therefore use a suitable *WHERE* conditional or *LIMIT 1*.

```
SET @varname = 3
SELECT @varname := 3
SELECT @varname := COUNT(*) FROM table
SELECT COUNT(*) FROM table INTO @varname
SELECT title, subtitle FROM titles WHERE titleID=... INTO @t, @st
```

Use of Variables

Once a variable has been defined, it can be used in any SQL command. Through MySQL 4.1 you have to pay attention to uppercase and lowercase distinction, but since MySQL 5.0, case distinction in variables no longer applies.

```
SELECT @varname
```

@varname‗‗‗‗
```
123
```

```
SELECT * FROM titles WHERE titleID=@varname
```

With variables, you can also perform simple calculations. The following example shows how you can determine, for the *bigvote* database, the percentage of participants who gave a particular answer in the survey (this database has the same structure as *test_vote* from Chapter 3, but it contains more entries):

```
USE bigvote
```

```
SELECT @total := COUNT(*) FROM votelanguage
```

@total := COUNT(*)
```
        4807
```

```
SELECT choice, COUNT(*) / @total * 100 AS percentage
FROM votelanguage GROUP BY choice ORDER BY percentage DESC
```

choice	percentage
4	49.19908466819
3	12.87705429581
1	11.75369253172
2	11.37923861036
5	7.53068441855
6	7.26024547534

In practice, however, such calculations are seldom used. Instead, for programming of complex query or insertion operations you should use a programming language such as PHP or Perl that makes variables available and therefore makes the use of MySQL variables unnecessary (see also the introductory example in Chapter 3).

IF Queries

With the function *IF* introduced earlier in this chapter, you can return one of two different results, depending on the evaluation of a condition:

```
IF(condition, result1, result2)
```

Of course, you can also nest *IF* queries:

```
IF(condition1, result1, IF(condition2, result2a, result2b))
```

If you wish to test whether a column contains *NULL,* you may use the function *ISNULL (expr).* In many cases, you can use *IFNULL* instead of a nesting of *IF* and *ISNULL.* The following expression returns *expr2* if *expr1* is *NULL,* and *expr1* otherwise:

```
IFNULL(expr1, expr2)   corresponds to   IF(ISNULL(expr1), expr2, expr1)
```

CASE Branching

The *CASE* construct has two syntactic variants. The first of these returns *result1* if *expr=val1,* *result2* if *expr=val2,* and so on:

```
CASE expr
  WHEN val1 THEN result1
  WHEN val2 THEN result2
  ...
  ELSE resultn
END
```

With the second variant, it is not a condition that is evaluated, but an arbitrary number of conditions. The result is *result1* if condition *cond1* holds, *result2* if condition *cond2* holds, and so on:

```
CASE
  WHEN cond1 THEN result1
  WHEN cond2 THEN result2
  ...
  ELSE resultn
END
```

The following example returns an alphabetical list of all English book titles (*langID=1*) from the *mylibrary* database. What is of interest here is that the articles *a, an,* and *the* are ignored in sorting. Thus *A Programmer's Introduction* will be found under the letter P, not A. To achieve this, sorting is not done directly by title, but using the *CASE* construct, which returns a truncated character string, with any article removed:

```
SELECT title FROM titles
WHERE langID=1
ORDER BY
  CASE
    WHEN LEFT(title,2)="A "   THEN MID(title,3)
    WHEN LEFT(title,3)="An "  THEN MID(title,4)
    WHEN LEFT(title,4)="The " THEN MID(title,5)
    ELSE title
  END
```

```
title_____
Darwin's Radio
The Definitive Guide to MySQL
Disgrace
A Guide to the SQL Standard
...
Practical UNIX & Internet Security
A Programmer's Introduction to PHP 4.0
```

In analogy to this example, you could do the same with articles in German (*der, die, das*), French (*le, la, les*), or Russian (just kidding, Russian has no articles). You could also filter out the www in web addresses or any other part of a character string.

■Note Please observe that such search criteria significantly slow the execution of SQL queries. MySQL must first create a list of all titles and then sort them. It is not possible to use the existing index of the *title* column.

Copying Data from One Table to Another

Creating a New Table by Copying

With the command *CREATE TABLE newtable SELECT … FROM oldtable* you can create a new table and insert into it all the records selected with a *SELECT* command. MySQL automatically generates all the necessary columns in *newtable* corresponding to the data selected by *SELECT*:

```
CREATE DATABASE newlibrary
USE newlibrary
CREATE TABLE publishers SELECT * FROM mylibrary.publishers
```

If you now look at the table definition with *SHOW CREATE TABLE oldtable* or *newtable*, you will discover that in the process of copying, the indexes and *AUTO_INCREMENT* attribute for the column *publID*, as well as some *TIMESTAMP* attributes, have gone missing. Furthermore, the table type has changed from *InnoDB* to *MyISAM*.

```
SHOW CREATE TABLE mylibrary.publishers      -- (original)
CREATE TABLE publishers(
  publID   INT(11) NOT NULL AUTO_INCREMENT,
  publName VARCHAR(60) COLLATE latin1_german1_ci NOT NULL default '',
  ts       TIMESTAMP NOT NULL DEFAULT CURRENT_TIMESTAMP
           ON UPDATE CURRENT_TIMESTAMP,
  PRIMARY KEY (publID),
  KEY publName (publName)
) ENGINE=InnoDB DEFAULT CHARSET=latin1 COLLATE=latin1_german1_ci

SHOW CREATE TABLE newlibrary.publishers       -- (new)
CREATE TABLE publishers (
  publID   INT(11) NOT NULL default '0',
  publName VARCHAR(60) CHARACTER SET latin1
           COLLATE latin1_german1_ci NOT NULL default '',
  ts       TIMESTAMP NOT NULL DEFAULT '0000-00-00 00:00:00'
) ENGINE=MyISAM DEFAULT CHARSET=latin1
```

To avoid such unwanted changes in the table structure, it is preferable first to create the new table just like the old one with a separate *CREATE TABLE* command and then use *INSERT INTO …SELECT …* to fill it with data. (*CREATE TABLE … LIKE* has been available since MySQL 4.1.)

```
USE newlibrary
CREATE TABLE publishers LIKE mylibrary.publishers
INSERT INTO publishers  SELECT * FROM mylibrary.publishers
```

■**Tip** Tables can also be copied and moved with the MySQL import and export commands. These commands are described in Chapter 14 in the discussion of backups.

Copying into Existing Tables

To copy data into an existing table, use the command *INSERT INTO ... SELECT*. You must make sure that the number of columns and their types match and that they are given in the correct order. If the source table has fewer columns than the target table, you can simply specify *NULL* or a fixed value for a column in the *SELECT* part, for example, *SELECT NULL, publID, publName, ts, 0, "abc"*:

```
INSERT INTO newlibrary.publishers
SELECT publID, publName, ts FROM mylibrary.publishers
```

The greatest source of problems with such commands is, yet again, *AUTO_INCREMENT* fields. If the source and target tables contain records with the same ID number, then an *INSERT* command results in an error (*Duplicate entry xy for key ...*). There are several ways of getting around this problem:

- You can use *INSERT IGNORE INTO ...*, which avoids the error message and leads to the affected records being simply not copied.

- You can use *REPLACE ...* instead of *INSERT INTO ...*, which results in the affected records being overwritten on copying.

- You can change the *publID* column in copying so that no conflicts arise. (This variant is possible only if no other records are referred to or if the foreign key field is also changed accordingly.)

  ```
  SELECT @maxid := MAX(publID) FROM newlibrary.publishers;
  INSERT INTO newlibrary.publishers
  SELECT publID + @maxid, publName, ts FROM mylibrary.publishers
  ```

Pivot Tables

Pivot tables collect information from a data source and arrange it in groups. The simplest way to understand these tables is by way of an example: In the *mylibrary* database, for each book title there can be stored a publisher, a category, and a language. Suppose we wish to know how many titles there are for every combination of category and language. Pivot tables provide a simple statistical evaluation of table data.

Many database systems offer special OLAP commands for creating pivot tables. OLAP stands for *online analytical processing* and includes special methods for the management and evaluation of multidimensional data, where here "multidimensional" refers to the several characteristics by which the data can be grouped. OLAP-capable database systems are often called *data warehouses*.

Unfortunately, MySQL does not support OLAP functions, except for *GROUP BY* (see Chapter 9). Therefore, you generally have to use external programs to create pivot tables. Especially well suited for this task is Microsoft Excel (see Chapter 7.)

In simple cases, you can make use of SQL functions in MySQL. Of particular practical use is the function *SUM* in combination with *IF*. *SUM* allows for the return of the sum of a grouped column.

With *IF*, the formation of the sum can be made dependent on a number of criteria. The following two examples show how to proceed.

Pivot Tables for Book Titles, Languages, and Categories

For our first example we use the *mylibrary* database. The goal is to return a table that tells how many titles there are in each combination of category and language (of course, only for those titles that have such information associated with them). The starting data looks like this:

```
USE mylibrary
SELECT title, langName, catName
FROM titles, categories, languages
WHERE titles.catID = categories.catID
  AND titles.langID = languages.langID
```

title	langName	catName
A Guide to the SQL Standard	english	SQL
Practical UNIX & Internet Security	english	Computer books
MySQL	english	MySQL
MySQL Cookbook	english	MySQL
PHP and MySQL Web Development	english	PHP
Visual Basic	deutsch	Programming
Excel 2000 programmieren	deutsch	Programming
LaTeX	deutsch	Computer books
Nennen wir ihn Anna	deutsch	Children's books
Mathematica	deutsch	Computer books
Jag saknar dig, jag saknar dig	svensk	Children's books
Hunderna i Riga	svensk	Literature and fiction
Ute av verden	norsk	Literature and fiction
...		

We will now group this list by category (*GROUP BY*). For each category we will use *SUM(IF(titles.langID=n, 1, 0))* to count the titles that appear in a particular language. *COUNT(*)* counts the titles in the category (independent of the category). *WITH ROLLUP* has the effect that *GROUP BY* also computes the sum of each column (the last row of the result):

```
SELECT catName,
       SUM(IF(titles.langID=1, 1, 0)) AS english,
       SUM(IF(titles.langID=2, 1, 0)) AS deutsch,
       SUM(IF(titles.langID=3, 1, 0)) AS svensk,
       SUM(IF(titles.langID=4, 1, 0)) AS norsk,
       COUNT(*)
FROM titles, categories, languages
WHERE titles.catID = categories.catID
  AND titles.langID = languages.langID
GROUP BY catName WITH ROLLUP
```

catName	english	deutsch	svensk	norsk	COUNT(*)
C#	0	1	0	0	1
Children's books	0	1	2	0	3
Computer books	1	5	0	0	6
Databases	0	1	0	0	1
LaTeX, TeX	0	2	0	0	2
Linux	0	3	0	0	3
Literature and fiction	2	7	9	1	19
MySQL	3	1	0	0	4

PHP	2	3	0	0	5
Programming	0	4	0	0	4
Relational Databases	0	1	0	0	1
Science Fiction	3	0	0	0	3
SQL	1	0	0	0	1
Visual Basic	0	1	0	0	1
Visual Basic .NET	0	2	0	0	2
NULL	12	34	11	1	58

There is an obvious problem with this query in the *SUM(...)* terms. What would happen if the *languages* column contained not four, but twenty or thirty languages? In such cases you would have to write the SQL code for the query in a client program (e.g., in a PHP script): First you would obtain a list of all languages, then for each language, add a *SUM(...)* term to the SQL query.

You can determine the number of titles in each language like this:

```
SELECT langName, COUNT(*)
FROM titles, categories, languages
WHERE titles.catID = categories.catID
  AND titles.langID = languages.langID
GROUP BY langName
```

langName	COUNT(*)
deutsch	15
english	5
norsk	1
svensk	5

Pivot Table Query Results by Month

Our second example evaluates the table *votelanguage*, with query results of a simple poll (see the example in Chapter 3). The goal is to display for each month the percentages of votes, in order to determine a change in opinion or to detect an attempt at manipulating the results. The starting data, about 3,300 records, look like this:

```
USE bigvote
SELECT * FROM votelanguage LIMIT 5
```

id	choice	ts
1	4	20010516083407
2	3	20010516083407
3	5	20010516083407
4	4	20010516083407
5	2	20010516083407

It is easy to determine the number of participants in the poll by month:

```
SELECT DATE_FORMAT(ts, '%Y-%m') AS mnth, COUNT(*)
FROM votelanguage
GROUP BY mnth
```

mnth	COUNT(*)
2001-05	214
2001-06	111
...	...

The number of votes for each programming language is again determined with *SUM(IF(...))*:

```
SELECT DATE_FORMAT(ts, '%Y-%m') AS mnth,
       SUM(IF(choice=1, 1, 0)) AS c,
       SUM(IF(choice=2, 1, 0)) AS java,
       SUM(IF(choice=3, 1, 0)) AS perl,
       SUM(IF(choice=4, 1, 0)) AS php,
       SUM(IF(choice=5, 1, 0)) AS vb,
       SUM(IF(choice=6, 1, 0)) AS other,
       COUNT(*)
FROM votelanguage
GROUP BY mnth
```

mnth	c	java	perl	php	vb	other	COUNT(*)
2001-05	20	24	30	110	16	14	214
2001-06	6	13	15	64	7	6	111
...							

If you now want to know the percentage distribution, you have to divide the *SUM* expressions by *COUNT(*)*. The results are then made readable by multiplying by 100 and using the *ROUND* function:

```
SELECT DATE_FORMAT(ts, '%Y-%m') AS mnth,
       ROUND(SUM(IF(choice=1, 1, 0)) * 100 / COUNT(*), 1) AS c,
       ROUND(SUM(IF(choice=2, 1, 0)) * 100 / COUNT(*), 1) AS java,
       ROUND(SUM(IF(choice=3, 1, 0)) * 100 / COUNT(*), 1) AS perl,
       ROUND(SUM(IF(choice=4, 1, 0)) * 100 / COUNT(*), 1) AS php,
       ROUND(SUM(IF(choice=5, 1, 0)) * 100 / COUNT(*), 1) AS vb,
       ROUND(SUM(IF(choice=6, 1, 0)) * 100 / COUNT(*), 1) AS other
FROM votelanguage
GROUP BY mnth
```

mnth	c	java	perl	php	vb	other
2001-05	9.3	11.2	14.0	51.4	7.5	6.5
2001-06	5.4	11.7	13.5	57.7	6.3	5.4
...						

SubSELECTs

MySQL has offered since version 4.1 the possibility of executing so-called sub*SELECT*s, a sort of collection of nested *SELECT* queries. (In most other database systems, sub*SELECT*s have always been taken for granted.

■**Tip** If you are working with an older version of MySQL, you can recast sub*SELECT* commands as a *JOIN* query. To do so, however, is not particularly intuitive. In the more complex cases it is also necessary first to create a temporary table for intermediate results.

Syntax Variants

There are many ways of formulating sub*SELECT*s. The following list gives the most important variants. Examples will follow in the next section.

SELECT ... WHERE col = [ANY/ALL] (SELECT ...): With this variant, the second *SELECT* query must return a single value (one row and one column). This value is used for the comparison *col=...*. (There are additional comparison operators available, such as *col>...*, *col<=...*, *col<>...*.)

A comparison can be modified using the keyword *ANY*, its synonym *SOME*, or *ALL*. In this case, the second *SELECT* query can return more than one value. *ANY/SOME* means that all suitable values should be considered. The total query might then return several results. The formulation *col = ANY...* means the same as *col IN ...* (see the next variant).

The effect of *ALL* is not so obvious: The expression *comparison operator ALL* has the value *TRUE* if the comparison is true for all the results of the second *SELECT* query or if the second *SELECT* query returns no result.

SELECT ... WHERE col [NOT] IN (SELECT ...): In this variant the second *SELECT* query may return an entire list of individual values. This list is then processed in the form *SELECT ... WHERE col IN (n1, n2, n3)*. In place of *IN*, one may use *NOT IN*.

SELECT ROW(value1, value2, ...) = [ANY] (SELECT col1, col2, ...): This query tests whether a record exists satisfying certain specified criteria. The possible results are *1* (true) and *NULL* (false). The main difference between this variant and the two previous ones is that the comparison criterion is not a single value, but a group of values.

MySQL compares the record *ROW(value1, value2, ...)* with the result of the second *SELECT* command, which must return precisely one data record. If the result record is the same as the *ROW* record, then the entire query returns *1*. Otherwise, it returns *NULL*.

If the optional keyword *ANY* or its synonym *SOME* is used, the second *SELECT* query may return more than one result. If at least one of them is identical to the *ROW* record, then the entire query returns the result *1*.

SELECT ... WHERE col = [NOT] EXISTS (SELECT ...): In this variant, the second *SELECT* query is executed for every record found in the first *SELECT* query. Only if this second query yields a result (that is, at least one record) does the record from the first *SELECT* query remain in the result list. In this variant, the negation operation *NOT* may be prefixed.

EXISTS constructions are generally useful only if the records of the two *SELECT* commands are joined with a *WHERE* condition (as with a *JOIN* operation).

SELECT ... FROM (SELECT ...) AS name WHERE ...: In this variant, which is seldom used in practice, first the *SELECT* command in parentheses is executed. It returns a table, which serves as the basis of the outer *SELECT* command. In other words, the outer *SELECT* command does not access a preexisting table, as is usually the case, but a table that is itself the result of a *SELECT* command. Such tables are called *derived tables*. The SQL syntax prescribes that such a table must be named using *AS name*.

SELECT commands may be nested within one another. However, such commands can be difficult to read and understand. *SELECT* commands can also be used within *WHERE* conditions of *UPDATE* and *DELETE* commands for determining which records have been changed or deleted.

■**Tip** You will find an interesting article on sub*SELECT* syntax at `http://dev.mysql.com/tech-resources/articles/4.1/subqueries.html`. Sub*SELECT*s are also extensively discussed in the MySQL documentation: `http://dev.mysql.com/doc/mysql/en/subqueries.html`

Limitations

MySQL is not yet capable of evaluating *LIMIT* in sub*SELECT* commands; for example, *SELECT ... WHERE ... IN (SELECT ... LIMIT 10)*. If you try to do this, you will receive the following error message: *ERROR 1235 (42000): This version of MySQL doesn't yet support 'LIMIT & IN/ALL ANY/SOME subquery'*.

If you use sub*SELECT*s to alter records (*DELETE, UPDATE*), the table to be updated and the sub*SELECT* table must be different.

It has been my experience that in many cases, sub*SELECT*s are executed extremely inefficiently. The reason is that sub*SELECT*s for MySQL seem to be much more difficult to optimize than ordinary *SELECT* command with *JOIN*s. In speed-critical applications it would be a good idea to use equivalent SQL commands without sub*SELECT*s.

SubSelects with Older Versions of MySQL

If you are working with an earlier version of MySQL (4.0 and earlier), it is often possible to reformulate a sub*SELECT* command as a *JOIN* query. However, to do so is not particularly intuitive.

The following two equivalent *SELECT* commands provide an example. Both commands return book titles whose *publID* is invalid (that is, not contained in the *publishers* table). Since in the *mylibrary* database there is an integrity rule between titles and publishers, such a case should never occur. Therefore, both commands return no resulting records. First as a sub*SELECT*:

```
SELECT * FROM titles
WHERE publID NOT IN
  (SELECT publID FROM publishers)
```

and then using *JOIN*:

```
SELECT titles.*
FROM titles LEFT JOIN publishers
ON titles.publID=publishers.publID
WHERE ISNULL(publishers.publID) AND NOT(ISNULL(titles.publID))
```

In more complex cases involving equivalents of sub*SELECT*s, it may be necessary to use a temporary table with intermediate results.

Examples

The following query returns all book titles whose publisher's name begins with "O." Then, a list of *publID* values for the key word *IN* is returned with a separate *SELECT* query.

```
USE mylibrary
SELECT title FROM titles WHERE publID IN
  (SELECT publID FROM publishers WHERE publName LIKE 'O%')
```

title
_____
MySQL & mSQL
Practical UNIX & Internet security
MySQL Cookbook
Comédia Infantil
Hunderna i Riga

You would also obtain this result if you were to execute the *publID* comparison with = *ANY*:

```
SELECT title FROM titles WHERE publID = ANY
  (SELECT publID FROM publishers WHERE publName LIKE 'O%')
```

Finally, you obtain the same result with the following command, which demonstrates the not particularly intuitive *EXISTS* syntax variant. Here the second *SELECT* command, the one in parentheses, is executed for every book title. A book title returned by the first *SELECT* command is considered only if this second command has a nonempty result. The condition *titles.publID* = *publishers.publID* creates the relation between the two *SELECT* queries:

```
SELECT title FROM titles WHERE EXISTS
  (SELECT * FROM publishers WHERE
    titles.publID = publishers.publID AND
    publName LIKE 'O%')
```

The following command tests whether the *title* table contains one or more books for which *title='Linux'* and *subtitle='Installation, Konfiguration, Anwendung'* are valid. The result is *1*. That is, there are such titles. Caution: Without *ANY*, the query would return *1* only if there existed precisely one such title.

```
SELECT ROW('Linux', 'Installation, Konfiguration, Anwendung') = ANY
  (SELECT title, subtitle FROM titles)
  1
```

The next command uses a *derived table*. The inner *SELECT* command returns a table with titles of books with more than one author. The outer *SELECT* command processes this result and sorts it in order of increasing number of authors:

```
SELECT * FROM
  (SELECT titles.titleID, title, COUNT(authID) AS authCount
  FROM titles, rel_title_author
  WHERE titles.titleID = rel_title_author.titleID
  GROUP BY rel_title_author.titleID
  HAVING authCount>1) AS titleAuthCount
ORDER BY authCount DESC
```

titleID	title	authCount
23	Maple	3
9	MySQL & mSQL	3
3	Client/Server Survival Guide	3
25	Linux für Internet und Intranet	3
69	Visual C#	2
2	The Definitive Guide to Excel VBA	2
59	PHP and MySQL Web Development	2
34	MySQL	2
...	...	

Ensuring the Integrity of Data

During the creation of a database project (database design, development of program code, and so on), it often happens that test data sets are incompletely deleted and some references to tables lead nowhere. Of course, programming errors can also lead to such problems in the actual operation of a database system, which is always an indication that somewhere or other there is an error in the code.

Whatever the cause, one of the burdensome tasks of database administration is to manage the integrity of the data and correct errors as they are discovered. In the following, you will find some tips for such error management. All the examples refer to the database *mylibrary*.

This section is also a good example of the application possibilities of sub*SELECT*s.

Searching for Titles Without Authors

Every title in the *mylibrary* database is required to have at least one author. The relationship between the tables *titles* and *authors* is via the table *rel_title_author*.

The following query tests each title in *titles* to see whether there is an entry in *rel_title_author* with a corresponding *titleID* number. Only the titles that do not have such an entry are displayed (due to *NOT EXISTS*):

```
SELECT title FROM titles WHERE NOT EXISTS
  (SELECT * FROM rel_title_author
  WHERE titles.titleID = rel_title_author.titleID)
```

Searching for Invalid Publisher Links: Invalid Records in 1 : *n* Relations

In an ideal world, all the records in the *titles* table should refer with *publID* to a publisher, or else the relevant field should contain *NULL*. But what happens if a publisher is inadvertently deleted? Then there are *titles* records with *publID*s that refer to a no longer existing publisher. (Similar problems can arise with other relations between other tables, with the *titles* table and the *catID* and *langID* fields. The following query thus does not find all *titles* records with incorrect cross references, but only those whose *publID* is invalid. Thus we are merely giving an example of how to find such records.)

■**Note** The *mylibrary* database certainly contains no invalid records, because all relations between tables have been ensured with foreign key rules.

Nonetheless, to simulate invalid records, an invalid record will be inserted in the *titles* table. (The command assumes that there is no publisher with *publID=9999*.) In order to make it possible for the *INSERT* command to be executed, the integrity rules must first be switched off (*SET ...*):

```
SET foreign_key_checks=0
INSERT INTO titles (title, publID) VALUES ('deleteme', 9999)
SET foreign_key_checks=1
```

The following query searches for titles whose *publID* value does not appear in the *publishers* table:

```
SELECT title, titles.publID  FROM titles
WHERE publID NOT IN (SELECT publID FROM publishers)
```

There are two ways to correct such errors: You can simply delete any invalid titles (which in this case is the called-for solution), or you can associate the title with a publisher (which you will have to create if the publisher does not already appear in the list of publishers):

```
DELETE FROM titles WHERE publID NOT IN
  (SELECT publID FROM publishers)
```

Searching for Invalid Links Between Authors and Titles (*n* : *m* Relation)

Somewhat more complicated is the search for *n* : *m* relations (such as in the title/author relationship). Now there are three sources of errors:

- Titles that refer via *rel_title_author* to nonexistent authors.

- Authors that refer via *rel_title_author* to nonexistent titles.

- Entries in *rel_title_author* for which both *titleID* and *authID* refer to invalid records. (If the search for illegal records is based on existing authors or titles, then this third source of errors remains unexposed.)

To simulate the error situation, three invalid records will be inserted into *rel_title_author*, covering all three error sources. The following instruction assumes that there exists an author with *authID=1* and a title with *titleID=1*, but no author or title with ID number *9999*:

```
SET foreign_key_checks=0
INSERT INTO rel_title_author (titleID, authID)
VALUES (1,9999), (9999,1), (9999, 9999)
SET foreign_key_checks=1
```

A simple sub*SELECT* command finds the relevant records:

```
SELECT titleID, authID FROM rel_title_author
WHERE authID  NOT IN (SELECT authID FROM authors) OR
      titleID NOT IN (SELECT titleID FROM titles)
```

authID	titleID
9999	1
1	9999
9999	9999

One can just as easily delete the invalid data:

```
DELETE FROM rel_title_author
WHERE authID NOT IN (SELECT authID FROM authors) OR
      titleID NOT IN (SELECT titleID FROM titles)
```

Tracking Down Duplicates

In database management, the problem repeatedly arises that data records are stored inadvertently in duplicate. As the following example involving the table *authors* and the database *mylibrary* shows, such records are easy to find. To this end, we form groups of identical author names and then display those groups with more than one member:

```
USE mylibrary
SELECT authName, COUNT(*) AS cnt
FROM authors
GROUP BY authName
HAVING cnt>1
```

In a second step, one could obtain all the *authID* numbers for these records. Then duplicate entries can be removed, and you should replace in the table *rel_title_author* the second *authID* number by the first, and then delete the second entry from the table *authors*.

For example, suppose that due to an input error the author Gary Cornell appears twice:

authID	authName
123	Cornell Gary
758	Cornell Gary

In the *titles* table there are two different books by Gary. The first of these, *The Sex Life of Unix*, is associated with *authID=123*, while the second book, *More Sex Life of Unix*, has *authID=758*. Gary has two *authID*s!

To alleviate this problem, we decide to use only *authID=123*, and so we change all *rel_title_author* entries with *758* to *123*:

```
UPDATE rel_title_authors SET authID=123 WHERE authID=758
```

Now all of Gary's books have *authID=123*. Finally, we delete the obsolete entry in the *authors* table:

```
DELETE FROM authors WHERE authID=758
```

In the *titles* table it is permitted for several books to have the same title. Therefore, several columns must be considered:

```
SELECT title, subtitle, edition, COUNT(*) AS cnt
FROM titles
GROUP BY title, subtitle, edition
HAVING cnt>1
```

It is more difficult to track down duplicates that involve typographical errors. With English words one can use *SOUNDEX*. This function returns a character string that corresponds to the pronunciation of the text. However, the result must be manually examined. *SOUNDEX* does not find all similar records, and it considers as duplicates names that are really different. The following query uses *MIN(authName)* to return the alphabetically first of the similar-sounding names:

```
SELECT SOUNDEX(authName) AS snd,
       COUNT(*) AS cnt,
       MIN(authName) AS firstname
FROM authors
GROUP BY snd
HAVING cnt>1
```

Bringing a Table into Normal Form

In Chapter 8 we described in detail the first three normal forms, which are considered the starting point for solid database design. In the best of all possible worlds, all design issues are dealt with at the outset, but in the world as we know it, it frequently happens that one comes to grips with these rules after it is too late.

But what does that mean, "too late"? The example of this section shows how you can move redundant information into a new table, thereby creating the third normal form after the fact.

The starting point for our example is the table *messages*, which contains a field *author* with the names of the contributors to an on-line discussion forum. Since many authors contribute multiple messages, their names appear repeatedly. This shortcoming will be corrected with the new table *users*, which is to contain a list of all the authors' names. In *messages*, the *author* column will be replaced by a *userID* column.

The first step is to create the new table *users*:

```
CREATE TABLE users (userID INT NOT NULL AUTO_INCREMENT,
                    username VARCHAR(60) NOT NULL,
                    PRIMARY KEY (userID))
```

With the command *INSERT INTO ... SELECT* introduced earlier in this chapter, all names can be inserted into the new *users* table. *SELECT* must be executed with the option *DISTINCT*, so that each name is inserted only once. For the *userID* column, the value *NULL* is passed. This leads to MySQL placing *AUTO_INCREMENT* numbers in the column automatically:

```
INSERT INTO users SELECT DISTINCT NULL, author FROM messages
```

Now the original table *messages* must be expanded to contain the new *userID* column:

```
ALTER TABLE messages ADD userID INT
```

Next, the *userID* column should be filled with data in such a way that the numbers refer to the corresponding entries in the *user* column. Note, please, that the *UPDATE* command in this form is valid only starting with version 4.0. Although *UPDATE* refers to both *messages* and *users*, it is only the former that is changed. (Only *messages.userID* is newly set by *SET*.)

```
UPDATE messages, users
SET messages.userID = users.userID
WHERE messages.author = users.username
```

Starting with MySQL 4.1, you can use the following sub*SELECT* command as an alternative to the above command. It has exactly the same effect, but it is easier to understand. Note that the inner *SELECT* command refers to the outer *SELECT* command through *messages.author*.

```
UPDATE messages SET userID=
  (SELECT userID FROM users WHERE users.username = messages.author)
```

A brief check shows that everything worked as planned:

```
SELECT messages.author, users.userName, users.userID
FROM messages, users
WHERE messages.userID = users.userID LIMIT 5
```

author	userName	userID
boehnke	boehnke	9
Michael	Michael	10
cjander	cjander	11
Frauke	Frauke	12
Bernd	Bernd	13

Now the column *messages.author* can be deleted; the information contained therein is recoverable via *messages.userID* and the new *users* table:

```
ALTER TABLE messages DROP author
```

Processing the First or Last *n* Records

All the examples of this section use the test database *myforum*.

Searching Data (SELECT)

The question repeatedly arises how to construct a list of the "top ten," or, better, the top *n*, which means the *n* first, the best, the worst, the oldest, or the most pleasing records in a data set. This question is easily answered: Use a *SELECT* command in combination with *ORDER BY* and *LIMIT*.

With *ORDER BY* you have to give a sort criterion, for example, a date. If you want not the first, but the last results, then reverse the sort order with *DESC*. (For example, *ORDER BY date DESC*, and *LIMIT* restricts the number of results to a particular value.)

The following query returns the last five entries in the *myforum* discussion groups. With *LEFT*, the *subject* text is reduced to twenty characters, to make the result easier to read:

```
USE myforum
SELECT LEFT(subject, 20) AS subj, forumID, ts
FROM messages ORDER BY ts DESC LIMIT 5
```

subj	forumID	timest
Re: Run-time error '	1001	20050124154825
Re: Re: Suche Erfahr	1	20050124132214
Re: Full text search	1006	20050124092312
Re: MySQL on ASP wit	1006	20050124052830
Full text searches	1006	20050123211616

Our second example searches not for arbitrary messages, but for those that start a new thread (*rootID=msgID*), and only for the forum 1006 (MySQL, English):

```
SELECT LEFT(subject, 20) AS subj, forumID, ts FROM messages
WHERE rootID=msgID AND forumID=1006
ORDER BY ts DESC LIMIT 5
```

subj	forumID	timest_____
Full text searches	1006	20050123211616
MySQL and ASP	1006	20051021223216
where do I save this	1006	20051016013629
samples do not work	1006	20051014151020
ASP and MySQL	1006	20050730224220

In our next example, the five longest threads are found (that is, the threads that have the largest number of contributions). For this, *COUNT* and *GROUP BY* are used to return to number of messages that have the same *rootID* number.

```
SELECT COUNT(*) AS answerCount, rootID FROM messages
GROUP BY rootID ORDER BY answerCount DESC LIMIT 5
```

answerCount	rootID
11	767
9	1392
8	1134
7	495
7	748

Unfortunately, with this query it was impossible to display the *subject*. The reason is that *GROUP BY* groups all the messages of a thread, and with *COUNT* the number of messages can be determined. But there is no string function that distinguishes the first of several *subject* texts. (With numerical values, one could use *MIN* or *MAX*.) A sub*SELECT* command is of no use here, since no *LIMIT* expressions are allowed within it. You must therefore work either with temporary tables or manually execute an additional query:

```
SELECT subject FROM messages WHERE msgID IN (767, 1392 ...)
```

Changing Records (UPDATE and DELETE)

Just as with *SELECT* you can select the first or last *n* records using *ORDER BY* and *LIMIT n*, you can as well change these records with *UPDATE* and *DELETE*.

The first of our two examples is rather trivial: To save space, *UPDATE* replaces the text of the oldest 100 messages with the bilingual notification *message no longer available/Nachricht steht nicht mehr zur Verfügung*. Important here is the instruction *ts=ts*, which ensures that *ts* is left unchanged. (Otherwise, the oldest 100 messages would suddenly seemingly become the newest.)

```
UPDATE messages
SET msgText="message no ... / Nachricht ...", ts=ts
ORDER BY ts LIMIT 100
```

It is even easier to delete the last 100 messages:

```
DELETE messages ORDER BY ts LIMIT 100
```

Both commands are easily understood, but they have the disadvantage that they destroy the threads. It can also happen that the start message of a thread is overwritten or deleted, while (newer) replies remain. That is not, of course, what we had in mind.

Delete All Threads Except the Last 500

The following commands delete complete threads except for the most recent 500. Unfortunately, the process is somewhat complex. The first command returns the time at which the oldest of the 500 most recent threads was begun. This time is stored in the variable *@oldtime*:

```
SELECT @oldtime := ts FROM messages
WHERE rootID=msgID ORDER BY ts DESC LIMIT 499,1
```

@oldtime := ts
       20050911093909

The next command tests how many threads exist that are even older. This information is not necessary for further processing, but it constitutes a sort of plausibility check:

```
SELECT COUNT(*) FROM messages WHERE ts<@oldtime AND rootID=msgID
```

COUNT(*)___
      117

Now we need to return a list of *msgID* numbers of the start messages of the threads that are to be deleted. This is written to a temporary table *rootIDs* using *CREATE … SELECT*. This table will be stored in RAM for reasons of efficiency (*ENGINE = HEAP*):

```
CREATE TEMPORARY TABLE rootIDs ENGINE=HEAP
SELECT rootID FROM messages WHERE ts<@oldtime AND rootID=msgID
```

The table *rootIDs* is now used to delete the old messages:

```
DELETE messages FROM messages, rootIDs
WHERE messages.rootID=rootIDs. rootID
```

Now the temporary table *rootIDs* can be deleted:

```
DROP TABLE rootIDs
```

Selecting Random Records

It is sometimes desirable to select data records at random, for example, to display images or advertisements on a website.

Selection Without a *random* Column

The easiest procedure is to obtain a random selection by selecting all records with *SELECT*, but executing *ORDER BY* with the addition of *RAND()*. This will yield a list sorted by random numbers. Then *LIMIT* can be used to select the first record.

The following example is based on a copy of the *titles* table from the *mylibrary* database. With two identical queries, two (possibly) different (randomly selected) titles are selected from the copy *titlescopy*:

```
USE mylibrary
CREATE TABLE titlescopy SELECT * FROM titles
SELECT titleID, title  FROM titlescopy
ORDER BY RAND() LIMIT 1
```

titleID title
     59 PHP and MySQL Web Development

```
SELECT titleID, title FROM titlescopy
ORDER BY RAND() random LIMIT 1
```

titleID title
    2 Definitive Guide to Excel VBA

If you wish to select two or more records randomly with only one *SELECT* query, then specify *LIMIT n* instead of *LIMIT 1*.

Selection with a *random* Column

The process just described has an obvious drawback: With large tables, it is extremely inefficient. All the records must be read into active memory, and there sorted by random numbers, all in order to select a single record.

For large tables it is therefore a good idea to provide the table with a column of random numbers at the time that the table is declared. Of course, the *random* column can also be created after the fact, as the following lines prove: The first *ALTER TABLE* command adds the column, while the second equips the column with an index. *UPDATE* then stores a random value in the new column for each existing record. (When a new record is added, you must then supply a new random number for the *random* column. Unfortunately, at present, MySQL does not allow a function such as *RAND* to be specified as a default value.)

```
ALTER TABLE titlescopy ADD random DOUBLE
ALTER TABLE titlescopy ADD INDEX (random)
UPDATE titlescopy SET random = RAND()
```

Now, to select a random record, use the following command:

```
SELECT titleID, title FROM titlescopy
WHERE random > RAND() ORDER BY random LIMIT 1
```

At first glance, this does not seem any more efficient than the previous example. In fact, however, MySQL now has selected only a single record from the table that satisfies the condition *random > RAND()*. Since an index was constructed for the *random* column, access is very efficient.

Do not forget *ORDER BY*! Otherwise, MySQL chooses any old record that satisfies *random > RAND()*, and not necessarily the one whose value is closest to the random number. The selection of a record would then no longer be purely random, but would depend on how the records are stored in the table.

Of course, the variant with the *random* column is not without its own drawbacks:

- More space on the hard drive is required to store the table (additional column plus index).

- Every change in the table is slower than previously (index for the *random* column).

- It is possible to select only a single random record. (If you use *LIMIT 5*, then you obtain five records to be sure, but it is always the same package of five records.)

- On inserting new records, you must always assign a random number to the *random* column.

Selection on the Basis of an *id* Column

Perhaps both of the solutions that we have offered seem unnecessarily complicated. We have only to read the *n*th of *nmax* records, where *nmax* can be easily obtained with *SELECT COUNT(*) FROM table*. Unfortunately, there is no SQL command to read the *n*th data record. MySQL decides the order in which the records are stored (for example, the table driver), and this cannot be controlled from outside.

One solution would be to use an *AUTO_INCREMENT* column. If the table contains 1,000 records, then the *id* column would have to contain the values from 1 to 1,000, and the selection would be possible with *WHERE id = CEILING(RAND()*1000)*. The problem, however, is that you cannot rely on the *id* column being filled without gaps. As soon as you delete records from the table, gaps arise that are never filled upon the addition of new records to the table.

Full-Text Search

If you are using SQL to search for a word in a character string, the query is often posed in the following form:

```
SELECT * FROM tablename WHERE column LIKE '%word%'
```

This query indeed achieves its goal. The only question is, when? There are few queries that are more time-consuming for MySQL to answer than this. (What is worse is searching for several words, perhaps in several columns.) It is not only that all the records of the table must be read. Additionally, many character string comparisons must be made. A traditional index cannot help you here.

Unfortunately, what is most difficult for the computer is simple for the user, who has become accustomed to using an Internet search engine to input a number of search terms without having to deal with complex search criteria.

If you wish to be able to process such queries efficiently in MySQL, you need a *full-text index*. This is a particular type of index, one that creates a list of all words that appear in a column of a table. MySQL has supported this type of index for MyISAM tables since version 3.23.23.

Fundamentals

Creating a Full-Text Index

To provide an existing table with a full-text index, you should execute the following command. You may specify arbitrarily many *xxxTEXT* and *(VAR)CHAR* columns.

```
ALTER TABLE tablename ADD FULLTEXT(column1, column2)
```

Of course, new tables can also be generated at once with a full-text index:

```
CREATE TABLE tablename (id INT NOT NULL AUTO_INCREMENT,
                        column1 VARCHAR(50), column2 VARCHAR(100),
                        PRIMARY KEY (id), FULLTEXT (column1, column2))
```

■Note A full-text index can currently be created only for MyISAM tables (not for InnoDB tables).
Words of three letters or fewer are not included in the full-text index and can therefore not be searched for. (You can change this default value by entering the setting *ft_min_word_len = 3* in the configuration file my.cnf or my.ni, restarting the server, and regenerating the index for the relevant tables with *REPAIR TABLE tablename QUICK*.)

Full-Text Search

For a full-text search, the SQL expression *MATCH AGAINST* is used:

```
SELECT * FROM tablename
WHERE MATCH(column1, column2) AGAINST('word1 word2 word3') > 0.001
```

The result is that all data records are found in which at least one of the three words *word1, word2, word3* is contained. The list of columns in *MATCH* must correspond exactly to the one with which the index was generated. There is no case distinction in the search criteria in *AGAINST*. The order of search criteria is also irrelevant. Words with three or fewer letters are generally ignored.

MATCH returns as result a floating-point number whose magnitude reflects the relevance of the result. If no words are found or if the search criteria appear in very many records and are therefore ignored, then *MATCH* returns 0.

The expression *MATCH ... > 0.001* excludes results for which *MATCH* returns very small values. (This gets rid of statistical outliers and inaccuracies due to floating-point representation.)

■**Note** For the above command *MATCH(title, subtitle)* to be able to be executed, a full-text index over exactly these two columns must exist. An index over more columns, or two full-text indexes each over one column (that is, one for *title* and one for *subtitle*) will not do.

Ordering Results

A *MATCH* expression can be used to order results. The following query returns the five best results. The condition must be formulated with *HAVING*, since *WHERE* does not accept the alias *mtch*:

```
SELECT *,
       MATCH(column1, column2) AGAINST('word1 word2 word3') AS mtch
FROM tablename
HAVING mtch > 0.001
ORDER BY mtch DESC
LIMIT 5
```

Boolean Search Expressions

By default, all search criteria specified in *AGAINST* are joined by a logical *OR*. Since MySQL 4.0, you can connect search criteria using a Boolean expression. For this, you must follow the search expression with *IN BOOLEAN MODE*. Furthermore, the special symbols shown in Table 10-3 can be used in the formulation of the expression.

Table 10-3. *Boolean Search Expressions (IN BOOLEAN MODE)*

Symbol	Meaning
+word	The word must be contained in the data record. Thus *AGAINST('+word1 +word2' IN BOOLEAN MODE)* corresponds to a Boolean *AND* in both search criteria.
-word	The word may not appear in the data record.
~word	The word should not appear in the record. In contrast to *-word*, such records are not completely excluded, but are given a lesser value. Thus *~word* is suited to eliminate "noise words," that is, expressions that are more hindrance than help in a search.
<word	Gives the word a lesser standing.
>word	Gives the word a greater standing.
word*	Searches for words that begin with *word* (e.g., *word, words, wordless*).
"word1 word2"	This exact word order should be searched. Case-insensitive.
()	Parentheses can be used to group expressions. *AGAINST('+mysql +(buch book)' IN BOOLEAN MODE)* searches for data records that contain *mysql* and either *buch* or *book*.

A Boolean full-text search might look like this:

```
SELECT * FROM tablename
WHERE MATCH(column1, column2)
    AGAINST('+word1 +word2 -word3' IN BOOLEAN MODE)
```

A significant drawback to Boolean search is that *MATCH* returns only 1 or 0, according to whether the search criteria were fulfilled or not. There is no longer an evaluation of relevance.

Note Observe that in a full-text search, search patterns like *LIKE* are not allowed. The only exception is the variant *word**, where the wild card * must be placed at the end of the word.

Full-Text Search over Several Tables

A full-text search can be defined only for a single table. To search for data in linked tables, you will have to equip both tables with a full index. The resulting SQL search queries are, however, complicated to formulate and difficult to optimize for the server. (There is an example in the following subsection on book search.)

Limitations

In order for full-text search to function, there must be at least three records in the table. Experiments with tables that contain only one or two records have ended in failure. In general, *MATCH* functions better with larger tables than with smaller, for which it occasionally returns results that are difficult to understand.

Full-text search is based on entire words. The slightest alteration (plurals, endings, etc.) is considered a different word. This makes searching at times more difficult.

To find all relevant records, variants have to be given in *AGAINST* (for example, *AGAINST('book books')* or *AGAINST('book books bookcase bookend')*) to obtain all records having to do with books. One way out is offered by the wild card *, which, however, can be used only in Boolean mode (*AGAINST('book*' IN BOOLEAN MODE)*).

A word in the sense of full-text search is considered to be a character string composed of letters, numbers, and the characters ' and _. Fortunately, letters with diacritical marks like *üàé* are considered letters. Note, however, that expressions like C++ are not considered words and therefore cannot be searched for.

Words must be at least four characters in length if they are to be considered. This makes the search for abbreviations like *SQL* impossible. (This limitation can be removed by a reconfiguration of the server; see below.)

Full-text search is case-insensitive (which usually makes sense, but sometimes is a bother).

Full-text search is currently available only for MyISAM tables (and not for InnoDB tables).

The creation of a full-text index is relatively slow. This affects not only the initial creation of an index, but all further changes in the table as well.

Full-Text Search for Words of Three Letters

As we have already mentioned, full-text search operates by default only for words of four or more letters. The reason for this is to avoid inflating the index with words like *a, and, the*, and the like. However, that makes the search for terms like *ADO* and *PHP* impossible.

With the configuration parameter *ft_min_word_len (mysqld)*, you can set the minimum length of words for the full-text index. To do this, enter the parameter into the MySQL configuration file (/etc/my.cnf or Windows \my.ini) in the section [mysqld]. For the setting to take effect, you will have to restart the MySQL server and regenerate the full-text index (the easiest way to do this is with *REPAIR TABLE tablename QUICK*).

Book Search

For the following examples, a new MyISAM table, *fulltitles*, was created in the *mylibrary* database, which otherwise consists exclusively of InnoDB tables. In doing so, a particular syntax variant of the *CREATE TABLE* command was used. MySQL first executes the *SELECT* command. Its results are then added to the new table. At the same time, the results determine the column names and column properties of the new table:

```
CREATE TABLE fulltitles ENGINE = MyISAM
SELECT titleID, title, subtitle FROM titles
```

Then the new table is supplied with a full-text index for the columns *title* and *subtitle*:

```
ALTER TABLE fulltitles ADD FULLTEXT(title, subtitle)
SELECT title,
       MATCH(title, subtitle) AGAINST('excel basic') AS fulltextmatch
FROM fulltitles
HAVING fulltextmatch > 0.001
ORDER BY fulltextmatch DESC
```

title	fulltextmatch
Visual Basic	2.7978503848587
Visual Basic Datenbankprogrammierung	2.7667480431589
VBA-Programmierung mit Excel 7	2.3731654830885
Definitive Guide to Excel VBA	2.3467841568515
Excel 2000 programmieren	2.3467841568515

In the above query, the condition *fulltextmatch > 0.001* was formulated with *HAVING*, since *WHERE* does not know the alias column name (that is, *AS fulltextname*). The following variant is a bit more efficient, but requires more typing:

```
SELECT title, MATCH(title, subtitle) AGAINST('excel basic') AS fulltextmatch
FROM fulltitles
WHERE MATCH(title, subtitle) AGAINST('excel basic') > 0.001
ORDER BY fulltextmatch DESC
```

Search by Title and Author

A full-text index can be defined only for a single table. If you wish to search for author and title simultaneously (such as *excel* and *kofler*), then you must equip all the tables with a full-text index and then in the query specify *MATCH* expressions for each index. However, the resulting queries are relatively inefficient (especially with large data sets).

```
CREATE TABLE fullauthors ENGINE = MyISAM
SELECT authName, authID FROM authors
ALTER TABLE fullauthors ADD FULLTEXT(authName)
SELECT title, authname FROM fulltitles, fullauthors, rel_title_author
WHERE fulltitles.titleID = rel_title_author.titleID
  AND fullauthors.authID = rel_title_author.authID
  AND MATCH(title, subtitle) AGAINST('excel kofler')
  AND MATCH(authName) AGAINST ('excel kofler')
```

title	*authname*
VBA-Programmierung mit Excel 7	Kofler Michael
Excel 2000 programmieren	Kofler Michael
Definitive Guide to Excel VBA	Kofler Michael

If *fulltitles* contained, say, 100,000 titles, and *fullauthors* as many author names, then the above query would be somewhat slow despite the full-text index. It would be more efficient to store the relevant data in a single table. In the following example *fulltitles* must be expanded to include an *authors* column with author names. (The author column must now be updated after each change, which is a significant disadvantage.) Subsequently, a new full-text index can be set up to encompass the columns *title*, *subtitle*, and *authors*:

```
ALTER TABLE fulltitles ADD COLUMN authors VARCHAR(255)
UPDATE fulltitles SET authors =
  (SELECT GROUP_CONCAT(authname SEPARATOR ', ')
   FROM authors, rel_title_author
   WHERE authors.authID = rel_title_author.authID
   AND   fulltitles.titleID = rel_title_author.titleID
   GROUP BY fulltitles.titleID)
ALTER TABLE fulltitles DROP INDEX title
ALTER TABLE fulltitles ADD FULLTEXT(title, subtitle, authors)
```

The search command can now be formulated thus:

```
SELECT title, authors FROM fulltitles
WHERE MATCH(title, subtitle, authors)
      AGAINST('+excel +kofler' IN BOOLEAN MODE)
```

Forum Search

The following examples relate to the table *messages* in the database *myforum*. The full-text index was created with the following command:

```
USE myforum
ALTER TABLE messages ADD FULLTEXT(msgText, subject)
```

There are almost 500 entries that deal with MySQL:

```
SELECT COUNT(*) FROM messages
WHERE MATCH(msgText, subject) AGAINST('mysql') > 0.001
```

COUNT(*)
464

MySQL believes that the following entries have the greatest relevance. This result should be taken with a grain of salt: The mechanism of full-text search is not blessed with clairvoyant insight, and the selection from among the many contributions is more or less random, reflecting generally the frequency with which the expression "MySQL" appears:

```
SELECT subject, msgID,
       MATCH(msgText, subject) AGAINST('mysql') AS mtch
FROM messages
ORDER BY mtch DESC
LIMIT 5
```

subject	msgID	mtch
help needed with figuring out error message	332	3.368218421936
where is MySQL database?	359	3.329582452774
MYSQL access ...	357	3.159619092941
An update to the first edition of MySQL?	775	3.151849031448
MySql ASP.NET & VB.NET sample code?	2585	3.133650779724

The search for the strings *mysql* and *odbc* gives 67 hits:

```
SELECT COUNT(*) FROM messages
WHERE MATCH(msgText, subject)
    AGAINST('+mysql +odbc' IN BOOLEAN MODE)
```

COUNT(*)
67

To obtain the five best hits, the query has to be changed a bit. As *WHERE* criterion we have the Boolean search expression *'+mysql +odbc'*, which, however, returns only the values 0 and 1. For sorting, we use instead the expression *'mysql odbc'*. The query is here additionally restricted by *forumID = 1006* to entries in the English-language MySQL forum:

```
SELECT LEFT(subject, 40) AS subj,
    msgID,
    MATCH(msgText, subject) AGAINST('mysql odbc') AS mtch
FROM messages
WHERE MATCH(msgText, subject) AGAINST('+mysql +odbc' IN BOOLEAN MODE)
AND    forumID=1006
ORDER BY mtch DESC
LIMIT 5
```

subj	msgID	mtch
Connecting ASP with MySQL	1975	5.6947469711304
MySQL on Visual Basic with ADO	1655	5.2777800559998
Access & MySQL	238	4.8645100593567
RecordCount with MySQL	2948	3.7673554420471
MySQL on ASP with ADO	1464	3.3525133132935

Locking

MySQL is a client/server database system. This means that several programs can simultaneously access the database, read data, and make changes. This can lead to problems when two programs (clients) change the same data at the same time.

Consider, for example, an airline flight reservation system: Two travel agencies check at the same time whether a particular flight has any available seats (e.g., *SELECT … WHERE flightnumber =…*). Both agents obtain the result *OK*, even though only a single seat is available. Based on these results, the agents each book the flight. If the airline's code for its booking system isn't a total basket case, only one agency will receive confirmation, and the other traveler will be out of luck. It would be a much worse situation if the reservation program relied on the validity of a *SELECT* result obtained milliseconds earlier; then both customers would receive confirmation and would have to fight over the seat at boarding time.

There are many solution procedures for such problems. The most elegant, and generally the most efficient, are transactions, which are dealt with in the following section. Transactions are available, however, only if you are using InnoDB tables. If you are using MyISAM tables, then you must rely on what is called *locking*. Locking means that one or more tables are reserved for a period of time for the exclusive use of a single program (client). Until the locking has been removed, other clients will be unable to make changes to the tables or even, depending on the type of locking, read them.

Syntax

To reserve tables for exclusive use, execute the command *LOCK TABLE[S]*:

```
LOCK TABLE table1 locktype, table2 locktype ...
```

The following lock variants (*locktypes*) are available:

READ: All MySQL users are allowed to read the table, but no one may make any changes (including the user who executed the *LOCK* command). A *READ LOCK* is granted only when the table is not blocked by any *WRITE LOCKs*.

READ LOCAL: Like *READ*, but *INSERT* commands are allowed if they don't alter any existing data records.

WRITE: The current user is permitted to read and change the table. All other users are completely blocked: They may neither read data in the table nor make changes to the data. A *WRITE LOCK* is permitted when the table is not blocked by any other *LOCKs* (*READ* or *WRITE*).

LOW PRIORITY WRITE: Like *WRITE*, but during the waiting time (that is, until all other *READ* and *WRITE LOCKs* are ended), other users receive as the need arises a new *READ LOCK*. However, this can increase the waiting time until the granting of a *WRITE LOCK*.

To end the locking, execute *UNLOCK TABLE[S]* without additional parameters. This will end all of the client's *LOCKs*. To block other clients as little as possible, *LOCKs* should be ended as soon as possible.

■**Tips** MySQL always executes individual commands in such a way that they cannot be influenced by other commands. Therefore, no locking is necessary for a single command *UPDATE … WHERE id=1234* or *DELETE … WHERE id=5678*.

You need to execute locking only if you are executing several interdependent commands during which another client should not alter the underlying data. Usually, that is the case when you first execute a *SELECT* command and then process the resulting data with an *UPDATE* or *DELETE* command.

LOCK and *UNLOCK* should not be used for InnoDB tables. With older versions of MySQL (< 4.0.22), the locking mechanisms of MySQL and InnoDB can get in each other's way. *LOCK* also ends the current transaction, which is often an undesired outcome. Instead, use transactions that block only individual records (instead of entire tables). If you really wish to block an entire InnoDB table, there is available a new command, since MySQL 5.0.3, namely, *LOCK TABLE[S] TRANSACTIONAL*.

GET_LOCK and RELEASE_LOCK

If you require locks only to secure communication between two processes, then instead of *LOCK/UNLOCK* you can use the functions *GET_LOCK* and *RELEASE_LOCK*. *GET_LOCK(name, time)* defines a lock with the name *name* for the time *time* (in seconds). The function is usually executed with *DO*, for example, *DO GET_LOCK('abc', 10)*. *RELEASE_LOCK(name)* released the lock on *name*.

Neither function actually executes a lock on the table; that is, neither MySQL nor a database nor a table is blocked. As long as a process has defined a lock with a certain name, no other process can obtain a lock with the same name. The second process is blocked by the call *GET_LOCK* until the first process has released the lock.

Transactions

Probably the most interesting feature of InnoDB tables is that in contrast to MyISAM tables, they support transactions. This means that several SQL commands can be encapsulated as a single operation. This section describes in detail why it is useful to use transactions, how to implement them, and what you have to watch out for when using them. This section also goes into how transactions are implemented in MySQL.

Why Transactions

Transactions can help in making the operation of a database system more efficient and secure: First of all, transactions ensure that a group of SQL commands that begin with *BEGIN* and end with *COMMIT* are executed either as a unit or not at all. Even if the connection with the server is dropped during the transaction, power goes out, or the computer crashes, it cannot happen that only some of the commands are executed.

Let's look at an example: You wish to transfer 100 dollars from account 123 to account 456. Therefore, you first execute

```
UPDATE tablename SET value=value-100 WHERE accountno=123
```

and then

```
UPDATE tablename SET value=value+100 WHERE accountno=456
```

If you are working without transactions and some misfortune occurs between the two commands, it can happen that 100 dollars was withdrawn from the first account but not deposited to the second. With transactions, that cannot occur: Either both commands are correctly executed, or neither of them.

Transactions also ensure that data cannot be simultaneously changed by two users. With MyISAM tables, you can achieve this result with *LOCK TABLE*. But that has the effect of blocking access to the entire table for all clients. With InnoDB tables, in contrast, only the affected records are blocked.

Finally, transactions make for easier programming. A transaction can be aborted at any time, which makes protecting against errors much simpler.

Acid Rules

The database-theoretic answer as to why one should use transactions can be summed up in one word: *ACID*. We are not talking about controlled substances here, but an acronym: *Atomicity, Consistency, Isolation, Durability*. Thus ACID encompasses four concepts that are considered in database theory to be the basis of secure simultaneous use of a database by multiple users. MySQL in combination with the InnoDB table driver passes the ACID test, adhering to its rules and regulations, which can be described in somewhat greater detail as follows:

Atomicity means that a transaction is indivisible. The database system must ensure that either all the commands of a transaction are correctly executed, or none of them. This holds even for such extreme cases as a crash during execution of the transaction.

Consistency requires that at the end of the transaction the database be in a consistent state. If a transaction were to lead to a violation of validity rules, then it must be broken off and undone (*ROLLBACK*). Validity rules include foreign key constraints, which are discussed in greater detail in Chapter 8.

Isolation means that several transactions can run independently and simultaneously without interfering with each other. Each transaction sees the entire database in the condition that it found it right up to the end of the transaction (other than those changes made by the transaction). If a transaction inserts, changes, or deletes records, a transaction running in parallel does not see this.

Complete fulfillment of the isolation requirement can be achieved only at great cost, and in practice, this means cost in speed. For this reason, the ANSI-92/SQL standard provides for four degrees of isolation, so that database programmers can decide on the appropriate level of security and the tradeoff against speed. The default isolation level depends on the database system, and for the InnoDB table driver it is *REPEATABLE READ*. We will have more to say later on isolation degree.

Durability requires that a transaction itself be preserved even if right after the end of the transaction there is a crash or other comparable problem. (The InnoDB table driver therefore writes changes first in a logging file. If a crash occurs, that is, before the changes can actually be made to the database, the changes can be reconstructed after restart of the MySQL server and transferred to the database.

Many database systems make compromises in their durability requirements to achieve improvements in speed. In the case of the InnoDB table driver, most significant in this regard is the option `innodb_flush_log_at_trx_commit`, which controls when transactions can be stored in the logging file.

Controlling Transactions

By default, MySQL is in auto commit mode. This means that every SQL command is executed in a single, small transaction. This has no effect on the use of transaction-capable tables.

There are two ways of executing several SQL commands together as a transaction:

- You can start an ad hoc transaction with *START TRANSACTION* or *BEGIN* and terminate it with *COMMIT* or *ROLLBACK*. *START TRANSACTION* or *BEGIN* deactivate the auto commit mode for this one transaction. If you subsequently wish to begin a transaction, then you must begin with another *BEGIN*.

- You can turn off auto commit mode. Then all the commands are considered together as a transaction until confirmed by *COMMIT* or aborted by *ROLLBACK*.

Again note that transactions are supported only for InnoDB tables, not for MyISAM tables.

BEGIN, COMMIT, and ROLLBACK

BEGIN or *START TRANSACTION* introduces a transaction, *COMMIT* ends it and stores all changes, and *ROLLBACK* aborts the transaction and stores no changes.

In InnoDB tables one may not have nested transactions. If you begin a new transaction with *BEGIN* while a previous transaction is still open, the open transaction is closed with *COMMIT*.

Transactions are managed by the client. If the connection is lost during a transaction, then all uncommitted changes are aborted (as with *ROLLBACK*).

Savepoints

Since MySQL 4.0.14, InnoDB has supported *savepoints*. This allows one to mark points within a transaction using *SAVEPOINT name. ROLLBACK TO SAVEPOINT name* ends the transaction, accepting all changes up to the *SAVEPOINT* and aborting all those that follow.

    *SAVEPOINT*s can be used only within a transaction, and at the end of the transaction, all *SAVEPOINT*s are deleted.

Automatic Transaction Termination

Transactions are also concluded automatically by the following commands (as with *COMMIT*): *ALTER TABLE, CREATE INDEX, CREATE TABLE, DROP DATABASE, DROP TABLE, LOCK TABLES, RENAME TABLE, SET AUTOCOMMIT = 1, TRUNCATE, UNLOCK TABLES.* On the other hand, transactions are not ended when an ordinary error occurs in the execution of an SQL command.

Setting Auto Commit Mode

The auto commit mode is deactivated with the SQL command *SET AUTOCOMMIT = 0.* Commands that relate to transaction-capable tables will now automatically be considered a transaction until they are ended with *COMMIT* or *ROLLBACK.* Then a new transaction begins automatically. (That is, you no longer need to execute *START TRANSACTION.* Just this convenience is often reason enough to work with *SET AUTOCOMMIT = 0.*)

    An important consequence of *AUTOCOMMIT = 0* is that if the connection is lost, whether or not intentionally, all SQL commands that have not been confirmed with a *COMMIT* are aborted.

    Note also that *AUTOCOMMIT = 0* can lead to very long transactions if you do not regularly execute *COMMIT* or *ROLLBACK.* The current state of auto commit can be determined with *SELECT @@autocommit.*

Controlling Transactions in Client Programming

Most libraries and APIs for MySQL programming (such as JDBC, ODBC, ADO, ADO.NET) provide special functions or methods for beginning and ending transactions. If these don't work, you can instead explicitly execute the commands *SET AUTOCOMMIT* and *START TRANSACTION/COMMIT/ROLLBACK.*

Trying Out Transactions

To try out transactions, you must establish two connections to the database. The simplest way to do this is to execute the monitor mysql in two windows. Then execute commands first in one window and then in the other. The following examples assume that there is a (still empty) table *table1* in the database *innotest.* (In practice, of course, you will have several records, but for the purposes of this first demonstration, even a single record suffices.)

```
CREATE DATABASE innotest
USE innotest
CREATE TABLE table1(colA INTEGER, colB INTEGER)
```

■**Note** This example shows the effect that transactions can have when data in a table are changed nearly simultaneously by two users. The example is very simple, and the simultaneity takes place in slow motion. Nonetheless, it should make you aware that in real applications it can certainly happen that database commands from two users or programs can be woven together as in the following example. If such an effect on the end result is possible, then you must exclude the possibility by the use of transactions or (if you wish to stick with MyISAM tables) by executing *LOCK TABLE.*

At time point 0, connection A begins a transaction (*BEGIN*) and changes, in the confines of this transaction, a record of the table *table1*.

At time point 1 (as indicated in the righthand column of Table 10-4) the contents of *table1* look different to the two different connections. For connection A, the record with *colA=1* already has *colB=11*. Since this transaction has not actually been executed, connection B sees the original value *colB=10* for the same record.

Table 10-4. *Two Parallel Transactions*

Connection A	Connection B	Time
USE innotest	USE innotest	
INSERT INTO table1 VALUES (1, 10)		

SELECT * FROM table1
  colA colB
   1 10		

START TRANSACTION		0
UPDATE table1 SET colB=11 WHERE colA=1		

SELECT * FROM table1
  colA colB
   1   11
	SELECT * FROM table1
	  colA colB
	   1 10
		1

	BEGIN	2
	UPDATE table1 SET colB=colB+3 WHERE colA=1	
COMMIT		3

SELECT * FROM table1
  colA colB
   1   11
	SELECT * FROM table1
	  colA colB
	   1 14
		4

	ROLLBACK	

SELECT * FROM table1
  colA colB
   1   11
	SELECT * FROM table1
	  colA colB
	   1 11
		5

At time point 2, B begins a transaction, in which *colB* of the data record with *colA=1* is to be increased by 3. The InnoDB table driver recognizes that it cannot execute this command at this time, and it blocks B, which then waits until A completes its transaction.

At time point 3, A completes its transaction with *COMMIT*, whereby *colB* attains the definitive value 11. And now B's *UPDATE* command can be completed.

At time point 4, A sees *colB=11*. For B things look as though *colB* already had the value 14.

Now B cancels its transaction. Then at time point 5 both A and B see the value actually stored, namely *colB=11*.

Transactions and Locking

The InnoDB table driver generally takes care of all necessary locking operations on its own, as soon as you execute your transactions. However, there are cases where the default behavior of InnoDB is not optimal. In such cases, InnoDB offers several possibilities of having its locking behavior altered.

SELECT ... LOCK IN SHARE MODE

A peculiarity of the InnoDB table driver is that *SELECT* commands are immediately executed even on blocked records. The results returned do not consider the possibility of open transactions of other clients (see connection B at time point 1 in the example above), and thus return potentially outmoded data.

If you execute the *SELECT* with the key word *LOCK IN SHARE MODE* appended, then when the command is executed, it is held pending until all transactions already begun have been terminated (of course, only to the extent that these transactions affect result records of the *SELECT* command). Thus if in the above example B were to issue the command

```
SELECT * FROM table1 LOCK IN SHARE MODE
```

at time 1, then a result would be displayed only when the transaction begun by A had been completed (time point 3).

If *SELECT ... LOCK IN SHARE MODE* is executed within a transaction, then additionally, all result records for all other clients will be locked until the end of the transaction. Such a lock is called a *shared lock*, whence the key word *SHARE*. With a shared lock you are assured that the records read during your transactions are not being changed or deleted by other clients.

With a shared lock, locked records can continue to be read by all clients, even if other clients are also using *SELECT LOCK IN SHARE MODE*. Any attempt by a client to change such records leads to the client being blocked until your transaction is completed.

SELECT ... FOR UPDATE

The key words *FOR UPDATE* also represent an extension of the normal *SELECT*. With this, all result records are provided an *exclusive lock*.

With a *shared lock*, locked records cannot be changed by other clients. They can continue to be read by all clients with a normal *SELECT* command, but not with *SELECT ... LOCK IN SHARE MODE*. The difference between a shared lock and an exclusive lock therefore relates only to whether other clients can execute *SELECT ... LOCK IN SHARE MODE*.

INSERT, UPDATE, DELETE

All three of these commands have the effect that changed records are locked by an exclusive lock until the end of the transaction. If links between tables must be checked (foreign key constraints) during the execution of an *INSERT, UPDATE,* or *DELETE* command, then the affected records of the linked tables will be locked by an *exclusive lock*.

Gap and Next Key Locks

InnoDB uses by default *gap* and *next key locks* when open conditions are used with *SELECT ... LOCK IN SHARE MODE, SELECT ... FOR UPDATE, UPDATE,* or *DELETE* (e.g., *WHERE id>100* or *WHERE id BETWEEN 100 AND 200*). The result is that not only the records currently affected by the condition are blocked, but also records that do not yet even exist that might be inserted by another transaction. (For which commands *next key locks* are used depends on the currently valid isolation degree; see the next section.)

Thus if you execute *SELECT ... WHERE id>100 FOR UPDATE* in a transaction, then no other user can input new records with *id>100* for the duration of the transaction.

Deadlocks

The InnoDB table driver automatically recognizes deadlock situations (that is, situations in which two or more processes block one another, each waiting for the other to finish, ad infinitum). In such situations an error occurs in the process that triggered the deadlock; SQL commands that are still open are aborted with a *ROLLBACK*.

Deadlocks that InnoDB doesn't know about can also arise when SQL commands affect both InnoDB tables and other tables as well. In order for the clients not to have to wait forever in such cases, the configuration setting innodb_lock_wait_timeout=n determines the maximum wait time (by default, 50 seconds).

Isolation Degree for Transactions

Before the start of a transaction, its isolation level can be defined:

```
SET [SESSION|GLOBAL] TRANSACTION ISOLATION LEVEL
  READ UNCOMMITTED | READ COMMITTED |
  REPEATABLE READ | SERIALIZABLE
```

SET can be executed in three different ways:

SET **without** *SESSION* **or** *GLOBAL:* In this case, the selected setting holds only for the next transaction. Note, please, that this behavior is different from that of the usual *SET* syntax, where *SET* works without the specification of what is to be set, as in *SET SESSION*.

SET SESSION: Here, the setting holds for the current connection until its termination or until another isolation degree is specified.

SET GLOBAL: Here, the setting holds for all new connections to MySQL (but not for the current connection).

The isolation degree influences the manner in which commands are executed within a transaction. In the following list, the isolation degrees are ordered according to increasing exclusivity. This means that you achieve the greatest access speed with *READ UNCOMMITTED* (no mutual blocking), while with *SERIALIZABLE*, you obtain the greatest security against simultaneous changes of data by clients. We now describe the four isolation degrees:

READ UNCOMMITTED: *SELECT* reads the current data and considers all changes arising from other running transactions. *SELECT* is therefore *not* isolated from other transactions. (The expression *read uncommitted* means that data of other transactions that are not yet completed with *COMMIT* can flow into the *SELECT* result.) If you execute the example from Table 10-4 in *READ UNCOMMITTED* mode, then at time point 1, transaction B sees *colA=1* and *colB=11*.

Please note that while *READ UNCOMMITTED* does not ensure isolation for *SELECT*, it does so for *UPDATE*. Even in *READ UNCOMMITTED* mode, the *UPDATE* command of transaction B is blocked at time point 2 until transaction A is finished. *UPDATE* is therefore correctly executed in *READ UNCOMMITTED* mode.

READ COMMITTED: *SELECT* takes into account changes by other transactions that have been confirmed with *COMMIT*. This means that one and the same *SELECT* command within a transaction can have different results if another transaction is closed in the intervening time. In comparison with *READ UNCOMMITTED*, the isolation for *SELECT* is somewhat better, but not perfect.

REPEATABLE READ: *SELECT* takes into account no changes by other transactions, regardless of whether these transactions have been confirmed with *COMMIT*. Thus the ACID isolation requirement for *SELECT* is satisfied for this isolation degree. One and the same *SELECT* command always returns one and the same result (as long, of course, as the transaction does not itself change data).

SERIALIZABLE: This mode functions much like *REPEATABLE READ*. The only difference is that ordinary *SELECT* commands are automatically executed as *SELECT … LOCK IN SHARE MODE*, and therefore supply all records with a shared lock.

By default, InnoDB uses the isolation level *REPEATABLE READ*. In most cases, this mode offers sufficient isolation for a variety of transactions without influencing transaction speed unduly. InnoDB is optimized for *REPEATABLE READ* mode and executes the required locks especially efficiently.

One can change the default setting in the MySQL configuration file with the option `transaction-isolation`. In setting the option, the names of the isolation levels consisting of more than one word must be separated by hyphens (thus, for example, `transaction-level = read-committed`).

You can determine the isolation level of a connection or of the server with the following command:

SELECT @@tx_isolation, @@global.tx_isolation

@@tx_isolation	*@@global.tx_isolation*
READ-UNCOMMITTED	REPEATABLE-READ

Isolation Level and Next Key Locks

As we have already mentioned, InnoDB supports *gap* and *next key locks*. This means that in open conditions (e.g., *WHERE id>100*), not only currently existing records are blocked, but also data that do not yet exist that would satisfy the condition.

InnoDB uses *gap* and *next key locks* only when open conditions appear in commands. Moreover, the locking is also dependent on the command being executed and on the isolation level. For the isolation degrees *REPEATABLE READ* and *SERIALIZABLE*, *gap* and *next key locks* are used for the following commands: *SELECT … LOCK IN SHARE MODE, SELECT … FOR UPDATE, UPDATE, DELETE*.

Error Protection

When you use transactions, you increase the odds of receiving certain error messages from the server. You should therefore always check in your code, even with apparently noncritical commands (such as *SELECT*), whether errors have occurred during execution.

While a transaction is open, another client cannot execute any operation that affects the records of the open transaction.

For example, Client A executes *BEGIN* and then *INSERT INTO table VALUES (1, 2)*. Client B attempts to execute *SELECT * FROM table*. This command is blocked until client A terminates its transaction with *COMMIT* or *ROLLBACK*.

Many clients, such as `mysql`, will wait forever for an open transaction to be completed (there is no timeout). But other clients can experience a timeout or other error. In sum, close your transactions as soon as possible.

Every transaction can be broken off due to a deadlock situation. (The InnoDB table driver automatically recognizes deadlock situations, that is, the situation in which two transactions mutually block each other. To avoid a permanent blocking of the server, one client's transaction will be terminated.)

CHAPTER 11

■■■■

Access Administration and Security

It is a fact of life, or at least of human social organization, that not all information is intended to be made available to all individuals. Thus with MySQL, a database is generally set up in such a way that not everyone can see all of the data (let alone change or delete it). In order to protect data from prying eyes (or unauthorized tampering), MySQL provides a dual access system. The first level determines whether the user has the right to communicate with MySQL at all. The second level determines what actions (such as *SELECT*, *INSERT*, *DROP*) are permitted for which databases, tables, or columns.

This chapter describes rather extensively the access system of MySQL, both its internal management and the tools that can assist you in changing access privileges.

Introduction

Communication Between the Client and the MySQL Server

Before any mechanisms for MySQL access administration can become effective, the client (for example, a Perl script, the command interpreter `mysql`, or the MySQL Query Browser) must be able to communicate with the MySQL server. This section summarizes the possible forms of communication.

If you wish to try out the various communication protocols, your best bet is to use the program `mysql`, introduced in Chapter 4, with the option `--protocol`. Allowable settings are `tcp`, `socket`, `pipe`, and `memory`. With the command *STATUS* you can determine the currently set communication protocol:

```
> mysql -u root -p --protocol=tcp
Enter password: xxx
mysql> status
...
Connection: localhost via TCP/IP
```

Communication over a Network

When the client and server are executed on different computers, the situation is simple: Communication between the two programs must take place over the network protocol TCP/IP. For this to happen, two conditions must be satisfied:

- The computers must be linked by TCP/IP. This can be easily checked with the command `ping computername`.

- Port 3306, used by default by MySQL, must not be blocked by a firewall.

Communication on a Local Computer (localhost)

When the client and server are running on the same computer, there are several possible variants:

TCP/IP: The network protocol can also be used for communication between programs running on a single computer. Under Windows, this is the usual case.

Socket file (Unix/Linux only): A socket file enables efficient communication under Unix/Linux between two programs. This is not a normal file (it contains no data and has length 0 bytes). Under Unix/Linux, local communication takes place over a socket file by default, since it is more efficient than TCP/IP.

Named pipes (only Windows 2000/XP): *Named pipes* are more or less the Windows answer to socket files under Unix/Linux. However, on the MySQL server, named pipes are deactivated by default and must be activated with the option enable-named-pipes. Moreover, the MySQL client program must support this communication variant. Since these conditions are seldom fulfilled, named pipes are hardly ever used in practice.

Shared memory (only Windows 2000/XP): *Shared memory* is another Windows alternative to the Unix socket file. Here client and server use the same region of memory for communication. In practice, however, shared memory is used as seldom as named pipes. This is because on the one hand, this form of communication can be used only when the configuration file of the MySQL server contains the option shared_memory (which is not the case by default). If this condition is satisfied, the client program must also support this communication variant, which is generally not the case. The command interpreter mysql is theoretically capable of this (option protocol=memory), but in practical tests it simply returns an error message: *Can't open shared memory; client could not create request event.*

In the further course of this book, only the two most common communication forms will be discussed, namely, TCP/IP and socket files.

Determining the Communication Forms Supported by the MySQL Server

Which communication variants your MySQL server offers depends on how the program was compiled and how it has been configured (see also Chapter 14). The current status of a running MySQL server can be determined with certain *SHOW VARIABLES* commands:

```
SHOW VARIABLES LIKE 'skip_net%'
skip_networking          OFF
SHOW VARIABLES LIKE 'port'
port                     3306
SHOW VARIABLES LIKE 'socket'
socket                   /var/lib/mysql/mysql.sock
SHOW VARIABLES LIKE 'named%'
 named_pipe              OFF
SHOW VARIABLES LIKE 'shared%'
      shared.memory          OFF
      shared_memory_base_name  MYSQL
```

These commands take care of the following: The MySQL server supports TCP/IP; that is, the network functions are not deactivated for security reasons via the option skip-networking. The TCP/IP communication uses port 3306.

The MySQL server supports communication over the socket file /var/lib/ mysql/mysql.sock. (The variable *socket* is available only with Unix/Linux versions of the MySQL server.)

The MySQL server supports neither named pipes nor shared memory. (The three variables *named_pipe*, *shared_memory*, and *shared_memory_base_name*) are available only under the Windows version of the MySQL server.)

Access Administration

Normally, it is undesirable to allow everyone to execute all database operations. To be sure, there must be one, or perhaps even several, administrators who have wide-ranging powers. However, it would be a great security risk to allow all users to act as they please in altering records or even deleting entire databases.

There can be many different degrees of access rights. In a company with an employee database, for example, it may make sense to allow all employees to read part of the database (for example, to find someone's telephone number), while other parts remain invisible (such as personnel records).

MySQL offers a finely meshed system for setting such access privileges. In the MySQL documentation this system is called the *access privilege system*, while the individual lists of the system are called *access control lists* (ACLs). The management of these lists is carried out internally in the tables of the *mysql* database, which will be described in detail.

This section assumes that communication between the client and the MySQL server is possible in principle.

Setting the Access Privileges

There are several ways to set access privileges:

- The simplest and most convenient way is to use an administration program with a graphical user interface. Two of these programs—MySQL Administrator and phpMyAdmin—were described in Chapters 5 and 6. Note, however, that even the most convenient user interface is of little help if you do not understand the concepts of MySQL access.

- You can change *mysql* directly with *INSERT* and *UPDATE* commands.

- You can use the SQL commands *GRANT* and *REVOKE*, which offer greater convenience.

- You can use the Perl script `mysql_setpermission.pl`. This script is even easier to use than *GRANT* and *REVOKE*, though it assumes, of course, that you have a Perl installation up and running.

User Name, Password, and Host Name

MySQL's access process has two phases. In the first phase, the question is whether the user is permitted to make a connection to MySQL at all. (Such does not imply the right to read or alter any databases, but nevertheless, such access provides the capability to pass SQL commands to MySQL. Then MySQL decides, based on its security settings, whether this command should actually be executed.)

While you are probably accustomed to providing a user name and password to enter the operating system of a multiuser computing system, MySQL evaluates a third piece of information: the name of the computer (host name) from which you are accessing MySQL. Since MySQL's entire security system is based on this informational triple, it seems not inappropriate to take a few moments now to explain what is going on.

User Name: The user name is the name under which you announce your presence to MySQL. The management of MySQL user names has nothing to do with login names managed by the operating system. It is, of course, possible, and indeed, it is often advisable, to use the same name for both purposes, but management of each of these names is independent of the other. There is no mechanism to synchronize these operations (such that, for example, a new MySQL user name is generated when the operating system generates a new user name).

The user name can be up to sixteen characters in length, and it is case-sensitive. In principle, such names do not have to be composed exclusively of ASCII characters. But since different operating systems handle special characters differently, such characters often lead to problems and therefore should be avoided.

Password: What holds for user names holds for passwords as well. There is no relation between the MySQL password and that used for the operating system, even if they are identical. Within MySQL, passwords are stored in 45-bit encrypted form, which allows passwords to be checked, but does not allow reconstruction of a password. Even if an attacker should gain access to the *user* table of MySQL, there is no way for the villain to determine the passwords.

■**Caution**   *For security reasons do not use the same password for MySQL as for the operating system!*
     MySQL passwords must often be supplied in plain text in script files, configuration files, and programs. Thus they are in danger of being intercepted. If an attacker who acquires such a password were to gain access not only to your database, but also discovers that the same password allows entry into the operating system, the villain will be very happy indeed.
     This warning is directed particularly at Internet service providers that allow their clients direct access to the computer (FTP, Telnet, SSH) in addition to access to a MySQL database. Be sure to give different passwords for these two different forms of access!
     Since version 4.1, MySQL has used a new authentication system and better-encrypted passwords. Older MySQL client programs are therefore no longer capable of establishing a connection to the MySQL server. Background information on suggested solutions to this authentication problem follow later in this chapter.

Passwords, like user names, are case-sensitive, and they can be of arbitrary length. Special characters outside of the ASCII character set are possible, but are not recommended.

Host Name: In establishing a connection, you must normally specify the computer on which the MySQL server is running. This computer name is generally referred to as *hostname*. The host name can be given as an IP number (e.g., 192.168.23.45). You can omit specification of the host name only if the MySQL server is running on the same computer as your client program.

When determining access rights, MySQL evaluates the information as to where the access request is coming from, that is, from what host name. When client and server are running on different computers, the evaluation of the host name can cause problems for two reasons:

- The MySQL server must be capable of resolving the computer name. In establishing a connection, the server first receives from the client its IP number. Then the server attempts to find the associated computer name (by contacting a *name server*). If that is unsuccessful, then the computer uses the IP number instead of the name for determining whether access should be allowed.

- Even if the name resolution succeeds, the name server can return the host name either with or without the domain name, depending on the configuration (e.g., *mars* or *mars.sol*). Only when the host name agrees exactly with the entry in the *mysql.host* table will access to MySQL be granted.

■**Note**   When the client and server are running under Unix/Linux on the same computer and are using a socket file for communication, the MySQL server uses for authentication not the local computer name, but the name *localhost* as host name. This means that the MySQL server distinguishes two different entries in the access system, according to whether communication takes place over TCP/IP or a socket file:

username1 / password1 / computername under TCP/IP

username2 / password2 / localhost under socket file

Extensive background information on these special cases and various other problems with host names and in establishing connections in general can be found later in this chapter.

Default Values: If no other parameters are given in establishing a MySQL connection, then under Unix/Linux the current login name is given as user name, while under Windows it is the character string *ODBC*. As password an empty character string is passed. The host name is *localhost*.

You can easily test this. Launch the program mysql and execute the command *status*. The current user name is displayed in the line *current user*. The following commands were executed under Linux:

```
kofler:~ > mysql -p
Enter password: xxx
Welcome to the MySQL monitor.
mysql> status
...
Current user:    kofler@localhost
Connection:      localhost via UNIX socket
```

If in establishing a connection you must provide a user name other than the login name, a host name, and a password, then the start of mysql looks something like this:

```
kofler:~ > mysql -u surveyadmin -h uranus.sol -p
Enter password: xxx
mysql> status
...
Current user:          surveyadmin@saturn.sol
Connection:            uranus.sol via TCP/IP
```

Here we have a TCP/IP connection between the client (computer *saturn.sol*) and the server (computer name *uranus.sol*).

MySQL recognizes the term *anonymous user*. This expression comes into play when any user name is permitted in establishing a connection to MySQL. In this case, *status* shows as *i* the user name used when the connection was established, but internally, an empty character string is used as user name. This is important primarily for the evaluation of additional access privileges. Further background information is contained later in this chapter, where the inner workings of the access system are discussed.

When a PHP script establishes the connection to the database and no other user name is supplied, then what is used as user name is the name of the account under which the PHP interpreter is executed. (As a rule, this is the same account under which Apache is also executed. Thus for security reasons, most Unix/Linux systems use an account that has few privileges, such as *apache* or *wwwrun*.)

Default Security Settings

Depending on how old your MySQL installation is and whether you installed MySQL under Windows or Linux, there are more or less (un)safe default settings for MySQL access administration.

Current Windows versions: Since versions 4.1.5 and 5.0.2, the MySQL server has been distributed together with a new installation program, which was described in Chapter 2. If you followed the instructions in that chapter, your MySQL installation is already relatively secure. The only user with unrestricted privileges is the system manager *root*, who, however, can gain access only from the local computer and must sign in with a password.

Older Windows versions: The default installation under older versions of Windows is much more insecure than the newer versions. Here *root* can log on both from the local computer and over the network, and can do so without a password. Moreover, *all* users of the local system can gain access without a password and have extensive privileges. For example, they can read all databases, alter them, and even completely delete them. Finally, anyone (arbitrary user name, arbitrary computer in the network) can gain access, even though such users have no privileges and cannot do much after establishing a connection.

Unix/Linux: The default settings under Unix/Linux are not as insecure as those under the old Windows installations, but they are by no means secure: *root* can gain access on the local computer without a password. Furthermore, all users on the local system (also with any user name) are permitted to access MySQL without a password; in contrast to *root*, these users have no rights whatsoever (they can't even execute a *SELECT* command). Access from an external computer is by default not allowed.

■**Caution** To make things perfectly clear: As long as *root* is not protected by a password, anyone can gain access to the MySQL server under this name and do whatever he wants with your databases. With old Windows installations it is not even necessary to use the local computer: A connection as *root* is possible over a network. In the next section, on first aid, you will learn how with a little effort you can replace this default setting with something more restrictive.

For those with little experience with Unix/Linux, *root* under Unix/Linux plays somewhat the same role as *Administrator* under Windows, that is, a superuser with almost unrestricted privileges. However, be advised that user names under MySQL have no connection with the login names for the operating system. Thus *root* has so many privileges under MySQL because the MySQL default setting was chosen, not because under Unix/Linux *root* has such privileges. It would have been possible to choose a name other than *root* for the MySQL user with administrative access privileges. In fact, in the interests of security it would be a good idea to replace *root* by a different user name.

You may perhaps be asking yourself where the default security settings come from. These settings are stored in the *mysql* database, which under Windows is created by the MySQL setup program. Under Unix/Linux, the script `mysql_install_db` is executed during RPM installation, which creates and sets up the *mysql* database.

Under Unix/Linux one can execute `mysql_install_db` manually, for example, to re-create the *mysql* database. To do this, the MySQL server must first be stopped. The script must be executed under the same account that is used for executing the MySQL server (usually *mysql*). You can execute `mysql_install_db` also as *root*, in which case you must be the owner of the *mysql* database directory and change the following files contained therein:

```
root# mysql_install_db
root# chown mysql -R /var/lib/mysql/mysql
```

Test Databases: Regardless of the operating system under which MySQL is installed, any user who connects to MySQL can create test databases. The only condition is that the name of the database must begin with *test*. Please note that not only can every MySQL user create such a database, in addition, every user can read, alter, and delete all data in such a database. In fact, anyone can delete the entire database. In short, the data in *test* databases are completely unprotected.

Tables 11-2, 11-3, and 11-5, which appear later in the chapter, depict this default setting. To understand these figures it is necessary that you understand the *mysql* table functions *user* and *db*, which are described in this chapter.

First Aid

Perhaps you are not quite ready to immerse yourself in the depths of SQL access management. In that case, this section provides a bit of first aid advice.

The instructions assume that you communicate with the MySQL server with the commands `mysql` and `mysqladmin` (see Chapter 4). You can, of course, execute equivalent commands with a graphical user interface.

Protecting the MySQL Installation

The following commands assume that you can sign into the MySQL server as *root*:

```
> mysql -u root
Welcome to the MySQL monitor. ...
```

If *root* has been secured with a password, then the above command fails. You must provide the option -p and then you will be asked for the *root* password:

```
> mysql -u root -p
Enter password: xxx
Welcome to the MySQL monitor. ...
```

All further commands relate to the database *mysql*, in which the user settings are stored. (If you execute the commands in mysql, don't forget to provide a semicolon at the end of each command.)

```
USE mysql
```

A *SELECT* command will give you a quick overview of all users. The results will of course probably look different on your computer. When a MySQL server has been in operation a long time and a variety of MySQL users have been defined, this list can be rather long.

```
SELECT user, host, password FROM user
```

user	host	password
root	localhost	
root	uranus.sol	
	uranus.sol	
	localhost	

This means that there are currently four users, none of whom is secured with a password. Here *uranus.sol* is the name of the local system. The following list presents possible steps to take for achieving security:

Set the root password: A simple *UPDATE* command defines a single password for all *root* users, regardless of from where they log on:

```
UPDATE user SET password = PASSWORD('secret') WHERE user = 'root'
```

Replace root with another name: By default, the MySQL user responsible for administration has the name *root*. If someone tries to attack your system, the first thing that will be attempted is to see whether a *root* login without a password is possible or whether the *root* password can be guessed. Therefore, you increase the security of your system considerably if you choose another name besides *root*:

```
UPDATE user SET user = 'myroot' WHERE user = 'root'
```

This has of course the consequence that you must always use this new name when you log in for system administrative tasks. Instead of mysql -u root -p, you must now call yourself mysql -u myroot -p.

Delete anonymous users: For the sake of security, you should delete all anonymous users, that is, those for whom the *user* column is empty. Only those explicitly registered in the MySQL *user* table should be able to log in:

```
DELETE FROM user WHERE user = ''
```

Set a password for every user: In general, the *user* table should contain no user without a password. As database administrator you can give every such user a password known to you with a single *UPDATE* command. This has the effect that the affected users can no longer log into the MySQL server. These users will contact you, and you can set a password for each such user:

```
UPDATE user SET password = PASSWORD(secret) WHERE password = ''
```

Deal with users who can log in from anywhere: A last source of insecurity is the existence of MySQL users who can log in from anywhere. You can recognize such users by the fact that the column *host* contains only a percent sign (%):

```
SELECT user, host, password FROM user WHERE host = '%'
```

There is no general rule for dealing with such users. In individual cases such a user could be allowed this privilege. However, often it would suffice to restrict the permissible network addresses to the local network or a range of IP numbers. (Note, however, that MySQL evaluates IP numbers only when it cannot determine the host names.) The following command allows logins only from the local network (which in this example has the name *sol*):

```
UPDATE user SET host = '%.sol' WHERE host = '%'
```

For all these commands to become effective, you must now execute the command *FLUSH PRIVILEGES*. MySQL keeps a copy of the *mysql* database in RAM, for speed optimization, which is updated via *FLUSH PRIVILEGES*:

```
FLUSH PRIVILEGES
```

Creating a New Database and User

Among the bread-and-butter tasks of a database administrator is setting up a new database and making it available to a user (who then can insert tables and fill them with data).

This task is easily accomplished. You have merely to execute the following two commands with `mysql`. The result is the creation of the database *forum*, to which the user *forumadmin* has been granted unrestricted access.

```
CREATE DATABASE forum
GRANT All ON forum.* TO forumadmin@localhost IDENTIFIED BY 'xxx'
```

It is often useful to create a second access to the database, one with fewer privileges (and therefore with fewer security risks):

```
GRANT Select, Insert, Update, Delete ON forum.*
  TO forumuser@localhost IDENTIFIED BY 'xxx'
```

Depending on the application, it can be a good idea to give ordinary users the ability to lock (*LOCK*) tables, create temporary tables, and execute stored procedures (since MySQL 5.0). The *IDENTIFIED* part was omitted. That is, the password of *forumuser* remains unchanged:

```
GRANT Lock Tables, Create Temporary Tables, Execute ON forum.*
  TO forumuser@localhost
```

When the MySQL server is running under Unix/Linux, *@localhost* allows only one local login over a socket file. If you also wish to allow a local login over TCP/IP (as is required for Java programs), you must also grant privileges (*ALL, SELECT, INSERT,* etc.) for *username@localcomputername*:

```
GRANT ALL            ON forum.* TO forumadmin@rechnername IDENTIFIED BY 'xxx'
GRANT privileges ... ON forum.* TO forumuser@rechnername IDENTIFIED BY 'xxx'
```

Creating New Users

After the database that we have just created, *forum*, has been in operation for a while, it turns out that another individual, operating from another computer, requires unrestricted access to this database. The following command gives user *forumadmin2* on computer *uranus.sol* full privileges:

```
GRANT ALL ON forum.* TO forumadmin2@uranus.sol IDENTIFIED BY 'xxx'
```

If you wish to allow *forumadmin2* to sign in from any computer, then the command looks like this:

```
GRANT ALL ON forum.* TO forumadmin2@'%' IDENTIFIED BY 'xxx'
```

If you wish to go so far as to allow *forumadmin2* access to all databases (and not just *forum*), the command is as follows:

```
GRANT ALL ON *.* TO forumadmin2@uranus.sol IDENTIFIED BY 'xxx'
```

In comparison to *root*, the only privilege that *forumadmin2* does not possess is the right to change access privileges. But a small change remedies the situation:

```
GRANT ALL ON *.* TO forumadmin2@uranus.sol
IDENTIFIED BY 'xxx' WITH GRANT OPTION
```

Now *forumadmin2* has the same privileges as *root*.

Granting the Right to Create One's Own Database

When there are many users each with his or her own databases (for example, on the system of an Internet service provider), it becomes increasingly burdensome for the administrator to create yet another database for a particular user. In such cases it would be a good idea to give this user the right to create databases. In order to prevent a jungle of databases from appearing with no clue as to which belongs to whom, it is usual practice to allow a user to create only databases that begin with that user's user name. That is, a user named, say, *kofler*, is allowed to create databases named, say, *kofler_test*, *kofler_forum*, *kofler1*, *koflerXy*, etc., but no databases whose names do not begin with *kofler*.

In the following, the way to proceed will be demonstrated for a user with the remarkable user name *username*. If this user is not yet known to MySQL, then first it must be created:

```
GRANT USAGE ON *.* TO username@localhost IDENTIFIED BY 'xxx'
```

Then, sad to tell, you must wrestle with an *INSERT* command, since the more convenient *GRANT* command does not, alas, permit wild cards in the specification of database names. Therefore, the necessary changes in the database *db* must be made directly. The allowable database names consist of *username* and arbitrary additional characters usually expressed with %. The relevant columns of the following command are shown in boldface:

```
INSERT INTO mysql.db (Host, Db, User, Select_priv, Insert_priv,
  Update_priv, Delete_priv, Create_priv, Drop_priv, Grant_priv,
  References_priv, Index_priv, Alter_priv, Create_tmp_table_priv,
  Lock_tables_priv, Create_view_priv, Show_view_priv)
VALUES ('localhost', 'username%', 'username', 'Y', 'Y', 'Y', 'Y',
  'Y', 'Y', 'N', 'Y', 'Y', 'Y', 'Y', 'Y', 'Y', 'Y')
```

For these changes to become effective, *FLUSH PRIVILEGES* must finally be executed:

```
FLUSH PRIVILEGES
```

Oops! I Forgot the root Password!

What do you do if you have forgotten the *root* password for MySQL (and there is no other MySQL user with sufficient administrative privileges and a known password to restore the forgotten password)?

Fear not, as the MySQL developers have thought about this possibility. The way to proceed is this: Terminate MySQL (that is, the MySQL server mysqld) and then restart it with the option skip_grant_tables. The result is that the table with access privileges is not loaded. You can now delete the encrypted password for *root*, terminate MySQL, and then restart without the given option. Now you can give the *root* user a new password.

In each case, we assume that you have system administrator privileges on the operating system under which MySQL is running.

The first step is to terminate MySQL. Under Windows, you end MySQL in the Service Manager (SETTINGS | CONTROL PANEL | ADMINISTRATIVE TOOLS | SERVICES). Under Unix/Linux, execute the following command:

```
root# /etc/rc.d/mysql stop
```

Now enter the option skip_grant_tables in the MySQL configuration file in the section [mysqld]. The configuration file is located here: under Unix/Linux, /etc/my.cnf; under Windows, C:\Programs\MySQL\MySQL Server n.n/my.ini:

```
# changes in my.cnf and my.ini
...
[mysqld]
skip_grant_tables
...
```

Then restart the MySQL server, under Windows in the Service Manager dialog mentioned previously, under Unix/Linux with the following command:

```
root# /etc/rc.d/mysql start
```

Now you can use mysql to reset the *root* password both for the host name *localhost* and the actual computer name (only Unix/Linux):

```
root# mysql -u root
Welcome to MySQL monitor.
mysql> USE mysql;
Database changed.
mysql> UPDATE user SET password=PASSWORD('new password')
    > WHERE user='root' AND host='localhost';
Query OK, 1 row affected (0.00 sec)
mysql> UPDATE user SET password=PASSWORD('new password'wort')
    > WHERE user='root' AND host='computername';
Query OK, 1 row affected (0.00 sec)
```

After these changes in the *mysql.user* table, stop the MySQL server again as previously described or else with the command mysqladmin shutdown. Delete again skip_grant_tables from the MySQL configuration database and restart the MySQL server.

■**Caution**   The procedures described here can, of course, be used by an attacker who wishes to spy on your data or manipulate it somehow. The only (fortunately, not easily achieved) condition is to acquire Unix/Linux *root* access (or *administrator* rights under Windows). This shows how important it is not only to secure MySQL, but also the computer on which MySQL is running. (The topic of security under Unix/Linux and Windows is, like any number of other topics, beyond the scope of this book.)

The Internal Workings of the Access System

You may be sorely tempted to skip over this foundational section, especially since the management of access privileges is rather complicated. However, I strongly suggest that you gird up your loins and make the effort to read through the description of the *mysql* tables. Regardless of the means that you use for setting up security on your system, it is helpful first to understand the inner workings of the system itself. This holds even for the case that you yourself are not the manager of access privileges, but that they are managed by a system administrator. It is only when you understand how it all works that you will be able to tell your system administrator just what your needs are.

Two-Tiered Access Control

Access control for MySQL databases is managed in two tiers: First, it is merely checked whether the user has the right to establish a connection to MySQL. This is accomplished by the evaluation of three pieces of information: user name, host name, and password.

Only if a connection can be established does the second level of access control come into play, which involves every single database command. For example, if a *SELECT* is executed, MySQL checks whether the user has access rights to the database, the table, and the column. If an *INSERT* is executed, then MySQL tests whether the user is permitted to alter the database, the table, and finally the column.

Privileges

How, then, does MySQL manage the information as to which commands can be executed? MySQL uses tables in which are stored *privileges*. If a user, let us call her *athena*, has a *Select* privilege for the database *owls*, then she is permitted to read all the data in *owls* (but not to change it). If *athena* has a global *Select* privilege, then it holds for all databases saved under MySQL.

The privileges recognized by MySQL are displayed in Table 11-1. Note that the names in the corresponding columns of *mysql* tables always end in *_priv*. The *Select* privilege is thus stored in the column *Select_priv*. In part, the column names are abbreviated (e.g., *Create_tmp_table* for the *Create Temporary Table* privilege).

■Caution In the past, new privileges were introduced with almost every version of MySQL. In comparison to version 3.23, MySQL 5.0 offers the following new privileges: *Alter Routine, Create Routine, Create Temporary Table, Execute, Lock Tables, Show Databases, Replication Client, Replication Slave, Super.* (A list of all available privileges together with a brief description can be obtained with the command *SHOW PRIVILEGES.*)

If you are updating an older MySQL installation, you must update the *mysql* tables as well so that you can use the new privileges. Under Unix/Linux, the script `mysql_fix_privilege_tables` will be of help, while under Windows, you can use the like-named SQL file (see also Chapter 14).

Table 11-1. *MySQL Privileges*

MySQL Privilege	Meaning
For Access to Tables	
Select	May read data (*SELECT* command).
Insert	May insert new records (*INSERT*).
Update	May change existing data records (*UPDATE*).
Delete	May delete existing records (*DELETE*).
Lock Tables	May lock tables (*LOCK*).
For Changing Databases, Tables, and Views	
Create	May create new databases and tables.
Create Temporary Table	May create temporary tables.
Alter	May rename tables and alter their structure.
Index	May add and delete table indexes.
References	Undocumented; perhaps will allow in the future to set up links between tables.
Drop	May delete existing databases and tables.
Create View	May define views (since MySQL 5.0).
Show View	May inspect view definitions with *SHOW CREATE VIEW* (since MySQL 5.0).
For Stored Procedures (since MySQL 5.0, see Chapter 13)	
Alter Routine	May change existing stored procedures.
Create Routine	May define new stored procedures.
Execute	May execute stored procedures.
For Data Access	
File	May read and alter files of the local file system.
Create User	May create new MySQL users (since MySQL 5.0.3).
For MySQL Administration	
Grant Option	May give other users one's privileges.
Show Databases	May see a list of all databases (*SHOW DATABASES*).
Process	May see the MySQL processes of other users (*SHOW PROCESSLIST*).
Super	May end the MySQL processes of other users (*KILL*), create SPs und triggers, and change and execute some administrative commands (*CHANGE/ PURGE MASTER, SET GLOBAL*).
Reload	May execute various commands (*reload, refresh, flush-xxx*).
Replication Client	May determine information about the participants in a replication system.
Replication Slave	May read data of the MySQL server via replication.
Shutdown	May shut down MySQL.

In the MySQL documentation, you will encounter (for example, in the description of the *GRANT* command) the privileges *All* and *Usage*. *All* means that all privileges should be granted with the exception of *Grant*. *Usage* means that all privileges should be denied.

All and *Usage* are thus themselves not independent privileges, but an aid in avoiding a listing of privileges in executing the *GRANT* command.

The meaning of most of the privileges should be clear without further explanation. For the not-so-clear privileges there will be some explanation in the coming paragraphs. *Replication Client* and *Replication Slave* are described in Chapter 14 in the discussion of replication.

Privileges are given in this book with an initial capital letter followed by lowercase letters in order to distinguish them from their like-named SQL commands (*Select* privilege and *SELECT* command). MySQL couldn't care less how you distribute uppercase and lowercase letters.

The Grant Option Privilege

The *Grant Option* privilege indicates that a MySQL user can dispense access privileges. (This is most easily accomplished with the SQL command *GRANT*, whence the name of the privilege.) However, the ability to dispense privileges is limited to the privileges possessed by the grantor. That is, no user can give privileges to another that he or she does not already possess.

■**Caution** The *Grant Option* privilege is an often overlooked security risk. For example, a test database is created to which all members of a team have unrestricted access. To this end, all the privileges in the relevant entry in the *db* table are set to *Y* (the *db* table will be described a bit later).

A perhaps unforeseen consequence is that everyone who has unrestricted access to this test table can give unrestricted access privileges (either to himself or to other MySQL users) for other databases as well!

The File Privilege

MySQL users with the *File* privilege may use SQL commands for direct access to the file system of the computer on which the MySQL server is running, for example, with the command *SELECT … INTO OUTFILE name* or the command *LOAD DATA* or with the function *LOAD_FILE*.

In the case of file access, it is necessary, of course, to pay heed to the access privileges of the file system. (Under Unix/Linux the MySQL server normally runs under the *mysql* account. Therefore, only those files that are readable by the Unix/Linux user *mysql* can be read.) Nevertheless, the *File* privilege is often a considerable security risk.

The Privileges Process and Super

The *Process* privilege gives the user the right to determine, using the command *SHOW PROCESSLIST*, a list of all processes (connections), including those of other users. (One may obtain a list of one's own processes without this privilege.)

The privilege *Super* permits the user to end both his own and others' processes with *KILL*. (If the *Super* privilege has not been granted, then only the current process can be ended.)

The *Super* privilege also permits the execution of some administrative commands: *CHANGE MASTER* for executing the client configuration of a replication system, *PURGE MASTER* to delete binary logging files, and *SET GLOBAL* for changing global MySQL variables.

Global Privileges Versus Object Privileges

In MySQL privileges can be chosen to be either global or related to a particular object. Global indicates that the privilege is valid for all MySQL objects (that is, for all databases, tables, and columns of a table).

The management of object-related privileges is somewhat more difficult, but it is also more secure. Only thus can you achieve, for example, that a particular MySQL user can alter a particular table, and not all tables managed under MySQL. An assumption in the use of object-related privileges is that the corresponding global privileges are not set. (What is globally allowed cannot be withheld at the object level.)

This hierarchical idea is maintained within the object privileges as well. First it is checked whether access to an entire database is allowed. Only if that is not allowed is it then checked whether access to the entire table named in the SQL command is allowed. Only if that is forbidden is it then checked whether perhaps access to individual columns of the table is allowed.

information_schema Tables

The virtual *information_schema* tables introduced in Chapter 9 are a special case of privilege administration. Everyone who is permitted to log into the MySQL server is permitted to execute *SELECT* queries for such tables. No *Select* privilege is required for this.

The mysql Database

It is not surprising that the management by MySQL of access privileges is carried out by means of a database. This database has the name *mysql*, and it consists of several tables, responsible for various aspects of access privileges.

■**Note** It is sometimes not entirely a simple matter to distinguish among the various uses to which the word "MySQL" is put. In this book we attempt to use different type styles to obtain some degree of clarity:

MySQL: the database system as a whole.

mysqld: the MySQL server (MySQL daemon).

mysql: the MySQL monitor (a type of command interpreter).

mysql: the database for managing MySQL access privileges.

The Tables of the Database mysql

The database *mysql* contains a large number of tables for various administrative tasks. Six tables are for managing access privileges. These tables are often referred to as *grant* tables. Table 11-2 provides an overview of the tasks of these *grant* tables.

Table 11-2. *mysql Tables for Administration of Access Privileges*

Name	Meaning
user	Controls who (user name) can access MySQL from which computer (host name). This table also contains global privileges.
db	Specifies which user can access which databases.
host	Extends the *db* table with information on the permissible host names (those that are not present in *db*).
tables_priv	Specifies who can access which tables of a database.
columns_priv	Specifies who can access which columns of a table.
func	Enables the management of UDFs (*user-defined functions*); this is still undocumented.
procs_priv	Specifies who is permitted to execute individual stored procedures.

When you newly install MySQL, the default values of *user* and *db* depend on the operating system. The contents of these two tables are displayed in Tables 11-4, 11-5, and 11-7, which appear later. The effect of these settings was discussed earlier. (The tables *host*, *tables_priv*, and *columns_priv* start off life empty.)

In MySQL's two-tiered access system, the table *user* is solely responsible for the first level (that is, for the connection to MySQL). The *user* table contains all global privileges.

For the second tier (that is, access to specific objects: databases, tables, and columns) it is the tables *db*, *host*, *tables_priv*, and *columns_priv* that are responsible, in addition to *user*.

The tables *db*, *host*, *tables_priv*, and *columns_priv* come into play in this order when the privileges for their respective tiers are set to *N* (which stands for "No"). In other words, if the *Select* privilege is granted to a user in *user*, then the other four tables will not be consulted in checking the permissibility of a *SELECT* command executed by that user.

The result is that if fine distinctions in access privileges are to be made, the global privileges in the *user* table must be set to *N*.

An Example

Before we attempt to describe the individual tables in detail, we present an example: Let us suppose that a particular MySQL user, let us call him *zeus*, is to be allowed to read a particular column of a particular table, and nothing else. Then *zeus* (with user name, host name, password) must be entered in the *user* table. There all of *zeus*'s global privileges will be set to *N*.

Furthermore, *zeus* (with user name, host name) must be registered in the *columns_priv* table as well. There it must also be specified which column *zeus* is permitted to access (database name, table name, column name). Finally, there the *Select* privilege (and only this privilege) must be activated. In the tables *db*, *host*, and *tables_priv* no entries for *zeus* are necessary.

The user Table

The *user* table (see Table 11-3) fulfills three tasks:

- This table alone regulates who has any access at all to MySQL.

- Global privileges can be granted through this table. Note that the column names of the table differ somewhat from those of the privileges (e.g., the *Create_tmp_table* column for the *Create Temporary Table* privilege).

- Since MySQL 4.0 the table contains several new columns for encrypted access via SSL (secure socket layer), for identity control in accordance with the X509 standard and for managing such control, and for the number of database connections, that is, the maximal number of updates and queries permitted to be executed per hour.

Table 11-3. *Schema of the user Table*

Field	Type	Null	Default
Host	char(60)	No	
User	char(16)	No	
Password	char(45)	No	
Select_priv	enum('N', 'Y')	No	N
Insert_priv	enum('N', 'Y')	No	N
Update_priv	enum('N', 'Y')	No	N

Continued

Table 11-3. *(Continued)*

Field	Type	Null	Default
Delete_priv	enum('N', 'Y')	No	N
Create_priv	enum('N', 'Y')	No	N
Drop_priv	enum('N', 'Y')	No	N
Reload_priv	enum('N', 'Y')	No	N
Shutdown_priv	enum('N', 'Y')	No	N
Process_priv	enum('N', 'Y')	No	N
File_priv	enum('N', 'Y')	No	N
Grant_priv	enum('N', 'Y')	No	N
Create_view_priv	enum('N', 'Y')	No	N
Show_view_priv	enum('N', 'Y')	No	N
References_priv	enum('N', 'Y')	No	N
Index_priv	enum('N', 'Y')	No	N
Alter_priv	enum('N', 'Y')	No	N
Show_db_priv	enum('N', 'Y')	No	N
Super_priv	enum('N', 'Y')	No	N
Create_tmp_table_priv	enum('N', 'Y')	No	N
Lock_tables_priv	enum('N', 'Y')	No	N
Execute_priv	enum('N', 'Y')	No	N
Alter_routine_priv	enum('N', 'Y')	No	N
Create_routine_priv	enum('N', 'Y')	No	N
Create_user_priv	enum('N', 'Y')	No	N
Repl_slave_priv	enum('N', 'Y')	No	N
Repl_client_priv	enum('N', 'Y')	No	N
ssl_type	enum('', 'ANY', 'X509', 'SPECIFIED')	No	0
ssl_cipher	blob	No	0
x509_issuer	blob	No	0
x509_subject	blob	No	0
max_questions	int	No	0
max_updates	int	No	0
max_connections	int	No	0
max_user_connections	int	No	0

Access Control (User, Host, and Password Columns)

For control over who can connect to MySQL there are three necessary identifiers—as we have mentioned already several times—that must be evaluated: user name, host name, and password. Here we shall say a few words about how this information is stored in the fields *User*, *Host*, and *Password*.

User Name: Access control is case-sensitive. In the *User* field no wild cards are allowed. If the *User* field is empty, then any user name is permitted for accessing MySQL. Then the user is considered to be an anonymous user. This means that in the second tier of access control the actual user name is not used, but rather an empty character string.

Password: The password must be stored in the column *Password* and there be encrypted with the SQL function *PASSWORD*. It is not possible to store a password in plain text. Furthermore, wild cards are not allowed. If the password field remains empty, then a connection can be made with no password whatsoever. (An empty password field thus does not mean that an arbitrary password can be given.)

With MySQL 4.1 the encryption of the *Password* column has changed. The encrypted code of the password contains 45 characters (in earlier versions of MySQL it was only 16 characters).

Be thou once more warned: For reasons of security you should never use as your MySQL password a password that you use to gain admittance to the operating system.

Host Name: The host name can be given either as a name or as an IP number. Here the wild cards _ (an arbitrary character) or % (zero or more characters) are permitted, for example, *192.168.37.%* or *%.myfavoriteenterprise.com*. In the case of IP numbers, the forms (which are equivalent to those of the first example) *192.168.37.0/255.255.255.0* and *192.168.37.0/24* are permitted. If the host name is given simply as the character %, a connection can be made from any computer. As with the user name, the host name is case-sensitive.

To enable access on the local computer, give *localhost* as the host name. When Unix/Linux users wish to obtain local access via TCP/IP (important for Java applications), then the actual computer name must be used as the host name. If both forms of access are to be enabled, then the user must be defined twice, once with the host name *localhost*, and once with *computername*.

■**Tip** Normally, the host name must be given together with the domain name. Thus if the computer *saturn.sol* wants to gain access from the network **.sol*, the column *Host* in the *user* table must contain the character string *saturn.sol* and not just *saturn*. Depending on your network configuration (file /etc/hosts or the configuration of an existing domain name server), it could be that one has to specify the host name without the domain name. Further details on this and other picky details will be discussed further along in this chapter.

The Order of Evaluation in the user Table

It often happens that in making a connection to MySQL several records match the given login data. If, for example, you log in as *root* from the local computer under the default settings of the *user* table for Windows (Table 11-5), then all four entries would match. MySQL then decides in favor of the most nearly exact description (thus in this case for *root/localhost* and not for "%). The reason for this is that with an exact match in the login one can expect more in the way of access privileges.

In order to speed up the selection of the correct record, the *user* table is sorted internally by MySQL. Here the field *Host* serves as the first sort criterion, and *User* as the second. In sorting, those character strings without the wild cards _ and % are given priority. Empty character strings and the character string % come in last in the sort order. Tables 11-4 and 11-5 show the default settings for the *user* table in their respective internal sort orders.

■**Caution** The order in which the entries in the *user* table are evaluated often leads to unexpected problems. Suppose that the MySQL default settings hold for user privileges and that you add a new user with *Host* = '%' and *User* = 'peter' in the *user* table. If *peter* now attempts to register from the local computer (that is, from *localhost*), it is not the entry %/'peter' that comes into play, but the entry from the default setting *Host* = 'localhost' and *User* = ''. The reason is that MySQL gives precedence to entries with a unique hostname (*Host* = 'localhost') over those with a wild card (*Host*='%').

The easiest and surest way out of this difficulty is to delete the entry *Host* = 'localhost' and *User* = '' from the *user* table. In general, for security, you should avoid entries whose *User* column is empty.

Privileges

The *user* table is responsible not only for access control for MySQL, but also for global privileges. To this end there are currently countless *xxx_priv* fields that take part, which can be set to *Y* or *N*. Since *Y* stands for "yes," this setting means that the associated privilege is set globally for the MySQL user (for all databases, tables, and columns). Contrariwise, *N* means "no" (or *non* in French, *nein* in German, *nyet* in Russian; you get the idea), and so such a setting means that the operation in question is not allowed globally, and therefore the tables *db*, *host*, *tables_priv*, and *columns_priv* will be consulted for object-specific privileges.

SSL Encryption and X509 Identification

To make communication between client and server particularly secure, the X509 standard can be used for user identification, and data transfer can be effected with SSL (secure socket layer) encryption. This requires a special compiled version of the MySQL server such as MySQL Max. (The SSL functions are not currently integrated into MySQL Standard.) Whether your version of MySQL supports SSL can be determined with the SQL command *SHOW VARIABLES LIKE 'have_openssl'*.

Note that the encryption of data affects the speed of the MySQL server and makes sense only if data transfer is taking place over the Internet, that is, if the MySQL server and the client are running on different computers.

The encryption of a local connection (if, for example, PHP/Apache accesses a MySQL server that is running on the same computer) does not increase the security of the application. In this case, the security is much more greatly determined by how communication between Apache and the web user takes place (e.g., encryption via HTTPS).

■**Tip** This book does not go into details of the configuration and application of SSL and X509. More extensive information can be found at http://dev.mysql.com/doc/mysql/en/secure-connections.html.

Restriction of MySQL Use

With the columns *max_questions* and *max_updates* you can specify how many queries (*SELECT* commands) and data changes (*INSERT* and *UPDATE*) are permitted to be executed per hour; *max_connections* specifies how many connections can be established per hour; *max_user_connections*, new in MySQL 5.0, limits the number of simultaneous connections that an individual user can have. The default setting 0 means that there are no restrictions.

Default Setting

As was described in the introduction to this chapter, after installation of MySQL there are various default settings of the *user* table that depend on the particular operating system. Tables 11-4 and 11-5 give these settings (for MySQL version 5.0.*n*).

Table 11-4. *Default Setting for the user Table under Unix/Linux*

Host	User	Password	Select_priv to Alter_priv	Super_priv to Repl_client_priv	ssl_xxx, x509_xxx	max_xxx
localhost	*root*		Y	Y	NULL	0
computername	*root*		Y	Y	NULL	0
localhost			N	N	NULL	0
computername			N	N	NULL	0

Table 11-5. *Default Setting for the user Table under Windows*

Host	User	Password	Select_priv bis Alter_priv	Super_priv bis Repl_client_priv	ssl_xxx, x509_xxx	max_xxx
localhost	*root*	xxxxxx	Y	Y	NULL	0

Note that Table 11-5 holds only for current MySQL installations, and then only if the installation was carried out as described in Chapter 2. For older MySQL installations under Windows, a default setting was used that was even more insecure than that under Unix/Linux.

The user.Host Column

As briefly mentioned in the previous section, the *Host* column of the *user* table specifies from which computer a particular user is to obtain access to the MySQL server. The computer name can be given with the wild card % or by an IP number.

What looks simple at first glance is, alas, in practice a source of numerous problems. Therefore, this section contains various pieces of background information and some tips for solving connection problems.

Note that the problems mentioned here do not always occur. It depends primarily on the network configuration, that is, on a factor outside of the MySQL server.

Host Name with or without Domain Name?

When you insert a new entry in the *user* table, the question arises whether the host name should appear with or without the domain name, that is, for example, *uranus* or *uranus.sol*. Which variant is correct depends on how the MySQL server resolves the network name. I have made the discovery that the probability of success is higher if you include the domain name. (The resolution of network names depends on the file /etc/hosts and, to the extent available, the configuration of a domain name server running in the local network, thus on factors that lie outside of MySQL.)

Depending on the network settings, it can happen that during installation of the MySQL server, the column *user.Host* is entered without domain name. This is due to the script mysql_install_db. If MySQL evaluates the complete network name in establishing a connection, then a local connection under TCP/IP is impossible. The problem is that mysql -u root is functioning, but mysql -u root -h *computername* is not.

In this case, you have to change the domain name explicitly. The necessary commands look like those below (of course, you will have to change *uranus.sol* and *uranus* to the names that apply in your situation):

```
root# mysql -u root
mysql> USE mysql;
mysql> UPDATE user SET host="uranus.sol"
WHERE host="uranus";
mysql> FLUSH PRIVILEGES;
```

computername Versus localhost Under Unix/Linux

When the MySQL server is executed under Unix/Linux, the default security settings provide two entries for local access to the server: *localhost* and *computername* (see Table 11-4). The reason for this dualism is that connections between the client program and the MySQL server running on the same computer can take place in two ways: over a socket file or via the network protocol TCP/IP.

If you launch the program mysql on the same computer as the MySQL server, you can test both connection options: If you do not specify a host name or if you give *localhost* as host name, the connection succeeds over the socket file (first and second commands below). The same holds as well if you use the option --protocol=socket (variant three).

If, on the other hand, you specify the actual computer name or the IP address, the connection proceeds over TCP/IP (fourth through eighth commands). You can use the command *status* to determine how the connection actually is made:

```
linux:~ $ mysql               -u root -p     via socket file (1)
linux:~ $ mysql -h localhost  -u root -p                     (2)
linux:~ $ mysql -h localhost  -u root -p --protocol=socket   (3)

linux:~ $ mysql -h uranus     -u root -p        via TCP/IP (4)
linux:~ $ mysql -h uranus.sol -u root -p                     (5)
linux:~ $ mysql -h 127.0.0.1  -u root -p                     (6)
linux:~ $ mysql -h 192.168.0.2 -u root -p                    (7)
linux:~ $ mysql -h uranus     -u root -p --protocol=tcp      (8)
Welcome to the MySQL monitor. ...
mysql> status
...
Connection:           uranus via TCP/IP
TCP port:             3306
```

localhost Problems with Red Hat Linux and Fedora Core

With Red Hat Linux and Fedora Core it can be necessary, in rare cases, to enter *localhost.localdomain* in the *Host* column of the *user* table for local TCP/IP connections (instead of the otherwise usual computer name). The reason is that with Red Hat, the IP address 127.0.0.1 is linked to the name *localhost.localdomain* (file /etc/hosts).

localhost Problems with SUSE

With SUSE as well there can be problems, in rare cases, with *localhost*. The reason is that after the execution of a network configuration, the line *127.0.0.2 computername* is entered in /etc/hosts. This line can cause confusion if *computername* is associated with a different IP address. Such problems generally occur in this case as well only when a local TCP/IP connection is sought. There are several options for alleviating this problem:

- As a first attempt, you should try to specify the complete computer name (including domain name) in the *Host* table. At least in my configuration, this was sufficient for establishing a local TCP/IP connection in spite of the 127.0.0.2 line in /etc/hosts.

- If that doesn't work, you can enter the IP number 127.0.0.2 in the *Host* column instead of the computer name. This should usually work, but it actually only alleviates the symptom, and does not get at the cause.

- A third variant is to specify the complete computer name in the *Host* column and to comment out the 127.0.0.2 line in /etc/hosts (by prefixing a # sign). Then you must restart the network and the MySQL server, so that the changes can take effect and so that the MySQL server will no longer use temporary storage for name resolution:

```
root# /etc/init.d/network restart
root# /etc/init.d/mysql    stop
```

The main disadvantage of this variant is that there can now be compatibility problems with other SUSE packages that may depend on the SUSE standard configuration.

Establishing the Host Name and IP Address Under Unix/Linux

You can determine the current computer name with the command hostname. With hostname -f you get the entire computer name, including the domain name. If you pass this computer name to the command host, the complete computer name (including domain name) and associated IP address will be returned. Conversely, host can return a computer name given an IP address:

```
linux:~ $ hostname
uranus
linux:~ $ hostname -f
uranus.sol
linux:~ $ host uranus.sol
uranus.sol. has address 192.168.0.2
linux:~ $ host 192.168.0.2
2.0.168.192.in-addr.arpa. domain name pointer uranus.sol.
```

In addition to host, you can also use the command resolveip, which is installed with MySQL. The MySQL server uses the same algorithm as resolveip in resolving network names and IP addresses. If resolveip and host give different results, there is a problem in the configuration. The most likely source of error is the file /etc/hosts or an incorrect configuration of the domain name server (DNS) if one is used in the local network:

```
linux:~ $ resolveip uranus
IP address of uranus is 192.168.0.2

linux:~ $ resolveip uranus.sol
IP address of uranus is 192.168.0.2

linux:~ $ resolveip 192.168.0.2
Host name of 192.168.0.2 is uranus.sol
```

■**Tip** The MySQL server takes care by default of the ordering of IP numbers and host names (so that repeated accesses can take place as rapidly as possible). If you change the network configuration, you must delete this temporary storage: root# **mysqladmin flush-hosts**.

Host Name or IP Address?

In principle, in the *Host* column you can specify the computer's IP address instead of the computer name. The advantage of IP numbers is that the numerous sources of error in name resolution no longer exist. However, this advantage is paid for in the drawback that in many networks, IP numbers frequently change (in some circumstances at each restart if the IP number is assigned dynamically by a DHCP server). Therefore, controlling access on the basis of IP addresses can succeed only if the management of IP addresses in your network is organized relatively strictly.

If there exist equivalent entries in the *user* table that differ only in that one has an IP number and the other an associated computer name, then the entry with the computer name takes precedence.

The db and host Tables

The db Table

The *db* table (see Table 11-6) contains information on which databases a particular user is permitted to read, edit, and delete. The function of this table is easy to understand: If user *u* located at computer *h* wishes to access database *d* by executing a *SELECT* command and does not possess a global *Select* privilege, then MySQL pores over the *db* table and looks for the first *User/Host/Db* entry for the triple *u/h/d*. (As we saw in the case of the *user* table, uniquely identifying entries take precedence over those with wild cards. The entries are case-sensitive.) If a matching entry is found, then all that must be checked is whether the column *Select_priv* contains the value *Y*.

Table 11-6. *The Schema for the db Table*

Field	Type	Null	Default
Host	char(60)	No	—
Db	char(64)	No	—
User	char(16)	No	—
Select_priv	enum('N', 'Y')	No	N
Insert_priv	enum('N', 'Y')	No	N
Update_priv	enum('N', 'Y')	No	N
Delete_priv	enum('N', 'Y')	No	N
Create_priv	enum('N', 'Y')	No	N
Drop_priv	enum('N', 'Y')	No	N
Grant_priv	enum('N', 'Y')	No	N
References_priv	enum('N', 'Y')	No	N
Index_priv	enum('N', 'Y')	No	N
Alter_priv	enum('N', 'Y')	No	N
Create_tmp_table_priv	enum('N', 'Y')	No	N
Lock_tables_priv	enum('N', 'Y')	No	N
Create_view_priv	enum('N', 'Y')	No	N
Show_create_priv	enum('N', 'Y')	No	N
Create_routine_priv	enum('N', 'Y')	No	N
Alter_routine_priv	enum('N', 'Y')	No	N
Execute_priv	enum('N', 'Y')	No	N

In order for security control to be executed quickly, MySQL maintains various *mysql* tables presorted in RAM. However, this has the consequence that direct changes in these tables become active only when MySQL is ordered to reread these tables with *FLUSH PRIVILEGES* or mysqladmin reload.

Practically the same rules as in the *user* table hold for the settings of *User* and *Host* in the *db* table. The only exception relates to the *Host* column: If this remains empty, then MySQL evaluates the *host* table as well (see the heading "The *host* Table").

Default Setting

After installation of MySQL, all users (those who are able to access MySQL) are permitted to set up, edit, and delete the database *test* as well as databases whose names begin with *test_*. (Under Windows, the underscore in the database name is not required.) This default setting is supposed to allow a non-bureaucratic testing of MySQL without the beleaguered system administrator having to set up such databases.

An obvious problem with this arrangement is that anyone with access to MySQL has the right to create a database and stuff it with data and then stuff it some more until the computer's hard drive is full.

Table 11-7 shows the default setting for the *db* table. Please note in particular that for *test* databases all privileges except for *Grant*, *Alter_routine*, and *Execute_priv* are set. *Grant='n'* is important, so that privileges from the *test* databases cannot be transferred to other databases.

Table 11-7. *Default Setting of the db Table*

Host	Db	User	Select_priv, Insert_priv, etc.	Grant_priv, Alter_routine, Execute_priv
%	test		Y	N
%	test_%		Y	N

■**Note** Have you understood the privileges system of MySQL? Then see whether you can answer the following question:

Can a MySQL user create and edit a *test* database even if all global privileges are set to *N*?

The answer is yes, of course. If all the global privileges are set to *N*, then the object-specific privileges are consulted (where every database that begins with *test* is considered an object). This is precisely the concept of the privilege system of MySQL.

The host Table

The *host* table (see Table 11-8) is an extension of the *db* table if the latter's *Host* field is empty. In this case, entries for the database in question are sought in the *host* table. If an entry that matches the computer name is found there, the privilege settings in *db* and *host* are joined with a logical *AND* (that is, privileges must be granted in both tables).

The *host* table is brought into play relatively rarely. (As a rule, the settings of the *db* table meet all requirements.) This is also expressed in the fact that the commands *GRANT* and *REVOKE*, introduced below, do not affect the *host* table. Thus the *host* table is empty in the default setting.

Table 11-8. *Schema of the host Table*

Field	Type	Null	Default
Host	char(60)	No	
Db	char(64)	No	
Select_priv	enum('N', 'Y')	No	N
Insert_priv	enum('N', 'Y')	No	N
...			
Show_create_priv	enum('N', 'Y')	No	N

The tables_priv and columns_priv Tables

With the tables *tables_priv* (see Table 11-9) and *columns_priv* (see Table 11-10) privileges can be set for individual tables and columns. For *Host* and *User* the same rules hold as for the *user* table. In the fields *Db*, *Table_name*, and *Column_name*, on the other hand, no wild cards are permitted. All the fields except *Column_name* are case-sensitive.

Table 11-9. *Schema of the tables_priv Table*

Field	Type	Null	Default
Host	char(60)	No	
Db	char(64)	No	
User	char(16)	No	
Table_name	char(64)	No	
Table_priv	set1	No	
Column_priv	set2	No	
Timestamp	timestamp	Yes	
Grantor	char(77)		

Table 11-10. *Schema of the columns_priv Table*

Field	Type	Null	Default
Host	char(60)	No	
Db	char(64)	No	
User	char(16)	No	
Table_name	char(64)	No	
Column_name	char(64)	No	
Column_priv	set2	No	
Timestamp	timestamp	Yes	
Grantor	char(77)		

In the undocumented column *Grantor* is stored information as to who has granted the access rights (for example, *root@localhost*).

Unlike the tables described above, these tables have their privileges managed by two sets. (Sets are a peculiarity of MySQL; see also Chapter 8. With sets an arbitrary combination of all character strings specified by set definitions can be stored.) The two sets for *tables_priv* and *columns_priv* look like this:

```
set1: SET('Select', 'Insert', 'Update', 'Delete', 'Create', 'Drop',
          'Grant', 'References', 'Index', 'Alter')
set2: SET('Select', 'Insert', 'Update', 'References')
```

Here *set2* contains only those privileges that hold for individual columns. (The *Delete* privilege is missing, because only an entire data record can be deleted, not an individual field of a record. This field can, of course, be set to *NULL*, 0, or ", but for that the *Update* privilege suffices.)

It is my sad duty to report that it is not documented as to when in the table *tables_priv* the field *Table_priv* is to be used and when the field *Column_priv*. If one considers how the fields are changed by the SQL command *GRANT*, one may venture the following hypotheses:

- Privileges that relate to the entire table are stored in the field *Table_priv*.

- Privileges that relate to individual columns are stored in the field *Column_priv*, as well as in the *tables_priv* and *columns_priv* tables. The *tables_priv* table is to a certain extent a conglomeration of all privileges for which there are additional details in the *columns_priv* table (perhaps divided over several data records). The reason for this is probably the idea that evaluating both tables leads to simplification or increased speed for MySQL.

If possible, use the commands *GRANT* and *REVOKE* for setting column privileges.

The procs_priv Table

The *procs_priv* table (Table 11-11) has been available since MySQL 5.0.3. It governs who can execute which stored procedures. The table is relevant only for users who have no privileges for executing and altering stored procedures on the global level (*user* table) or the table level (*db* table). In such cases the *procs_priv* table offers the possibility to allow a user to execute or change particular stored procedures.

Table 11-11. *The Schema of the procs_priv Table*

Field	Type	Null	Default
Host	char(60)	No	
Db	char(64)	No	
User	char(16)	No	
Routine_name	char(64)	No	
Proc_priv	set('Execute', 'Alter Routine', 'Grant')	No	
Timestamp	timestamp(14)	Yes	
Grantor	char(77)		

Tools for Setting Access Privileges

One can edit the tables of a database (assuming, of course, that you have the appropriate access privileges) with the usual SQL commands *INSERT*, *UPDATE*, and *DELETE*. However, that is a tiring and error-prone occupation. It is much more convenient to use the commands *GRANT* and

REVOKE, which are the centerpiece of this section. More convenient are graphical user interfaces such as MySQL Administrator and phpMyAdmin, described in Chapters 5 and 6.

■**Caution** MySQL maintains, for reasons of speed optimization, copies of the *mysql* tables in RAM. Direct changes to the tables are effective only if they are explicitly reread by MySQL via the SQL command *FLUSH PRIVILEGES* or the external program `mysqladmin reload`. (With *GRANT* and *REVOKE* this rereading takes place automatically.)

Changing Access Privileges with GRANT and REVOKE

The syntax of the *GRANT* and *REVOKE* commands, in simplified form, is as follows:

```
GRANT    privileges
ON       [database.]table  or  database.spname
TO       user@host [IDENTIFIED BY 'password']
[WITH GRANT OPTION]
REVOKE privileges
ON       [database.]table  or  database.spname
FROM     user@host
```

If you wish to change the access privileges for all the tables of a database, the correct form to use is *ON database.**. If you wish to alter global privileges, then specify *ON *.**. It is not allowed to use wild cards in database names.

For *user* you can specify *"* to indicate all users on a particular computer (for example, *"@computername*). On the other hand, for *host* you must use *'%'* (for example, *username@'%'*).

Depending on their function, these commands change the *mysql* tables *user*, *db*, *tables_priv*, *columns_priv*, and *procs_priv*. (The *host* table remains untouched.)

■**Tip** The complete syntax of *GRANT* and *REVOKE* is given in Chapter 21. However, you can get a fairly good feel for these commands from the following examples.

Registering New Users

All users with the computer name **.myorganization.com* are permitted to link to MySQL if they know the password *xxx*. The privilege *Usage* means that all global privileges have been set to *N*. The users thereby at first have no privileges whatsoever (to the extent that so far no individual databases, tables, or columns have been made accessible to all users who can log into MySQL):

```
GRANT Usage ON *.* TO '@'%.mycompany.com' IDENTIFIED BY 'xxx'
```

The following command gives the user *admin* on the local computer unrestricted privileges. All privileges (including *Grant*) are set:

```
GRANT All ON *.* TO admin@localhost IDENTIFIED BY 'xxx'
WITH GRANT OPTION
```

Enabling Access to a Database

The following command gives the user *peter* on the local computer the right to read and alter data in all tables of the database *mylibrary*. If *peter@localhost* is unknown to the *user* table of the *mysql* database, then this name is added without a password. (If there is already a *peter@localhost*, then the password is not changed.)

```
GRANT Select, Insert, Update, Delete
ON mylibrary.* TO peter@localhost
```

If you wish to add to *peter*'s privileges the right to lock tables, create temporary tables, and execute stored procedures (which is useful in many applications), the command looks like this:

```
GRANT Select, Insert, Update, Delete, Create Temporary Tables,
    Lock Tables, Execute
ON mylibrary.* TO peter@localhost
```

Prohibiting Changes in a Database

The next command takes away from *peter* the right to make changes to *mylibrary*, but *peter* retains the right to read the database using *SELECT* (assuming that the command of the previous example was just executed).

```
REVOKE Insert, Update, Delete
ON mylibrary.* FROM peter@localhost
```

Enabling Access to a Table

With the following command the user *kahlila* on the local computer is given the right to read data from the table *authors* in the database *mylibrary* (but not to alter it):

```
GRANT Select ON mylibrary.authors TO kahlila@localhost
```

Enabling Access to Individual Columns

The access privileges for *katherine* are more restrictive than those for *kahlila*: She is permitted only to read the columns *title* and *subtitle* of the table *books* in the database *mylibrary*.

```
GRANT Select(title, subtitle) ON mylibrary.books TO kathrine@localhost
```

Granting Database Access to All Local Users

All users on the local computer can read and edit data in the *mp3* database:

```
GRANT Select, Insert, Delete, Update ON mp3.* TO ''@localhost
```

Viewing Access Privileges with SHOW GRANT

If you have lost track of which privileges a particular user has, the command *SHOW GRANTS* is just what you need:

```
SHOW GRANTS FOR peter@localhost
  Grants for peter@localhost:
  GRANT SELECT ON mylibrary.* TO 'peter'@'localhost'

SHOW GRANTS FOR testuser@localhost
  GRANT USAGE ON *.* TO 'testuser'@'localhost'
    IDENTIFIED BY PASSWORD 'xxxxxxxxxxxxxxxxxx'
  GRANT SELECT, INSERT, UPDATE, DELETE,
    CREATE TEMPORARY TABLES, LOCK TABLES
    ON 'myforum'.* TO 'ptestuser'@'localhost'
```

Changing a Password with mysqladmin

The program mysqladmin carries out various administrative tasks (see also Chapters 4 and 14). Although this program does not offer any immediate assistance in managing access privileges, it enables changing a password. This gives ordinary MySQL users without *root* privileges a simple way to change their passwords. (Of course, the current password must be known.)

```
> mysqladmin -u peter -p password newPW
Enter password: oldPW
```

The above command changes the password for the user *peter* on the computer *localhost*. Please note that the new password is passed as a parameter, while the old password is entered on request. (This order, first the new and then the old, is rather unusual.)

If the MySQL server is running under Unix/Linux and the test user *peter* has local access via TCP/IP, then you must also change the password for the computer name. (As already mentioned, *mysql.user* contains, under Unix/Linux, two entries from local users, one as *hostname='localhostl'* for the socket file, and one as *hostname='computername'* for TCP/IP.)

```
> mysqladmin -u peter -p -h uranus.sol password newPW
Enter password: oldPW
```

Since MySQL 4.1, the MySQL server has used a new procedure for password encryption, which will be described in the following section. If for reasons of compatibility you wish to use the old encryption method, then use mysqladmin old-password:

```
> mysqladmin -u peter -p old-password newPW
Enter password: oldPW
```

Secure Password Authentication Since MySQL 4.1

Since MySQL 4.1, the MySQL server uses by default an improved method for password encryption. The text length of the *password* column in the table *mysql.user* has been enlarged to 45 characters (previously 16). The number of characters refers to the encrypted code, and not the password itself. In the *password* column the password is not stored in plain text, but in an encrypted form.

At the same time, the authentication protocol has changed by which the client program transmits the password to the MySQL server. This transmission of the password now takes place in encrypted form, while previously, it was in plain text.

Both of these measures improve the security of the MySQL authentication. However, they are also the reason that countless MySQL applications suddenly fail to function properly after a MySQL server update. The error message is the typical: *Client does not support authentication protocol requested by server.*

In this section I will describe various possibilities for getting around this difficulty. Further information can be found at http://dev.mysql.com/doc/mysql/en/old-client.html.

Updating the Client Libraries

The best solution to the problem consists in installing a new version of the client libraries. However, this recommendation is easier to state than to carry out: With Linux installations, manual intervention into the PHP or Perl installation is very difficult when the distributor does not offer a suitable update, and that is seldom the case. If you don't want to migrate to a newer distribution, you can attempt to install a package from another distribution. But this can result in unavoidable dependency conflicts in the Linux package management, whose solution requires a great deal of Linux know-how. The other alternative consists in compiling the program in question. Only Linux pros will be able to do so.

The following list tells from which version on, the various programming languages are compatible with the new MySQL authentication:

C: You need `libmysqlclient` from version 14.

Perl: You need the module `perl-DBD-MySQL` in version 2.9004 or higher.

PHP with mysql interface: PHP 5.0.3.

PHP with mysqli interface: PHP 5.0.0.

Java: You must use Connector/J at least version 3.1.

ODBC: You must use Connector/ODBC at least version 3.51.10.

Furthermore, the client libraries are capable of communicating with newer MySQL servers (that is, they manage both the old and the new authentication). Therefore, an update is backward compatible.

old-passwords Mode

If an update of the client libraries is impossible, you can run the MySQL server in *old-passwords* mode. To do so, enter in the MySQL configuration file `my.cnf` or `my.ini` the option `old-passwords` in the section [`mysqld`]. After a restart, the MySQL server behaves as though it were version 4.0:

- The function *PASSWORD* encrypts passwords according to the old algorithm.

- The SQL command *GRANT* uses the old algorithm for encryption.

- The MySQL server accepts the old authentication protocol for logins.

Note that this option holds only for the definition of new passwords. Existing passwords remain unchanged and must be re-created. (If that is not done, the MySQL server demands, despite the *old-passwords* mode, an authentication based on the new protocol.)

Parallel Operation with Old and New Passwords

The *old-passwords* mode has the obvious drawback that the security improvements of MySQL 4.1 go unused. If on your system only a few users rely on the old authentication protocol, while the rest of the users are able to use other programming languages and the new authentication method, then a parallel operation with both the old and new passwords recommends itself. In that case, no change in `my.cnf` or `my.ini` is required, and thus the option `old-passwords` must not be used.

The MySQL server decides, based on the length of the password, whether the old or new authentication protocol is to be used. For passwords whose encrypted code is only sixteen characters long, the old method is used, while for longer passwords, it is the new one.

The only problem with parallel operation is that you, as database administrator, must take care how you define passwords. For users who rely on the old method, you must define passwords with the function *OLD_PASSWORD('secret')* or `mysqladmin old-password`. If you use the SQL command *GRANT*, then leave out the part *IDENTIFIED BY* and insert the password manually. The following lines demonstrate how this is done:

```
GRANT ALL ON databasename.* TO newuser@localhost
UPDATE mysql.user SET password = OLD_PASSWORD('secret')
WHERE user='newuser' AND host='localhost'
FLUSH PRIVILEGES
```

Problems with Establishing a Connection

If you experience connection problems, regardless of what programming language you are using, you should first perform a test interactively with the program mysql to determine whether you can establish a connection. Only when that succeeds is it worthwhile pursuing a search for the cause of the error in the program that you are using or developing.

Changes to access privileges or to the *mysql* database become effective only after *FLUSH PRIVILEGES* is executed (or after a restart of the MySQL server). Many administration programs with dialogs for user management do not automatically execute *FLUSH PRIVILEGES*.

Therefore, if you have changed access privileges but see no result, execute in mysql as *root* the command *FLUSH PRIVILEGES* (or the equivalent mysqladmin flush-privileges).

In the case of an existing connection, changes made may take effect in part only after a new login, despite the execution of *FLUSH PRIVILEGES*. The following rules are in effect:

- Changed global privileges will go into effect only after a new connection is made.

- Changed database privileges go into effect only after the command *USE table* is executed.

- Changed table and column privileges go into effect at the next SQL command.

Possible Causes of the Connection Difficulty

The following list gives the typical causes of problems in establishing connections. Note that a particular error message can arise from one of several different causes.

The MySQL server does not run: If you attempt a connection with mysql, you obtain error 2002 (*Can't connect to MySQL server on 'hostname'*) or error 2003 (*Can't connect to local MySQL server through socket /var/lib/mysql/mysql.sock*).

Under Windows, you can tell whether the server is running by looking in the task manager, while under Unix you use the command ps | grep -i mysql. As result, a list of processes should appear (since the server divides itself into a number of processes for reasons of efficiency). If that does not occur, then the server must be started (under Linux with the command /etc/init.d/mysql[d] start).

The client program does not find the socket file: Under Unix/Linux, communication takes place mostly over a socket file if server and client are running on the same computer. For this to function, both programs must agree on the location of this file. When problems arise, you should ensure that there is an entry socket=filename in the configuration file /etc/my.cnf in the section [client], where filename specifies the actual location of the socket file. Normally, this file has the name /var/lib/mysql/mysql.sock.

The client program cannot access the socket file (SELinux): Many Linux distributions (e.g., RHEL 4) are configured in such a way that Apache cannot access files outside the htdocs directory. Therefore, PHP or a Perl CGI script cannot use the MySQL socket file. The previously mentioned error 2002 is triggered. The remedy: Communicate via TCP/IP or deactivate SELinux for Apache (under RHEL with system-config-security).

The network connection between client and server is broken: If your program is running on a different computer from that of the MySQL server, execute on the client computer the command ping serverhostname to test whether a connection to the server computer exists. If that is not the case, you must first repair the network configuration.

MySQL accepts no connections over the network (over TCP/IP): This can be achieved with the option *–skip-networking* or a corresponding setting in my.cnf. This setting is often chosen to give MySQL maximum security. A database connection is then available only from the local computer and only via a socket file.

The problem is generally recognizable from error 2003 (*Can't connect to MySQL server*). A solution is to remove the option my.cnf from the start script.

MySQL accepts no connections from your computer: This problem generally arises when the MySQL server is running on the computer of an Internet service provider. There the server is generally so configured that only connections from local computers (or a local network) are allowed. For administration you must therefore either create a telnet/ssh connection or use a program that is executed locally on the server and is served via the internet (e.g., phpMyAdmin).

Name resolution of host names does not work correctly: In establishing a connection over a network, error 1130 arises (*Host n.n.n.n' is not allowed to connect to this MySQL server*). The most likely cause of this error is either the incorrect specification of the host name in the *mysql.user* table or an incorrect name-server configuration. Depending on the network configuration, the host names must be given in the column *user.Host* with or (more seldom) without domain name.

A solution is to add domain names to the host names in the *mysql.user* table (*uranus* ➤ *uranus.sol*) or to remove this (*uranus.sol* ➤ *uranus*) and try again. (Do not forget *FLUSH PRIVILEGES*.)

If that does not work, you can test with the commands hostname, host, and resolveip whether there are problems with name resolution. An emergency solution that almost always works (but is inflexible) is to give the IP number instead of the host name in the *user.Host* column. There are many other suggestions about dealing with host-name problems earlier in this chapter.

User name or password is incorrect: Watch out for typos! Note as well that not only user name and password must correspond, but the host name as well. (Thus a connection is usually possible only from certain specific computers.) Also, read the previous point relating to resolution of the host name; perhaps that is where the problem resides.

Note that the *user.Password* column does not contain passwords in plain text, but in encrypted form. If you wish to change a password with SQL commands, you must use the function *PASSWORD("xxx")*.

The client program uses an old MySQL library for password authentication: The error message *Client does not support authentication protocol requested by server* results from an attempt to create a connection to a MySQL server 4.1 or higher while your client program is geared to a MySQL server 4.0 or below. With MySQL 4.1 an improved password encryption algorithm and new authentication protocol were introduced, which unfortunately are incompatible with the old protocol. The solution is to update the client program and its MySQL library or to use the MySQL server option old-passwords. Details on this appear in the previous section.

An incorrect entry was used in the mysql.user table: When user *x* attempts to register with computer *y*, the MySQL server compares the entries in the *user* table in a particular order: First, entries are considered whose *Host* character string is unique, and only then *Host* entries with wild cards (% and _). Within these two groups, again unique *User* strings are preferred to those with wild cards.

The result of this order of precedence is that user *abc* on the local computer (*localhost*) will be unable under certain circumstances to register, although in the *user* table there is an entry *Host='%'* / *User='abc'*. The reason is that in the default setting of access privileges there is also an entry *Host='localhost'* / *User=''*. This entry is given precedence to the first one because there the host name is given explicitly.

To solve the problem, either add a second entry *Host='localhost'* / *User='abc'* to the *user* table or delete the entry *Host='localhost'* / *User=''*. I recommend the second variant, since an entry with *user=''* always represents a security risk.

No user name was specified: If you do not specify a user name in your program for making a connection, then the login name of the account under which the program was launched is given automatically. In programs that are launched interactively, this is your login name.

With programs that run over a web server (PHP or JSP scripts, Perl CGI files, etc.), the account name of the web server is used. For security reasons the web server usually runs not as *root* (Linux) or with administrator privileges (Windows), but in a separate account, such as *wwwrun* or *apache*. The problem is now that in the *mysql* access tables, the user *wwwrun* or *apache* is unknown. Therefore, access to the database is denied. Therefore, do not forget in script files to specify the user name for the connection to MySQL explicitly.

The connection succeeds, but access to the database is impossible: This error occurs immediately if you specify the desired database during the establishment of the connection. However, the error cannot occur until you select the desired database (*USE dbname*). Error message 1045 is, for example, *Access denied for user ... to database ...*.

The most likely cause of the error is that the user in fact does not have access rights to the database. Perhaps in *GRANT* you have specified only the *Usage* privilege (which allows a login, but not the actual use of a database). Execute the command *GRANT SELECT, INSERT ... ON dbname.* TO name@hostname* to allow database access to *dbname*.

If the MySQL server is running on the computer of an Internet service provider (ISP), then the server is generally so configured that only local access is possible. In other words, your PHP or Perl scripts run without problems (because they are executed on the same computer), but you cannot access your databases from home, say, with MySQL Administrator.

Here the issue is the correct (because secure) setting of the access privileges. You will find scarcely an ISP that allows MySQL connections from an arbitrary computer on the Internet. You must therefore use programs for administration that run locally on the computer of the ISP (e.g., phpMyAdmin).

It is impossible to create a local TCP/IP connection: This problem usually occurs under Unix/Linux. A local connection succeeds only if with option -h no computer name or IP number is specified. The most likely cause is a problem with the resolution of the host name. As a rule, you must add the domain name in the column *user.Host*, and then it works. Another cause can be the local network configuration (file /etc/hosts). We have already given some tips in this chapter especially for Red Hat Fedora and SUSE Linux.

The local connection fails for Java programs: This problem is usually connected with the previous point, since Java programs, in contrast to most other MySQL clients, generally use TCP/IP (and not a socket file). Have a look in Chapter 17, where there are some troubleshooting tips.

Another cause of error can be the incorrect installation of Connector/J (see Chapter 17), but then an error occurs in the attempt to use JDBC (*java.lang.ClassNotFoundException: com.mysql.jdbc.Driver*).

Port 3306 is blocked: Between the MySQL server and your program there is a firewall that is blocking port 3306. This problem can occur only when your program and the MySQL server are running on different computers. If you manage the firewall yourself, you must clear port 3306; otherwise, you must ask the administrator to do so.

An update of the MySQL server causes problems: In all previous updates of MySQL (from 3.23 to 4.0 to 4.1 to 5.0) the *mysql* tables of the security system were greatly expanded. If you carry out an update of the MySQL server, you must be sure to bring the *mysql* tables into conformity with the new security system. For this, the script mysql_fix_privilege_tables is provided (see also Chapter 14). This script creates all new columns in the *mysql* tables, but retains the default setting *N* for these columns. You may need to take a close look at the new access privileges and explicitly grant certain individual new privileges. I have already mentioned the authentication problems caused by changing from version 4.0 to version 4.1 or newer.

■**Tip** An additional list of possible causes of errors and some tips for alleviating them can be found in the MySQL documentation: http://dev.mysql.com/doc/mysql/en/access-denied.html.

Further Tips for Error-Checking

If you believe that your *mysql* database is properly configured, yet database access fails nonetheless, stop the MySQL server, add temporarily *skip-grant-tables* to the [mysql] section in my.cnf or my.ini and restart the server. Now everyone has access to all data. If access now succeeds, you at least know with certainty that the problem resides in the *mysql* tables. Do not forget to remove *skip-grant-tables* from the configuration file.

MySQL manages temporary storage (cache) with a list of most recently used IP addresses and associated host names. This cache has the effect that the usually time-consuming process of name resolution is necessary only on first access. However, if you change your network configuration without restarting the MySQL server, it can happen that this cache contains incorrect, that is, no longer valid, entries. To run the MySQL server without this cache, add skip-host-cache in the [mysql] section of my.cnf or my.ini and restart the server.

Unfortunately, there is no way to make the MySQL server save precise information as to why a login attempt failed. In the error log (file hostname.err; see Chapter 14) is mentioned only the IP address of the login attempt, but not the course of name resolution, which entries in the *mysql* tables were looked at, etc.

System Security

Up to this point we have dealt in this chapter with issues of security from the point of view of the MySQL user and access administration. In reality, of course, your data within a MySQL database are only as secure as the database server and the underlying operating system.

Security at the System Level

To secure your MySQL database system you should begin by asking the following questions:

- Are there security loopholes that would place an attacker in a position to log in as *root* (Unix/Linux) or with administrator privileges (Windows 2000/XP)?

  To minimize such risks, you should employ as secure an operating system as possible, carry out routine security updates, institute a firewall, and so on. (However, system security is not the subject of this book.)

- Are the logging files secured? There, for example, the passwords can be found in plain text.

- Are script files containing passwords in plain text adequately secured? (And if full-fledged security is impossible, is it ensured that the user name/password combination in these files is provided with minimal access privileges? Is it ensured that the given password can really be used only for this MySQL login, that for convenience the same password as for *root* was not used?)

Security Measures in the Storage of Critical Data

An additional issue concerns the data within a database. You should prepare yourself for the worst-case scenario—the possibility that an attacker gains access to your data—by encrypting key information within the database:

- If you store login information in the database (for example, the login information for users of your web site), then do not store the passwords in plain text, but only as MD5 check sums. These check sums are sufficient to verify a password. (The drawback is that a forgotten password cannot be restored from the check sum.)

- If you store even more sensitive data (credit card information, say, to take a particularly relevant example), such data should be encrypted. You should ask whether MySQL is a suitable database system for managing such data. If you store such critical data, you should engage security experts to make your system as secure as possible. Anything less should be considered gross negligence.

The MySQL Server as Security Risk

The MySQL server itself can present a security risk. Since errors in the code of the MySQL server are continually being discovered and corrected, it is absolutely necessary to carry out regular updates to the most recent version of MySQL. (With many Linux distributions this happens automatically via the update system.)

For example, at the beginning of 2005, security holes were found in the area of user-defined functions (UDFs). These holes were able to be exploited by a worm (a type of virus), because countless MySQL Windows installations were running without a password or with one that was easy to guess. Since then, the UDF implementation has been changed to prevent such misuse. More details are available at `http://dev.mysql.com/tech-resources/articles/security_alert.html` and `http://dev.mysql.com/doc/mysql/en/udf-security.html`.

Note as well that a MySQL user with *File* privileges can read and alter files in the local file system. The extent of this ability depends on how the file system itself is secured (access privileges for directories and files) and under what account the MySQL server (and thus `mysqld`) is running.

Running the MySQL Server Without root or Administrator Privileges

In no case should the MySQL server be run as *root* under Unix/Linux or with administrator privileges under Windows, since then, every MySQL user with *File* privileges would have the run of the entire file system.

Linux: With all current Linux distributions MySQL is already correctly configured. You can check this with the following command:

```
root# ps au | grep mysqld
root   ... /bin/sh /usr/bin/mysqld_safe ...
mysql  ... /usr/sbin/mysqld ...
mysql  ... /usr/sbin/mysqld ...
...
```

This means that the script mysqld_safe is executed by *root*, but the various threads of the MySQL server mysqld are executed by the user *mysql*. (The script mysqld_safe must be executed by *root*. It serves only to start mysqld. It runs until the MySQL server is explicitly shut down. The script restarts mysqld automatically if the server crashes.)

If mysqld is executed as *root*, the following entry in /etc/my.cnf can help:

```
# file /etc/my.cnf
[mysqld]
user = mysql
```

Windows: Under Windows, the MySQL server unfortunately runs by default in the account *System* and thereby has unrestricted privileges. Moreover, it is difficult to achieve a secure configuration, which requires the creation of a new user, changing all the access privileges to all the MySQL directories, etc. How to proceed is detailed in the article at http://dev.mysql.com/tech-resources/articles/security_alert.html previously mentioned (see step 9 in the article).

Network Security, Firewall

Under Unix/Linux, the MySQL server is frequently used exclusively by local programs over a socket file. That is the case, for example, when only PHP scripts on the local web server or local administration programs access the database server. In this case, it is most secure to deactivate completely the network functions of the MySQL server with the option skip-networking in /etc/my.cnf (section [mysqld]).

If you set up MySQL as a database server only within a local network, the use of skip-networking is not possible. However, you should at least close the IP port 3306 with an IP packet filter (firewall). The MySQL server uses this port by default for TCP/IP communication. By closing this port you make the MySQL server inaccessible from outside the network.

Internet access over dynamic web sites is still possible in spite of all security measures, since dynamic web sites are generated from the locally running web server (which in turn calls a script interpreter). The MySQL server is thus addressed locally, and external communication is accomplished not via port 3306, but via the HTTP protocol (normally port 80). If there is a security loophole there, then closing port 3306 will not be of any help.

■■■

## CHAPTER 12

GIS Functions

Geographic information systems (GIS for short) are software packages that allow for the processing of spatial data. Such programs are as a rule included in database systems that can directly manage and process geographic data. MySQL has offered such functions since version 4.1.

These functions are of interest not only for those seeking to realize a complete GIS, but also for those wishing to manage geographic data. Even if you don't have much to do with geography, you would be surprised to learn what sorts of data involve spatial considerations. Just think, for example, about the images inside your digital camera. Each photo was taken at a particular location. Why not consider sorting the pictures by geographic coordinates? You could then later execute queries along the lines of, "show all pictures taken within ten kilometers of my house."

The current implementation of geometric functions in MySQL is not as well developed as in many commercial products (for example, Oracle Spatial and DB2 Spatial). Moreover, the GIS implementation of MySQL is limited to two-dimensional vectorial data. However, the GIS functions of MySQL are sufficient for many tasks, and they open a whole new world of possibilities.

■**Note** Parts of this chapter were written by Bernd Öggl for our jointly written book *PHP 5 and MySQL 5*. Thanks to his educational studies in geography and his professional qualifications as an instructor in GIS systems and databases, he has considerably more experience in the realm of GIS than I do. I am very grateful to him for allowing me to use his work for this book.

If you are looking for more information on MySQL GIS functions, then you should take a look at the relevant chapter of the MySQL documentation: `http://dev.mysql.com/doc/mysql/en/spatial-extensions-in-mysql.html`. The article `http://dev.mysql.com/tech-resources/articles/4.1/gis-with-mysql.html` provides some ideas for using geometric data in nongeographic applications.

GIS Data Formats

Before we go into a description of the GIS functions of MySQL, it would be well to consider the current standards for geographic data. This section summarizes some of the important concepts and data formats. This information is particularly indispensable if you are going to be importing or exporting geographic data.

Specifying Coordinates

You have likely encountered coordinate specifications of the form *N47 16 06.6 E11 23 35.9*. A geographic position is specified in degrees, minutes, and seconds. In this case, the location in question is to be found at 47 degrees, 16 minutes, 6.6 seconds north latitude and 11 degrees, 23 minutes,

35.9 seconds east longitude. Such data are called *geographic coordinates.* A drawback to such notation is the difficulty in calculation by human beings, who have become accustomed to the decimal system. Since the coordinates describe a position on the ellipsoid of revolution Earth, in calculating distances, one must also take into account the curvature of the planetary surface.

To simplify matters, *projective coordinates* are generally used in practice, whereby the ellipsoid is cut into strips on which distance between points is measured linearly. Until recently, there was a large number of projective coordinate systems competing with one another. Many countries had their own system, optimized for local considerations.

UTM format: A unified format, called *UTM,* should simplify matters when it becomes the standard for geographic coordinates. It divides the planet into 60 strips of 6 degrees of longitude each. It is valid from 84 degrees north latitude to 80 degrees south latitude. In each of these zones, positions are described with a value to the right and a value upward, in meters.

All UTM coordinates relate to a specific *datum.* A datum tells which model of ellipsoid should be used and where the source should be set relative to the center of the earth.

For converting from traditional coordinates into UTM coordinates there are freely available programs and libraries on the Internet. A good starting point is the site `http://www.remotesensing.org/`.

An example: The following lines contain the UTM coordinates of some locations in the Austrian Tirol:

```
681547.32, 5237595.88, Innsbruck
680397.55, 5233845.59, Mutters
685271.40, 5239558.18, Rum
685387.69, 5235857.76, Aldrans
679141.11, 5233807.33, Natters
```

Of course, one must know the coordinate system that is being used. The UTM system used here describes data with rightward and upward values in meters. One can read off that Innsbruck is 3,750 meters higher (that is, more northerly) and about 1,150 meters to the right (eastward) of Mutters. Tirol is in UTM zone 32, and therefore the specified data are to be found in UTM 32, datum WGS84.

Well-Known Text, Well-Known Binary (OpenGIS)

For depicting lines and polygons one requires rules of syntax. In the past, countless formats were developed. The formats *Well-Known Text* (WKT) and *Well-Known Binary* (WKB) are an attempt to replace these formats with an open standard. Both formats are directly supported by MySQL.

Open GIS Consortium (OGC)

Behind these formats stands the *Open Geospatial Consortium,* or *Open GIS Consortium* (OGC). This is a consortium of businesses, research institutes, universities, and public authorities. Among the 266 members are to be found major corporations, universities, and NGOs.

In 1997, the OGC published the document *OpenGIS Simple Features Specifications for SQL.* It describes how geographic data can be stored and managed in relational database systems. The specification comprises data types, text format, and binary format for representing geometric data as well as a large number of functions for processing geometric data and for performing calculations and geometric analysis. Additional details can be found at `http://www.opengis.org/docs/99-049.pdf`.

WKT and WKB Formats

Well-Known Text is a format for the textual representation of geometric objects. The UTM coordinates of Innsbruck in WKT format look like this:

POINT(681547.32 5237595.88)

Note that the pair of coordinates are separated by a space. Lines consist of two or more points separated by commas:

LINESTRING(681547.32 5237595.88, 685387.69 5235857.76)

Table 12-1 provides a brief summary of WKT elements.

Table 12-1. *Well-Known Text Representation of Various Geometric Objects*

WKT Example	Description
POINT(1 1)	Point with coordinates $x = 1$ and $y = 1$.
LINESTRING(0 0, 1 1, 3 3)	Line with two segments.
POLYGON((0 0, 5 0, 5 5, 0 5, 0 0))	Rectangular drawing.
MULTIPOINT(1 1, 5 5)	Multipoint with two points.
MULTILINESTRING((0 0, 5 5), (10 10, 20 20, 40 20), (10 10, 2 0))	Three lines in a *multilinestring* element.
MULTIPOLYGON(((0 0, 5 0, 5 5, 0 5, 0 0)), ((10, 10, 30 30, 30 10, 10 10)))	Two polygonal drawings.
GEOMETRYCOLLECTION(POINT(100 100), POINT(10 10), LINESTRING(1 1, 100 1, 100 100))	Two points and a line in a geometry collection field.

You may perhaps have noticed that two sets of parentheses are used in defining a polygon for bounding the coordinates. This is not a typographical error. As you will see in the following section, a polygon can contain holes in its interior. To define such forms, additional closed *LINESTRING* objects can be specified inside the outer parentheses. For example, the following polygon has a hole in the middle:

POLYGON((1 1, 9 1, 9 9, 1 9, 1 1),(3 3, 3 6, 6 6, 6 3, 3 3))

The WKT format is the primary means of importing spatial data into a MySQL database.

The *WKB format* is the binary translation of Well-Known Text. All coordinates are given as double-precision values (64-bit floating-point numbers). The MySQL server uses WKB internally for storing geometric data.

MySQL's GIS Implementation

The GIS functions in MySQL have been available since version 4.1. Geometric data can at present be stored only in MyISAM tables, and not in InnoDB or other types of tables. The MySQL GIS implementation is oriented toward the OpenGIS standard previously mentioned. MySQL does not currently implement all the functions envisioned in this standard.

Data Types

The geometric data types in MySQL are based on the OGC specifications and ordered in the hierarchy shown in Figure 12-1.

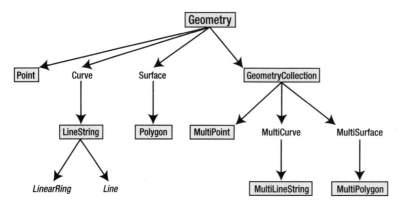

Figure 12-1. *Hierarchy of geometric objects in MySQL*

The objects shown in the figure with a gray background are the data types that you can use in MySQL. *LinearRing* and *Line* are described in the OGC specification, but they do not function in the current implementation of MySQL. In practice, this causes no limitation, since you can always use the *LineString* type. *Curve, MultiCurve, Surface,* and *MultiSurface* are abstract classes that currently have only a single derived class. Table 12-2 shows the types that take one object per cell.

Table 12-2. *Geometric Types in MySQL That Store Exactly One Object*

Geometric Type	Description
GEOMETRY	Geometric type, not further specified.
POINT	A point in the coordinate system; zero-dimensional.
LINESTRING	One or more linear segments joining two points; one-dimensional.
POLYGON	A closed *LINESTRING*; two-dimensional.

Points, lines, and polygons can be stored in a *Geometry* table column. The OGC specification does not provide for these classes being used in this way, but nevertheless, they function in MySQL. As a rule, however, one should try to limit columns to a single geometric type. In application development this also results in a clearer picture of what is going on.

The *POLYGON* object requires further explanation. According to the definition, a MySQL polygon consists of an outer closed ring, within which additional rings may appear that represent holes. These holes may touch at a point, but not otherwise overlap. What is important here is that holes inside a polygon are not part of the surface of the object. An example of this appears in the next section.

The following example shows several geometric types in a table:

```
CREATE TABLE glacier (
  id      INT NOT NULL PRIMARY KEY,
  border  POLYGON NOT NULL,
  ela     LINESTRING,
  ref     POINT)
ENGINE=MyISAM DEFAULT CHARSET=latin1
```

The geometric types can be used in the MySQL *CREATE* instruction just like standard SQL types (*INTEGER, VARCHAR, …*).

■**Note** There is currently no GIS support for a number of MySQL user interfaces. Therefore, for example, with phpMyAdmin 2.6 you cannot create tables of geometric data types. The only current exception is MySQL Administrator. You can use the `mysql` command interpreter, which accepts every SQL command that adheres to MySQL syntax.

MySQL also offers types that can store a collection of like objects in a cell. These are shown in Table 12-3.

Table 12-3. *Geometric Types in MySQL That Store Several Objects in a Single Cell*

Geometric Type	Description
GEOMETRYCOLLECTION	A variety of geometric objects.
MULTIPOINT	One or more *POINT* types.
MULTILINESTRING	One or more *LINESTRING* types.
MULTIPOLYGON	One or more *POLYGON* types.

These types are oriented to the specifications of OGC as set out in the *OpenGIS Simple features for SQL*. There is also a hierarchical structure in which geometric data can be depicted. Somewhat simplified, this means that there is a base class (*Geometry*) and the derived classes of points, lines, and polygons. Each type offers certain functions for querying information about an object of that type. They will be described in the following section.

Simple Geometric Functions

Functions for Converting the Geometric Format

There are several functions available in MySQL for conversion between the internal geometric format and WKT and WKB. These are shown in Table 12-4.

Table 12-4. *Functions for Converting MySQL Geometric Data*

Function	Description
ASTEXT	Returns a geometry type as Well-Known Text.
ASBINARY	Returns a geometry type as Well-Known Binary.
GEOMFROMTEXT	Creates the internal MySQL *GEOMETRY* format from a WKT string.
GEOMFROMWKB	Creates the internal MySQL *GEOMETRY* format from a WKB string.

For example, to store a point from the table *mountain*, you might use

```
INSERT INTO mountain(pt) VALUES(GEOMFROMTEXT('POINT(681547 5237595)'))
```

Moreover, for each data type there is an available conversion function from the WKT or WKB format. Thus, for example, there exist *POINTFROMTEXT*, *LINESTRINGFROMTEXT*, and *POLYGONFROMTEXT*. However, you achieve the same result with the *GEOMFROMTEXT* function.

SRID: With each of the functions *xxxFROMTEXT* and *xxxFROMWKB* you can use an optional SRID (spatial reference system identifier) value. This value denotes a coordinate system for the geometric object. This makes it theoretically possible to store within a table geometric objects whose points are specified in different coordinate systems.

In the current version, however, MySQL ignores SRID information; all geometric calculations are carried out as though a planar Cartesian coordinate system were being used.

Functions in the Geometry Class

All geometric objects in MySQL support these functions. As parameter, a suitable geometric object is passed to the SQL functions, as displayed in Table 12-5.

Table 12-5. *Functions for All Geometric Objects in MySQL*

Function	Description
DIMENSION	Returns the dimension of the object. Possible results: -1 for an empty object 0 for a point (length = 0, width = 0) 1 for a line (length > 0, width = 0) 2 for a polygon, etc. (length > 0, width > 0)
ENVELOPE	Returns the bounding box of the geometric object. The result has the data type *POLYGON*.
GEOMETRYTYPE	Returns the type of the geometric object as a character string (*POINT*, *LINESTRING*, *POLYGON*, …).
SRID	Returns the identifier of the coordinate system. (MySQL stores a coordinate system identifier for every geometric object; however, it does not evaluate this information.)

The bounding box is called a *minimal bounding rectangle* (MBR) and is defined as the smallest rectangle that encloses the geometric form. With compound geometric types this rectangle contains all the constituent objects. In the following example, the variable *@mp* is assigned a *Multipoint* object with three points:

```
SET @mp = GEOMFROMTEXT('MULTIPOINT(1 1, 10 99, 0 5)')
SELECT ASTEXT(ENVELOPE(@mp))
ASTEXT(ENVELOPE(@mp))
POLYGON((0 1,10 1,10 99,0 99,0 1))
```

The *ASTEXT* function specifies the bounding box in WKT format:

```
SELECT GEOMETRYTYPE(@mp)
GEOMETRYTYPE(@mp)
MULTIPOINT
```

Functions for Point Objects

In addition to the functions of the geometry class, two additional methods can be applied to points: *X(pt)* and *Y(pt)*. They return the coordinates of the point as a floating-point number:

```
SET @pt = GEOMFROMTEXT('POINT(33.2 99.9)')
SELECT X(@pt), Y(@pt)
X(@pt)    Y(@pt)
 33.2      99.9
```

Functions for Line Objects

LINESTRING objects offer somewhat more functionality than points. Table 12-6 provides an overview of these geometric functions.

Table 12-6. *Geometric Functions for Line Objects*

Function	Description
GLENGTH	The length of the line (as a floating-point number).
ISCLOSED	1 if the starting point is the same as the ending point; otherwise 0.
NUMPOINTS	The number of points that the line comprises.
STARTPOINT	The first point.
ENDPOINT	The last point.
POINTN(g, N)	The point at location *N*.

A common application is the calculation of the length of a route.

```
SET @ls = GEOMFROMTEXT('LINESTRING(2 2, 9 0, 9 9)')
SELECT GLENGTH(@ls)
GLENGTH(@ls)
16.280109889281
```

To specify the start and terminal points in Well-Known Text format, a simple *SELECT* query will suffice:

```
SELECT ASTEXT(STARTPOINT(@ls)), ASTEXT(ENDPOINT(@ls))
ASTEXT(STARTPOINT(@ls))   ASTEXT(ENDPOINT(@ls))
POINT(2 2)                POINT(9 9)
```

In contrast, only two functions can be used with *MULTILINESTRING* objects: *GLENGTH* and *ISCLOSED*. The result of *GLENGTH* is the sum of the lengths of all the components, and *ISCLOSED* returns *TRUE (1)* if all segments are closed. Note that a closed line of type *LINESTRING* is not a polygon. If you use a polygon function such as *AREA*, you will always obtain *NULL* as result.

■**Note** The OpenGIS standard provides the names *LENGTH* and not *GLENGTH* for the length function. But in MySQL, the function *LENGTH* returns the number of bytes of a character string.

Functions for Polygon Objects

Table 12-7 shows the functions that can be used with polygon objects.

Table 12-7. *Geometric Functions for Polygon Objects*

Function	Description
AREA	Area of the polygon.
EXTERIORRING	Outer ring of the polygon as *LINESTRING*.
INTERIORRINGN(g, N)	Inner ring of the polygon as *LINESTRING*.
NUMINTERIORRINGS	Number of inner rings (holes).

In calculating areas (*AREA*), all holes in a polygon are subtracted out. In the following example, the quadrilateral *@po* has a hole of size 3×3:

```
SET @po = POLYFROMTEXT('POLYGON((1 1, 9 1, 9 9, 1 9, 1 1),
        (3 3, 3 6, 6 6, 6 3, 3 3))')
SELECT AREA(@po), NUMINTERIORRINGS(@po)
AREA(@po)   NUMINTERIORRINGS(@po)
     55                 1
SELECT ASTEXT(INTERIORRINGN(@po, 1))
ASTEXT(INTERIORRINGN(@po, 1))
LINESTRING(3 3,3 6,6 6,6 3,3 3)
```

If the *AREA* function is applied to a *MULTIPOLYGON* object, the individual areas are added.

Functions for GeometryCollection Objects

Table 12-8 shows the functions for *GeometryCollection* objects.

Table 12-8. *Geometric Functions for GeometryCollection Objects*

Function	Description
GEOMETRYN(g, N)	Returns the geometric object at position *N*.
NUMGEOMETRIES(g)	Number of objects in a collection.

A *GeometryCollection* can hold any number of objects in a cell. After you have fetched the desired object with *GEOMETRYN* from a collection, you can process it further with various functions. In the following example, the length of a *LineString* is sought:

```
SET @gc = GEOMFROMTEXT('GEOMETRYCOLLECTION(
        POINT(10 10), POINT(0 100), POINT(40 40),
        LINESTRING(10 0, 10 10, 20 10))')
SELECT GLENGTH(GEOMETRYN(@gc, 4))
GLENGTH(GEOMETRYN(@gc, 4))
            20
```

Function for Spatial Analysis

In addition to the geometric functions described in the previous section, the *OpenGIS Simple Features for SQL* provides for a series of functions for spatial analysis. The current GIS implementation of MySQL supports only calculations based on the bounding box of a geometric object. Thus well-known functions from GIS systems such as *Buffer, Distance, Intersection, Union, ConvexHull,* and *SymDifference* cannot be used.

The active analysis functions are collected in Table 12-9. Each function receives two geometric objects as parameters. The result is either *1* for *TRUE* or *0* for *FALSE*.

Table 12-9. *Bounding Box Functions*

Function	Description
MBRCONTAINS(G1,G2)	*TRUE* if the bounding box of *G2* is completely within the bounding box of *G1*.
MBRWITHIN(G1,G2)	*TRUE* if the bounding box of *G1* is completely within the bounding box of G2.
MBREQUAL(G1,G2)	*TRUE* if the bounding boxes are identical.
MBRINTERSECTS(G1,G2)	TRUE if the bounding boxes of *G1* and *G2* touch or overlap.
MBROVERLAPS(G1,G2)	*TRUE* if the bounding boxes of *G1* and *G2* overlap.
MBRTOUCHES(G1,G2)	*TRUE* if the bounding boxes of *G1* and *G2* touch.
MBRDISJOINT(G1,G2)	*TRUE* if the bounding boxes of *G1* and *G2* neither touch nor overlap.

In the following, some examples involving three rectangles *@r1*, *@r2*, and *@r3* will be presented. A schematic representation of these three objects appears as Figure 12-2.

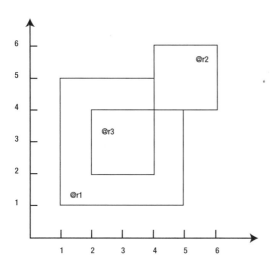

Figure 12-2. *Schematic representation of the bounding boxes of three rectangles*

The following SQL commands can be input directly into an SQL text field in phpMyAdmin. You can use any database. Of course, you could also use the command interpreter mysql:

```
SET @r1 = GEOMFROMTEXT('POLYGON((1 1, 5 1, 5 5, 1 5, 1 1))')
SET @r2 = GEOMFROMTEXT('POLYGON((4 4, 6 4, 6 6, 4 6, 4 4))')
SET @r3 = GEOMFROMTEXT('POLYGON((2 2, 4 2, 4 4, 2 4, 2 2))')
SELECT MBROVERLAPS(@r1,@r2), MBRINTERSECTS(@r1,@r2)
```

MBROVERLAPS(@r1,@r2)	*MBRINTERSECTS(@r1,@r2)*
1	1

```
SELECT MBRINTERSECTS(@r1,@r3), MBRCONTAINS(@r1,@r3)
```

MBRINTERSECTS(@r1,@r3)	*MBRCONTAINS(@r1,@r3)*
1	1

```
MBRTOUCHES(@r2,@r3), MBROVERLAPS(@r2,@r3)
```

MBRTOUCHES(@r2,@r3)	*MBROVERLAPS(@r2,@r3)*
1	0

Functions for querying the relations among precise geometric boundaries of objects are not yet implemented in MySQL. The OGC specification prescribes a number of functions that exist in MySQL (see Table 12-10) but are applied only to the bounding box. In the current version of MySQL it doesn't matter whether you use *CONTAINS* or *MBCONTAINS*.

Table 12-10. *Geometric Functions (Return Only Bounding Box Results in MySQL)*

Function	Description
CONTAINS(G1,G2)	*TRUE* if *G2* is completely within the bounding box of *G1*.
WITHIN(G1,G2)	TRUE, if *G1* is completely within the bounding box of *G2*.
CROSSES(G1,G2)	*G1* and *G2* do not cross (see the online documentation).
EQUALS(G1,G2)	*TRUE* if the objects are identical.
INTERSECTS(G1,G2)	*TRUE* if *G1* and *G2* touch or overlap.
OVERLAPS(G1,G2)	*TRUE* if *G1* and *G2* overlap.
TOUCHES(G1,G2)	*TRUE* if *G1* and *G2* touch.
DISJOINT(G1,G2)	*TRUE* if *G1* and *G2* neither touch nor overlap.

The functions *DISTANCE* and *RELATED* provided in the OpenGIS standard are entirely absent in the current version of MySQL. Later in the chapter I will present an example that shows how you can get around this issue.

Indexing Geometric Data

With any database query, the speed of execution depends to a great extent on whether an index is present, and spatial data are no exception. The good news for MySQL databases is that spatial indexes are supported, and they are also very easy to set up:

```
CREATE TABLE mountain (
    id INT NOT NULL AUTO_INCREMENT PRIMARY KEY,
    pt POINT NOT NULL,
    SPATIAL INDEX(pt) )
```

The geometric column *pt* is thereby provided with a spatial index. However, you could also add the index to an existing table after the fact. To do so, use *ALTER TABLE* with *ADD SPATIAL INDEX* or the *CREATE* command:

```
ALTER TABLE mountain ADD SPATIAL INDEX(pt)
CREATE SPATIAL INDEX pt ON mountain(pt)
```

MySQL uses an *R-tree* index for indexing spatial data, where "R" stands for "region." The regions that are pictured in the tree structure contain either the bounding box of the geometric objects to be indexed or a reference to *R-tree* rectangles in the next-lower level. In MySQL these *R-trees* are managed using quadratic splitting.

Accelerated access in queries comes at the cost of speed in insertions and storage requirements. For example, the *cities* table introduced in this chapter requires for the spatial index half again as much space as the data set itself.

If you wish to check the magnitude of the difference in speed with and without an index, you can explicitly suppress the index in a query: *IGNORE INDEX(pt)* shuts off the geometric index for the column *pt*.

To check whether MySQL actually has built the index in the query, you can follow the execution of the query with *EXPLAIN SELECT*:

```
EXPLAIN SELECT city FROM cities WHERE MBRCONTAINS ...
```

In the output of this SQL query you will see which indexes MySQL has available, which it uses, and how many rows can be excluded by use of the index. In the following example you will have the possibility of using *EXPLAIN SELECT* on a complex query.

SQL Examples (the Database glacier)

This section presents an example of the use of a GIS database. Here you will find mainly SQL code, which you can try out for yourself. The data are represented in Figure 12-3, displayed as two highly stylized glaciers, showing the *border*, the line between the accumulation and ablation regions (*ela*, shown as a dashed line), and a reference point (*ref*). One of the glaciers contains a rock island that is not covered by ice and therefore does not belong to the glacier's polygonal surface (shown in gray in the figure).

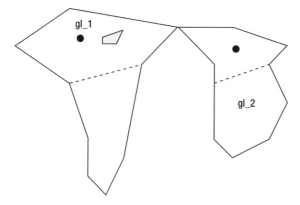

Figure 12-3. *The graphical representation of the data for an SQL example*

Creating the Table

The following commands show how you can generate the table *glacier* and fill it with data. If you wish to save yourself the trouble typing in commands, create a new database with mysqladmin and then using mysql import the file glacier.sql, which you will find in the directory databases of the example files for this book.

```
CREATE TABLE glacier (
        id      INT NOT NULL PRIMARY KEY,
        border  POLYGON NOT NULL,
        ela     LINESTRING NOT NULL,
        ref     POINT NOT NULL,
        name    VARCHAR(20),
        SPATIAL KEY(border),
        SPATIAL KEY(ela),
        SPATIAL KEY(ref) )
```

Inserting the Data

```
INSERT INTO glacier VALUES ( 1,
      GEOMFROMTEXT('POLYGON(
         (2500 1500,1000 2500,2500 3500,3000 5000,3000 6000,
          3500 6500,4000 5500,4500 3000,5500 2000,2500 1500),
         (3395 2827,3861 2840,4094 2374,3395 2594,3395 2827)
      )'),
      GEOMFROMTEXT('LINESTRING(2500 3500, 4500 3000)'),
      GEOMFROMTEXT('POINT(2850 2350)'), 'gl_1')
INSERT INTO glacier VALUES ( 2,
      GEOMFROMTEXT('POLYGON((7000 2000,5500 2000,6500 3000,
         6500 5000,7000 5500,8000 5000,8500 4000,8000 3000,
         8500 2500,7000 2000))'),
      GEOMFROMTEXT('LINESTRING(6500 3500, 8000 3000)'),
      GEOMFROMTEXT('POINT(7250 2750)'), 'gl_2')
```

When you store this table with mysqldump, the geometric data will be output in WKB format, not WKT.

Querying the Data

After the data have been input, you should check whether they were imported correctly. The simplest way of checking the geometric data is with the *asText* function:

```
SELECT name, ASTEXT(ref), ASTEXT(ela) FROM glacier
```

name	ASTEXT(ref)	ASTEXT(ela)
gl_1	POINT(2850 2350)	LINESTRING(2500 3500,4500 3000)
gl_2	POINT(7250 2750)	LINESTRING(6500 3500,8000 3000)

You can also query the length of the lines:

```
SELECT name, GLENGTH(ela),GLENGTH(border) FROM glacier
```

name	GLENGTH(ela)	GLENGTH(border)
gl_1	2061.5528128088	NULL
gl_2	1581.1388300842	NULL

The result is somewhat surprising, since the length of the bounding polygon is *NULL*. In fact, polygons have no length, only an area. If you wish to determine the length of the outer polygon, you need to use the *EXTERIORRING* function:

```
SELECT name,AREA(border), GLENGTH(EXTERIORRING(border)) FROM glacier
```

name	AREA(border)	GLENGTH(EXTERIORRING(border))
gl_1	8933474	15016.935459803
gl_2	5875000	11263.66792108

Note that the area of the first glacier is automatically diminished by the area of the rock island.

The area of the island can also be determined with the following trick: The following command transforms the geometric object into a textual representation, replaces *LINESTRING* with *POLYGON*, transforms the result back into a geometric object, and then returns its area:

```
SELECT AREA(GEOMFROMTEXT(
      CONCAT(REPLACE(
         ASTEXT(INTERIORRINGN(border, 1)),
            'LINESTRING(', 'POLYGON((' ),
      ')') )) AS innerArea
   FROM glacier WHERE id = 1
```

innerArea
191526

Here the function *INTERIORRINGN* returns a type *LINESTRING*. To calculate the area, however, a *POLYGON* is needed. Unfortunately, there is no way to convert between these two types, and therefore a textual replacement must be carried out using the *REPLACE* function. Additionally, the *CONCAT* function is used to insert the closing parentheses.

That the two geometric objects (or their bounding boxes) touch is shown by the *TOUCHES* function:

```
SELECT TOUCHES(g1.border,g2.border)
    FROM glacier AS g1 , glacier AS g2
    WHERE g1.id=1 AND g2.id=2
```
TOUCHES(g1.border,g2.border)
1

For the two objects to be compared, the table must be referenced twice in *FROM*. In the *WHERE* condition, for *g1* the first record is selected, and for *g2* the second. A further value of interest is the total area of the glacier. Nothing could be simpler:

```
SELECT SUM(AREA(border)) FROM glacier
```
SUM(AREA(border))
14808474

Or perhaps you would like to know the total length of the glacier's border:

```
SELECT SUM(GLENGTH(EXTERIORRING(border))) FROM glacier
```
SUM(GLENGTH(EXTERIORRING(border)))
26280.603380883

Glaciologists would certainly like to know how much area is in the accumulation region (that is, above the dashed line) and how much lies below. Here, alas, MySQL must take a pass, since spatial operators such as intersection, union, and difference are not yet implemented in MySQL.

One could formulate additional queries, for example, regarding the position of the reference points. The smaller the *x* values, the farther to the west the glacier lies. To find the most westerly and easterly points on the glacier, use the following command:

```
SELECT MIN(X(ref)), MAX(X(ref)) FROM glacier
```
MIN(X(ref))	*MAX(X(ref))*
2850	7250

You can also collect several geometric columns of a table into a *GEOMETRYCOLLECTION*:

```
SELECT ASTEXT(GEOMFROMTEXT(
        CONCAT('GEOMETRYCOLLECTION(',
            ASTEXT(border),',', ASTEXT(ref), ')')))
        AS collection FROM glacier
```
collection
GEOMETRYCOLLECTION(POLYGON((2500 1500,1000 2500,2500 3500,
3000 5000,3000 6000,3500 6500,4000 5500,4500 3000,
5500 2000,2500 1500),
(3395 2827,3861 2840,4094 2374,3395 2594,3395 2827)),
POINT(2850 2350))
GEOMETRYCOLLECTION(POLYGON((7000 2000,5500 2000,6500 3000,
6500 5000,7000 5500,8000 5000,8500 4000,8000 3000,
8500 2500,7000 2000)),
POINT(7250 2750))

In this example, renewed use is made of *CONCAT*. In order that *GEOMFROMTEXT* function correctly and create a *GEOMETRYCOLLECTION*, the corresponding character string must stand at the beginning of the parenthesized expression. Furthermore, the individual objects within the parentheses must be separated by commas. These are supplied by the *CONCAT* function.

The bounding box of each geometric object is always a rectangle, which in MySQL is represented as a *POLYGON*. In the special case of a *POINT* object, the polygon is reduced to a single point:

```
SELECT ASTEXT(ENVELOPE(ela)) FROM glacier
```
ASTEXT(ENVELOPE(ela))
POLYGON((6500 3000,8000 3000,8000 3500,6500 3500,6500 3000))
POLYGON((2500 3000,4500 3000,4500 3500,2500 3500,2500 3000))

```
SELECT ASTEXT(ENVELOPE(ref)) FROM glacier
```
ASTEXT(ENVELOPE(ref))
POLYGON((7250 2750,7250 2750,7250 2750,7250 2750,7250 2750))
POLYGON((2850 2350,2850 2350,2850 2350,2850 2350,2850 2350))

```
SELECT ASTEXT(ENVELOPE(border)) FROM glacier
```
ASTEXT(ENVELOPE(border))
POLYGON((1000 1500,5500 1500,5500 6500,1000 6500,1000 1500))
POLYGON((5500 2000,8500 2000,8500 5500,5500 5500,5500 2000))

SQL Examples (the Database opengeodb)

The *opengeodb* example database consists of a single table, *cities*. This table contains locations in Austria, Germany, and Switzerland, together with their coordinates (in the UTM system, zone 32U), postal code (*zip*), and other data. The following command displays ten randomly selected records:

```
SELECT id, ASTEXT(pt), zip, country AS cnt, state AS st, city, district
FROM cities ORDER BY RAND() LIMIT 10
```

id	ASTEXT(pt)	zip	cnt	st	city	district
3357	POINT(863667 5784840)	15848	DE	BB	Friedland	
7249	POINT(320685 5500822)	54441	DE	RP	Mannebach	
14857	POINT(605034 5213504)	6555	AT	7	Kappl	
16458	POINT(588645 5122467)	7747	CH	GR	Viano	
9104	POINT(702844 5728043)	6388	DE	ST	Piethen	
2231	POINT(501094 5976100)	25709	DE	SH	Diekhusen-...	
13113	POINT(726772 5656658)	6712	DE	ST	Würchwitz	
10491	POINT(474289 5403425)	75328	DE	BW	Schömberg	
13518	POINT(421059 5942907)	26409	DE	NI	Wittmund	Berdum
12622	POINT(396497 5621193)	57635	DE	RP	Werkhausen	

Table 12-11 summarizes the column properties of the table. Note that a spatial index has been defined for the *pt* column.

Table 12-11. *Properties of the cities Table*

Field	Data Type	Attribute	Index
id	INT	NOT NULL AUTO_INCREMENT	PRIMARY KEY
pt	POINT	NOT NULL	SPATIAL KEY
zip	INT	NULL	KEY
country	VARCHAR(10)	NULL	KEY
state	CHAR(2)	NULL	
city	VARCHAR(100)	NULL	KEY
district	VARCHAR(100)	NULL	

In comparison with the tiny *glacier* table, *cities* comprises almost 18,000 records. The volume of data is about 1MB, and the indexes require an additional 1.2 megabytes. Thus this table is useful not only for trying out various SQL commands, but also for efficiency tests (such as searching for coordinates with and without an index).

Data Source and Import

The example database opengeodb.sql is based on the like-named OpenGeoDB project. This is an initiative in German-speaking countries to create a freely available database with the names of locations with their geographic positions. The database is available at the following location for download (LGPL license; that is, even commercial use of the data is permitted): http://opengeodb.de/download/.

The quality of the data is good, but not perfect. OpenGeoDB notes that the data have been only moderately checked, and errors may well be present. In the following examples we will be concerned not with a concrete application, but with testing the GIS functions of MySQL with real data.

Import

The initial data are in the form of a CSV (comma-separated values) file, not in the form of an SQL file that can be directly read in by MySQL. The following lines show some entries from this text file:

```
30443; AT; 3; -; -; -; Zwingendorf; -; -; 48.7; 16.2333; -; 2063
30444; CH; AG; -; -; -; Aarau; -; -; 47.3833; 8.05; -; 5000,5004,5001
30445; CH; AG; -; -; -; Aarburg; -; -; 47.3167; 7.9; -; 4663
30446; CH; AG; -; -; -; Aettenschwil; -; -; 47.1833; 8.36667; -; 5645
```

The coordinates of the locations appear in columns 10 and 11 and are given in degrees latitude and longitude. This coordinate system is, however, unsuitable for MySQL. Fortunately, there is an open source library, *Proj.4*, available on the Internet for conversion from decimal degrees into the projective UTM system. Binary packages for Windows and for Linux can be found at http://www.remotesensing.org/proj/.

From this package, the executable cs2cs is used to transform from one coordinate system into the other. The following example shows the transformation of a coordinate pair from the *latlong* system into the UTM system in Zone 32U:

```
user@host > echo "11.4 47.2667" | cs2cs +proj=latlong +to +proj=utm +zone=32U
681547.32       5237595.88 0.00
```

■**Note** Parts of this chapter were written by Bernd Öggl (Innsbruck, Austria). Thanks to his educational studies in geography and his professional qualifications as an instructor in GIS systems and databases, he has considerably more experience in the realm of GIS than I do. I am very grateful to him for allowing me to use his work for this book.

Radial Search

Imagine the following scenario: You wish to develop a trading community in which you can specify a maximal spatial separation of product groups. A typical search might be to locate all used washing machines within a radius of 30 kilometers of your location. The *cities* table offers the necessary basis for such searches.

To start with, we need the coordinates of the base point (which is Innsbruck in the following example). These coordinates are stored with a simple *SELECT* command in the variables @x0 and @y0 (in the case of large cities, it is better to work with the comparison *zip=...* rather than *city=...*):

```
SELECT X(pt), Y(pt) FROM cities
WHERE city='Innsbruck' LIMIT 1 INTO @x0, @y0
SELECT @x0, @y0
```

@x0	@y0
681547.32	5237595.88

Now we have to search for locales in the *cities* table whose location falls within a certain distance from @x0 and @y0. Since the MySQL GIS implementation does not yet support a *DISTANCE* function, the distance must be calculated using the Pythagorean theorem (the square root of the sum of the squares of the distances between the respective *x* and *y* coordinates). The result is then divided by 1,000 and rounded, yielding the distance in kilometers:

```
SELECT ROUND(SQRT(POW(@x0 - X(pt), 2) + POW(@y0 - Y(pt), 2)) / 1000) AS distance,
       city FROM cities
HAVING distance<=30 ORDER BY distance
```

distance	city
0	Innsbruck
4	Rum
4	Natters
4	Mutters
4	Aldrans
5	Sistrans
5	Völs
...	...
29	Wallgau
29	Pertisau
30	Tux

49 rows in set (0.15 sec)

Speed Optimization

The result is correct, but it is bothersome that the query took relatively long to execute. The reason is that MySQL must compute the distance for all 17,000 records without being able to use the spatial index for the column *pt*. The query can be executed considerably faster if first, a sub*SELECT* command is used to determine all records that lie within 30 kilometers of the start point. The condition of this sub*SELECT* command uses the function *MBRCONTAINS*, which MySQL can execute much more efficiently thanks to the *pt* index.

However, to do this, some preparations are necessary. First, a geometric object (variable *@bbox*) must be created that describes the square 30 kilometers around the starting point. This is difficult to do in pure SQL code. (The two *SELECT* commands show the intermediate results and serve to clarify the code, but they are not necessary. If you develop your application with PHP or another programming language, the assembling of the *MULTIPOINT* string is much simpler.)

```
SET @d0 = 30000
SET @str = CONCAT('MULTIPOINT(', @x0-@d0, ' ', @y0-@d0, ', ',
                  @x0+@d0, ' ', @y0+@d0, ')')
SET @bbox = ENVELOPE(GEOMFROMTEXT(@str))
SELECT @str
```

@str
MULTIPOINT(651547.32 5207595.88, 711547.32 5267595.88)

```
SELECT ASTEXT(@bbox)
```

ASTEXT(@bbox)
POLYGON((651547.32 5207595.88, 711547.32 5207595.88,
711547.32 5267595.88, 651547.32 5267595.88,
651547.32 5207595.88))

Using the *POLYGON* object in the variable *@bbox*, all points that reside within can easily be determined. (Note that processing time is 0.00 seconds, that is, too short to measure with mysql.)

```
SELECT city, X(pt), Y(pt) FROM cities
WHERE MBRCONTAINS(@bbox, pt)
```

city	*X(pt)*	*Y(pt)*
Farchant	659311.95	5266601.84
Krün	671959.24	5263256.57
...		
Mittenwald	669666.07	5255771.14
Scharnitz	672340.12	5250287.98

54 rows in set (0.00 sec)

Now from these results we can remove all cities whose distance is greater than 30 kilometers. (The rectangular *POLYGON* object with length 60 kilometers is larger than a circle with a radius of 30 kilometers.) In the following sub*SELECT* command, the inner command returns all such cities. The outer command calculates the actual distances and excludes the cities that are too far away. Note that the entire time for execution of this command is only 0.01 seconds, thus much less than in the first version of our radial search.

```
SELECT ROUND(SQRT(POW(@x0 - sub.x, 2) + POW(@y0 - sub.y, 2)) / 1000) AS distance,
       sub.city
FROM (SELECT city, X(pt) AS x, Y(pt) AS y FROM cities
      WHERE MBRCONTAINS(@bbox, pt)) AS sub
HAVING distance<=30 ORDER BY distance
```

distance	*sub.city*
0	Innsbruck
4	Rum
...	...
30	Tux

49 rows in set (0.01 sec)

CHAPTER 13

■ ■ ■

Stored Procedures and Triggers

Stored procedures (SPs) are the most significant innovation in MySQL 5.0. These are custom SQL procedures or functions that are stored and executed directly by the MySQL server. With SPs you have an SQL-based programming language at your service. SPs make it possible to store part of the logic of a client-server database application.

In this chapter you will learn why SPs are a good idea (greater speed, greater data security, less code redundancy, etc.). The following sections describe details about the SP implementation in MySQL and provide several application examples.

A *trigger* is the automatic calling of SQL commands or SPs before or after *INSERT*, *UPDATE*, or *DELETE* commands. For example, you can test for every *UPDATE* operation whether the altered data obey certain conditions. The trigger implementation in MySQL 5.0 is unfortunately not very complete. Triggers will probably not be of practical use until version 5.1. Nevertheless, this chapter provides an introduction to the use of triggers.

■**Tip** Further information on SPs and triggers can be found, as usual, at the MySQL website: `http://dev.mysql.com/doc/mysql/en/stored-procedures.html`, `http://dev.mysql.com/doc/mysql/en/triggers.html`, `http://dev.mysql.com/tech-resources/articles/`, `mysql-storedprocedures.pdf`.

Why Stored Procedures? Why Triggers?

Stored procedures are a collection of SQL commands that are stored and executed in the MySQL server. Depending on the application, the following advantages can accrue:

Greater speed: It often happens that in carrying out a database operation, a large amount of data must be transported back and forth between the PHP program and the database server: The PHP program executes a *SELECT* command, processes the result, executes an *UPDATE* command based on the results, and returns *LAST_INSERT_ID*, etc. If all of these steps can be executed on the server in an SP, a great deal of overhead in data transmission can be saved.

SPs have the additional advantage that the database server can preprocess the code (this is similar to a compiler, which creates a binary file from source text). However, the extent to which such optimizing functions are available under MySQL and whether they provide a measurable increase in speed is not documented.

Note that the use of SPs is no guarantee of improved speed. You will achieve a speed advantage only if the SP's code is efficient. Since SQL is a much more primitive program than PHP, it is not always possible to achieve optimal code in an SP.

The use of SPs has the result that the MySQL server is more greatly burdened, while the opposite is the case for the web server with PHP. Whether the net result is positive or negative depends on the entire configuration. If the MySQL server and the web server are running on different computers and the MySQL server is the bottleneck, then the intensive use of SPs can worsen the situation, even if the web server carries less of a load.

Avoidance of code redundancy, better maintenance: It is frequently the case that several applications access the same database. Then generally there are identical or similar code segments in each application for checking the input values, inserting new data records, updating tables, etc. If such code can be offloaded to an SP, then not only is code redundancy avoided, but all the affected applications are easier to maintain. When the database schema is changed, often only a single SP needs to be changed, and not the code in every conceivable application.

Increase in database security: In many security-critical industries, such as banking, it is undesirable for user programs to be able to access tables directly. Instead, the client programs must use SPs for all database operations. There are thus SPs for obtaining data (*SELECT*), inserting new data, changing existing data, etc. At first glance, this seems rather complicated, and indeed, the creation and maintenance of a large number of SPs is a considerable task. The advantage for the database administrator, however, is that every data access can be monitored, and logged if necessary. Therefore, one can institute security rules of arbitrary stringency.

Of course, stored procedures do not offer only advantages. Among the greatest drawbacks is that SPs normally cannot be easily ported from one database system to another. The reason for this is that (almost) every database system uses a different syntax or syntax extensions for SPs. Therefore, it is an enormous task to port SPs for the Microsoft SQL server or for Oracle to MySQL. (The same holds of course in the other direction.)

Triggers

Triggers make it possible to execute a set of SQL commands or a stored procedure automatically after or before *INSERT*, *UPDATE*, or *DELETE* commands. For example, you can test every *UPDATE* operation to see whether the altered data conform to a particular set of rules. Other possible applications include changes to logging and updating variables or columns in other tables.

Since trigger code is automatically executed at each change in the table, complex triggers can result in sharply diminished data throughput. This is particularly true when a command changes a large number of records (*UPDATE table SET columnA = columnA + 1*); the trigger code must be executed for each data record.

Hello, SP World!

The best way to begin to understand the world of stored procedures is by means of a small example. The function *shorten* reduces character strings to a prescribed maximum length. For example, *shorten("abcdefghijklmnopqrstuvwxyz", 15)* returns the string *"abcde ... vwxyz"*.

■Note There are two types of stored procedures: procedures and functions. The two types differ in a number of details that will be discussed in the following sections. For now, suffice it to say that functions can return values, while procedures support reference parameters and a greater variety of SQL commands (e.g., *SELECT* and *INSERT*). Procedures must be called with *CALL*, while functions can be embedded in ordinary SQL commands. The example in this section shows the definition of a function.

In early 2005, there were only two programs that could be used for inputting and testing functions: the command interpreter `mysql` and MySQL Query Browser. Other administrative tools such as phpMyAdmin 2.6 were offering no support for SPs, a situation that will change soon, and may well have done so by the time you are reading this book. If that is not yet the case, you might consider making use of SP Administrator, a small tool that will be introduced in Chapter 15 as an example of PHP programming. With SP Administrator you can conveniently create, edit, test, and archive SPs (backup and restore).

The Command Interpreter mysql

To launch the command interpreter, execute under Linux the command `mysql -u root -p` in a console window and provide the required password. Under Windows, execute Programs | MySQL | MySQL Server | MySQL Command Line Client.

Defining an SP: In `mysql`, make *mylibrary* the active database and change the delimiter character from ; to *$$*. These two characters indicate the end of input. Since the code of an SP might use the semicolon, it is an unsuitable character for termination. Keep in mind that all input must now be terminated by *$$*:

```
mysql> use mylibrary
mysql> delimiter $$
```

The next step is to define the new function *shorten*. Try to avoid typos! When `mysql` encounters an error, you can, of course, correct it, but the process is highly counterintuitive.

The code of *shorten* should be easy to understand. Two parameters are passed to the function: a string *s* and an integer *n* representing the maximum length of the result. The function returns a string (data type *VARCHAR(255)*). If *n* is less than 15, then oversized strings are converted to the desired length using the SQL string function *LEFT*. If *n* is greater than or equal to 15, then oversized strings are shortened so that the resultant string contains the first *n – 10* and the last 5 characters, with the string " ... " in between.

```
mysql> CREATE FUNCTION shorten(s VARCHAR(255), n INT)
    ->     RETURNS VARCHAR(255)
    -> BEGIN
    ->    IF ISNULL(s) THEN
    ->      RETURN '';
    ->    ELSEIF n<15 THEN
    ->      RETURN LEFT(s, n);
    ->    ELSE
    ->      IF CHAR_LENGTH(s) <= n THEN
    ->        RETURN s;
    ->      ELSE
    ->        RETURN CONCAT(LEFT(s, n-10), ' ... ', RIGHT(s, 5));
    ->      END IF;
    ->    END IF;
    -> END$$
Query OK, 0 rows affected (0.00 sec)
```

■**Tip** Instead of typing the code directly into `mysql`, you could as well use a text editor. The text file should comprise the following commands:

```
- file sp.sql
DROP FUNCTION IF EXISTS shorten;
DELIMITER $$
CREATE FUNCTION shorten ... $$
```

Now you can read in the text file with the command `mysql` and thereby define the function:

> **mysql -u root -p mylibrary < sp.sql**

If an error occurs, simply edit the file in the editor and try again. Note that it is impossible to read in the text file in interactive `mysql` mode using the command *source filename*, since *source* requires the commands to be separated by semicolons, and it does not accept the command *delimiter*.

Trying out the SP: After having successfully defined the function, you can now try it out. Observe that your custom functions can be implemented with ordinary SQL commands:

```
mysql> SELECT shorten("abcdefghijklmnopqrstuvwxyz", 15)$$
  abcde ... vwxyz
mysql> SELECT title, shorten(title, 20) FROM titles LIMIT 10$$
  A Guide to the SQL Standard        A Guide to ... ndard
  A Programmer's Introduction to PHP 4.0   A Programm ... P 4.0
  Alltid den där Annette             Alltid den ... nette
  Anklage Vatermord                  Anklage Vatermord
  Apache Webserver 2.0               Apache Webserver 2.0
  Client/Server Survival Guide       Client/Ser ... Guide
  Comédia Infantil                   Comédia Infantil
  CSS-Praxis                         CSS-Praxis
  Dansläraren Återkomst              Dansläraren ... komst
  Darwins Radio                      Darwins Radio
```

If the command termination string *$$* bothers you, then put `mysql` back into default mode:

```
mysql> delimiter ;
```

The MySQL Query Browser

Instead of the command interpreter `mysql`, you can use the MySQL Query Browser. As of March 2005 its functions were not yet fully mature, but in any case, it offers more convenience than the command interpreter `mysql`.

Defining an SP: First select the database *mylibrary* via FILE | SELECT SCHEMA and then execute the command SCRIPT | CREATE STORED PROCEDURE. After you have specified the desired name and type (procedure or function), the Query Browser presents a template for you to complete with code (see Figure 13-1). When you are finished, store the new SP with EXECUTE. If you have committed a syntax error, you must halt execution with STOP. Correct the error and try again.

Testing the SP: To try out your new function, execute FILE | NEW QUERY TAB, give the command *SELECT shorten(title, 20), title FROM titles*, execute it with EXECUTE (see Figure 13-2).

Editing an SP: While you have the dialog for defining the function *shorten* open, you can easily edit it. (Don't forget to execute EXECUTE.)

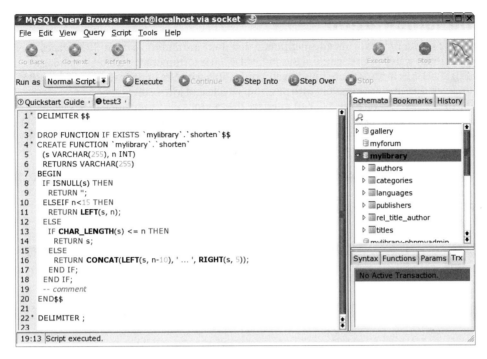

Figure 13-1. *Definition of a custom function in the MySQL Query Browser*

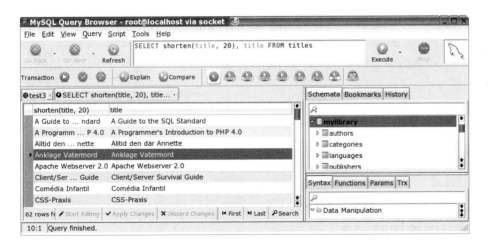

Figure 13-2. *Testing a function in the MySQL Query Browser*

If you have already closed the dialog, editing after the fact is difficult. The Query Browser provides only the command SCRIPT | EDIT ALL STORED PROCEDURES. That should open a new dialog containing the code of all SPs in the current database. (In the tested version 1.1.5 of the Query Browser this did not function, though it did with older versions.) Now you can copy the *DELIMITER* instructions at the beginning and end as well as the *DROP* and *CREATE* commands of your SP into a new script dialog (FILE | NEW SCRIPT TAB). There you can edit your code and then execute EXECUTE.

SP Implementation

The SQL 2003 standard: I have already mentioned that there are almost as many SP syntaxes as there are database systems. The syntax of SPs in MySQL 5.0 is fortunately based on a standard, namely SQL:2003. SPs in MySQL are thus largely compatible with SPs in the database system IBM DB/2. However, they are incompatible with SPs from Oracle and Microsoft SQL Server.

In the future, MySQL will likely offer an interface that permits the formulation of SPs using external programming languages (e.g., PHP and Perl). That would open up attractive programming opportunities for PHP programmers in particular, since SPs can use all of the features of PHP. How all this would affect the speed of SPs remains to be seen.

Internal storage of SPs: MySQL stores SPs in the table *mysql.proc*. In the columns of this table are stored the name of the underlying database, the name and type (*PROCEDURE* or *FUNCTION*) of the SP, the parameters, the actual code, and various other attributes (see Figure 13-3). Note that every SP is associated with a particular database.

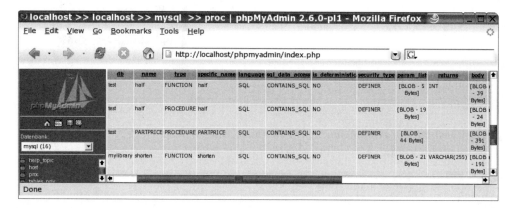

Figure 13-3. *MySQL internal storage of stored procedures*

■**Caution** SPs can be stored only if the table *mysql.proc* actually exists. If you did not do a clean install of MySQL 5.0 but used an earlier version of MySQL and upgraded to version 5.0, the database *mysql* may have been left unchanged and thus be without the *proc* table. Instructions for creating this table after the fact can be found at http://dev.mysql.com/doc/mysql/en/upgrading-grant-tables.html.

SP Administration

This section describes the SQL commands for administration of SPs. These allow you to create, edit, and delete SPs. The direct application of these commands is relatively tedious. Unfortunately, in March 2005 there were still no usable administrative tools to simplify working with SPs. Such tools are to be expected in the near future. As a transitional aid, you can use the SP Administrator, introduced in Chapter 15.

Creating, Editing, and Deleting SPs

Creating SPs

As the Hello SP World example demonstrated, new SPs are created using *CREATE FUNCTION* or *CREATE PROCEDURE*. You need the privilege *Create Routine* in order to be able to execute these commands. The following lines summarize the syntax for these commands:

```
CREATE FUNCTION name ([parameterlist]) RETURNS datatype
[options] sqlcode
CREATE PROCEDURE name ([parameterlist])
[options] sqlcode
```

Both commands associate the SP with the current database. It is allowable for a function and a procedure to have the same name. In the definition, the following options can be specified:

LANGUAGE SQL: The only permissible setting for the option *LANGUAGE* is currently *SQL*. This setting holds by default. Future versions of MySQL will likely offer the option of defining SPs in other programming languages.

[NOT] DETERMINISTIC: An SP is considered to be deterministic when it always returns the same result with the same parameters. (SPs whose result depends on a database table are thus not deterministic.)

By default, SPs are nondeterministic. However, deterministic SPs can be executed with greater efficiency. (For example, it is possible to store the result of an SP for particular parameters in a cache.) At the moment, however, the MySQL *DETERMINISTIC* option is ignored.

SQL SECURITY DEFINER or *INVOKER:* The *SQL SECURITY* mode specifies the access privileges with which an SP is to be executed. Details will be given later in the chapter.

COMMENT 'text': The comment *text* is stored together with the SP.

Semicolons separate individual commands within an SP. These semicolons can cause problems with the execution of *CREATE* commands. If you use the command interpreter mysql, you must set a different separator using *DELIMITER*, as described earlier in this chapter. Additional details on the definition of a parameter list and on SP syntax rules for the actual code follow in the next section.

Deleting SPs

The following two commands delete an existing procedure or function. The optional key words *IF EXISTS* have the effect that the command is executed without triggering an error even if the SP to be deleted does not exist. You need the privilege *Alter Routine* to execute the command. The creator of the function or procedure (that is, the user who executed *CREATE FUNCTION/PROCEDURE*) has this privilege automatically.

```
DROP FUNCTION  [IF EXISTS] name
DROP PROCEDURE [IF EXISTS] name
```

Changing SPs

With *ALTER* you can change the name of an SP and some of its options. You need again the *Alter Routine* privilege to execute this command:

```
ALTER FUNCTION/PROCEDURE name
  [NAME newname]
  [SQL SECURITY DEFINER/INVOKER]
  [COMMENT 'newcomment']
```

> ■**Note** MySQL currently (version 5.0.3) offers no way of changing the code of an existing SP. If that is what you would like to do, then you must first delete the SP with *DROP*, and then create it anew with *CREATE*.

Determining Existing SPs

The two commands *SHOW PROCEDURE STATUS* and *SHOW FUNCTION STATUS* return a list of all defined procedures and functions. Using *LIKE pattern* you can limit the output to those procedures/functions whose names correspond to a given search pattern. In any case, you will obtain the SPs of all databases (not only the current database). In the following example, the return columns *Modified* and *Created* have been left out:

```
SHOW FUNCTION STATUS
```

Db	Name	Type	Definer	Security_type	Comment
mylibrary	faculty	FUNCTION	root@192.168.80.1	DEFINER	
mylibrary	shorten	FUNCTION	root@192.168.80.1	DEFINER	
mylibrary	shortentest	FUNCTION	root@localhost	DEFINER	
mylibrary	swap_name	FUNCTION	root@192.168.80.1	DEFINER	
test	test	FUNCTION	root@localhost	DEFINER	

More complete information is provided by the table *information_schema.routines*. It contains all data of the table *mysql.proc*, though in part it employs different column names:

```
SELECT routine_name, routine_type, created
FROM information_schema.routines
WHERE routine_schema='mylibrary'
```

routine_name	routine_type	created
categories_insert	PROCEDURE	2005-01-31 11:29:16
...		
test	FUNCTION	2005-02-06 10:43:11
titles_insert_all	PROCEDURE	2005-01-31 11:29:17

Determining the Code of an SP

If you know the name of an SP, you can access its code. Execute the command *SHOW CREATE FUNCTION/PROCEDURE name*:

```
SHOW CREATE FUNCTION shorten
```

Function	sql_mode	Create Function
shorten		CREATE FUNCTION mylibrary.shorten(s VARCHAR(255), n INT) RETURNS VARCHAR(255) BEGIN IF ISNULL(s) THEN RETURN ''; ELSEIF n<15 THEN RETURN LEFT(s, n); ELSE IF CHAR_LENGTH(s) <= n THEN RETURN s; ELSE RETURN CONCAT(LEFT(s, n-10), ' ... ', RIGHT(s, 5)); END IF; END IF; END

Security

Only users possessing the above-mentioned privileges *Create Routine* and *Alter Routine* may create, change, or delete SPs. The privilege *Execute* determines which MySQL users are allowed to execute SPs. All three privileges can be set via user administration (see Chapter 11).

Even if the current user has the right to execute SPs, the question remains open which database operations for the SP are allowed. (For example, can a record be deleted from a table via a particular SP?) MySQL distinguishes two variants:

SQL SECURITY INVOKER: SPs that are defined with this option have the same access privileges as the MySQL user who executes the SP. (The SP is allowed to delete records if the user who launched the SP is allowed to.)

SQL SECURITY DEFINER: In this case, the SP has the same privileges as the MySQL user who defined the SP. This security mode holds by default; that is, if the option *SQL SECURITY INVOKER* is not taken, then *DEFINER* holds. (Caution: SPs defined by *root* have unrestricted privileges in all databases.)

Backup and Restoration of SPs

The usual mechanisms for creating database backups unfortunately continue to ignore SPs. This holds, for example, for the version of MySQL Administrator that was available in March 2005, for the command `mysqldump`, and the export tool of phpMyAdmin 2.6.

To carry out a backup of all SPs for all databases, your best bet is to back up the table *mysql.proc*, for example:

```
> mysqldump -u root -p mysql proc > backup.sql
```

However, this method has two significant drawbacks:

- You must have access privileges to *mysql.proc*. Normally, this is possessed only by *root*, not an ordinary user.

- It is impossible to back up SPs only from a particular database. This makes it impossible as well to read in the SPs of a particular database without simultaneously overwriting the SPs of all other databases.

You can also execute a backup manually by executing *SHOW CREATE FUNCTION/PROCEDURE* for all the SPs in a database and saving the result to a file. A particularly convenient approach is to perform an SP backup using SP Administrator, introduced in Chapter 15.

SP Syntax and Language Elements

SPs consist primarily of a collection of ordinary SQL commands, such as those that you have come to know from Chapters 9 and 10. In addition, however, there are some additional commands available to SPs, such as those that allow you to create loops and conditional branches, and to run through all the records in a table (*cursor functions*). These SP-specific commands are the focus of this section.

As has been mentioned repeatedly, there are two types of SPs: procedures and functions. Table 13-1 summarizes the most important differences between the two.

Table 13-1. *Differences Between Procedures and Functions*

	Procedures	Functions
Calling	Only with *CALL*	Possible in all SQL commands, e.g., in *SELECT* and *UPDATE* commands.
Return	Can return one or more SELECT results	Returns a single value (command *RETURN*); the data type of the return value must be specified in the declaration with *RETURNS*.
Parameters	Value and reference parameters possible (*IN, OUT, INOUT*)	Only value parameters allowed, thus no identification with *IN*, etc.
Commands allowed in the code	All SQL commands, including *SELECT, INSERT, UPDATE, DELETE, CREATE TABLE*	No commands that access tables.
Calling other functions and procedures	May call other procedures and functions	May call only functions, not procedures.

General Syntax Rules

These are the most important syntax rules for SPs:

Semicolon: SPs can consist of arbitrarily many SQL commands. The commands must be separated by semicolons. Even control structures for branches and loops must be terminated with a semicolon.

BEGIN–END: Several commands that do not fall between key words (for example, between *THEN* and *END IF*) must be placed between *BEGIN* and *END*. For this reason, the code of every SP that consists of more than one instruction must be introduced by *BEGIN* and terminated by *END*.

New lines: A new line in the code has the same syntactic effect as a space character. It thus doesn't matter whether an *IF–THEN–ELSE–END-IF* construction is divided over several lines or placed all on one line.

Variables: Local variables (SP-internal variables) and parameters are used without a prefixed @ character. Within an SP you can access ordinary SQL variables, which as usual must be identified with the @ character.

Case distinction: There is no case distinction in the definition or invocation of SPs. It is all the same whether you write *shorten, SHORTEN*, or *Shorten*.

For this reason, it is impossible to define a number of functions or procedures whose names are the same except for case.

It is, however, permitted to have a function and a procedure with the same name, since when it is called, MySQL can tell whether a function or a procedure is being invoked.

Special characters: Avoid the use of international characters such as ä, à, ñ in SP names. MySQL accepts such characters in the *CREATE* command, but you may experience problems in administering and using functions and procedures with such characters in their names.

Comments: Comments are introduced with a double hyphen (—) and extend to the end of the line.

Calling SPs (CALL)

Functions and procedures have different ways of being invoked. SPs are associated with a database. If you wish to execute an SP belonging to another database, you must prefix the name of the database, e.g., *CALL dbname.spname()*.

Functions

Functions, like the predefined SQL functions, are integrated into ordinary SQL commands. For example, the *shorten* function from the "Hello World" section can be called thus:

```
SELECT shorten("a very long character string", 15)
SELECT shorten(title, 30), shorten(subtitle, 20) FROM titles
UPDATE titles SET title = shorten(title, 70)
WHERE CHAR_LENGTH(title)>70
```

With *SET* or *SELECT INTO* you can store the result of a function in an SQL variable, which you can then place in other SQL commands:

```
SET @s = " a very long character string "
SET @a = shorten(@s, 15)
SELECT shorten(@s, 10) INTO @b
SELECT @s, @a, @b
```

@s	@a	@b
a very long character string	a ver ... tring	a very lon

Procedures

Procedures must be called with *CALL*. You can return as result a table (as with a *SELECT* command). It is impossible to link procedures to SQL commands in any other way.

The following examples use the procedures *get_title* and *half*:

```
PROCEDURE mylibrary.get_title(IN id INT)
BEGIN
  SELECT title, subtitle, publName
  FROM titles, publishers
  WHERE titleID=id
  AND titles.publID = publishers.publID;
END
PROCEDURE mylibrary.half(IN a INT, OUT b INT)
BEGIN
  SET b = a/2;
END
```

Here *get_title* behaves like a *SELECT* command, which is not surprising, since that is what the procedure contains.

```
CALL get_title(1)
```

title	subtitle	publName
Linux	Installation, Konfiguration, Anwendung	Addison-Wesley

In the case of procedures with reference parameters (*OUT* or *INOUT*), the result can be evaluated only if an SQL variable is passed as parameter.

```
CALL half(10, @result)
SELECT @result
```

result
5

Recursion

In the code of a procedure, other functions and procedures can be called, while in the code of a function, only other functions (and not procedures) can be called. Functions and procedures can even call themselves. This makes possible the realization of recursive algorithms. The following lines show the standard example of recursion: evaluation of the factorial function (1*2*3*4, etc.):

```
CREATE FUNCTION factorial(n BIGINT) RETURNS BIGINT
BEGIN
  IF n>=2 THEN
    RETURN n * factorial(n-1);
  ELSE
    RETURN n;
  END IF;
END
SELECT factorial(6)
factorial(6)
      720
```

Parameters and Return Values

For functions and procedures there is a slightly unusual rule for the declaration of parameters and for the ways of returning results. This section discusses the relevant syntax variants.

Parameters of Procedures

Procedures are created by the command *CREATE PROCEDURE*. A parameter list is optional. Note, however, that you must provide a pair of parentheses even if there are no parameters.

```
CREATE PROCEDURE name ([parameterlist])
[options] sqlcode
```

If there is more than one parameter, they must be separated by commas. Each parameter is specified as follows:

```
[IN or OUT or INOUT] parametername datatype
```

The keywords *IN*, *OUT*, and *INOUT* determine whether the parameter is to be used only for input, only for output, or for data transport in both directions. (The default is *IN*.)

All data types from MySQL are allowed, such as *INT* and *VARCHAR(n)* and *DOUBLE*. However, in contrast to the definition of table columns, it is impossible to provide additional attributes to the data type such as *NULL* and *NOT NULL*. MySQL currently does not attempt to do type checking when it passes parameters, but that may change in future versions.

▮**Caution** Be careful to give your parameters names that differ from those of your columns and tables. Otherwise, ambiguity can enter into the formulation of SQL commands in procedure code.

Results of Procedures (SELECT)

Unlike functions, procedures cannot return a single value. In procedures, however, one may use ordinary *SELECT* commands. It is even allowed for a procedure to execute several *SELECT* commands in sequence. The procedure then returns several result tables. However, only those programming languages that support the *MULTI_RESULT* mode are capable of evaluating several results. If you are working with PHP, you must use the method *multi_query* of the *mysqli* interface.

Function Parameters

The *CREATE* command for creating new functions looks very much like that for procedures:

```
CREATE FUNCTION name ([parameterlist]) RETURNS datatype
[options] sqlcode
```

A significant difference, however, is that functions do not support reference parameters. For this reason, the keywords *IN*, *OUT*, and *INOUT* are not permitted in the parameter list.

Function Results

Functions can return a value with the command *RETURN*, which also terminates the function execution. *RETURN* can be used only in functions, not in procedures. The data type of the return value must be specified in the parameter list with *RETURNS*.

Encapsulation of Commands (BEGIN-END)

Every procedure or function that consists of more than one SQL command must be introduced with *BEGIN* and terminated with *END*. *BEGIN–END* constructs are also possible within the code, for example in an *IF* conditional or in a loop if local variables, conditions, *handlers*, or *cursors* are to be declared. (The following sections will reveal the meaning of the terms *handler* and *cursor*.)

Within the *BEGIN–END* block a particular order must be adhered to:

```
BEGIN
  DECLARE variables;
  DECLARE cursors;
  DECLARE conditions;
  DECLARE handler;
  other SQL commands;
END;
```

Before the *BEGIN*, an optional label can be given. The same name must then appear after the *END*. Naming a block makes sense if the block may be exited early with *LEAVE*. The following lines show the syntax of such a construction:

```
blockname: BEGIN
  commands;
  IF condition THEN LEAVE blockname; END IF;
  further commands;
END blockname;
```

Variables

There are two types of variables to consider:

Ordinary SQL variables: Such variables are prefixed with the @ character. These variables can be used in SPs just as they are in ordinary SQL commands (see Chapter 10). They maintain their contents until the termination of the connection to the MySQL server.

Local variables and parameters: These variables are used without the @ character. They must be declared with *DECLARE* before they are used. The content of a local variable is lost as soon as the procedure or function terminates.

Variables are local within the *BEGIN–END* group in which they are defined. This means that within a procedure several like-named variables can coexist within different levels of definition (see the following example). In the case of a recursive SP call, each instance of the SP has its own variables that are independent of those of the other instances (as in PHP).

Which type of variables you use in an SP is up to you. To avoid side effects, local variables are generally preferable. On the other hand, ordinary variables can be advantageous with recursive functions, since they maintain their value through all function and procedure calls.

Declaration (DECLARE)

The declaration of local variables must take place within a *BEGIN–END* group and before other commands in the group. The syntax of variable declaration looks like this:

```
DECLARE varname1, varname2, ...  datatype [DEFAULT value];
```

As you can see, you must provide the data type for all local variables. Local variables contain *NULL* by default, unless you initialize them with another value.

█Caution Be very careful not to give your variables names that coincide with those of columns or tables that you use in your SP. It is allowed syntactically, but it frequently leads to hard-to-detect errors (which can be revealed, for example, in that a variable, despite an assignment otherwise, always contains *NULL*).

The following example demonstrates the levels of definition of local variables. There are three variables, all called *x*, but declared in different levels of the code and therefore independent of one another. When you call the procedure, three results are returned, 2, 1, and then 0.

```
CREATE PROCEDURE test()
BEGIN
  DECLARE x INT DEFAULT 0;
  BEGIN
    DECLARE x INT DEFAULT 1;
    IF TRUE THEN
      BEGIN
        DECLARE x INT DEFAULT 2;
        SELECT x;
      END;
    END IF;
    SELECT x;
  END;
  SELECT x;
END
```

Variable Assignment

Variable assignments of the form $x = x + 1$ are not permitted in SQL. Instead, you must use either *SET* or *SELECT INTO*. The latter is a variant of *SELECT*, in which the command ends with *INTO varname*. This variant is permitted only for *SELECT*s that return a single data record (not several records). In functions, only *SET* can be used, since there the use of *SELECT* and various other SQL commands is not allowed.

```
SET var1=value1, var2=value2, var3=value3 ...
SELECT var:=value
SELECT 2*7 INTO var
SELECT COUNT(*) FROM table WHERE condition INTO var
SELECT title, subtitle FROM titles WHERE titleID=...
INTO mytitle, mysubtitle
```

Branching

IF–THEN–ELSE Branching

The SQL syntax for *IF* branching looks like this:

```
IF condition THEN
  commands;
[ELSE IF condition THEN
 commands;]
[ELSE
 commands;]
END IF;
```

As already mentioned, the use of *BEGIN* and *END* within a control structure is not necessary. The condition can be formulated as with *WHERE* or *HAVING* in *SELECT* queries.

Instead of the *IF* structure presented here, in simple cases you may use the *IF* function that was introduced in Chapter 10.

CASE Branching

CASE is a syntactic variant of *IF* that is particularly useful when all the branch decisions depend on the value of a single expression.

```
CASE expression
WHEN value1 THEN
      commands;
[WHEN value2 THEN
 commands;]
[ELSE
 commands;]
END CASE;
```

Loops

MySQL offers a host of variants for constructing loops. The future holds out the offer of a *FOR* loop, which in MySQL 5.0.3 has not yet been implemented and whose syntax is not yet documented.

REPEAT–UNTIL

The instructions between *REPEAT* and *UNTIL* are executed until the condition is first satisfied. Since the condition is not evaluated until the end of the loop body, there is always at least one pass through the loop.

The loop can be given an optional label. The same loop name must then appear at the end of the loop. Naming a loop can be useful if you exit the loop prematurely with *LEAVE* or wish to repeat a loop iteration with *ITERATE* (more on this soon).

```
[loopname:] REPEAT
    commands;
UNTIL condition
END REPEAT [loopname];
```

The following lines show an example of a *REPEAT–UNTIL* loop. Here *test(n)* returns a string that contains the * character *n* times. (This could, of course, have been accomplished much more simply. The purpose here is to demonstrate the syntax.)

```
CREATE FUNCTION test(n INT) RETURNS TEXT
BEGIN
  DECLARE i INT DEFAULT 0;
  DECLARE s TEXT DEFAULT '';
  myloop: REPEAT
    SET i = i+1;
    SET s = CONCAT(s, "*");
  UNTIL i>=n END REPEAT;
  RETURN s;
END
SELECT test(5)
test(5)
*****
```

WHILE

The instructions between *DO* and *END WHILE* are executed as long as the condition is satisfied. Since the condition is evaluated at the beginning of the loop, it can happen that the loop is not executed even once (namely, when the condition is not satisfied on its initial evaluation). If you wish to use *LEAVE* or *ITERATE*, you must provide the loop with a label.

```
[loopname:] WHILE condition DO
    commands;
END WHILE [loopname];
```

LOOP

The instructions *LOOP* and *END LOOP* are executed until the loop is exited with *LEAVE loopname*. It is not syntactically required that the loop be given a name, but in practice, it is usually done (unless you wish to create an infinite loop).

```
loopname: LOOP
  commands;
END LOOP loopname;
```

The following lines give an example of a *LOOP*. Here *test(n)* returns once again a string with *n* asterisks.

```
CREATE FUNCTION test (n INT) RETURNS TEXT
BEGIN
  DECLARE i INT DEFAULT 0;
  DECLARE s TEXT DEFAULT '';
  myloop: LOOP
    SET i = i+1;
    SET s = CONCAT(s, "*");
    IF i>=n THEN LEAVE myloop; END IF;
  END LOOP myloop;
  RETURN s;
END
```

LEAVE and ITERATE

LEAVE loopname aborts execution of a loop. *LEAVE* can also be used to break off a *BEGIN–END* block prematurely.

ITERATE loopname has the effect that the commands of the loop body are executed once again. In contrast to *LEAVE*, *ITERATE* cannot be used with a *BEGIN–END* block.

Error Handling (Handlers)

Errors may occur during the execution of SQL commands within an SP. SQL therefore provides a mechanism using *handlers* to react to such errors.

A handler must be defined after the declaration of variables, cursors, and conditions but before the SQL commands of a *BEGIN–END* block. Here is the syntax:

```
DECLARE type HANDLER FOR condition1, condition2, condition3, ... command;
```

> *type*: Allowable types are currently *CONTINUE* and *EXIT*. The former means that program execution simply continues with the next command after the occurrence of an error. *EXIT* means that the *BEGIN–END* block is exited and the program continued after that point. (Future versions of MySQL will support a third variant: *UNDO*.)
>
> *condition*: The condition or conditions enumerate under what conditions the handler should be activated. There are several ways of formulating the conditions:
>
>> *SQLSTATE 'errorcode'*: Specifies a particular error code.
>>
>> *SQLWARNING*: Encompasses all 01*nnn SQLSTATE*s.
>>
>> *NOT FOUND*: Encompasses all other errors (hence *SQLSTATE*s that do not begin with 01 or 02).
>>
>> *mysqlerrornumber*: Specifies the MySQL error number instead of the *SQLSTATE* code.
>>
>> *conditionname*: Refers to a condition that was formulated with *DECLARE CONDITION* (more below).
>
> *command*: This command is executed when an error occurs. Usually, a variable is used that is evaluated in the following code. The command must be present (in the case of *DECLARE EXIT HANDLER* as well).

■**Tip** An example of error handling can be found in the next section. The difference between MySQL error numbers and *SQLSTATE* values is that the former are MySQL-specific, while the latter are standardized. For example, MySQL error 1329 (*No data to fetch*) corresponds to *SQLSTATE* error code *'02000'*. A list of all MySQL error codes and the associated *SQLSTATE* values can be found in the online MySQL documentation at http://dev.mysql.com/doc/mysql/en/error-handling.html.

Conditions

Conditions make it possible to give certain error codes a clear name. A condition must be defined before a handler. The name of the condition can then be used in the handler. The syntax of a condition looks like this:

```
DECLARE name CONDITION FOR condition;
```

The condition can be formulated with *SQLSTATE 'errorcode'* or *mysqlerrornumber* (see above). The following example shows the declaration of a variable, a condition, and a handler for the error *duplicate key*.

```
DECLARE dupkey VARCHAR(100);
DECLARE duplicate_key CONDITION FOR SQLSTATE '23000';
DECLARE CONTINUE HANDLER FOR duplicate_key SET myerror='dupkey';
```

Triggering Errors

Sometimes it would be helpful if you could trigger an error in an SP when a certain situation occurs (such as passing an invalid parameter). IBM DB/2 provides the SQL command *SIGNAL SQLSTATE xxx* for this purpose. Unfortunately, there is no such command (yet) in MySQL.

The only current option is to deliberately execute an invalid command. In a procedure, you could execute, for example, *SELECT `errorreport`* or *SET `errorreport`=0*. The backward apostrophes normally indicate the name of a database, table, or column. This command will trigger the error *Unknown column 'errorreport' in 'field list'*. This is a bit confusing, but it has the advantage that your error report is part of the MySQL error announcement.

In functions the execution of *SELECT* is not allowed. Here you can use *RETURN `errorreport`*. This leads to the error *Unknown column 'errorreport' in 'order clause'*.

Searching for Errors

Handlers and conditions help in protecting SPs in the case of errors. It is often much more difficult to localize errors made during the development of an SP. MySQL has no debugger for SPs, and the error reports are often of little assistance. To get at least an idea during the execution of an SP of the value of a variable or which code segment is being executed, in a procedure you can misuse a *SELECT* command to output variables or text. (Simply place a *SELECT varname;* in a loop.)

Cursors

From your everyday life you know the concept of a cursor, mouse, and places within a text document that allow for textual input. In database jargon, a cursor is something else: a pointer to a particular record in a table. Cursors offer the possibility of looping through all the records of a table. Typical applications are the selective copying of modified data from a table into a second table, and changes to the content of an extensive table that could be formulated with difficulty if at all using an *UPDATE* command.

The efficacy of the use of cursors is disputed: Cursor advocates maintain that they are a practical tool for executing particular operations with extreme ease. Opponents claim that the use of cursors is a sign of bad programming practice and maintain that almost every problem has a cursorless solution whose code is not only more elegant, but also more efficient. But in the end, no one can take from you the choice whether to use cursors. Yet if you are processing large amounts of data, you should not blindly assume that an algorithm with cursors will operate more efficiently than one without. Try both and see for yourself.

Syntax

The use of cursors involves several steps: First, you declare the cursor with *DECLARE cursorname CURSOR FOR SELECT ...;*. You may use any *SELECT* command. Then you must activate the cursor with *OPEN cursorname*.

Now you have available the command *FETCH cursorname INTO var1, var2, ...*, where the first column of the record is stored in *var1*, the second in *var2*, and so on. (The variables must have been previously declared and of the correct type. Note that the variables must not have the same names as the columns, since that can lead to problems.)

The question now arises, what happens after *FETCH* has read all the *SELECT* results? The answer is simple: MySQL error 1329 is triggered (*No data to fetch*), which corresponds to *SQLSTATE* 02000. This error is unavoidable, but it can be caught with a handler (see the previous section). For this reason, error-handling is a necessary part of every SP that uses cursors. Usually *NOT FOUND* is used as the error condition, where all *SQLSTATE* values 02*nnn* are encompassed.

The cursor can be ended with *CLOSE cursorname*. But this is usually not done, since the cursor declaration is automatically terminated together with the *BEGIN–END* block.

Limitations

The following limitations exist for cursors in MySQL 5.0:

- Cursors are *read-only*. That is, you can only read data, not alter it.

- Cursors are *forward-only*. That is, data must be processed in the order in which it is delivered by the MySQL server.

- Cursors are *asensitive*. It is therefore not permitted to change a cursor's underlying tables while you are reading the cursor's records. If you do so anyway, the MySQL server guarantees no consistent behavior.

An Example

The following lines show a simple application of a cursor. A procedure runs through all records of the *titles* table and sums the number of characters for title and subtitle. This sum is divided by the number of records, which yields the average length of title plus subtitle. The cursor commands and error-handling are highlighted in boldface:

```
CREATE PROCEDURE mylibrary.cursortest(OUT avg_len DOUBLE)
BEGIN
  DECLARE t, subt VARCHAR(100);
  DECLARE done INT DEFAULT 0;
  DECLARE n BIGINT DEFAULT 0;
  DECLARE cnt INT;
  DECLARE mycursor CURSOR FOR
    SELECT title, subtitle FROM titles;
  DECLARE CONTINUE HANDLER FOR NOT FOUND SET done=1;
  SELECT COUNT(*) FROM titles INTO cnt;
  OPEN mycursor;
  myloop: LOOP
    FETCH mycursor INTO t, subt;
    IF done=1 THEN LEAVE myloop; END IF;
    SET n = n + CHAR_LENGTH(t);
    IF NOT ISNULL(subt) THEN
      SET n = n + CHAR_LENGTH(subt);
    END IF;
  END LOOP myloop;
  SET avg_len = n/cnt;
END
```

The following lines show the procedure call and evaluation of the result, which is written using a reference parameter in the variable *@result*.

```
CALL cursortest(@result)
SELECT @result
@result
  29.47
```

Of course, this result could have been obtained much more efficiently without an SP using a simple SQL command:

```
SELECT (SUM(CHAR_LENGTH(title)) + SUM(CHAR_LENGTH(subtitle))) COUNT(*) AS avg_len
FROM titles
avg_len
  29.47
```

SP Examples

This section illustrates the application possibilities of SPs using a number of examples. All the examples are based on the database *mylibrary*, introduced in Chapter 8.

Adding a Category

The following procedure adds a new category to the *categories* table. The new category name and the *parentCatID* number must be passed to the procedure, which returns the new *catID* number, making it possible to avoid the otherwise usual determination of *last_insert_id*. If invalid data are sent to the procedure (empty string, *NULL*, incorrect *parentCatID* number), the return value is −1. If there is already a like-named category within the group specified by *parentCatID*, the procedure does not add a new category and returns the *catID* number of the existing category.

This example also shows that a well-programmed *insert* SP can do much more than a simple *INSERT* command. Depending on the application, of course, all conceivable tests are possible, such as whether a value is contained within a permissible range. If you as database administrator do not give your users the *Insert* privilege but instead force them to insert all data via *INSERT* SPs, you can avoid many erroneous entries in your tables. (Of course, you should make available a corresponding *UPDATE* SP so that invalid entries don't creep into the database in this way.)

The code consists of ordinary SQL commands in combination with some *IF* queries, and it should be easy to understand. The *BEGIN–END* block has the name *proc*. This makes it possible to abort code execution with *LEAVE proc*. Note that in the tested version of MySQL the system variable *@@last_insert_id* contains obsolete values, while the function *LAST_INSERT_ID()* does not.

```
CREATE PROCEDURE categories_insert
  (IN newcatname VARCHAR(60), IN parent INT, OUT newid INT)
proc: BEGIN
  DECLARE cnt INT;
  SET newid=-1;
  - validation
  SELECT COUNT(*) FROM categories
  WHERE parentCatID=parent INTO cnt;
  IF ISNULL(newcatname) OR TRIM(newcatname)="" OR cnt=0 THEN
    LEAVE proc;
  END IF;
  - Test whether the category already exists
  SELECT COUNT(*) FROM categories
  WHERE parentCatID=parent AND catName=newcatname
  INTO cnt;
  IF cnt=1 THEN
    - determine the existing catID number
    SELECT catID FROM categories
    WHERE parentCatID=parent AND catName=newcatname
    INTO newid;
    LEAVE proc;
  END IF;
  - insert new category
  INSERT INTO categories (catName, parentCatID)
  VALUES (newcatname, parent);
  SET newid = LAST_INSERT_ID();
END proc
```

The procedure is used thus:

```
CALL categories_insert('Microsoft Access', 2, @catid)
SELECT @catid
@catid
90
```

Adding a Title

With the following procedure you can insert a book title together with the author and publisher into the *mylibrary* database. If a book has more than one author, they must be separated by semicolons. The call to *titles_insert_all* might look like this:

```
CALL titles_insert_all(
  'Programmieren mit der .NET-Klassenbibliothek',
  'Addison-Wesley', 'Eller Frank;Schwichtenberg Holger', @newID)
```

Noteworthy in the procedure is that it involves four tables: The title is stored in the *titles* table, while the author goes into the *authors* table and the publisher into *publishers* if said publisher is not there already. Furthermore, the cross-reference between the new title and the author goes into *rel_title_authors*.

The procedure *titles_insert_all* recognizes existing authors even if the first and last name are reversed, say if you specified *Stephen King* instead of *King Stephen*. This is accomplished by comparing existing authors with both *author* and *swap_name(author)*. (The code for *swap_name* appears a bit later.)

This precaution ensures that obvious duplicates do not end up in the *authors* table (one *Stephen King* and one *King Stephen*). The correct author format, family name first, cannot thereby be ensured, but at least a later correction is easy. (If some titles are associated with the correctly spelled author, and others with the incorrect one, then correction becomes more complex.)

Of course, one could think of various improvements, such as additional parameters for the remaining columns of the *titles* table, better parameter validation, and so on. But the idea of the procedure should be clear.

This example also makes clear that SP code can often be complicated and difficult to read. The same algorithm in PHP would not occupy fewer lines, but it would be more understandable and therefore easier to maintain over the long term. (This also suggests a reason why many database administrators warn against the overuse of SPs. The maintenance of a large number of SPs can become a nightmare.)

```
CREATE PROCEDURE titles_insert_all
  (IN newtitle VARCHAR(100), IN publ VARCHAR(60),
   IN authList VARCHAR(255), OUT newID INT)
proc: BEGIN
  DECLARE cnt, pos INT;
  DECLARE aID, pblID, ttlID INT;
  DECLARE author VARCHAR(60);
  SET newID=-1;
  - Search for/store publisher
  SELECT COUNT(*) FROM publishers WHERE publname=publ INTO cnt;
  IF cnt=1 THEN
    SELECT publID FROM publishers WHERE publname=publ INTO pblID;
  ELSE
    INSERT INTO publishers (publName) VALUES (publ);
    SET pblID = LAST_INSERT_ID();
  END IF;
```

```
  - store the title
  INSERT INTO titles (title, publID) VALUES (newtitle, pblID);
  SET ttlID = LAST_INSERT_ID();
  - loop over all authors in authList
  authloop: WHILE NOT (authList="") DO
    SET pos = LOCATE(";", authList);
    IF pos=0 THEN
      SET author = TRIM(authList);
      SET authList ="";
    ELSE
      SET author = TRIM(LEFT(authList, pos-1));
      SET authList = SUBSTR(authList, pos+1);
    END IF;
    IF author = "" THEN ITERATE authloop; END IF;
    - search for/store author
    SELECT COUNT(*) FROM authors
    WHERE authName=author OR authName=swap_name(author)
    INTO cnt;
    IF cnt>=1 THEN
      SELECT authID FROM authors
      WHERE authName=author OR authName=swap_name(author)
      LIMIT 1 INTO aID;
    ELSE
      INSERT INTO authors (authName) VALUES (author);
      SET aID = LAST_INSERT_ID();
    END IF;
    - update rel_title_authors
    INSERT INTO rel_title_author (titleID, authID)
    VALUES (ttlID, aID);
  END WHILE authloop;
  - return value
  SET newID=ttlID;
END proc
CREATE FUNCTION swap_name(s VARCHAR(100)) RETURNS VARCHAR(100)
BEGIN
  DECLARE pos, clen INT;
  SET s = TRIM(s);
  SET clen = CHAR_LENGTH(s);
  SET pos =  LOCATE(" ", REVERSE(s));
  IF pos = 0 THEN RETURN s; END IF;
  SET pos = clen-pos;
  RETURN CONCAT(SUBSTR(s, pos+2), " ", LEFT(s, pos));
END
```

Determining Parent Categories

The procedure *get_parent_categories* takes a *catID* number and returns a table with all the parent categories. Let us consider an example:

```
CALL get_parent_categories(57)
```

catID	catName
11	All books
1	Computer books
56	Operating Systems
57	Linux

The procedure creates a temporary *HEAP* table (which is located in RAM, not on the hard drive) and stores all the categories there. The column *level* serves only to store the order in which the categories are entered. The result table is sorted in the reverse order.

If the *startid* number is valid, the corresponding category data are read into the variables *id*, *pid*, and *cname*. The counter *i* as well as *id* and *cname* are inserted into the new table *__parent_cats*.

In the following loop, the parent category is searched for until *parentCatID* has the value *NULL*. Here as well the data found are inserted into *__parent_cats*.

After the end of the loop, the contents of the temporary table are output via *SELECT*. This output is the result of the procedure. The temporary table, no longer needed, is deleted.

```
CREATE PROCEDURE get_parent_categories(startid INT)
BEGIN
  DECLARE i, id, pid, cnt INT DEFAULT 0;
  DECLARE cname VARCHAR(60);
  DROP TABLE IF EXISTS __parent_cats;
  CREATE TEMPORARY TABLE __parent_cats
    (level INT, catID INT, catname VARCHAR(60)) ENGINE = HEAP;
  main: BEGIN
    - check startid
    SELECT COUNT(*) FROM categories WHERE catID=startID INTO cnt;
    IF cnt=0 THEN LEAVE main; END IF;
    - insert the startid category into __parent_cats
    SELECT catID, parentCatID, catName
    FROM categories WHERE catID=startID
    INTO id, pid, cname;
    INSERT INTO __parent_cats VALUES(i, id, cname);
    - loop for searching for parent categories
    parentloop: WHILE NOT ISNULL(pid) DO
      SET i=i+1;
      SELECT catID, parentCatID, catName
      FROM categories WHERE catID=pid
      INTO id, pid, cname;
      INSERT INTO __parent_cats VALUES(i, id, cname);
    END WHILE parentloop;
  END main;
  SELECT catID, catname FROM __parent_cats ORDER BY level DESC;
  DROP TABLE __parent_cats;
END
```

During execution of the procedure a warning will normally be triggered. This comes from *DROP TABLE*, which notes that the table to be deleted does not exist.

Producing a List of Hierarchically Ordered Categories

In the previous example, all parent categories were sought. In this example, *get_subcategories* lives up to its name by delivering all subcategories. This is a more complex task, since subcategories can be branched. Therefore, *get_categories* calls the recursive procedure *find_subcategories*, which finds all subcategories of a given category.

Like *get_parent_categories*, the procedure *get_subcategories* uses a temporary table for storing its results. A significant difference, though, is that this time, the table is not deleted. It remains as the result of the procedure call. As the following examples show, it can be used in a variety of useful ways by the client program.

The start category is passed to *get_subcategories*. The procedure then writes in the second parameter how many subcategories it found (including the start category).

```
CALL get_subcategories(1, @result)
SELECT @result
```
@result
26

In addition to this result, the table *subcats* is available with the results of the search. In addition to the columns *catID* and *catName*, the table contains two more columns: *rank* gives the row number and is used for sorting the data; *level* gives the hierarchical level of the category (where for the start category, we have *level=0*). The following command indents the categories according to their hierarchical placements.

```
SELECT rank, level, catID,
       CONCAT(SPACE(level*2), catname)
FROM __subcats ORDER BY rank
```

rank	level	catID	CONCAT(SPACE(level*2), catname)
0	0	1	Computer books
1	1	2	Databases
2	2	69	IBM DB/2
3	2	86	Microsoft Access
4	2	67	Microsoft SQL Server
5	2	34	MySQL
6	2	5	Object-oriented databases
7	2	68	Oracle
8	2	77	PostgreSQL
9	2	4	Relational Databases
10	2	8	SQL
11	1	36	LaTeX, TeX
12	1	56	Operating Systems
13	2	57	Linux
14	2	58	Mac OS
15	2	59	Windows
16	1	3	Programming
17	2	54	C
18	2	53	C#
19	2	55	C++
20·	2	50	Java
21	2	7	Perl
22	2	6	PHP
23	2	52	VBA
24	2	51	Visual Basic
25	2	60	Visual Basic .NET

The *__subcats* table can also be used to search for book titles within these categories:

```
SELECT title FROM titles, __subcats
WHERE titles.catID = __subcats.catID
ORDER BY title;
```
title
A Guide to the SQL Standard
A Programmer's Introduction to PHP 4.0
Apache Webserver 2.0
Client/Server Survival Guide
...

When the result table is no longer needed, it is simply deleted. (If the user of the procedure neglects to do so, the table will be deleted at termination of the MySQL connection. There is thus no danger that memory will be clogged up with temporary tables.)

```
DROP TABLE __subcats
```

Program Code

The procedure *get_categories* creates a temporary table, tests whether *startid* is valid, and if so, enters the first record into *__subcats*. Then the procedure *find_subcategories* is called. After that call terminates, the number of records in *__subcats* is determined and returned in the parameter *n*.

```
CREATE PROCEDURE get_subcategories(IN startid INT, OUT n INT)
BEGIN
  DECLARE cnt INT;
  DECLARE cname VARCHAR(60);
  DROP TABLE IF EXISTS __subcats;
  CREATE TEMPORARY TABLE __subcats
    (rank INT, level INT, catID INT, catname VARCHAR(60))
    ENGINE = HEAP;
  SELECT COUNT(*) FROM categories WHERE catID=startID INTO cnt;
  IF cnt=1 THEN
    SELECT catname FROM categories WHERE catID=startID INTO cname;
    INSERT INTO __subcats VALUES(0, 0, startid, cname);
    CALL find_subcategories(startid, cname, 1, 0);
  END IF;
  SELECT COUNT(*) FROM __subcats INTO n;
END
```

The procedure *find_subcategories* uses a cursor to run through all subcategories. All categories found are entered into *subcats*, and the *INOUT* parameter *catrank* is increased by 1. Then *find_subcategories* is called recursively, and *catlevel* is also increased by 1.

```
CREATE PROCEDURE find_subcategories
  (IN id INT, IN cname VARCHAR(60), IN catlevel INT,
   INOUT catrank INT)
BEGIN
  DECLARE done INT DEFAULT 0;
  DECLARE subcats CURSOR FOR
    SELECT catID, catName FROM categories WHERE parentCatID=id
    ORDER BY catname;
  DECLARE CONTINUE HANDLER FOR NOT FOUND SET done=1;

  OPEN subcats;
  subcatloop: LOOP
    FETCH subcats INTO id, cname;
    IF done=1 THEN LEAVE subcatloop; END IF;
    SET catrank = catrank+1;
    INSERT INTO __subcats VALUES (catrank, catlevel, id, cname);
    CALL find_subcategories(id, cname, catlevel+1, catrank);
  END LOOP subcatloop;
  CLOSE subcats;
END
```

Triggers

Triggers are used for the automatic calling of SQL commands or SPs before or after *INSERT, UPDATE,* and *DELETE* commands. For example, you could test for each *UPDATE* operation whether the altered data conform to certain conditions.

This section provides a first introduction to the trigger implementation of MySQL 5.0. Note, however, that triggers are currently (MySQL 5.0.3) implemented only half-heartedly. In contrast to SPs, they are not really ready for practical application. The MySQL online documentation promises more trigger functionality for version 5.1. Until this version appears, you can execute only rather trivial tasks with triggers, as demonstrated by the example at the end of this section.

Creating a Trigger

You create a new trigger with the command *CREATE TRIGGER*. Only MySQL users with the *Super* privilege can execute this command.

```
CREATE TRIGGER name  BEFORE|AFTER   INSERT|UPDATE|DELETE
ON tablename FOR EACH ROW code
```

You can define up to six triggers for each table, whose code is to be executed before or after each *INSERT, UPDATE,* or *DELETE* command. If the command encompasses more than one record, the trigger will be executed for each record.

Currently (MySQL 5.0.3), each trigger must have a unique name within a table. In the future, trigger names will be valid for the entire database.

There are similar syntax rules for trigger code as for SPs. In particular, the code must be introduced with *BEGIN* and terminated with *END* if it contains more than one command. All SP language elements are available for triggers. However, there are many restrictions as to which SQL commands may be used in trigger code (more on this below).

Within the trigger code you can access the columns of the current record:

OLD.*columnname* returns the content of an existing record before it is changed or deleted (*UPDATE, DELETE*).

NEW.*columnname* returns the content of a new or altered record (*INSERT, UPDATE*).

You may change *NEW.columnname* in *BEFORE INSERT* triggers and *BEFORE UPDATE* triggers.

Deleting a Trigger

To delete a trigger, execute *DROP TRIGGER*. You need to specify the table and trigger names. The option *IF EXISTS* is not yet supported.

```
DROP TRIGGER tablename.triggername
```

In contrast to SPs, there are not yet any administrative commands like *ALTER TRIGGER, SHOW CREATE TRIGGER,* or *SHOW TRIGGER STATUS*. It is not currently clear whether, when, and with what syntax such commands will be implemented.

Implementation Details and Administrative Assistance

Currently (MySQL 5.0.3), MySQL trigger code is stored in the text file `tablenname.TRG` in the directory of the database. One can guess that this location will change in future versions of MySQL. Probably, triggers, like SPs, will be managed in a table of the *mysql* database.

Furthermore, there is currently nothing in the way of administrative help: MySQL Query Browser, MySQL Administrator, phpMyAdmin, etc., know nothing about triggers. To execute the *CREATE TRIGGER* command you must use the command interpreter `mysql`, where, as in the case of SPs, you must change the delimiter character.

Even `mysqldump` has not yet heard about triggers. If you wish to execute a backup of defined triggers, you should back up the `*.TRG` files in the database directory.

Functional Limitations

Alas, there are at present many restrictions on triggers that make practical application of them well nigh impossible:

- One cannot access tables in trigger code, not even the table for which the trigger was defined. As with SP functions, the commands *SELECT, UPDATE, INSERT*, etc., are unavailable.

- There are no commands or language elements to cancel the *DELETE, UPDATE*, or *INSERT* command from within a trigger or to raise an error.

- Trigger code cannot call an SP with *CALL*.

- No transaction commands can be called in trigger code.

An Example

The two triggers presented here ensure that you can place only floating-point numbers between 0 and 1 in the column *percent* of the table *test*. (Numbers that are too large or too small are replaced with the value *NULL*.)

```
USE test
CREATE TABLE test (id SERIAL, percent DOUBLE)
DELIMITER $$
CREATE TRIGGER test_before_insert
  BEFORE INSERT ON test FOR EACH ROW
BEGIN
  IF NEW.percent < 0.0 OR NEW.percent > 1.0 THEN
    SET NEW.percent = NULL;
  END IF;
END$$
CREATE TRIGGER test_before_update
  BEFORE UPDATE ON test FOR EACH ROW
BEGIN
  IF NEW.percent < 0.0 OR NEW.percent > 1.0 THEN
    SET NEW.percent = NULL;
  END IF;
END$$
DELIMITER ;
```

The following commands prove that the triggers work as advertised with *INSERT* and *UPDATE* commands.

```
INSERT INTO test (percent) VALUES (-1), (0.3), (1.5)
SELECT * FROM test
```

id	percent
1	NULL
2	0.3
3	NULL

```
UPDATE test SET percent = 1.7 WHERE id =2
SELECT * FROM test
```

id	percent
1	NULL
2	NULL
3	NULL

CHAPTER 14

■■■

Administration and Server Configuration

This chapter describes the administration and configuration of the MySQL server. Among the most important themes that we treat are backups, logging files, migration of databases from one computer to another (or from one version of MySQL to a newer one), and import/export of text files. This chapter also goes specifically into the maintenance of MyISAM and InnoDB tables.

Some advanced topics are treated in this chapter: Whether you set up a replication system or wish to achieve greater processing speed, this chapter gives the relevant introductions and tips.

Finally, this chapter goes into the painful question of the various options for administration of databases that are present at an Internet service provider. (The problem is that in such a case you are not the database administrator and thus have very limited access rights.)

■**Tip** Additional topics on administration of MySQL appear in the following chapters: Chapters 4 through 6 discuss the use of user interfaces for administration (`mysql`, MySQL Administrator, etc.). Chapter 11 goes into security and user administration as well as the *mysql* database. Chapter 22 contains a reference on `mysqld`, `mysql`, `mysqladmin`, etc.

First Steps

This section summarizes information on the elementary steps for administration and points to other places in the book where you can find further details.

Using Administrative Tools

With MySQL you get a number of administrative tools (such as `mysqladmin` and `myisamchk`), some of which are described in some detail in this chapter. A common feature of all these tools is that they are command-oriented programs. That is, there is no graphical user interface, and the tool is used with options and commands.

Under Unix/Linux the tools are executed in a shell window, while under Windows they are executed in a command window. Chapter 4 contains tips on the optimal configuration of the command window as well as the proper setup of the Windows system variable *PATH*.

Most of the administrative tools can be used with their full functionality only if you sign in as *root* and provide your password. To do this you specify the options -u and -p at launch of `mysqld`.

With `command help` (`mysql --help` for example) you can obtain a brief overview of the available options and commands. Some of the commands described in this chapter, generally those involving shell or Perl scripts, are available only under Unix and Linux, and not under Windows.

mysqladmin

As the name of the program implies, `mysqladmin` assists in the execution of a variety of administrative tasks:

- Create and delete databases
- Change a user's password
- Input again the privileges database *mysql*
- Update database and logging files (clear buffer or intermediate storage)
- Determine status information and variables of the MySQL server
- List and store MySQL processes
- Test connection to MySQL server (*ping*)
- Shut down the MySQL server (*shutdown*)

The following examples demonstrate a few possible applications:

```
> mysqladmin -u root -p create newDatabaseName
Enter password: xxx
> mysqladmin -i 5 ping
mysqld is alive
mysqld is alive
...
 > mysqladmin status
Uptime: 435152  Threads: 2       Questions: 26464  Slow queries: 3
Opens:  140     Flush tables: 1  Open tables: 0
Queries per second avg: 0.061
> mysqladmin -u root -p processlist
Enter password: xxx
Id   User Host        db      Command Time  State  Info
1    ODBC localhost   books3  Sleep   7
196  root localhost           Query   0            show processlist
...
```

Each time `mysqladmin` is called, only one operation can be executed. Most `mysqladmin` operations can be carried out as well with SQL commands (for example, with `mysql` or with a client program). The advantage of `mysqladmin` is that the program is easily adapted to the automation of administrative tasks.

A reference to all `mysqladmin` options and commands can be found in Chapter 22.

Setting the root Password

The first and most important administrative task after a new installation of MySQL is to secure the MySQL user *root* with a password. If you did not do so during installation, as described in Chapter 2, you will find in Chapter 11 a detailed description of the MySQL access system and a general introduction to securing the MySQL server (not only for *root*). Here we offer a brief summary:

Unix/Linux: Execute the following two commands. You must give the complete network name of the computer, e.g., *uranus.sol*.

```
root# mysqladmin -u root -h localhost password xxx
root# mysqladmin -u root -h computername  password xxx
```

Windows: Execute START | PROGRAMS | MYSQL | MYSQL SERVER N.N | MYSQL SERVER INSTANCE CONFIG WIZARD. This program takes you step by step through the basic configuration. Simply leave the default settings unchanged. Of particular interest here is the step PLEASE SET THE SECURITY OPTIONS. Here you should give *root* a password, activate the option ROOT MAY ONLY CONNECT FROM LOCALHOST, and deactivate the option CREATE AN ANONYMOUS ACCOUNT.

MySQL Server Configuration File

If you followed the installation instructions in Chapter 2, the MySQL server `mysqld` should be running and should perform without problems for most application situations. If you have particular wishes, such as changing the logging or optimizing performance, you can specify a number of options in the MySQL configuration file. Table 14-1 shows where that file is to be found.

Table 14-1. *Files for Setting Global and Local Options*

Type of Options	Windows	Unix/Linux
Global options (both for `mysqld` and for some client programs)	Current MySQL versions: `C:\Programs\MySQL\ MySQL Server n.n\my.ini` Older MySQL versions: `C:\my.cnf or Windows\ my.ini`	`/etc/my.cnf`
User-specific options (only for client programs)		`/.my.cnf`

The server-specific options in the configuration file begin with the line `[mysqld]`. The following option has the effect that new tables are created by default as InnoDB tables (not as MyISAM tables).

```
# Example of the server-specific part of
# /etc/my.conf (Linux) or my.ini (Windows)
[mysqld]
default-storage-engine=INNODB
```

Some important options will be introduced in this chapter. A reference on options appears in Chapter 22.

Restarting the MySQL Server

Changes in the configuration files take effect only after a restart of the affected files. This holds as well for the MySQL server. If you change any server-specific options, you must then restart the server.

Under Windows, the easiest way to do so is with MYSQL SYSTEM TRAY MONITOR. This is a small icon at the right or lower border of the toolbar, in which you can execute the commands SHUTDOWN INSTANCE (shut down the server) or START INSTANCE with the right mouse button. If the SYSTEM TRAY MONITOR is not running, launch the program in the menu START | PROGRAMS | MYSQL. If the program is running but is not displayed in the toolbar, the problem is usually the toolbar settings. Click on the toolbar with the right mouse button, execute the command PROPERTIES, and deactivate the option HIDE INACTIVE ICONS.

Under Unix/Linux things are much simpler. A brief command accomplishes what in Windows necessitated a complex search in the user interface. To restart, use the appropriate Init V script, which you execute first with the parameter *stop* and then with *start*.

Red Hat:

```
root# /etc/init.d/mysqld stop
root# /etc/init.d/mysqld start
```

SUSE:

```
root# /etc/init.d/mysql stop
root# /etc/init.d/mysql start
```

Basic Configuration of the MySQL Server

This section introduces some elementary options for the MySQL configuration file my.cnf/my.ini. The settings become effective after the MySQL server is restarted. With these options, the hyphen (-) and underscore (_) have the same effect. Thus, for example, skip_networking and skip-networking are equivalent.

Directories

After being started, the MySQL server has to locate the directories in which the MySQL programs and databases are located. Under Linux it is usual to specify these directories using options in the Init V file (e.g., /etc/init.d/mysql). Under Windows, the relevant options are set in my.ini; basedir gives the installation path, while datadir provides the path to the database files.

```
# in /etc/my.conf (Linux) or my.ini (Windows)
[mysqld]
basedir=C:/Programs/MySQL/MySQL Server 5.0/
datadir=C:/Programs/MySQL/MySQL Server 5.0/Data/
```

In the course of this chapter you will become acquainted with additional options for setting the location of logging files, InnoDB masterspace files, etc. If these options are not set explicitly, then basedir and datadir hold as default settings.

Communication Settings

The MySQL server can communicate in up to four different ways with client programs, depending on the operating system. Which variants are actually active and which parameters are valid are set with options.

TCP/IP: Communication over TCP/IP is active by default and uses port 3306. You can set a different port with the option port.

skip-networking stops all communication over TCP/IP. This option is often used for reasons of security. Clients can then communicate with the server only from the local computer over a socket file (Unix/Linux) or *named pipes* or *shared memory* (both Windows).

Socket file (Unix/Linux only): The option socket specifies the location of the socket file. The option should be given in both the section [mysqld] and the section [client], since communication succeeds only if both client and server are in agreement as to this location.

Named pipes (Windows only): The option enable-named-pipes activates *named pipes*. With socket you can specify the name of the *named pipe* (by default it is *MySQL*).

Shared memory (Windows only): The option shared-memory activates communication over a common memory block. The option shared-memory-base-name gives the memory block a name (by default it is *MYSQL*).

```
# in /etc/my.conf (Linux) or my.ini (Windows)
[mysqld]
# TCP/IP
port   = 3306
# skip-networking
```

```
# Socket File (Unix/Linux)
socket = /var/lib/mysql/mysql.sock
# Named Pipe (Windows)
enable-named-pipes
socket = MySQL
# Shared memory (Windows)
shared_memory
shared_memory_base_name = MYSQL
[client]
socket = /var/lib/mysql/mysql.sock
```

Default Table Format

As described in Chapter 8, MySQL supports a variety of table types. If you create a new table with *CREATE TABLE*, the option *ENGINE name* determines the table type. If this option is lacking, then the MySQL server uses the default table type that was set with `default-storage-engine`.

```
# in /etc/my.conf (Linux) or  my.ini (Windows)
[mysqld]
default-storage-engine=INNODB
```

Default Character Set and Sort Order for New Tables

As described in Chapter 8, starting with MySQL 4.1, you can specify for each database, each table, and indeed for each column of a table an arbitrary character set and a corresponding sort order. The following settings in the MySQL configuration file hold only for the case that no character set was specified in the *CREATE* command.

Note that `character-set-server` replaces the option `default-character-set` known from earlier versions of MySQL. Although `default-character-set` is still supported for reasons of compatibility, it is considered *deprecated*.

```
# in /etc/my.cnf (Linux) or my.ini (Windows)
[mysqld]
character-set-server = latin1
collation-server     = latin1_german1_ci
```

Note that the character set for communication between client and server is independent of `character-set-server`. In some programming languages and client programs you must set the desired character set with the option `default-character-set=xxx` or via *SET NAMES 'xxx'*. This holds, for example, for C, PHP, Perl, and command tools such as `mysql` and `mysqldump`.

Time Zones

At launch, the MySQL server takes on the time zone of the computer on which it is running. A different time zone can be set in the configuration file with the option `default-time-zone`. Under Windows, the time zone must be specified in terms of the offset from Coordinated Universal Time (UTC), for example, +1:00 for Berlin and -5:00 for New York. Under Linux you can also use the usual international denotations for time zones or their abbreviations, provided that the MySQL table *mysql.time_zone* has been previously initialized (more on this in the next subsection).

```
# in /etc/my.cnf (Linux)
[mysqld]
default-time-zone = Europe/London
```

Initializing Time Zone Tables

Since MySQL 4.1.3 several *time_zone* tables are located in the *mysql* database, which contains among other things all information on access privileges. By default, these tables are empty. To fill the tables with data, execute under Unix/Linux the following command, where instead of /usr/share/zoneinfo, you may have to specify a different directory in which time zone files are located on your computer. The MySQL server must be running when the command is executed:

```
root# mysql_tzinfo_to_sql /usr/share/zoneinfo | mysql -u root -p mysql
Password: xxxxxxxx
```

The table *mysql.time_zone_name* now contains a long list with all the time zone names. (In my Linux installation the table has 1600 entries.)

```
SELECT name FROM mysql.time_zone_name LIMIT 5
name
Africa/Abidjan
Africa/Accra
Africa/Addis_Ababa
Africa/Algiers
Africa/Asmera
```

Under Windows there is no such possibility to initialize the time zone table. For this reason, with MySQL servers that are running under Windows, time zones must be specified as offsets from the UTC, that is, in the form '+1:00'.

Background information on time zone management in MySQL, on the possibility of setting the time zone for a MySQL connection locally, and on SQL functions for calculating with dates and times is to be found in Chapter 10.

The Language for Error Messages

If you would like MySQL to report errors to you in German, French, or some other language, you have merely to set the option language in one of the configuration files. The language chosen will also be used for entries in the error logging file hostname.err.

MySQL currently supports 20 languages. A look at the directory mysql\share\ (Windows) or /usr/share/mysql (Linux) will let you know which they are. If, for example, you prefer German error messages, then execute the following change in the MySQL configuration file:

```
# in /etc/my.cnf or my.ini (Windows)
[mysqld]
language = german
```

If MySQL cannot find the language file, then provide the complete path, for example language = /usr/share/mysql/danish.

SQL Mode

Since version 4.1, the MySQL server can be run in several different modes. The desired mode is set with the option sql-mode, where several modes can be named simultaneously if they are compatible. The modes must be separated by commas. The mode can be changed while the server is running with *SET [GLOBAL] sql_mode='mode1,mode2'*.

The following list briefly describes the most important modes. Note that ansi, db2, maxdb, mssql, mysql323, mysql40, oracle, and postgresql are simply abbreviations for various other options. For example, ansi corresponds to the modes real_as_float, pipes_as_concat, ansi_quotes, ignore_space, and only_full_group_by.

ansi: The MySQL server conforms as closely as possible to the ANSI SQL standard.

`db2, maxdb, mssql, mysql323, mysql40, oracle, postgresql:` The MySQL server conforms as closely as possible to the given database system.

allow_invalid_dates: The MySQL server accepts obviously incorrect dates, such as 30.2.2005. This had been the default behavior since MySQL 4.1 and was replaced in MySQL 5.0 with a check on the validity of dates.

ansi_quotes: Character strings must be enclosed within simple apostrophes (e.g., 'I am a string'), object names in double quotes (e.g., "tablename").

error_for_division_by_zero: This setting triggers an error on division by zero. (The default behavior of the MySQL server is to return the value *NULL* and post a warning.)

ignore_space: In a function call, the MySQL server accepts spaces between the function name and the parentheses (e.g., *SQRT (3)*). By default, that is an error, since it could lead to ambiguity.

no_zero_date: The MySQL server considers 0000-00-00 an invalid date and triggers an error. (The default behavior is to store such a date as is, which is often useful as a way of storing the information *date unknown.*)

no_zero_in_date: The MySQL server considers 00 for the month or day as an error. (The default behavior is to accept dates such as 2005-12-00. This allows the recording of a partial date, here without the day of the month.)

only_full_group_by: The MySQL server considers *GROUP BY* expressions as invalid if the grouping column was not named with a *SELECT* command.

pipes_as_concat: The MySQL server considers | | as an operator for concatenating character strings (like the function *CONCAT*). By default, | | is equivalent to the *OR* operator.

real_as_float: The MySQL server considers *REAL* a synonym for *FLOAT* (8 digits). By default, *REAL* is a synonym for *DOUBLE* (16 digits).

strict_all_tables: The MySQL server triggers an error if you insert data with an *INSERT* command and don't specify the value for a column without a default value. (By default, the MySQL server provides a possibly suitable value, for example 0 for numeric columns.)

strict_trans_tables: This setting is similar to `strict_all_tables`. In this setting, however, the MySQL server distinguishes different table types. With transaction-capable tables (e.g., InnoDB), an invalid *INSERT* command is always aborted, while with other tables (MyISAM), the command is aborted only if the error affects the first record inserted with *INSERT*. If, on the other hand, more than one record is entered simultaneously and the error occurs only at the *n*th record, the entire command is executed, and suitable default values are inserted.

A detailed description of all these modes can be found at `http://dev.mysql.com/doc/mysql/en/server-sql-mode.html`. This book describes the MySQL server in default SQL mode (that is, without the option `sql-mode` being set).

■**Note** In connection with the SQL mode, the MySQL server notes the valid SQL mode at the time of the definition of a stored procedure. When the stored procedure is later executed, the SQL mode valid at the time of definition is used. An informative and readable article on the topic of when MySQL behaves other than as a normal database system can be found at `http://sql-info.de/mysql/gotchas.html`.

Backups

Backups are undoubtedly one of the most important tasks of a database administrator. MySQL offers a variety of methods for executing a backup.

- The classical way, so to speak, uses the command mysqldump. This command returns a file with SQL commands for generating the tables of the database and filling them anew with data. Backups using mysqldump are comparatively slow, but they offer maximal portability. Therefore, mysqldump is used for database migration (for example, to copy a database from one MySQL installation to another).

  The command mysql is used to re-create the database.

- Significantly faster is simply to copy the database directories at the system level. This is efficient and secure if the MySQL server is stopped for this purpose. However, if the server is to continue running, then it must be ensured that during the copying process no changes are allowed to be made in the database. This task is taken care of under Unix/Linux by the script mysqlhotcopy.

  To re-create the database it is necessary merely to copy the backed-up directory into the MySQL database directory. Note that this form of backup is possible only for MyISAM tables, and not for InnoDB tables.

- One can use logging files in combination with regular backup files for incremental backups. However, that is practicable only as long as the number of changes in the database is not too large. Backup strategies based on logging files are not handled in this section, but in the section on logging.

- Another variant of securing data is replication. This mechanism allows a database to be synchronized on two different computers. For databases that are changed frequently this can result in a high demand on communication between the computers. If you really want nothing more than to keep two copies of your database on two different hard drives, then it is more efficient to mirror a hard drive using RAID. Replication is not dealt with in this section, but in the section of this chapter on replication.

Hot Backups: Both the execution of mysqldump and the copying of database directories can take place while the database is in operation. However, the integrity of the backup is ensured only if *read lock* is executed during the backup for the affected tables.

The result is, on the one hand, that the backup can be executed only when the table is not blocked by a *write lock*. On the other hand, no client can access the tables during the execution of the backup. Since the backup of large databases can take a relatively long time (especially if you use mysqldump), blocking is quite burdensome.

To circumvent this problem, commercial database systems offer *hot backup* mechanisms that permit a backup while the system is running without the complete blocking of entire tables. For MyISAM tables, MySQL is unfortunately incapable of this (despite the promises of mysqlhotcopy). If you use InnoDB tables, however, you can execute hot backups with the supplementary program InnoDB Hot Backup (see http://www.innodb.com/order.php).

Backing Up Databases (mysqldump)

The command mysqldump returns a long list of SQL commands required for the exact recreation of a database. Normally, the program returns a *CREATE TABLE* command for each table in order to generate the table together with indexes, as well as numerous *INSERT* commands (one for each record). The following example shows the result of mysqldump for the *authors* table of the *mylibrary* database presented in Chapter 8.

A couple of brief comments are called for: Lines that begin with -- are considered comments in SQL. In addition, as in C, /* introduces a comment. A MySQL-specific form of comment is introduced by /*!*n*, where *n* is the MySQL version number. If the MySQL server version is less than *n*, then everything up to the closing */ is considered a comment. However, if the server version number is greater than or equal to *n*, then the instructions contained in the comment are in fact executed. This prevents syntax errors from being triggered in older MySQL versions.

The various *SET* commands store the current character set settings and reset the character set to Unicode. (The following commands thus use the UTF8 character set.) Moreover, *unique* and *foreign key* tests are deactivated so that the commands can be more efficiently executed.

The actual backup begins with the command *DROP TABLE*, which deletes the table *authors* if it exists. Then the table is created anew with *CREATE TABLE* and filled with data using *INSERT*. At the end of the output are some instructions that restore the most recently valid settings (character set, foreign key tests, etc.).

```
> mysqldump -u root -p mylibrary authors
Enter password: xxx
-- MySQL dump 10.9
-- Host: localhost     Database: mylibrary
-- Server version       5.0.2-alpha-standard-log
/*!40101 SET @OLD_CHARACTER_SET_CLIENT =@@CHARACTER_SET_CLIENT */;
/*!40101 SET @OLD_CHARACTER_SET_RESULTS=@@CHARACTER_SET_RESULTS */;
/*!40101 SET @OLD_COLLATION_CONNECTION =@@COLLATION_CONNECTION */;
/*!40101 SET NAMES utf8 */;
/*!40014 SET @OLD_UNIQUE_CHECKS=@@UNIQUE_CHECKS,
         UNIQUE_CHECKS=0 */;
/*!40014 SET @OLD_FOREIGN_KEY_CHECKS=@@FOREIGN_KEY_CHECKS,
         FOREIGN_KEY_CHECKS=0 */;
/*!40101 SET @OLD_SQL_MODE=@@SQL_MODE,
         SQL_MODE="NO_AUTO_VALUE_ON_ZERO" */;
--
-- Table structure for table `authors`
--
DROP TABLE IF EXISTS `authors`;
CREATE TABLE `authors` (
  `authID` int(11) NOT NULL auto_increment,
  `authName` varchar(60) collate latin1_german1_ci NOT NULL default '',
  `ts` timestamp NOT NULL default   CURRENT_TIMESTAMP
                       on update CURRENT_TIMESTAMP,
  PRIMARY KEY  (`authID`),
  KEY `authName` (`authName`)
) ENGINE=InnoDB DEFAULT CHARSET=latin1 COLLATE=latin1_german1_ci;
--
-- Dumping data for table `authors`
--
/*!40000 ALTER TABLE `authors` DISABLE KEYS */;
LOCK TABLES `authors` WRITE;
INSERT INTO `authors` VALUES
  (1,'Kofler Michael','2004-12-02 18:36:51'),
  (2,'Kramer David','2004-12-02 18:36:51'),
  (3,'Orfali Robert','2004-12-02 18:36:51'),
...
```

Usually, it makes sense to direct the output of mysqldump not to the screen, but to a backup file using > filename.

```
> mysqldump -u root -p mylibrary authors > backup.sql
```

Backup of All Databases

The following command creates a backup of all databases managed by MySQL and stores these in a single file. During the backup, the database is blocked for all write operations:

```
> mysqldump -u root --all-databases > backup.sql
```

Syntax of mysqldump

The general syntax of mysqldump is the following:

```
mysqldump [options] dbname [tables] > backup.sql
```

If no tables are specified, then mysqldump writes all the tables of the database *dbname* into the file backup.sql. Optionally, the backup can be limited to specific tables. If you wish to back up more than one database or even all of them, then the following syntax variants are what you use:

```
mysqldump [options] --databases  dbname1 dbname2 ...
mysqldump [options] --all-databases
```

The details of the backup can be controlled by a large number of options. An extensive description and reference to all the options appears in Chapter 22. To execute a simple backup, the default settings generally suffice. They have the following effect:

- During the backup *read lock* is executed for each table.

- The resulting backup file is as small as possible (one *INSERT* command for multiple records of the table).

- The resulting file contains *DROP TABLE* commands to delete existing tables when the database is restored.

- All features of the database are retained (including MySQL-specific features that could interfere with migration to a different database system).

- The backup is created in UTF8 format and contains necessary SQL commands for resetting the character set when the data are read back into the database.

The default settings are not recommended for backing up InnoDB tables if individual tables could be changed during the backup, thus jeopardizing the integrity of the backup, or when the resulting files should be backward compatible or as compatible as possible to other database servers. In such cases, you must set additional options. In many cases it is even necessary to deactivate all settings with skip-opt and then set each option individually. In the following you will find two suggestions for options in the case of unusual requirements.

Secure backup of a MyISAM database: In the default setting, individual tables are protected against changes during backup, but it can happen that table B is changed during the backup of table A. This could have the consequence that backed-up table A refers to a record of table B that was deleted just before it was backed up. The solution is the option --lock-all-tables:

```
> mysqldump -u root -p --lock-all-tables databasename > backup.sql
```

Backup of InnoDB databases: With InnoDB tables, *LOCK* commands solve nothing. The option --single-transaction, however, executes the backup within a transaction. Since --single-transaction is incompatible with the default settings, you must use --skip-opt and set a large number of other options. The resulting command is divided over three lines here in order to fit it on the page:

```
> mysqldump -u root -p --skip-opt --single-transaction --add-drop-table \
        --create-options --quick --extended-insert \
        —set-charset —disable-keys databasename > backup.sql
```

Views and Stored Procedures

You can back up the definitions of *views* with `mysqldump`, but backing up stored procedures is not supported. If you wish to execute an ordinary backup with `mysqldump`, the stored procedures belonging to the database will not be backed up. There is currently no backup tool that can simply back up the stored procedures of a particular database. You can execute

```
> mysqldump -u root -p mysql proc > backup.sql
```

to back up the table *mysql.proc*, but the backup will contain the SPs of all databases. That makes reading in the backup at a later time problematic.

You can achieve a usable result if you restrict the backup of the *proc* table to the records belonging to the database you wish to back up. To do so, supply a condition with the option `--where`: here *db* is the column within the *proc* table that contains the database names, and `--no-create-info` keeps the *proc* table from being re-created and thereby destroying the existing stored procedures of other databases.

```
> mysqldump -u root -p "--where=db='dbname'" --no-create-info \
  mysql proc > backup.sql
```

Before using `backup.sql`, you must delete any existing SPs of the table *dbname*. If you forget to do so, when you attempt to overwrite existing SPs with the backup you will trigger an error.

DELETE FROM `mysql.proc` **WHERE** `db='dbname'`

Until there is an official backup tool for stored procedures, you can execute your backups with the example program SP Administrator; see Chapter 15.

mybackup

The Perl script `mybackup` is currently not included with MySQL. However, you can find it on the Internet: `http://www.mswanson.com/mybackup/`.

The script `mybackup` uses `mysqldump`. The advantage over `mysqldump` is that the backup files (one per database) are written into a specified directory and there immediately compressed with `gzip` and if required, broken up into pieces of size 2GB.

Restoring a Database (mysql)

There is no direct inverse operator for `mysqldump`, simply because the old workhorse `mysql` is completely satisfactory for this purpose.

The re-creation of a database works even if you use a different (newer) version of MySQL or if MySQL is running on a different computer (under a different operating system). On the other hand, the attempt to read in a backup onto an older version of MySQL can be problematic. If the backup database uses functions or data types that the old MySQL version is unaware of, difficulties are unavoidable.

Restoring a Single Database

If `backup.sql` contains only a single database, then the restore command looks like this:

```
> mysql -u root -p databasename < backup.sql
Enter password: xxx
```

The database *databasename* must already exist. If that is not the case, then you can easily create it with `mysqladmin create databasename`.

Restoring Several Databases

If several databases were backed up with mysqldump, then backup.sql contains the requisite *CREATE DATABASE* commands for creating the databases anew if they do not yet exist. There is no necessity to create the databases first. You also do not need to specify a database when mysql is called.

```
> mysql -u root -p < backup.sql
Enter password: xxx
```

Reading In Databases and Tables Interactively

You can read in *.sql files interactively in the program mysql, that is, without restarting this program each time. For this, you use the command *SOURCE* or its abbreviated form /. and specify the file name of the *.sql file. (Under Windows, directories can be separated with either / or \. The file name does not need to be placed in quotation marks.)

Now mysql executes every SQL command in the file. However, the many outputs to the monitor (*Query OK, 1 row affected*) that are normally displayed are burdensome. They can be prevented by launching mysql with the option --silent:

```
> mysql -u root -p --silent
Enter password: xxx
mysql> USE dbname
mysql> \. /tmp/backup.sql
```

Problems with Character Sets

Backups made with a current version of mysqldump use by default the UTF8 character set. However, since the backup file also contains all necessary commands for using this character set, there is no problem in restoring a backup.

But when a backup is made with an older version of mysqldump or with some other backup program entirely, the situation is different. In restoring the backup with mysql, you absolutely must specify the required character set with --default-character-set:

```
> mysql -u root -p --default-character-set=latin1 mylibrary < mylibrary.sql
```

Fast Backups (mysqlhotcopy)

For a considerable time, the Perl script mysqlhotcopy has been provided with the Unix/Linux version of MySQL. This script is supposed to help in improving the speed of backups executed with mysqldump. The basic idea of the program is first to execute a *read lock* for the specified databases and then with *FLUSH TABLES* to ensure that the database files are actually in their current versions. Then the database files are directly copied.

■**Caution** mysqlhotcopy creates a direct copy of table files. Therefore, the command can be used only with MyISAM tables, not InnoDB tables. Beware: With InnoDB tables you will receive no error message, but the backup will be unusable.

The documentation to mysqlhotcopy is obtained with the following command. Instead of /usr/local/bin you may have to give another path: user$ perldoc /usr/local/bin/mysqlhotcopy.

Making a Backup

In the simplest case, the use of mysqlhotcopy is as follows:

```
root# mysqlhotcopy dbname1 dbname2 dbname3 backup/
```

With this the databases *dbname1*, *dbname2*, and *dbname3* are copied into the specified backup directory. (This backup directory must already exist.) Each database is copied into a subdirectory named for the database; mysqlhotcopy must be capable of reading the MySQL database files that usually are located in /var/lib/mysql/dbname/.

Options

Table 14-2 gives merely the most important options. A full description of all the options can be found in the documentation.

Table 14-2. *mysqlhotcopy Options*

Option	Meaning
--allowold	overwrites existing backup files.
--keepold	archives existing backup files into the directory dbname_old. If this directory already exists, then its contents are overwritten.
--flushlog	has the effect that MySQL changes made in the databases after the backup are written to a new logging file. This option makes sense only if the logging files are to be used for an incremental backup.
--noindices	copies for (My)ISAM tables only the actual data, not the index files. (More precisely, the first 2KB of the index files are copied. This makes possible an uncomplicated, though slow, restoration of the index files with myisamchk -r. But the backup can be executed more quickly, because fewer data must be copied.)

The options -u, -p, -P, and -S, as well as --user=, --password=, --port=, and --socket=, function as they do with all MySQL tools, but with one exception. In the case of -p, the password must be given here (while all other tools provide interactive password input, which is more secure).

Restoring a Database

To restore a database you simply copy the relevant database directory into MySQL's data directory. If you execute this operation as *root*, you must then specify the owner of the database files with chown. (The owner must have the same account under which mysqld is running, usually *mysql*.)

```
root# chown -R mysql.mysql /var/lib/mysql/dbname
```

■**Caution** If the database to be restored already exists, the files involved in an operational MySQL cannot simply be overwritten. First execute *DROP DATABASE*.

It is possible to re-create data only if the version of MySQL that is running is compatible with the version under which the backup was executed. (With each change in the main version number the format of database files can conceivably change.)

Database Migration

The term "migration" applied to databases denotes the transport of a database from one system to another. There are many reasons that can account for the migratory instinct appearing in a database:

- installation of a new database server
- transfer of a development system (for example, on a local computer) to a production system (on the ISP's computer)
- a MySQL update (for example, from version 4.1 to 5.0)
- a change in database system (for example, from Microsoft SQL Server to MySQL)

Transfer of Databases Between MySQL Systems

Migration between MySQL systems is generally carried out with the backup tools mysqldump and mysql, which we have previously described. In other words, with the old MySQL server you make a complete backup using mysqldump, install the new MySQL server, and read in the saved databases with mysql.

If the tables are in MyISAM format and compatible versions of MySQL are running on both computers (say, 5.0.n), then the migration can be effected by simply copying the database files. This holds even if MySQL is running under different operating systems.

The main advantage of direct copying of MyISAM tables as opposed to the use of mysqldump/ mysql is, of course, the much greater speed.

MySQL guarantees compatibility of database files only within main versions (such as from 5.0.17 to 5.0.18), and not between major updates (such as from 3.23 to 4.0 or 4.0 to 4.1). In such cases it is safer to use mysqldump and mysql. With InnoDB tables, there is no provision for direct copying of the so-called *masterspace* files, and so there is no avoiding mysqldump.

In migrating with mysqldump/mysql, you do not necessarily have to create (possibly enormous) files. You can pass the output of mysqldump directly to mysql.

The following command demonstrates the usual way of proceeding. It assumes that the command is executed on the computer with the source database and that the data are transported to a second computer (host name *destinationhost*). There the database in question must already exist, and the access privileges must allow access to the source computer. For space considerations the command is broken over two lines:

```
root# mysqldump -u root --password=xxx dbname | \
      mysql -u root --password=yyy -h destinationhost dbname
```

If you wish to change only the format of database files, say from MyISAM to InnoDB, then you do not need to go through any migration process at all. The command *ALTER TABLE tablename TYPE=newtype* will be adequate to meet your needs. If you wish to convert a large number of tables, then under Unix/Linux the Perl script mysql_convert_table_format will save you a great deal of effort. (The script assumes that a connection to the MySQL server can be established.)

■Tip A special case of migration, namely, setting up a database on an ISP, is described toward the end of this chapter. The usual problem in doing this is the possession of inadequate access privileges to the ISP computer.

If you copy databases from Windows to Unix/Linux, there can arise problems with the case-sensitivity of file extensions. The Perl script mysql_fix_extensions solves this problem (see Chapter 22).

MySQL Server Update

Usually, an update to the MySQL server (such as from 5.0.7 to 5.0.8) is done in such a way that the server is stopped, the old version deinstalled, and the new version installed. (Although an update usually causes no problems, it is recommended before any server update to create a complete backup with `mysqldump` of all databases. Better safe than sorry!)

This simple process is possible in updating from 4.*n* to 5.*n*. However, there are also some details to keep track of:

Installation directory: Under Windows, the default location of the MySQL installation has changed. While the server previously was usually installed in the directory `c:\mysql`, now by default the directory `C:\Programs\MySQL\MySQL Server` *n.n* is used. All database files must be copied before server startup into the new directory.

Also, the location of the configuration file has changed. While previously under Windows the MySQL server evaluated the file `Windows\my.ini`, now it reads `C:\Programs\MySQL\ MySQL Server` *n.n*`\my.ini`.

mysql database: If you wish to continue to use the *mysql* database with its information on access administration, you must back up this database before installation and then read it in after installation. This can be problematic in that the *mysql* database was expanded to include additional tables and columns.

Under Unix/Linux you can simply update the database *mysql* restored from an earlier version using the script `mysql_fix_privilege_tables`. To execute the script, you must give the *root* password.

Under Windows, this script is unavailable. Instead, you must execute the file `scripts/ mysql_fix_privilege_tables.sql` with the `mysql` command interpreter. (The following command must be given on a single line.)

```
> mysql -u root -p mysql <
  "c:\programs\MySQL\MySQL Server 5.0\scripts\mysql_fix_privilege_tables.sql"
```

In my experience, many problems and errors have arisen in attempting to adapt old *mysql* tables to the new MySQL conventions. Furthermore, all passwords remain in the old format, so that the security advantage of the new authentication system goes unused (see Chapter 11).

If you must migrate very large MySQL user tables, it is often simpler to migrate the access data manually from the old *mysql* tables into the new ones. Here it can be helpful to install, parallel to the new *mysql* database, the old version under another name (e.g., *oldmysql*).

Further information on executing MySQL server updates can be found at `http://dev.mysql.com/ doc/mysql/en/upgrade.html`.

Changing the Database System

For migrating to MySQL from another database system or vice versa there is no universal solution. Almost every database system offers a tool, comparable to `mysqldump`, that represents the contents of the database as an SQL file. The problem is that the resulting files are seldom precisely compatible (for example, due to different column types or lack of ANSI SQL/92 conformity). With *Find and Replace* you can solve some of these problems. Under Unix/Linux the tools `awk` and `sed` can be helpful.

I have developed a small script especially for migration from the Microsoft SQL server to MySQL that in many cases is helpful (see Chapter 19). For other database systems you will find suitable converters at `http://solutions.mysql.com/` and `http://solutions.mysql.com/software/`.

If you are working under Windows, then ODBC is often helpful. For example, you can use Access to import a database of an ODBC-compatible system and then export it to MySQL. Do not expect, however, that all the details of the definition of the columns will remain intact.

Importing and Exporting Text Files

Sometimes, the contents of a table should be written as efficiently as possible into a text file or read from such a file. MySQL offers several ways of doing this:

- The SQL command *LOAD DATA* reads in a text file and transfers the contents into a table.

- With `mysqlimport` there is a command available that is equivalent to *LOAD DATA*. It is especially well suited for automating the importation of a script file.

- The SQL command *SELECT ... INTO OUTFILE* writes the result of a query into a text file.

- If you wish to automate exportation with a script, then the command `mysqldump` is to be recommended. Its functionality is similar to that of *SELECT ... INTO OUTFILE*.

- In many cases you can use the universal tool `mysql` for implementing text, HTML, or XML exportation.

If none of the above commands suits your needs, then you will have to write your own script to assist you in importing or exporting. The programming language Perl was made for such tasks.

Special Characters in the Imported or Exported File

A common feature of *LOAD DATA*, *SELECT ... INTO OUTFILE*, `mysqlimport`, and `mysqldump` is the set of options for handling special characters in a text file. There are four options for this purpose, which as SQL commands look like this:

```
FIELDS TERMINATED BY 'fieldtermstring'
       ENCLOSED BY 'enclosechar'
       ESCAPED BY 'escchar'
LINES TERMINATED BY 'linetermstring'
```

fieldtermstring specifies the character string that separates the columns within the row (for example, a tab character).

enclosechar specifies a character that is permitted to appear in the text file before and after individual entries (usually a single or double quote character for character strings). If an entry begins with this character, then that character is deleted at the beginning and end. (The end of a column is recognized by *fieldtermstring*.)

escchar specifies the escape character that is to be used to indicate special characters (the default is the backslash). This is necessary if special characters appear in character strings of the text file that are also used for separating rows or columns. Moreover, MySQL expects code 0 in the form \0 (where the backslash is to be replaced by *escchar*).

linetermstring specifies the character string with which a row is terminated. With DOS/Windows text files the character string '\r\n' must be used.

Working with Character Strings, Numbers, Dates, and BLOBs

For all the commands introduced in this section there is a data format that must be followed exactly. In particular, for importation you must hold to the format expected by MySQL. For exportation you have somewhat more leeway, in that you can use SQL functions for formatting data in the *SELECT* command (such as *DATE_FORMAT* for formatting dates and times).

Moreover, there are four options that you can use to determine how rows and columns should be separated and how character strings and special characters should be indicated. (Details can be found in Chapter 21 under *LOAD DATA* and *SELECT ... INTO OUTFILE*.)

Numbers: For very large and very small numbers in the *FLOAT* and *SINGLE* formats one has the use of scientific notation in the form *-2.3e-037*.

Character Strings: Strings are not changed in importation and exportation. Special characters contained in the character string are marked by default with the backslash in order to distinguish these from the characters used for separation (e.g., *tab, carriage return, linefeed*).

BLOBs: Binary objects are treated byte for byte like character strings. Neither in importing nor exporting is there the possibility of using hexadecimal character strings (0x123412341234 …).

Date and Time: Dates are treated as character strings of the form *2005-12-31*, and times as character strings of the form *23:59:59*. Timestamp values are considered integers of the form *20051231235959*.

NULL: The treatment of *NULL* is problematic. The following text assumes that the backslash is used as the escape character for special characters and the double quote character for indicating a character string. If you use other characters (options *FIELDS ESCAPED BY '?' ENCLOSED BY '?'*), then you will have to reconfigure the following paragraphs.

In exporting with escape characters, *NULL* is represented by \N. In exporting without escape characters *NULL* is simply represented by the four characters *NULL*. However, *NULL* or \N is placed between double quote characters (though not if they are in a text or BLOB field) and can therefore be distinguished from character strings.

In importing with escape characters, MySQL accepts *NULL*, \N, and *"\N"* as *NULL*. However, *"NULL"* is interpreted as a character string (consisting of the four characters *NULL*).

■**Caution** If you use neither escape characters for special characters nor "enclose" characters for character strings in importing and exporting, then the condition *NULL* cannot be distinguished from the character string *NULL*. In the character string \N the *N* must be uppercase. Note that \n is the newline character.

Importing with LOAD DATA INFILE

The syntax of *LOAD DATA* is as follows:

```
LOAD DATA [loadoptions]  INFILE 'filename.txt'  [duplicateoptions]
    INTO TABLE tablename [importoptions] [IGNORE ignorenr LINES]
    [(columnlist)]
```

The result is that the file `filename.txt` is imported into the table *tablename*. There are various options (see the SQL reference in Chapter 21) that can be given, as well as the column names for the table. To execute the command you need the *File* privilege (so that files can be read).

If the MySQL server and the *LOAD DATA* command are executed on different computers, *LOAD DATA* reads the file from the file system of the MySQL server. This is generally not correct. To read the file from the local file system, the variant *LOCAL INFILE* … must be used.

If the text file to be imported contains characters outside the ASCII character set, you must set the character set of the text with *SET NAMES* before the command *LOAD DATA*.

Example 1

The following example assumes that the table *importtable1* in the database *exceptions* already exists. The table consists of five columns: one *AUTO_INCREMENT* column (*id*) and the columns *a_double*, *a_datetime*, *a_time*, and *a_text*. The column name refers to its data type.

The text file `import1-latin1.txt` is to be imported into this table. In the following expression, ➤ represents the tab character. The file uses the character set *Latin1*, separates the lines in the Windows-typical way with *carriage return* and *line feed*, and furthermore contains some stumbling blocks, such as decimal numbers and dates in various notations.

```
12.3      ➤ 12/31/1999  ➤ 17:30  ➤ text
-0.33e-2  ➤ 2000/12/31  ➤ 11:20  ➤ "text in quotes"
1,23      ➤ 31.12.2001  ➤ 0:13   ➤ "german text with äöüß"
```

Before the importation, any existing records from *importtable1* are deleted, and the character set is set to *Latin1*.

```
USE exceptions
DELETE FROM importtable1
SET NAMES 'latin1'
```

The import command looks like this:

```
LOAD DATA INFILE 'c:/import1-latin1.txt'
  INTO TABLE importtable1
  FIELDS TERMINATED BY '\t'
        ENCLOSED BY '\"'
  LINES TERMINATED BY '\r\n'
  (a_number, a_date, a_time, a_string)
  Query OK, 3 rows affected (0.00 sec)
  Records: 3  Deleted: 0  Skipped: 0  Warnings: 3
```

SHOW WARNINGS returns a list of warnings that report on various importation problems:

```
SHOW WARNINGS
Level    Code   Message
Warning  1264   Out of range value adjusted for column 'a_date' at row 1
Warning  1265   Data truncated for column 'a_number' at row 3
Warning  1264   Out of range value adjusted for column 'a_date' at row 3
```

The following *SELECT* command shows that the importation was only partially successful. In both the first and third lines, the date has been incorrectly interpreted. Moreover, in the third line the decimal number with the German comma for a decimal point has caused problems; namely, the part to the right of the decimal point has gone missing. In sum, take care to obey the MySQL formatting rules to the letter when preparing a file for importation.

If you execute the *SELECT* command with `mysql` in an input or console window, you must, before execution of the *SELECT* command, set the character set valid in the window (e.g., *cp850* under Windows, *utf8* in most current Linux distributions).

```
SET NAMES utf8
SELECT * FROM importtable1
id  a_number  a_datetime            a_time     a_string
1      12.3   0000-00-00 00:00:00   17:30:00   text
2    -0.0033  2000-12-31 00:00:00   11:20:00   text in quotes
3         1   0000-0000  00:00:00   00:13:00   german text with äöüß
```

Example 2 (BLOB, NULL)

The starting point for our second example is the table *importtable2* with columns *id* and *a_blob*. The second column is allowed to contain *NULL*.

The following Unix text file is to be imported into this table (again, ➤ represents a tab character):

```
1  ➤ NULL
2  ➤ "NULL"
3  ➤ \N
4  ➤ "\N"
5  ➤ \n
6  ➤ "\n"
7  ➤ 0x414243
8  ➤ "0x414243"
9  ➤ blob blob
10 ➤ "blob blob"
```

The text file is imported with the following command. (By default, the backslash serves as escape character, and the tab sign as column separator.) *REPLACE* means that existing data records are to be replaced.

```
USE exceptions
LOAD DATA INFILE '/tmp/import2.txt' REPLACE
INTO TABLE importtable2
FIELDS ENCLOSED BY '\"'
  Query OK, 20 rows affected (0.01 sec)
  Records: 10  Deleted: 10  Skipped: 0  Warnings: 0
```

In order to analyze the result of the importation in more detail, we shall use *SELECT* * and add the additional columns *LENGTH(a_blob)* and *ISNULL*. This enables us to distinguish the state *NULL* (length *NULL*) from the character string *NULL* (length 4):

```
SELECT *, LENGTH(a_blob), ISNULL(a_blob) FROM importtable2
```

id	a_blob	LENGTH(a_blob)	ISNULL(a_blob)
1	NULL	NULL	1
2	NULL	4	0
3	NULL	NULL	1
4	NULL	NULL	1
5		1	0
6		1	0
7	0x414243	8	0
8	0x414243	8	0
9	blob blob	9	0
10	blob blob	9	0

We see that in the first six records, *NULL* was treated correctly in only the first, third, and fourth records. In the second record, the character string *"NULL"* was stored, while in the fifth and sixth records a newline character was stored.

The attempt to read in a hexadecimal number as a binary object fails. Both times, 0x414243 is interpreted as the character string "0x414243" (and not, as intended in record 7, as hex code for the character string "ABC").

CSV Import

Sometimes, one wishes to import data into MySQL from a spreadsheet program like Excel. Such programs generally offer the possibility to store tables in CSV (comma-separated values) format. In principle, the importation of such files proceeds effortlessly. For files that were created with Excel under Windows, suitable import options look like this:

```
FIELDS TERMINATED BY ',' ENCLOSED BY '\"'
LINES TERMINATED BY '\r\n'
```

In practice, importation usually runs into trouble with the formatting of dates (usually in the form 12/31/2003, about which MySQL is clueless). In particular, with Microsoft software, the automatic country-specific formatting of numbers can cause problems when, for example, Excel suddenly represents a decimal number with a comma instead of a period for the decimal point. In such cases one can get help from a special import script for MySQL (or else you can program your own export filters for Excel).

Importing with mysqlimport

If you wish to execute *LOAD DATA* not as an SQL command but through an external program, then MySQL offers the tool `mysqlimport`. (It relies on *LOAD DATA*.)

```
mysqlimport databasename tablename.txt
```

The command reads the specified file into a like-named table of the database *databasename*. (The table name is thus taken from the file name, with the file identifier being eliminated. Thus `mysqlimport db1 authors.txt` imports the data into the table *authors* of the database *db1*.)

Please note that the file normally is read from the file system of the MySQL server. If you are working at another computer and wish to read a file that is located there, you must use the option `--local`. The character set of the text file is set as usual with `--default-character-set=`.

The options `--fields-terminated-by`, `--fields-enclosed-by`, `--fields-escaped-by`, and `--lines-terminated-by` correspond to the SQL options described at the beginning of this section. These options should be placed in quotation marks, for example, `"--fields-enclosed-by=+"`.

To carry out the importation demonstrated in the previous section (example 2) with `mysqlimport`, the file to be imported must first be renamed to correspond with the table name in `importtable2.txt`. Then the following command is necessary, here separated onto two lines with `\` for space reasons:

```
root# mysqlimport --local "--fields-enclosed-by=\"" \
      exceptions /tmp/importtable2.txt
```

Under Windows (that is, for importing a Windows text file), the command would look like this (broken into two lines here for reasons of space):

```
> mysqlimport --local "--fields-enclosed-by=\"" \
    "–lines-terminated-by=\r\n" exceptions C:\importtable2.txt
```

Exporting with SELECT … INTO OUTFILE

With the command *SELECT … INTO OUTFILE* we are dealing with a garden-variety *SELECT*, where before the *FROM* part, *INTO OUTFILE* is used to specify a file name and several possible options:

```
SELECT [selectoptions] columnlist
INTO OUTFILE 'filename.txt' exportoptions
FROM ... WHERE ... GROUP BY ... HAVING ... ORDER BY  ... LIMIT ...
```

The result of the query is thus stored in the file `filename.txt`. With *exportoptions* various options can be specified for dealing with special characters (see the SQL reference in Chapter 21).

Example

The following example assumes that there exists a table *exporttable* in the current database that has the following contents (note in particular the field *a_char* in the second data record):

```
SELECT * FROM exporttable
id   a_char        a_text        a_blob       a_date       a_time    ...
1    char char     text text     blob blob    2001-12-31   12:30:00
2    ' " \ ; +     adsf          NULL         2000-11-17   16:54:54
...  a_timestamp        a_float      a_decimal    a_enum    a_set
     20001117164643     3.14159          0.012    b         e,g
     20001117165454    -2.3e-037       12.345     b         f,g
```

The data types of the columns are taken from the column names. The following lines show the result of an *OUTFILE* exportation without special options. The tab character is again indicated by a hooked arrow. The resulting file has two lines, which for reasons of space are here distributed over five lines:

```
SELECT * INTO OUTFILE '/tmp/testfile.txt'
FROM exporttable
1 ➤ char char ➤ text text ➤ blob blob ➤ 2001-12-31 ➤ 12:30:00 ➤ 20001117164643 ➤ ➥
3.14159 ➤ 0.012 ➤ b ➤ e,g
2 ➤ ' " \\ ; + ➤ adsf ➤ \N ➤ 2000-11-17 ➤ 16:54:54 ➤
20001117165454 ➤ -2.3e-037 ➤ 12.345 ➤ b ➤ f,g
```

In the second attempt a semicolon is used as column separator. All fields are enclosed at beginning and end with a double quote character. As escape character, the backslash, is used (the default setting). Of particular interest is the behavior in the field *a_char*:

```
' " \ ; +    becomes      "' \" \\ ; +"
```

The semicolon within the character string remains untouched, since it is clear on account of the double quote character where *a_char* ends. However, the double quote becomes a backslash to ensure that the character is not misinterpreted at the end of the character string.

Please note also that *NULL* is represented as \\N, and in fact, without being enclosed in double quotes.

```
SELECT * INTO OUTFILE '/tmp/testfile.txt'
FIELDS TERMINATED BY ';' ENCLOSED BY '\"'
FROM exporttable
1;"char char";"text text";"blob blob";"2001-12-31";"12:30:00";
20001117164643;3.14159;0.012;"b";"e,g"

2;"' \" \\ ; +";"adsf";\N;"2000-11-17";"16:54:54";
20001117165454;-2.3e-037;12.345;"b";"f,g"
```

In our third attempt, a semicolon is again used as a column separator. The plus sign (+) is used as optional field identifier (that is, only with character strings, dates, times, and BLOBs, and not with numbers). Finally, the exclamation mark (!) is used as escape character. Again the most interesting feature is the transformation of *a_char*:

```
' " \ ; +    becomes    +' " \ ; !++
SELECT * INTO OUTFILE '/tmp/testfile.txt'
FIELDS TERMINATED BY ':' OPTIONALLY ENCLOSED BY '+' ESCAPED BY '!'
FROM exporttable
```

Now *NULL* becomes *!N* (that is, for *NULL*, too, the changed escape character is used).

```
1;+char char+;+text text+;+blob blob+;+2001-12-31+;+12:30:00+;
20001117164643;3.14159;0.012;+b+;+e,g+

2;+' " \ ; !++;+adsf+;!N;+2000-11-17+;+16:54:54+;
20001117165454;-2.3e-037;12.345;+b+;+f,g+
```

Basically, the data stored in a text file with *LOAD DATA* can be read again into a table unchanged if the same options are used as with *SELECT ... INTO OUTFILE*.

Exporting with mysqldump

As an alternative to *SELECT ... INTO OUTFILE* there is the auxiliary program mysqldump. This program is actually primarily a backup program (see also earlier in this chapter and Chapter 22).

The program mysqldump always stores entire tables (and not the result of a particular *SELECT* query). A further difference is that mysqldump normally does not return a text file with the raw data, but entire *INSERT* commands. The resulting file can then later be read in with mysql. To use mysqldump for text exportation you must specify the option --tab:

```
mysqldump --tab=verz [options] databasename tablename
```

With --tab a directory is specified. In this directory mysqldump stores two files for each table: tablename.txt and tablename.sql. The *.txt file contains the same data as after *SELECT ... INTO OUTFILE*. The *.sql file contains a *CREATE TABLE* command, which allows the table to be re-created.

As with mysqlimport, the representation of special characters can be controlled with four options: --fields-terminated-by, --fields-enclosed-by, --fields-escaped-by, and --lines-terminated-by. These options are analogous to the SQL options described at the beginning of this section. They should be set in quotation marks (for example, "--fields-enclosed-by=+"). In the following example, the command is divided over two lines:

```
C:\> mysqldump -u root -p --tab=C:\tmp "--fields-enclosed-by=\""
        exceptions exporttable
Enter password: ******
```

XML Exporting with mysqldump

If you execute mysqldump with the option --xml, you obtain as result an XML file. By default, the Unicode character set (UTF8) is used. With --default-character-set you can switch to another character set.

```
root# mysqldump -u root -p --xml mylibrary > /tmp/mylibrary.xml
Enter password: ******
```

Exporting with mysql in Batch Mode

The universal tool mysql can be used to execute SQL commands in batch mode and store the results in a text file. In contrast to mysqldump, mysql is distinguished in that the resulting file is actually more or less readable—for human beings, that is. (However, there is no attempt to make the file suitable for a later reexportation.)

In the simplest case, execute mysql in the following form (here once again divided over two lines with \):

```
> mysql -u root --password=xxx --batch --default-character-set=latin1 \
  "--execute=SELECT * FROM authors;" mylibrary > output.txt
```

The SQL command is passed with the option --execute, where the entire option must be placed in quotation marks. In the resulting text file output.txt the columns are separated by tab characters. The first line contains the column headings.

Exchanging Rows and Columns

If a table has many columns, then mysql returns very long rows, which can be difficult to interpret. In this case, instead of --batch you can use the option --vertical. Then each record is divided over several lines, where in each row only one data item is given (this command must be typed on one line).

```
> mysql -u root -p =xxx --vertical
    "--execute=SELECT * FROM titles;" \
  mylibrary > test.txt
```

The resulting file looks like this:

```
*************************** 1. row ***************************
 titleID: 1
   title: Linux, 5th ed.
subtitle: NULL
 edition: NULL
  publID: 1
   catID: 1
  langID: NULL
    year: 2000
    isbn: NULL
 comment: NULL
*************************** 2. row ***************************
 titleID: 2
   title: Definitive Guide to Excel VBA
...
```

Generating HTML Tables

If instead of --batch the option --html is used, then mysql generates an HTML table with column headers (see Figure 14-1). However, the resulting file does not contain any HTML headers. The text uses the character set specified by --default-character-set. The following command must be given on a single line.

```
> mysql -u root -p=xxx --html
    "--execute=SELECT * FROM titles;" \
  --default-character-set=latin1 mylibrary > test.html
```

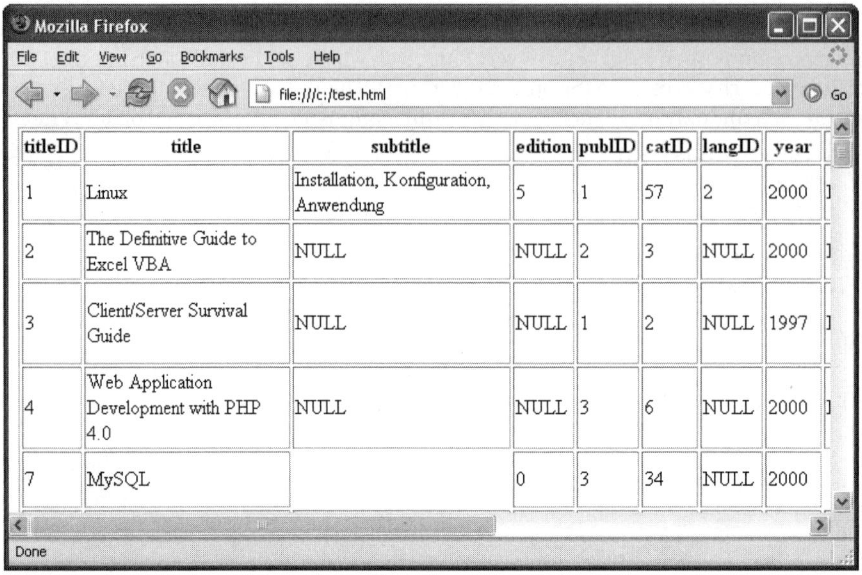

titleID	title	subtitle	edition	publID	catID	langID	year
1	Linux	Installation, Konfiguration, Anwendung	5	1	57	2	2000
2	The Definitive Guide to Excel VBA	NULL	NULL	2	3	NULL	2000
3	Client/Server Survival Guide	NULL	NULL	1	2	NULL	1997
4	Web Application Development with PHP 4.0	NULL	NULL	3	6	NULL	2000
7	MySQL		0	3	34	NULL	2000

Figure 14-1. *A table created with mysql*

XML Exporting with mysql

Like `mysqldump`, `mysql` is also capable of creating XML files. The following command must be input in a single line:

```
> mysql -u root -p --xml --default-character-set=utf8
    "--execute=SELECT * FROM titles;" mylibrary > C:\test.xml
```

Logging

The term *logging* generally denotes the recording of each change in a database. (As you will see in the course of this section, there are other items that can be recorded as well.) Thus, if a MySQL client program executes the command

```
INSERT INTO mydatabase.mytable (col1, col2) VALUES (1, 'xy')
```

then MySQL changes the table *mydatabase.mytable* accordingly. If logging is activated, then the command itself is also saved in the logging file.

Tip In the MySQL documentation you will find a great deal of information on the subject of logging: `http://dev.mysql.com/doc/mysql/en/log-files.html`.

Why Logging?

There are various goals that can be achieved through logging:

Security: It is not possible to execute backups uninterruptedly. Thus, for example, if you make a backup every night, and then the next day your hard drive crashes, all that day's changes would be lost. If you have a logging file (naturally, on a different hard drive), then you can re-create the lost data.

Logging files also help in determining who has used the database when, at what times an unusually large number of failed attempts to access MySQL were made, etc.

Monitoring: Normally, you know only the current state of the data. If your tables contain *TIMESTAMP* columns, then the time of the last change can easily be determined. But it is impossible to determine who made this change. If such information is important for your system, if it should be possible to find out who changed what data when, then you can activate an expanded logging protocol that will capture this additional information.

Optimization: Often, it is difficult to determine which queries are most burdensome to a database system. Therefore, MySQL offers the possibility to log all queries whose execution takes a particularly long time.

Replication: Replication denotes the process of synchronizing databases on several computers. For replication it is required that logging be carried out on the *master* computer. (Details on replication follow in the next section of this chapter.)

Transactions: Logging is also carried out with transaction-capable tables (such as InnoDB). In this case, logging files ensure that completed transactions can be executed even after a crash of the database. (Details on transaction logging for InnoDB tables appear later in this chapter.)

Based on the various purposes that it fulfills, MySQL supports various types of logging, which are presented in this section. As long as logging is activated, the logging files are stored in the same directory in which the directories of the various MySQL databases are located. There is, however, the possibility of using various options to change the location. If you value maximum speed and security, the logging files should reside on a different hard drive from that on which the database files are located.

Drawbacks

In the default setting almost all logging variants are deactivated. (The only exception is the logging of errors.) The main reason for this deactivation is speed: Logging slows down the operation of MySQL considerably. How great the losses in speed are depends on which logging variants are activated and which SQL commands are typically executed. For example, in *update log*, only those commands that change a database are logged (but no *SELECT* commands).

The second drawback is the tendency of logging files rapidly to consume more and more space on your hard drive. In particular, with database systems in which data are frequently altered, logging files often require significantly more space than the actual database.

Logging Changes (update log)

The *update log* is responsible for the logging of changes to a database. In the past, MySQL could carry out this logging in two ways: in text form (log-update) and in binary format (log-bin). Since version 5.0, this form of logging can be done only in binary form; that is, the option log-update is no longer available. The reason for this change is the numerous advantages of the binary format:

- The logging file contains more information, such as the time of each change and the client thread ID number. (If you wish to know the users behind the ID numbers, you must activate an additional logging file with the option log, in which each login to the MySQL server is recorded.)

- Transactions are handled correctly. (The commands of a transaction are recorded only after a *COMMIT*.)

- The logging files are significantly smaller.

- Writing the logging files is more efficient.

- The logging files can be used as the basis for replication.

- According to the MySQL documentation, binary logging slows operation of the MySQL server by only one percent. (To be sure, it is not indicated under what circumstances this value holds. If the database operation consists overwhelmingly of changes, the speed advantage could diminish sharply.)

The only drawback to binary logging is that the logging files cannot be viewed with an ordinary text editor; however, they can be viewed with the auxiliary program mysqlbinlog.

The internal format of the binary logging files has changed with every principal version number of MySQL (3.*n*, 4.*n*, 5.*n*). New MySQL server versions and new versions of mysqlbinlog cannot cope with the old formats, but that is not true in the opposite direction.

Activating Binary Update Logging

Binary logging is activated by the line log-bin in the configuration file. MySQL must then be restarted so that the change can become effective.

```
# in /etc/my.cnf (Unix/Linux) or \my.ini (Windows)
[mysqld]
log-bin [=name]
```

MySQL now creates two new files, name-bin.001 and name-bin.index, in the directory in which the database directories are located. If no name is given in the log-bin option, MySQL uses the computer name. The file name-bin.index contains a directory of all logging files. (At each server start a new logging file is begun.)

If you are using replication (see the next section), you should by all means specify a name with log-bin. If you do not do so and the network name of the computer on which the MySQL server is running changes at a later date, the names of the logging files will change, which could cause problems with replication.

MySQL also logs in name-bin.n all changes to the contents and structure of all databases (thus, for example, the generation of a new table, adding a new column). MySQL logs only actual changes. *SELECT* and *UPDATE* commands that leave the data unchanged will not be logged.

The logging files can be viewed with mysqlbinlog; they look somewhat like the following example (where we have broken long lines and provided some comments):

```
> mysqlbinlog saturn-bin.002 | less
#050222 16:52:19 server id 1  end_log_pos 53492
#         Query   thread_id=20   exec_time=0    error_code=0
SET TIMESTAMP=1109087539;
SET ONE_SHOT CHARACTER_SET_CLIENT=33,COLLATION_CONNECTION=33,
  COLLATION_DATABASE=8,COLLATION_SERVER=8;
# at 53492
#050222 16:52:19 server id 1  end_log_pos 53601
#         Query   thread_id=20   exec_time=0    error_code=0
```

```
SET TIMESTAMP=1109087539;
/*!40000 ALTER TABLE "languages" ENABLE KEYS */;
# at 53601
#050222 16:52:19 server id 1  end_log_pos 53763
#          Query    thread_id=20    exec_time=0      error_code=0
SET TIMESTAMP=1109087539;
SET ONE_SHOT CHARACTER_SET_CLIENT=33,COLLATION_CONNECTION=33,
  COLLATION_DATABASE=8,COLLATION_SERVER=8;
# at 53763
#050222 16:52:19 server id 1  end_log_pos 54171
#          Query    thread_id=20    exec_time=0      error_code=0
SET TIMESTAMP=1109087539;
CREATE TABLE "publishers" (
  "publID" int(11) NOT NULL auto_increment,
  "publName" varchar(60) collate latin1_german1_ci NOT NULL default '',
  "ts" timestamp NOT NULL default CURRENT_TIMESTAMP
                        on update CURRENT_TIMESTAMP,
  PRIMARY KEY  ("publID"),
  KEY "publName" ("publName")
) ENGINE=InnoDB DEFAULT CHARSET=latin1 COLLATE=latin1_german1_ci;
```

Starting New Logging Files

When you stop and restart the MySQL server, the server automatically begins to fill the next logging file with data (name-bin.000002, .000003, etc.). A change in the logging file can, of course, be effected without a server restart, and in fact, with the SQL command *FLUSH LOGS* or with mysqladmin flush-logs. Furthermore, MySQL automatically begins a new logging file when the current file exceeds size max_binlog_size (1GB by default).

A suitable time to begin filling new logging files is after the execution of a complete backup. (The new logging file can help later to reconstruct all changes that occurred after the backup.)

Deleting Logging Files

Logging files that are no longer needed should be deleted with *PURGE MASTER LOGS TO*. This command is described later in this chapter when we discuss replication. If you would like to delete all update logging files, execute *RESET MASTER*.

Restoring a Database on the Basis of a Logging File

If, perish the thought, misfortune should visit you, then the reconstruction of your database begins with the last full backup to restore the database. Then you employ all your logging files made since the last backup. The SQL commands contained therein are simply executed with mysql. (Be careful to follow the correct order. The oldest logging file must be executed first.)

```
root# mysqlbinlog name-bin.000031 | mysql -u root -p
root# mysqlbinlog name-bin.000032 | mysql -u root -p
root# mysqlbinlog name-bin.000033 | mysql -u root -p
```

Determining the Location of the Logging File

You can determine the location of the logging file yourself. (For reasons of security and speed the logging files should be located on a different hard drive from that on which the database resides.) For this you specify the file name with the option log-bin. MySQL extends the file name with .nnn (that is, with a three-digit running integer).

Please make sure that the MySQL server, which under Unix/Linux is usually executed as user mysql, has writing privileges in the specified directory (here /var/log/mysql):

```
# in /etc/my.cnf or \my.ini (Windows)
[mysqld]
log-bin = /var/log/mysql/myupdatelog-bin
```

Logging Files for Various Table Types

The logging procedure described in this section works for all table types (it is independent of type). However, some table types require their own logging files. Information on logging files for InnoDB appears later in this chapter.

Halting Logging Temporarily

If you wish to execute SQL commands that are not to be logged, execute *SET SQL_LOG_BIN=0*. (To do so, you need to have the *Super* privilege.) Logging is reactivated with *SQL_LOG_BIN=1*.

Further Logging Options

There are numerous additional logging options for restricting logging to individual databases, excepting certain databases from logging, limiting the maximal size of files, and improving the synchronization of files (less speed, greater security). A reference to these options appears in Chapter 22, and there is much more information at http://dev.mysql.com/doc/mysql/en/binary-log.html.

Errors, Logins, and Slow Queries

Logging Errors (error log)

MySQL automatically logs each launch and shutdown of the MySQL server as well as all server error messages in the file hostname.err in the database directory. (Instead of hostname, the actual computer name is used.) *FLUSH LOGS* renames the file name.old and begins a new error logging file.

There is no option whereby this error logging can be prevented. With the option log-error, however, you can set the name and location of the file:

```
# in /etc/my.cnf or my.ini (Windows)
[mysqld]
log-error=/var/log/mysql/mysqlerrorlog
```

Logging Logins and Operations (general query log)

With the option log you can enable the logging of each connection to MySQL as well as every command. If you do not specify a file name, then MySQL creates the file hostname.log in the database directory, where instead of hostname, the actual computer name is used. The resulting file is not for the purpose of restoring data but for keeping track of which users are looking at and changing what data, etc.

```
# in /etc/my.cnf or my.ini (Windows)
[mysqld]
log
```

The following lines show a small section of such a log:

```
/usr/sbin/mysqld, Version: 5.0.2-alpha-standard-log. started with:
Tcp port: 3306  Unix socket: /var/lib/mysql/mysql.sock
Time              Id Command    Argument
050222 11:18:58    1 Connect    root@localhost on
                   1 Query      SET SESSION interactive_timeout=1000000
                   1 Query      SET SESSION sql_mode=''
                   1 Query      SET NAMES utf8
                   1 Query      SHOW VARIABLES LIKE 'datadir'
                   1 Query      SHOW VARIABLES LIKE 'log_error'
050222 11:19:09    1 Query      show databases
050222 11:22:45    1 Query      /*!40101 SET @OLD_SQL_MODE=@@SQL_MODE,
                                             sql_mode='' */
                   1 Query      SELECT count(*) FROM `mylibrary`.`authors`
                   1 Query      SHOW CREATE DATABASE
                                WITH IF NOT EXISTS `mylibrary`
                   1 Query      SET SQL_QUOTE_SHOW_CREATE=1
                   1 Query      SHOW CREATE TABLE `mylibrary`.`authors`
                   1 Query      SELECT /*!40001 SQL_NO_CACHE */ *
                                FROM `mylibrary`.`authors`
                   1 Query      SELECT count(*)
                                FROM `mylibrary`.`categories`
```

In comparison to *update logging*, here all commands are logged immediately, as soon as they are passed to the server. This holds as well for transactions, independent of whether they are later completed with a *COMMIT*. In contrast to *update logging*, all commands are actually logged, even those that do not alter any data.

Logging Slow Queries

If MySQL is becoming painfully slow due to the burden of complex queries, it is often useful to undertake an analysis to find out which *SELECT* queries are actually causing the greatest delays. To do this, use the option log-slow-queries. Then MySQL will create a logging file with the name hostname-slow.log.

All queries whose execution takes longer than ten seconds will be logged. You can change this default time limit by setting the variable long_query_time. By setting the option log-long-format you can have all queries logged, even those that must be carried out without the use of an index (e.g., *SELECT * ... WHERE txtcolumn LIKE '%abc%'*):

```
# in /etc/my.cnf or my.ini (Windows)
[mysqld]
log-slow-queries
long_query_time=5
log-queries-not-using-indexes
```

Administration of Logging Files

Logging files are like children: It is easier to create them than to take care of them, and furthermore, they grow on you. And just as children will take over your life if you aren't careful, your logging files will very quickly fill even the largest hard drive if you don't take prophylactic measures. Therefore, do not log more than is absolutely necessary.

Update Logs and Error Logging

With `mysqladmin flush-logs` or the SQL command *FLUSH LOGS*, MySQL closes the currently active logging file and begins a new update logging file (with a new running number). At the same time, the error logging file `name.err` will be renamed `name.old` and a new error logging file will be started.

You have unrestricted access to all update logging files with the exception of the currently active file. You can thus move these files to another directory, compress them, and even delete them (for example, if they exceed a certain age or if they are older than the last complete backup). Under Unix/Linux you can develop a `cron` job to automate this task.

Logins and Slow Queries

With logging files for logins and operations (option `log`) and for slow queries (option `log-slow-queries`) there is a problem in that there is only one file, which gradually grows larger and larger. The MySQL documentation recommends that you simply rename these files while MySQL is running and then execute `mysqladmin flush-logs` or *FLUSH LOGS*:

```
root# cd logpath
root# mv hostname.log hostname.log.old
root# mv hostname-slow.log hostname-slow.old
root# mysqladmin flush-logs
```

The `*.old` files can now be compressed and eventually deleted.

Error Logging

Alas, neither `mysqladmin flush-logs` nor *FLUSH LOGS* has any effect on the logging file for error messages (`hostname.err`). Therefore, it is impossible to manipulate this file while MySQL is running. If this file becomes too large (which is seldom the case), you must stop MySQL, rename the file, and then restart MySQL.

Replication

Introduction

Replication makes it possible to synchronize two or more MySQL servers running on different computers.

Different database systems employ differing methods of establishing replication. If you are familiar with replication from another database system, you should not expect MySQL to exhibit the exact same properties.

MySQL currently supports master/slave replication exclusively. There is one master system (*read/write*). This system is responsible for all changes to data. Additionally, there are one or more slave systems (*read-only*) on which, perhaps after a brief delay, exactly the same data are available as on the master system.

The exchange of data between the master and slaves is accomplished via binary logging files belonging to the master. The slaves remain in contact with the master and synchronize their databases by taking the requisite SQL commands from the logging files.

Replication functions even when the computers are running under different operating systems. (For example, the master can be running under Linux and a slave under Windows.)

■**Tip** In addition to the information of this section, in Chapter 21 you will find a reference to all SQL commands for running replication, and in Chapter 22 there is a reference to all `mysqld` options related to replication.

Further information can be found in the MySQL documentation, the section "Replication in MySQL": `http://dev.mysql.com/doc/mysql/en/replication.html`.

Why Replication?

There are two reasons that argue in favor of setting up a replication system: security and speed.

Security: Thanks to replication, your database is available on several computers. If a slave computer goes off-line, the entire system can continue to run without interruption. (A new slave system can later synchronize itself.)

If the master computer goes off-line, then the preservation of the data can be taken over by a slave computer. Alternatively, the entire system can be reconfigured so that a slave computer takes over the role of the master. In either case, though, the entire system is available as *read-only*.

If you are considering replication for reasons of security only, you should also consider a RAID system, whereby the contents of two (or more) hard drives are synchronized. A RAID system, however, protects only against a hard-drive crash, and not against an operating system crash, power outage, or the like.

Note that replication can also be used as a substitute for conventional backups. (Thanks to replication, the backup is always current. If you also require a conventional backup, you can execute it on the slave computer without involving the master computer.)

Speed: If the speed of a database system is limited primarily by many read-only queries (and not by a large number of alterations to the data), then a replication system can gain you great savings in time: The expensive queries are divided among several slave systems, while the master system is used exclusively or primarily for updates. (Of course, part of the theoretical increase in speed is lost due to the increased communication overhead.)

Please note that you can gain speed only if the programming of the client is compatible with your system. The client programs must divide your queries according to a load-balancing procedure (or simply at random) among all available slave systems. MySQL itself provides no mechanism for this purpose.

If your interest in replication is motivated by performance problems, you should consider alternative performance-enhancing measures, in particular, better hardware (in the following order: more RAM, a faster hard drive, a RAID system, a multiprocessor system).

Limitations

- MySQL currently supports replication only in the form of a master/slave system (*one-way replication*). All changes in data must be carried out on a single master system. The slave systems can be used only for database queries (*read-only*).

  It is not currently possible for a slave system to take over the role of the master automatically if it should go out of service (*fail-safe replication*). Thus replication can produce a system that is secure against breakdowns for database queries, but not for alterations to the data. Fail-safe replication is planned for MySQL 5.1.

  It is also impossible to synchronize changes to several systems (*multiple-master replication*). That would lead to problems, for example, with *AUTO_INCREMENT* values. It is therefore impossible, for example, to execute changes in a MySQL database on a notebook computer and later bring these into balance with the master system on another computer.

- If possible, the same MySQL version should run on the master and slave computers. Replication usually works if the version number on the slave is higher than that on the client.

- In older versions of MySQL there were many commands that caused problems with replication. Most of these problems have been solved in MySQL 5.0. Therefore, use the most current MySQL version that you can.

Setting Up the Replication Master System

This section describes the preparatory work for setting up a replication system on the master computer. Note, please, that this introduction does not show the only way to proceed. There are even several ways for transferring the start data to the slave. (One variant will be shown a bit later in this chapter.)

This section and the next assume that the database *mysql*, too, is to be replicated with its access privileges. This is usually a good idea, so that all users who are permitted to read data from the master system will be able to read data from the slaves with the same access information.

This method of proceeding is, however, burdened with some drawbacks. Everyone who is permitted to change the master is now permitted to do the same to the slaves. However, changes to data should fundamentally be made to the master, for otherwise, replication falls apart. If you thus wish to exclude data alteration on the slaves, you (as database administrator) must exclude the *mysql* database from replication (`binlog-ignore-db=mysql`), and instead, manage the *mysql* databases separately for the master and all of the slaves. However, that causes synchronization problems. For example, if a user obtains a new password on the master, the changed password must be entered on all the slaves.

Setting Up the Replication User

The first step consists in setting up a new user on the master system that is responsible for communication between master and client. The user name is irrelevant, and in this section we will use the name *replicuser*.

This user requires the *Replication Slave* privilege for access to the binary logging files. Instead of *slavehostname*, specify the complete computer name or IP number of the slave computer. For security reasons you should use as password a combination of characters that is in use neither in the operating system nor in the database:

```
GRANT REPLICATION SLAVE ON *.*
  TO replicuser@slavehostname IDENTIFIED BY 'xxx'
```

If you have in mind to use the commands *LOAD TABLE FROM MASTER* and *LOAD DATA FROM MASTER*, then you must also grant *replicuser* the privileges *Select, Reload*, and *Super*. These commands are conceived primarily as aids for the MySQL developer and experts; they can help in setting up and managing a replication system.

If the replication system is to have several slaves, then you must execute *GRANT* for all the slave computers. Alternatively, you can permit access for all computers in the local system (e.g., *replicuser@'%.netname'*). This can simplify administration, though at the cost of introducing an unnecessary security risk.

On the slave system, use `mysql -u replicuser -p -h masterhostname` to test whether it is possible to establish a connection. This has only the effect of ruling out possible errors that have nothing to do with replication.

Shutdown

In setting up the slave (see the next section) you must specify the position in the logging files at which the slave is to begin reading. You can determine this position with the following command:

```
FLUSH TABLES WITH READ LOCK
SHOW MASTER STATUS
File                Position   Binlog_do_db  Binlog_ignore_db
saturn-bin.000005   375344
```

You must note the information from the first two columns (*file* and *position*). If *SHOW MASTER STATUS* returns no result (*empty set*), then binary logging is not yet activated. Next, shut down the MySQL server, for example, with `mysqladmin shutdown` or with an Init V script such as `/etc/init.d/mysql stop`.

Creating a Snapshot

Now you create a copy (called a *snapshot*) of all the databases. You will need this snapshot for the installation of the initial state of all the databases on the slave computers.

Under Windows use WinZip or another compression program; under Unix/Linux your best bet is to use `tar`. The archive should contain only the database directories, not the various logging files that are also usually found at this location.

```
root# cd mysql-data-dir
root# tar vczf snapshot.tgz
```

If you are using InnoDB tables on the master, the snapshot must also contain the InnoDB *tablespace* files (`ibdata`):

```
root# tar vczf snapshot.tgz ibdata* */*
```

You can also create the snapshot with `mysqldump --all-databases --master-data` (with InnoDB tables with the additional option `--single-transaction`). However, the resulting snapshot file is then considerably larger, and moreover, the creation of the snapshot and the later reading on the slave computer by `mysql` take longer.

Server Configuration

In order for the MySQL server to be able to function as a replication master, you must associate a unique ID number with the server, using the option `server-id`. (Every computer in the replication system must be so designated.) Moreover, you must activate binary logging with the option `log-bin`. Here you should provide a name for the logging files (here *mysqlmaster*). If you do not do so, the MySQL server automatically chooses the name of the computer plus `bin`. If the computer name should change due to a change in the network configuration, replication could fall apart.

```
# master configuration
# in /etc/my.cnf or my.ini (Windows)
[mysqld]
log-bin=mysqlmaster
server-id=1
```

Then restart the server. You can again use the server in normal fashion. All changes to the database will now be recorded in the binary logging file. As soon as a slave system goes online, it will automatically synchronize its database based on the logging files.

■**Tip** A brief description of additional master options can be found in the `mysqld` reference in Chapter 22. For example, you can restrict the replication to individual databases (option `binlog-do-db`) or exclude several databases from the replication (`binlog-ignore-db`).

Setting Up the Replication Slave System

Setting Up the Databases (Snapshot)

If the MySQL server is already using replication that is no longer to be used but is to be replaced by a new configuration, then execute *RESET SLAVE*. With this, the server forgets the old replication configuration.

Now stop the slave server. If there were already databases there, move their files into a backup directory (better safe than sorry).

Then copy the database files of the snapshot into the database directory with WinZip or `tar xzf`. Make sure that the files can be read and written by the MySQL server. Under Unix/Linux you do this by executing `chown -R mysql.mysql` (Red Hat) or `chown -R mysql.daemon` (SUSE).

The following commands summarize the process under Linux. It is assumed here that the MySQL data directory is `/var/lib/mysql`:

```
root# cd /var/lib/
root# mv mysql/ mysql-bak/          creates a backup of /var/lib/mysql
root# mkdir mysql                   creates an empty mysql directory
root# cd mysql
root# tar xzfv snapshot.tgz         opens the snapshot there
root# cd ..
root# chown mysql.daemon -R mysql/  change owner of mysql/
```

Configuration File

With the slave system as well, the configuration file must be changed a bit. With `server-id` each slave system also obtains a unique identification number. With `master-host`, `master-user`, and `master-password` you specify how the slave system is related to the master.

■Note If InnoDB files were in the snapshot, then the configuration file of the slave must have exactly the same InnoDB options as that of the master so that the InnoDB *tablespace* files can be correctly recognized when the server is started. The logging of all changes (i.e., update logging) is not necessary for the slaves and should be deactivated for speed optimization. A short description of additional slave options can be found in the `mysqld` option reference in Chapter 22.

```
# slave configuration
# in /etc/my.cnf or my.ini (Windows)
[mysqld]
server-id=2
innodb_xxx = <as with the  master>
```

Now the slave system can be brought on-line. Start the server. If problems arise, look at the error log (file `hostname.err`).

A useful additional option in the configuration file might be `read-only`. This option has the effect that the slave system is unable to execute SQL commands on its own. This ensures that no changes can be made on the slave that are unknown to the master.

Starting Replication

To start replication between slave and master, execute the following command. The slanted text should be replaced by the configuration data of the master:

```
CHANGE MASTER TO
  MASTER_HOST =      'master_hostname',
  MASTER_USER =      'replication user name',
  MASTER_PASSWORD = 'replication password',
  MASTER_LOG_FILE = 'log file name',
  MASTER_LOG_POS =   log_offset
```

If the master is running on the computer *saturn.sol* and all other specifications are the same as those of the previous section, then the command would look like this:

```
CHANGE MASTER TO
  MASTER_HOST =      'saturn.sol',
  MASTER_USER =      'replicuser',
  MASTER_PASSWORD = 'xxx',
  MASTER_LOG_FILE = 'saturn-bin.000005,
  MASTER_LOG_POS =   375344
```

If binary logging was not instituted before replication was set up or the name of the logging files was changed during the setup of the master, then specify *MASTER_LOG_FILE* = '' and *MASTER_LOG_POS* = 0.

Now to start the replication slave system, you need only the command

```
START SLAVE
```

First Test

With mysql create a connection to the master system and add a new data record to the table of your choice. Then use mysql to establish a connection to a slave system and test whether the new record appears there. If that is the case, then rejoice, for your replication system is working. (Of course, you could also generate and then delete new tables and even entire databases on the master. The slave system understands and carries out these commands as well.)

Take a look, too, into the logging file hostname.err on the slave system. There you should see entries on the status of the replication, for example in the following form:

```
050317 18:49:24 [Note] Slave SQL thread initialized, starting replication
  in log 'FIRST' at position 0,
  relay log './uranus-relay-bin.000001' position: 4
050317 18:49:24 [Note] Slave I/O thread: connected to master
  'replicuser@merkur1.sol:3306',
  replication started in log 'FIRST' at position 4
```

As a further test you can shut down the slave system, make changes in the master system, and then start up the slave system again. The databases on the slave system should be automatically synchronized within a couple of seconds.

Setting Up a Replication System with LOAD DATA

A replication system can be set up much more easily if one makes use of the command *LOAD DATA FROM MASTER*. A couple of conditions must be satisfied first:

- On the master, MyISAM tables must be used exclusively.

- The *mysql* database should not be replicated. (*LOAD DATA* ignores the *mysql* database. Therefore, this database must already exist on the slave system.)

- The MySQL configuration file of the master should contain `log-bin` and a unique `server-id` setting.

- The MySQL configuration file of the slave should also contain `log-bin` and a unique `server-id` setting.

Master: If these conditions are satisfied, then setting up the replication system is child's play. You set up the replication user on the master, to which you grant the privileges *Select*, *Reload*, and *Super*.

```
GRANT SELECT, RELOAD, SUPER, REPLICATION SLAVE ON *.*
  TO replicuser@slavehostname IDENTIFIED BY 'xxx'
```

If the databases on the master are already filled in, then the variables *net_read_timeout* and *net_write_timeout* should have their values increased. (The default value is 30. The variables should be reset to the default after the replication system has been set up.)

```
SET GLOBAL net_read_timeout=600
SET GLOBAL net_write_timeout=600
```

Slave: On the slave, set the host name and user name and password for the replication process:

```
CHANGE MASTER TO
  MASTER_HOST =      'saturn.sol',
  MASTER_USER =      'replicuser',
  MASTER_PASSWORD = 'xxx'
```

On the slave as well, *net_read_timeout* and *net_write_timeout* should be increased:

```
SET net_read_timeout=600
SET net_write_timeout=600
```

The following command transfers all the databases and tables from master to slave and starts the replication system:

```
LOAD DATA FROM MASTER
```

If an error occurs in executing this command, then life becomes complicated: You must stop the slave server, delete all (partially) transferred database directories, and then begin again. Possible sources of the problem are too-small values of *net_read_timeout* and *net_write_timeout* (from master and/or slave) as well as the presence of InnoDB tables. *LOAD DATA FROM MASTER* looks at the configuration settings `replicate_ignore_xxx`, with which individual tables or entire databases can be excluded from replication (see Chapter 22).

Inside Replication

The master.info file (Slave)

At the initial startup of replication, the slave system will have the file `master.info` added to its database directory. In this file MySQL keeps track of which binary logging file is currently being used, to what point this file has been evaluated, how the master can be contacted (host name, user name, password), etc. This file is absolutely necessary for the operation of replication. The MySQL documentation naturally emphatically recommends that you not mess around with this file:

```
14
masterbinlogname.000007
265
saturn.sol
replicuser
saturn
3306
60
0
```

■**Note** The content of `master.info` can also be determined with the SQL command *SHOW SLAVE STATUS*. Changes can be carried out with *CHANGE MASTER TO*. Both of these commands will be described in the SQL reference in Chapter 21.

Relay Files (Slave)

Once replication is running on the slave computer, the files `relay-log.info`, `hostname-relay-bin.index`, and `hostname-relay-bin.nnn` appear in the data directory. These files are created by a separate IO thread (subprocess) on the slave server, using a copy of the binary logging files on the master. The sole task of the IO thread is to copy these data from master to slave. A second SQL thread then executes the SQL commands contained in the logging files.

By default, commands that have already been processed are automatically deleted from the relay files. If that is not your wish, use the option `relay-log-purge=0`.

Excluding Databases and Tables from Replication

If you do not want all of the databases or tables of the master replicated, there are two ways of excluding some of them: You can exclude databases from logging in the master configuration file (`binlog-ignore-db`), or you can exclude databases and tables from replication in the slave configuration file (`replicate-ignore-table`, `replicate-wild-ignore-table`, `replication-ignore-db`).

Turning Off Replication Temporarily (Master)

If you wish to execute an SQL command on the master that is not to be replicated on the slave, then first execute the command *SQL_LOG_BIN=0* and then the command *SET SQL_LOG_BIN=1*. (For this, the *Super* privilege is necessary.)

Ending the Master and Slave Servers

Master and slave servers run independently of each other, and they can be stopped and restarted independently and in either order without loss of data. If the slave is unable to make a connection to the master, or to reconnect, then it attempts a connection every 60 seconds. As soon as the connection is reestablished, all outstanding changes are read from the binary logging files and executed on the slave. This works even if the slave was down for a long time and has a great deal of catching up to do.

Several Slaves, Replication Chains

One may have an arbitrary number of slaves, all accessing the same master. From the master's point of view, nothing is different (except for the additional burden of accesses).

In addition, MySQL offers the possibility of creating replication chains of the form $A \succ B \succ C$. Here B would be a slave with respect to A, but a master with respect to C. This generally increases the overhead and is therefore not worthwhile. However, a possible scenario is a slow network connection between A and B (say, one server is in Europe and the other in the USA) and a fast connection between B and C. On computer B, the configuration log-slave-updates must be used.

Replication and Transactions

Transactions are not executed on the slave systems until they have been terminated on the master by *COMMIT*. On the other hand, if a transaction on the master is terminated by *ROLLBACK*, then the affected SQL commands are neither logged in the logging files nor executed on the slave system.

It is even possible to use a transaction-capable table format (InnoDB) on the master system, while using an ordinary MyISAM table on the slave. Since transaction management takes place entirely on the master, it is unnecessary to have slave support on the slave. However, it is necessary to have the slave properly set up before replication begins. (If the tables in the start state come from a file snapshot, then they are in the same format as those of the master and must be explicitly transformed on the slave to MyISAM tables. Note that changes in the format of a table are replicated from master to slaves.)

Client Programming

If the goal of a replication system is to ensure against system failure or to increase speed by dividing up the queries among several systems, then changes are necessary to the client as well.

In establishing the connection, a distinction must be made as to whether data are going to be queried only or whether changes are required as well. If *INSERT*, *UPDATE*, or *DELETE* commands are to be executed, then a connection to the master system must be made.

On the other hand, if data are to be queried only, then the connection should be made to the server that is currently the least burdened. Since the client program as a rule has no way of determining this, the *Connect* function should randomly select a computer from a predetermined list of computer names or IP numbers and attempt to make a connection. If this does not succeed (because this server is currently unreachable), then *Connect* should make an attempt to connect to another server.

Random Server Selection

The following example in the programming language PHP assumes that you wish to read (and not alter) data and to select the server randomly to improve efficiency. To do this you define in *mysqlhosts[]* an array of all the server names (or IP addresses) and use *rand(min, max)* to select an element of the array.

After the connection has been established, the single query mysql_list_dbs is executed (corresponding to the SQL command *SHOW DATABASES*):

```
<html><head><title>test</title></head><body>
<?php
  $mysqlhosts[0]="venus.sol";            // list of all servers
  $mysqlhosts[1]="mars.sol";             // of the replication system
  $mysqlhost=$mysqlhosts[rand(0,1)];     // select the server randomly
  $mysqluser="user";                     // user name
  $mysqlpasswd="xxx";                    // password
  $connID=mysql_connect($mysqlhost, $mysqluser, $mysqlpasswd);
  ...
?>
</body></html>
```

Crashproof Server Selection

The starting point for our second example is similar. However, now our goal is to make the connection process immune to a connection failure. The following lines demonstrate a possible procedure whereby at most ten connection attempts are made.

```
$tries=0;
  while($tries<10 && !$connID) {
    $mysqlhost=$mysqlhosts[rand(0,1)];
    $connID = @mysql_connect($mysqlhost, $mysqluser, $mysqlpasswd);
    $tries++;
  }
  if(!$connID) {
    echo "<p>Sorry, no database server found.\n";
    echo "</body></html>";
    exit();
  }
```

Administration of MyISAM Tables

As we have already mentioned in Chapter 8, MyISAM tables are stored in the files dbname/tablename.MYD (data) and dbname/tablename.MYI (indexes). This allows the simple copying and moving of tables and databases. However, such operations are allowed only if the server is not using the databases (the best procedure is to stop the server for this purpose).

In rare cases, it may be necessary to work with the MyISAM table files directly, such as to restore indexes or repair damaged files. This section offers the tools that you will need.

myisamchk

The command myisamchk is, in a sense, a universal tool for the maintenance of MyISAM tables. With this command you can accomplish the following:

- Check the integrity of MyISAM tables.
- Repair damaged MyISAM table files (e.g., after a power outage).
- Release unused storage space in MyISAM files.
- Re-create the index to MyISAM tables.

Instead of myisamchk, you can also use the following SQL commands:

ANALYZE TABLE provides information about internal index management.

CHECK TABLE tests the table file for errors in consistency.

OPTIMIZE TABLE optimizes the use of storage space in tables.

REPAIR TABLE attempts to repair defective tables.

OPTIMIZE and *REPAIR TABLE* work only for MyISAM tables. The advantage of the SQL commands over myisamchk is that you do not need to worry about the MySQL server and myisamchk interfering with each other. The disadvantage is that the MySQL server must be running (which may be problematic after a crash), that under some circumstances not all errors can be corrected, that there are fewer options for control of the process, and that the SQL commands are somewhat slower in their execution.

An extension to myisamchk is the command myisampack, with which MyISAM tables can be compressed. In this way, a great deal of space can be saved. However, only *read* access to such tables is then possible. At the end of this section we shall have more to say about myisampack.

■Tip A reference to all options of myisamchk and myisampack can be found in Chapter 22. Further information on the use of myisamchk, particularly for the repair of defective table files, can be found in the MySQL documentation: http://dev.mysql.com/doc/mysql/en/table-maintenance.html.

Using myisamchk

The syntax of the myisamchk command is as follows:

```
myisamchk [options] tablename1 tablename2 ...
```

The table names are given as complete file names, either with or without the ending *.MYI (but, surprisingly, not with *.MYD). Depending on the options specified, however, both MyISAM files, that is, name.MYD (data) and name.MYI (indexes), are analyzed or changed.

To check on the integrity of all tables in the database *mydatabase* you should execute the following command. (You must, of course, replace /var/lib/mysql with your actual database directory.)

```
root# myisamchk /var/lib/mysql/mydatabase/*.MYI
```

You can use myisamchk independently of the MySQL server (the server may be running, but it does not have to be). If the server is running, then mysqladmin flush-tables or the SQL command *FLUSH TABLES* must be executed first.

■Caution If myisamchk actually changes MyISAM files and not just checks them, it must be ensured that the MySQL server does not change any data during this time.

Therefore, you must execute if necessary the SQL command *LOCK TABLE name* with mysql, followed by myisamchk, and then, finally, *UNLOCK TABLES*. You must not leave mysql during this time, since otherwise, the *LOCK*s would end.

Speed Optimization, Memory Usage

In the case of large tables, the analysis, and even more the repair, of tables is a very costly operation. The speed of myisamchk depends greatly on the amount of available RAM.

The memory usage of myisamchk is set by four variables. In the default setting, myisamchk requires about 3MB of RAM. If you have more memory to squander, then you should raise the values of the appropriate variables, since then myisamchk will execute much more quickly for large tables. The MySQL documentation recommends the following values:

```
root# myisamchk -sort_buffer=64M -key_buffer=64M   \
                -read_buffer=1M  -write_buffer=1M ...
```

Furthermore, for repairing database files myisamchk requires a huge amount of space on the hard drive (among other reasons, because a copy of the database file is first made). A copy of the file is placed in the directory specified by the environment variable TMPDIR. You can also specify this directory via --tmpdir.

Shrinking and Optimizing MyISAM Tables

The MyISAM table driver attempts, normally, to keep table files as small as possible. However, if you delete a large number of records from your tables or if you often carry out changes to records with columns of variable size (*VARCHAR*, *xxxTEXT*, *xxxBLOB*), then the optimization algorithm runs up against its limit. In the worst case, the database files are significantly larger than necessary. Moreover, the data are scattered throughout the file, which slows down access to the database.

The following command provides some assistance. It regenerates the database file and optimizes the index file in view of providing the speediest access to the database. With the option `--set-character-set` the character set is specified for the sort order. The effect of `--check-only-changed` is that only those tables are processed that were changed since the last processing by `myisamchk`. (For space reasons, the command has been split using a backslash over two lines.)

```
root# myisamchk --recover --check-only-changed --sort-index \
      --analyze databasepath/*.MYI
```

■Tip If you would like to check the performance of `myisamchk`, create a test database and then delete at random about half of the data records: `DELETE FROM testtable WHERE RAND()>0.5`.

Repairing MyISAM Tables

For me, this section is largely of a theoretical nature, because fortunately, I have thus far had no problems with corrupt MyISAM tables. Corrupted files can arise when the database is stopped by a power failure, when MySQL or the operating system crashes, or if the MyISAM table driver contains errors.

Damaged MyISAM files make themselves known in MySQL service by error messages like *Index-file/Record-file/Table is crashed* or *No more room in index/record file*. In such a case, `myisamchk` will not, of course, be able to work a miracle. Data that for some reason are no longer available or have been overwritten cannot be restored. However, `myisamchk` can repair the database to the extent that at least all other records can again be read:

```
root# myisamchk --recover databasepath/*.MYI
```

If you suspect that only the index file has been affected, then execute `myisamchk` with the additional option `--quick` (which is considerably faster). In this case `myisamchk` regenerates the index file.

In particularly difficult cases, that is, when `myisamchk --recover` fails, you can attempt recovery with `--safe-recover`. However, that will take much longer than `--recover`.

Compressing MyISAM Tables (myisampack)

If you exclusively read (but do not change) large tables, then it is a good idea to compress your files. Not only does this save space, but in general, it speeds up access (since larger portions of the table can reside in the file buffer of the operating system):

```
root# myisampack databaspath/*.MYI
```

Although with `myisampack` the identifier `*.MYI` is specified for the index file, the command changes only the data file `*.MYD`. To uncompress compressed table files, you should execute `myisamchk` with the option `--unpack`.

Administration of InnoDB Tables

While InnoDB tables offer, in comparison to MyISAM tables, a number of additional functions (transactions and integrity rules), they make administration a bit more complex. This section provides some tips for managing *tablespace* and logging files, copying and moving InnoDB tables, and the optimal configuration of the MySQL server.

■Tip A quick overview of the most important InnoDB parameters can be obtained with the command *SHOW VARIABLES LIKE 'innodb%'*. A summary of the InnoDB configuration parameters for the MySQL server can be found in Chapter 22.

Tablespace Administration

While MyISAM files and indexes are stored in their own files within a directory with the name of the database (e.g., data/dbname/tablename.myd), all InnoDB tables and indexes are stored in a virtual file system, which in the InnoDB documentation is called the *tablespace*. The *tablespace* itself can be composed of a number of files.

You can use InnoDB tables without any particular configuration settings, in which case at the first start of the MySQL server the file ibdata1, of size 10MB, is created for the *tablespace* and can be enlarged repeatedly by 8MB as required.

A peculiarity of *tablespace* files is that they cannot be made smaller. Thus when you delete tables or records, the space in the *tablespace* is released and can be used for new tables, but the size of the *tablespace* file is unchanged.

A significant innovation since MySQL 4.1 is that with a suitable configuration, a separate *tablespace* file is created for each table (instead of storing all tables in a single giant *tablespace* file). Details on this will be discussed shortly.

Determining the Space Requirements of InnoDB Tables

The *tablespace* is more or less a black box that you cannot see into. For example, there is no command to return any sort of directory of the *tablespace*. The command *SHOW TABLE STATUS* does give information about how much space the individual InnoDB tables and their indexes require within the *tablespace* and how much space is available before the *tablespace* will have to be enlarged. In what follows, only the relevant columns of the *SHOW* command are displayed. The storage of tables and indexes is managed in 16KB blocks, which is why *SHOW* always returns integer multiples of 16,384:

```
SHOW TABLE STATUS FROM mylibrary
Name        Engine    Data_Length   Index_Length   Comment
authors     InnoDB       16384         16384        InnoDB free: 3072 kB ...
categories  InnoDB       16384         49152        InnoDB free: 3072 kB ...
```

In general, the space requirement for the *tablespace* file is significantly greater in MySQL 4.*n* than for an equivalent MyISAM table file. The situation has improved since version 5.0.3 through a more compact table format, which is used automatically within the *tablespace* files. The storage requirement is reduced by about 20 percent, but remains greater than for MyISAM tables. However, the new format brings with it no speed disadvantage.

Apparently, beginning with MySQL 5.1 the InnoDB table driver will offer the possibility of transparently compressing individual pages within the *tablespace*. This will cause the memory requirement to go down significantly, though at the cost of greater demand on CPU.

Individual tablespace Files for Each Table

Since MySQL 4.1 there has been the option of creating an individual *tablespace* file for each table. This has a host of advantages over the exclusive use of a central *tablespace* file, and so we shall describe this variant first.

Individual *tablespace* files are currently not the default, but are activated via the option innodb_file_per_table. Even after a server restart, this setting holds only for newly created tables. Existing tables remain in the central *masterspace*.

Note that despite individual *tablespace* files, there must always be a central *masterspace* file (which the MySQL server automatically creates at initial startup without any particular configuration).

```
# in /etc/my.cnf or my.ini (Windows)
[myslqd]
innodb_file_per_table
```

The MySQL server now creates, for every new InnoDB table, a file with the name databasename/ tablename.ibd. This file begins life at size 64KB and grows as necessary. It contains table data and all indexes.

To migrate existing tables from the central *tablespace* to individual *tablespace* files, you must make a backup of these tables (mysqldump), delete the tables, and then re-create the backup by reading the tables back in.

If you should later remove the option innodb_file_per_table from the configuration file, the individual *tablespace* files remain active. New tables, however, will be stored in the central *tablespace*. The migration of individual tables into the central *tablespace* is precisely as in the opposite direction: backup, delete tables, restore backup.

To determine which tables are stored in individual files and which in the central *tablespace*, you must look in the MySQL data directory to see what dbname/tablename.ibd files exist. *SHOW TABLE STATUS* gives no information, and moreover, the MySQL server currently offers no way of determining this information.

Pluses and minuses: According to an email from the InnoDB developer Heikki Tuuri in the *mysql* mailing list, individual *tablespace* files are only marginally slower than the exclusive use of a central *tablespace*. The significant disadvantage is that when a table is deleted, the corresponding *tablespace* file is also deleted. In contrast to the use of a central *tablespace* file, *DROP TABLE* immediately creates space on the hard drive.

Note that (in contrast to MyISAM tables) it is not permitted to move or copy individual *tablespace* files from one directory to another or from one MySQL server installation to another. You must adhere to the rules outlined later in this chapter (see the section "Copying, Deleting, and Moving InnoDB Tables").

Configuration of the Central Tablespace

By default (that is, without any particular configuration settings), the MySQL server creates at initial startup a 10MB file ibdata1 that is increased as needed in 8MB increments. The following remarks are of interest only if you wish to manage the location and size of the files of the central *tablespace* yourself. For this there exist the parameters innodb_data_home and innodb_data_file_path. The former specifies the directory in which all InnoDB files are stored (by default the MySQL data directory), and the latter contains the names and sizes of the *tablespace* files. A possible setting in the configuration file before the first startup of the MySQL server is the following:

```
# in /etc/my.cnf or my.ini (Windows)
[mysqld]
innodb_data_home = D:/data
innodb_data_file_path = ibdata1:1G;ibdata2:1G:autoextend:max:2G
```

This means that the *tablespace* consists of the files D:\data\ibdata1 and D:\data\ibdata2. If these files do not exist, they will be created, of size 1GB each. If the InnoDB tables require more space while the server is running, then ibdata2 will be enlarged automatically in 8MB increments (to a maximum of 2GB).

In the management of the *tablespace* files you should observe the following:

- The MySQL server requires *write* privileges for the innodb_data_home directory so that it can create and alter the *tablespace* files.

- If you do not use the autoextend attribute, as administrator you must enlarge the *tablespace* in good time (that is, before reaching the limits of a *tablespace* file). If the InnoDB driver determines in a transaction that the *tablespace* is full and cannot be enlarged any further, the transaction will be aborted with *ROLLBACK*.

Using Hard Drive Partitions Directly

InnoDB also offers the option of using an entire hard drive partition directly (that is, without a file system managed by the operating system). For this, instead of specifying the file name, you give the device name of the partition and append the exact size specification (newraw). The partition size must be an integer multiple of 1MB. (The following example uses the Linux device notation.)

```
innodb_data_home_dir=
innodb_data_file_path=/dev/hdb1:61440Mnewraw
```

After the partition has been initialized by MySQL, you must stop the MySQL server and replace newraw by raw. (The former is necessary only if you are adding a new partition.)

```
innodb_data_home_dir=
innodb_data_file_path=/dev/hdb1:61440Mraw
```

The InnoDB documentation unfortunately contains no information about whether better performance can be obtained by the direct use of hard drive partitions (one suspects that it can) and if so, how much. I have been able to obtain little concrete information from the MySQL mailing list.

Enlarging the Central Tablespace

In principle, the files of the central *tablespace* cannot be enlarged. The one exception is the autoextend attribute, which, however, can be specified only for the last *tablespace* file in innodb_data_file_path. To enlarge the amount of space available in the central *tablespace*, you must therefore add an additional file to innodb_data_file_path. The process looks in detail like this:

- Stop the MySQL server.
- If the size of the last *tablespace* file was variable due to autoextend, you must determine its actual size in megabytes (the number of bytes according to DIR or ls divided by 1,048,576). The resulting size must be specified in the innodb_data_file_path setting.

  If innodb_data_file_path does not yet exist in the configuration file, then previously, ibdata was used as the default file, and you must determine and specify its size.

- Add one or more new files to innodb_data_file_path.

  By default, all files must be located in the one directory (or in directories relative to it). If you wish to divide the *tablespace* files among several partitions, hard drives, etc., then you must specify an empty character string for innodb_data_home, and in innodb_data_file_path you must use absolute file names.

  Note that the order of the files specified up to now in innodb_data_file_path cannot be changed (and that of course, none of the previous files may be missing).

- Restart the MySQL server. If the server does not detect an erroneous configuration, it will generate the new *tablespace* files. This process will also log any errors in the file `hostname.err`.

Let us suppose that the previous setting looks like the following and that `ibdata2` has current size of 1904MB:

```
innodb_data_file_path = ibdata1:1G;ibdata2:1G:autoextend
```

You now want to increase the size of the *tablespace* to 4GB. The new setting must look like the following:

```
innodb_data_file_path = ibdata1:1G;ibdata2:1904M;ibdata3:1100MB:autoextend
```

If you use individual *tablespace* files, you save all this trouble. In the central *tablespace* are stored only relatively few (temporary) data, for which reason its size can remain relatively small. And the individual *tablespace* files grow automatically.

Shrinking the Tablespace

It is, unfortunately, impossible to make the files of the central *tablespace* smaller. If you delete large InnoDB tables or change them into another table format, the space within the *tablespace* is freed up, but the *tablespace* files cannot be made smaller. The only way to shrink them is by the following process:

- Make a backup of all InnoDB tables with `mysqldump`.
- Delete all InnoDB tables (*DROP TABLE ...*).
- Stop the MySQL server (`mysqladmin shutdown`).
- Delete the current *tablespace* files (ibdata...). If you have enough space, it is, of course, more secure first to move the files into another directory.
- Change `innodb_data_file_path` in the MySQL configuration file.
- Restart the MySQL server. New *tablespace* files corresponding to the `innodb_data_file_path` setting will be created.
- Re-create all your InnoDB tables from your backup files.

Copying, Deleting, and Moving InnoDB Tables

From your experience with MyISAM tables you are accustomed to the fact that (after a server shutdown) you can simply copy or move all files `dbname.tablename`. The MySQL server recognizes at restart which tables are to be found where. This is very practical for backups or making a copy of a table or database.

If you use InnoDB tables, none of this is possible, not even if you use an individual *tablespace* file for each table.

Moving tables: To move a table from one database into another, execute *RENAME dbname.tablename TO dbnamenew.tablenamenew*.

Copying tables: To copy a table, you must either create a new table and copy the data with *INSERT ... SELECT*, or you must make a backup of the table (`mysqldump`) and then create the table under another name.

Deleting tables: *DROPTABLE tablename* deletes the given table. If the table was located in an individual *tablespace* file, this file is deleted as well. If the table was, on the other hand, in the central *tablespace*, then the space it occupied is given up. However, the *tablespace* files are not made smaller.

*.frm files: Caution is necessary with the `*.frm` files. These files give the structure of a table and are located in the relevant database directory (even with InnoDB tables!). The `*.frm` files and associated tables stored in *tablespace* must always be synchronized. You must not simply delete `*.frm` files. If you wish to delete a table, execute *DROP TABLE*; then the `*.frm` file will be deleted.

Making a Backup

There are several ways of making a backup of InnoDB tables:

- The most elegant way is to use *InnoDB Hot Backup*. This auxiliary program makes the backup while the server is running, without blocking tables. However, *InnoDB Hot Backup* is a commercial program and is not freely available; see `http://www.innodb.com/order.php`.

- Of course, you can always use `mysqldump`. The command must be used with `single-transaction`.

- If you are prepared to stop the MySQL server, you can simply copy the *tablespace* files. Note, though, that you must use the exact same `innodb_data_file_path` setting as well as all `*.frm` files. On the other hand, you do not require the transaction logging files. If the server was properly shut down, these files no longer contain any relevant data.

Migrating the tablespace

According to the MySQL documentation, the *tablespace* files are independent of the operating system. Only the CPU's floating-point representation must be correct. If those conditions are satisfied, then the *tablespace* files can be moved without problem between, say, Windows and Linux. Of course, you must take care here, too, that the `innodb_data_file_path` setting is correct and that all `*.frm` files are moved as well. (In practice, it will usually be the case that both MyISAM and InnoDB tables are to be copied. For this, all database directories and all *tablespace* files are simply copied.

The InnoDB documentation contains no information as to whether the *tablespace* file format is dependent in any way on the version. Heikki Tuuri, the developer of the InnoDB table driver, has promised forward compatibility for all present and future versions. (It has always been a tradition with MySQL that database files be able to be moved without difficulty to a new version.)

In general, an occasional backup with `mysqldump` is a good idea. The backup file then exists in text format, which is immune against possible compatibility problems.

Logging Files

Transaction Logging

InnoDB logs all changes in logging files with the names `ib_logfile0`, `ib_logfile1`, etc. The purpose of these logging files is to make large transactions possible as well as to restore InnoDB data after a crash.

If MySQL is properly configured and there is sufficient memory, then most of the currently needed data should reside in RAM. To improve speed, changes to data are first made only in RAM, and not in the actual data files (that is, in the case of InnoDB, in the *tablespace*).

Only when a transaction is completed with *COMMIT* are the changes in data actually stored on the hard drive, and then first in the InnoDB logging files `ib_logfile0`, `ib_logfile1`, etc. The changed parts of the *tablespace* are only gradually transferred to the hard drive, all this for reasons of efficiency. If a crash occurs during these proceedings, then the *tablespace* can be restored with the help of the logging files.

The logging files `ib_logfile0`, etc., have two purposes. On the one hand, they satisfy the ACID condition of durability, so that transactions that have been carried out are not endangered even if there is a crash immediately after the transaction has been completed. On the other hand, the logging files enable transactions of almost unlimited size, even those for which it is not possible to hold all pending (but not yet confirmed) changes in RAM.

The InnoDB logging files are filled in order. When the last file is full, the InnoDB table driver begins writing data to the first logging file. Therefore, the entire size of all logging files limits the quantity of *tablespace* changes that can be temporarily stored before a *COMMIT*. The maximum size of all logging files is currently limited to 4GB.

The transaction logging files are necessary only while the MySQL server is running. As soon as the MySQL server has been properly shut down, these files are no longer needed. For example, if you make a backup with `ibdata` files, you do not need to copy the logging files.

Size and Location of the Logging Files

The proper dimensioning of the logging files has a great influence on the speed of MySQL/InnoDB. The location, size, and number of logging files are determined by the configuration parameters `innodb_log_group_home`, `innodb_log_files_in_group`, and `innodb_log_file_size`. By default, two logging files of size 5MB each are created in MySQL's data directory.

The InnoDB documentation recommends that the total size of the logging files be about the size of the buffer (parameter `innodb_buffer_pool_size`, which is 8MB by default). If the buffer is larger than the logging files, then it can happen that the InnoDB table driver will have to make a so-called *checkpoint*, involving temporary storage of uncommitted changes.

If you wish to change the location, size, or number of logging files, you must stop the MySQL server. Now delete the existing logging files `ib_logfilen` (only when you are sure that shutdown took place without error) and change `/etc/my.cnf` or `my.ini`. New logging files will be created at the subsequent restart of the MySQL server.

■Note If you value maximal speed, then you should have the logging files stored on a different hard drive from that on which the *tablespace* files reside. If the MySQL server finds logging files when it is started up that do not correspond to the `innodb_log_` parameters, then the startup process is broken off. You will find error messages in the error logging file `hostname.err`. The creation of new logging files (even if there is no error) is also logged in `hostname.err`.

Logging Synchronization

The configuration parameters `innodb_flush_log_at_trx_commit` and `innodb_flush_method` tell when (how often) and how logging files are synchronized. For `innodb_log_at_trx_commit` there are three settings, which allow one to make tradeoffs between speed and security:

- The setting 0 means that the data are written about once per second into the current logging file, and then the file is synchronized. (Writing means here that the data are passed to an I/O function of the operating system. Synchronization means that changes are actually physically written to the hard drive.)

  If there is a crash during the time between the *COMMIT* and the synchronization of the logging file, the transaction is lost and cannot be reconstructed at a later restart. Therefore, `innodb_flush_log_at_trx_commit=0` is a strike against the ACID durability condition.

- More secure is the default setting 1. Now writing and synchronization take place with each *COMMIT*. The drawback is that if you make mostly small transactions, then the hard drive limits the number of possible transactions per second. (For a hard drive with 7200 revolutions per minute, that is, 120 per second, at most 120 transactions can be executed per second, a theoretical limit that is never reached in practice.)

- The setting 2 is a good compromise. Here the writing takes place at each *COMMIT*, but the synchronization only about once per second. If the MySQL server crashes, then immediately terminated transactions are not lost (since the synchronization can take place after a crash). However, if the operating system crashes (power outage, for example), then transactions are lost as with setting 0.

The parameter `innodb_flush_method` determines whether the operating system function *fsync* (the default) or *O_SYNC* (setting O_DSYNC) is used for synchronizing the logging files. With many Unix versions, *O_SYNC* is faster.

Caution Even in the most secure setting, the security of data is dependent on how the operating system actually carries out the synchronization of the logging files. If after a power failure the logging file is defective or synchronization is only partially successful, there can be problems with the reconstruction of data at the next startup. Precisely this happened to `wikimedia.org` in February 2005. Read the following article. You will learn a great deal about how (in)secure database files are despite all security measures, logging, etc.: `http://meta.wikimedia.org/wiki/February_2005_server_crash` and `http://lists.mysql.com/mysql/180326`.

Archive Logging

The transaction logging files are conceived only for internal data management, not for backups. If you require a record of all changes to data since a particular time (since the last complete backup), then you must use MySQL binary logging, which functions entirely independently of the InnoDB table driver. (See the discussion earlier in this chapter.)

InnoDB can, in principle, also carry out such logging. This type of logging is called *archive logging* in the InnoDB documentation. However, *archive logging* makes sense only if InnoDB is used independently of MySQL.

Should you wish for some reason to use *archive logging*, it can be activated with `innodb_log_archive`.

Tips for Speed Optimization

This section offers some tips for speed optimization. The information here is relevant only if you are using primarily InnoDB tables and are working with large data sets.

Tip Look at the section "Performance Tuning Tips" in the InnoDB documentation: `http://dev.mysql.com/doc/mysql/en/innodb-tuning.html`. In optimizing for speed there is also useful information in the InnoDB status information, which can be retrieved with *SHOW INNODB STATUS*.

Buffer Settings

Perhaps the most important parameter for influencing the speed of the InnoDB table driver is `innodb_buffer_pool_size`. This parameter specifies how much RAM should be used for temporary storage of InnoDB tables and indexes. The more such data is available in RAM, the less often access must be made to the hard drive in *SELECT* commands. By default, the InnoDB table driver reserves only 8MB as a buffer. Larger values (the InnoDB documentation recommends up to 80 percent of main memory for a dedicated database server) can dramatically increase the speed of *SELECT* queries. (The total size of the transaction logging files should be as large as the buffer storage.)

Depending on the application, two additional parameters influence what data are stored temporarily in RAM: `innodb_log_buffer_size` sets the size of the buffer for transaction logging, while `innodb_additonal_mem_pool_size` determines how much space in RAM is reserved for various other information such as metadata on open tables. This buffer (by default 1MB) should be enlarged if you are dealing with a large number of InnoDB tables.

Block Operations

If you are carrying out extensive block operations (such as importing a table with a million data records or changing from MyISAM to InnoDB format), you can speed up the process with a few tricks:

- Use the setting *SET unique_checks=0*. Then no check is made whether the data of a *UNIQUE* column or the primary index column are actually unique. Of course, you should use this setting only if you are absolutely sure that there are, in fact, no duplicates!

- Use the setting *SET foreign_key_checks=0*. With this setting you achieve that the integrity conditions are not checked. Of course, here, too, this setting should be used only if you are convinced of the integrity of your data (e.g., in restoring backup data).

- Execute all the *INSERT* commands for a table as a single transaction. Usually, importation consists of countless *INSERT* commands, which by default (*auto commit*) are all carried out in separate transactions. With *SET AUTOCOMMIT=0*, all *INSERT* commands are collected into a single transaction. Keep in mind that this transaction must be confirmed with a *COMMIT*.

  This technique works only if the transaction logging files are large enough. Note that with large transactions, a *ROLLBACK* can be unusually long, even taking hours. Note as well that *CREATE TABLE* has the effect of *COMMIT*. Therefore, it is impossible to read in several tables in a single transaction.

Logging Settings

In the previous section we made reference to the possible settings of the logging parameters. Here is a brief summary:

- `innodb_flush_log_at_trx_commit=2` is useful is you wish to execute as many (small) transactions per second as possible and are prepared to lose the last few seconds of data in case of a crash.

- Ideally, the logging files should be located on a different hard disk from those of the *tablespace* files.

- Depending on the operating system, `innodb_flush_method=O_DSYNC` may speed up logging.

Server Tuning

Server tuning refers to the optimal configuration of the MySQL server so that it uses hardware as efficiently as possible and executes SQL commands with maximum efficiency.

Server tuning is worthwhile, as a rule, only if very large databases are involved (in the gigabyte range), many queries per second are to be processed, and the computer is serving primarily as a database server.

This section provides merely a first introduction to this topic and is restricted primarily to the correct configuration of the buffer storage and the use of the query cache. Note, however, that server tuning is only a component of the larger topic that perhaps might be called *optimization of database applications*. On this theme one could easily write an entire book, which would, among other things, answer the following questions:

- What possibilities are there to optimize the database design in such a way that the most frequently used commands are executed with maximum efficiency? Were the optimal indexes set up? The correct database design is assuredly the most important and undervalued component of speed optimization. Fine tuning the server for a poorly designed database is like hitching a racehorse to a carriage with square wheels. (See also Chapter 8.)

- What is the best hardware for the task (within a given price range)?

- What is the best operating system (if there is a choice)?

- What is the optimal table format?

- Can the burden of many *SELECT* queries be divided among a number of computers?

Tip Many questions will go here unanswered, not least because I myself have too little experience with very large database applications. Further information can be found in the MySQL documentation: `http://dev.mysql.com/doc/mysql/en/mysql-optimization.html`.

A wealth of tuning information is contained in the book, the website, and the news and mailing list contributions of the MySQL guru Jeremy Zawodny. Do a Google search or have a look at the following site: `http://jeremy.zawodny.com/mysql/`.

Finally, of particular worth is the following presentation in OpenOffice/Star Office format. It is a lecture on performance tuning for MySQL/InnoDB by Peter Zaitsev: `http://dev.mysql.com/tech-resources/presentations/` and `http://dev.mysql.com/Downloads/Presentations/OSCON-2004.sxi`.

Optimal Memory Management

MySQL reserves at startup a portion of main memory for certain tasks, such as a cache for data records and a location for sorting data. The size of this buffer is controlled by options in the configuration file and generally cannot be altered while the server is in operation. It can happen that MySQL leaves a great deal of RAM unused, even though there was sufficient memory available and MySQL could make use of it.

The setting of the parameters takes place in the `mysqld` section of the MySQL configuration file. Memory sizes can be abbreviated by K (kilobytes), M (megabytes), and G (gigabytes). The following lines clarify the syntax.

```
# in /etc/my.cnf or my.ini (Windows)
[mysqld]
key_buffer_size = 32M
```

In the following, various important configuration parameters will be introduced (though not all of them by a long shot). Unfortunately, one cannot say which parameter settings should be changed and to what, it all depends heavily on the specific application. However, first attempts should include `key_buffer_size` and `table_cache`:

- The parameter `key_buffer_size` (default 8M) tells how much storage is to be reserved for index blocks. The higher the value, the more rapid is table access to columns for which there is an index. On dedicated database servers it can make sense to increase `key_buffer_size` up to one-fourth of the available RAM.

- The parameter `table_cache` (default 64) specifies how many tables can be open at one time. The opening and closing of table files costs time, and so a larger value of the parameter can increase parallel access to many tables. On the other hand, open tables cost RAM, and the number is also limited by the operating system. The number of tables open in MySQL can be determined with *SHOW STATUS* (variable *open_tables*).

- The parameter `sort_buffer` (default 2M) specifies the size of the sorting buffer. This buffer is used in *SELECT* commands with *ORDER BY* or *GROUP BY* if there is no index available. If the buffer is too small, then a temporary file must be used, which is, of course, slow. The default value of 2MB should suffice for many purposes.

- The parameter `read_buffer_size` (formerly `record_buffer`, default 128K) specifies how much memory each thread reserves for reading sequential data from tables. The parameter should not be unnecessarily large, since this memory is required for each new MySQL connection (thus for each MySQL thread, not only once for the entire server). It is best to increase the parameter only when it is needed for a particular session with *SET SESSION read_buffer_size=n*.

- The parameter `read_rnd_buffer_size` (default 256K) has an effect similar to that of `read_buffer_size`, except that it is valid for the case in which the records are to be read out in a particular order (as with *ORDER BY*). A larger value can avoid search operations on the hard disk, which can slow things down considerably with large tables. As with `read_buffer_size`, `read_rnd_buffer_size` should be increased only as needed with *SET SESSION*.

- The parameter `bulk_insert_buffer_size` (default 8M) specifies how much memory is reserved for the execution of *INSERT* commands in which many records are to be inserted simultaneously (such as *INSERT ... SELECT ...*). This parameter can also be changed for individual connections with *SET SESSION*.

- The parameter `join_buffer_size` (default 128K) specifies how much memory is to be used for *JOIN* operations when there is no index for the *JOIN* columns. (For tables that are frequently linked there should definitely be an index for the linking field. This will contribute more to speed efficiency than increasing this parameter.)

- The parameter `tmp_table_size` (default 32M) specifies how large temporary *HEAP* tables can get. If this size is exceeded, then the tables are transformed into MyISAM tables and stored in a temporary file.

- The parameter `max_connections` (default 100) gives the maximum number of database connections that can be open at one time. The value should not be unnecessarily high, since each connection requires memory and a file descriptor. On the other hand, persistent connections profit from a larger number of allowed connections, since then it is less frequent that a connection is closed and a new one has to be opened. (With *SHOW STATUS* you can determine `max_used_connections`. This is the maximum number of connections that were open simultaneously up to a particular time.)

Tip You can get a look at the most important current settings with the command *SHOW VARIABLES LIKE '%size%*.

If you use InnoDB tables, you should definitely look also at the InnoDB options; see the previous section of this chapter.

A brief description of all available parameters of the MySQL server can be obtained by launching `mysqld` with the option `--help`. A more complete description is given in the MySQL documentation: `http://dev.mysql.com/doc/mysql/en/show-variables.html`.

Query Cache

The query cache is a new function in MySQL 4.0. The basic idea of the query cache is to store the results of SQL queries. If later this exact same query is to be executed, then the stored result can be used instead of having to search through all the affected tables.

The query cache is no panacea, though, for speed optimization. In particular, queries must be deleted from the query cache as soon as the underlying tables are altered:

- The query cache is therefore useful only if the data change relatively seldom (thus many *SELECT* commands in relation to the number of *UPDATE*, *INSERT*, and *DELETE* commands), and it is expected that particular queries will be frequently repeated (which is frequently the case with web applications).

- The *SELECT* commands must be exactly the same (including spaces and case), so that the query cache knows that they are, in fact, the same.

- The *SELECT* commands cannot contain user-defined variables and cannot use certain functions, the most significant of which are *RAND, NOW, CURTIME, CURDATE, LAST_INSERT_ID*, and *HOST*.

If these conditions are not satisfied, then the query cache *SELECT* queries will, in the worst case, slow the system down somewhat (due to the management overhead).

Activating the Query Cache

By default, the query cache is deactivated (due to the default setting `query_cache_size=0`). To activate the query cache, execute the following changes to the MySQL configuration file:

```
# in /etc/my.cnf or my.ini (Windows)
[mysqld]
query_cache_size = 32M
query_cache_type = 1     # 0=Off, 1=On, 2=Demand
query_cache_limit = 50K
```

Now 32MB of RAM is reserved for the query cache. In the cache are stored only *SELECT* results that require less than 50KB. (This avoids the situation in which a few large query results force all other results out of the cache.)

After a server restart, the cache is automatically active. For MySQL applications nothing changes (except that the reaction time to repeated queries is less).

Demand Mode

The query cache can also be run in demand mode. In this case, only those *SELECT* queries are considered that are executed with the option *SQL_CACHE*, as in *SELECT SQL_CACHE * FROM authors*. This mode is useful if you wish to control which commands use the cache.

No Temporary Storage of SQL Query Results

If you wish to prevent a *SELECT* command from using the active query cache (query_cache_type=1), then simply add the option *SQL_NO_CACHE*. This makes sense with commands about which one is certain that they will not soon be repeated and would therefore take up space unnecessarily in the query cache.

Turning the Query Cache On and Off for a Connection

You can change the mode of the query cache for a particular connection. Just execute *SET query_cache_type = 0/1/2/OFF/ON/DEMAND*.

Determining the Status of the Query Cache

If you wish to know how well the query cache is functioning, whether its size is well chosen, etc., then execute the command *SHOW STATUS LIKE 'qcache%'*. As result you receive a list of status variables, whose meaning is briefly described in Table 14-3.

Table 14-3. *Query Cache Status Variables*

Status Variable	Meaning
Qcache_queries_in_cache	Tells how many queries have results in the cache.
Qcache_inserts	Tells how many queries have been cached up to now. This value is generally greater than *Qcache_queries_in_cache*, since results are removed from the cache due to lack of space or changes to tables.
Qcache_hits	Tells how often a query was able to be answered directly from the cache.
Qcache_lowmem_prunes	Tells how many results were deleted from the cache because it was full. (If this value is high, that is an indication that the cache size is too small.)
Qcache_not_cached	Tells how many queries were not accepted into the cache (e.g., because a function like *RAND* or *NOW* or the option *SQL_NO_CACHE* was used).
Qcache_free_memory	Tells how much memory is currently free in the cache.

With *FLUSH QUERY CACHE* you can defragment the cache (which, the MySQL documentation states, makes possible improved memory usage, but it does not empty the cache). *RESET QUERY CACHE* deletes all entries from the cache.

ISP Database Administration

Up to now we have assumed that you have installed MySQL on your own computer and have unrestricted access to the server. And indeed, this is the usual starting point for every database administrator.

However, with MySQL the situation can be a bit different. Often, your database is located on the computer of an Internet service provider. There you have almost no administrative privileges. That is, the ISP administers MySQL on its own. (If you have a responsible ISP, it will automatically carry out backups of your databases, but don't count on it.) Nonetheless, you will have to carry out certain administrative tasks:

- Create new databases (provided that the ISP permits this).

- Execute backups. (Even if your ISP does this regularly, it is good to be able to be responsible for your own data.)

- Execute a database upload. (For example, you have developed a database application on your own computer and now wish to transfer the completed database to the ISP computer.)

Working with ssh

Administration is at its simplest when your ISP provides you with ssh access. Then you can log into the ISP's computer and use all of the commands introduced in this chapter. Needless to say, with commands such as mysqldump you can access only your own databases. But that should suffice. For moving files between your local computer and that of the ISP, you can use ftp.

Unfortunately, not all ISPs offer their clients access via ssh, since this means extra work for the ISP and greater security risks.

Working via phpMyAdmin

Probably the most popular solution to this administrative problem is offered by phpMyAdmin, a collection of PHP scripts installed in a www directory on the ISP's computer (see Chapter 6). In principle, phpMyAdmin is suited for all the administrative tasks mentioned above. In practice, however, there is usually a problem.

For the execution of PHP scripts—and thus for phpMyAdmin as well—there is a time limit. If the execution of a script exceeds the allotted time, the script is automatically terminated. In most cases this limit represents a sensible protective measure against programmer error (such as infinite loops), but unfortunately, it makes the backup of a large database impossible.

Implementing Custom PHP Scripts for Administration

Instead of working with phpMyAdmin, you can, of course, program your own PHP scripts for administration and store them in a directory on your web site. For example, you can execute a backup of a database with a PHP file of the following design:

```
<?php system("/usr/bin/mysqldump --host=hostname --user=username " .
          "--password=xxx dbname > backup.sql");  ?>
```

Instead of /usr/bin you may have to specify a different path (for example, /usr/local/bin). In some circumstances things will work without a path name being specified. As hostname you can use *localhost* if the web server and MySQL are running on the same computer.

After you have loaded the page via your web browser (and thereby executed the script), you can transfer the file backup.sql, which is located in the same directory as the script, to your computer, again via the web browser or FTP.

Note With an ISP the web server (and thus the PHP script as well) is usually executed under the account *nobody* or *apache*. This user usually has writing privileges in your directories.

mysqldump works only if you have granted extensive *write* privileges for the directory in which the PHP script is located. For this the command chmod a+w directory would be necessary, but you might not be able to execute it without ssh. Instead, use your FTP client to set the directory's access privileges.

Conversely, for an upload you first transfer via FTP the file upload.sql generated on your computer into the directory in which your PHP administration scripts are located. Then you execute a script via your web browser according to the following pattern:

```
<?php system("/usr/bin/mysql --host=hostname --user=username " .
          "--password=xxx dbname < upload.sql");   ?>
```

For the upload to succeed, the specified database must already exist. If that is not the case, you can first create the database with mysqladmin (which you also execute in the PHP script via *system*).

If you have previously created upload.sql with mysqldump, then the database at the ISP may not contain the tables defined in upload.sql. If necessary, you must insert some *DROP TABLE IF EXISTS* commands in upload.sql.

In comparison to phpMyAdmin, the advantage of this way of proceeding is that no time is lost in the transfer of the database files over the Internet. Instead, the upload file is read from the local computer, or the download file is written there. However, this does not change anything in regard to the time limit for PHP scripts. Of course, you can transport somewhat larger databases with the method presented here than with phpMyAdmin, but sooner or later you will find yourself nose to nose with the PHP time limit.

Do not forget to secure access to the directory with your administrative scripts with .htaccess. The use of .htaccess is described in Chapter 2.

Custom Perl Scripts for Administration

What works with PHP works also, of course, with Perl, and often better. The advantage of Perl is that in the execution of CGI scripts there is often no time limit. (But this depends on the provider.)

In Perl, too, there is a *system* function for calling external commands. In the lines below there is also code added that evaluates and displays the return value of this function. The mysqldump and mysql commands look exactly the same in the PHP scripts presented above. Even the preparatory work is identical:

```
#!/usr/bin/perl -w
use CGI qw(:standard);
use CGI::Carp qw(fatalsToBrowser);
print header(), start_html("Backup");
if(system("/usr/bin/mysqldump --host=hostname --user=username " .
          "--password=xxx dbname > backup.sql")) {
  print p(), "failed", end_html(); }
else {
  print p(), "done", end_html(); }
```

PART 4

■■■

Programming

CHAPTER 15

■ ■ ■

PHP

PHP stands for *PHP: Hypertext Preprocessor* (a typical recursive abbreviation in the world of Unix). PHP is a script programming language for HTML pages. The code embedded in an HTML file is executed by the server. (The *Active Server Pages* of Microsoft also follow this plan.)

When a programming language is brought into play with MySQL, that language is almost always PHP. The reason for this is that PHP and MySQL offer almost ideal conditions for building dynamic websites: simple deployment, high speed, and unbeatable price (free). This is the reason that this PHP chapter is much more extensive than the following chapters, which deal with other programming languages.

Since PHP 5 there are two interfaces available for MySQL programming: The *mysql* functions are known to many PHP programmers from earlier versions of PHP. New since PHP 5 is the object-oriented interface *mysqli*, which enables more elegant programming features and access to new MySQL functions (e.g., the particularly efficient execution of SQL commands with parameters using *prepared statements*). However, *mysqli* assumes that you have available versions PHP 5 and MySQL 4.1 or newer.

After an introduction to the most important *mysqli* functions, classes, methods, and properties, I will introduce several examples of elementary programming techniques, for example the paged representation of search results, the processing of hierarchical data, and working with Unicode character strings.

Assumptions: This chapter assumes that PHP and MySQL have been correctly installed and configured (see Chapter 2). Most of the examples are based on the newer *mysqli* interface and use the database *mylibrary*, which was presented in Chapter 8. Note that you must synchronize the login and password strings in the files `mysql-intro.php`, `mysqli-intro.php`, and `password.php` for the examples to work properly. Read as well the `readme` file in the directory containing the example files for this chapter.

mysql Functions

The *mysql* functions are not an integral part of PHP, but an extension. In order for this extension to be used, PHP under Linux must have been compiled with the option *—with-mysql*. With the Windows version of PHP, the corresponding extension is provided as a DLL. However, the extension must be activated in `php.ini`, and PHP must find all the requisite DLLs (see also Chapter 2).

You can find out whether the PHP version you are using recognizes the *mysql* functions with a minimal PHP script, which contains the line *<?php phpinfo() ?>*. The result of this script is a long table containing available PHP functions. The *mysql* part of the output should look something like Figure 15-1.

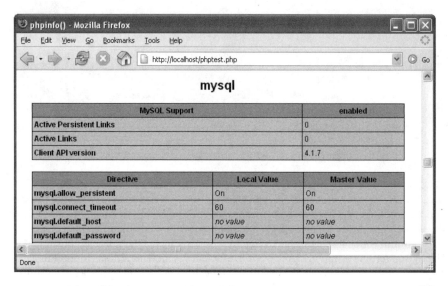

Figure 15-1. *PHP recognizes the mysql functions.*

Establishing a Connection

To establish a connection, execute *mysql_connect*, where you need to pass three pieces of information: the computer name (hostname) of the MySQL server, the MySQL user name, and the password. If MySQL is running on the same computer as the PHP script, the computer name should be *localhost*.

```
$conn = mysql_connect("localhost", "username", "xxx");
```

With RHEL and Fedora, SELinux is configured in such a way that Apache and PHP are not permitted to access the MySQL socket file. Therefore, instead of *localhost*, the actual name of the computer must be given. Communcation with the MySQL server now takes place via TCP/IP instead of the socket file.

The function returns an identification number. You will need this number in the future only if you open more than one connection to MySQL. (As long as there is only one connection to MySQL, this connection is the default connection. The ID number therefore does not need to be given in calling various *mysql_xxx* functions.)

With an optional fourth parameter you can specify whether, in the case of multiple executions of *mysql_connect* with the same connection data, only a link to the existing connection should be returned (the default is *false*) or a new connection should be established (*true*). The format *mysql_connect($host, $name, $pw, true)* is thus absolutely necessary if you need several distinct connections.

In the optional fifth parameter you can pass client flags. A possible constant is *MYSQL_CLIENT_COMPRESS* (if the data exchange should be compressed).

If problems occur, the variable *conn* contains the value *FALSE*. Moreover, *mysql_connect* sends an error message to the web server, so that in the resulting HTML document an unattractive error message appears. To avoid this message, the character @ must be placed before *mysql_connect*. (This character generally inhibits the display of error messages in PHP function calls.)

If you wish to provide the PHP code for establishing the connection itself with a readable error message, the necessary code looks something like this:

```
$conn = @mysql_connect("localhost", "username", "xxx");
if($conn == FALSE) {
  echo "<p>error message ...</p>\n";
  exit();
}
```

As soon as a connection has been made, you can execute SQL commands with various *mysql_xxx* functions and much else besides. In order to avoid having to specify the desired database every time, you can select a default database with *mysql_select_db*. (This corresponds to the SQL command *USE databasename.*)

```
mysql_select_db("mylibrary");
```

The functions *mysql_get_client_info*, *mysql_get_host_info*, *mysql_get_proto_info*, and *mysql_get_server_info*, as well as *mysql_client_encoding*, *mysql_stat*, and *mysql_thread_id* provide precise information about the current connection: the version of the client library, the type of connection to the server, the version number of the protocol, the server version, the valid character set, the current status of the server, and the thread number of the MySQL server process.

You close the connection to MySQL with *mysql_close*.

Executing SQL Commands

To execute SQL commands, you pass them as a character string to the function *mysql_query*. If the command is not intended for the current database, you can add the name of the desired database using *mysql_db_query*. With both of these functions an optional final parameter can be given: the ID number of the connection (that is, the return value of *mysql_connect*) if there is more than one connection to MySQL.

```
$result = mysql_query("SELECT COUNT(*) FROM titles");
$result = mysql_db_query("mylibrary", "SELECT COUNT(*) FROM titles");
```

Every type of SQL command can be executed with *mysql_query*: queries with *SELECT*; changes to data with *INSERT, UPDATE*, and *DELETE*; changes to the database structure with *CREATE TABLE*; etc.

■**Caution** The SQL command must not be terminated with a semicolon. (That would be an SQL syntax error.) It is impossible to pass several commands simultaneously. If you wish to execute more than one command, you must execute *mysql_query* once for each command.

After *INSERT, UPDATE*, and *DELETE* commands (and all other commands that change data records) you can determine with *mysql_affected_rows* how many records were changed. This function is also useful after *CREATE TABLE ... SELECT ...* for determining how many records were inserted into the newly created table.

Moreover, after an *INSERT* command you can determine with *mysql_insert_id* the *AUTO_INCREMENT* value that was used for the last new record to be inserted.

```
$n = mysql_affected_rows();  // number of changed records
$new_id = mysql_insert_id(); // ID number of the last AUTO_INCREMENT record
```

Since PHP 4.3, the function *mysql_info* has offered additional information about the last *ALTER TABLE, CREATE TABLE, INSERT INTO, LOAD DATA,* and *UPDATE* command. The returned string contains, for example, information on duplicates and warnings. For example, if you execute the command *CREATE TABLE backup SELECT * FROM table*, then *mysql_info* returns a string of the form *"Records: nnn Duplicates: nnn Warnings: nnn"*.

If an SQL command can be correctly executed, *mysql_query* returns a nonzero value. If the command involved a query, the return value of *mysql_query* is a reference to a PHP resource (e.g., a character string of the form *"Resource id #2"*). The return value can be used in various other functions (e.g., *mysql_fetch_row*) to evaluate individual fields of the table. In the examples of this chapter, the return value will generally be stored in a variable called *result*. (The use of *SELECT* results will be described in detail in the following section.)

On the other hand, if an SQL command cannot be executed, *mysql_query* returns the result *FALSE* (i.e., 0). Moreover, an error message is displayed, which you can suppress by executing *mysql_query* with a prefixed @ character. (The cause of the error can be determined by evaluating *mysql_errno* and *mysql_error*. More information on error evaluation will be given shortly.)

Evaluating SELECT Results

When you execute a *SELECT* query with *mysql_query*, you obtain as result a reference to a table with *rows* rows and *cols* columns:

```
$result = mysql_query("SELECT * FROM titles");
$rows = mysql_num_rows($result);
$cols = mysql_num_fields($result);
```

This is also the case in two special situations:

- If the query returns only a single value (e.g., *SELECT COUNT(*) FROM table*), the table has only one row and one column.

- If the query returns no result at all (e.g., when there is no record that satisfies a *WHERE* condition), the table has 0 rows. This case can be recognized only by evaluating *mysql_num_rows*.

Only when an SQL query is syntactically incorrect or there is a problem communicating with MySQL will you get no result whatsoever (that is, the return value of *mysql_query* is *FALSE*).

The simplest, but slowest, access to the individual fields of a table is offered by *mysql_result*. In two parameters you give the desired row and column numbers. (The count begins at 0, as with all PHP/MySQL functions.) Instead of the column number, you can also give the column name (or an alias, if you processed the SQL query with *AS alias*).

```
$item = mysql_result($result, $row, $col);
```

It is much more efficient to evaluate the result row by row. For this there are three functions:

```
$row = mysql_fetch_row($result);
$row = mysql_fetch_array($result);
$row = mysql_fetch_assoc($result);
$row = mysql_fetch_object($result);
```

- *mysql_fetch_row* returns a record in the form of a simple array. Access to the columns is via *$row[$n]*.

- *mysql_fetch_array* returns a record in the form of an associative array. Access to the columns is via *$row[$n]* or *$row[$colname]* (so, for example, *$row[3]* or *$row["publName"]*). The column name is case-sensitive.

- *mysql_fetch_assoc* (available since PHP 4.0.3) also returns an associative field, which can be read in the form *$row[$colname]*. In contrast to *mysql_fetch_array*, one is not allowed to give the column number as parameter.

- *mysql_fetch_object* returns a data record as object. Access to the column is via *$row->colname*.

A common feature of all four functions is that with each call, the next record is automatically returned (or *FALSE* if the end of the list of data has been reached). If this specified order should be changed, the currently active record can be changed with *mysql_data_seek*:

```
mysql_data_seek($result, $rownr);
```

PHP stores query results until the end of the script. If a query result must be released earlier (for example, if you have executed a large number of queries in a script and don't want to waste memory), you can release the result early with *mysql_free_result*. This is particularly useful if the script contains a loop that executes SQL queries.

```
mysql_free_result($result);
```

An Example with SELECT

The following lines should clarify the interplay among the various functions. After the connection, protected with an *if*, the program executes the query *SELECT * FROM titles* for the database *mylibrary* and displays the titles (and subtitles, when present) found in rows. *htmlspecialchars* ensures that any special characters in a book title (e.g., <, >, ') are coded in conformity to HTML. After the output, the result object is deleted and the connection ended.

```
// example mysql-intro.php
if($conn = @mysql_connect("localhost", "root", "xxx")) {
  mysql_select_db("mylibrary");
  if($result=mysql_query("SELECT * FROM titles ORDER BY title")) {
    printf("<p>Number of records: %d</p>\n", mysql_num_rows($result));
    printf("<p>Number of columns: %d</p>\n",
      mysql_num_fields($result));
    while($row = mysql_fetch_object($result)) {
      if($row->subtitle)
        printf("<br />%s -- %s\n",
          htmlspecialchars($row->title), htmlspecialchars ($row->subtitle));
      else
        printf("<br />%s\n", htmlspecialchars($row->title));
    }
    mysql_free_result($result);
  }
} else {
  printf("<p>Sorry, could not connect to MySQL server! %s</p>\n",
    mysql_error());
}
```

The output is shown in Figure 15-2.

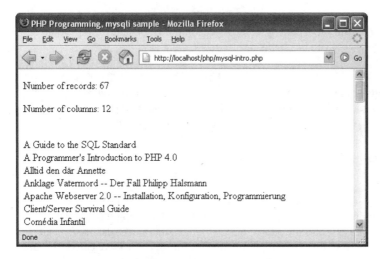

Figure 15-2. *The mylibrary title list as result of the example program*

Column Names and Metainformation

If you are processing generally valid queries and wish to display the results, you need not only the data themselves, but also metainformation about the nature of the data, such as the names of the columns and their data types.

mysql_field_name returns the name of the specified column. *mysql_field_table* gives in addition which table the data come from (important in queries that collect data from several tables). *mysql_field_type* gives the data type of the column as a string (e.g., *"BLOB"*). *mysql_field_len* gives the maximum length of the column (of particular interest with the data types *CHAR* and *VARCHAR*).

```
$colname    = mysql_field_name($result, $n);
$tblname    = mysql_field_table($result, $n);
$typename   = mysql_field_type($result, $n);
$collength  = mysql_field_len($result, $n);
```

Even more detailed information on a column is given by *mysql_field_flags* and *mysql_fetch_field*: The function *mysql_field_flags* returns a string in which the most important attributes of the column are given (e.g., *"not_null primary_key"*). The properties are separated by spaces; the evaluation proceeds most simply with *explode*.

mysql_fetch_field, on the other hand, returns an object that provides some of the same information as that in the string of *mysql_field_flags*. Evaluation takes place in the form *colinfo->name*, *colinfo->blob*, etc.

```
$colflags = mysql_field_flags($result, $n);
$colinfo  = mysql_fetch_field($result, $n);
```

Queries with mysql_unbuffered_query

You can also execute *SELECT* queries with *mysql_unbuffered_query* (instead of with *mysql_query*). This has the effect that the query results are not transferred at once into the memory of the PHP interpreter, but only as needed (that is, when individual result records are read). That yields the following consequences:

- The data remain on the server until they are fetched by the PHP script. This means that during this time, resources are blocked on the MySQL server. (The PHP interpreter must reserve only a very small amount of memory for this intermediate storage.)

- You must read in the found records, one after the other, with *mysql_fetch_row*, *mysql_object*, *mysql_assoc*, or *mysql_array* (*forward only*). On the other hand, the functions *mysql_fetch_result* and *mysql_data_seek* are unavailable. Already read records cannot be read a second time, because only one record at a time is present in the memory of the PHP interpreter.

- You may not execute a new SQL command for the given MySQL connection before you have read all the records of the *SELECT* result. If you nevertheless wish to do so, either you need an additional connection to the MySQL server or you must explicitly release the *SELECT* command with *mysql_free_result($result)*.

- You can determine the number of found records only by running through all the result records. You cannot use *mysql_num_rows*.

- *mysql_buffered_query* is designed only for *SELECT* queries (and not for commands that return no result, such as *INSERT* or *DELETE*).

The function *mysql_unbuffered_query* is especially suitable when very large *SELECT* results are to be processed record by record without much client memory being reserved for the purpose. Since it is in the nature of PHP pages to process mostly very small amounts of data, and since the execution time of PHP code is limited (via the setting *max_execution_time* in php.ini), there are few situations in which this function has real advantages over *mysql_query*.

Transactions

There are no functions for managing transactions. If you wish to execute several SQL commands as a transaction, then first execute *mysql_query("BEGIN")*. With *mysql_query("COMMIT")* you confirm the transaction, and with *mysql_query("ROLLBACK")* you can undo all the commands of the transaction. Note that at present, MySQL supports transactions only for InnoDB tables.

Error Handling and Search

All *mysql_xxx* functions return *FALSE* if an error occurs during execution. Information on the nature of the error is obtained by evaluating the functions *mysql_errno* (returns an error number) and *mysql_error* (error message).

Many *mysql* functions themselves write error messages to the HTML output. If you wish to suppress that, you must call the function with a prefixed @ character or use the setting *display_errors = Off* in php.ini.

```
$result = @mysql_query($sql);
if(!$result) {
  printf("<p>error: %d -- %s</p>\n", mysql_errno(),
    htmlspecialchars(mysql_error()));
}
```

In general, you must always count on there being errors, especially in the execution of SQL commands that alter data. A possible cause of error can be connection problems with the MySQL server.

In searching for errors, the function *mysql_query_test* can be useful. It is seen as a replacement for *mysql_query*, and it displays every executed SQL command in blue. If an error occurs, the error message is displayed at once.

```
function mysql_query_test($sql) {
  echo '<p><font color="#0000ff"> SQL:', htmlspecialchars($sql),
    "</font></p>\n";
  $result = mysql_query($sql);
  if($result) return $result;
  echo '<p><font color="#ff0000">Error: ',
    htmlspecialchars(mysql_error()), "</font></p>\n";
  die();
}
```

■**Tip** What should you do if an example from this book fails to function properly? The error message, if one is displayed, often does not indicate a clear cause of the problem.

The cause of problems is almost always database access: The PHP script cannot, for example, read the data in the database and therefore returns incorrect data or no data at all. There are many possible reasons for this, but they almost always have to do with access privileges: incorrect password, no password when one was required. Only when MySQL is not secured at all will access from the local computer be possible with the combination *name = "root" and password = ""*.

---

mysqli Classes, Methods, and Properties

The *mysqli* interface is considered, at least by developers of MySQL applications, to be among the most important innovations in PHP 5. This interface makes possible object-oriented programming of database access with MySQL and is thus a great help in the creation of readable code.

A second advantage of *mysqli* in comparison to the older *mysql* interface is that with it, SQL commands with parameters can be executed very efficiently (*prepared statements*). Such commands have been possible only since MySQL 4.1. They offer somewhat greater efficiency when several equivalent SQL commands are to be executed that differ only in their parameters.

If you are using stored procedures, there is a second argument in favor of *mysqli*: With *multi_query* you can execute stored procedures that return not one, but several records (thus the results of several *SELECT* commands). To do so is much more complicated with the *mysql* interface.

The *mysqli* interface can be used in both an object-oriented and procedural manner. However, this book describes only the object-oriented approach. If you prefer to work procedurally, then use the interface *mysql* introduced in the previous section.

Which Will It Be: mysql or mysqli?

With two interfaces available, the following question naturally arises: Which interface is better, and which one should I use?

In favor of *mysqli* one can say that it is the more modern interface. It offers more functions, leads usually to simpler code, and in many instances promises greater speed. For this reason, all the remaining sections of the chapter are based on *mysqli*.

Against *mysqli* one may say that this interface assumes PHP 5 and MySQL 4.1 (or newer versions). If you are writing code that must be compatible with PHP 4.*n* or MySQL 4.0, you should stick with *mysql*.

Although you may freely install the newest program versions on your development computer, many Internet service providers are very conservative as regards migrating to new versions of software. Stability and maturity generally count for more than new functionality. Thus the *mysql* interface will surely justify its existence for a few more years.

Availability Tests

The *mysqli* interface is, like the *mysql* interface, not an integral component of PHP, but an extension. For this extension to be usable, PHP must be compiled under Linux with the option *—with-mysqli*. With the Windows version of PHP the corresponding extension is provided as a DLL, and the extension must be activated in php.ini, and PHP must be able to find all requisite DLLs (see also Chapter 2).

You can most easily determine whether the version of PHP that you are using recognizes the *mysqli* interface with a minimal PHP script, containing simply the line *<?php phpinfo(); ?>*. The result of this script is a long table of the available PHP functions. The *mysqli* part of the output should look something like that in Figure 15-3.

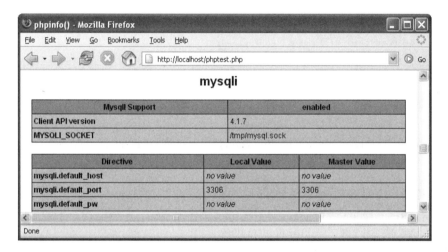

Figure 15-3. *PHP recognizes the mysqli interface.*

Overview of Classes

mysqli makes three classes available:

> **mysqli:** Objects of this class control the connection to the MySQL server. To establish a connection, you use a constructor. The most important method is called *query*, and its purpose is to execute SQL queries. With *SELECT* queries you obtain as result a *mysql_result* object.
>
> **mysqli_result:** Objects of this class contain the result of *SELECT* queries.
>
> **mysqli_stmt:** With objects of this class you can define and execute parameterized SQL commands. You create *mysqli_stmt* objects with *$mysqli ->prepare*.

Making the Connection

To create a new connection to the MySQL server, pass to the *mysqli* constructor the name of the server (or *localhost* if the MySQL server is running on the local computer), the user name, and the password. Three additional parameters are optional: the name of the database that you wish to use, the port number of the MySQL server (by default 3306), and the name of the socket file or named pipe. You can later change the default database for the active connection with the method *select_db*.

With RHEL and Fedora, SELinux is configured in such a way that Apache and PHP are not permitted to access the MySQL socket file. Therefore, instead of *localhost*, the actual name of the computer must be given. Communcation with the MySQL server now takes place via TCP/IP instead of the socket file.

As a rule, the constructor returns a *mysqli* object. However, you must test with the function *mysqli_connect_errno* whether an error occurred in building the connection. The associated error message is returned by *mysqli_connect_error*.

With various methods and properties such as *client_info, character_set_name, get_client_info, get_host_info, get_server_info,* and *stat* you can determine characteristics of the database connection.

When you no longer need the connection to the database, you should explicitly close the *mysqli* object with *close*.

```
// create connection to the database
$mysqli = new mysqli("localhost", "user", "password", "mylibrary");
// test whether connection OK
if(mysqli_connect_errno()) {
  echo "<p>Sorry, no connection! ", mysqli_connect_error(), "</p>\n";
  exit();
}
// use connection
...
// close connection
$mysqli->close();
```

All further examples in this section assume that *$mysqli* is an object with an active MySQL connection.

Establishing the Connection with real_connect

The establishment of a connection with the *mysqli* constructor as described above has the drawback that you cannot set any MySQL-specific connection options. If that is necessary (even if seldom), this is how you can make the connection:

```
$mysqli = mysqli_init();  // create mysqli object
$mysqli->options(...);     // set additonal options (optional)
$mysqli->ssl_set(...);     // set SSL options (optional)
// create connection to MySQL server
$mysqli->real_connect("localhost", "user", "password", "mylibrary");
// test whether OK
if(mysqli_connect_errno()) {
  echo "<p>Sorry, no connection! ", mysqli_connect_error(), "</p>\n";
  exit(); }
```

Additional Connection Options

The methods *options* and *ssl_set* are optional. With *options* you can set various MySQL options, for example to set the timeout period for a connection or to execute an SQL command directly after the connection is made:

```
$mysqli->options(MYSQLI_OPT_CONNECT_TIMEOUT, 10);
$mysqli->options(MYSQLI_INIT_COMMAND, "SQL command ...");
```

With *ssl_set* you can set the keys and other parameters for SSL encryption:

```
$mysqli->ssl_set("key", "cert", "ca", "capath", "cipher");
```

In the optional fifth through seventh parameters you can pass to the method *real_connect* the IP port number of the MySQL (generally 3306), the server's socket file for internal Unix/Linux communication, as well as some flags with specific connection attributes. Some allowable flags are *MYSQLI_CLIENT_COMPRESS* and *MYSQL_CLIENT_SSL,* if all transmitted data is to be respectively compressed or encrypted via SSL.

```
$mysqli->real_connect("localhost", "user", "password", "mylibrary",
  3306, "/var/lib/mysql/mysql.sock", MYSQLI_CLIENT_COMPRESS);
```

Executing SQL Commands

The *mysqli* interface offers a number of ways to execute SQL commands, but the most frequently used is the method *query.* With SQL commands that don't return data (e.g., *INSERT, UPDATE, DELETE*), *query* normally returns *TRUE.* In addition, *$mysqli->affected_rows* returns the number of changed records. *$mysqli->insert_id* returns the *AUTO_INCREMENT* value generated from the last *INSERT* command.

```
if($mysqli->query("INSERT ...")) {
  echo "<p>changed records: ", $mysqli->affected_rows, "</p>\n";
  echo "<p>new ID value: ",      $mysqli->insert_id, "</p>\n";
}
```

With *SELECT* commands, query returns a *mysqli_result* object. *$result->num_rows* gives the number of found records, and *$result->field_count* the number of result columns.

```
if($result = $mysqli->query("SELECT ...")) {
  echo "<p>found records: ", $result->num_rows, "</p>\n";
  echo "<p>number of columns: ",  $result->field_count, "</p>\n";
  ...
  $result->close();
}
```

If an error occurs in the execution of a command, the *query* return value is *FALSE.* More precise information about the error can be obtained with *$mysqli->errno* and *$mysqli->error.*

■**Tip** Note that you can pass only a single command to *query.* If you wish to execute several commands simultaneously, you must use the method *multi_query*, which will be described shortly.

If you wish to execute the same SQL command several times with different parameters, then your most efficient option is first to prepare the command and then execute it. The use of such *prepared statements* is the subject of the next major section of this chapter.

A third alternative to *query* is the method *real_query*, which executes an SQL command without transmitting the result. The method returns *TRUE* or *FALSE*, depending on whether the SQL command was executed without error. If the command returns records, they must be processed with the methods *store_result* and *use_result*. (Caution: If you do not read the resulting records with *store_result* or *use_result*, then all following SQL commands will result in an *out-of-sync* error.)

Evaluating SELECT Results (mysqli_result)

By default, *query* transfers all result data from the server to the client and makes them available as a *mysqli_result* object. If you want the results to remain on the server, to be read as needed record by record, than pass to *query* the additional parameter *MYSQLI_USE_RESULT.* This is useful when you are processing large data sets that should not be brought over to the client all at once. (In other words, the client would be burdened, and so the server must keep *SELECT* results longer in memory.) A disadvantage of *MYSQLI_USE_RESULT* is that you can determine the number of records only by reading all the records.

As in the *mysql* interface, *mysqli* also offers four methods similar to one another for reading the result row by row:

```
$row = $result->fetch_row();
$row = $result->fetch_array();
$row = $result->fetch_assoc();
$row = $result->fetch_object();
```

- *fetch_row* returns a record in the form of a simple array. Access to the columns is via *$row[$n]*.

- *fetch_array* returns a record in the form of an associative array. Access to the columns is via *$row[$n]* or *$row[$colname]* (e.g., *$row[3] oder $row["publName"]*). The column name is case-sensitive.

- *fetch_assoc* also returns an associative field, which can be read in the form *$row[$colname]*. In contrast to *fetch_array*, here it is not permitted to pass the column number as a parameter.

- *fetch_object* returns a record as an object. Access to the columns is via *$row->colname*, where the column names are case-sensitive.

A common feature of all four methods is that with each call, the next record is automatically retrieved (or *FALSE* if the end of the data list is reached). If the specified order is to be changed, the currently active record can be changed with *$result->data_seek*.

```
$result->data_seek($rownr);
```

The fetch *methods* automatically change SQL *NULL* values into the PHP constant *NULL*. The following lines show the application of *fetch_assoc* in outputting the content of a simple *SELECT* query. The function *htmlspecialchars* ensures that any special characters stored in the database (e.g., <, >, ", &) are transformed to the correct HTML code.

```
// example mysqli-intro.php
if($result = $mysqli->query("SELECT title, subtitle FROM titles")) {
  while($row = $result->fetch_assoc()){
    if($row["subtitle"]==NULL)
      printf("<br />%s\n", htmlspecialchars($row["title"]));
    else
      printf("<br />%s -- %s\n", htmlspecialchars($row["title"]),
        htmlspecialchars($row["subtitle"]));
  }
  // release content of result
  $result->close();
}
```

Metadata on the SELECT Result

The already mentioned properties *$result->num_rows* and *$result->field_count* give the number of found records as well as the number of columns. *$result->lengths* returns an array whose elements contain the number of characters in each column for the last record read with *fetch_xxx*.

If you require more precise data about the nature of the query results, you should evaluate *$meta=$result->fetch_fields()*. This method returns an object array. Each object contains, among other things, the following data:

```
$meta[$n]->name        name of the column
$meta[$n]->table       name of the underlying table
$meta[$n]->max_length  longest string in the SELECT result
$meta[$n]->type        data type ID (Integer)
```

The following lines show how to evaluate the object array in a loop:

```
foreach($result->fetch_fields() as $meta)
  printf("<br />Name=%s Table=%s Len=%d Type=%s\n",
    $meta->name, $meta->table, $meta->max_length, $meta->type);
```

Executing Several SQL Commands at Once

With *query* you can execute only a single SQL command. Sometimes, however, it is useful to execute several commands simultaneously. To do so, pass a character string to the method *multi_query* containing the commands, separated by semicolons. The method returns *TRUE* if the first command was executed without error. Otherwise, it returns *FALSE*. (The return value *TRUE* gives no information as to whether the remaining commands were executed without error; see the remark below.)

Since each command can return results, the use of *multi_query* also changes how you evaluate results: The result of the first command can be read with the method *use_result* or *store_result*. The difference between the two methods is that in using *use_result*, the result remains on the server and is transferred to the client record by record. With *store_result*, all results are immediately transferred to the client, which in general is more efficient.

You can test whether there are additional results with *more_results*. This method returns *TRUE* or *FALSE* as result. If you want to process the next result, execute *next_result*. This method also returns *TRUE* or *FALSE*, depending on whether there are further results. If there are, they must be read with *use_result* or *store_result*.

The following lines show a typical application of these methods: With the first SQL command the variable *@a* is initialized. This variable is passed to a stored procedure (that is, a user-defined SQL function). Then the values of *@a* and *@b* are output with *SELECT*. Each result object is displayed with the function *show_result*, which formats the result as a table. The code of *show_result* appears later in the chapter. (In this example the third SQL command simply returns a result.)

```
$sql = "SET @a=12; CALL mysp(@a, @b); SELECT @a, @b";
$ok = $mysqli->multi_query($sql);
if($ok)
  do {
    $result = $mysqli->store_result();
    if($result) {
      show_table($result);
      $result->close();
    }
  } while($mysqli->next_result());
```

■**Caution** The methods *multi_query* and *next_result* are problematic if errors occur during the processing of commands. The return value of the method *multi_query* and the *mysqli* properties *errno*, *error*, *info*, and *warning_count* relate to only the first SQL command. There is no way of determining errors from the second command on.

The source of this problem is the implementation of the method *next_result*, which in PHP 5.0.3 returns only *TRUE* or *FALSE*. However, the underlying C-API function *mysql_next_result* distinguishes three variants (further results, no further results, and error).

SQL Commands with Parameters (Prepared Statements)

With many PHP pages, similar queries must be executed that differ only in the values of individual parameters. In such cases, MySQL, from version 4.1, provides *prepared statements*: The complete command is sent to the MySQL server only once; thereafter, only the parameters vary. This reduces considerably the amount of data to be transmitted and also makes the processing of the commands more efficient, since the MySQL server must analyze the structure of the command only once.

From the point of view of PHP programming, the greatest advantage of prepared statements is that the code is much more elegant and understandable. It is no longer necessary to compose a valid command out of the individual parameters (including the quoting of character strings and BLOBs). Instead, it suffices to store the parameters in simple PHP variables and then execute *execute*.

Before you do so, some preparations are required. First you must specify the SQL command with *$mysqli->prepare*. In the command you place question marks in place of the parameters. As result, you obtain a *mysqli_stmt* object, which becomes the basis for all further operations. The following text assumes that this object has been stored in the variable *$stmt*.

Then, with *$stmt->bind_param* you bind the parameters to the PHP variables. (Take care to place things in the correct order.) Each parameter's data type must be specified by the appropriate character, as shown in Table 15-1.

Table 15-1. *Data Types for bind_param*

Character	Meaning
i	whole number (*integer*)
d	floating-point (*double*)
s	character string (*string*)
b	binary data (BLOBs, *binary*)

In order actually to execute the SQL command, store the desired values in the PHP variables and then execute *$stmt->execute*. You can repeat the process as often as you like. When you no longer need the *mysqli_stmt* object, you should release it explicitly at once. You thereby not only free the object from local memory, you also signal the MySQL server that no further commands are to follow and it can therefore delete the prepared statement.

The following example clarifies the process:

```
// example mysqli-prepared.php
// prepare SQL command with parameters
$stmt = $mysqli->prepare(
  "INSERT INTO titles (title, subtitle, langID) VALUES (?, ?, ?)");
$stmt->bind_param('ssi', $title, $subtitle, $langID);
// execute command multiple times
$title = "new Linux title 1";
$subtitle = "new subtitle 1";
$langID = 1;
$stmt->execute();
$title = "new MySQL title 2";
$subtitle = "new subtitle 2";
$langID = 2;
$stmt->execute();
// release command
$stmt->close();
```

After *INSERT, UPDATE,* and *DELETE* commands, *$stmt->affected_rows* returns the number of changed records. *$mysqli->insert_id* (not *$stmt->insert_id!*) returns the last-generated *AUTO_INCREMENT* value.

Evaluating SELECT Results (Prepared Statements)

Unlike *$mysqli->query*, *$stmt->execute* does not return a *mysqli_result* object. Instead, the *mysqli_stmt* object offers a significantly more elegant way of evaluating *SELECT* results: After carrying out the query, use *$stmt->bind_result* to bind the columns of the result to PHP variables. Then *$stmt->fetch* moves the next data record into these variables. *fetch* returns the value *TRUE* or *FALSE*, depending on whether a record was found or all records have been processed.

By default, the *SELECT* results remain on the MySQL server and are transmitted to the client by *fetch* record by record. If you wish to have all the results transferred to the client at once, then execute *$stmt->store_result*. This is more efficient and relieves the server if you need to read all the records. In the additional code for reading the data, *store_result* changes nothing. That is, the method is optional.

```php
// example mysqli-prepared.php
// execute query
$stmt = $mysqli->prepare("SELECT titleID, title FROM titles");
$stmt->execute();
// transfer all results to the client (optional!)
$stmt->store_result();
// bind SELECT result to variables
$stmt->bind_result($titleID, $title);
// loop through all results
while($stmt->fetch())
  printf("<br />%d %s\n",
    htmlspecialchars($titleID), htmlspecialchars($title));
$stmt->close();
```

If you wish to know how many records the *SELECT* command has returned, you can retrieve that number with *$stmt->num_rows*. However, this property functions only if you first execute *$stmt->store_result*.

Of course, you can combine the method *bind_result* presented here with the method *bind_param* presented in the previous section, for example if you wish to execute a command of the form *SELECT ... FROM ... WHERE column = ?* several times. The following lines provide an example.

```php
// example mysqli-prepared.php
// preparation
$stmt = $mysqli->prepare(
  "SELECT titleID, title FROM titles WHERE title LIKE ?");
$stmt->bind_param('s', $pattern);
// first SELECT command
$pattern="%Linux%";
$stmt->execute();
$stmt->store_result();
$stmt->bind_result($titleID, $title);
echo "<p></p>\n";
while($stmt->fetch())
  printf("<br />%d %s\n", $titleID, htmlspecialchars($title));
// second SELECT command
$pattern="%MySQL%";
$stmt->execute();
$stmt->store_result();
$stmt->bind_result($titleID, $title);  // possibly unnecessary
echo "<p></p>\n";
while($stmt->fetch())
  printf("<br />%d %s\n", $titleID, htmlspecialchars($title));
// clean up
$stmt->close();
```

Unfortunately, it cannot be determined from the PHP documentation whether it is sufficient to execute *bind_result* after the first call of the *execute* method, or whether *bind_result* must be executed after every query. The above example worked in my tests even without the second *bind_result* call. It is unclear whether one can rely on such behavior. You will be safer (and not lose too much time) if you use *execute* and *bind_result* in pairs.

Transactions

The *mysqli* interface currently has no method corresponding to the SQL commands *BEGIN TRANSACTION* and *START TRANSACTION*. If you have to use transactions, then you must first deactivate auto commit mode with *$mysqli->autocommit(0)*. (There is also no method or property that gives information on the current commit mode. You must execute a query with *SELECT @@autocommit*. Note that at present, MySQL supports transactions only for InnoDB tables.)

Once autocommit has been deactivated, all the SQL commands form a transaction, which you can close with the *mysqli* method *commit* or abort with *rollback*. The next transaction begins along with *commit* or *rollback*. Caution: If you forget *commit* or if an error occurs or a break in the connection interrupts before *commit*, then all SQL commands in the current transaction are rolled back.

Instead of the methods *autocommit, commit,* and *rollback,* you could simply execute the corresponding SQL commands with *real_query*, for example *$mysqli ->real_query("START TRANSACTION")*.

Outsourcing Database Functions into a Class

Most PHP projects consist of a large number of PHP files, and in most of the files the same code fragments appear again and again: building a connection to the MySQL database, executing simple queries, etc. Such a way of doing things is impractical for a variety of reasons:

Redundancy: Redundant code is generally to be avoided. If you discover an error, you may have to correct it dozens of times. The same is true when access data change due to a change in provider, and you have to change user name and password in dozens of files.

Security: For reasons of security, the MySQL user name and password should never appear in plain text in a PHP file that is directly accessible over the web.

Error-handling: For convenience, and to achieve the most compact and readable code possible, one is tempted to minimize error handling routines or to avoid them altogether.

The solution to all three problems is to store all the MySQL access data as well as all functions that are used repeatedly in a separate PHP file. This file can then be included in every project file.

More Security with a Separate Password File

Theoretically, visitors to your website should never see any of your PHP source code. (The code is evaluated by the web server, but the user normally sees only the resulting HTML document.) But there are some possible errors that can allow visitors to read a PHP file in plain text:

- The web server (for example, during an update) is unconfigured or incorrectly configured, and it displays the PHP file without evaluating it.

- The PHP page is accessible via anonymous FTP. (That is a serious configuration error! If there is a directory for anonymous FTP, it must be kept separate from the directory with HTML and PHP files!)

- When a PHP page is changed, a backup copy is stored (for example, under the name name.php~ or name.php.bak). This file is not processed by the PHP interpreter due to its file identifier being different from *.php. An attacker can easily determine by poking around whether any such files exist.

To make it unlikely that strangers will obtain your MySQL password, you should store the MySQL login information in a separate file. This information might look like this:

```php
<?php
  // file password.php
  $mysqluser="user";          // user name for MySQL access
  $mysqlpasswd="xxx";         // password
  $mysqlhost="localhost";     // name of the computer on which MySQL is running
  $mysqldb="mylibrary";       // name of the database
?>
```

Where you should store this file to keep it secure depends on the configuration of the web server. On my website I have created a directory htdocs/_private/ and secured access to that directory with a .htaccess file. Therefore, you can access the address http://www.kofler.cc/_private/password.php only if you specify the HTTP user name given in .htaccess and the password stored in encrypted form in the associated authentication file. And even then, you will see in the web browser only an empty file.

■Tip Use the file identifier *.php (and not *.inc) for your password and other include files. This will ensure that the file is executed by the PHP interpreter in case of direct HTTP access.

Loading a Password File

The password file must be loaded into the PHP file in which the connection to MySQL is to be made using the *require_once* function. This function has the effect that the file is loaded only once, even if the *require_once* command appears in several PHP files that mutually call each other. If the password file is not found, then *require_once* leads to an error and the abortion of the script.

If you suppose, for example, that the files intro.php and password.php are located in the directories /www/user1234/htdocs/php-example/general/intro.php and /www/user1234/htdocs/_private/password.php, then the *require_once* instruction in intro.php must look like the following. In the path specification the two periods .. mean that a subdirectory should be used. Depending on how the directories with the PHP scripts and the include file are placed relative to one another, you will of course have to change the path specification with *require_once*. (The example in the files for this book always read the password file from the local directory. This simplifies the installation of the example files, but is of course less secure.)

```php
// file intro.php
require_once("../../_private/password.php");
$mysqli = new mysqli($mysqlhost, $mysqluser, $mysqlpasswd, $mysqldb);
...
```

Security and Convenience with the MyDb Class

After the storage of the MySQL access data, one can certainly go a step further and store all the code necessary for database access in a separate PHP file. This file thus encapsulates all MySQL functions that you frequently need in your project. In the process, you can use the new possibilities for object-oriented programming offered by PHP 5 and formulate the code in its own class.

The following lines give an example of how such a class might look. The example uses the *mysqli* interface; the code can also be realized analogously with the *mysql* interface.

```php
// example file mydb.php
class MyDb {
  protected $mysqli;
  // constructor (create an object of this class)
  function __construct() {
    require_once('password.php');
    $this->mysqli = @new mysqli($mysqlhost, $mysqluser,
      $mysqlpasswd, $mysqldb);
    // test whether connection OK
    if(mysqli_connect_errno()) {
      printf("<p>Sorry, no connection! %s\n</p>",
        mysqli_connect_error());
      // add any needed HTML code to conclude the code
      // (</body></html> etc.)
      $this->mysqli = FALSE;
      exit();
    }
  }
  // destructor (delete object)
  function __destruct() {
    $this->close();
  }
  // explicitly terminate object/connection
  function close() {
    if($this->mysqli)
      $this->mysqli->close();
    $this->mysqli = FALSE;
  }
  // execute SELECT return object field
  function queryObjectArray($sql) {
    if($result = $this->mysqli->query($sql)) {
      if($result->num_rows) {
        while($row = $result->fetch_object())
          $result_array[] = $row;
        return $result_array; }
      else
        return FALSE;
    } else {
      printf("<p>Error: %s</p>\n", $this->mysqli->error);
      return FALSE;
    }
  }
  // execute SELECT return individual value
  // Note: return value for error is -1 (not 0)!
  function querySingleItem($sql) {
    if ($result = $this->mysqli->query($sql)) {
      if ($row=$result->fetch_array()) {
        $result->close();
        return $row[0];
      } else {
        return -1;
      }
```

```
  } else {
    printf("<p>Error: %s</p>\n", $this->mysqli->error);
    return -1;
  }
}
// execute SQL command without result (INSERT, DELETE, etc.)
function execute($sql) {
  if ($this->mysqli->real_query($sql)) {
    return TRUE;
  } else {
    print $this->mysqli->error;
    return FALSE;
  }
}
// return insert_id
function insertId() {
  return $this->mysqli->insert_id;
}
}
```

Debugging and Error Search with MyDb

Variables are a very practical extension to this class. They govern whether all executed SQL commands and all error messages are to be output to the HTML document. To do so is practical during code development and simplifies the identification of errors (see Figure 15-4). The following code segment shows the required changed to the function *execute*.

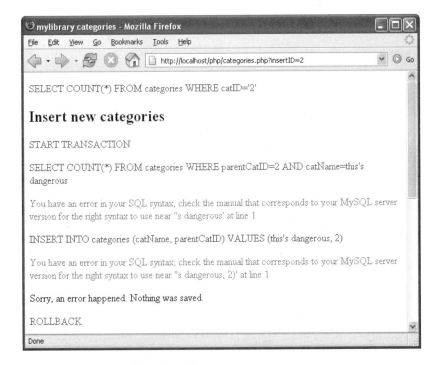

Figure 15-4. *Error search made easy!*

```
class MyDb {
  protected $mysqli;
  protected $showerror = TRUE;    // display error message
  protected $showsql   = FALSE;   // display SQL code
  function execute($sql) {
    $this->printsql($sql);
    if($this->mysqli->real_query($sql))
      return TRUE;
    else {
      $this->printerror($this->mysqli->error);
      return FALSE;
    }
  }
  ...
  private function printsql($sql) {
    if($this->showsql)
      printf("<p><font color=\"#0000ff\">%s</font></p>\n",
        htmlspecialchars($sql)); }
  private function printerror($txt) {
    if($this->showerror)
      printf("<p><font color=\"#ff0000\">%s</font></p>\n",
        htmlspecialchars($txt));     }
}
```

■**Tip** Later in this chapter I will describe some extensions to the MyDb class that help in optimizing PHP pages for efficiency. The method *showStatistics* displays how many SQL commands have been executed thus far, how many records have been returned, how much time has elapsed, etc.

Application of the MyDb Class

PHP code based on a *MyDb* object is normally very compact, as the following lines show:

```
// example file test-mydb.php
require_once("mydb.php");
$db = new MyDb();
// query for single value
if(($n = $db->querySingleItem("SELECT COUNT(*) FROM titles"))!=-1)
  printf("<p>number per title: %d</p>\n", $n);
// SELECT
if($result = $db->queryObjectArray("SELECT * FROM titles")) {
  foreach($result as $row)
    printf("<br />TitleID=%d Title=%s Subtitle=%s\n",
      $row->titleID, $row->title, $row->subtitle);
}
```

Numerous examples in the following sections of this chapter use the *MyDb* class.

Displaying a SELECT Result As a Table

The following example shows how the result of a simple query (*SELECT * FROM titles*) can be displayed in an HTML table (see Figure 15-5). The code for table output is contained in the function *show_table*. All character strings are translated correctly into HTML code with the PHP function *htmlspecialchars*. This function ensures that even strings with HTML special characters, such as

< and >, are correctly represented. The structure of the table is limited to a minimum. With little effort, you can customize the layout of the table with the CSS file `table.css` to your own specifications.

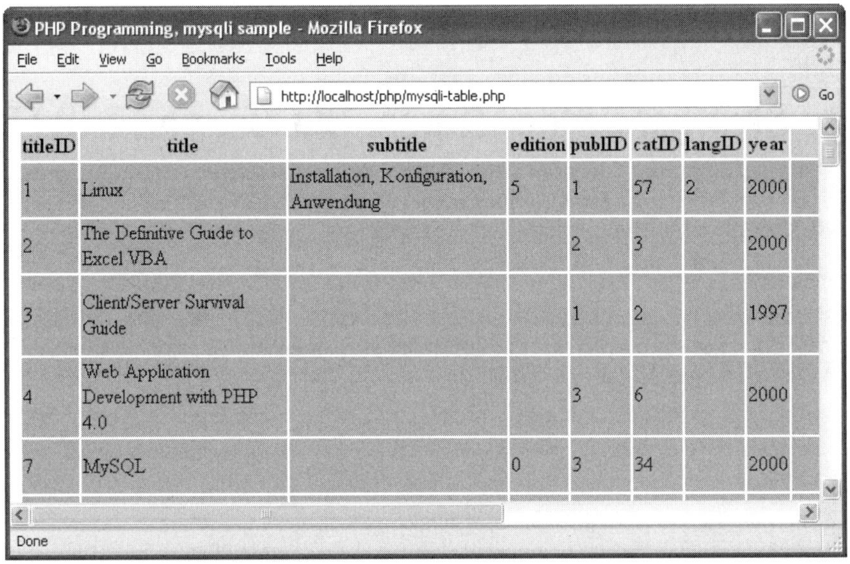

titleID	title	subtitle	edition	publID	catID	langID	year
1	Linux	Installation, Konfiguration, Anwendung	5	1	57	2	2000
2	The Definitive Guide to Excel VBA			2	3		2000
3	Client/Server Survival Guide			1	2		1997
4	Web Application Development with PHP 4.0			3	6		2000
7	MySQL		0	3	34		2000

Figure 15-5. *Displaying a simple query as a table*

```
// example file mysqli-table.php
// displays the result of a query as an HTML table
function show_table($result) {
  if(!$result) {
    echo "<p>No valid query result.</p>\n";
    return;
  }
  if($result->num_rows>0 && $result->field_count>0) {
    echo "<table>";
    // column labels
    echo "<tr>";
    foreach($result->fetch_fields() as $meta)
      printf("<th>%s</th>", htmlspecialchars($meta->name));
    echo "</tr>\n";
    // table content
    while($row = $result->fetch_row()) {
      echo "<tr>";
      foreach($row as $col)
        printf("<td>%s</td>", htmlspecialchars($col));
      echo "</tr>\n";
    }
    echo "</table>\n";
  }
}
```

The application of this function looks like this:

```
if($result = $mysqli->query("SELECT * FROM titles")) {
  show_table($result);
  $result->close();
}
```

Character Strings, Dates, Times, BLOBs, and NULL

When you are reading and outputting data from a MySQL table, you must adhere to the HTML syntax rules. Likewise, you must adhere to the MySQL syntax when you are assembling *INSERT* and *UPDATE* commands. This section offers some tips on handling such situations.

Tip If you are using the *mysqli* interface, you can use prepared statements with bound parameters and bound result variables (see the discussion earlier in the chapter). This has the advantage that PHP then takes care that character strings, BLOBs, and dates are correctly formatted.

Storing Data

To change records in the database, you must pass the necessary SQL commands as a character string to *mysql_query* or *$mysqli->query*. The following lines show how an *INSERT* command can be formulated:

```
$sql = "INSERT INTO tablename (column, column2, ...) "
    . "VALUES($data1, $data2, ...);
```

Reading Data

To read data, execute a query with *mysql_query* or *$mysqli->query* and then evaluate the result *$result* with *mysql_fetch_xxx* or *$resul ->fetch_xxx*.

```
$result = mysql_query("SELECT ...");
$row = mysql_fetch_row($result);
$data = $row[0];
```

Character Strings and BLOBs

Storing Character Strings in MySQL

In SQL commands, a character string must be placed within quotation marks, where there is a choice between double "and single 'quotes. Problems arise when the string itself contains quotation marks or other characters (\) impermissible in SQL. This can easily lead to syntax errors:

```
$data = "O'Reilly";
$sql  = "INSERT INTO publishers (publName) VALUES('$data')";
```

The resulting (invalid) SQL command looks like this:

```
INSERT INTO publishers (publName) VALUES('O'Reilly')
```

Help is provided by the function *mysql_real_escape_string* and the method *$mysqli ->escape_string*. This replaces ', ", \, and 0 bytes with \', \", \\, and \0. (This process is often called quoting.)

```
$sql  = "INSERT INTO publishers (publName) VALUES('"
      . $mysqli->escape_string($data) . "')";
```

Now the SQL command is correct:

```
INSERT INTO publishers (publName) VALUES('O\'Reilly')
```

■**Note** If the data to be stored come from an HTML form and the PHP configuration variable *magic_quotes_gpc* is set to *On*, then the data are already quoted. In this case of course, no additional quoting should be done. Further information on *Magic Quotes* appears in Chapter 5.

Outputting Character Strings

In outputting character strings to an HTML document you should generally use the function *htmlspecialchars* or *htmlentities*. *htmlspecialchars* replaces the characters <, >, ", and & with *<*, */>*, */"*, and */&*. Additionally, *htmlentities* replaces a large number of special characters with HTML code, for example, *ä* with *ä*. This is necessary in particular when the character set of the HTML document does not provide for the direct representation of the special characters.

Two optional parameters can be passed to *htmlspecialchars* and *htmlentities*. The first parameter determines whether the characters 'and "should be replaced. Possible settings are *ENT_QUOTES* ('and "are replaced), *ENT_NOQUOTES* ('and "remain unchanged), and *ENT_COMPAT* ("is replaced, 'is unchanged). By default, *ENT_COMPAT* holds.

The second parameter determines the character set of the output string. By default, both functions assume that the output string is in the *Latin1* character set (ISO-8859-1). Alternative settings include *iso-8859-15*, *utf-8*, and *cp1252*.

For example, if Unicode strings are stored in your database, the correct call to *htmlentitites* looks like this:

```
printf("<p>%s</p>\n",
       htmlentities($data, ENT_COMPAT, "UTF-8"));
```

Further tips on dealing with Unicode character strings appear later in this chapter.

BLOBs

Binary data (BLOBs) are treated exactly like character strings. PHP, in contrast to C, has no problem with zero bytes/0 codes.

Dates and Times

Storing Dates and Times in MySQL

To format a date or time according to MySQL rules, you can use PHP functions such as *date* and *strftime*. If the data come from user input, you must, of course, carry out the usual validation tests. (MySQL does only a cursory validation check and stores many dates that could not possibly exist.)

On the other hand, if you wish to store a PHP timestamp in a *MySQL TIMESTAMP* column, you should use the MySQL function *FROM_UNIXTIME* in an *INSERT* or *UPDATE* command.

```
$data = time();  // data contains the current time as a Unix timestamp
$sql = "INSERT INTO table (column) VALUES (FROM_UNIXTIME($data))";
```

Reading Dates and Times from MySQL

When you read dates and times from a *DATETIME* column, you receive a character string of the form *2005-12-31 23:59:59*. With *DATE* columns, the time is of course not included. In many cases it is most practical for the further processing of dates in PHP to use the MySQL function *UNIX_TIMESTAMP*. You thereby obtain a 32-bit integer that gives the number of seconds elapsed since 1.1.1970.

```
$sql = "SELECT UNIX_TIMESTAMP(column) FROM table WHERE ...";
$result = $mysqli->query($sql);
$row = $result->fetch_row();
$ts = $row[0];
```

You can obtain a desired format using the MySQL function *DATE_FORMAT*. The following SQL command returns a string of the form *December 31 2005*.

```
SELECT DATE_FORMAT(column, '%M %d %Y') FROM table
```

With a *TIME* column you obtain a string of the form *23:59:59*. If you do not wish to extract hours, minutes, and seconds from this string, the MySQL function *TIME_TO_SEC* provides the number of seconds since 00:00:00. In addition, there are many MySQL functions for processing times. Warning: *UNIX_TIMESTAMP* does not work with *TIME* columns!

With *TIMESTAMP* columns, MySQL returns a string of the form y*yyy-dd-mm hh:mm:ss*. If instead you desire a PHP-compatible timestamp value, then use the MySQL function *UNIX_TIMESTAMP* in your SQL query.

```
SELECT UNIX_TIMESTAMP(column) FROM table
```

NULL

Storing NULL

To store *NULL* in a column, simply pass the string *NULL* to the SQL command without quotation marks:

```
INSERT INTO table (column) VALUES (NULL)
```

If you wish to store *NULL* in place of empty character strings, the following is recommended:

```
$sql = "INSERT INTO table (column) VALUES (";
if(isset($data)
  $sql .= "'" . $mysqli->escape_string($data) . "')";
else
  $sql .= "NULL)"
NULL-Test
```

When you are reading data from a MySQL column that allows the value *NULL*, you must query this value before further processing of the data. If you are using the *mysql* interface, execute *isset($data)* for this purpose. The function returns *FALSE* if the underlying data had the value *NULL*. Similar tests for data type can be made with *is_numeric*, *is_string*, etc. Note, however, that tests with the function *empty* lead to incorrect results when applied to character strings: *empty* returns the result *TRUE* for *NULL* and the empty string *""*.

The *mysqli* interface offers much greater convenience for the programmer: the *fetch_xxx* methods automatically convert MySQL *NULL* values to the PHP value *NULL*. You can also simply execute a query of the form *if($data == NULL)*.

Inserting Linked Data Records

To insert a record into a table, simply execute an *INSERT* command. Things become more difficult when several tables are linked. Then you must worry about the correct key when executing the *INSERT* command.

As a rule, an *AUTO_INCREMENT* column is responsible for the link between two tables. With *$mysqli->insert_id* (*mysqli*) or *mysql_insert_id* (*mysql*) you can determine the ID value of the most recently stored record.

The following lines show how a new book title, including two authors, is stored in the *mylibrary* database. Note that three ID values must be stored during the process in order to insert the record in the *rel_title_author* table. It is assumed that the publisher (here Addison-Wesley) has already been stored as *publID=1* in the database.

```
$mysqli->query("INSERT INTO titles (title, publID, year)
                VALUES ('A Guide to the SQL Standard', 1, 1997)");
$titleID = $mysqli->insert_id;
$mysqli->query("INSERT INTO authors (authName)
                VALUES ('Date Chris')");
$author1ID = $mysqli->insert_id;
$mysqli->query("INSERT INTO authors (authName)
                VALUES ('Darween Hugh')");
$author2ID = $mysqli->insert_id;
$mysqli->query("INSERT INTO rel_title_author (titleID, authID)
                VALUES ($titleID, $author1ID),
                       ($titleID, $author2ID)");
```

In practice, that is, when data are given interactively, the storage of new entries becomes more complicated. For example, you have to check whether an author already exists in the database. If so, its ID must be stored in *rel_title_author*, and otherwise, a new author must be registered. (Or was there a typo? To minimize such an eventuality, some similar-sounding or -looking names could be displayed and offered as alternatives.)

Processing Input from Forms

The following example describes the code for managing a form for input or for changing data in the *mylibrary* database (see Figure 15-6). The resulting code is relatively extensive. Some intensive involvement with this example is worth the effort due to its general nature: In almost every database application you have to evaluate, validate, and store form input or transfer existing data into a form in order to alter or delete it. This example has the added feature that the form data are not associated with a single table but are distributed over several linked tables.

Not much need be said about using the form. Most of the input fields are optional, with only title and author being mandatory. If there are several authors of a book, their names can be separated with semicolons. With the input fields *publisher* and *language* you can either select an existing entry or input a new publisher or language. The button Delete title is visible only if the form is used to change an existing title.

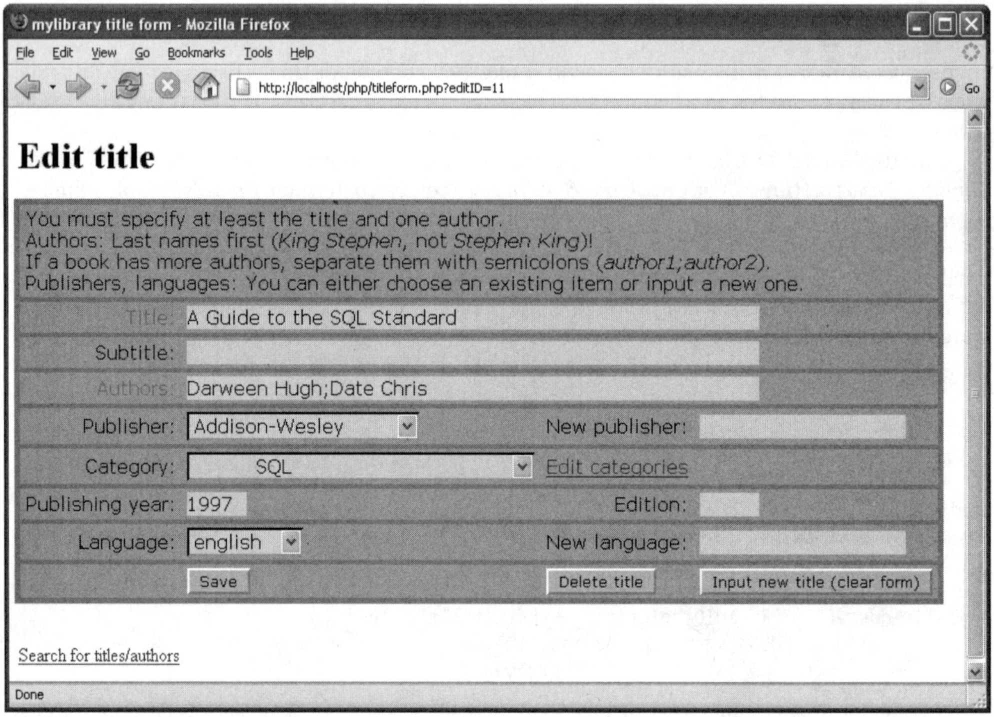

Figure 15-6. *Title input form for mylibrary*

Code Structure

The code is divided among the following files:

formtitle.php	Main code
mydb.php	Class *MyDb* with database methods
mylibraryfunctions.php	Auxiliary functions
formfunctions.php	Functions for output of a form
form.css	CSS file for formatting the form

Two mechanisms are used for data transfer when a page is changed:

POST	Form data in the form of a field (*form["title"), form["authors"]*, etc.)
REQUEST	URL parameter (*editID* gives the ID number of the title to be changed)

■Note formtitle.php is related to the two pages find.php and categories.php, which are described in the following sections. These three pages, together with formtitle.php, form a complete example: title input, title search, and category management. All three pages access the classes and functions of mydb.php, mylibraryfunctions.php, and formfunctions.php.

The additional file deletegarbage.php is contained in the source code for ths book. It deletes authors without titles, titles without authors, publishers without books, etc., from *mylibrary*. This page is also useful for deleting incomplete or invalid data, perhaps resulting from testing, from *mylibrary*.

Of central importance in the evaluation of these data is the tiny yet indispensable function *array_item*, which is defined in the file mylibraryfunctions.php. *array_item($x, "abc")* returns *$x["abc"]* if such an element exists, and otherwise *FALSE*. Since it is not always clear in advance what elements a field contains, *array_item* spares you burdensome warnings such as that an element doesn't exist or error messages that such a field doesn't exist.

```
function array_item($ar, $key) {
  if(is_array($ar) && array_key_exists($key, $ar))
    return $ar[$key];
  else
    return FALSE; }
```

Code Management

The central management of titleform.php is effected with relatively few lines of code, which are reproduced in the following. All the remaining code is to be found in functions and in the *MyDb* class. Depending on what data are passed to the page, there are two basic cases:

An existing title is to be processed (editID=...): In this case, the *titleID* number is to be passed to the function *read_title_data*. This retrieves all the data (title, subtitle, authors, publisher, etc.) and returns them as a field. This field has the same structure as that of the form data.

Form data are to be processed: Depending on the button with which the form was terminated, a title is to be stored or deleted, or else the form is simply to be emptied (in order to input a new title). The form data are located in the field *formdata*, from whose elements any existing *Magic Quotes* are removed.

The title is stored only if validation with *validate_data* is successful. Then *formdata* is deleted and an empty form for the input of the next title is displayed. If *validate_data* discovers an error, then first error messages are displayed and then the form with the old data is displayed again.

The title is deleted after a query. The query form is output with the function *build_delete_form*. Its DELETE button has the name *btnReallyDelete*.

The storage and deletion functions are executed in memory within a transaction. Only if the function is executed without error is the transaction confirmed with *COMMIT*.

Finally, the form is refreshed and displayed, either with existing data for correction or else empty for input of a new title. The form is not displayed if *$showform==FALSE* is in effect. (That is the case only if the delete query is displayed.)

█Note This is not a book on PHP, but it won't hurt to include here a bit of background information on *Magic Quotes*. With *Magic Quotes* the developers of PHP hoped to make the programmer's job easier. Special characters in strings coming from external sources (a form sent with *GET* or *POST* or from a cookie) are automatically provided with back-slashes. This avoids problems with such characters, such as in compound SQL commands. In principle, then, *Magic Quotes* should be of great use. Unfortunately, that is not always the case.

The problem is that *Magic Quotes* are turned on and off in the PHP configuration file php.ini (variable *magic_quotes_gpc*). If your PHP scripts are running on an ISP, you generally have no control over the PHP configuration. This means that every time form data are processed, you must first test whether *Magic Quotes* are active. In the examples of this chapter, any existing quoting will be deleted (see the following code listing).

```php
$db = new MyDb();    // establish connection to MySQL
$showform=TRUE;      // should the form be displayed at the end?

if(($editID = array_item($_REQUEST, 'editID'))
  && is_numeric($editID))
  // case 1: process existing title
  $formdata = read_title_data($editID);

else {
  // case 2: process form data
  $formdata = array_item($_POST, "form");
  if(is_array($formdata)) {
    if(get_magic_quotes_gpc())  // eliminate Magic Quotes
      while($i = each($formdata))
        $formdata[$i[0]] = stripslashes($i[1]);

    // respond depending on button
    if(array_item($formdata, "btnClear"))
      // clear form
      $formdata = FALSE;

    elseif(array_item($formdata, "btnDelete")) {
      // query whether title really should be deleted
      if(build_delete_form($formdata))
        $showform = FALSE; }

    elseif(array_item($formdata, "btnReallyDelete")) {
      // delete title
      $db->execute("START TRANSACTION");
      if(delete_title($formdata))
        $db->execute("COMMIT");
      else
        $db->execute("ROLLBACK");
      $formdata = FALSE; }

    elseif(validate_data($formdata)) {
      // check data and store if ok
      $db->execute("START TRANSACTION");
      if(save_data($formdata))
        $db->execute("COMMIT");
      else
        $db->execute("ROLLBACK");
      $formdata = FALSE; }
  }
}
```

```
if($showform) {
  // alter data or input new?
  if(array_item($formdata, "titleID"))
    echo "<h1>Edit title</h1>";
  else
    echo "<h1>Input new title</h1>";

  // display form
  build_form($formdata);
}
```

Creating the Form

You will have a better grasp of the processing of the form if you understand its internal structure. Therefore, the following lines show some of the HTML code of the form. Important for the evaluation are the element names *form[title]*, *form[publisher]*, etc. (in boldface). A table with four columns is used to format the form.

```
<table class="myformtable">
<form method="post" action="titleform.php">
<tr><td class="myformtd" colspan="4" >explanation ...</td></tr>
<tr><td align="right" class="myformtd">
     <span class="red">Title:</span></td>
     <td class="myformtd" colspan="3" >
     <input class="mycontrol" name="form[title]" size="60"
      maxlength="100" value="Client/Server Survival Guide"/></td>
</tr>
...
<tr><td align="right" class="myformtd">Publisher:</td>
    <td class="myformtd">
    <select class="mycontrol" name="form[publisher]" >
      <option value="none">(choose)</option>
      <option value="1" selected="selected" >Addison-Wesley</option>
      ...
    </select></td>
    <td align="right" class="myformtd">New publisher:</td>
    <td class="myformtd">
      <input class="mycontrol" name="form[newpubl]"
       size="20" maxlength="40" /></td>
</tr>
...
<tr><td align="right" class="myformtd"></td>
    <td class="myformtd">
      <input class="mybutton" type="submit" value="Save"
      name="form[btnSave]" /></td>
    <td class="myformtd">
      <input class="mybutton" type="submit" value="Delete title"
      name="form[btnDelete]" /></td>
    <input type="hidden" name="form[titleID]" value="3" />
    <td class="myformtd">
      <input class="mybutton" type="submit"
      value="Input new title (clear form)"
      name="form[btnClear]"  /></td>
</tr>
</form></table>
```

The layout of the table, its cells and controls, is determined by several CSS definitions in
form.css:

```
/* example file form.css */
.myformtable {
  font-family: Verdana, Arial, Helvetica, sans-serif;
  border: 5px solid #9090e0;
  border-spacing: 0px;
  border-collapse: collapse; }
.myformtd {
  background-color: #b0b0ff;
  border-width: 4px 0px;
  border-style: solid;
  border-color: #9090e0;
  padding: 3px 5px; }
.mycontrol {... }
.mybutton { ... }
.red { color: red; }
```

Display the Input Form

A field with any existing form data is passed to the function *build_form* (if data are to be corrected
or changed). These data are inserted into the corresponding form elements (*value="..."*).

The creation of HTML forms with PHP code is a task that comes up often and is liable to error.
In this and some additional examples in this book this task is therefore relegated to auxiliary functions, which appear in formfunctions.php (see the following topic).

```
// example file titleform.php
function build_form($formdata) {
  global $db;   // database access
  form_start("titleform.php");
  // input field for book title
  form_new_line();
  form_label("Title:", TRUE);
  form_text("title", array_item($formdata, "title"), 60, 100, 3);
  form_end_line();
  // input field for subtitle and author names
  ... and so on
```

From the database point of view, things become interesting when a selection list for the publishers
is to be displayed. The list is created with an SQL query and passed in the form of a two-dimensional
field to *form_list*. The third parameter of this function specifies the list element that is selected.

```
// selection list for publisher
form_new_line();
form_label("Publisher:");
$sql = "SELECT publName, publID FROM publishers ORDER BY publName";
form_list("publisher", $db->queryArray($sql),
  array_item($formdata, "publisher"));
form_label("New publisher:");
form_text("newpubl", array_item($formdata, "newpubl"), 20, 40);
form_end_line();
```

Things get more complicated with the list for categories. Here we are dealing with a hierarchical
structure whose list elements must be appropriately indented. Such a field is created in the function
build_category_array (file mylibraryfunctions.php). Details on this recursive function appear later in
this chapter, whose general theme is dealing with hierarchical data.

```
// selection list for category
form_new_line();
form_label("Category:");
// determine all categories
$sql = "SELECT catName, catID, parentCatID FROM categories " .
       "ORDER BY catName";
$rows = $db->queryObjectArray($sql);
// form two associative fields
//    subcats[catID]  contains a field with sub-catIDs
//    catNames[catID] contains the name
foreach($rows as $row) {
  $subcats[$row->parentCatID][] = $row->catID;
  $catNames[$row->catID] = $row->catName; }
// form hierarchical category list
$rows = build_category_array($subcats[NULL], $subcats, $catNames);
form_list("category", $rows , array_item($formdata, "category"));
form_url("categories.php", "Edit categories", 2);
form_end_line();
```

After some further text input and labeling fields we finally come to the buttons. The *Delete* button is displayed only if an existing title is displayed in the form. In this case the *titleID* number is passed in an invisible element, so that this number is in any case contained in the form data.

```
// buttons
form_new_line();
form_label("");
form_button("btnSave", "Save");
// delete button for existing title
if(array_item($formdata, "titleID")) {
  form_button("btnDelete", "Delete title");
  form_hidden("titleID", $formdata["titleID"]); }
else
  form_empty_cell(1);
form_button("btnClear", "Input new title (clear form)");
form_end_line();
// end of the form
form_end();
}
```

Auxiliary Functions for Form Creation

The auxiliary functions used in *build_form* are located in formfunctions.php. In the following, some functions are presented as examples. These functions are used as well in numerous examples in this book.

```
// example file formfunctions.php
// start and end form
function form_start($action) {
  echo '<table class="myformtable">', "\n";
  echo '<form method="post" ',
    html_attribute("action", $action), ">\n"; }
function form_end() {
  echo "</form></table>\n\n"; }
// start and end one line of the form
function form_new_line() {   echo "<tr>"; }
function form_end_line() {   echo "</tr>\n\n"; }
// auxiliary function, returns $name="value"
function html_attribute($name, $value) {
  return $name . '="' . htmlspecialchars($value) . '" '; }
```

A table is used for formatting the form. The number of columns in this table is not specified. You must simply take care to use the same number of columns in each line. Most of the functions use a cell (thus *<td>* through *</td>*) for their output. With some of the functions, the output can extend over several columns using an optional parameter (attribute *colspan*).

The function *form_label* writes text right justified in a cell. Thus the function is well suited for labeling the subsequent input and control elements. The optional parameter *emphasize* tells whether the label should be colored.

```php
// label cell
function form_label($caption, $emphasize =FALSE) {
  echo '<td align="right" class="myformtd">';
  if($emphasize )
    echo '<span class="red">', htmlspecialchars($caption), '</span>';
  else
    echo htmlspecialchars($caption);
  echo '</td>', "\n";   }
```

The function *form_text* creates a text input field, while *name* determines the name of the element (the result is then *form["name"]*), *value* the default value, *size* and *maxlength* the desired size.

```php
// create a one-cell text input field
function form_text($name, $value,
                   $size=40, $maxlength=40, $colspan=1) {
  if($colspan>1)
    echo '<td class="myformtd" ',
      html_attribute("colspan", $colspan), '>';
  else
    echo '<td class="myformtd"> ';
  echo '<input class="mycontrol" ',
    html_attribute("name", "form[$name]"),
    html_attribute("size", $size),
    html_attribute("maxlength", $maxlength);
  if($value)
    echo html_attribute("value", $value);
  echo ' /></td>', "\n";
}
```

The function *form_list* creates a selection list, and *name* determines the name of the control element; *rows* contains a two-dimensional list, where *row[n][0]* must contain the list entry and *row[n][1]* the associated value. The function *selected* can contain the value of the selected list element.

```php
// create selection list (<option>-Tag)
function form_list($name, $rows, $selected=-1) {
  echo '<td class="myformtd">';
  echo '<select class="mycontrol" ',
    html_attribute("name", "form[$name]"), '>', "\n";
  echo '<option value="none">(choose)</option>';
  foreach($rows as $row) {
    echo '<option ', html_attribute("value", $row[1]);
    if($selected==$row[1])
      echo 'selected="selected" ';
    $listentry = str_replace(" ", " ", htmlspecialchars($row[0]));
    echo ">$listentry</option>\n";
  }
  echo '</select></td>', "\n";
}
```

Validation of Form Data

When the form data are passed to `titleform.php`, *validate_data* checks whether the data contained in the field (*array*) are correct. Depending on the result, the function returns *TRUE* or *FALSE*. Then depending on this result, the data are either stored or displayed again in the form to be corrected.

Error messages are passed to *show_error_msg*. This function is located in `formfunctions.php` and returns the text as a paragraph colored red.

```
// example file titleform.php
function validate_data($formdata) {
  $result = TRUE;
  if(trim($formdata["title"])=="") {
    show_error_msg("You must specify a title!");
    $result = FALSE; }
  if(trim($formdata["authors"])=="") {
    show_error_msg("You must specify at least one title!");
    $result = FALSE; }
  $year = $formdata["publyear"];
  if(!empty($year) && ((!is_numeric($year)) || $year<1000
      || $year>2100)) {
    show_error_msg("Publishing year must be a four-digit number " .
      "(or empty).");
    $result = FALSE; }
  if(!empty($edition) && ((!is_numeric($edition)) || $edition<1
      || $edition>100)) {
    show_error_msg("Edition must be a number <= 100 (or empty).");
    $result = FALSE; }
  return $result;
}
```

Storing the Form Data

The most interesting function in this example from the database point of view is *save_data*. It stores the data passed to the field *formdata* in various tables of the *mylibrary* database. Depending on whether new data were entered or existing data altered, the title must be stored with *INSERT* or *UPDATE*. (Which in this case is recognized by *save_data* based on the existence of *$formdata[titleID]*.)

In addition, various special cases must be taken into consideration, such as the search for existing authors and storing new authors, publishers, and languages. Furthermore, the link between title and author must be created or corrected in the table *rel_title_author*.

If no error occurs during storage, the function returns the result *TRUE*. The return value is used to confirm or abort the transaction started before the function call.

```
// example file titleform.php
function save_data($formdata) {
  global $db;

  // search for and store authors
  $authors = explode(";", $formdata["authors"]);
  foreach($authors as $author) {
    $author = trim($author);
    $sql = "SELECT authID FROM authors WHERE authName = " .
      $db->sql_string($author);
    $rows = $db->queryObjectArray($sql);
    if($rows)
```

```
      // note IDs of existing authors
      $authIDs[] = $rows[0]->authID;
    else {
      // also note new author and ID
      $sql = "INSERT INTO authors (authName) " .
        "VALUES (" . $db->sql_string($author) . ")";
      if(!$db->execute($sql))
        return FALSE;
      $authIDs[] = $db->insertId();
    }
  }

  // store new publisher or note ID of selected publisher
  if($formdata["newpubl"]) {
    $sql = "SELECT publID FROM publishers WHERE publName = " .
      $db->sql_string($formdata["newpubl"]);
    $rows = $db->queryObjectArray($sql);
    if($rows)
      // publisher already exists
      $publID = $rows[0]->publID;
    else {
      // store new publisher
      $sql = "INSERT INTO publishers (publName) " .
        "VALUES (" . $db->sql_string($formdata["newpubl"]) . ")";
      if(!$db->execute($sql))
        return FALSE;
      $publID = $db->insertId();
    }
  }
  else
    // read publID from selection list
    $publID = $formdata["publisher"];

  // analogous procedure for languages (language) --> $langID
  ...

  // update existing title (UPDATE)
  if(array_item($formdata, "titleID")) {
    $titleID = array_item($formdata, "titleID");
    $sql = "UPDATE titles SET " .
      "title="    . $db->sql_string($formdata["title"]) . ", " .
      "subtitle=" . $db->sql_string($formdata["subtitle"]) . ", " .
      "langID="   . ID_or_NULL($langID) . "," .
      "publID="   . ID_or_NULL($publID) . "," .
      "catID="    . ID_or_NULL($formdata["category"]) . "," .
      "year="     . num_or_NULL($formdata["publyear"]) . ", " .
      "edition="  . num_or_NULL($formdata["edition"]) . " " .
      "WHERE titleID=$titleID";
    if(!$db->execute($sql))
      return FALSE;
    // delete exising rel_title_author entry
    $sql = "DELETE FROM rel_title_author WHERE titleID=$titleID";
    if(!$db->execute($sql))
      return FALSE;
  }
```

```
else {
  // store new title (INSERT)
  $sql = "INSERT INTO titles (title, subtitle, " .
    "langID, publID, catID, year, edition) VALUES (" .
    $db->sql_string($formdata["title"]) . ", " .
    $db->sql_string($formdata["subtitle"]) . ", " .
    ID_or_NULL($langID) . "," .
    ID_or_NULL($publID) . "," .
    ID_or_NULL($formdata["category"]) . "," .
    num_or_NULL($formdata["publyear"]). "," .
    num_or_NULL($formdata["edition"]) . ") ";
  if(!$db->execute($sql))
    return FALSE;
  $titleID = $db->insertId();
}

// create link between title and authors
foreach($authIDs as $authID) {
  $sql = "INSERT INTO rel_title_author (titleID, authID) " .
    "VALUES ($titleID, $authID)";
  if(!$db->execute($sql))
    return FALSE;
}

// output confirmation of success as link
echo "<p>Title ",
  build_href("titleform.php", "editID=$titleID",
    $formdata['title']),
  " has been saved.</p>\n";
return TRUE;
}
```

The confirmation of success for the storage process is output as a link (*titleform.php?editID=nnn*). With a simple click, the user can see the title again and make corrections as necessary.

Auxiliary Functions

In creating the SQL commands, the auxiliary functions *ID_or_NULL* and *num_or_NULL* as well as the method *sql_string* are used:

```
// example file titleform.php
function num_or_NULL($n) {
  if(is_numeric($n))  return $n;
  else                return 'NULL'; }
function ID_or_NULL($id) {
  if($id=="none")
    return 'NULL';
  else
    return $id; }
// example file mydb.php
function escape($txt) {
  return trim($this->mysqli->escape_string($txt)); }
function sql_string($txt) {
  if(!$txt || trim($txt)=="")
    return 'NULL';
  else
    return "'" . $this->escape(trim($txt)) . "'";
}
```

In creating the link, we use the function *build_href*.

```
// example file mylibraryfunctions.php
function s($url, $query, $txt) {
  if($query)
    return "<a href=\"$url?" . $query . "\">" .
           htmlspecialchars($txt) . "</a>";
  else
    return "<a href=\"$url\">" . htmlspecialchars($txt) . "</a>"; }
```

Deleting a Title

Before an existing title can be deleted, a query must be answered (see Figure 15-7). This form is output with the function *build_delete_form*.

Figure 15-7. *Query before a title is deleted*

The function *delete_title* is responsible for the file deletion. It deletes not only the title, but also the entries that are no longer needed in the table *rel_title_author*.

```
// example file titleform.php
function delete_title($formdata) {
  global $db;
  if((!$titleID = array_item($formdata, "titleID"))
     || !is_numeric($titleID))
    return FALSE;
  $sql = "DELETE FROM rel_title_author WHERE titleID=$titleID";
  if(!$db->execute($sql))
    return FALSE;
  $sql = "DELETE FROM titles WHERE titleID=$titleID LIMIT 1";
  if(!$db->execute($sql))
    return FALSE;
  echo "<p>One title has been deleted.</p>\n";
  return TRUE;
}
```

Room for Improvement

If you are motivated to work on this example, here are some suggestions for improving it:

Titles: In storing new titles, there is no check as to whether the title already exists. To institute such a control is complicated by the fact that a simple comparison of titles does not suffice, since there can easily be two books with the same title, such as *Linux*. The ISBN could be used as a unique identifier, but its presence in the form is not required. However, a simple query whether a book with the same title and author already exists should catch most errors.

Authors: Author names in the *authors* table always begin with the family name, since that is the only sorting criterion that makes sense. In addition, titleform.php expects input in this form (thus *Kofler Michael* and not *Michael Kofler*). Problems occur when the user does not adhere to this rule.

One possible improvement would be to provide separate fields for given name and family name. That would make the input of multiple authors more complicated.

One could also consider a test in storing new names whether the name in the reverse order already appears in the *authors* table. That would help prevent duplicates.

Categories: There is no way in the form to define a new category. Rather, the category must be summoned from the page categories.php. Then the title input must be redone, since the category list cannot be updated.

It would be more convenient if as with publishers and languages, a new category could be placed directly in the form. In that case, the relevant parent category should be selected in a category selection field. The danger of erroneous input would be rather great.

Delete titles: The function *delete_title* deletes only the title (entries in the tables *titles* and *rel_title_author*). One could also delete authors and publishers if they were no longer associated with any titles.

Pagewise Representation of Search Results

There is a search option on almost every dynamic website. If there are more than *n* search results, only the first *n* are displayed. Buttons or links make it possible to go to the next page. Relevant programming techniques are demonstrated in the file find.php.

The program find.php makes it possible to search the *mylibrary* database for titles and authors. Using the program is easy: For a title search, specify the first letters of the title and/or select a category (Figure 15-8). The program searches for titles that fulfill both criteria. For an author search you specify the first letters of the author name (family name).

■**Tip** This example does not provide for full-text search. Nevertheless, you can search in this example for books in which the search string appears somewhere in the title (that is, not necessarily at the beginning). To do so, simply preface the search string with the percent sign %. Thus *%mysql* finds not only *MySQL Cookbook*, but also *PHP 5 and MySQL 5*.

The search results (Figure 15-9) are ordered alphabetically and contain links to find.php, for finding all titles by a given author, all titles of a category, and detailed information about a particular title. If there are more search results than *$pagesize* (this variable is declared at the beginning of find.php), there appear after the search results links to the following and previous pages.

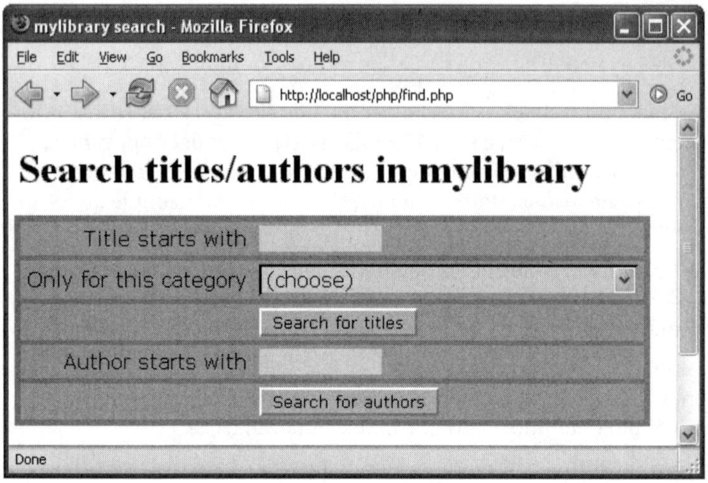

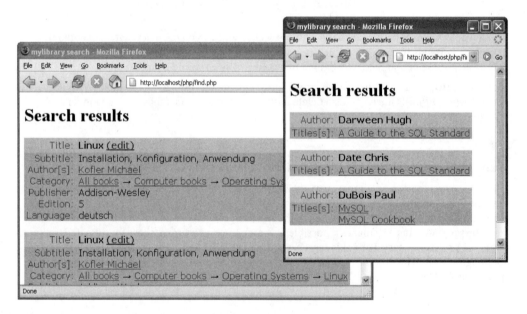

Figure 15-8. *Search form for mylibrary*

Figure 15-9. *The search results of a title search (left) and an author search (right)*

Code Structure

The code is divided among the following five files:

find.php	Main code
mydb.php	Class *MyDb* with database methods
mylibraryfunctions.php	Auxiliary functions
formfunctions.php	Functions for output of a form
form.css	CSS file for formatting the form
resulttable.css	CSS file for formatting the search result

Two mechanisms are used for providing the data when a page is changed:

POST	Contains the input from the search form in the form of a field: *form["title"), form["authors"], form["btnAuthor"]*, etc.
REQUEST	Contains URL parameters: *titleID*: Display this title *titlePattern*: Display titles corresponding to the search pattern *authID*: Display this author *authPattern*: Display authors matching the search pattern *catID*: Display all titles of this category *page*: Display this page

Code Flow

The greater portion of the code is in functions, some of which will be presented in the following sections. The control of the code takes place in the following lines.

First, the parameters passed to the page are evaluated. Here the function *array_item* from the file mylibraryfunctions.php introduced in the previous section comes into play. The parameters *titlePattern* and *authPattern* must be coded within the URL so that any special characters that might be present will not cause any problems. This encoding is decoded with *urldecode*.

```php
// example file find.php
$db = new MyDb();  // connection to MySQL
$pagesize = 5;     // search results per page
// evaluate URL parameters
$titleID     = array_item($_REQUEST, 'titleID');
$authID      = array_item($_REQUEST, 'authID');
$catID       = array_item($_REQUEST, 'catID');
$authPattern = urldecode(array_item($_REQUEST, 'authPattern'));
$titlePattern = urldecode(array_item($_REQUEST, 'titlePattern'));
$page        = array_item($_REQUEST, 'page');
// validation control
if(!$page || $page<1 || !is_numeric($page))   $page=1;
elseif($page>100)                             $page=100;
if(!is_numeric($catID))   $catID = FALSE;
if(!is_numeric($authID))  $authID = FALSE;
if(!is_numeric($titleID)) $titleID = FALSE;
```

Any *Magic Quotes* are removed from the form data. A percent character is appended to the search pattern for titles and authors. This character is necessary for the later formation of a *SELECT* command. (*WHERE title LIKE 'abc%'* searches for titles beginning with *abc*.)

```
// form data
$formdata = array_item($_POST, "form");
if(is_array($formdata)) {
  // remove Magic Quotes
  if(get_magic_quotes_gpc())
    while($i = each($formdata))
      $formdata[$i[0]] = stripslashes($i[1]);
  $authPattern = array_item($formdata, "author") . "%";
  if(!array_item($formdata, "btnAuthor")) {
    $catID       = array_item($formdata, "category");
    $titlePattern = array_item($formdata, "title") . "%"; }
}
```

After these preparations, we come to the nitty gritty. If *titlePattern*, *titleID*, or *catID* contains values, then three functions are called one after the other: *build_title_query*, to formulate the SQL command; *show_titles*, to represent the search result; and finally *show_page_links*, to display links to the previous and following pages as necessary. The code for author search is completely analogous. If there are no data to be searched for, an empty form is displayed with *build_form*.

```
if($titlePattern || $titleID || $catID) {
  // title search
  $sql = build_title_query($titlePattern, $titleID, $catID,
    $page, $pagesize);
  $rows = $db->queryObjectArray($sql);
  show_titles($rows, $pagesize);
  $query = "catID=$catID&titleID=$titleID&titlePattern=" .
    urlencode($titlePattern);
  show_page_links($page, $pagesize, sizeof($rows), $query);
  echo '<p><a href="find.php">Back to search form</a></p>', "\n";
}
elseif($authPattern || $authID) {
  // author search, analogous code
  ...
}
else {
  // display search form
  echo "<h1>Search titles/authors in mylibrary</h1>\n";
  build_form(); }
```

Author Search

The SQL command for author search is formulated in the function *build_author_query*. If *authID* contains an author ID number, the command is simply the following:

```
SELECT authID, authName FROM authors WHERE authID=...
```

On the other hand, if the search is for authors whose name corresponds to a pattern, then the SQL code is somewhat more complicated:

```
SELECT authID, authName FROM authors
WHERE authName LIKE 'abc%'
ORDER BY authName
LIMIT 20, 11
```

Of greatest interest here is the *LIMIT* part, which restricts the result to a given size. *LIMIT 20, 11* means that the *SELECT* command should return the twentieth through thirtieth results (thus the third page if *size=10*).

You may be wondering why 11 authors are being sought when the size is 10. The reason is that in this way it can be determined whether there are any additional search results. (In any case, only ten results are displayed. If the query returns 11 authors, then the function *show_page_links*, described below, will create a link to the next page.)

```php
// example file find.php
function build_author_query($pattern, $authID, $page, $size) {
  global $db;
  $sql = "SELECT authID, authName FROM authors ";
  if($authID)
    return $sql . "WHERE authID = $authID";
  else
    return $sql ."WHERE authName LIKE " . $db->sql_string($pattern) .
      " ORDER BY authNAME " .
      "LIMIT " . (($page-1) * $size) . "," . ($size + 1);
}
```

Title Search

The function *build_title_query* is analogous to *build_author_query*. The only difference is that in some situations, two search criteria must be considered, that is, the category and the search pattern for a title. Therefore, two conditions are set, which are then combined in the form *WHERE cond1 AND cond2*. If no category or search pattern is specified, that criterion is simply set to *TRUE*.

In the category search the condition *catID=n* is insufficient: Indeed, with *subcategory_list* a list is created that contains all subcategories of the given category. (If you are searching for *Computer books*, you also want to see results in the categories *Databases, Programming*, etc.) The function *subcategory_list* is located in mylibraryfunctions.php and will be described in the next section of this chapter.

```php
// example file find.php
function build_title_query($pattern, $titleID, $catID,
                           $page, $size) {
  ... analogous to build_author_query
  if($catID && $catID!="none") {
    $catsql = "SELECT catID, parentCatID FROM categories";
    $rows = $db->queryObjectArray($catsql);
    foreach($rows as $row)
      $subcats[$row->parentCatID][] = $row->catID;
    $cond1 = "catID IN (" .
      subcategory_list($subcats, $catID) . ") ";    }
  else
    $cond1 = "TRUE";
  if($pattern)
    $cond2 = "title LIKE " . $db->sql_string($pattern) . " ";
  else
    $cond2 = "TRUE";
  $sql .= "WHERE " . $cond1 . " AND " . $cond2 .
    " ORDER BY title ";
  ... and so on, as in build_author_query
}
```

Displaying Search Results

The functions *show_authors* and *show_titles* are passed fields whose elements contain *authID* and *authName* for any authors found, and *titleID* and *titleName* for found titles. All further author and title data are returned within the *show_* functions in one or two additional SQL queries. In *show_authors* the query for titles that the authors have written looks like this:

```
SELECT title, rel_title_author.titleID, authID
FROM   titles, rel_title_author
WHERE  titles.titleID = rel_title_author.titleID
  AND  rel_title_author.authID IN (1, 2, 3, ...)
ORDER BY title
```

Then it is a matter of presenting this information in a visually appealing manner. This example uses a table, whose cells are structured by the CSS file resulttable.css.

```php
// example file find.php
function show_authors($authors, $pagesize) {
  global $db;
  echo "<h1>Search results</h1>\n";
  if(!$authors) {
    echo "<p>Sorry, no authors found.</p>\n";
    return; }
  // create string with authIDs
  $items = min($pagesize, sizeof($authors));
  for($i=0; $items; $i++)
    if($i==0)
      $authIDs = $authors[$i]-authID;
    else
      $authIDs .= "," . $authors[$i]->authID;
  // return titles that these authors have written ermitteln
  $sql = "SELECT title, rel_title_author.titleID, authID " .
    "FROM titles, rel_title_author ".
    "WHERE titles.titleID = rel_title_author.titleID " .
    "AND rel_title_author.authID IN ($authIDs) " .
    "ORDER BY title";
  $rows = $db->queryObjectArray($sql);

  // display all authors
  echo '<table class="resulttable">', "\n";
  for($i=0; $items; $i++) {
    echo td1("Author:", "td1head"),
      td2($authors[$i]-authName, "td2head");
    // show all titles for each author
    $titles=0;
    foreach($rows as $row)
      if($authors[$i]->authID == $row->authID) {
        if($titles==0)
          echo td1("Titles[s]:");
        else
          echo td1("");
        echo td2url($row->title, "find.php?titleID=$row->titleID");
        $titles++;
      }
    // blank line before next title
    echo td1("", "tdinvisible"), td2asis(" ", "tdinvisible");
  }
  echo "</table>\n";
}
```

The auxiliary functions *td1* and *td2xxx* are used for output of the table cells:

```
function td1($txt, $class="td1") {
  echo "<tr><td class=\"$class\">",
    htmlspecialchars($txt), "</td>\n"; }
function td2($txt, $class="td2") {
  echo "<td class=\"$class\">",
    htmlspecialchars($txt), "</td></tr>\n"; }
function td2asis($txt, $class="td2") {
  echo "<td class=\"$class\">$txt</td></tr>\n"; }
...
```

The code for *show_titles* is much more extensive, since for each title much more information must be displayed. However, the principle is the same as in *show_authors*, and so I will not discuss its code further.

Links to Additional Pages

There are two ways that you might display links to additional pages:

- You could begin by determining the total number of search results using a command of the form *SELECT COUNT(*) ... WHERE*. Then you could easily compute how many pages are necessary for displaying the results and create links to all these pages.

- The other variant is simply to test when a page is created whether there are any additional search results (by passing as second parameter to *LIMIT* not *pagesize*, but *pagesize+1*). This information is sufficient for setting a link to the next page if there is one.

The function *show_page_links* is based on the second alternative. Four parameters are passed to the function: the current page number, the number of results per page, the number of most recently found search results, and in *query* the list of parameters that should be passed in the link to the next or previous page (e.g., *authPattern=abc*).

The function *show_page_links* first creates the links to previous pages (if *page>1*), and then links to the following page (if *results>pagesize*). For creating the links, the auxiliary function *build_href* from `mylibraryfunctions.php` is used.

```
// example file find.php
function show_page_links($page, $pagesize, $results, $query) {
  if(($page==1 && $results<=$pagesize) || $results==0)
    return;
  echo "<p>Goto page: ";
  if($page>1) {
    for($i=1; $i<$page; $i++)
      echo build_href("find.php", $query . "&page=$i", $i), " ";
    echo "$page "; }
  if($results>$pagesize) {
    $nextpage = $page + 1;
    echo build_href("find.php", $query . "&page=$nextpage",
      $nextpage);  }
  echo "</p>\n";
}
```

Managing Hierarchical Data

It is quite easy to express hierarchies in a table: an additional column with a reference to the parent element suffices. It is thus, for example, that the book categories in the *mylibrary* database (see Chapter 8) are managed. Additional application domains include managing the personnel hierarchy in a corporation (at the top is the chief executive, then the division heads, followed by the group leaders, etc.) and genealogical trees (first Adam and Eve, and so on).

As easy as the construction of such hierarchies is, the evaluation of hierarchical tables is correspondingly difficult. One generally requires recursive functions (that is, functions that call themselves) to determine all elements ordered above or below a particular point in the hierarchy.

This section takes as an example the *categories* table of the *mylibrary* database to demonstrate some programming techniques that you can use, with the necessary modifications, in managing your own hierarchical data.

The greatest portion of the functions discussed here are to be found in `categories.php`. This page assists in the management of book categories (see Figure 15-10). It is easy to use: a click of the mouse deletes existing categories or creates new subcategories (see as well Figure 15-12 further along in this section).

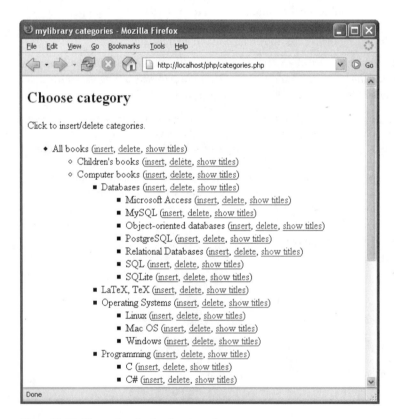

Figure 15-10. *Managing the book categories*

When a category is deleted, all of its subcategories are deleted as well (but only if these categories are not in use). The link *SHOW TITLES* leads to *find.php?catID=…* (see the previous section) and displays all titles associated with a particular category, including all of its subcategories.

With MySQL 5.0, you can also use stored procedures for processing tables with hierarchical data. Examples of such a nature can be found in Chapter 13.

Code Structure

The code is divided among the following files:

categories.php	Main code
mydb.php	Class *MyDb* with database methods
mylibraryfunctions.php	Auxiliary functions

Two mechanisms are used for data transfer when a page is changed:

POST	Contains the new categories from the input form (*submitbutton*, *subcategories*)
REQUEST	Contains URL parameters: *insertID*: Insert subcategories to this category *deleteID*: Delete this category

Code Flow

The majority of the code is contained in functions, some of which will be described in the following sections. The control of the code is managed in the following lines:

```
// example file categories.php
$db = new MyDb(); // connection to MySQL
$insertID      = array_item($_REQUEST, 'insertID');
$deleteID      = array_item($_REQUEST, 'deleteID');
$submitbutton  = array_item($_POST, 'submitbutton');
$subcategories = array_item($_POST, 'subcategories');
if(get_magic_quotes_gpc())    // no magic quotes
  $subcategories = stripslashes($subcategories);
```

The functions *delete_ new_categories* and *insert_new_categories* are executed in transactions. Depending on the function's return value, the transaction is confirmed or aborted. This ensures that either the complete deletion or insertion operation was executed without error or the category list was left unchanged.

```
// delete category
if($deleteID) {
  $sql = "SELECT COUNT(*) FROM categories WHERE catID='$deleteID'";
  if($db->querySingleItem($sql)==1) {
    $db->execute("START TRANSACTION");
    if(delete_category($deleteID)===-1)
      $db->execute("ROLLBACK");
    else
      $db->execute("COMMIT");   }}
// store or insert new categories
if($insertID) {
  $sql = "SELECT COUNT(*) FROM categories WHERE catID='$insertID'";
  $n = $db->querySingleItem($sql); }
if($insertID && $n==1) {
  echo "<h2>Insert new categories</h2>\n";
```

```
  // store new categories
  if($subcategories) {
    $db->execute("START TRANSACTION");
    if(insert_new_categories($insertID, $subcategories))
      $db->execute("COMMIT");
    else
      $db->execute("ROLLBACK"); }
  // input form
  print_category_entry_form($insertID);  }
// display complete list of all categories
else {
  echo "<h2>Choose category</h2>\n";
  echo "<p>Click to insert/delete categories.</p>\n";
  ... details in the next section
  print_categories($rows, NULL);  }
```

Displaying the Category Tree

To represent the category tree (see Figure 15-10), first all the categories are determined with a single SQL query. Then in the next step, these data are used to create two additional fields. The purpose of these fields is to avoid searching for field elements in the function *print_categories*. Instead of running through all categories in a loop to find those for which *parentCatID==n* holds, the desired categories are immediately available as *subcats[catID]*. (More precisely, the search is delegated to PHP's internal operations: when you access *array[key]*, PHP must look for the element with the key *key*. PHP carries out this search very efficiently.)

The significance of the field *catNames* should be clear at first glance. *catName[catID]* simply contains the category names for the category selected with *catID*.

On the other hand, *subcats* is somewhat more difficult to understand: every element *subcats[catID]* again contains a field whose elements contain the *catID* numbers of all subcategories. However, the elements are inserted with a somewhat inverted logic: in the *foreach* loop, *parentCatID* serves as key, while *catID* is the value that is added to the field. Fortunately, the special case *parentCatID==NULL* does not require special handling. PHP also accepts *NULL* as the key in a field. Note that *subcats[n]* contains the subcategories in alphabetical order, since the initial data were sorted in *rows* with *ORDER BY catName*.

The PHP syntax *array[] = abc* means that *abc* is inserted as a new element in the field *array*. If *array* does not yet exist, a new field is created in which *abc* is the first element.

```
// preparations for calling print_categories
// determine all categories
$sql = "SELECT catName, catID, parentCatID " .
       "FROM categories ORDER BY catName";
$rows = $db->queryObjectArray($sql);
// create fields subcats and catNames
foreach($rows as $row) {
  $subcats[$row->parentCatID][] = $row->catID;
  $catNames[$row->catID] = $row->catName; }
// display categories beginning with the root element
print_categories($subcats[NULL], $subcats, $catNames);
```

In the first paramenter, a field with the root element(s) is passed to the function *print_categories* (*subcats[NULL]*). Then these elements are looped through and output. The field *catNames* is used for determining the category names. If there are subcategories (test with *array_key_exists($catID, $subcats)*), these are simply passed with *$subcats[$catID]* in a recursive call to *print_categories*.

```
function print_categories($catIDs, $subcats, $catNames) {
  echo "<ul>";
  foreach($catIDs as $catID) {
    printf("<li>%s (%s, %s, %s)</li>\n",
      htmlspecialchars($catNames[$catID]),
      build_href("categories.php", "insertID=$catID", "insert"),
      build_href("categories.php", "deleteID=$catID", "delete"),
      build_href("find.php", "catID=$catID", "show titles"));
    if(array_key_exists($catID, $subcats))
      print_categories($subcats[$catID], $subcats, $catNames);
  }
  echo "</ul>\n";
}
```

Selection List for Catagories (for titleform.php, find.php)

The two pages titleform.php and find.php contain a listbox for selecting a category. In this field the list entries are indented to indicate the hierarchical structure (see Figure 15-11).

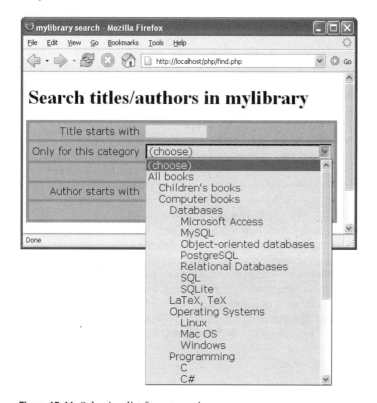

Figure 15-11. *Selection list for catagories*

To create such list fields, the pages titleform.php and find.php use the functions *build_category_array* (file mylibraryfunctions.php) and *form_list* (file formfunctions.php). *build_category_array* returns a two-dimensional field. Each entry contains two elements: the category text and the *catID* number. *form_list* then uses these data to create the listbox.

In principle, *build_category_array* is structured like the function *print_categories* shown above, and it expects the same parameters (in particular the fields *catNames* and *subcats*). What is new is the fourth, optional, parameter *indent*, which contains the current indentation level.

The function inserts the categories passed in the first parameter into the field *tmp*. If this category possesses subcategories, then these are also inserted via a recursive call to the function (shown in boldface).

The field *tmp* is declared to be static, so that its value is not lost in the call to *build_category_array*. (Normally, functions are declared to be local within a function; that is, each function call contains its own independent variables.) At the first call to *build_category_array* with *indent==0*, the content of *tmp* is cleared. Note that the usual function *unset* cannot be used here, since it does not work as desired with static variables (a PHP-specific problem).

To indent the list entries correctly, *build_category_array* governs the current indentation level in the parameter *indent*. The list entries are prefixed with *indent*3* spaces. In *form_list* these entries are replaced by the HTML special character * * (that is, by fixed spaces that are not treated as whitespace and can therefore be properly represented by the browser).

```
// example file mylibraryfunctions.php
function build_category_array($catIDs, $subcats, $catNames, $indent=0) {
  static $tmp;
  if($indent==0)
    $tmp = FALSE;  // clear tmp
  foreach($catIDs as $catID) {
    $pair[0] = str_repeat(" ", $indent*3) . $catNames[$catID];
    $pair[1] = $catID;
    $tmp[] = $pair;
    if(array_key_exists($catID, $subcats))
      build_category_array($subcats[$catID], $subcats, $catNames, $indent+1); }
  if($indent==0)
    return $tmp;   }
```

The function *build_category_array* will appear again in the next section, where the topic is speed optimization.

Inserting Subcategories

When you click on an INSERT link, first the function *build_category_entry_form* is called. It returns a reduced representation of the hierarchy tree containing only the categories directly above and below the selected category. A small form consisting of a text field and a button allows for the input of new categories (see Figure 15-12). We will not go more deeply into this function for reasons of space. Furthermore, the function offers nothing new in the way of programming techniques.

The insertion of new categories is managed by the function *insert_new_categories*. Two parameters are passed to the function: the *catID* number of the category of which the new category is to define as a subcategory, and a character string with one or more new category names (separated by semicolons).

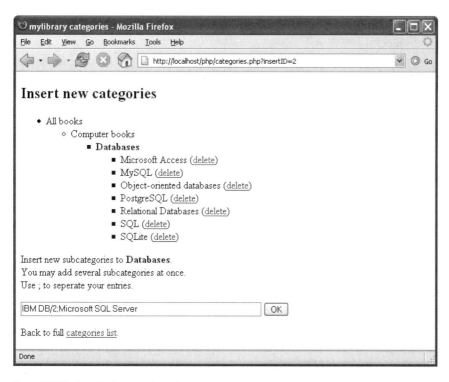

Figure 15-12. *Input of new categories*

The function *insert_new_categories* uses *explode* to split the string into several field elements and then for each field element calls *insert_new_category*. If an error occurs in storing a category (return value *-1*), the function call is aborted.

```
// example file categories.php
function insert_new_categories($insertID, $subcategories) {
  global $db;
  $subcatarray = explode(";", $subcategories);
  $count = 0;
  foreach($subcatarray as $newcatname) {
    $result = insert_new_category($insertID, trim($newcatname));
    if($result == -1) {
      echo "<p>Sorry, an error happened. Nothing was saved.</p>\n";
      return FALSE; }
    elseif($result)
      $count++;      }
  if($count)
    if($count==1)
      echo "<p>One new category has been inserted.</p>\n";
    else
      echo "<p>$count new categories have been inserted.</p>\n";
  return TRUE;
}
```

The function *insert_new_category* stores a new category. First a test is made whether this category already exists. The function returns one of three values: *1* (the category was deleted), *0* (the category was not deleted), *-1* (an SQL or database error occurred).

```
function insert_new_category($insertID, $newcatName) {
  global $db;
  // newcatName is empty
  if(!$newcatName) return 0;
  $newcatName = $db->sql_string($newcatName);
  // newcatName already exists
  $sql = "SELECT COUNT(*) FROM categories " .
         "WHERE parentCatID=$insertID " .
         "  AND catName=$newcatName";
  if($db->querySingleItem($sql)>0) {
    return 0; }
  $sql = "INSERT INTO categories (catName, parentCatID) " .
         "VALUES ($newcatName, $insertID)";
  if($db->execute($sql))
    return 1;
  else
    return -1;
}
```

Deleting Categories and Subcategories

A category can be deleted only after all of its subcategories have been deleted. Therefore, *delete_category* calls itself recursively (shown in boldface in the listing). There is an additional condition that must be fulfilled before deletion can take place: There can be no titles that belong to such a category.

```
// example file categories.php
function delete_category($catID) {
  global $db;
  // search out and delete subcategories
  $sql = "SELECT catID FROM categories " .
         "WHERE parentCatID='$catID'";
  if($rows = $db->queryObjectArray($sql)) {
    $deletedRows = 0;
    foreach($rows as $row) {
      $result = delete_category($row->catID);
      if($result==-1)
        return -1;
      else
        $deletedRows ++;
    }
    // if not all subcategories can be deleted,
    // then do not delete this category
    if($deletedRows != count($rows))
      return 0;
  }
  // if category is being used, do not delete
  $sql = "SELECT COUNT(*) FROM titles WHERE catID='$catID'";
  if($n = $db->querySingleItem($sql)>0) {
    $sql = "SELECT catName FROM categories WHERE catID='$catID'";
    $catname = $db->querySingleItem($sql);
    printf("<br />Category %s is used in %d titles. " .
           "You cannot delete it.\n", $catname, $n);
    return 0;
  }
```

```
  // delete category
  $sql = "DELETE FROM categories WHERE catID='$catID' LIMIT 1";
  if($db->execute($sql))
    return 1;
  else
    return -1;
}
```

Searching for Parent Categories

In the search results of find.php, not only a link to the category is displayed, but also links to all the subcategories (see Figure 15-13). That makes the search for related titles particularly easy.

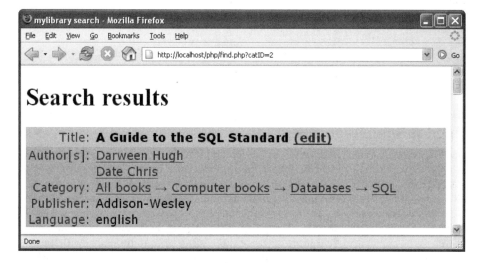

Figure 15-13. *Links to the book's category as well as all its subcategories*

Of interest here is of course the search for the parent categories. To this end, *show_titles* uses the function *build_cat_string*, which returns a string with all the requisite links. Three parameters are passed to *build_cat_string*: the fields *catNames* and *catParents* and the *catID* number of the current category.

First the two fields are initialized. *catNames* contains the category name for each *catID* index. The field *catParents* contains the *catID* number of the parent category.

```
// example file find.php
function show_titles($titles, $pagesize) {
  ...
  // determine all categories
  $sql = "SELECT catName, catID, parentCatID FROM categories";
  $rows = $db->queryObjectArray($sql);
  // form associative fields for category names and parentCatID
  foreach($rows as $cat) {
    $catNames[$cat->catID] = $cat->catName;
    $catParents[$cat->catID] = $cat->parentCatID; }
  ...
```

```
// loop over all titles
foreach($titlerows as $title) {
  ... display various title information
  // display category and subcategories
  if($title->catID)
    echo td1("Category:"), td2asis(
      build_cat_string($catNames, $catParents, $title->catID));
```

The function *build_cat_string* first creates a link to the category specified by *catID*. Then it runs through a loop to search for all categories lying above it in the hierarchy. Links are created to these categories as well. Rightward-pointing arrows between the links are provided by *→*. The function *build_href* from mylibraryfunctions.php is used, as in many other examples in this book, for forming the link (hence *<a href="link?query"> txt</a>*).

```
function build_cat_string($catNames, $catParents, $catID) {
  $tmp = build_href("find.php", "catID=$catID", $catNames[$catID]);
  while($catParents[$catID] != NULL) {
    $catID = $catParents[$catID];
    $tmp = build_href("find.php", "catID=$catID", $catNames[$catID]) .
      " &rarr; " . $tmp; }
  return $tmp;
}
```

Searching for Subcategories

You can specify a category as search criterion in the search form find.php. If you now select the criterion *Databases*, you expect, of course, that the result will also contain the titles of the subcategories *MySQL, SQL*, etc. Therefore, it is insufficient to use *catID=nnn* as search criterion in the *SELECT* query. First you must compile a list of ID numbers of all the subcategories and then use that list as *SELECT* criterion, that is, *catID IN (n1, n2, n3 ...)*.

Such a list is returned by the function *subcategory_list*. It expects as parameters the initial category as well as the associative field *subcats*, where *subcats[catID]* contains a field with the *catID* numbers of all subcategories. The following lines show the formation of *subcats* and then the call to *subcategory_list* within *build_title_query*.

```
// example file find.php
function build_title_query(...) {
  ...
    $catsql = "SELECT catID, parentCatID FROM categories";
    $rows = $db->queryObjectArray($catsql);
    foreach($rows as $row)
      $subcats[$row->parentCatID][] = $row->catID;
    $cond1 = "catID IN (" .
      subcategory_list($subcats, $catID) . ") ";
```

The function *subcategory_list* stores *catID* in the temporary variable *lst*. If there are subcategories (that is, if the field *subcats* contains an element with the key *catID*), then *subcategory_list* is called recursively for all subcategories. The result is added to *lst*.

```
function subcategory_list($subcats, $catID) {
  $lst = $catID;
  if(array_key_exists($catID, $subcats))
    foreach($subcats[$catID] as $subCatID)
      $lst .= ", " . s($subcats, $subCatID);
  return $lst;
}
```

Speed Optimization

When you test your PHP pages on your local system, you are likely to be satisfied with the speed at which things take place. However, when later the project can be reached over the Internet, things can suddenly slow considerably: Most Internet service providers run several websites on a single server. The greater the number of simultaneous hits to these sites, the slower each site becomes.

Furthermore, many database applications become slower as the database grows in size. That is true particularly if your program code has not been optimized so that it is miserly with respect to resources in working with large data sets (memory, CPU cycles, database accesses, data transfer over the network).

For these reasons it is desirable, even for simple projects, to pay attention to writing well thought out and efficient code. This section provides some tips and examples. Also take a look at Chapter 14, where the issue was discussed of configuring the MySQL server as efficiently as possible (query cache, etc.), independently of PHP.

Ground Rules for Efficient Code Execution

Database design: The most important principle for the efficient construction of a dynamic website is a good database design. If the structure of the data does not correspond to your requirements, then all attempts at optimization are doomed.

From the point of view of efficiency, the design is good if the following rules for efficiency are easy to fulfill. (Note that such optimized databases do not generally meet all the criteria of normal forms, since, for example, they contain redundant data. Database theoreticians may not be happy with such databases, but you can often gain speed with redundancy.)

One aspect of database design is the correct use of indexes. All columns that are frequently searched by content (*WHERE column = …*) should be equipped with an index. Note, however, that too many indexes is not a good thing: they increase the memory requirement for each table and slow down changes to the data.

As few SQL queries as possible per page: Every SQL command that is sent from the PHP interpreter to the MySQL server results in a considerable expense of resources: transferring a command, executing a command on the server, transferring the result. Therefore, the fewer SQL commands needed for constructing a page or in general performing an action, the better.

This old piece of database wisdom holds also for the combination PHP/MySQL, even if with certain restrictions: If the MySQL server is properly configured, then frequently used tables should be contained completely in RAM. And if Apache and MySQL are running on the same computer (which is often the case), then the network ceases to be a brake on speed. The overhead due to an SQL command is then rather small. For example, if you can avoid a costly PHP loop by using an additional SQL command, the overall performance can increase. In sum, avoid unnecessary SQL commands, but don't avoid them at any price.

Keep SELECT results as small as possible: One should almost always avoid a query that returns 1,000 records. The great cost of such queries often is caused not by the actual execution of the query, but by its transmission to the PHP interpreter and the subsequent evaluation with PHP code. Filter the data on the MySQL server by providing your *SELECT* queries with suitable conditions.

The most efficient possible PHP code (few loop passes, etc.): Many problems can be solved in ways that are more or less efficient. Attempt in particular to avoid search and sort procedures in PHP by building the necessary criteria and sorting rules into your *SELECT* command. (MySQL is optimized for such tasks, in contrast to your code.)

You will note that these rules partially contradict one another. Often it can be determined with concrete tests whether it is more efficient to execute a single *SELECT* query that returns 1,000 records (greater cost from transferring larger data sets) or 20 *SELECT*s that each return 100 records (greater cost because the PHP interpreter must contact the MySQL server 20 times and wait for its answer).

■**Tip** Before you begin with your optimization, consider which pages will be called frequently. Often, pages with read and search access are called more frequently than those that alter data. Optimize the pages that are needed most frequently. Optimize the database design so that frequently occurring tasks are executed efficiently.

Let us suppose that search queries and data changes occur in the frequency 100 to 1. If you are able to execute search queries twice as fast as previously, but with the result that data changes, due to the changed design, now take three times as long, you will have reaped an enormous increase in efficiency.

If you are working on a website like Yahoo! or GMX, where millions of accesses per day are to be expected, efficiency of the code occupies a place of supreme importance. However, optimally efficient code is often complex, difficult to maintain, and error-prone. For websites that experience many fewer hits, the priorities should be directed toward making the code clear, simple, and easy to maintain.

Statistical and Benchmarking Help

If you have encapsulated database access (for example, with the previously introduced *MyDb* class), it is easy to determine the number of SQL commands, the number of returned records, the time for the execution of the SQL commands, and the total time for creating the class as well as the time since the last reset. At the end of the page, output this basic information with a call to *$db->showStatistics()*.

This information will at least give you a first impression of the cost of creating the page from the database point of view (see also Figure 10-14). Note, however, that the times given are strongly dependent on what else the computer was doing when you were testing your page, whether the data sought were already in the cache of the MySQL server, etc. Therefore, apply a certain amount of skepticism to the results.

To determine the exact time, the PHP function *microtime* is used. The function *microtime_float* changes its result into a floating-point number. The extensions to the class file mydb.php look in part like this:

```php
// example file mydb.php
class MyDb {
   ...
   protected $sqlcounter = 0;     // counter for SQL commands
   protected $rowcounter = 0;     // counter for SELECT records
   protected $dbtime     = 0;     // time elapsed for SQL commands
   protected $starttime;          // total time
   // constructor
   function __construct() {
      ...
      $this->starttime = $this->microtime_float();
   }
   function queryObjectArray($sql) {
      $this->sqlcounter++;
      $this->printsql($sql);
      $time1  = $this->microtime_float();
      $result = $this->mysqli->query($sql);
      $this->dbtime += ($time2 - $this->microtime_float());
```

```
    if($result) {
      if($result->num_rows) {
        while($row = $result->fetch_object())
          $result_array[] = $row;
        $this->rowcounter += sizeof($result_array);
        return $result_array; }
      else
        return FALSE;
    } else {
      $this->printerror($this->mysqli->error);
      return FALSE;
    }
  }
  ...
  function showStatistics() {
    $totalTime = $this->microtime_float() - $this->starttime;
    printf("<p><font color=\"#0000ff\">SQL commands: %d\n",
      $this->sqlcounter);
    printf("<br />Sum of returned rows: %d\n", $this->rowcounter);
    printf("<br />Sum of query time (MySQL): %f\n", $this->dbtime);
    printf("<br />Processing time (PHP): %f\n",
      $totalTime - $this->dbtime);
    printf("<br />Total time since MyDb creation / " .
      "last reset: %f</font></p>\n", $totalTime);    }
  function resetStatistics() {
    $this->sqlcounter = 0;
    $this->rowcounter = 0;
    $this->dbtime     = 0;
    $this->starttime = $this->microtime_float();  }
  private function microtime_float() {
    list($usec, $sec) = explode(" ", microtime());
    return ((float)$usec + (float)$sec);    }
}
```

Example: Generating the Category List Efficiently

In the previous section the function *build_category_array* from `mylibraryfunctions.php` was introduced. This function returns a field from which the category selection list is created.

This section compares three variants of this function and shows how a function can be optimized step by step. The complete code can be found in `optimize/show_categories_list.php`. The speed difference between the slowest and fastest variants is hardly noticeable with a small number of categories. But it grows dramatically as the number of categories grows (by a factor of 50 with more than 1,000 elements).

Creating the Test Data

The starting point for the following tests if a category list built from random data with about 1,000 entries. To create a corresponding *categories* table, call once the page `optimize/create_categories_test.php`. The code contained there resolves the integrity rules for *titles.catID*, renames the *categories* table *oldcategories*, and then creates a new *categories* table with random data. To restore the status quo, call `optimize/remove_categories_test.php`.

Variant 1: One SQL Query, Worse PHP Code

The function *build_category_array1* expects as parameter a sorted field with all categories as well as the *parentCatID* number of the initial element (*parentCatID=NULL* means that the entire tree, beginning with the root element, is to be displayed). The category list is determined before the call to *build_category_array1* through a single *SELECT* command.

Now the function searches through the entire *rows* field for entries with the matching *parentCatID* and adds these to the static field *tmp*. For each found category, *print_categories* is called recursively to take care of the category's subcategories.

```
// example file optimize/show_categories_list.php
$sql = "SELECT catName, catID, parentCatID FROM categories ORDER BY catName";
$categories = $db->queryObjectArray($sql);
$rows = build_category_array1($categories);
...
function build_category_array1($rows, $parentCatID=NULL, $indent=0) {
  static $tmp;
  if($indent==0)
    $tmp=FALSE;  // unset does not work with static variables
  foreach($rows as $row)
    if($row->parentCatID==$parentCatID) {
      $pair[0] = str_repeat(" ", $indent*3) . $row->catName;
      $pair[1] = $row->catID;
      $tmp[] = $pair;
      build_category_array1($rows, $row->catID, $indent+1);
    }
  if($indent==0)
    return $tmp;
}
```

Result: There turn out to be exactly n^2 passes through *build_category_array1*. That explains why the first variant becomes unbearably slow as the number of categories grows. On the other hand, the code is easy to understand.

Variant 2: Many Small SQL Queries

The function *build_category_array1* is so slow because it searches for each category by a simple pass through the entire list of categories. To avoid that, *build_category_array2* determines only the subcategories of the given category.

In other words, instead of one query with many results, now many queries must be executed, each of which, however, returns only a few results. (For 1,000 categories, 1,000 queries are required, which return all the categories. Thus the same amount of data is transferred from the MySQL server in both cases, but the overhead is greater in this variant.)

In constructing the recursive function, not much is changed in comparison to *build_category_array1*. Only in creating the SQL query, now only one case distinction is necessary: whether the parameter *parentCatID* contains *NULL*. In this case, the condition must be formulated with *ISNULL(catID)*, since *catID=NULL* is not permitted in SQL.

```
function  b($parentCatID=NULL, $indent=0) {
  global $db;
  static $tmp;
  if($parentCatID==NULL) {
    $tmp = FALSE;  // delete tmp
    $sql = "SELECT catName, catID FROM categories " .
           "WHERE ISNULL(parentCatID) ORDER BY catName"; }
```

```
    else
      $sql = "SELECT catName, catID FROM categories " .
             "WHERE parentCatID=$parentCatID ORDER BY catName";
  if($rows = $db->queryObjectArray($sql))
    foreach($rows as $row) {
      $pair[0] = str_repeat(" ", $indent*3) . $row->catName;
      $pair[1] = $row->catID;
      $tmp[] = $pair;
      build_category_array2($row->catID, $indent+1);
    }
  if($parentCatID==NULL)
    return $tmp;
}
```

Result: The more categories there are, the faster variant 2 is in comparison to variant 1. This result proves that in many instances, it is better to pay the price of more SQL queries than to process enormous lists of *SELECT* results with inefficient PHP code. (With small category lists, variant 2 is somewhat slower than variant 1.)

Figure 15-14 shows, however, that while the total time for creating the selection list has gone down, the burden on the MySQL server is much higher than it was in the first variant (2.26 vs. 0.04 seconds).

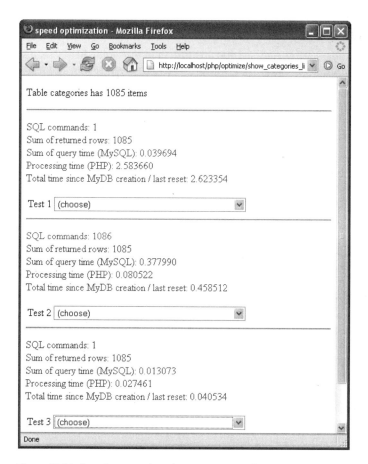

Figure 15-14. *Speed comparison in constructing the category selection list*

> **■Note** You may be wondering why no prepared statements were used here. The answer is simple: Because of the recursive nature of *build_category_array2*, the use of prepared statements is relatively difficult here and would not lead to a significant increase in speed. Prepared statements are more suitable when one and the same query is executed repeatedly in a loop.

Variant 3: One SQL Query, Optimized PHP Code

Variant 3 returns to the initial situation of variant 1: first all categories are determined with a single SQL query. But now, instead of blindly beginning to search through the category field for individual elements, two additional fields, *catNames* and *subcats*, are created, for which *catID* and *parentCatID* are used as index (key). This then enables direct access to the needed data, that is, without lengthy search loops. Details on the code appeared earlier in the chapter, under the heading "Displaying the Category Tree."

Result: Variant 3 is faster than the previous two variants with large category lists. Even with small category lists the additional time for creating the fields *catNames* and *subcats* is made up for. The only drawback of this variant is that it requires some mental effort to understand the code. This makes it difficult to make changes later (in particular if they are to be carried out by another programmer).

Other Possibilities for Improvement

The results achieved by the third variant are already so good that further optimization hardly seems necessary. Nevertheless, if we assume that the category list will be changed relatively seldom but read very often, then two further improvements come to mind:

Use of an auxiliary table: Every time a category selection field is displayed, the category list must be sorted and ordered by hierarchy with indentation. The results of this task could well be stored in a table.

Before this table is output, it would have to be tested whether any categories had changed in the meantime. Criteria could be the number of elements and the time of the last change. This point in time can be determined relatively easily if the *categories* table has been equipped with a supplementary *TIMESTAMP* column (*SELECT MAX(ts) FROM categories*). If *categories* has changed, the auxiliary table would have to be re-created.

A different table design: More elegant than a supplementary table that has to be updated continually is to enlarge the *categories* table by two columns: *indent* gives the indent level of the associated entry, and *position* the position of the element in the hierarchically ordered list. *SELECT catName, catID, indent FROM categories ORDER BY position* then returns the categories in the order needed for creating the listbox.

Of course, there are disadvantages with this variant as well: The additional columns run contrary to the normalization rules, since they contain redundant data. Moreover, the storage space for the table increases (though only minimally). And finally, the insertion of new categories is considerably more complex, since the correct positional value must be determined for the new element; furthermore, *position* must be increased for all categories beneath the new one in the hierarchy.

From the point of view of efficiency, these drawbacks may be overlooked, since they take effect only rarely (when changes are made). However, the PHP code for inserting new records would become more extensive and thereby more error-prone.

Unicode

By default, PHP serves up HTML documents in the *Latin1* character set (ISO-8559-1). Setting a different character set directly in PHP code is currently not provided for. (Such functions may well be offered in a forthcoming version) Nevertheless, PHP is in principle already capable of creating HTML documents in almost any other character set. Functions such as *echo* and *print* output strings without change, and thus do not concern themselves with the character set.

The actual problem is that all PHP string functions assume that the character strings employ the *Latin1* character set (1 byte per character). If the strings are encoded in UTF-8, then each character has a code consisting of up to 3 bytes. The consequences are these:

- *strlen* returns the number of bytes instead of the number of characters.

- You can no longer rely on the results of case operators.

- You can no longer reliably sort arrays of strings.

- Important functions such as *stripslashes*, *substr*, and *split* can cause problems.

The situation is not entirely hopeless: PHP offers the functions *utf8_encode* and *utf8_decode* for converting strings between UTF-8 and ISO-8859-1. If PHP is compiled with the *iconv* extension or if the extension module is activated (under Windows *extension= php_iconv.dll* in php.ini), then in addition to the standard string functions, there are some *iconv* variants available. For example, *iconv_strlen($s, "UTF-8")* determines the actual number of characters in a UTF-8 character string. Even more supplementary functions are offered by the *mbstring* extension. With these you can use regular expressions with multibyte strings, send email, etc.

In sum, if *Latin1* suffices for your purposes, then use that character set. That will keep your problems to a minimum. On the other hand, if the requirements of your program demand that you use the Unicode character set, look in the remainder of this section for some tips as to what you need to watch out for in your programming.

Setting the HTML and HTTP Coding

Meta-Tag: According to the HTML standard, all documents without a specified character set use *Latin1* (that is, ISO-8859-1). You can specify the character set to be used at the beginning of an HTML document in a *<meta>* tag. In HTML code it looks like this:

```
<!DOCTYPE HTML PUBLIC "-//W3C//DTD HTML 4.01 Transitional//EN"
  "http://www.w3.org/TR/html4/loose.dtd">
<html><head>
<meta http-equiv="Content-Type"
      content="text/html; charset=utf-8" />
...
```

Allowable *charset* settings are *utf-8*, *iso-8859-1*, *iso-8859-15*, etc. However, there is a problem in that many web browsers simply ignore this information and instead rely on the HTTP header.

Header information: The HTTP protocol defines how a web browser and web server communicate with each other. In addition to the HTML *<meta>* tag, this protocol offers a second way of setting the character set. Most web browsers rely on the information in the HTTP protocol and ignore the character set specification in the *<meta>* tag.

What determines the character set is the header information about the document type. The HTTP header is sent before the actual HTML document and is therefore not part of the HTML code. Some web browsers, however, offer a command for displaying page information or properties from which the header information follows (with Firefox it is Tools | Page Info; see Figure 15-15).

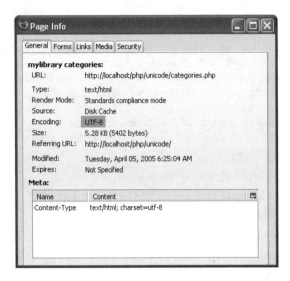

Figure 15-15. *Determining the character set of an HTML document*

So where does the Header information about the document type and character set come from? There are several possibilities. (When there are several mutually contradictory settings, the first-named points in the following list have precedence.)

- The PHP code of the page in question

  ```
  <?php header("Content-Type: text/html; charset=utf-8"); ?>
  ```

- The PHP default setting (*default_charset="utf-8"* in php.ini)
- The Apache directory configuration (*AddDefaultCharset* in .htaccess)
- The Apache default setting (*AddDefaultCharset utf-8* in httpd.conf)

If your entire website consists of Unicode documents, it is most convenient to change the Apache configuration file. If you have no influence over the Apache and PHP configuration (such as when your website is located at an ISP), it is most secure to insert the *header* function with all of your PHP scripts. Note that the *header* function must be called before each HTML output.

MySQL

Neither the *mysql* nor *mysqli* interface offers functions or methods for setting the character set. However, a simple SQL command suffices to inform the MySQL server that the SQL commands to come are encoded in UTF-8 and that you want *SELECT* results in this encoding as well.

SET NAMES 'utf8'

Execute this command with *mysql_query* or *$mysqli->query*.

Note that *SET NAMES* governs only the character set for communication between MySQL and your PHP script. *SET NAMES* has no influence over the character set in which data are actually stored in MySQL tables. (That character set is determined when the table is created with *CREATE*

TABLE.) MySQL automatically converts all character strings from the table character set to the processing character set. But watch out! If in the process characters appear that are not representable in the second character set, such characters are replaced with a question mark. (Such characters also lead to loss of information.)

PHP Character Set Functions

Almost every PHP script employs string functions. By default, these functions assume that each character is represented by a single byte. However, that is not the case with UTF-8 strings, in which a character has length from 1 to 3 bytes. The following recommendations should help in porting code:

- Output functions such as *printf* and *echo* are usually unproblematic.

- The concatenation of strings with . causes no trouble.

- Sorting strings should generally be left to MySQL.

- The functions *htmlentities* and *htmlspecialchars* can be called in a form that is compatible with UTF-8:

```
echo htmlspecialchars($txt, ENT_COMPAT, "UTF-8");
echo htmlentities($txt, ENT_COMPAT, "UTF-8");
```

- Some elementary string functions can be replaced with equivalent functions from the already mentioned PHP extensions *iconv* and *mbstring*. (Unfortunately, these extensions do not provide a UTF-8–compatible replacement for all string functions, not by a long shot.)

Example

In the directory unicode in the PHP example files you will find a UTF-8–compatible variant of the *mylibrary* example scripts that were described in the previous three sections of this chapter. The Unicode transformation of this example was by and large without problems. The following points summarize the changes that were made:

- A *header* function was inserted at the beginning of the files find.php, titleform.php, and categories.php to change the HTTP coding to Unicode:

```
<?php header("Content-Type: text/html; charset=utf-8"); ?>
```

- A *<meta>* tag was inserted in the header of these files to set the HTML coding to Unicode. (As we have said, this information is ignored by many browsers. Nonetheless, they should be given so that the HTML syntax rules are adhered to.)

```
<meta http-equiv="Content-Type" content="text/html; charset=utf-8" />
```

- After the connection to the MySQL server was made, communication was changed over to Unicode with *SET NAMES 'utf8'*:

```
$db = new MyDb();
$db->execute("SET NAMES 'utf8'");
```

- All calls to *htmlspecialchars($txt)* were replaced by *htmlspecialchars($txt, ENT_COMPAT, "UTF-8")*. To minimize typing, the new function *htmlspecial_utf8* was defined in mylibraryfunctions.php.

```
function htmlspecial_utf8($txt) {
  return htmlspecialchars($txt, ENT_COMPAT, "UTF-8"); }
```

Open problems: In the example code, there are some string functions that are incompatible with UTF-8. Particularly problematic is the function *explode* in titleform.php, which decomposes a string of several authors (e.g., *"name1;name2"*) into individual names. When the user inputs an author name whose UTF-8 encoding contains a byte with the code 59 (the ASCII code for the semicolon character), the name will be broken into two pieces at that point. Unfortunately, such invalid UTF-8 strings may well exist. (Not every random sequence of byte codes yields a valid UTF-8 string.)

In my tests such an error did not occur. However, if you fancy using titleform.php for the input of Japanese or Chinese book titles with several authors, sooner or later such an error will occur. Here the function *mb_split* from the *mbstring* extension would come to your aid.

Another problematic function is *stripslashes*, though in our example it should not lead to any errors. It is used in the example a number of times to remove the backslash escape character from form data. (Depending on the configuration, PHP inserts backslashes automatically. Further information can be found in any good PHP book under the heading *Magic Quotes*.)

The function *stripslashes* is not UTF-8 compatible, but that is true also of the automatic quoting by *Magic Quotes*, so any errors should cancel themselves out. However, most secure would be to deactivate *Magic Quotes* by setting *magic_quotes_gpc = Off* in php.ini.

The character set in the mylibrary database: All tables of the *mylibrary* database use the *Latin1* character set (see also Chapter 8, where the design of the database is described in detail). At first sight it might seem surprising that converting the tables to UTF-8 is not absolutely necessary. Yet the example works at the first try, since the MySQL server automatically converts all strings between UTF-8 (PHP code) and *Latin1* (database). However, a loss of information can occur if a user inputs Unicode characters that cannot be represented in the *Latin1* character set.

Thus it makes sense to convert a PHP project to UTF-8 only if the underlying database is converted to UTF-8. To convert existing table data, use the following SQL command:

```
ALTER TABLE tblname CONVERT TO CHARACTER SET 'utf8' [COLLATE 'utf8-...']
```

Binary Data (BLOBs) and Images

One of the most frequently raised questions in PHP and MySQL newsgroups and discussion forums is this: How can I give visitors to my website the ability to upload images that later can be displayed? In this section I will answer the question using an example project (see Figure 15-16) that demonstrates the required programming techniques.

Figure 15-16. *Storing and displaying images*

Fundamentals and Programming Techniques

Database Design

The starting point for our example is the database *testimages* with the table *images*. The *CREATE TABLE* command shows the structure of the table:

```
CREATE TABLE images (
  id    BIGINT        NOT NULL AUTO_INCREMENT,
  name  VARCHAR(100)  NOT NULL,
  type  VARCHAR(100)  NOT NULL,
  image LONGBLOB      NOT NULL,
  ts    TIMESTAMP     NOT NULL,
  PRIMARY KEY  (id))
```

The *images* table contains in addition to the usual primary index *id* the column *name* for describing the image, *type* for storing the image format (e.g., *"JPEG IMAGE"*), *image* for storing the image data, as well as *ts* for logging the time of insertion.

■**Caution** From the point of view of efficiency, it is not a good idea to store images or other large binary data sets in a database. For such purposes, a traditional file system is much more suitable. Databases with many BLOBs suffer a loss of speed, above all because it is difficult for the database system to store needed data and indexes temporarily in RAM. It is therefore more efficient to store images as normal files and store only the file names in the database.

In practice, however, the storage of binary in BLOBs is relatively common, for two reasons: First, managing data (e.g., backups, migrating the server) is easier when all the data are stored in a central location; and second, many ISPs do not allow local files to be created and read with PHP scripts or other programming code.

The HTML Form for File Transfer

To offer an HTML page the possibility of transferring a file to a web server, you need a specially constructed form. Most important is that the attributes *method* and *enctype* be correctly set. The input field for the file name (which the browser automatically equips with the Browse button) is formed of an *<input>* field with the attribute *type = "file"*.

If you wish to limit the file size, you can do so with a hidden field with the attribute *name="MAX_FILE_SIZE"*. The following lines show the code for the upload form, where the file size is restricted to 200KB. The form is formatted as a table for easier viewing. The layout of the table elements is accomplished by the file table.css.

```
<form method="post" action="filename.php"
      enctype="multipart/form-data" >
  <input type="hidden" value="204800" name="MAX_FILE_SIZE" />
  filename: <input name="imgfile" type="file" />
  <input type="submit" value="OK" name="submitbtn" />
</form>
```

PHP Evaluation of the $_FILES Field

The PHP script that is called with the form data contains the usual form fields as usual in the *$_POST* field (i.e., *$_POST['descr']* with the description of the image as well as *$_POST['submitbtn']* with the string *'OK'*). The information on the file to be transferred is to be found in the *$_FILES* field. Access is in accord with the example form shown above via the key *'imgfile'* (see the *name* attribute with *<input type="file">*), and it returns again a field. Its elements give information on the transferred file:

```
$imgfile = $_FILES['imgfile'];
$name    = $imgfile['name'];      // file name (without volume/path)
$type    = $imgfile['type'];      // file type, e.g., "image/gif"
$size    = $imgfile['size'];      // file size in Bytes
$uperr   = $imgfile['error'];     // error number (0 = no error)
$tmpfile = $imgfile['tmp_name'];  // name of the local temporary file
```

The transferred file is stored by the web server in a temporary file (file name *$tmpfile*). This file can be read by the PHP script, for example with the functions *fopen* and *fread*. Note that this file is automatically deleted after the execution of the PHP script.

The file transfer is a relatively dangerous operation from a security point of view. Therefore, it is recommended to validate the code for further processing of the file. The following query tests whether *$tmpfile* is empty, whether a transmission error has occurred, or whether the specified file is not a file that has been transferred (*is_uploaded_file*) but is a local file. This validation is necessary so that an attacker cannot attempt to evaluate a local system file (e.g., the Unix/Linux password file /etc/passwd). Such cases have occurred in the past.

```
if(!$tmpfile or $uperr or !is_uploaded_file($tmpfile))
  echo "<p>error ...</p>\n";
else {
  ... // read and process the temporary file
}
```

Optionally, you could also evaluate the file type and size in the validation query.

Storing the Transferred File in the MySQL Database

To store the transferred file in the MySQL database, read the entire file into a variable and execute an *INSERT* command. In the simplest case, the code looks like this:

```
$file = fopen($tmpfile, "rb");  // open file (read-only, binary)
$imgdata = fread($file, $size); // read file
fclose($file);
$mysqli->query(
  "INSERT INTO images (image) " .
  "VALUES ('" . $mysqli->escape_string($imgdata) . "')");
```

In the code of the example program presented further below, the *INSERT* command is somewhat more complicated, since in addition to the MIME type of the image (e.g., *"GIF image"*) the file name or an image description is to be stored.

Displaying Images from a MySQL Database

It is somewhat more complicated to read an image out of a MySQL database and display it within an HTML document. Basically, it is impossible to create an HTML document in a PHP script (which is the usual task of such a script) and at the same time generate the data for representing an image. The two tasks must be separated into two PHP scripts.

The first (usual) script creates the HTML page including the *<img>* tag for the image. However, the name of the local image file is not specified in this tag, as is otherwise usual, but instead, the name of the second PHP script together with the ID number of the image.

```
// PHP-Script pictures.php
echo "<img src=\"showpic.php?id=$id"\" />";
```

The browser gets to see, for example, the tag *<img src="showpic.php?id=3" />* and it now calls the second script showpic.php?id=3. Its code looks like this (somewhat simplified):

```
// PHP-Script showpic.php
$result = $mysqli->query("SELECT image FROM images WHERE id = $id");
$row = $result->fetch_object();
header("GIF image");  // file type
echo $row->image;
```

Actually, a bit more code is required to create the database connection, determine *$id*, and protect the script against possible errors. If the image database contains not only GIF images but also bitmaps in other forms, the file type, set by *header*, must also be determined from the database. What is crucial at this point is that the second PHP script not create a second HTML file and not create any output with *echo* before the *header* function is called. This function advises the PHP interpreter to create not the usual HTML text file, but an image file.

Processing Large Files

If you wish to allow for the transfer of very large files, you should pay attention to several factors:

- The limit for the maximal size of a transferred file must be set sufficiently high. The limit is set in the PHP configuration file php.ini with the variable *upload_max_filesize* (default value 2MB).

- The limit for *POST* transfers must also be sufficiently great (php.ini, variable *post_max_size*, default value 8MB).

- The PHP interpreter must be capable of reserving enough memory to process files of the maximal size envisioned (php.ini, variable *memory_limit*, default value 8 MByte).

- The PHP interpreter must give the script sufficient time for processing the data (php.ini, variable *max_execution_time*). The default value of 30 seconds is generally too small for large files.

- The variable *max_input_time* may have to be increased (default value 60 seconds). This variable specifies how much time is to be taken for the the transfer of data over the Internet.

- For the transfer of an image between the PHP script and MySQL server to succeed, the maximal packet size (which limits the *INSERT* command, for example) must be sufficiently large. The MySQL variable *max_allowed_packet* can be changed either in the MySQL configuration file (/etc/my.cnf or my.ini) or with the SQL command *SET max_allowed_packet=n*. The default value is a measly 1MB!

Program Code

The entire code of the example project consists of the following files, which are to be found in the directory images:

connect.php	Offers the functions *connect_to_picdb* and *array_item*.
images.php	Displays a table with the last ten images and a form for transferring additional images. The script contains as well the code for evaluation of the form.
showpic.php	Displays a single image.
table.css	CSS file for formatting tables.

connect.php

This file contains two functions: *connect_to_picdb* creates a connection to the MySQL database *testimages*, while *array_item* reads an element from a PHP field (if it exists).

```
// example file images/connect.php
function connect_to_picdb() {
  $mysqluser = "root";        // user name
  $mysqlpw   = "xxxx";        // password
  $mysqlhost = "localhost";   // name of the computer on which MySQL is running
  $mysqldb   = "testimages";  // name of the database
  $mysqli = new mysqli($mysqlhost, $mysqluser, $mysqlpw, $mysqldb);
  if(mysqli_connect_errno()) {
    echo "<p>Sorry, no connection to database ...",
         "</p></body></html>\n";
    exit();  }
  return $mysqli;
}
```

images.php

The code in images.php is divided into three parts. The first part is responsible for processing the form data. When a file has been transferred without error, the contents of the table *images* are stored.

The *switch* construction evaluates the type of the transferred file and then returns a new MIME string. (MIME stands for *multipurpose internet mail extensions.* Originally, MIME was used only for email attachments, but now MIME also controls how a web browser with a variety of data types should behave.) The MIME type must be specified when an image is displayed and is therefore stored together with every image in the *images* table. Unfortunately, the *type* information after a file transfer does not correspond to MIME, but instead uses other strings (which in addition depend on the web browser).

```php
<!DOCTYPE HTML PUBLIC "-//W3C//DTD HTML 4.01 Transitional//EN"
  "http://www.w3.org/TR/html4/loose.dtd">
<html><head> ... </head><body>
<?php    // images/images.php
include("connect.php");
$mysqli = connect_to_picdb();
// Part I: store the image
$submitbtn = array_item($_POST,  'submitbtn');
$descr =     array_item($_POST,  'descr');
$imgfile =   array_item($_FILES, 'imgfile');
// are there form data to be processed?
if($submitbtn == 'OK' and is_array($imgfile)) {
  $name    = $imgfile['name'];
  $type    = $imgfile['type'];
  $size    = $imgfile['size'];
  $uperr   = array_item($imgfile, 'error');
  $tmpfile = $imgfile['tmp_name'];
  if(!$descr) $descr = $name;
  switch ($type) {
  case "image/gif":
    $mime = "GIF Image";  break;
  case "image/jpeg":
  case "image/pjpeg":
    $mime = "JPEG Image"; break;
  case "image/png":
  case "image/x-png":
    $mime = "PNG Image";  break;
  default:
    $mime = "unknown";    }
  if(!$tmpfile or $uperr or $mime == "unknown" or
     !is_uploaded_file($tmpfile))
    echo "<p>error message ...</p>\n";
  else {
    // read file and store it in the database
    $file = fopen($tmpfile, "rb");
    $imgdata = fread($file, $size);
    fclose($file);
    if(!$mysqli->query(
        "INSERT INTO images (name, type, image) " .
        "VALUES ('" . $mysqli->escape_string($descr) . "', " .
        "         '$mime', " .
        "         '" . $mysqli->escape_string($imgdata) . "')"))
      printf("<p>error message ...: %s</p>\n", $mysqli->error);
  }
}
```

The second code segment serves to read the last ten images from the database and display them in a table. As described earlier, the actual display of the images is delegated to the script showpic.php.

```php
// Part II: Display the most recently inserted images
echo "<h2>last inserted images ...</h2>\n";
$sql =
  "SELECT id, name, " .
  "DATE_FORMAT(ts, '%Y/%c/%e %k:%i') AS dt " .
  "FROM images ORDER BY ts DESC LIMIT 10";
$result = $mysqli->query($sql);
if($result->num_rows==0)
  echo "<p>There are no more images ...</p>\n";
else {
  // display the images in a table
  while($row = $result->fetch_object())
    $rows[] = $row;
  echo "<table>\n<tr>";
  for($i=0; $i<sizeof($rows); $i++)  // first line: images
    echo "<th>",
      "<img src=\"showpic.php?id=" .
      $rows[$i]->id . "\" /></th>";
  echo "</tr>\n<tr>";
  for($i=0; $i<sizeof($rows); $i++)  // second line: text
    echo "<td>", htmlspecialchars($rows[$i]->name), "</td>";
  echo "</tr>\n<tr>";
  for($i=0; $i<sizeof($rows); $i++)  // third line: date
    echo "<td>", $rows[$i]->dt, "</td>";
  echo "</tr>\n</table>\n";
}
```

The third part of images.php contains the HTML code for the form for transferring additional images. The form is contained within a table that helps with the formatting.

```php
// Part III: represent the form
?>
<h2>image upload</h2>
<p>maximal file size: 200 kByte.
   allowed formats: PNG, JPEG, and GIF.</p>
<table>
<form method="post" action="images.php"
      enctype="multipart/form-data">
  <input type="hidden" value="204800" name="MAX_FILE_SIZE" />
  <tr><td>description (optional):</td>
      <td><input name="descr" type="text" /></td></tr>
  <tr><td>file name:</td>
      <td><input name="imgfile" type="file" /></td></tr>
  <tr><td></td>
      <td><input type="submit" value="OK"
          name="submitbtn" /></td></tr>
</form>
</table>
</body></html>
```

Stored Procedures

Fortunately, there is little to write on the subject of stored procedures: calling SQL commands that call or changes stored procedures (*CREATE FUNCTION*, etc.) is done via the usual *mysqli* methods. The following points show the possible cases.

Calling a stored procedure that returns no records: For this you can use either *$mysqli->real_query* or *$mysqli->query*.

```
$sql = "CALL categories_insert('abc', 123, @newcatID)";
$ok = $mysqli->real_query($sql);
```

Calling a stored procedure that returns records (one *SELECT* command): For such commands you would generally use *$mysql->query*, since this method immediately returns the result.

```
$sql = "CALL categories_select(123)";
$result = $mysqli->query($sql);
```

Calling a stored procedure that returns several records (several SELECTs) or calling several SQL commands: If several *SELECT* commands are executed in a stored procedure, the procedure returns several lists of records. For these to be processed, the command must be executed with *$mysqli->multi_query*. To read the list of records, use *use_result* or *store_result*, and for navigation to the next record list, use *next_result*.

```
$sql = "CALL many_selects(123)";
$ok = $mysqli->multi_query($sql);
```

You can also use *multi_query* when you wish to execute several SQL commands simultaneously (regardless of how many lists of records you expect as result). The SQL commands must be separated by semicolons.

```
$sql = "SET @myvar=1;
        CALL complicated_calculation(123, @myvar);
        SELECT * FROM table WHERE id=@myvar";
$ok = $mysqli->multi_query($sql);
```

Definition of a new stored procedure (CREATE command): In most PHP applications it is seldom necessary to define new stored procedures. If that is the case, however, you must use *real_query* or *query* to execute *CREATE FUNCTION* or *CREATE PROCEDURE*, and never *multi_query*. The reason is that *multi_query* interprets the semicolon as a separator between commands. But semicolons also appear in the code of stored procedures. If you wish to execute a *DROP* command before a *CREATE* command, the two commands must be executed separately.

```
$sql = "DROP PROCEDURE IF EXISTS mysp";
$ok  = $mysqli->real_query($sql);
$sql = "CREATE PROCEDURE mysp (OUT abc DOUBLE)
    BEGIN
      DECLARE t, subt VARCHAR(100);
      ...
    END";
$ok  = $mysqli->real_query($sql);
```

Note You can also use stored procedures if you use the older *mysql* interface for PHP programming. The only restriction involves the *mysqli* method *multi_query*, for which there is no equivalent *mysql* function. Strings containing several commands must therefore be split up and the commands executed separately.

SP Administrator

As of March 2005, the available MySQL user interfaces were unsuitable for convenient processing, administration, and testing of stored procedures (SPs). Until professional tools for this purpose appear, the program SP Administrator introduced here is a good stopgap. At the same time, it can serve as a PHP example program of independent interest.

Though SP Administrator does not distinguish itself through an elegant interface, such as phpMyAdmin will probably offer in the near future, the program does take care of the following everyday SP tasks efficiently and effortlessly:

- Create new SPs (with code template)

- Edit SPs

- Execute and test SPs, clear display of arbitrarily many *SELECT* results

- Delete SPs

- Back up and restore all SPs in a database

The program demonstrates some interesting programming techniques and various aspects of how to use SPs with PHP.

Installation

The code of SP Administrator is located in the directory spadmin with the example files. The file password.php needs to be modified. If the user specified there is not *root*, that user needs privileges to define and execute SPs (*Execute* privilege).

Using the Program

The program's entire user interface is on the page spadmin.php. There you must first select a database. Then in a second form you can choose the action that you wish to take (see above). With some operations (*ALTER, CALL, DROP*) you must also select the desired SP. (Caution: Deletion of SPs is carried out without preliminary warning.) Figure 15-17 shows the program processing an SP.

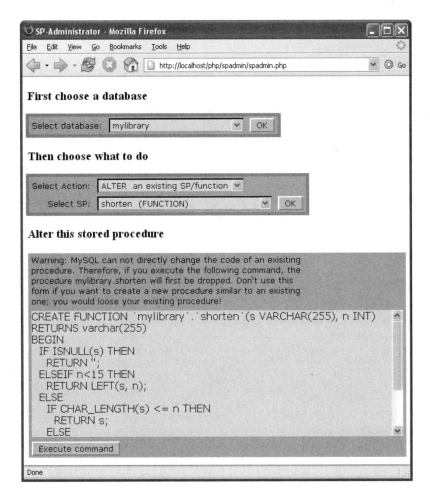

Figure 15-17. *Changing an SP*

Trying Out SPs

If you select the action *CALL A PROCEDURE,* you can specify several commands in the input region, which then will all be executed. All *SELECT* results that arise will be output one after the other (see Figure 15-18).

Figure 15-18. *Trying out an SP*

Backing Up and Restoring SPs

When you execute the action BACKUP ALL SPs, most browsers should display a dialog for storing the resulting file sp.sql. This file contains SQL instructions to re-create all the SPs in the current database. The following lines show in part what such a file looks like:

```
DELIMITER $$
DROP PROCEDURE IF EXISTS mylibrary.cursortest$$
CREATE PROCEDURE `mylibrary`.`cursortest`(OUT avg_len DOUBLE)
BEGIN
  DECLARE t, subt VARCHAR(100);
  ...
  SET avg_len = n/cnt;
END$$
DROP FUNCTION IF EXISTS mylibrary.faculty$$
CREATE FUNCTION `mylibrary`.`faculty`(n BIGINT) RETURNS BIGINT
BEGIN
  ...
END$$
DELIMITER ;
```

Restore SPs leads to a form in which you can read in the backup file. The file must be in the form given above.

■**Caution** The *restore* function ignores the *DELIMITER* instructions in the backup file and always uses $$ as the separator between SQL commands.

SP Administrator is unable to set the character set for backup and restore. It always uses *Latin1*.

The backup format is chosen in such a way that the backup file can be restored with the command mysql:

```
user$ mysql -u root -p --default-characterset=latin1 databasename < sp.sql
Password: *******
```

Code

The code is divided among the following files:

---

spadmin.php	Start page
spfunctions.php	Auxiliary functions
backup.php	Transfers the text file sp.php with the backup of all SPs to the browser (file download)
password.php	MySQL login data
formfunctions.php	Functions for output of a form
sp.css	CSS file for formatting forms and tables

The program uses a host of session variables, within which the inputs of all three forms are stored, so that they are available again after a page change. The evaluation of the form data and management of the session variables is accomplished with the code in spadmin.php. The actual work is done by functions in spfunctions.php, and in what follows we shall present the most interesting of them.

Form for SP Selection

The function *show_sp_form* displays the form for selecting an SP and an action (e.g., *ALTER*). The function *show_sp_form* accesses various *form_xxx* functions from formfunctions.php. The list of available SPs is determined by a *SELECT* query for the table *information_schema.routines*, where the procedure or function name and the type are concatenated into a character string of the form *name_type* with *CONCAT*. This string is entered as a *value* attribute in the elements of the listbox and decomposed into its components when an SP is selected (variables *spname* and *type*).

```
// example file spfunctions.php
function show_sp_form($mysqli, $formdata, $dbname) {
  form_start("spadmin.php");
  form_new_line();
  form_label("Select Action:");
  $rows = array(array('ALTER  an existing SP/function', 'alter'),
                array('CALL   a procedure/function', 'call'),
                ...
                array('Restore SPs', 'restore'));
```

```
    form_list("action", $rows, $formdata["action"],
      "[choose an action]");
    form_empty_cell();
    form_end_line();
    form_new_line();
    form_label("Select SP:");
    $sql = "SELECT CONCAT(routine_name, '  (', routine_type, ')')
                AS displayname,
              CONCAT(routine_type, '_', routine_name) AS internalname
            FROM information_schema.routines
            WHERE routine_schema = '$dbname'
            ORDER BY displayname";
    $rows = queryArray($mysqli, $sql);
    form_list("spname", $rows, array_item($formdata, "spname"),
            "[choose a SP]");
    form_button("btnAction", "OK");
    form_end_line();
    form_end();
}
```

Executing and Testing SPs

To test an SP, the user can specify arbitrary SQL commands in the form provided for this purpose (see Figure 15-18). These are passed in the variable *cmd* to the function *test_sp*. This function displays the SQL code (auxiliary function *printsql* in spfunctions.php) and then executes *$mysqli->multi_query*.

   If PHP detects an error during command execution (which at present is the case only if the error occurs in the first SQL command), *printerror* steps in to display various error messages. Then all available results are read with *store_result* and *next_result* and then output with *show_table* in attractive tables. (*printerror* and *show_table* are auxiliary functions that are defined in spfunctions.php.)

```
// example file spfunctions.php
function test_sp($mysqli, $dbname, $cmd) {
  echo "<h3>Results of SQL command(s)</h3>\n";
  $mysqli->select_db($dbname);
  printsql($cmd);
  $ok = $mysqli->multi_query($cmd);
  if($mysqli->info)
    printerror("Info: " . $mysqli->info);
  if($mysqli->warning_count)
    printerror("Warnings: " . $mysqli->warning_count);
  if($mysqli->errno)
    printerror("Error: " . $mysqli->error);
  if($ok) {
    do {
      $result = $mysqli->store_result();
      if($result) {
        show_table($result);
        $result->close();
      }
    } while($mysqli->next_result());
  }
}
```

Backing Up SPs (File Download)

The function *backup_sps* returns a string with the SQL commands for an SP backup. The function first returns a list of all SPs (functions and procedures) and then executes *SHOW CREATE* for each function. The results of these commands are then collected in the variable *result*. In the process, each *CREATE* command is prefixed by a *DROP IF EXISTS*, so that any existing SPs are first deleted without an error message and then redefined.

```
// example file spfunctions.sp
$separator = "$$";
function backup_sps($mysqli, $dbname) {
  global $separator;
  $sep    = $separator . "\n";
  $result = "DELIMITER $sep";
  $sql    = "SELECT routine_name, routine_type
             FROM information_schema.routines
             WHERE routine_schema = '$dbname'";
  $rows   = queryArray($mysqli, $sql);
  foreach($rows as $row) {
    $spname = $row[0];
    $type = $row[1];
    if($type=="FUNCTION") {
      $sql     = "SHOW CREATE FUNCTION $dbname.$spname";
      $create  = queryArray($mysqli, $sql);
      $result .= "DROP FUNCTION IF EXISTS $dbname.$spname" . $sep .
                 $create[0]["Create Function"] . $sep;
    }
    else {
      $sql     = "SHOW CREATE PROCEDURE $dbname.$spname";
      $create  = queryArray($mysqli, $sql);
      $result .= "DROP PROCEDURE IF EXISTS $dbname.$spname" . $sep .
                 $create[0]["Create Procedure"] . $sep;
    }
  }
  $result .= "DELIMITER ;\n";
  return $result;  }
```

The function *backup_sps* is called by the page backup.php?dbname=name. How a file download is realized is demonstrated by backup.php. Instead of creating an HTML page, as is usual, three *header* calls have the effect that the browser recognizes the data as a text file (type *text/plain*) and treats it as an attachment. The data are therefore not displayed in the browser, but instead, a Save dialog appears. The *Expires* instruction makes it clear to the browser and any intermediate web proxy that this file is not suitable for temporary cache storage. After these preparations, the actual backup data are simply output with *echo*.

```
// example file backup.php
require_once 'spfunctions.php';
require_once 'password.php';
$dbname = array_item($_REQUEST, 'dbname');
if(!$dbname)
  exit;
else
  $dbname = urldecode($dbname);
$mysqli = @new mysqli($mysqlhost, $mysqluser, $mysqlpasswd);
```

```
if(mysqli_connect_errno()) {
  html_start('MySQL connection error');
  printerror("Sorry, no connection!");
  html_end();
  exit(); }
header('Content-Type: text/plain');
header('Content-Disposition: attachment; filename="sp.sql"');
header('Expires: ' . gmdate('D, d M Y H:i:s') . ' GMT');
echo backup_sps($mysqli, $dbname);
```

It remains to discuss how the page backup.php is called. This step takes place in spadmin.php during the evaluation of the form data. The name of the database that is to be stored is coded by *urlencode*, so that any special characters that might be present will not cause any problems.

```
// example file spadmin.php
if($action=='backup') {
  header("Location: " . baseurl() . "/backup.php?dbname=" .
    urlencode($dbname));
  exit; }
```

Restoring an SP (File Upload)

While a backup is involved in transferring data from the server to the client, now the data transport goes in the opposite direction. A form with an *<input>* of type *file* is used for selecting the file in the client file system. In addition to such fields, the browser displays a SEARCH button. If this button is clicked, a file-selection dialog appears. The form is created with *show_restore_form*, which we do not show here. The following lines show instead the form code (without layout elements for the sake of clarity).

```
<form  method="post" action="spadmin.php"
        enctype="multipart/form-data" >
<input type="hidden" name="MAX_FILE_SIZE" value="100000" />
<input type="file" size="40" name="spfile" />
<input type="submit" value="Restore" name="form[btnRestore]" />
</form>
```

The evaluation of the form data takes place in spadmin.php. If the data seem to be error-free, the contents of the file are read into the variable *sql* and passed to the function *restore_sps*.

```
// example file spadmin.php
$formdata = array_item($_POST, "form");
if(array_item($formdata, 'btnRestore')) {
  $spfile  = array_item($_FILES, 'spfile');
  if($spfile && is_array($spfile)){
    $uperr   = $spfile['error'];    // error number (0 = no error)
    $tmpfile = $spfile['tmp_name']; // local, temporary file
    $size    = $spfile['size'];
    if(!$uperr && $size>0 && $tmpfile && is_uploaded_file($tmpfile)) {
      $file = fopen($tmpfile, "rb");  // open file
      $sql  = fread($file, $size);    // read file
      fclose($file);
      restore_sps($mysqli, $sql);
}}}
```

The function *restore_sps* decomposes the string with *explode* into separate SQL commands, where *separator* is used as a separator. Then each command that is not empty or contains *DELIMITER* is executed.

The function *restore_sps* uses two auxiliary functions whose code is also located in sp-functions.php: *printsql* outputs the code of the command to the website (as feedback), and *execute* executes *$mysqli->real_query* and displays if necessary an error message.

```
// example file spfunctions.php
function restore_sps($mysqli, $sql) {
  global $separator;
  echo "<h3>Restore SPs</h3>\n";
  $cmds = explode($separator, $sql);
  foreach($cmds as $cmd)
    if(trim($cmd)!="" && strpos($cmd, "DELIMITER")===FALSE) {
      printsql($cmd);
      $ok = execute($mysqli, $cmd);
      if($ok) echo "<font color=\"#00cc00\">OK</font>\n";}
}
```

CHAPTER 16

■■■

Perl

For many years, Perl has been the best-beloved scripting language in the Unix/Linux universe. Moreover, Perl continues to play an important role as a programming language for CGI scripts, by which dynamic websites can be realized. This chapter gives a brief introduction to MySQL database access with Perl and shows, by means of a few examples, the considerable bandwidth of possible applications.

Programming Techniques

This chapter assumes that Perl and the modules *DBI* and *DBD::mysql* are installed on your computer and that they are functioning properly. An introduction to the installation procedure can be found in Chapter 1.

Further information on both Perl modules can be found in the official MySQL documentation (the chapter "MySQL APIs"). Furthermore, the command perldoc nets you extensive on-line help:

```
perldoc DBI
perldoc DBI::FAQ
perldoc DBD::mysql
```

HTML versions of these three help pages can be found at, for example, http://search.cpan.org/. Finally, a compact reference to DBI functions and methods can be found in Chapter 23.

The Modules DBI and DBD::mysql

Access to MySQL is carried out in Perl via the modules *DBI* and *DBD::mysql*. (The abbreviation "DBI" stands for *database interface*, while "DBD" stands for *database driver*.) *DBI* is a general interface for database programming, independent of particular database systems. Thus DBI can be used for database programming with Oracle, DB2, etc. Ideally, the code is the same in every case; that is, you can switch database systems without changing the Perl code (with the exception of *datasource* character strings for establishing the connection).

DBD::mysql is used by *DBI* to communicate with MySQL. (There exist comparable driver modules for a host of other database systems.) Which driver module *DBI* must use is determined by the character string specified when the connection is established (method *connect*). Therefore, the instruction *use DBI* at the beginning of the Perl script suffices for incorporating the DBI module.

Although *DBI* actually follows a process that is independent of the database, *DBD:: mysql* makes available a number of MySQL-specific functions. The reason for this is that DBI constitutes the greatest common denominator of all database systems, and thus is relatively small. The use of MySQL-specific functions simplifies MySQL programming with Perl considerably, but leads, of course, to the result that the code can be ported to another database system only with difficulty.

DBI and *DBD* are object-oriented modules. For this reason, most of their functions are available in the form of methods, which are applied to objects (which in Perl are represented by *handles*). For example, *DBI->connect* returns a handle to a *database* object (which is usually stored in the variable *$dbh*). Various functions that affect the database can now be executed as methods of this object, for example, *$dbh->do("INSERT ...")*, for executing an SQL command.

Establishing a Connection to the Database

The database connection is established with the DBI method *connect*. The first parameter to this method is a character string specifying the type of the database and the name of the computer (or *localhost*). The syntax of the character string can be deduced from the following example. The next two parameters must contain the user name and password.

A fourth, optional, parameter can be used to specify numerous attributes. For example, *'RaiseError'=>1* has the effect that the Perl script is ended with an error message if the connection to the database cannot be established. A reference to additional connection attributes for the fourth parameter can be found in Chapter 23.

```
use DBI;
$datasource   = "DBI:mysql:database=mylibrary;host=localhost";
$user = "root";
$passw = "xxx";
$dbh = DBI->connect($datasource, $user, $passw,
  {'RaiseError' => 1});
```

With RHEL and Fedora, SELinux is configured in such a way that Apache and PHP are not permitted to access the MySQL socket file. Therefore, instead of *localhost*, the actual name of the computer must be given. Communication with the MySQL server now takes place via TCP/IP instead of the socket file.

■Tip Note that older versions of DBD::mysql do not support the new password system since MySQL 4.1 (error message *Client does not support authentication protocol requested by server*). If the installation of a newer version of DBD::mysql is impossible, you must launch the MySQL server with the option --old-passwords or insert entries with the SQL function *OLD_PASSWORD*. More detail on this can be found in Chapter 11.

Specifying the Configuration File (Unix/Linux Only)

If you are working under Unix/Linux, you can you may specify the name of a configuration file in which the user name, password, and possible additional connection options are specified in the *datasource* character string. This is practical if such configuration files are stored in the home directories of the users. (Information on creating configuration files can be found in Chapter 22.)

In the following example, the option *mysql_read_default_file* specifies the location of the configuration file (relative to the home directory from the environment variable *HOME*). The option *mysql_read_default_group* specifies the group *[mygroup]* within the configuration file. If this option is not used, then *connect* automatically evaluates the group *[client]*. The second and third parameters to the method *connect* are both specified as *undef*, to make it clear that the user name and password are specified in another location:

```
$datasource = "DBI:mysql:database=mylibrary;" .
    "mysql_read_default_file=$ENV{HOME}/.my.cnf;" .
    "mysql_read_default_group=mygroup";
$dbh = DBI->connect($datasource, undef, undef, {'RaiseError' => 1});
```

The associated configuration file ~/.my.cnf might look like the following:

```
[mygroup]
user=root
password=xxx
host=uranus.sol
```

Please note that access rights to this file are set in such a way that only the user is allowed to read it.

Under Windows, I was unable to evaluate a configuration file with *DBI->connect()*. This function appears to be available only under Unix/Linux (though such a restriction is not explicitly documented).

Terminating the Connection

All accesses to the database are attained via the variable *$dbh* (or from variables derived from it). When the connection to the database is no longer needed, it should be closed with *disconnect*:

```
$dbh->disconnect();
```

Persistent Connections

The Perl DBI module itself offers no possibility of making use of persistent connections in order to minimize the time for repeated establishment of a connection to the database. You can, however, achieve persistent connections by a slight detour.

If you execute CGI Perl scripts via the Apache module *mod_perl* (which is recommended for reasons of efficiency), you achieve by use of the Perl module *Apache::DBI* that MySQL connections remain after the script has ended and are reused when another script requires the same type of MySQL connection. To use the module you have merely to insert *use Apache::DBI* before all *use DBI* commands in your script. No other changes are necessary. (*Apache::DBI* replaces the *connect* method of *DBI* with its own version.) Additional information on *Apache::DBI* can be found at the following location: http://search.cpan.org/~abh/Apache-DBI/DBI.pm.

Note, however, that persistent connections have some drawbacks: They take over the connection in an unknown state; it could happen that the most recently executed script has changed some (system) variables, that the autocommit mode has been set in some undesired way, and so on.

Executing SQL Commands

SQL Commands Without Record List As Result

SQL commands that do not return a list of records are generally executed by means of *do*:

```
$n = $dbh->do("INSERT INTO authors (authName) " .
              "VALUES ('New author')");
```

Normally, *do* returns the number of altered data records. Other possible return values are as follows:

"0E0" means that no record has been changed. This character string can be changed into a number by means of an arithmetic operation (i.e., *$n+=0*).

-1 means that the number of changed records is unknown.

undef means that an error has occurred.

Determining AUTO_INCREMENT Values

After *INSERT* commands it is frequently necessary to determine the *AUTO_INCREMENT* value of the newly inserted data record. For this task, the attribute *mysql_insertid* of *DBD::mysql* is helpful:

```
$id = $dbh->{'mysql_insertid'};
```

■**Note** The attribute *mysql_insertid* is not portable; that is, it is available only for MySQL databases. In porting the code to another database system you will have to find another way of proceeding.

SELECT Queries

SQL commands that return a list of records (typically *SELECT* commands) cannot be executed with *do*. Instead, the query must first be prepared with *prepare*.

Since version 4.1, MySQL has been capable of executing prepared statements quite efficiently. However, only the current versions of *DBD::mysql* use the new MySQL functions. While *prepare* is available in older versions of *DBD::mysql*, it is somewhat slower.

The return value of *prepare* is a *statement handle*, which must be used for all further operations with the query, even for the method *execute*, in order actually to execute the query. (If an error occurs in the execution of the query, the return value is *undef*.)

```
$sth = $dbh->prepare("SELECT * FROM titles LIMIT 5");
$sth->execute();
```

Then the resulting records can be output with *$sth*, about which we shall have more to say in the next section. When the evaluation is complete, the resources bound to *$sth* should be released with *finish*:

```
$sth->finish();      # delete query object
```

SQL Queries with Wild Cards for Parameters

It often happens that the same type of query needs to be executed over and over with varying parameters (*WHERE id=1, WHERE id=3*, etc.). In such cases, *DBI* offers the possibility of replacing the parameters in *prepare* by a question mark, which serves as a wild card. Each question mark corresponds to a parameter, whose value must subsequently be specified with *execute*. Note that in *execute*, the correct order of the parameters must be adhered to. The following lines demonstrate how to proceed:

```
$sth = $dbh->prepare("SELECT * FROM titles " .
                     "WHERE catID=? AND publID=?");
$sth->execute(1, 1);  # titles with catID=1 und publID=2
...                   # evaluate results
$sth->execute(1, 2);  # tites with catID=1 und publID=2
...                   # evaluate results
$sth->finish();       # delete query object
```

In working with wild cards a few points should be noted: First of all, wild cards must be given in SQL commands unquoted (even if it is a character string). Secondly, the value passed to *execute* by the *DBI* module is dealt with automatically with *quote*, which places character strings in single quotation marks and prefixes a backslash to the apostrophe and backslash characters. If you wish to pass *NULL* to an SQL command, you must specify the value *undef*, which *quote* turns into *NULL*.

If you execute the commands

```
$sth = $dbh->prepare("INSERT INTO publishers (publName)" .
                     "VALUES (?)");
  $sth->execute("O'Reilly");
```

with Perl, then it is the following SQL command that is actually executed in MySQL:

```
INSERT INTO publishers (publName) VALUES ('O\'Reilly')
```

This example shows that *prepare* and *execute* are suitable not only for *SELECT* queries, but also for all SQL queries that need to be executed a number of times.

■Tip Wild cards can also be used when SQL commands are executed with *do*. This does not contribute to increased speed, but it does generally improve readability, since *DBI* takes care of both single quotation marks and *quote*:

```
$dbh->do("INSERT INTO table (cola, colb)
         VALUES (?, ?), undef, ($data1, $data2)");
```

Evaluating SELECT Queries

Provided that no error occurs in a query (test by *if(defined($sth))*), the resulting records can be read via the *statement handle* (i.e., *$sth*). There are several different methods for accomplishing this.

Reading Data Records with fetch Alias fetchrow_array

The two equivalent methods *fetch* and *fetchrow_array* return an array with the values of the next record. Within the array, the value *NULL* is expressed by *undef*. When the end of the record list is reached or if an error occurs, the array is empty. (To distinguish between these two cases, *$sth->err()* must be evaluated.) The following lines execute a query and display the results line by line. Here *NULL* is represented as a character string *<NULL>*:

```
$sth = $dbh->prepare("SELECT * FROM titles LIMIT 5");
$sth->execute();
while(@row = $sth->fetchrow_array()) {  # process all records
  foreach $field (@row) {               # each field
    if(defined($field)) {               # test whether NULL
      print "$field\t";
    } else {
      print "<NULL>\t";
    }
  }
  print "\n";
}
$sth->finish();
```

The evaluation of the columns in a *foreach* loop is rather the exception. To be sure, the individual columns could also be selected in the form *$row[n]*, where *n=0* must be specified for the first column. A further variant consists in assigning all the columns at once to the variables in question. Then, of course, the correct order of the variables must be heeded:

```
($titleID, $title, ...) = @row;
```

Selecting Individual Values

It is often clear from the outset that a query will return only a single value (e.g., *SELECT COUNT(*) FROM …*). In this case, neither a loop over all records nor an evaluation of all elements of an array is necessary. Instead, simply assign *fetchrow_array* to a scalar variable:

```
$sth = $dbh->prepare("SELECT COUNT(*) FROM titles");
$sth->execute();
$result = $sth->fetchrow_array();
print "$result\n";
$sth->finish();
```

■**Caution** You can use *fetchrow_array* in the scalar context (*$field = $sth->fetchrow_array()*) only if the *SELECT* result contains only one column. If the result has more than one column, the scalar result of *fetchrow_array* is undefined. It could be the first or equally the last column.

But in addition, the scalar evaluation of *fetchrow_array* is not without its problems. There are now three reasons for which *$field* can contain the value *undef*. The column contains *NULL* in the record in question, the last record was reached, or an error has occurred.

Instead of the code given above, you could use the following shorthand version:

```
$result = $dbh->selectrow_array("SELECT COUNT(*) ... ");
```

Binding Columns to Variables

In processing a *SELECT* command, instead of transmitting every data record manually in variables, you can automate this step and at the same time increase the efficiency and readability of your program a bit. To do this you bind the column of the query with *bind_col* to individual variables. Each time that *fetchrow_array* is executed, the associated variables contain the value of the new record. It is necessary that *bind_col* be executed after *execute*. The return value of *bind_col* is *false* if an error occurs. Please note that column numbering begins with 1 (not, as is usual in Perl, with 0):

```
$sth = $dbh->prepare("SELECT titleID, title FROM titles");
$sth->execute();
$sth->bind_col(1, \$titleID);
$sth->bind_col(2, \$title);
while($sth->fetchrow_array()) {
  print "$title $titleID\n";
}
$sth->finish();
$dbh->disconnect();
```

Instead of binding the variables individually, you can do this for all columns at once with *bind_columns*. Please observe the correct sequence and number of variables:

```
$sth->bind_columns(\$titleID, \$title);
```

Determining the Number of Data Records

The *DBI* module provides no possibility of determining the number of records returned by a *SELECT* command. (This has to do with the fact that with many database servers the records are transmitted to the module only when they are needed.) If you wish to know how many resulting records there are, you have the following options:

- You can count during the evaluation. (This variant is ruled out if you wish to know the number of records in advance.)

- You can execute the second query with *SELECT COUNT(*)* . . . . Depending on the application, this can be relatively costly.

- You may use the *DBI* method *fetchall_arrayref* (see below). Thereby all resulting records are transmitted together into a local array, so that the number can easily be determined.

- You may use the method *$sth->rows()*. This method can be evaluated after *execute()*. At first glance, this seems the obvious solution, but it has, in fact, a number of drawbacks:

    First, the method is not portable. (According to the *DBI* documentation, *rows* may be used to determine the altered records, say after *UPDATE* or *DELETE*, but not for investigating records read with *SELECT*.)

    Second, the method is itself available in conjunction with the *DBD::mysql* driver only when queries are evaluated without the attribute *mysql_use_result*. That is indeed the default setting, but it is not always particularly efficient.

Determining Column Names and Other Metainformation

If you wish to program a generally valid function for representing tables, you need not only the data themselves, but also metainformation about the data (column names, data types, etc.). This information is made available by *DBI* via various attributes of *$sth*:

$sth->{'NUM_OF_FIELDS'} returns the number of columns.

$sth->{'NAME'}* returns a pointer to an array with the names of all columns. The same holds for *$sth->{'NAME_lc'} and *$sth->{'NAME_uc'}*, but with the names all in lowercase or uppercase, respectively.

$sth->{'NULLABLE'} returns a pointer to an array whose values tell whether a column can contain *NULL*.

$sth->{'PRECISION'}* and *$sth->{'SCALE'} return pointers to arrays with the maximum number of characters and the number of decimal places, respectively.

$sth->{'TYPE'} returns a pointer to an array with numerical values that permit one to determine the data types of the columns.

The following loop demonstrates the evaluation of this information:

```
$sth = $dbh->prepare("SELECT * FROM testall");
$sth->execute();
for($i=0; $i < $sth->{'NUM_OF_FIELDS'}; $i++) {
  print @{$sth->{'NAME'}}[$i] . " " .
        @{$sth->{'TYPE'}}[$i] . "\n";
}
```

■**Tip** *DBD::mysql* makes available some additional attributes with MySQL-specific information. These attributes are presented in their own subsection of this chapter, together with other MySQL-specific (and therefore nonportable) extensions of the *DBI* module.

Reading Data Records with fetchrow_arrayref

The functioning of *fetchrow_arrayref* is similar to that of *fetchrow_array*. The sole difference is that now pointers (references) to arrays instead of the arrays themselves are returned. This method returns *undef* if the end of the data list is reached or an error has occurred.

```
while(my $arrayref = $sth->fetchrow_arrayref()) {
  foreach $field (@{$arrayref}) {
    ... as before
}
```

Reading Data Records with fetchrow_hashref

The method *fetchrow_hashref* returns an associative array (*hash*) with the values of the next data record. It returns *undef* if the end of the record list has been reached or an error has occurred.

Access to the individual columns is effected with *$row->{'columnname'}*. In providing the *columnname*, attention must be paid to case-sensitivity. The following lines demonstrate its application:

```
$sth = $dbh->prepare("SELECT title, titleID FROM titles LIMIT 5");
$sth->execute();
while($row = $sth->fetchrow_hashref()) {
  print "$row->{'title'}, $row->{'titleID'}\n";
}
$sth->finish();
$dbh->disconnect();
```

If *fetchrow_hashref* is called with the optional parameter *"NAME_lc"* or *"NAME_uc"*, then all the hash keys are transformed into lowercase or uppercase, respectively.

Reading All Data Records with fetchall_arrayref

A drawback to all the access methods described above is that the data records must be read sequentially, and thereafter, they are no longer available. It is thus impossible to move about to your heart's content in the list of data records. (Depending on the database system, this has at least the advantage that it is miserly with resources. Under MySQL, *fetchall_arrayref* does not exhibit this advantage because by default, all records that are found are immediately transmitted to the client. This can be avoided only by using the attribute *mysql_use_result*. More about *mysql_use_result* can be found further along in this section.)

If you wish to access all records in an arbitrary order and to do so multiple times, you could output the entire result of the query *fetchall_arrayref*. As result you obtain an array with pointers to the individual records, which themselves are arrays. Access to an individual element is then accomplished via *$result->[$row][$col]*, where the indices begin with 0:

```
$sth = $dbh->prepare("SELECT titleID, title FROM titles");
$sth->execute();
$result = $sth->fetchall_arrayref();
print "$result->[2][5]\n";  # third record, sixth column
$sth->finish();
$dbh->disconnect();
```

The number of records and columns can be determined as follows:

```
$rows = @{$result};
$cols = @{$result->[0]};
```

An optional parameter can be passed to *fetchall_arrayref*, which influences both the columns to be read and the organization of the data. The following command reads only the first, fourth, and last columns:

```
$result = $sth->fetchall_arrayref([0,3,-1]);
```

The following command reads all columns, but returns a pointer to an array that contains pointers to hashes. Access to individual elements is via *$result->[$row]->{'columnname'}*, as in, for example, *$result->[3]->{'titleID'}*:

```
$result = $sth->fetchall_arrayref({});
```

Our last example again returns hashes, but this time only for columns with the names *titleID* and *title*:

```
$result = $sth->fetchall_arrayref({titleID=>1, title=>1});
```

In general, it makes better sense to limit the number of columns in the *SELECT* command, instead of waiting for *fetchall_arrayref* to do so, after all the data have been extracted from the database. The method *fetchall_arrayref* can be executed only once per query. If you would like to execute the method more than once, you must execute *execute* before each call.

If the query has returned no result, then *fetchall_arrayref* returns a pointer to an empty array. If an error occurs during data selection, then *$result* contains all data read to that point. If in any event you are working without *'RaiseError' => 1*, then after *fetchall_arrayref*, you should see to it that *$sth->err()* is evaluated.

Instead of the three methods *prepare*, *execute*, and *fetchall_arrayref*, you can also use the shorthand form *$dbh->selectall_arrayref($sql)*.

Character Strings, BLOBs, DATEs, SETs, ENUMs, and NULL

Altering Data

To alter data records in your database you must transmit the relevant SQL commands as character strings to *do*. The structure of this character string must conform to the syntax of MySQL (see Chapter 21).

The starting point for the following description of the various data types is the variable *data*, which contains the data to be stored. The contents of this variable should be placed in an *INSERT* command, which is stored temporarily in the variable *sql*. In the simplest case, it goes like this:

```
$sql = "INSERT INTO tablename VALUES('$data1', '$data2', ...);
```

Dates and times: To format a date or time according to the MySQL official regulations, you must use the corresponding Perl function or module (for example, *gmtime()* or *TIME::Local*).

Timestamps: Perl and MySQL timestamps have the same meaning, but different formats. A Perl timestamp (function *time()*) is simply a 32-bit integer that gives the number of seconds since 1/1/1970. MySQL, on the other hand, expects a timestamp in the form *yyyy-dd-mm hh:mm:ss*.

As a rule, timestamps are used to mark the time of the most recent change. In such a case, you simply pass *NULL*, and MySQL automatically takes care of proper storage:

```
$sql .= "NULL";
```

On the other hand, if you would like to store a Perl timestamp as a MySQL timestamp, then you should use the MySQL function *FROM_UNIXTIME* in your *INSERT* or *UPDATE* command:

```
$data = time();  // data contains the current time as a Unix timestamp
$sql .= "FROM_UNIXTIME(" . $data . ")";
```

Character strings and BLOBs: If special characters occur in a character string or BLOB, then there are frequently problems with quotation. SQL requires that the single-quote, double-quote, 0-byte, and backslash characters be prefixed by a backslash.

If you place value on the portability of your Perl code, then you should use the method *$dbh->quote()* for quoting character strings. This method not only adds \ or \0 to the character string, but also encloses the character string in single quotation marks. Thus *$dbh->quote("ab'c")* returns *'ab\'c'*. (If you execute an SQL command with wild cards, *quote()* will be used automatically.)

```
$sql .= $dbh->quote($data);
```

In putting together SQL commands, the Perl construct *qq{}*, which returns the specified character string, is often useful. Within *qq{}*, variables are replaced by their contents (but not quoted). The advantage of *qq{}* over a direct concatenation of character strings with *$sql="INSERT ..."* is that within *qq{}* the single- and double-quote characters may be used:

```
$data = $dbh->quote($data);
$sql = qq{INSERT INTO table (col1, col2, col3)
        VALUES ($data, 'abc', PASSWORD("abc"))};
```

NULL: I am pleased to be able to inform you, dear reader, that *$dbh->quote()* also treats the value *undef* correctly, and in this case returns *NULL* (without a single quote):

```
$sql .= $dbh->quote($data);
```

If you do not wish to use *quote()*, then you might try the following:

```
$sql .= defined($data) ? "'$data'" : "NULL";
```

Please note that within an SQL character command you do not place *NULL* in quotation marks as if it were a character string.

Reading Data

The starting point for the following considerations is the variable *$data*, which contains a data field. For example, *$data* can be initialized as follows:

```
$sth = $dbh->prepare("SELECT * FROM titles");
$sth->execute();
@row = $sth->fetchrow_array();
$data = $row(0);
```

Timestamps: Timestamps in the form of a character string of the form 2005-12-31 23:59:59 are contained in *data*. This won't get you very far in Perl. If you want to work with the timestamp value in Perl, then use the MySQL function *UNIX_TIMESTAMP* and formulate the corresponding *SELECT* query. Then for the above date *data* contains the value 20051231235959:

```
SELECT ..., UNIX_TIMESTAMP(a_timestamp) FROM ...
```

Date: For a *DATETIME* column, *data* contains a character string of the form 2005-12-31 23:59:59. For *DATE* columns, the time information is lacking. For the further processing of dates in Perl, it is practical in many cases here, too, to use the function *UNIX_TIMESTAMP*. You can obtain any format you like with the MySQL format *DATE_FORMAT*. The following instruction results in *data* containing a character string of the form *'December 31 2005'*.

```
SELECT ..., DATE_FORMAT(a_date, '%M %d %Y')
```

Time: For a *TIME* column, *data* contains a character string of the form 23:59:59. If you do not wish to extract hours, minutes, and seconds from this character string, then the MySQL function

TIME_TO_SEC can be used to return the number of seconds since 00:00:00. Additionally, you can, of course, use any of the numerous MySQL functions for processing times. Warning: *UNIX_TIMESTAMP* does not work for *TIME* columns.

■**Tip** In Chapter 21 you will find an overview of the MySQL functions for processing and converting dates and times.

NULL: Since *$data* is as yet undefined, it contains *undef.* Whether *$data* contains *NULL* can be determined with the Perl function *defined($data)*. (Do not compare *$data* with " " or *0* to detect *NULL.* Both comparisons return *True*, though preceded by a Perl warning.)

Character strings and BLOBs: Perl, in contrast to C, has no difficulties with binary data; that is, even 0-bytes within a character string are correctly handled. Thus *data* truly contains the exact data from the database.

If you wish to output character strings read from tables into HTML documents, as a rule you must use the function *escapeHTML.*

If problems arise in reading large BLOBs because the maximum amount of data per field is limited, then this limit can be set (before *execute*) with *$dbh->{'LongReadLen'}=n*. The value *n* specifies the maximum number of bytes.

Take note that 0 means that long fields will not be read at all. In this case, *$data* contains the value *undef*, which cannot be distinguished from *NULL.*

Determining Elements of an ENUM or SET

The use of *ENUM*s and *SET*s presents no problems in and of itself: The values are passed in both directions as simple character strings. Note that with *ENUM*s no empty spaces are permitted between the comma-separated items.

When in a Perl program you wish to display the character strings of an *ENUM* or *SET* for selection (in an HTML listbox, for example), you must determine the definition of this field with the SQL command *DESCRIBE tablename columnname*:

```
USE exceptions
DESCRIBE test_enum a_enum
Field   Type                    Null  Key ...
a_enum  enum('a','b','c','d','e')  YES      ...
```

The column *Type* of the result table contains the required information. In the following lines of code, the character string *enum('a', 'b', 'c')* will first be decomposed step by step and then displayed line by line. (The algorithm assumes that the *SET* or *ENUM* character string contains no commas.)

```
$sth = $dbh->prepare("DESCRIBE test_enum a_set");
$sth->execute();
$row = $sth->fetchrow_hashref();
$tmp = $row->{'Type'};          # enum(...) or set(...)
($tmp) = $tmp =~ m/\((.*)\)/;   # xyz('a','b','c') --> 'a','b','c'
$tmp =~ tr/'//d;                # 'a','b','c' --> a,b,c
@enums = split(/,/, $tmp);      # @enums[0]=a, @enums[1]=b ...
foreach $enum (@enums) {        # output all values
  print "$enum\n";
}
```

DBD::mysql-specific Methods and Attributes

Whereas the *DBI* module represents the greatest common denominator of all database APIs, *DBD::mysql* contains as well various MySQL-specific functions. Their application leads to Perl code that can be transferred to other database systems only with difficulty. However, such code is often more efficient.

This section introduces only the most important MySQL-specific methods and attributes. Chapter 23 contains a complete reference of *DBD::mysql* extensions.

Using rows to Determine the Number of Records Found with SELECT

The method *$sth->rows()*, which was mentioned previously, is, in fact, not MySQL-specific. But only with the *DBD::mysql* driver does this method return, after *execute*, the number of records found. This holds only if queries are executed without the attribute *mysql_use_result*.

Determining the AUTO_INCREMENT Value

The *$dbh* attribute *mysql_insertid* has also been mentioned. It enables you to determine the *AUTO_INCREMENT* value of the most recently inserted data record after an *INSERT* command:

```
$id = $dbh->{'mysql_insertid'};
```

Determining Additional Column Information

DBI makes a number of *$sth* attributes available that make it possible to determine information about the columns of a *SELECT* result (for example, *$sth-> {'NAME'}*). *DBD::mysql* adds some additional attributes, such as *'MYSQL_IS_BLOB'*, to establish whether a column contains *BLOB*s; or *'MYSQL_TYPE_NAME'*, to determine the name of the data type of the column.

mysql_store_result Versus mysql_use_result

If a *SELECT* command is executed with *prepare* and *execute*, then usually, *DBD::mysql* calls the C function *mysql_store_result*. This means that all the data records found have been transmitted at once to the client and retained there in memory until *$sth->finish()* is executed.

If between *prepare* and *execute* you set the attribute *mysql_use_result* to 1, then *DBD::mysql* uses the C function *mysql_use_result* for transmitting the records. This means that records are brought from the server to the client only when they are needed. In particular, in processing large amounts of data the memory requirement can be greatly lowered on the client side. (This advantage is lost if you use *fetchall_arrayref*.)

```
$sth = $dbh->prepare("SELECT * FROM table");
$sth->{'mysql_use_result'}=1;
$sth->execute();
```

A summary of the difference between *mysql_store_result* and *mysql_use_result* is shown in Table 16-1.

Table 16-1. *mysql_store_result Versus mysql_use_result*

	mysql_store_result (default)	mysql_use_result
$sth->rows();	This function returns the number of records found.	This function returns 0 or the number of records transmitted thus far.
Locking	The *READ-LOCK* time is minimal.	If locking is used, the table is blocked until the last record is read.
Client Memory Requirement	All found records are stored at the client.	Only one record is stored at the client at one time.
Speed	Access to the first record is comparatively slow (since all records are transmitted to the client); it is very fast thereafter.	Access to the first record is very rapid; further access is slower than with *mysql_store_result.*

Unicode

There are several things you need to consider when you are processing Unicode with a Perl script:

- You must inform the MySQL server that communication is to take place in UTF-8.

```
$dbh->do("SET NAMES 'utf8'");
```

  Instead of *'utf8'*, other character set names supported in MySQL are allowed, such as *'latin1'*. The default character set that MySQL uses depends on the configuration. Therefore, do not rely on a particular character set being active in every MySQL installation, not even *'latin1'*.

  Note that *SET NAMES* governs only the character set for communication between MySQL and your Perl program. *SET NAMES* has no influence over the character set in which data are stored in MySQL tables. (That character set is determined when the tables are defined with *CREATE TABLE*.) MySQL automatically converts all character strings from the table character set to the processing character set. But be careful. If characters are present that are not representable in the second character set, then these characters are replaced by the *?* character. (This also results in a loss of information.)

- Strings that you obtain from MySQL are now UTF-8 encoded. For Perl to interpret such strings correctly, you must inform Perl of the situation. To do so, use the function *decode("utf8", ...)* from the module *Encode*.

```
use Encode;   # makes Encode and Decode functions available
...
$utf8data = decode("utf8", $data_from_mysql);
```

- If your Perl script produces output, you must inform Perl that the results are to be in UTF-8 encoding.

```
binmode(STDOUT, ":utf8");    # set output to be in UTF8
```

- If your Perl script itself contains strings in UTF-8, then you must set *use utf8*.

```
use utf8;
$utf8data = "äöüß";
```

- With CGI scripts you must specify in the HTTP header that the output is to be in UTF-8:

```
print header(-type => "text/html",  -charset => "utf-8");
```

Depending on the particular applications that you foresee for your script, some of the above points may not be applicable. Under Unix/Linux the Perl interpreter often recognizes from the environment variable *$LANG* that it is being executed in a UTF-8 system and then processes Unicode correctly by default. But my experience indicates that one cannot rely on this always to be the case.

■Tip Later in this chapter you will find two CGI Perl scripts that process Unicode. In these a number of Unicode programming techniques are demonstrated. There is no space here for going into the fine points of Perl and Unicode, for which you should obtain a current book on Perl or look at the following web pages, which offer a good introduction to Perl and Unicode (and MySQL):

```
http://www.perldoc.com/perl5.8.0/pod/perluniintro.html
http://perlwelt.horus.at/Beispiele/Magic/PerlUnicodeMysql/
http://lists.mysql.com/perl/3312
```

Transactions

Even in transaction-capable tables (e.g., InnoDB), database commands are executed by default individually. To form a transaction out of several commands, you must first turn off autocommit mode with the instruction *$dbh->{'AutoCommit'}=0*. If you are not working with *{'RaiseError'=>1}* (see below), you should check whether the change in autocommit mode was accepted.

From now on, all SQL commands will form a transaction, which is eventually confirmed with *$dbh->commit()* or aborted with *$dbh->rollback()*. At the same time, the next transaction begins. The Perl code for this looks as follows:

```
$dbh->{'AutoCommit'} = 0;      # turn of autocommit mode
if($dbh->{'AutoCommit'}) {     # test whether it worked
  print "transaction error\n";
  exit(); }

$dbh->do("SQL-Kommando");      # all SQL commands form a transaction
$dbh->do("SQL-Kommando");
...
$dbh->commit();                # confirm transaction
$dbh->rollback();              # or abort transaction
```

Error-Handling

There are several possibilities for Perl script error-handling. The most convenient way (especially during program development) is to specify the option *{'RaiseError'=>1}* in establishing the connection. The result is that an error message is automatically displayed at each error. Additionally, the Perl program is terminated immediately. (This holds not only for errors during the connection, but also for all additional errors that occur in the execution of DBI methods.)

For many administrative tasks this sort of error-handling is sufficient. However, once you employ Perl for programming dynamic web pages, the termination of a script (and perhaps the display of a cryptic error message) is quite the opposite of what one might call user-friendly.

You can achieve more refined error-handling by turning off *DBI*'s automatic response to errors and executing *connect()* with *{'PrintError'=>0}*. Now you must consistently evaluate the two DBI methods *err()* and *errstr()*. The first of these contains the error number, or 0 if no error has occurred, while *errstr()* contains the error text corresponding to the last error to have occurred.

■**Note** DBI methods return *undef* if an error has occurred. However, individual DBI methods sometimes also return *undef* in the course of their normal operation (such as when a data field contains *NULL*). For this reason, a simple evaluation of the return value is usually insufficient.

The methods *err()* and *errstr()* can also be applied to the DBI handles *$dbh* and *$sth* (depending on the context in which the method that caused the error was executed). Immediately after the connection has been established, *err()* or *errstr()* must be applied to *DBI* (since *$dbh* cannot be used after an unsuccessful connection attempt).

Example

The following lines show error-handling for Perl DBI code. In this example, the reaction to an error is always that the script is terminated, but of course, you can execute other instructions. Note particularly how *err()* and *errstr()* are applied to the objects *DBI*, *$dbh*, and *$sth*.

The code contains something particular to MySQL: With the *SELECT* command, error-handling occurs only after *execute*. With many other database systems an error can be recognized after *prepare*.

```
$datasource   = "DBI:mysql:database=exceptions;host=localhost;";
$user  = "root";
$passw = "xxx";
$dbh = DBI->connect($datasource, $user, $passw,
  {'PrintError' => 0});
if(DBI->err()) {
  print "connection error: " . DBI->errstr() . "\n";
  exit(); }
$dbh->do("INSERT INTO testall (a_float) VALUES (10.0)");
if($dbh->err()) {
  print "error wth INSERT command: " . $dbh->errstr() . "\n";
  exit(); }
$sth = $dbh->prepare("SELECT * FROM test_blob");
$sth->execute();
if($sth->err()) {
  print "error in SELECT execute: " . $sth->errstr() . "\n";
  exit(); }
while(my $hashref = $sth->fetchrow_hashref()) {
  if($sth->err()) {
    print "error in SELECT fetch: " . $sth->errstr() . "\n";
    exit(); }
  print length($hashref->{'a_blob'}) . "\n";
}
$sth->finish();
$dbh->disconnect();
```

Logging (trace)

If you suspect that the cause of an error is not in your code, but in MySQL, *DBI*, *DBD::mysql,* or some other origin, it can help to display internal DBI logging information or to write it to a file. This is enabled by *trace()*, which, like *err()* and *errstr()*, can be applied to all *DBI* objects (including *DBI* itself).

Expected as parameters are the desired logging level (0 = none, 9 = maximal logging) and an optional file name. Without a file name, the logging data are sent to *STDERR* (under Windows, to the standard output *STDOUT*):

```
DBI->trace(2);  # activate logging globally for the DBI module
$sth->trace(3, 'c:/dbi-trace.txt'); # logging for $sth methods only
```

Example: Deleting Invalid Data Records (mylibrary)

After months-long experiments with the database *mylibrary*, a variety of invalid records have accumulated. This is a scenario well known to many database developers, and one often forgets to clean house after the testing is complete.

In the case of the *mylibrary* database, the script `delete-invalid-entries.pl` offers help in most cases. It takes care of the following cases:

- Book titles, authors, and publishers whose names begin with *test* are deleted. (To avoid violation of the foreign key rules, for titles and authors, first the corresponding entries are deleted from *rel_title_author*, and only then are the entries deleted from *titles* and *authors*.

- In the same way, orphaned book titles, authors, and publishers are deleted. "Orphaned" refers to entries that are not part of complete book information, such as authors without any books, publishers without any books, or books without any authors.

Of course, the script could be enlarged, for example to delete orphaned categories and languages. On the other hand, there is no point in searching for invalid relations between tables, since foreign key rules see to it that such a situation does not arise. Thus it cannot happen that the *titles* table refers to a publisher that does not exist.

Program Code

The script begins as usual with establishing a connection to the database. If an error occurs (then or later), the script, on account of *{'RaiseError' => 1}*, is simply terminated with an error message:

```perl
#!/usr/bin/perl -w
# delete-invalid-entries.pl
use strict;
use DBI;
# declare variables
my($datasource, $user, $passw, $dbh, $sth, $n, $row);
# create connection to database
$datasource  = "DBI:mysql:database=mylibrary;host=localhost;";
$user = "root";
$passw = "xxx";
$dbh = DBI->connect($datasource, $user, $passw,
  {'RaiseError' => 1);
```

The following *SELECT* command searches for books whose title or subtitle begins with *test*. In the loop that follows, the found titles are deleted first from *rel_title_author* and then from *titles*.

```perl
# delete test titles
$sth = $dbh->prepare(
  "SELECT DISTINCT title, titles.titleID " .
  "FROM titles, rel_title_author " .
  "WHERE titles.titleID = rel_title_author.titleID " .
  "  AND (title LIKE 'test%' OR subtitle LIKE 'test%')");
$sth->execute();
while($row = $sth->fetchrow_hashref()) {
  print "Delete title: $row->{'title'}\n";
  $dbh->do("DELETE FROM rel_title_author " .
          "WHERE titleID=$row->{'titleID'}");
```

```
$dbh->do("DELETE FROM titles " .
        "WHERE titleID=$row->{'titleID'}");  }
$sth->finish();
# delete test authors
# code similar to the above ...
# delete test publishers
# code similar to the above...
```

The following *DELETE* command uses the sub*SELECT*s available since MySQL 4.1. It deletes all titles that have a *titleID* number that does not appear in *rel_title_author*. Orphaned authors are handled similarly.

```
# delete orphaned titles
$n = $dbh->do(
  "DELETE FROM titles WHERE titleID NOT IN " .
  "  (SELECT titleID FROM rel_title_author)");
if($n>0) {
  print "Deleted $n orphaned titles\n"; }
# delete orphaned authors
# code similar to the above ...
```

For orphaned publishers, in the sub*SELECT* command the case that *publID* has the value *NULL* must be excluded, since that value is allowed for the *publID* column. However, *NULL* is not a suitable value in the comparison *NOT IN* ....

```
# delete orphaned publishers
$n = $dbh->do(
  "DELETE FROM publishers " .
  "WHERE publID NOT IN " .
  "  (SELECT DISTINCT publID FROM titles " .
  "    WHERE NOT publID IS NULL)");
if($n>0) {
  print "Deleted $n orphaned publishers\n"; }
# end of program
$dbh->disconnect();
```

CGI Example: Library Management (mylibrary)

Access to the database looks the same in CGI scripts as it does in Perl programs, which for administrative purposes are usually executed as *stand alone*. One must, however, note in the output of data from the database that special characters in character strings are coded with *escapeHTML* according to the HTML syntax.

This section introduces two small Perl programs that access the *mylibrary* database:

- `mylibrary-simpleinput.pl` enables the input of new book titles.
- `mylibrary-find.pl` enables the search for book titles.

Book Search (mylibrary-find.pl)

The script `mylibrary-find.pl` assists in locating books in the *mylibrary* database. The initial letters of the title are given in the search form. Clicking the OK button leads to an alphabetical list of all titles found, together with their authors, publisher, and year of publication (see Figure 16-1).

Figure 16-1. *Searching for book titles*

Program Structure

The script my library-find.pl looks after the display of a simple form as well as the evaluation of that form (including the display of search results). The method *param()* of *CGI* is used to evaluate the form variable *formSearch*.

Program Code

The code begins with the declaration of modules and variables. The combination of *strict* and *my* helps in discovering typographical errors in variable names; *DBI* enables access to the database; *CGI* assists in the output of HTML structures; *CGI::Carp* displays error messages in the resulting HTML document, which is especially practical in searching for errors.

```
#!/usr/bin/perl -w
# mylibrary-find.pl
use strict;
use DBI;
use CGI qw(:standard);
use CGI::Carp qw(fatalsToBrowser);
# declaration of variables
my($datasource, $user, $passw, $dbh, $search, $sql, $sth, $result,
    $rows, $i, $row);
```

Establishing the connection to the database offers nothing new over our previous examples in this chapter. If an error occurs, an error message (in the form of an HTML document) is displayed, and the script is terminated. If the connection succeeds, then the HTML document is opened with several methods from the *CGI* module:

```
# create connection to database
$datasource   = "DBI:mysql:database=mylibrary;host=localhost;";
$user  = "root";
$passw = "xxx";
$dbh = DBI->connect($datasource, $user, $passw,
  {'PrintError' => 0});
# display error message and end script if necessary
if(DBI->err()) {
  print header(),
    start_html("Sorry, no database connection"),
    p("Sorry, no database connection"), end_html();
  exit();
}
```

```
# inform MySQL that communication will be in the Latin-1
# character set
$dbh->do("SET NAMES 'latin1'");
# introduce HTML document
print header(-type => "text/html",  -charset => "latin-1"),
    start_html("Perl programming, search form for the ",
               "mylibrary database"), "\n",
    h2("Search for titles in the mylibrary database"), "\n";
```

Evaluate Form, Display Search Results

If the script is called with form data, then the form variable *formSearch* is evaluated with *param*. The special characters _ and % are removed from the character string. If the variable *search* is not empty, then in *sql* an extensive *SELECT* command is assembled and executed. The results are transmitted with *fetchall_arrayref* into a two-dimensional array.

Some notes on the *SELECT* query: *GROUP_CONCAT* in combination with *GROUP BY titleID* creates a sorted string with all the authors of the given title. *LEFT JOIN* makes a connection between the tables *titles* and *publishers*, which is valid even if no publisher is specified for the title.

```
# process form data
$search = param('formSearch');
# delete characters _ and %
$search =~ tr/%_//d;
if($search) {
  print p(), b("Titles beginning with ", encode_entitiesescapeHTML($search));
  # Titelsuche
  $sql = "SELECT titles.titleID, title, year, publName, " .
         "         GROUP_CONCAT(authname ORDER BY authname SEPARATOR ', ') " .
         "           AS authors " .
         "FROM titles, authors, rel_title_author " .
         "  LEFT JOIN publishers ON titles.publID = publishers.publID " .
         "WHERE titles.titleID = rel_title_author.titleID " .
         "  AND authors.authID = rel_title_author.authID " .
         "  AND title LIKE '$search%' " .
         "GROUP BY titles.titleID " .
         "ORDER BY title " .
         "LIMIT 100";
  $sth = $dbh->prepare($sql);
  $sth->execute();
  $result = $sth->fetchall_arrayref({});
  $sth->finish();
```

The evaluation of the array begins with a test as to whether any book titles were found at all. In the following loop the title information is output, with any HTML special characters being transformed with *escapeHTML* into the correct HTML code.

```
# were titles found?
  $rows = @{$result};
  if($rows==0) {
    print p(), "Sorry, no titles found."; }
  # display titles
  else {
    # loop over all records
    for($i=0; $i<$rows; $i++) {
      $row = $result->[$i];
```

```
print p(),
        b(escapeHTML($row->{'title'})), ": ",
        i(escapeHTML($row->{'authors'})), ". ",
        escapeHTML($row->{'publName'}), " ",
        $row->{'year'}, ".";
  }
    print p(), hr(), p(), "New search:", p();
  }
}
```

Display the Form

```
# display the form
print start_form(),
    p(), "Search for title beginning with ... ",
    textfield({-name => 'formSearch', -size => 20,
              -maxlength => 20}), " ",
    submit({-name => 'formSubmit', -value => 'OK'}),
    end_form();
print end_html();
# program ends
$dbh->disconnect();
```

Ideas for Improvements

The code as it stands permits only a search based on the initial letters of a title. It would be desirable, of course, to allow a search by author(s), categories, and so on, ideally in the form of a full-text search. (A somewhat more refined example of book search in *mylibrary* was presented in Chapter 15, where PHP was used as the programming language. That program offers pagewise representation of the search results as well as cross references between results, for example to display all titles written by a particular author.)

Simple Input of New Books (mylibrary-simpleinput.pl)

This section presents a minimalist input form for new books (see Figure 16-2). In two input fields are placed the new book title and a list of authors. The script then tests which if any of the authors are already stored in the database. All as yet unknown authors are added with *INSERT*. Then the new title is stored as well as the requisite entries in *rel_title_author* for relating title and authors.

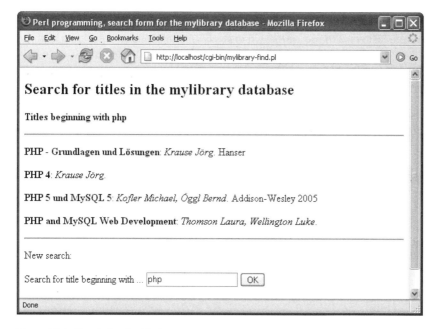

Figure 16-2. *Simple book title input*

Program Structure

The script `mylibrary-simpleinput.pl` displays a simple form and then evaluates it when OK is clicked. The method *param()* of the *CGI* module is used to transmit the two form variables: *formTitle* with the title, and *formAuthors* with the list of authors.

Program Code

As with `mylibrary-find.pl`, the code begins with the declaration of modules and variables:

```
#!/usr/bin/perl -w
# mylibrary-simpleinput.pl
use strict;
use DBI;
use CGI qw(:standard);
use CGI::Carp qw(fatalsToBrowser);
# declaration of variables
my($datasource, $user, $passw, $dbh, @row,
   $formTitle, $formAuthors, $titleID, $authID, $author);
```

The next lines of code are similar to those of the script `mylibrary-find.pl`, which we have just seen, and so we do not reproduce the code:

```
# create connection to database
... as with mylibrary-find.pl
# if an error occurs, display error message, end script
... as with mylibrary-find.pl
# introduce HTML document
... as with mylibrary-find.pl
```

Storing a Book Title and Its Authors

If the script is called with form data (these are located in *param()*), there follows a quick test as to whether a title and author list have been specified. If that is not the case, then an error message is displayed. The program is continued below with the redisplay of the form:

```
# evaluate form data
if(param()) {
  $formTitle = param('formTitle');
  $formAuthors = param('formAuthors');
  # were both title and authors given?
  if($formTitle eq "" || $formAuthors eq "") {
    print p(), b("Please specify title and at least one author!"); }
```

For storing the book title in the *titles* table, the *INSERT* command with one parameter is passed to *do*. As parameter, *$formTitle* is passed. The effect of this way of proceeding is that *$formTitle* (with a minimal amount of typing) is placed in single quotation marks, and all special characters are handled correctly:

```
# form data are correct; store
  else {
    # store title
    $dbh->do("INSERT INTO titles (title) VALUES (?)",
             undef, ($formTitle));
    $titleID = $dbh->{'mysql_insertid'};
```

The list of authors is processed in a *foreach* loop. For each author, a test is made as to whether the author already resides in the *authors* table. If that is indeed the case, then *authID* is read from the *authors* table. Otherwise, the new author is stored, and the new *authID* value is determined with *mysql_insertid*. Finally, the combination of *titleID* and *authID* must be stored in the table *rel_title_author*:

```
# store authors
    foreach $author (split(/;/, $formAuthors)) {
      # does the author already exist?
      @row = $dbh->selectrow_array("SELECT authID FROM authors " .
                                   "WHERE authName = " .
                                   $dbh->quote($author));
      # yes: determine existing authID
      if(@row) {
        $authID = $row[0]; }
      # no: store new author, determine new authID
      else {
        $dbh->do("INSERT INTO authors (authName) VALUES (?)",
                 undef, ($author));
        $authID = $dbh->{'mysql_insertid'};
      }
      # store entry in in rel_title_author table
      $dbh->do("INSERT INTO rel_title_author (titleID, authID) " .
               "VALUES ($titleID, $authID)");
    }
```

In the HTML document a brief announcement is made that the new title was successfully stored. Then the form variables are deleted so that the next title can be input in the form:

```
# feedback
    print p(), "Your last input has been saved.";
    print br(), "You may now continue with the next title.";
    # delete form variables (for the next input)
    param(-name=>'formTitle', -value=>'');
    param(-name=>'formAuthors', -value=>'');
  }
}
```

Displaying the Form

The remaining lines of code serve to display the form and close the HTML document:

```
print start_form(),
    p(), "Title:",
    br(), textfield({-name => 'formTitle', -size => 60,
                     -maxlength => 80}),
    p(), "Authors:",
    br(), textfield({-name => 'formAuthors', -size => 60,
                     -maxlength => 100}),
    br(), "(Last name first! If you want to specify more ",
          "than one author, use ; to separate them!)",
    p(),  submit({-name => 'formSubmit', -value => 'OK'}),
    end_form();
print end_html();
# program end
$dbh->disconnect();
```

Ideas for Improvements

The script `mylibrary-simpleinput.pl` does not permit one to specify subtitle, publisher, category, etc. Furthermore, it is as good as completely unprotected against input errors. It is impossible to make changes to titles already stored. Thus there is enormous potential to improve this script! (A much more satisfactory input form was presented in Chapter 15. There, to be sure, the programming language PHP was used. Nonetheless, many of the techniques employed there could easily be ported to Perl.)

CGI Unicode Example

This section uses the two scripts from the previous section and presents the two Unicode variants `mylibrary-find-utf8.pl` and `mylibrary-simpleinput-utf8.pl`. The code of the two scripts is similar to the previous code, as was to be expected, and for that reason, this section will be limited to pointing out the differences. These code fragments will be emphasized in boldface type.

■**Note** Please note that older browsers have difficulties on occasion with Unicode HTML documents. This is particularly true, as in the following examples, when form data are processed. The examples were successfully tested with two modern browsers (Internet Explorer 6.0 under Windows XP SP2 and Firefox 1.0 under Windows and Linux); Unicode incompatibilities with older browsers are nonetheless a real possibility.

Book Search (mylibrary-find-utf8.pl)

In the first part of the script there are two new instructions: *use Encode qw (decode)* enables the function *Encode::decode*, while *binmode* informs Perl that output is to be produced in the Unicode character set (UTF-8).

   SET NAMES 'utf8' has the effect that communication with the MySQL server takes place in the Unicode character set. The options *-charset=>"utf-8"* and *-encoding=>'utf-8'* are passed to the functions *header* and *start_html*. This is necessary so that the browser recognizes that the HTML document is UTF-8 encoded. One does not need to use *use utf8*, because the script contains no Unicode characters.

```
#!/usr/bin/perl -w
# mylibrary-find-utf8.pl
...
use Encode qw(decode);
binmode(STDOUT, ":utf8");
# definition of variables as in mylibrary-find.pl ...
# connection to the database as in mylibrary-find.pl ...
# inform MySQL that communication
# is in the Latin-1 character set
$dbh->do("SET NAMES 'utf8'");
# introduce HTML document
print header(-type => "text/html",  -charset => "utf-8"),
    start_html(-encoding => 'utf-8',
      "Perl programming, search form for the mylibrary database"), "\n",
    h2("Search for titles in the mylibrary database"), "\n";
```

   If a search string from the form is passed to the script, it must be transformed from the UTF-8 format into the internal Perl character set format. (If you neglect this step, Perl considers the form input to be a Latin-1 string.)

   The code for searching for suitable titles is no different from the example of the previous section. However, in outputting the results you must again think about applying the *decode* function to inform Perl that it is dealing with UTF-8 strings.

```
$search = decode('utf8', param('formSearch'));
# title search as in mylibrary-find.pl ...
# output results
...
        print p(),
          b(escapeHTML( decode("utf8", $row->{'title'})    )), ": ",
          i(escapeHTML( decode("utf8", $authors)            )), ". ",
            escapeHTML( decode("utf8", $row->{'publName'}) ), " ",
          $row->{'year'}, "\n";
```

   In connection with the search results, the search form is displayed with the previous input, which happens automatically. However, Perl does not recognize the UTF-8 character set for input and messes up all non-ASCII characters. To prevent this, the form parameter *formsearch* must be assigned the previously UTF-8 decoded variable *search*.

   The HTML form option *accept-charset ="utf-8"* should make it clear to the browser that UTF-8 input is expected. (However, the browsers that I tested worked fine without this option.)

```
# display search form
param('formSearch', $search);
print start_form('-accept-charset' => 'utf-8'),
  ... and so on as in mylibrary-find.pl
```

Input of New Books (mylibrary-simpleinput-utf8.pl)

The changes in mylibrary-simpleinput-utf8.pl with respect to the Latin-1 variant in the previous section look similar to those in mylibrary-find-utf8.pl. The function *binmode(STDOUT, ":utf8")* is not required, since the script processes only input and produces no (Unicode) output.

```perl
#!/usr/bin/perl -w
# mylibrary-simpleinput-utf8.pl
...
use Encode qw(decode);
# definition of variables as in mylibrary-simpleinput.pl ...
# connection to database as in mylibrary- simpleinput.pl ...
# inform MySQL that communication is
# to be in the Latin-1 character set
$dbh->do("SET NAMES 'utf8'");
# HTML/HTTP header as in mylibrary-find.pl ...
# form data are in the UTF-8 character set
if(param()) {
  $formTitle   = decode('utf8', param('formTitle'));
  $formAuthors = decode('utf8', param('formAuthors'));
  ...
  # and so on, as in mylibrary-find.pl ...
```

CHAPTER 17

■■■

Java (JDBC and Connector/J)

This chapter describes the development of MySQL applications with the programming language Java. As an interface to MySQL we will use JDBC in combination with the driver *Connector/J*.

All the tests for this chapter were carried out under Windows XP (with Sun JDK 1.5.0) and under SUSE Linux 9.2 (with Sun JDK 1.4.2, package `java-1_4_2-sun-devel`). The connection to MySQL was made in each case with Connector/J 3.1.7 and 3.2.0 alpha.

Introduction

The Java Installation

To develop your own Java programs you need the Java Software Development Kit (Java SDK, or simply JDK). The most widely distributed JDK is from Sun (the creator of Java); however, there are Java implementations available from other developers, such as IBM. This chapter focuses primarily on the Sun implementation.

JDK is bundled with many Linux implementations and can be simply installed with the package manager. For Linux distributions without Java, or for working under Windows, you can download the JDK without charge from `java.sun.com/downloads` (about 40 megabytes). The official name is *Java 2 Platform Standard Edition n SDK* (or J2SE *n* SDK for short), where *n* is the current version number.

After installation you have to complete the environment variable *PATH* to the `bin` directory of the Java installation. To do this, modify the file `autoexec.bat` under Windows 9x/ME. Under Windows NT/2000/XP, open the dialog CONTROL PANEL | SYSTEM | ADVANCED | ENVIRONMENT VARIABLES (see Figure 17-1). The components of *PATH* are separated by semicolons.

```
C:\> PATH
PATH=C:\Programs\Perl\bin\;C:\WINDOWS\system32;C:\WINDOWS;
C:\WINDOWS\System32\Wbem;C:\programs\mysql\mysql server 5.0\bin;
C:\Programs\Java\jdk1.5.0_01\bin
```

With SUSE 9.2, Java is located in the directory `/usr/lib/jvm/java-1.4.2-sun`, where additionally, there are two links from `/usr/lib/jvm/jre` to `/etc/alternatives/jre` and from `/etc/alternatives/jre` to `/usr/lib/jvm/java-1.4.2-sun`. (These links make it possible to install different Java implementations in parallel and to switch between them.) The content of the *PATH* variables looks like this:

```
linux:~ $ echo $PATH
  /home/suse/bin:/usr/local/bin:/usr/bin:/usr/X11R6/bin:/bin:
  /usr/games:/opt/gnome/bin:/opt/kde3/bin:/usr/lib/jvm/jre/bin/
```

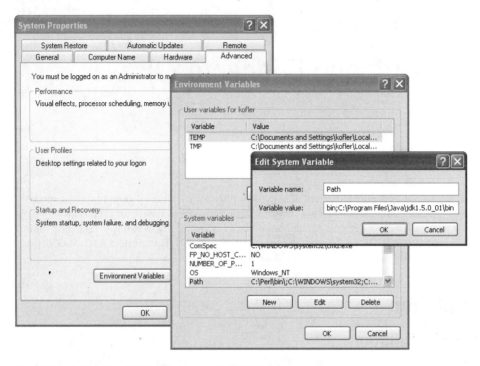

Figure 17-1. *Setting the PATH variables under Windows XP*

After installation, under Windows you can test in the command window, or under Linux in a console window, whether everything proceeded properly:

```
C:\> java -version
java version "1.5.0_01"
Java(TM) 2 Runtime Environment, Standard Edition (build 1.5.0_01-b08)
Java HotSpot(TM) Client VM (build 1.5.0_01-b08, mixed mode, sharing)

linux:~ # java -version
java version "1.4.2_06"
Java(TM) 2 Runtime Environment, Standard Edition (build 1.4.2_06-b03)
Java HotSpot(TM) Client VM (build 1.4.2_06-b03, mixed mode)
```

Hello, World!

To try out the Java compiler, create the following file Hellow.java. Note that the file name must match that of the class *Hellow* defined in the code exactly, including case distinction:

```
/* example file Hellow.java */
public class Hellow
{
  public static void main(String[] args)
  {
    System.out.println("Hello, world!");
  }
}
```

To compile, change to the directory of the file `Hellow.java` and execute the following command:

```
> javac Hellow.java
```

As result, you obtain the file `Hellow.class`. This program is executed as follows:

```
> java Hellow
Hello World!
```

Note that you must not specify the `.class`. If you do, `java Hellow.class` doesn't work.

Connector/J Installation

Connector/J is a JDBC driver for MySQL. JDBC is a collection of classes that help in the programming of database applications with Java. JDBC is independent of specific database systems. Therefore, to create a connection to a database system via JDBC, a driver specific to the database must be used. For MySQL database systems this driver is Connector/J.

Versions

Connector/J is a so-called type-4 driver, which means that it is implemented completely in Java. Connector/J assumes JDBC 2.0 (that is, at least Java 2, version 1.2). There are currently three versions of Connector/J in circulation.

- Connector/J 3.0 is especially for MySQL 3.23 and 4.0.

- Connector/J 3.1 can be used in combination with all currently available versions of MySQL. This version supports in particular the new features of MySQL 4.1: new password authentication, Unicode character sets, and prepared statements.

- Connector/J 3.2 was available in alpha version in March 2005. Among the new features is the support of new MySQL 5.0 cursor functions. Until Connector/J 3.2 reaches maturity, you should use version 3.1 (even in combination with MySQL 5.0).

■**Note** Earlier versions of Connector/J had the name MM.MySQL. After the programmer Mark Matthews moved over to the MySQL team, the driver was called Connector/J and is now officially supported by MySQL.

Connector/J is available under the GPL. If you wish to use Connector/J in commercial applications, the MySQL server used must be properly licensed.

Installation

The installation of Connector/J was briefly described in Chapter 7. This section returns to the topic, but with more technical detail and with reference to a variety of installation possibilities.

Connector/J is available for download at `www.mysql.com` as a `*.zip` (Windows) or `*.tar.gz` file. Both archives contain exactly the same files. (Java is platform-independent.) To install, unpack the contents of the archive into the directory of your choice. Under Windows, use Windows Explorer or the program WinZip, and under Linux the following command:

```
linux:~ # tar -xzf mysql-connector-java-n.tar.gz
```

Table 17-1 summarizes the most important files and directories of the archive:

Table 17-1. *Directories and files of the Connector/J archive*

Directory/File	Content
mysql-connector-java-n.n.n/	Directory of the actual library files; all further entries of this table are in relation to this directory.
/mysql-connector-java-n.jar	All Java classes of the driver as a Java archive file; this file is the actual driver.
/com/*	All Java classes of the driver as individual files.
/docs/*	Extensive documentation in PDF and HTML format.
/org/*	The Java start class of the driver under the old driver name (org.gjt.mm.mysql.Driver).

The crucial point here is that the Java runtime environment should be able to find the new library when executing programs. To ensure this state of affairs, there are several possibilities:

- The simplest solution is generally to copy the file mysql-connector-java-n.jar into the Java installation directory jre\lib\ext, which is automatically checked during the execution of Java programs. Now there remains the question of where Java is installed on your computer. Typical paths are C:\Programs\Java\jre1.5.0_01\lib\ext under Windows and /usr/lib/jvm/jre-1.4.2-sun/lib/ext under SUSE.

- Alternatively, you can set the environment variable *CLASSPATH*. This variable specifies all directories in which there are classes that should be taken into account when Java programs are executed. So that Connector/J will be considered, you must add the directory in which mysql-connector-java-n.jar is located to *CLASSPATH*. Note that for the execution of Java programs from the current directory, *CLASSPATH* must also contain the path "." (that is, a period, which denotes the current directory).

  Under Windows, you can set *CLASSPATH* temporarily with the DOS command *SET var=xxx*. To set it permanently, use the dialog CONTROL PANEL | SYSTEM | ADVANCED | ENVIRONMENT VARIABLES under Windows 2000/XP, or under Windows 9x/ME, the file autoexec.bat. Components of *CLASSPATH* are separated by semicolons.

  Under Linux, you can set *CLASSPATH* with the command *export var=xxx* or permanently in /etc/profile. The specified directories in *CLASSPATH* are separated with colons.

- For initial testing there is also the option of copying the com and org directories from Connector/J into the local directory (that is, into the directory in which the program that you have developed resides).

You can test whether the installation of Connector/J was successful with the following miniprogram. It should run without reporting any errors:

```
/* example file HelloMySQL.java */
import java.sql.*;
public class HelloMySQL {
  public static void main(String[] args) {
    try {
      Driver d = (Driver)
        Class.forName("com.mysql.jdbc.Driver").newInstance();
      System.out.println("OK"); }
    catch(Exception e) {
      System.out.println("Error: " + e.toString()); }
  }
}
```

And If It Doesn't Work?

If something goes wrong, then the usual suspect is that the Connector/J classes have not been found. The error message usually looks something like this: *java.lang.ClassNotFoundException: com.mysql.jdbc.Driver*. Here are some of the possible sources of error:

- If you have copied `mysql-connector-java-n.n.n.jar` into the directory `jre\lib\ext`, then it is possible that more than one Java interpreter resides on the computer. (It is also possible that a run-time version and a development version have been installed in parallel.) You have apparently copied `mysql-connector-java-3.0.n.jar` into the directory of an interpreter that is not the active one. Try again with a different directory.

  Under Linux you can determine the correct directory easily with `which  java`. With some distributions what is returned in only a link pointing to the actual file. Under SUSE Linux you must actually follow two links before you get to the location of the interpreter.

  ```
  linux$ which java
  /usr/bin/java
  linux$ ls -l /usr/bin/java
  ... /usr/bin/java -> /etc/alternatives/java
  linux$ ls -l /etc/alternatives/java
  ... /etc/alternatives/java -> /usr/lib/jvm/jre-1.4.2-sun/bin/java
  ```

  Unfortunately, there is not a comparable option under Windows, since the relevant settings are located in the somewhat opaque registration database. However, you can determine with START | SETTINGS | CONTROL PANEL | ADD/REMOVE HARDWARE which Java versions are already installed and when installation took place.

- If you have edited *CLASSPATH*, then perhaps Java is having no trouble locating Connector/J's classes, but is unable to locate the classes of your own program (error message *java.lang. NoClassDefFoundError*). If *CLASSPATH* is defined, then it must also point to the current directory.

  Under Windows, you can determine the contents of *CLASSPATH* in a command window with `echo %CLASSPATH%`, and under Linux in a console window with `echo  $CLASSPATH`. Under Windows, the components of *CLASSPATH* are separated with semicolons, while under Linux it is colons that do the separation. The following commands show possible settings (where, of course, you must adapt the configuration to your own installation):

  ```
  > ECHO %CLASSPATH%
  .;C:\Programs\mysql-connector-java-3.0.3-beta

  linux: $ echo $CLASSPATH
  .:/usr/local/mysql-connector-java-3.0.3-beta/
  ```

Programming Techniques

The following examples assume that Java SDK and Connector/J have been correctly installed. All example programs run only in text mode. Of course, Java programs with an AWT or Swing interface will look more attractive, but for demonstrating programming techniques, text mode is completely satisfactory and offers the advantage that the code remains compact and easy to read.

■Tip Additional information on Connector/J can be found in the associated online documentation, which is available in HTML and PDF format as well as being readable over the Internet: http://dev.mysql.com/doc/connector/j/en/index.html.

Every Java program that uses Connector/J is actually a JDBC program. (JDBC is the database interface of Java. Only relatively few details of a MySQL JDBC program are actually MySQL-specific.)

This section provides only a first introduction to JDBC programming. More advanced information is to be found in books on Java that discuss JDBC.

A First Example

The following example offers a first impression of the construction of a JDBC program. The use of *import java.sql* facilitates access to the JDBC interfaces and classes. The Connector/J driver is loaded with *Class.forName("…\nolinebreak").newInstance()*. (This must take place before a connection is established.)

The connection is established with the method *DriverManager.getConnection*, where the most important parameters (driver name, host name, and database name) are passed in the form of a URL; details to follow.

Before you can execute an SQL command, a *Statement* object must be created, whose method *executeQuery* returns a *ResultSet* object, which contains the result of the query. In the following example, all data records are read through (method *next*), selectively chosen (*getInt*, *getString*, etc.), and output to the console window:

```
/* example file SampleIntro.java */
import java.sql.*;
public class SampleIntro
{
  public static void main(String[] args)
  {
    try {
      Connection conn;
      Statement stmt;
      ResultSet res;
      // load the Connector/J driver
      Class.forName("com.mysql.jdbc.Driver").newInstance();
      // establish connection to MySQL
      conn = DriverManager.getConnection(
        "jdbc:mysql://uranus/mylibrary", "username", "xxx");
      // execute SELECT query
      stmt = conn.createStatement();
      res = stmt.executeQuery(
        "SELECT publID, publName FROM publishers " +
        "ORDER BY publName");
      // process results
      while (res.next()) {
        int id = res.getInt("publID");
        String name = res.getString("publName");
        System.out.println("ID: " + id + "  Name: " + name);
      }
      res.close();
    }
```

```
    catch(Exception e) {
      System.out.println("Error: " + e.toString() );
    }
  }
}
```

Upon execution, the program returns the following result:

```
ID: 1  Name: Addison-Wesley
ID: 2  Name: Apress
ID: 9  Name: Bonnier Pocket
ID: 5  Name: Hanser
```

Establishing the Connection

Establishing the Connection with DriverManager.getConnection

As already mentioned in our introductory example, the Connector/J driver must be loaded before the connection is established. For this, execute the method *Class.forName* and pass the name of the driver. The method returns a *Driver* object, which you generally will not need. More to the point is that Connector/J is registered as a result of this call as a JDBC driver, which now can be used:

```
// SampleConnection1.java
// load Connector/J driver
Class.forName("com.mysql.jdbc.Driver").newInstance();
```

For further programming, what is much more important is the *Connection* object that you create with the method *DriverManager.getConnection*. To this method you usually pass three character strings, containing the basic information about the database, as a URL (uniform resource locator), the user name, and the password:

```
// connection to MySQL
Connection conn = DriverManager.getConnection(
  "jdbc:mysql://uranus/mylibrary", "username", "password");
```

The construction of the URL looks like this (here split into two lines):

```
jdbc:mysql://[host1][,host2...][:port]/
  [dbname][?para1=val1][&para2=val2][&para3=val3]...
```

Tables 17-2 and 17-3 describe the components of the connection URL and the most important optional connection parameters. A complete list of parameters can be found in the Connector/J Readme file.

Table 17-2. *Components of the Connection URL*

Component	Function
jdbc:mysql://	Selects the driver.
host1	Specifies the host name (*localhost* if a server on the local computer is to be accessed).
host2, host3	Specifies additional (optional) host names, to be used only if the connection the previously named host is unsuccessful.
:port	Specifies the port number (by default, 3306).
/dbname	Specifies the default database.
?para1=value1	Specifies the first optional parameter (see Table 17-3).
&para2=value2	Specifies all additional optional parameters.

Table 17-3. *Optional Parameters in the Connection URL (with Default Settings)*

Parameter	Function
allowMultiQueries=false	Specifies whether several SQL commands can be executed at once. If this option is used, the SQL commands must be separated by semicolons. This option has been available since Connector/J 3.1.1.
autoreconnect=false	Specifies whether the driver should attempt on its own to reconnect if the connection is broken.
connectTimeout=0	Specifies in milliseconds the wait time for a connection to be established. A setting of 0 means that no timeout is used. This setting functions only since Java 2, version 1.4.
initialTimeout=2	Specifies in seconds the time between attempts at reestablishing a broken connection. This time does not hold for the first connection.
maxReconnects=3	Specifies the maximum number of reconnects.
useCompression=false	Compresses communication between the Java program and the MySQL server.
relaxAutoCommit=false	Specifies whether the driver is to accept *COMMIT* and *ROLLBACK* commands without reporting an error even if MySQL supports no transactions for the affected tables (for example, because the tables are in MyISAM format).
useTimezone=false	Specifies whether times should be converted between the client and server time zones.

All further database operations proceed from the *Connection* object. If you wish to close the connection at the end of the program, simply use the method *close* on the *Connection* object.

Establishing the Connection with DataSource.getConnection

Since Java 2, version 1.4, in addition to the method *DriverManager.getConnection*, which we have already described, there is an alternative way to establish a database connection: the *DataSource* class (package *javax.sql*). The JDBC documentation recommends this way, because it allows for the use of advanced functions, such as connection pooling and the execution of distributed transactions (that is, database operations that process data from several databases).

The following lines do not go into these additional possibilities, but simply show the principles of establishing the connection. To do this, you generate an object of the class *com.mysql.jdbc.jdbc2.optional.MysqlDataSource* and with the methods *setServerName* and *setDatabaseName*, set the host and database names. The actual connection is then established with *getConnection*, where you have to pass only the user name and password. This method returns a *Connection* object, which in the *DriverManager* variant is the starting point for all further database operations.

If you wish to set additional connection parameters, you can use the method *setURL* (the format of the URL, as described previously) or pass a *Properties* field to *getConnection*:

```
// SampleConnection2.java
import java.sql.*;
import javax.sql.*;  // for DataSource
public class SampleConnection2
{
  public static void main(String[] args)
  {
    try {
      com.mysql.jdbc.jdbc2.optional.MysqlDataSource ds;
      Connection conn2;
```

```
      // create connection with a DataSource object
      ds = new com.mysql.jdbc.jdbc2.optional.MysqlDataSource();
      ds.setServerName("uranus");
      ds.setDatabaseName("mylibrary");
      conn2 = ds.getConnection("root", "xxxx");
      // and so on, as before ...
    }
    catch(Exception e) {
      System.out.println("Error: " + e.toString() );
    }
  }
}
```

■**Tip** If you wish to use more advanced JDBC functions, you should look at the Connector/J driver directory `com\mysql\jdbc\jdbc2\optional`. There you will find, for example, the Java source texts for the Connector/J classes *MysqlPooledConnection* and *MySQLConnectionPoolDataSource*.

Problems in Establishing a Connection

Normally, the connection between a client program and the MySQL server is established via TCP/IP when the programs are running on different computers. On the other hand, if both programs are running on the same computer and a Linux/Unix system is being used, then the connection is established over a socket file, which is more efficient than TCP/IP.

However, Java does not support sockets, and so the connection is always over TCP/IP. The importance here is that in MySQL access control, the name *localhost* is not used as host name, but instead, the actual name of the computer. This state of affairs frequently leads to difficulties, with an error message that usually looks something like this:

```
linux:~/ java SampleConnection1
Error: java.sql.SQLException: Server configuration denies access
to data source
```

What is particularly irritating is that a local connection using the same access information (e.g., with `mysql -h localhost -u name -p`) works just fine. The reason is that `mysql` deals with local access by default over socket files, but Java does not.

The following points should help you in solving such problems. (Additional tips for solving access problems—independent of Java—can be found in Chapter 11.) The starting point for our example is a MySQL server that is running on the computer *uranus.sol* with IP number 192.168.0.2. The Java program is to run on the same computer.

- It can be that for security reasons, every network connection to the MySQL server is forbidden. (For this, at server start the option `--skip-networking` must be passed, or else this option must be entered in `my.cnf`.) Whether such is the case can be determined with the following command:

  ```
  linux~/$ mysql -h uranus.sol -u name -p databasename
  Enter password: xxxxx
  ERROR 2003: Can't connect to MySQL server
  ```

  The only solution is to remove this option.

- It can also be the case that network access is indeed allowed, but the table *mysql.user*, which is responsible for access control, contains an invalid entry in the column *hostname*. This case can also be recognized with `mysql`. (Note that this time, the error message is different.)

```
linux~/$ mysql -h uranus.sol -u name -p databasename
Enter password: xxxxx
ERROR 1130: Host '192.168.0.2' is not allowed to connect
to this MySQL server
```

With the command `resolveip 192.168.0.2` you can determine which host name is expected by MySQL for this address. (On my computer, the command returns the result *uranus.sol*.) Then you can check whether the table *mysql.user* contains a corresponding entry (and not, say, simply *uranus*).

- Another possible cause is that there is a correct entry in *mysql.user*, but the specified user name and password do not match. Note that this time, the error message looks different:

```
linux~/$ mysql -h uranus.sol -u name -p databasename
Enter password: xxxxx
ERROR 1045: Access denied for user: 'root@192.168.0.2'
(Using password: YES)
```

Once you have succeeded in gaining access to the MySQL server with the program `mysql` by giving the computer name, the Java program should generally run if the same user name and password are used.

Executing SQL Commands

Before you can execute SQL commands, you need a *Statement* object. You obtain it with *conn.createStatement*:

```
Statement stmt = conn.createStatement();
```

If you have in mind executing *SELECT* queries, then you can use two optional parameters to select the cursor type and specify whether the data resulting from *SELECT* are able to be changed:

```
stmt = conn.createStatement(resultcursortype, resultconcurrency);
```

By default, the cursor type is *forward only*, and the data are *read only*. Additional details to follow. The *Statement* class now offers a selection of various *execute* methods:

executeUpdate: for *INSERT, UPDATE,* and *DELETE* commands;

executeQuery: for *SELECT* queries;

executeBatch: for executing several commands that have been previously specified with *addBatch* as a block (which can increase efficiency);

execute: to execute an arbitrary SQL command (where it is not known in advance what sort of command it will be).

In the following pages we shall look more closely at the variants *executeUpdate, executeQuery,* and *executeBatch*.

Executing INSERT, UPDATE, and DELETE Commands

The execution of an *INSERT, UPDATE,* or *DELETE* command is quite simple: You simply pass the SQL command as a character string to the method *executeUpdate*:

```
stmt.executeUpdate(
  "INSERT INTO publishers (publName) VALUES ('new publisher')");
```

The method *executeUpdate* returns an *int* value that specifies how many records were changed by the command.

If you wish to pass strings to the SQL command that contain special characters like ', ", \, and so on, you should use prepared statements, which will be discussed shortly.

With the method *getWarnings* you can determine the warnings that occurred during the execution of the SQL command (corresponds to *SHOW WARNINGS*). The method returns an *SQLWarning* object until all warnings have been processed.

Determining ID Numbers from a New Data Record (AUTO_INCREMENT)

There are several ways of determining the *AUTO_INCREMENT* number of newly created records. Which variant is to be preferred depends on the version of Java that you are using.

Variant 1: Starting with Java 1.4, the method *getGeneratedKeys* has been available. If you are working with a current version of Java, then *getGeneratedKeys* represents the best, most efficient, and most portable option. The method returns a *ResultSet* object (which will be described later when we discuss the evaluation of *SELECT* queries).

If there is precisely one new record, then the *ResultSet* object contains only one record with the sought ID number. To evaluate, execute first the method *next* (to address the first record of the *ResultSet* object) and then read the ID number with the method *getInt(1)* (the index 1 denotes the column of the record):

```
// SampleGetID1
stmt.executeUpdate("INSERT ...");
ResultSet newid = stmt.getGeneratedKeys();
newid.next();
int id = newid.getInt(1);
```

Furthermore, *getGeneratedKeys* should return a complete list of new ID numbers when *INSERT* commands were executed that generate several new data records. In order for JDBC to take note of new ID numbers, the optional parameter *Statement.RETURN_GENERATED_KEYS* must be passed to *executeUpdate*.

```
stmt.executeUpdate(
  "INSERT INTO publishers (publName) VALUES ('publisher1'), ('publisher2')",
  Statement.RETURN_GENERATED_KEYS);
ResultSet newids = stmt.getGeneratedKeys();
while(newids.next()) {   // returns the IDs of publisher1 and publisher2
  System.out.println("ID: " + newids.getInt(1));
}
```

Variant 2: If you are working with an older version of Java, you can use the method *getLastInsertID* of the *Statement* object to obtain the last *AUTO_INCREMENT* value. However, this method is defined specifically only for the *Statement* class of Connector/J, not for the *Statement* interface from *java.sql*. Therefore, you must transform the *Statement* object, via a cast operation, into an object of the class *com.mysql.jdbc.Statement* before you can use the method. (This works for *PreparedStatement* objects as well, which will be described further on.)

The principal disadvantage of *getLastInsertID* is that the resulting code is not portable, functioning only for MySQL in combination with the Connector/J driver:

```
// SampleGetID2.java
Statement stmt = conn.createStatement();
stmt.executeUpdate(
  "INSERT INTO publishers (publName) VALUES ('new publisher')");
long id = ((com.mysql.jdbc.Statement)stmt).getLastInsertID();
```

Variant 3: A third possibility (the slowest!) is to execute the additional SQL command *SELECT LAST_INSERT_ID()* after the *INSERT* command. However, you must see to it that this command is executed in the same MySQL connection *and* within a transaction. If you are working with InnoDB tables, you must set *conn.setAutoCommit(false)* and close the transaction with *conn.commit()*:

```
// SampleGetID3.java
conn.setAutoCommit(false);
stmt.executeUpdate(
  "INSERT INTO publishers (publName) VALUES ('new publisher')");
ResultSet newid = stmt.executeQuery("SELECT LAST_INSERT_ID()");
if(newid.next()) {
  id = newid.getInt(1);
  System.out.println("new ID = " + id); }
conn.commit();
```

Evaluating SELECT Queries

In order to be able to evaluate the results of a *SELECT* query, you must execute the SQL command with *executeQuery*. This method returns a *ResultSet* object:

```
Statement stmt = conn.createStatement();
ResultSet res = stmt.executeQuery(
  "SELECT publID, publName FROM publishers " +
  "WHERE publID < 10 ORDER BY publName");
```

■**Caution** If you have already developed JDBC programs with database drivers other than Connector/J, you should take note of the default properties of *ResultSet* objects:

By default, the *ResultSet* object cannot be edited (read only).

By default, the *ResultSet* object supports free navigation. This has the consequence that all data are immediately transferred from MySQL server to client, even with large query results. This behavior differs from that of many other JDBC drivers, for which the *ResultSet* is *forward only* by default and is transferred only as required.

If you wish to have *ResultSet* properties that differ from the default behavior, then you must specify this in the creation of *Statement* objects for the query. More details to follow (see the headings *Forward-Only ResultSets* and *Variable ResultSets*).

Immediately after the execution of *executeQuery*, no record is active. To address the first record, the method *res.next()* must be executed. All further records will be run through with *next()* until this method returns the result *false*.

For the currently active record, the individual columns can be selected with the methods *getInt*, *getString*, etc. Optionally, this method can be passed the column number (e.g., *res.getInt(1)* for the first column) or the column name (e.g., *res.getInt("publID")*. The latter variant leads to more readable code, but is slower.

The following loop selects all found records from the previously given *SELECT* query and displays them in the console window:

```
while (res.next()) {
  int id = res.getInt("publID");
  String name = res.getString("publName");
  System.out.println("ID: " + id + "  Name: " + name);
}
```

Invalid and Empty Queries

If the syntax of an SQL command is invalid, then the execution of *executeQuery* throws an *SQLException* exception.

If the query returns no result (zero records), then *executeQuery* returns simply an empty *ResultSet* object (not *NULL*). The only way to determine whether a *SELECT* query has returned results is by executing *res.next()*. Once this method has returned the value *false*, the *ResultSet* object is empty.

Checking for NULL

Methods such as *getInt* and *getFloat* that return elementary Java data types are incapable of differentiating 0 and *NULL*. To determine whether the last selected data field contained *NULL*, one has the method *wasNull*:

```
int n = res.getInt(1);
if(res.wasNull)
  System.out.println("n = [NULL]");
else
  System.out.println("n = " + n);
```

With character strings, the use of *wasNull* is unnecessary, since in *String* variables, the state *null* can be stored. You can therefore execute *String s = res.getString(…)* and then test whether *s == null*.

Character Strings/Unicode

Internally, all character strings in Java are stored in the Unicode format. Connector/J and the MySQL server automatically take care of conversion of strings into the character set of the table. However, this has worked only since MySQL 4.1 and Connector/J 3.1. If you are working with older versions, you can select the desired character set with parameters of the JDBC connection URL.

Navigating in the ResultSet

In addition to the method *next*, there are several additional methods for selecting the currently active data record: *previous* activates the previous record, while *first* and *last* activate the records that their names imply. With these methods, the data record pointer is directed to the place before the first or after the last record. You can test with *isFirst* and *isLast* whether the beginning or end of the record list has been reached. The method *getRow* returns the number of the current record (1 for the first); *absolute* activates a record that is specified by its number.

Determining the Number of Found Records

Since Connector/J returns by default navigable *ResultSet*s, it is rather simple to determine the number of records: With *last*, the last record is activated, and then with *getRow* its number is determined:

```
res.last();
int n = res.getRow();
```

If you then wish to run a loop over all records, you must set the record pointer to the beginning:

```
res.beforeFirst();
while(res.next()) ...
```

If you also want to determine the number of columns, you need a *ResultSetMetaData* object, which we discuss in the next section.

Determining Metadata About the ResultSet

If you do not know in advance which data your *SELECT* query returns (for example, if you wish to write a program that can work with arbitrary tables), you can employ the class *ResultSetMetaData* to return all relevant information about the *SELECT* result: the number of columns (*getColumnCount*), their names (*getColumnName*), their data types (*getColumnType* and *getColumnTypeName*), and the number of decimal places (*getPrecision, getScale*). With methods such as *isNullable, isAutoIncrement*, and *isSigned*, you can find out additional properties of each column. All of these methods require as parameter the column number about which you want information.

You obtain a *ResultSetMetaData* object with the method *getMetaData*, which is applied to a *ResultSet* object. The following lines show a simple application of *ResultSetMetaData*:

```
int i, n;
ResultSetMetaData meta = res.getMetaData();
n = meta.getColumnCount();
System.out.println("number of columns: " + meta.getColumnCount());
for(i=1; i<=n; i++) {
  System.out.println("column " + i + ": " +
    " Name: " + meta.getColumnName(i) +
    " datatype: " + meta.getColumnTypeName(i));
}
```

Forward-Only ResultSets

By default, *ResultSets* are freely navigable; that is, you can change the currently active record at will using *previous, next*, etc. This is convenient, but it has the drawback that when you execute *executeQuery*, all data records that are found must be transferred from the MySQL server to the Java program. This can involve not only large data sets, but also the need for the Java program to reserve a large amount of memory. When you are processing numerous data sequentially, this is not the optimal way to proceed.

If you wish to transfer the records individually, you must define the *Statement* object for your *SELECT* query as follows. (*Integer.MIN_VALUE* is the smallest representable integer. Connector/J requires that exactly this value be passed.)

```
Statement stmt = conn.createStatement(
  java.sql.ResultSet.TYPE_FORWARD_ONLY,
  java.sql.ResultSet.CONCUR_READ_ONLY);
stmt.setFetchSize(Integer.MIN_VALUE);
ResultSet res = stmt.executeQuery("SELECT ...");
```

■**Caution** Note that you can use only *next()* for navigation in the *ResultSet* (that is, navigation is *forward-only*). Note as well that you can execute a further SQL command for the existing connection (*Connection* object) only when you have completely run through the *ResultSet* or have closed the connection with *close*. (You may, of course, have a second connection open.)

Variable ResultSets

If you want to edit the data in a table, you generally execute *INSERT, UPDATE*, and *DELETE* commands. However, JDBC offers another possibility: You can insert, edit, and delete data records directly in a *ResultSet* object; these changes are then executed in the underlying table. However, for this to function, certain conditions must be satisfied:

- The *Statement* object must be opened with the additional parameter
  ResultSet.CONCUR_UPDATABLE.

- The *SELECT* query can encompass only one table (no *JOIN*s), may not use any *GROUP*
  functions, and must include the primary index.

If these conditions are satisfied, you can delete the current record from the *ResultSet* and the
database with *deleteRow.*

To edit the current record, execute the methods *updateInt(n, 123), updateString(n, "new text"),*
etc. You must then confirm these changes with *updateRow.*

To insert a new record, first execute *moveToInsertRow.* Now specify the value to be stored with
updateXxx methods and confirm the insertion operation with *insertRow.*

If you wish to know the ID number of the new record (*AUTO_INCREMENT*), execute *last.* This
ensures that the new record is also the active record. You can then select the ID column with *getInt(n).*

The following program first selects all records from the *publisher* table of the *mylibrary* database. Then a new record is inserted, after which it is edited and then deleted. Records inserted into
a *ResultSet* can no longer be edited. Therefore, in our example program, the *ResultSet* is first input
anew.

```java
// SampleChangeResultSet.java
stmt = conn.createStatement(ResultSet.TYPE_SCROLL_SENSITIVE,
                            ResultSet.CONCUR_UPDATABLE);

// insert new publisher; then display all publishers
res = stmt.executeQuery(
  "SELECT publID, publName FROM publishers ORDER BY publID");
res.moveToInsertRow();
res.updateString(2, "New publisher");
res.insertRow();
res.last();
int newid = res.getInt(1);
res.beforeFirst();
while (res.next())
  System.out.println(res.getString(1) + " " + res.getString(2));
res.close();

// change previously inserted new publisher
res = stmt.executeQuery(
  "SELECT publID, publName FROM publishers WHERE publID = " + newid);
res.next();
res.updateString(2, "new with another name");
res.updateRow();

// ... and delete
res.last();
res.deleteRow();
res.close();
```

Closing a ResultSet Object

If you no longer need a *ResultSet* object, you should close it explicitly with *close.* This allows
reserved memory to be returned earlier than otherwise. In the case of incompletely run-through
forward-only *ResultSet*s, the result is the release of resources blocked by the MySQL server.

Prepared Statements

Prepared statements make it possible to formulate an SQL command with placeholders. Before the execution of the command, the placeholders must be passed. The advantage of this way of proceeding is that JDBC looks after the transformation of character strings and binary data into a MySQL-compatible syntax. This includes both the addition of quotation marks at the beginning and end of strings and the transformation of special characters such as ' into \' and \ into \\.

Prepared statements can also offer an advantage in speed, since the SQL code must be transferred only once to the database server.

The starting point for prepared statements is a *PreparedStatement* object, which is generated with the method *prepareStatement*. Note that character-string parameters may not be enclosed in quotation marks, which is usually the case with strings (that is, *VALUES (?)* and not *VALUES('?')*).

To pass parameters, use methods such as *setString*, *setInt*, *setNull*, *setDate*, and *setBinaryStream*. (A complete reference is given in the class description of *PreparedStatement*.)

To execute the SQL command, use, depending on the type of command, the familiar methods of the *Statement* class, for example, *executeUpdate*, *executeQuery*, *addBatch*, and *executeBatch*. What is new is that you can no longer pass parameters to these methods: The SQL command was already defined in *prepareStatement*, and the parameters are set with *setXxx* methods.

In the following example, two new publishers are inserted into the *publisher* table of the *mylibrary* database:

```
// SamplePreparedStatement.java
PreparedStatement pstmt = conn.prepareStatement(
  "INSERT INTO publishers (publName) VALUES (?)");
pstmt.setString(1, "O'Reilly");    // inserts O'Reilly
pstmt.executeUpdate();
pstmt.setString(1, "\\abc\"efg");  // inserts \abc"efg
pstmt.executeUpdate();
```

Transactions

JDBC supports transactions via the *Connection* object. Of course, transactions are possible only if your MySQL tables are in a format that supports transactions (generally InnoDB).

By default, JDBC is in AutoCommit mode; that is, every SQL command is considered a separate transaction and is executed immediately. You can determine the mode with *getAutoCommit* and change it with *setAutoCommit*. At the same time, the starting point for the first transaction is specified by *setAutoCommit(false)*, which you can either confirm with *commit* or abort with *rollback*. These two commands simultaneously start the next transaction.

The following lines show a simple application. Several *INSERT* commands are executed within a *try* block. If an error occurs, the entire transaction is aborted:

```
// no AutoCommit after every command
conn.setAutoCommit(false);

// execute several commands
try {
  stmt.executeUpdate("INSERT INTO table1 ...");
  stmt.executeUpdate("INSERT INTO table2 ...");
  conn.commit();
}
catch(Exception e) {
  conn.rollback();
}
```

Batch Commands

JDBC offers the possibility of executing several SQL commands as a block. Such command blocks are called *batches* in the database community. The advantage over the individual execution of SQL commands is somewhat greater efficiency (depending on the application).

Batch commands are formed in two parts: First, all commands to be executed are passed with *addBatch* to a *Statement* or *PreparedStatement* command. Then the commands thus collected are executed with *executeBatch*.

The method *executeBatch* returns an *int* field, which for each SQL command specifies how many records were changed (a number greater than or equal to 0). If this number could not be determined, but the command was executed without error, then the return value is *SUCCESS_NO_INFO*. If an error did occur, then the return value is *EXECUTE_FAILED*. (Note, however, that with syntax errors, the execution of the batch command is broken off with an exception.)

The following lines show the execution of a simple batch command:

```
int i;
stmt = conn.createStatement();
stmt.addBatch("INSERT INTO publishers (publName) VALUES ('publ1')");
stmt.addBatch("INSERT INTO publishers (publName) VALUES ('publ2')");
stmt.addBatch("INSERT INTO publishers (publName) VALUES " +
              "('publ3'), ('publ4')");
int[] n = stmt.executeBatch();
for(i=0; i < n.length; i++)
  System.out.println(
    "Recordsets changed by batch command no " + (i+1) + ": " + n[i]);
```

If no errors occur during execution, the following text appears in the console window:

```
Recordsets changed by batch command no 1: 1
Recordsets changed by batch command no 2: 1
Recordsets changed by batch command no 3: 2
```

■**Note** Do not confuse batches with transactions. Batches are appropriate only if you do not need to read in your altered data in the confines of the batch. Thus you can execute a series of *INSERT* or *UPDATE* commands within a batch only if you do not determine any *AUTO_INCREMENT* values or execute any *SELECT* queries in between. Moreover, batches offer no mechanism for error handling. If an error occurs within a batch, then all SQL commands executed to that point remain valid, while all further commands will be rejected.

Batches are thus a simple aid in executing a large number of *INSERT* or *UPDATE* commands efficiently. The goal of a transaction, on the other hand, is to obtain greater data security. For example, transactions ensure that either all commands of a transaction are correctly executed, or none of them.

Of course, a batch can be executed within a transaction.

Working with Binary Data (BLOBs)

JDBC offers several ways of dealing with binary data:

- When the task at hand is to read data from a file or to store data to a file, the methods *ResultSet.getBinaryStream* and *PreparedStatement.setBinaryStream* are to be recommended. In the first case, you can read the binary data from the database with the aid of an *InputStream*. In the second case, you pass an existing *InputStream* object (e.g., that of a file) to transfer its data into a parameter of an SQL command.

- With BLOBs that contain Unicode text you will find *getCharacterStream* and *setCharacterStream* helpful. You can use *java.io.Reader* objects with them to select text at the character level.

- If you wish to process data as a *byte* array, you can use the methods *getBytes* and *setBytes*.

- Finally, JDBC offers the interfaces *Blob* and *Clob* (character large object): With *Blob* objects you can conveniently read and edit data byte by byte with the methods *getBytes* and *setBytes*. *Clob* objects offer a character-oriented approach with methods such as *getAsciiStream* and *getCharacterStream*. The passing of *Blob/Clob* objects takes place with the methods *getClob*, *setBlob*, *setClob*, and *getBlob*.

An Example

The following example shows the application of the methods *getBinaryStream* and *setBinaryStream*. The program loads the content of the file test.jpg, stores it in a new record in the database exceptions (table *a_blob*), reads it from there, and stores the data thus obtained in the new file test-copy.jpg. Then the new record in *a_blob* is deleted.

The SQL commands are executed with *PreparedStatement* objects that are created at the beginning of the program excerpt reproduced here. For transferring the file into the *a_blob* table, a *FileInputStream* object with *setBinaryStream* as parameter is simply passed to the first *PreparedStatement* object.

It is somewhat more complicated to read the data from the *a_blob* table and store it in a file. The *BinaryStream* object obtained from the *ResultSet* object via *getBinaryStream* must be read in a loop and copied with the help of a buffer into a *fileOutputStream* object:

```
// example SampleBlob.java
import java.sql.*;
import java.io.*;
...

// make connection
Connection conn = DriverManager.getConnection(
  "jdbc:mysql://uranus/exceptions", "root", "uranus");

// create three PreparedStatement objects
PreparedStatement pstmt1, pstmt2, pstmt3;
pstmt1 = conn.prepareStatement(
  "INSERT INTO test_blob (a_blob) VALUES(?)");
pstmt2 = conn.prepareStatement(
  "SELECT a_blob FROM test_blob WHERE id=?");
pstmt3 = conn.prepareStatement(
  "DELETE FROM test_blob WHERE id=?");

// read file test.jpg and store in a BLOB field
File readfile = new File("test.jpg");
FileInputStream fis = new FileInputStream(readfile);
pstmt1.setBinaryStream(1, fis, (int)readfile.length());
pstmt1.executeUpdate();
fis.close();

// determine id of the new records
long id = ((com.mysql.jdbc.Statement)pstmt1).getLastInsertID();
```

```
// create new, empty file copy-test.jpg
File writefile = new File("copy-test.jpg");
if(writefile.exists()) {
  writefile.delete();
  writefile.createNewFile(); }
FileOutputStream fos = new FileOutputStream(writefile);

// read BLOB field from the database
pstmt2.setLong(1, id);
ResultSet res = pstmt2.executeQuery();
res.next();
InputStream is = res.getBinaryStream(1);

// store binary data in the new file
final int BSIZE = 2^15;
int n;
byte[] buffer = new byte[BSIZE];
while((n=is.read(buffer, 0, BSIZE))>0)
  fos.write(buffer, 0, n);

// close open objects
is.close();
fos.close();
res.close();

// delete the new record
pstmt3.setLong(1, id);
pstmt3.executeUpdate();
```

Peculiarities of Large BLOBs

BLOBs are always transferred in their entirety between MySQL and the Java program. Connector/J is incapable of piecewise transfer. For this reason, the Java virtual machine (JVM) must be so configured that it can reserve enough space to hold the entire BLOB in local memory.

Moreover, the MySQL server must allow the transfer of large data packets (variable *max_allowed_packet*; see Chapter 22). If necessary, you can increase the value of the variable on the client side by executing the following command:

```
SET max_allowed_packet=16000000
```

CHAPTER 18

■■■

C

This chapter gives a first introduction to programming MySQL applications with the programming languages C. In particular, we will introduce the client library libmysqlclient, which is a part of MySQL. This chapter considers programming only under Unix/Linux, and not under Windows.

As test system for this chapter I have used SUSE Linux Professional 9.2 with the compiler gcc 3.3 and the MySQL package (version 5.0.*n*) downloaded from mysql.com. If you are working under another Linux distribution or operating system, you will require different paths and other settings.

The C API (libmysqlclient)

The C application programming interface (API) is the most elementary interface to MySQL. All other APIs, such as those for PHP, Perl, and C++, are based on the C API. Thus a knowledge of the C API will facilitate learning about the other APIs. The API functions constitute a component of the library libmysqlclient. Every C program that wishes to use MySQL functions must therefore have access to this library.

Please note that there are several versions of libmysqlclient in use: version 10 for MySQL 3.23.*n*, version 12 of MySQL 4.0.*n*, and finally, version 14 for MySQL 4.1.*n* and beyond. (This chapter is based on version 14.)

These libraries are largely compatible in their basic functions and differ primarily in the supplementary functions that have been added to newer versions. However, there is an important exception: beginning with MySQL 4.1, the internal encryption of MySQL passwords has changed. That necessitated changes in the C API, which were instituted in version 14. For communication with a MySQL server from version 4.1 on, libmysqlclient is necessary. (An emergency solution to difficulties is to start the server with the option --old-passwords; then the older libmysqlclient version can be used.)

Tip An extensive syntax reference for the data structures and functions from the library libmysqlclient mentioned in this chapter appears in Chapter 23.

Hello, World!

Assumptions

For developing C programs under Linux or a comparable Unix system, you will need, of course, the usual equipment, in particular, a C compiler (generally gcc) and the program make. Furthermore, all the necessary include and library files for compiling and linking must be installed. With many distributions (such as SUSE, Red Hat), certain packages must be installed as well, ending with -devel (e.g., `glicb-devel`). It might be a good idea to test out your installation by executing a very simple C program.

For the development of MySQL programs you will need, in addition, the MySQL developer files, consisting of include files and libraries. These files usually are located in the package `MySQL-Devel-n`. This chapter assumes that the developer files are located in the following places: include files at `/usr/include/mysql`, and libraries at `/usr/lib/mysql`.

If these files are located elsewhere on your system, then the compile and link options will have to be changed accordingly.

Introductory Example

Perhaps a small and simple program will help develop some intuition in the direction of MySQL programming with C. The following example assumes that the database *mylibrary* has been installed on the local computer (see Appendix B). Furthermore, in the code you must change, in the function call *mysql_real_connect*, the user name (*"root"*) and password *("XXX")*. The code is documented to the extent that it should give at least some idea of what is going on. Details on the use of MySQL functions appear later.

```c
// example file hellow/main.c
#include <stdio.h>
#include <mysql.h>  // functions from libmysqlclient
int main(int argc, char *argv[])
{
  int i;
  MYSQL *conn;         // connection
  MYSQL_RES *result;   // result of the SELECT query
  MYSQL_ROW row;       // a record of the SELECT query

  // create connection to MySQL
  conn = mysql_init(NULL);
  if(mysql_real_connect(
       conn, "localhost", "root", "XXX",
       "mylibrary", 0, NULL, 0) == NULL) {
    fprintf(stderr, "sorry, no database connection ...\n");
    return 1;
  }

  // only if Unicode output (utf8) is desired
    mysql_query(conn, "SET NAMES 'utf8'");

  // create list of all pulishers and number of titles published for each pulisher
  const char *sql="SELECT COUNT(titleID), publName \
                   FROM publishers, titles \
                   WHERE publishers.publID = titles.publID \
                   GROUP BY publishers.publID \
                   ORDER BY publName";
  if(mysql_query(conn, sql)) {
    fprintf(stderr, "%s\n", mysql_error(conn));
    fprintf(stderr, "%s\n", sql);
    return 1;
  }
```

```
  // process result
  result = mysql_store_result(conn);
  if(result==NULL) {
    if(mysql_error(conn))
      fprintf(stderr, "%s\n", mysql_error(conn));
    else
      fprintf(stderr, "%s\n", "unknown error\n");
    return 1;
  }
  printf("%i records found \n", (int)mysql_num_rows(result));

  // loop over all records
  while((row = mysql_fetch_row(result)) != NULL) {
    for(i=0; i < mysql_num_fields(result); i++) {
      if(row[i] == NULL)
        printf("[NULL]\t");
      else
        printf("%s\t", row[i]);
    }
    printf("\n");
  }

  // release memory, sever connection
  mysql_free_result(result);
  mysql_close(conn);
  return 0;
}
```

If you execute the program, you should get the following result:

```
uranus:~/hellow-c $ ./hellow
13 records found
23      Addison-Wesley
4       Apress
1       Bonnier Pocket
1       Diogenes Verlag
1       dpunkt
1       Galileo
1       Hanser
2       Markt und Technik
2       New Riders
3       O'Reilly & Associates
2       Ordfront förlag AB
1       Sybex
1       Zsolnay
```

Compiling and Linking

To compile and link the example program just presented under Linux or comparable Unix system, execute the following command:

```
$ gcc -o hellow -I/usr/include/mysql -lmysqlclient main.c
```

In detail, the components of the command have the following meaning:

gcc	The GNU C and C++ compiler
-o hellow	The name of the executable
-I/usr/include/mysql	The location of the MySQL include files (in particular mysql.h)
-lmysqlclient	Link the executable to the MySQL client library
main.c	The code file

Depending on the system configuration, the location of the MySQL include files can be different from those presented here (e.g., /usr/local/include/mysql).

Makefile

Assembling the input for the command for compiling and linking a program is generally rather labor-intensive (especially when a project consists of several files). Therefore, it is a good idea to create a file with the name Makefile that contains all necessary instructions in the syntax of the make command. To compile, you simply input make, which decides on its own which parts of the program need to be recompiled.

As starting point for creating your own projects, you can use the following example. Note that the make syntax for the indentation requires tabs (not spaces):

```
# example file hellow/Makefile
CC = gcc
INCLUDES = -I/usr/include/mysql
LIBS = -lmysqlclient

all:hellow

main.o: main.c
        $(CC) -c $(INCLUDES) main.c

hellow: main.o
        $(CC) -o hellow main.o $(LIBS)

clean:
        rm -f hellow main.o
```

Static Binding of MySQL Functions

With the Makefile presented here, the library libmysqlclient is linked to the program dynamically if the *shared* library libmysqlclient.so can be found in one of the usual places (under Linux in the directory /lib or /usr/lib).

If this fails (because the library was not found) or if you wish that all MySQL API functions should be integrated directly into the executable (static instead of dynamic binding), you must specify the location of the static library variant libmysqlclient.a. This is generally in the directory /usr/lib/mysql.

Furthermore, you must now specify the additional option -lz. This permits the library libz to be consulted during linking. It contains functions accessed by libmyssqlclient for compressing data exchange between client and server (when that is desired):

```
$ gcc main.c -I/usr/include/mysql -L/usr/lib/mysql -lmysqlclient \
    -lz -o hellow
```

If you are using make, you need to change only the *LIBS* variable:

```
LIBS =  -L/usr/lib/mysql -lmysqlclient -lz
```

It can happen (depending on the Unix system and on which libmysqlclient functions you use) that in addition to libz, you will require other libraries. Table 18-1 summarizes the options that might be necessary:

Table 18-1. *Options for Static Linking of MySQL Programs*

Option	Meaning
-L/usr/lib/mysql	location of the static MySQL libraries (libmysqlclient.a)
-lc	basic libraries with basic functions (libc)
-lcrypt	library with cryptographic functions (libcrypt)
-lm	library with mathematical functions (libm)
-lnsl	library with *name service* functions (libnsl)
-lnss_files and -lnss_dns	library with name service switch functions; further information from man nsswitch.conf
-lz	library with compression functions (libz)

The static variant has the advantage that all libmysqlclient functions that the program uses are compiled directly into the executable. This allows the program to run on a computer that does not have the libmysqlclient library installed.

However, this advantage is paid for by a larger executable than that in the dynamic version. The difference in size depends on how many functions you use from libmysqlclient. In our "Hello World" program, the dynamic executable is only 11KB, while the static variant weighs in at around 1MB. (Note that only the MySQL functions are statically bound, not all functions from all other libraries.)

You can easily determine which dynamic libraries a program must access during execution with the command ldd. In the static variant of the "Hello World" program, the result looked as follows on my test system:

```
$ ldd hellow
        linux-gate.so.1 =>  (0xffffe000)
        libz.so.1 => /lib/libz.so.1 (0x4002b000)
        libc.so.6 => /lib/tls/libc.so.6 (0x4003c000)
        /lib/ld-linux.so.2 => /lib/ld-linux.so.2 (0x40000000)
```

In the dynamic variant, the list of libraries is much longer. It contains, in addition to libmysqlclient, all libraries that are accessed by libmysqlclient:

```
$ ldd hellow
(0xffffe000)
        libmysqlclient.so.14 => /usr/lib/libmysqlclient.so.14 (0x4002b000)
        libc.so.6 => /lib/tls/libc.so.6 (0x4012d000)
        libcrypt.so.1 => /lib/libcrypt.so.1 (0x40243000)
        libnsl.so.1 => /lib/libnsl.so.1 (0x40275000)
        libm.so.6 => /lib/tls/libm.so.6 (0x4028b000)
        libz.so.1 => /lib/libz.so.1 (0x402ae000)
        libnss_files.so.2 => /lib/libnss_files.so.2 (0x402bf000)
        libnss_dns.so.2 => /lib/libnss_dns.so.2 (0x402c9000)
        libresolv.so.2 => /lib/libresolv.so.2 (0x402d0000)
        /lib/ld-linux.so.2 => /lib/ld-linux.so.2 (0x40000000)
```

Establishing the Connection

Before establishing a connection, you must initialize a data structure of type *MYSQL* with *mysql_init*. The connection is then established with *mysql_real_connect*, where a parameter, a pointer to the *MYSQL* structure, as well as the usual connection data must be specified: the host name (or *"localhost"*) or the IP number of the server, the user name, password, name of the default database, the socket number (or 0 for the default value), the name of the socket file (or *NULL* for the default socket file), as well as certain flags that describe particular properties of the connection.

A flag such as *CLIENT_COMPRESS* is involved if the data should be transmitted in compressed form. *CLIENT_MULTI_STATEMENTS* makes it possible to execute several commands at a time; such commands must be separated by semicolons. *CLIENT_MULTI_RESULTS* enables the processing of several *SELECT* results, which is required when a stored procedure is called. (A list of more constants can be found in Chapter 23.)

```
MYSQL *conn;
unsigned long flags;
flags = CLIENT_MULTI_STATEMENTS | ...;
conn = mysql_init(NULL);
if(mysql_real_connect(conn, "hostname", "username", "password",
                      "databasename", 0, NULL, flags) == NULL) {
    fprintf(stderr, "error messages ...\n");
```

Once the connection is no longer needed, it should be closed with *mysql_close*.

```
mysql_close(conn);
```

Evaluation of the Configuration File my.cnf

If in establishing the connection you wish to have the settings in the configuration file my.cnf automatically evaluated (e.g., connecting over a nonstandard port number or socket file), then add a call to the function *mysql_options* between *mysql_init* and *mysql_real_connect*. The following instruction yields the result that all configuration settings of the group *[client]* are considered, to the extent that *NULL* or 0 is passed for the corresponding parameters in the following *mysql_real_connect* call. (This holds for user name and password as well.)

```
conn = mysql_init(NULL);
mysql_options(conn, MYSQL_READ_DEFAULT_GROUP, "");
mysql_real_connect(...);
```

If in addition to the *[client]* options, you also want a further options group to be considered, then you should give its name in the last parameter of *mysql_options*:

```
mysql_options(conn, MYSQL_READ_DEFAULT_GROUP, "mygroup");
```

Evaluation of Options in the Command Line

With many standard MySQL programs (such as mysql, mysqladmin, mysqldump), you can send a connection parameter in a uniform format in the command line, for example, -hname or --host==name. An evaluation of this command parameter is especially sensible if you are developing administration programs in C that are to be applied to arbitrary databases. Unfortunately, the MySQL library does not offer a convenient means of doing so like *mysql_options*. Instead, it must be done by hand. The following points sketch the way to proceed:

- Instead of *mysql_options*, you call the unfortunately undocumented MySQL function *load_defaults* to read the settings from my.cnf and to copy them into the field of the command parameters (*argc* and *argv* of *main*). This has the advantage that all settings, whether they come from my.cnf or were passed as parameters, can be processed uniformly. Also, the string field *groups* specifies which options groups from my.cnf should be read and copied into *argv*.

```
const char *groups[] = {"mygroup", "client", NULL};
load_defaults("my", groups, &argc, &argv);
```

- Now create a loop and evaluate, with the standard function *getopt_long* (include file getopt.h), all parameters from *argv* and initialize variables for the host name, user name, etc. If a password is to be passed in the command line, you should overwrite it with blank characters for reasons of security. For interactive input of a password you can use the function *get_tty_password*.

- Finally, pass the values thus determined to *mysql_real_connect*.

■**Tip** This way of proceeding is described in full in the chapter "The MySQL C API" in the book *MySQL* by Paul DuBois. This chapter can also be found as a sample chapter on the author's website, most recently at the following address: http://www.kitebird.com/mysql-book/.

Executing SQL Commands

Simple Commands

To execute an SQL command, pass it as a character string to the function *mysql_query*. The string must generally contain only one SQL command, and it may not end with a semicolon. There is more information on executing several commands at once in Chapter 18.

The function *mysql_query* returns 0 if the SQL command was accepted by the server. (The return value allows one to draw conclusions only about whether the command was syntactically correct, not about whether the command changed data or whether, say, a *SELECT* command returned results.)

After *DELETE*, *INSERT*, or *UPDATE* commands, you can use *mysql_affected_rows* to determine how many records were changed as a result of the command. The result has the data type *my_ulonglong*. This data type is defined in the MySQL library; it describes a 64-bit unsigned integer.

If you have inserted a new record—perhaps with *INSERT*—into a table with an *AUTO_INCREMENT* column, you can determine the value of the *AUTO_INCREMENT* field with the function *mysql_insert_id*. This function also returns a result in the form of a *my_ulonglong* integer:

```
mysql_query(conn, "INSERT INTO publishers (publName) \
                VALUES ('publisher')");
printf("publID = %i\n", (int)mysql_insert_id(conn));
```

Evaluating SELECT Results

After a *SELECT* command executed with *mysql_query*, you can process the expected results with either *mysql_store_result* or *mysql_use_result*. Both functions return a *MYSQL_RES* structure, from which you will be able to read out all the records with *mysql_fetch_row* one after another. The following lines show the general way of proceeding:

```
MYSQL_RES *result;  // result of a SELECT query
MYSQL_ROW row;      // a record of the result
...
result = mysql_store_result(conn);
if(result==NULL)
  fprintf(stderr, "%error ...\n");
else {
  while((row = mysql_fetch_row(result)) != NULL) {
    // process each record
  }
  mysql_free_result(result);  // release result
}
```

The *MYSQL_RES* structure for the results should then be released as soon as possible with *mysql_free_result* in order to keep memory requirements in the client (*mysql_store_result*) and resource demands on the server (*mysql_use_result*) as small as possible.

As Table 18-2 shows, *mysql_store_result* and *mysql_use_result* differ fundamentally internally. If you expect smaller rather than larger *SELECT* results, then *mysql_store_result* is the better choice. It makes less of a demand on the server and offers more convenience for client programming. Only when you expect large quantities of data (in the megabyte quantity) should you consider *mysql_use_result*.

Table 18-2. *Internal Management of SELECT Results*

mysql_store_result	mysql_use_result
All found records are immediately transmitted to client memory. With large record lists, this can result in large memory requirements for the client.	At first, no records are transmitted; that is, the data remain on the server. This means that the server is responsible for record management. Until this process is complete, resources on the server are occupied.
The records can be addressed in any order and as often as desired (function *mysql_data_seek*).	The records must be processed one at a time, and can be read only once.
The number of records found by *SELECT* can be determined immediately with *mysql_num_rows*.	The number of found records is known only after all records have been run through with *mysql_fetch_row*.

Once you have read a record with *mysql_fetch_row* into a *MYSQL_ROW* structure, you can access the individual fields (columns) easily with *row[n]*. All results are passed as 0-terminated strings (including numbers, dates, *TIMESTAMP*s, etc.). For fields that are empty in the database (*NULL*), *row[n]* also contains *NULL*. One must be careful in the evaluation of binary data, as we shall discuss a bit later.

The following loop runs through all records and outputs the individual columns, separated by tab characters, in the console window:

```
int i;
while((row = mysql_fetch_row(result)) != NULL) {
  for(i=0; i < mysql_num_fields(result); i++) {
    if(row[i] == NULL)
      printf("[NULL]\t");
    else
      printf("%s\t", row[i]);
  }
  printf("\n");
}
```

If you are developing a program to read arbitrary tables, that is, if you do not know in advance how many columns the result will include and what data types were originally in the MySQL database, you can use *mysql_num_fields* to determine the number of columns, and *mysql_fetch_fields* to get metainformation about each column (data type, maximum number of characters and digits, etc.). These functions are described in greater detail in Chapter 23.

Executing Several Commands at a Time

Normally, you can execute only a single SQL command with *mysql_query*. A semicolon can appear in such a command only when it is syntactically allowed, and that is normally not the case! In particular, SQL does not allow for a command to end in a semicolon. (The C API will raise an error if you attempt to do so.)

The commands *CREATE PROCEDURE, CREATE FUNCTION, CREATE TRIGGER,* and the like are exceptions when they define a stored procedure or trigger: In such commands the semicolon serves as a separator between the SQL instructions that are part of the stored procedure or trigger. Such commands can be executed without problem.

MULTI_STATEMENTS Mode

Starting with MySQL version 4.1, the C API offers the additional option of executing several SQL commands at a time. To do so, you must explicitly activate the *MULTI_STATEMENTS* mode. There are two ways of doing this:

- Pass to *mysql_real_connect* the option *CLIENT_MULTI_STATEMENTS* in the last parameter:

```
mysql_real_connect(conn, "localhost", "username", "xxx",
        "dbname", 0, NULL, CLIENT_MULTI_STATEMENTS);
```

- Set *MULTI_STATEMENTS* mode after the fact with *mysql_set_server_option*. Note that the *MULTI_STATEMENTS* constant has another name here.

```
mysql_set_server_option(conn, MYSQL_OPTION_MULTI_STATEMENTS_ON);
```

You are then allowed to send several SQL commands at a time to *mysql_query*. The commands must be separated by semicolons:

```
mysql_query("command1; command2; command3");
```

Status information: If you wish to determine after an *INSERT, UPDATE,* or *DELETE* command how many records were changed, you can execute as the first command *mysql_affected_rows* as usual. For the additional commands you must first execute *mysql_next_result* (see below).

Error handling: If an error occurs in the execution of the first command, MySQL ignores the rest of the commands; *mysql_query* returns an error number, while *mysql_error* and *mysql_errno* provide any necessary additional information on the underlying problem.

It is more difficult to detect an error that occurs in the SQL commands after the first: *mysql_query* returns 0 (OK) as return value even when execution ended with an invalid SQL command. You can tell that an error occurred only if you run through all the results with *mysql_next_result* (see below). An error number is returned by *mysql_next_results* for the invalid command. Then you can obtain the related error text with *mysql_error*.

MULTI_RESULTS Mode (Evaluating Several SELECT Results)

It is permissible in stored procedures to execute *SELECT* multiple times. A single command (*CALL spname*) can thereby return several results. For the results to be processed, *MULTI_RESULTS* mode must be activated. To do so, pass to *mysql_real_connect* the option *CLIENT_MULTI_RESULTS*. Moreover, *MULTI_RESULTS* mode is automatically activated when *MULTI_STATEMENTS* mode is used.

In *MULTI_RESULTS* mode you can immediately, as usual, evaluate the first *SELECT* result after the execution of an SQL command (*mysql_store_result*, etc.). You can test whether there are additional results with *mysql_more_results*. If that is the case, you can activate the next result with *mysql_next_result*, which can return three different types of value:

0 (OK, there are additional results);

-1 (OK, there are no additional results);

> 0 (error number).

After the execution of *mysql_next_result* you can evaluate the *SELECT* result with *mysql_use_result* or *mysql_store_result*. Furthermore, functions such as *mysql_error*, *mysql_warning_count*, and *mysql_affected_rows* provide status information on the command in question.

Example

The following example shows the execution of several commands and the evaluation of the results. The SQL command was divided over several lines with a backslash to increase the readability of the code.

```c
// example file multi/main.c
#include <stdio.h>
#include <mysql.h>

int main(int argc, char *argv[])
{
  int        i, next;
  MYSQL      *conn;    // connection to the MySQL server
  MYSQL_RES *result;  // manage SELECT results
  MYSQL_ROW row;      // process data record

  // create connection
  conn = mysql_init(NULL);
  mysql_options(conn, MYSQL_READ_DEFAULT_GROUP, "");
  if(mysql_real_connect(
       conn, "localhost", "root", "uranus",
       "mylibrary", 0, NULL, 0) == NULL) {
    fprintf(stderr, "sorry, no database connection ...\n");
    return 1;
  }
  mysql_set_server_option(conn, MYSQL_OPTION_MULTI_STATEMENTS_ON);

  // execute SQL commands
  const char *sql="SELECT * FROM categories LIMIT 5;\
              INSERT INTO categories (catName) \
                VALUES ('test1'), ('test2');\
              SELECT 1+2+dummy;\
              DELETE FROM categories WHERE catName LIKE 'test%';\
              DROP TABLE IF EXISTS dummy";
  if(mysql_query(conn, sql)) {
    fprintf(stderr, "MySQL error: %s\n", mysql_error(conn));
    fprintf(stderr, "MySQL error number: %i\n", mysql_errno(conn));
  }
```

```
  do  // loop over all results
  {
    printf("\n-------------------------------------------------\n\n");
    printf("Affected rows: %i\n", mysql_affected_rows(conn));
    if(mysql_warning_count(conn))
      fprintf(stderr, "MySQL warnings: %i\n", mysql_warning_count(conn));

    result= mysql_store_result(conn);
    if(result) {
      // display SELECT results
      while((row = mysql_fetch_row(result)) != NULL) {
        printf("result: ");
        for(i=0; i < mysql_num_fields(result); i++) {
          if(row[i] == NULL)
            printf("[NULL]\t");
          else
            printf("%s\t", row[i]);
        }
        printf("\n");
      }
      mysql_free_result(result);
    } else
      printf("no result\n");

    // read next result
    next = mysql_next_result(conn);
    if(next>0) {
      printf("\n-------------------------------------------------\n\n");
      printf("mysql_next_result error code: %i\n", next);
      if(mysql_errno(conn))
          fprintf(stderr, "MySQL error: %s\n", mysql_error(conn));
    }
  } while (!next);

  // close connection
  mysql_close(conn);
  return 0;
}
```

When you execute the program, you obtain the following output:

```
user:~/c/multi> ./multi
-----------------------------------------------
Affected rows: -1
result: 1       Computer books                  11      2004-12-02 18:37:20
result: 2       Databases                       1       2004-12-02 18:37:20
result: 3       Programming                     1       2004-12-02 18:37:20
result: 4       Relational Databases            2       2004-12-02 18:37:20
result: 5       Object-oriented databases       2       2004-12-02 18:37:20
-----------------------------------------------
Affected rows: 2
no result
-----------------------------------------------
Affected rows: -1
result: 3
-----------------------------------------------
```

```
Affected rows: 2
no result
-----------------------------------------------
Affected rows: 0
MySQL warnings: 1
no result
```

Prepared Statements

In many applications, a number of similar queries must be executed that differ only in the values of certain parameters. For such cases, MySQL since version 4.1 has offered *prepared statements*. The entire SQL command is transported to the MySQL server only once, and thereafter only the varying parameter values need to be sent. This not only reduces somewhat the amount of data to be transported, it also makes the processing of the command more efficient, since the MySQL server needs to analyze the structure of the command only once.

An additional advantage of prepared statements is that numbers, times, and dates are passed not as strings, but as buffer variables in a suitable C data type (e.g., *int* for MySQL *INT* numbers). However, this requires a relatively complex initialization of various data structures, which must take place before execution of the first command.

Executing a Command Multiple Times

In the following example, the command *INSERT INTO titles (title, subtitle, langID) VALUES (?, ?, ?)* is to be executed several times with varying parameters. To accomplish this, first create a *MYSQL_STMT* data structure with *mysql_stmt_init* and initialize it with *mysql_stmt_prepare*. You simply pass a string with the SQL command to this function, where each parameter is represented by a question mark.

The three parameters (two strings, one integer) are described by a *MYSQL_BIND* field, whose elements are overwritten with zeros before initialization (*memset*). At least the data type and a buffer variable must be specified for each parameter. In executing the SQL command the data are read from the buffer. A reference to all allowable data types (*buffer_type*) can be found in Chapter 23. After initialization of the field elements, these are appended to the command with *mysql_bind_param*.

Now the command can be executed as often as you like with *mysql_stmt_execute*, with the parameters being set first. If the value *NULL* is to be passed in a parameter, the variable to which *bind[n].is_null* points must be set to 1. This is demonstrated in the following code, in the second execution of the command for the parameter *langID*. With character strings, the actual number of characters must be specified. (For this, the variables *strlen_title* and *strlen_subtitle* were bound to the length element of the *MYSQL_BIND* structure.)

```c
// example file prepare1/main.c
#include <stdio.h>
#include <mysql.h>

int main(int argc, char *argv[])
{
  MYSQL *conn;        // connection to MySQL server
  MYSQL_STMT *stmt;   // data structure for the prepared statement
  MYSQL_BIND bind[3]; // description of the parameters

  char *insert =
    "INSERT INTO titles (title, subtitle, langID) VALUES (?, ?, ?)";
  char title_buf[256];
  char subtitle_buf[256];
  unsigned long title_len, subtitle_len;
  int langID;
  my_bool langID_is_null;
```

```c
    // connection to MySQL
    conn = mysql_init(NULL);
    mysql_options(conn, MYSQL_READ_DEFAULT_FILE, "");
    if(mysql_real_connect(
          conn, "localhost", "root", "uranus",
          "mylibrary", 0, NULL, 0) == NULL) {
      fprintf(stderr, "sorry, no database connection ...\n");
      return 1;
    }

    // create statement structure
    stmt = mysql_stmt_init(conn);

    // initialize prepared statement
    mysql_stmt_prepare(stmt, insert, strlen(insert));

    // define parameters of the prepared statement
    memset(bind, 0, sizeof(bind));
    bind[0].buffer_type   = FIELD_TYPE_STRING;
    bind[0].buffer        = title_buf;
    bind[0].buffer_length = 256;
    bind[0].length        = &title_len;

    bind[1].buffer_type   = FIELD_TYPE_STRING;
    bind[1].buffer        = subtitle_buf;
    bind[1].buffer_length = 256;
    bind[1].length        = &subtitle_len;

    bind[2].buffer_type   = FIELD_TYPE_LONG;
    bind[2].buffer        = (gptr) &langID;
    bind[2].is_null       = &langID_is_null;
    mysql_stmt_bind_param(stmt, bind);

    // execute command for the first time
    strcpy(title_buf, "title1");
    title_len = strlen(title_buf);
    strcpy(subtitle_buf, "test prepared statements");
    subtitle_len = strlen(subtitle_buf);
    langID=1;
    langID_is_null = 0;
    mysql_stmt_execute(stmt);
    printf("new title with titleId=%d has been inserted\n",
          (int) mysql_insert_id(conn));

    // execute again
    strcpy(title_buf, "title2");
    title_len = strlen(title_buf);
    strcpy(subtitle_buf, "test prepared statements");
    subtitle_len = strlen(subtitle_buf);
    langID_is_null = 1;       // langID = NULL
    mysql_stmt_execute(stmt);
    printf("new title with titleId=%d has been inserted\n",
          (int) mysql_insert_id(conn));

    // close statement and connection
    mysql_stmt_close(stmt);
    mysql_close(conn);
    return 0;
}
```

Evaluate SELECT Results

When you execute *SELECT* commands as prepared statements, you must correlate the buffer variables to the columns of a *SELECT* result. In this way, mechanisms similar to those for parameter passing can also be used in reading results. The advantage over the previously described functions *mysql_store_result* and *mysql_fetch_row* is that you receive numbers and dates not in the form of character strings, but as *int* variables, *MYSQL_TIME* structures, etc. This greatly simplifies further processing.

The following example reads some records from the *titles* table (columns *title*, *titleID*, *catID*, and *ts*). The connection between the result columns and corresponding C variables is again via a *MYSQL_BIND* field, which this time is processed with *mysql_stmt_bind_result*. Note that this function can be called only after *mysql_stmt_prepare*.

After execution of the SQL command via *mysql_stmt_execute*, you can transfer all the resulting records to the client using *mysql_stmt_store_result*. Calling this function is optional, but it simplifies evaluation of the result, since you now can use functions such as *mysql_stmt_num_rows* and *mysql_stmt_data_seek*. (If you call *mysql_stmt_store_result*, MySQL behaves as with the function *mysql_store_result*. Avoid *mysql_stmt_store_result*, whose behavior is like that of *mysql_use_result*. Further details can be read in Table 18-2.)

Now the individual records are transferred via *mysql_stmt_fetch* into the variables specified in the *MYSQL_BIND* field. The function returns zero if there are no more results. *mysql_stmt_fetch* functions independently of whether *mysql_stmt_result* was previously executed. In one case the records are read from the local buffer, in the other case from the server.

You can determine the number of result records with *mysql_stmt_num_rows*. If you want to read the records in any order, call the function *mysql_stmt_data_seek* before *mysql_stmt_fetch*. Metadata on the results can be obtained with *mysql_stmt_result_metadata*.

You must always check in the output of results whether the value is *NULL*. In such a case, the variable to which *bind[n].is_null* refers contains the value 0. In the following example, such a test is carried out for *catID*, since this is the only column of the *SELECT* command for which *NULL* is a permissible value.

This example also demonstrates the use of date and time values. The column *titles.ts* contains the *TIMESTAMP* value of the most recent change. The corresponding data type for *MYSQL_BIND* is *FIELD_TYPE_TIMESTAMP*. The time value is transferred into a *MYSQL_TIME* variable, from which the individual components can easily be read out (*.year*, *.month*, etc.).

```
// example file prepare2/main.c
#include <stdio.h>
#include <mysql.h>

int main(int argc, char *argv[])
{
  MYSQL      *conn;      // connection to MySQL server
  MYSQL_STMT *stmt;      // prepared statement
  char       *cmd =
    "SELECT title, titleID, catID, ts \
     FROM titles ORDER BY RAND() LIMIT 5";

  MYSQL_BIND   bind[4]; // result column
  char         title_buf[256];
  unsigned long title_len;
  int          titleID, catID;
  my_bool      catID_is_null;
  MYSQL_TIME   ts;

  int          err;      // for the return value of the mysql functions
```

```
    // create connection to MySQL
    .. see the previous example

    // for UTF-8 outputs
    mysql_query(conn, "SET NAMES 'utf8'");

    // initialize and prepare prepared statement
    stmt = mysql_stmt_init(conn);
    mysql_stmt_prepare(stmt, cmd, strlen(cmd));

    // declare result columns
    memset(bind, 0, sizeof(bind));
    bind[0].buffer_type = FIELD_TYPE_VAR_STRING; // title
    bind[0].buffer = title_buf;
    bind[0].buffer_length = 256;
    bind[0].length = &title_len;

    bind[1].buffer_type = FIELD_TYPE_LONG;      // titleID
    bind[1].buffer =  (gptr) &titleID;

    bind[2].buffer_type = FIELD_TYPE_LONG;      // catID
    bind[2].buffer =  (gptr) &catID;
    bind[2].is_null = &catID_is_null;

    bind[3].buffer_type = FIELD_TYPE_TIMESTAMP; // ts
    bind[3].buffer = (gptr) &ts;

    // bind result columns to variables
    mysql_stmt_bind_result(stmt, bind);

    // execute command
    err = mysql_stmt_execute(stmt);
    if(err) {
      fprintf(stderr, "sorry, an error happened ...\n");
      return 1;  }

    // read all results of the MySQL command
    mysql_stmt_store_result(stmt);

    // loop through all result records
    while(!mysql_stmt_fetch(stmt)) {

      printf("titleID=%d \t", titleID);
      if(catID_is_null)
        printf("catID=NULL \t");
      else
        printf("catID=%d \t", catID);
      printf("timestamp=%d-%02d-%02d %02d-%02d-%02d\t",
            ts.year, ts.month, ts.day,
            ts.hour, ts.minute, ts.second);
      printf("title=%s\n", title_buf);
    }

    // end
    mysql_stmt_close(stmt);
    mysql_close(conn);
    return 0;
}
```

Character Set Settings (Unicode)

As a programming language, C does not distinguish among the various character sets. Any string that ends with a zero byte is considered a character string. The meaning of the individual bytes is of no interest to the C program. It simply transmits the sequence of bytes further.

If you execute your program in a console window, then it is necessary for correct processing of character strings that in communication with the MySQL server, the character set be used that is valid in the console window. Normally, the client program uses the default character set of the MySQL server, generally *latin1*. If you wish to use a different character set, then set it using *SET NAMES*:

```
mysql_query(conn, "SET NAMES 'utf8'");
```

Of course, instead of *'utf8'* you could use any other character set supported by MySQL, for example *'latin1'*. If you want your programs to be compatible with a variety of character sets, you can control the setting of *SET NAMES* with an option or evaluate the Unix/Linux environment variables *LANG* and *LC_xxx*.

Note that only the character set for communication between MySQL and your C program is governed by *SET NAMES*. *SET NAMES* has no influence over which character set is used for the storage of data in MySQL tables. (This character set is determined when the table is defined with *CREATE TABLE*.) MySQL converts all character strings from the table character set to the processing character set automatically. But watch out! If characters appear in one character set that cannot be represented in the other, they are replaced by question marks. (This can lead to loss of information.)

Working with Binary Data and Special Characters

Particular care needs to be taken in executing SQL commnds that contain 0 bytes or special characters (such as the processing of BLOBs) or in situations in which you expect such data as the result of a *SELECT* query.

The function *mysql_real_escape_string* serves to mark problematic characters with a backslash (\0, \b, \t, \", \', etc.). This is accomplished by copying the starting character string into a new string, for which sufficient memory must be reserved in advance:

```
// char *s1              target string
// char *s2              initial string (may contain 0 bytes)
// unsigned long len2   the length of s2
mysql_real_escape_string(conn, s1, s2, len2);
```

The function *mysql_real_escape_string* should be used in assembling SQL commands when individual strings can contain special characters. The following lines give an example of how an *INSERT* command can be correctly assembled. (The resulting command looks like this: *INTO publishers(publName) VALUES ('O\'Reilly')*.)

The example also shows the use of the auxiliary function *strmov*, which is also available from the MySQL library. It does the same thing as *strcpy*, but it returns a pointer that points to the end of the copied character string. Thus *strmov* is particularly well suited for assembling strings piece by piece (which under C is a particularly tiresome chore). To use *strmov*, it is necessary that *include* instructions for my_global.h and m_string.h be added (and in fact, in the order given below).

If you alter the code given below, you should ensure that the string buffer *tmp* is large enough for your requirements. Insert the requisite checks:

```
#include <my_global.h>  // necessary so that strmov works
#include <m_string.h>   // necessary so that strmov works
#include <mysql.h>
...
```

```
char tmp[1000], *tmppos;
char *publname = "O'Reilly";
tmppos = strmov(tmp, "INSERT INTO publishers (publName) VALUES ('");
tmppos += mysql_real_escape_string(
  conn, tmppos, publname, strlen(publname));
tmppos = strmov(tmppos, "')");
*tmppos++ = (char)0;
mysql_query(conn, tmp);
```

To execute SQL commands that contain 0 bytes, instead of *mysql_query*, you must use the function *mysql_real_query*. The difference is that the length of the SQL string is no longer determined by the first 0 byte, but is given explicitly:

```
// sql points to the string with the SQL command
// n gives the length of the string
mysql_real_query(conn, sql, n);
```

The reading of binary data also poses problems, since the string functions usually used assume that the data in *row[i]* end with the first 0 byte. If it is not certain that such is the case with your data, then you must determine the actual size of the data with a call to the function *mysql_fetch_lengths*. This function returns an *unsigned long* field whose values specify the size for every column of the current record. The following example shows how the function is used.

■Tip You can also transfer binary data within the framework of a prepared statement. While this increases the effort in initialization, it saves on burdensome composition of SQL commands using *mysql_real_escape_string*.

An additional advantage of prepared statements is in the function *mysql_stmt_send_long_data*. It allows you to transfer BLOBs piece by piece to the server, thereby minimizing storage requirements for the client. An example of the use of this function can be found at http://dev.mysql.com/doc/mysql/en/mysql-stmt-send-➡ long-data.html. Unfortunately, there is no equivalent function for reading BLOBs piece by piece.

Storing Binary Data in a Database and Reading It

With the following lines, the content of the file test.jpg from the current directory is stored in the table *test_blob* of the database *exception* (see Chapter 8). Then this record is read from the table and the result stored in a new file, test-copy.jpg. The new record can now be deleted. (Note that for the sake of simplicity, the program uses a fixed buffer of 512KB for transferring data to the database. There is no check whether test.jpg is smaller than this buffer. In a real application, you should, of course, adapt the memory size dynamically.)

```
// example file blob/main.c
#include <stdio.h>
#include <my_global.h>  // for strmov
#include <m_string.h>   // for strmov
#include <mysql.h>
int main(int argc, char *argv[])
{
  int id;
  FILE *f;
  MYSQL *conn;        // connection to MySQL
  MYSQL_RES *result;  // SELECT result
  MYSQL_ROW row;      // a record of the SELECT result
  size_t fsize;
  char fbuffer[512 * 1024];  // file size maximum 512 kByte
  char tmp[1024 * 1024], *tmppos;
  unsigned long *lengths;
```

```
// create connection
conn = mysql_init(NULL);
if(mysql_real_connect(
        conn, "localhost", "root", "uranus",
        "exceptions", 0, NULL, 0) == NULL) {
    fprintf(stderr, "sorry, no database connection ...\n");
    return 1;
  }

// read file test.jpg and store in exceptions.test_blob
f = fopen("test.jpg", "r");
fsize = fread(fbuffer, 1, sizeof(fbuffer), f);
fclose(f);
tmppos = strmov(tmp, "INSERT INTO test_blob (a_blob) VALUES ('");
tmppos += mysql_real_escape_string(
  conn, tmppos, fbuffer, fsize);
tmppos = strmov(tmppos, "')");
*tmppos++ = (char)0;
mysql_query(conn, tmp);
id = (int)mysql_insert_id(conn);
// read the new record and store the data in the
// new file test-copy.jpg
f = fopen("test-copy.jpg", "w");
sprintf(tmp, "SELECT a_blob FROM test_blob WHERE id = %i", id);
mysql_query(conn, tmp);
result = mysql_store_result(conn);
row = mysql_fetch_row(result);
lengths = mysql_fetch_lengths(result);
fwrite(row[0], 1, lengths[0], f);
fclose(f);

// delete the new record
sprintf(tmp, "DELETE FROM test_blob WHERE id = %i", id);
mysql_query(conn, tmp);

// release resources
mysql_free_result(result);
mysql_close(conn);
return 0;
}
```

Error Handling

Most MySQL functions return an error number, or else 0 if no error occurred. With some functions that return data structures (e.g., *mysql_store_result, mysql_fetch_row*) it is the other way around. Now the return value *NULL* means that there were problems during execution.

The functions return respectively zero and an empty string "" if no error occurred.

```
if(mysql_query(conn, sql)) {
  fprintf(stderr, "%s\n", mysql_error(conn));
  fprintf(stderr, "Fehlernummer %i\n", mysql_errno(conn));
  ...
}
```

Many SQL commands can also return warnings. The number of warnings can be determined after execution of the command with *mysql_warning_count*. To see the warnings themselves, you must execute the command *SHOW WARNINGS* and process its result as you would a *SELECT* result.

## CHAPTER 19

Visual Basic 6/VBA

This chapter concerns itself with the programming of MySQL applications with the programming languages Visual Basic 6 and VBA (the latter is part of all Microsoft Office components). The central feature is the application of the database library ADO in combination with the MySQL driver Connector/ODBC. In addition to a number of small examples, this chapter introduces the program `mssql2mysql`, which translates databases from Microsoft SQL Server to MySQL.

In certain speed-critical applications it can be useful to use `VBMySQLDirect` instead of ODBC and ADO. This library will therefore be briefly introduced.

Fundamentals and Terminology

ODBC (Open Database Connectivity) is a popular mechanism under Windows for standardized access to a great variety of database systems. The only condition on ODBC for it to be used to access MySQL is the installation of Connector/ODBC, the ODBC driver for MySQL. (In earlier versions, Connector/ODBC was called MyODBC.)

■**Tip** This chapter is based on the assumption that you have installed Connector/ODBC as described in Chapter 7. There is extensive documentation for Connector/ODBC, and most recently it was available at `http://dev.mysql.com/doc/mysql/en/odbc.html`. There is also a Connector/ODBC mailing list, which can be found at `http://lists.mysql.com/myodbc`.

Determining the Connector/ODBC Version Number

To determine whether Connector/ODBC is installed on your computer (and in what version), execute START | SETTINGS | CONTROL PANEL | ADMINISTRATIVE TOOLS | DATA SOURCES (ODBC) and search in the DRIVERS dialog sheet of the ODBC dialog for the Connector/ODBC driver.

This chapter is based on Connector/ODBC 3.51.n. (I ran my tests using version 3.51.11.) Note that you will need at least Connector/ODBC version 3.41 for database connections to the MySQL server 4.1 or later. Older versions of the ODBC driver do not support the new passwords of MySQL 4.1/5.0.

A new and greatly revised version 3.52.n has been announced for over a year, but in March 2005 it was not yet available even in a beta version.

A Small Glossary from the World of Microsoft Databases

If you are new to the world of Microsoft databases, then ODBC is not the only abbreviation that is going to confuse you. Here is a brief overview:

ODBC (Open Database Connectivity): ODBC is a popular, primarily Windows, mechanism for integrated access to a variety of database systems. ODBC is rather old, but it is supported by countless old and new database systems and libraries and will therefore likely be the most important producer-independent standard for communication and programming with database systems under Windows for a long time to come. ODBC is also available under Unix, but is seldom used in that context.

DSN (Data Source Name): With many programs with an ODBC interface (e.g., Access, Excel) you cannot directly select a database. Instead, you must first define a DSN for the database in the ODBC manager (see Chapter 7).

If you access MySQL via a programming language, you can set up database access without a DSN. Later in this chapter we will look at both variants (access with and without a DSN) in the context of ADO programming.

OLE-DB: OLE-DB was designed as the successor to ODBC, but it never achieved such an important role in the database world. Since Microsoft in the meantime has developed a new database technology (ADO.NET as part of the .NET framework), OLE-DB has lost even more significance, while ODBC continues to be considered a standard.

OLE-DB was developed primarily with a view to working with ADO (see the next glossary entry). For MySQL there is at present no mature OLE-DB driver. However, there is an ODBC interface for OLE-DB, by means of which all ODBC-compatible databases without their own OLE-DB drivers can be addressed.

ADO (ActiveX Data Objects): ADO is a collection of objects that are used in the programming languages Visual Basic, VBA, Delphi, etc., for creating database programs. ADO stands between the programming language and OLE-DB. For programmers, the object-oriented ADO library offers much more convenience than direct access to the database via OLE-DB functions. Later in the chapter, we provide information on ADO programming with Visual Basic for accessing MySQL databases.

ADO.NET: ADO.NET is the database interface of the new Microsoft .NET Framework. (This framework is an enormous class library that can be used only by .NET-compatible programming languages such as Visual Basic .NET and C#.) ADO.NET has a name similar to that of ADO, but internally it has little in common with it; the two are completely incompatible.

If you wish to develop applications with ADO.NET-MySQL, you can use Connector/ODBC, since ADO.NET ODBC is also compatible. However the use of a direct ADO.NET driver for MySQL is more efficient. There are several such drivers available. One of these, Connector.NET, which is officially supported by MySQL, will be described in detail in the next chapter.

MDAC (Microsoft Data Access Components): MDAC is the general term for the countless Microsoft database components and libraries (including ADO and OLE-DB). Various MDAC versions are installed as parts of Windows, Office, Internet Explorer, etc. The most current versions can be found (at no cost) at the following address: http://msdn.microsoft.com/data/downloads/updates/default.aspx.

DAO, RDO: DAO and RDO are similar to the ADO libraries for database programming. These are precursors to ADO and are now supported by Microsoft only half-heartedly. DAO and RDO are not discussed further in this book.

Connector/ODBC Options

The behavior of an ODBC connection to the MySQL server can be controlled by a number of options. These options can be selected in the ODBC-DSN dialog (see Figure 19-1) or as a numerical value in

ADO program code. For this reason, the numerical values of the options are placed in parentheses in the following list, which describes the most important options, presented in the order of the DSN dialog.

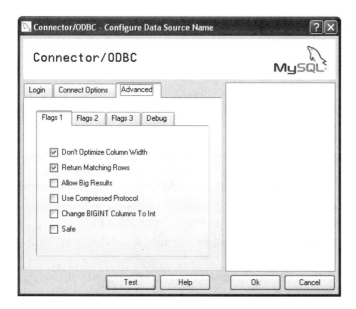

Figure 19-1. *Setting Connector/ODBC options in the DSN dialog*

Don't Optimize Column Width (1): If the query *SELECT col FROM table* returns character strings with a maximal length of n characters, and n is smaller than the maximal string length for this column, then Connector/ODBC returns n as the optimal column width. The option *Don't Optimize Column Width* avoids such problems.

Return Matching Rows (2): With many commands (e.g., *UPDATE*), the MySQL server can return the number of affected data records (*affected rows*). However, many ODBC clients are incapable of interpreting this information correctly. If this option is used, Connector/ODBC returns *found rows* instead of *affected rows* (thus 0 in the case of *UPDATE* commands). This option must be set for Connector/ODBC to be able to function in combination with a number of programs (including Microsoft Access and Visual Basic/VBA with ADO).

Allow Big Results (8): With this option, the size of packets that are transmitted between an ODBC program and the server is unlimited. This option must be used if large *SELECT* commands are anticipated or large BLOB fields are to be processed.

Use Compressed Protocol (2048): Data transmission between the ODBC program and MySQL is in compressed form, thus reducing the amount of network traffic. However, the cost is more CPU time on both client and server, since all data must be compressed and decompressed.

Change BIGINT Columns to Int (16384): Most Microsoft libraries are unable to deal with 64-bit integers. This option has the effect that MySQL *BIGINT* fields are automatically reduced to 32 bits upon transmittal. This option is necessary in particular for ADO programming with Visual Basic/VBA. Be thou warned, however: The most-significant 32 bits will be lost.

Safe (131072): This option has the effect that Connector/ODBC makes some additional checks. This option should be used when an ODBC client experiences problems in the processing of MySQL data. (The documentation does not offer a more precise description.)

Don't Prompt Upon Connect (16): This option prevents the DSN dialog from being displayed during the establishment of a connection due to the lack of relevant information. (Even if this option is activated, the dialog will appear if the database login is unsuccessful on account of an incorrect or missing user name or password.)

Enable Dynamic Cursor (32): With this option, Connector/ODBC supports the cursor type *Dynamic*. The cursor is made available by the ODBC driver, not directly by the MySQL server. By default, the *Dynamic* option is deactivated for the sake of efficiency. (In this connection, a *cursor* describes the internal management of *SELECT* results. Further details are available in the ADO documentation of the properties *CursorLocation* and *CursorType*.)

Don't Cache Results (1048576): Normally, all results of a *SELECT* command are transmitted as a block from server to client. This option prevents that. It makes sense only when huge (millions of records) *SELECT* results are being processed. This option takes effect only if in ADO programming a *forward only* cursor is used.

Force Use of Named Pipes (8192): This option results in *named pipes* (instead of TCP/IP) being used in communication between client and server. This is possible only under Windows NT/2000/XP, and only if the MySQL server supports *named pipes*, which is not the default behavior.

Force Use of Forward Only Cursors (2097152): This option has the effect that the driver always returns a *forward only* cursor (even when another cursor type is requested by ADO).

Trace Driver Calls To myodbc.log (4): This option has the effect that a log of all called ODBC functions is saved to the file `C:\myodbc.log`. This is often helpful in debugging.

Save Queries To myodbc.log (524288): This option results in a log of all executed SQL commands being saved to the file `C:\myodbc.sql`.

In many cases it suffices to activate only the options *Don't Optimize Column Width* and *Return Matching Rows*.

■Tip A complete list of all options and further information on Connector/ODBC can be found at `http://dev.mysql.com/doc/mysql/en/connection-parameters.html`.

ADO Programming and Visual Basic/VBA

Introduction

In this section we describe access to MySQL databases via program code, where we use Visual Basic 6 or VBA as our programming language. We use ADO as our database library. The actual access to the database is effected by means of Connector/ODBC, where between ADO and Connector/ODBC we have OLE-DB and the ODBC driver for OLE-DB. Thus communication takes place in the following way: VB/VBA ➤ ADO ➤ OLE-DB ➤ ODBC driver for OLE-DB ➤ Connector/ODBC ➤ MySQL.

If MySQL is running on a computer as a Visual Basic program, then the first five stages of this communication chain take place on the client computer. It is Connector/ODBC that first communicates over the network with the MySQL server.

■**Tip** In this book we are assuming that the reader has basic knowledge of ADO. If you know nothing much about ADO, what *Connection* and *Recordset* objects are, or the purpose of bound controls, then you should consult the literature on ADO programming before you read further, since we are not making much ado about nothing.

The code presented here was tested with Connector/ODBC 3.51.11, Visual Basic 6, and ADO 2.8. The code should function as well with VBA 6 and older versions of ADO (e.g., ADO 2.1, which is installed together with Office 2000), except as it involves ADO controls.

Of course, you can also work with a scripting variant of Visual Basic, for example, if you wish to develop Active Server Pages (ASP) or programs for the Windows Scripting Host (WSH). In that case you must leave out *As typename* in the variable declaration and create ADO objects according to *Set conn = CreateObject(`ADODB.Connection")*.

Assumptions and Limitations

MySQL tables: Tables that you wish to alter via ADO *Recordset*s or in bound controls (*Insert, Update, Delete*) must have a primary index and a *TIMESTAMP* column.

Connector/ODBC options: In the configuration of a DSN, the options *Don't optimize column width, Return matching rows,* and *Change BIGINT into INT* must be selected. If the connection is made without a DSN, then instead, the equivalent setting *Options=16387 (1 + 2 + 16384)* must be specified. If you wish to use a dynamic server cursor in your ADO program (*CursorType= adOpenDynamic, CursorLocation=adUseServer*), then the correct *Options* setting is *16419 (1 + 2 + 32 + 16384)*.

Changing data with Recordsets and bound controls: If the above conditions have been satisfied, you can use *Recordset*s and bound controls to read, display, and alter data.

This last point can often cause problems. Storing altered data (whether via a *Recordset* object or a bound control) functions properly in many simple cases, but in more complex applications it often leads to problems that are difficult to resolve. These problems do not always have to do with MySQL or Connector/ODBC, but with the vagaries of OLE-DB/ADO. Many experienced ADO programmers therefore do without bound controls, even if a Microsoft database system is used as the data source.

For this reason you will continually find in MySQL newsgroups and mailing lists the recommendation to use *Recordset*s and bound controls exclusively for reading or displaying data. If you wish to alter data, then you should formulate a traditional SQL command (*UPDATE ...*) and execute it with *conn.Execute*. Even if both methods are demonstrated in this chapter (both the convenient editing of data with a *Recordset* object and the variant with SQL commands), the second variant is nonetheless recommended.

Speed: Because of the many layers and libraries between Visual Basic and MySQL, and also because of the lower speed in the processing of character strings with Visual Basic, solutions using Visual Basic and MySQL tend to be comparatively slow. Better performance is promised by the *VBMySQLDirect* library, which establishes a direct connection between Visual Basic and MySQL (without ODBC).

Example Programs

As with the other chapters in this book, there are extensive examples available at www.apress.com. These examples assume that you have Visual Basic 6. Most of the examples also assume previous installation of the *mylibrary* database.

Note that at the beginning of the program (usually in *Form_Load*), you must set the connection parameters (computer name, user name, password) in accord with the settings of your system. In the example programs, the computer name is *localhost*, the user name is *root*, and the password is *uranus*.

Establishing the Connection

Establishing the Connection with a DSN

The following lines show a code outline for establishing a connection to MySQL based on a DSN and for executing a simple *SELECT* query. The resulting record list can then be processed with the properties and methods of the *rec* object:

```
Dim conn As Connection
Dim rec As Recordset
Set conn = New Connection
conn.ConnectionString = "DSN=mysql-mylibrary"
conn.Open
Set rec = New Recordset
rec.CursorLocation=adUseClient
rec.Open "SELECT * FROM tablename", conn
...        'process record list
rec.Close  'close record list
conn.Close 'close connection
```

The only really interesting code line is the one for setting the *ConnectionString* property. In the simplest case you specify the DSN. Optionally, you can also specify the user name and password. These parameters must be separated by semicolons. The *ConnectionString* character string looks like this:

```
conn.ConnectionString = "DSN=mysql-mylibrary;UID=root;PWD=xxx"
```

The *UID* and *PWD* settings have precedence over the DSN settings.

Table 19-1 shows the *ConnectionString* parameters for establishing a connection with a DSN.

Table 19-1. *ConnectionString Parameters (Connection with DSN)*

Parameter	Meaning
DSN=name	Name of the data source (*Data Source Name*)
UID=name	User name for the MySQL connection
PWD=password	Password for the MySQL connection

Establishing a Connection Without a DSN

With Visual Basic you can also establish a connection to a MySQL database without previously having defined a DSN. (This is particularly practical if you wish to develop a program to access an arbitrary MySQL database.) The *ConnectionString* character string looks like this:

```
conn.ConnectionString = "Provider=MSDASQL;" + _
  "DRIVER={MySQL ODBC 3.51 Driver};" + _
  "Server=localhost;UID=username;PWD=xxx;" + _
  "database=databasename;Option=16387"
```

Table 19-2 shows the *ConnectionString* parameters for establishing a connection without a DSN.

Table 19-2. *ConnectionString Parameters (Connection Without DSN)*

Parameter	Meaning
Provider=MSDASQL	Name of the ODBC driver for OLE-DB (Microsoft Data Access SQL)
Driver=MySQL ODBC 3.51 Driver	Name of the MySQL-ODBC driver
Server=name	Name or IP address of the computer on which the MySQL server is running
Port=n	IP port of the MySQL server (by default 3306)
UID=name	User name for the MySQL connection
PWD=password	Password for the MySQL connection
Database=name	Name of the database
Prompt=noprompt/complete	Display Connector/ODBC dialog if the connection fails
Option=n	Connector/ODBC options

Prompt=complete leads to the program automatically displaying the ODBC connection dialog depicted in Figure 7-2. This dialog can be used, for example, to provide a missing or an incorrect password. Moreover, an arbitrary character string must be specified in the field WINDOWS DSN NAME so that the dialog can be exited.

Since the dialog is not particularly user-friendly (the many choices are more confusing than helpful), it is better to do without *Prompt=complete*. (The default setting is *noprompt*.)

Instead, execute *On Error Resume Next* before establishing the connection and test after establishing the connection whether an error has occurred. If this is the case, display your own dialog, in which the user can input other connection parameters as necessary and from which the program can then construct a new *ConnectionString* character string.

Options enables the setting of a number of Connector/ODBC connection options. The required value is determined from the sum of the values of the individual options. For Visual Basic/ADO programs, the value *16387 = 1 + 2 + 16384* must generally be specified, corresponding to the options *Don't optimize column width*, *Return matching rows*, and *Change BIGINT into INT*.

Establishing the Connection with the DataEnvironment

If you are working with Visual Basic Professional or Enterprise version 6, then you have *DataEnvironment* available for setting connection properties.

In the properties dialog for the *Connection* object, in the dialog sheet PROVIDER, the entry MICROSOFT OLE-DB PROVIDER FOR ODBC DRIVERS. You can then choose, in the dialog sheet CONNECTION (see Figure 19-2), an already defined DSN or assemble an equivalent character string with the required connection properties with the button BUILD. (This button leads to the familiar ODBC dialogs. However, the result of the setting is copied as a character string into the *DataEnvironment* dialog, where it can be edited as necessary.)

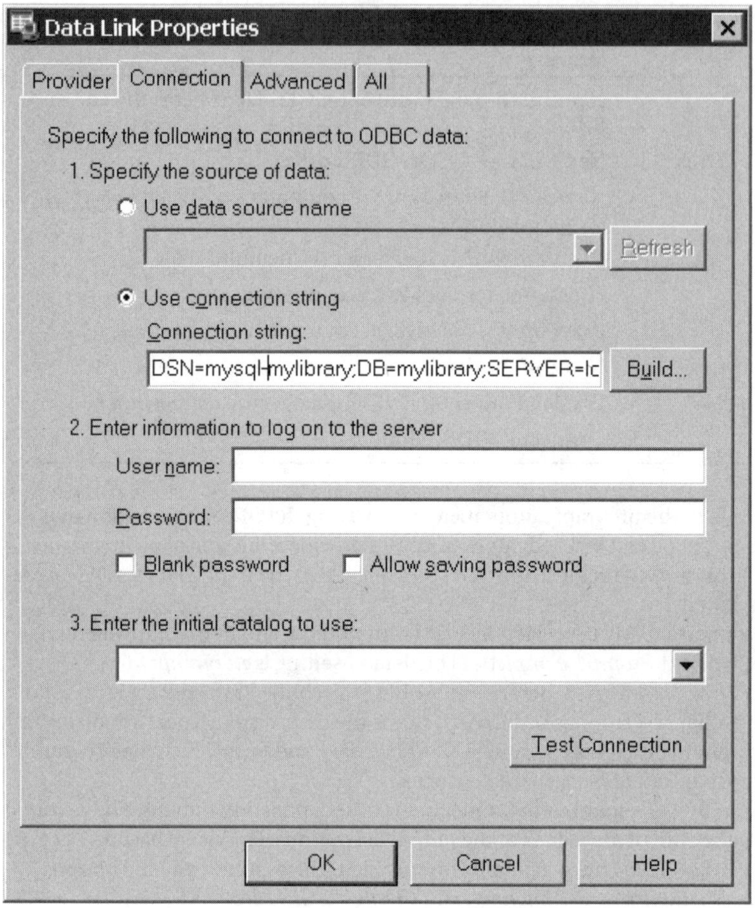

Figure 19-2. *DataEnvironment dialog for setting connection properties*

In the further program code you can now access the *Connection* object. (The following lines assume that the *DataEnvironment* object has the name *DE* and the *Connection* the name *Conn*.)

```
Dim rec As Recordset
Set rec = New Recordset
If DE.Conn.State = adStateClosed Then
  DE.Conn.Open
End If
rec.CursorLocation=adUseClient
rec.Open "SELECT * FROM database", DE.Conn
...
```

The *DataEnvironment* helps not only in setting the connection data, but also in the development of SQL queries. With the SQL generator you have a convenient tool for this purpose. You can then access the query in code via the *Command* object.

Connection Properties

The *ConnectionString* parameters described in this section represent only a small part of the available parameters. For those parameters that are not specified, ADO/ODBC simply uses various default settings.

Sometimes, it is useful to know how these parameters are set. The property *ConnectionString*, which is changed in establishing the connection (and then no longer contains the character string originally set), provides our first overview. Here most of the parameters are collected into a sort of superparameter called *Extended Properties*:

```
conn.ConnectionString = "Provider=MSDASQL;Driver=MySQL;Server=..."
conn.Open
Debug.Print conn.ConnectionString
  Provider=MSDASQL.1;Extended Properties=
  "DRIVER={MySQL ODBC 3.51 Driver};DESC=;DATABASE=mylibraryodbc;
   SERVER=localhost;UID=root;PASSWORD=uranus;PORT=;
   OPTION=16387;STMT=;"
```

Considerably more information is provided by the *Properties* enumeration of the *Connection* object. Moreover, the values saved there can be more easily extracted:

```
Debug.Print conn.Properties("Max Columns in Index")
  32
```

A complete list of all properties and their values can be obtained with the following loop:

```
Dim p As Property
For Each p In conn.Properties
  Debug.Print p.Name & " = " & p.Value
Next
```

ADO Programming Techniques

Recordsets with Client-Side Cursors

Recordset objects are opened on the basis of an existing *Connection* object (see the previous section). In all the examples in this chapter the variable name for this object is *conn*.

Since ADO provides a server-side cursor as the default cursor position, a client-side cursor must be set before the *Open* method. The following lines demonstrate how this is done:

```
Dim rec As Recordset
rec.CursorLocation = adUseClient  'client-side cursor
rec.Open "SELECT ... FROM ... WHERE ...", _
        conn, adOpenStatic, adLockReadOnly
```

We note the following about the parameters of *Open*: In the first parameter, the SQL code is expected; in the second, the *Connection* variable. The third parameter describes the desired cursor type. Since for client-side cursors only the type *adOpenStatic* is supported, it doesn't matter what is given here. The fourth parameter specifies whether the data in the *Recordset* are read-only (*adLockReadOnly*) or whether changes are permitted (*adLockOptimistic*). ADO provides the locking types *adLockPessimistic* and *adLockBatchOptimistic* as well, which, however, I have not tested.

With the *Open* method, all the data encompassed by the SQL query are transmitted to the program. (This can take considerable time with large data sets.) You can then apply all *Recordset* properties and methods to run through the data (*MoveNext*, etc.), to search (*Find*), to sort locally (*Sort*), to change (*column="new value"*: *rec.Update*), etc.

Recordsets with Server-Side Cursor

You can open a *Recordset* with a server-side cursor with the property *CursorType = adForwardOnly*. You can thereby move through and read all the records of the query with *MoveNext*, and also change them (unless you are operating with *LockType = adLockReadOnly*):

```
Dim rec As Recordset
rec.CursorLocation = adUseServer
rec.Open "SELECT ... FROM ... WHERE ...", _
        conn, adOpenForwardOnly, adLockOptimistic
```

The only navigation method allowed is *MoveNext*. You cannot use *Bookmarks*. You cannot determine the number of records without running through all of them. (You would do better to use a separate query with *SELECT COUNT(*) FROM ....*)

In spite of all these restrictions, in a few cases it can make sense to use a server-side cursor, namely, when large quantities of data are to be read sequentially. The drawbacks of the client-side cursor are thereby avoided (namely, that all the records are transmitted at once to the client).

Possible Recordset Properties

ADO provides for an almost endless number of combinations of properties of a *Recordset*. But the *Recordset* does not always contain the properties requested by *Open*. If a given driver does not support a particular cursor type, then ADO automatically chooses another.

As a way of testing which properties a *Recordset* actually possesses, you can use the program `Cursortypes.vbp` (see Figure 19-3). With a click of the mouse you can set the desired properties. The program then opens the *Recordset*, determines the actual properties, and then displays them. (Note, please, that the results of the program are not always correct for a server-side cursor. In particular, the *Recordset* method *Supports(...)* sometimes returns completely incorrect results.)

In sum, ADO + Connector/ODBC supports the following cursor combinations:

CursorLocation = Client

CursorType = Static

LockType = ReadOnly or *Optimistic* or *BatchOptimistic*

CursorLocation = Server

CursorType = ForwardOnly/ Static/ Dynamic

LockType = all

In the case of *CursorLocation=Server*, the ODBC option *Enable dynamic cursor (32)* determines whether you obtain a dynamic or static cursor.

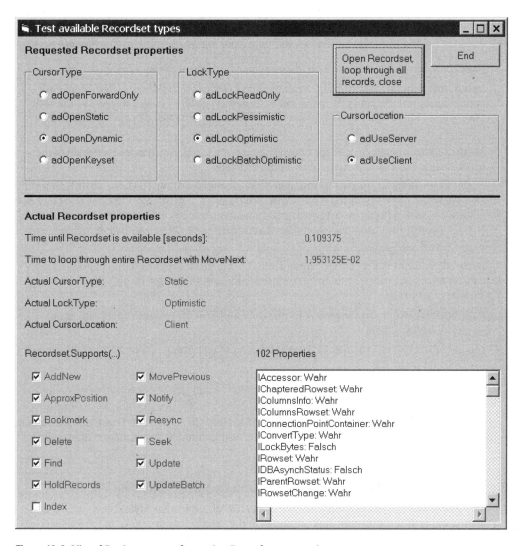

Figure 19-3. *Visual Basic program for testing Recordset properties*

Opening a Variable Recordset Object

If you don't bother to set the cursor properties, you receive by default an invariable *Recordset* object (*CursorLocation = Server, CursorType = ForwardOnly, LockType = ReadOnly*). If you wish to change data in the *Recordset,* you must specify the desired cursor properties explicitly. Typically, the code for opening a variable *Recordset* object looks like this:

```
Dim rec As New Recordset
rec.CursorLocation = adUseClient
rec.Open "SELECT cola, colb FROM table", conn, _
  adOpenStatic, adLockOptimistic
```

Behavior of Recordsets with Null, Dates and Times, and Suchlike

The following list describes how various MySQL data types are represented in ADO *Recordset*s:

Null: The value *Null* in a column of a *Recordset* can be determined with *IsNull(rec!column)*.

Date/Time: Columns in the MySQL formats *DATE, TIME, DATETIME,* and *TIMESTAMP* are automatically transformed into the Visual Basic data type *Date.* Please exercise caution with *TIME* values: These values are supplemented with the current date. (For example, from 9:00 you may get 2005/3/17 9:00.)

BLOBs: *BLOB*s are transformed into *Byte* arrays. Access to individual bytes is effected in the manner *rec!a_blob(n),* here *n=0* addresses the first byte.

A *Byte* array can be interpreted by Visual Basic as a character string. However, again caution is advised: Since internally, Visual Basic works with Unicode, a *BLOB* with 512 bytes corresponds in Visual Basic to a character string with 256 Unicode characters. For bytewise evaluation of the character string, the Visual Basic functions *AscB, ChrB, LenB, MidB, LeftB, RightB, InStrB,* etc., must be used.

Decimal: Columns in the MySQL format *DECIMAL* are metamorphosed into the Visual Basic data type *Decimal,* which is not to be confused with *Currency.* It is to be thought of more as a subtype of *Variant.*

Sets/Enums: Columns in the MySQL formats *SET* and *ENUM* are transformed into garden-variety character strings.

Character strings: MySQL-specific special characters in strings (\, ', ", and 0-byte) are correctly handled automatically.

Character Strings

Within Visual Basic, character strings are represented in Unicode. Connector/ODBC and the MySQL server automatically take care of converting character strings into the appropriate character set for a given table.

Storing and Reading BLOBs from Variables (AppendChunk and GetChunk Methods)

If you wish to store binary data, then you must use *BLOB* columns in the MySQL table. You can use the method *AppendChunk* to store data contained in the variable *bin,* as shown in the following code segment. (This works only if you are using client-side cursors.)

```
Dim rec As New Recordset
rec.CursorLocation = adUseClient
rec.Open "SELECT * FROM test LIMIT 1", conn, adOpenStatic, _
  adLockPessimistic
rec.AddNew
rec!blobcolumn.AppendChunk bin
rec.Update
```

With *GetChunk* you can read the data. You have to use *ActualSize* to determine the size of the data:

```
bin = rec!blobcolumn.GetChunk(rec!blobcolumn.ActualSize)
```

You can also transmit the data piecewise (by executing *AppendChunk* and *GetChunk* repeatedly). This is of particular utility in managing large data sets.

Storing and Reading BLOBs as Files

The *Stream* class from the ADO library (version 2.5 and higher) offers an elegant way to store and read BLOBs directly to and from files. The following lines show how you can open a file with *Load-FromFile* as a binary stream and store it in the field *rec!pic* (*rec* is a *Recordset* object, and *pic* is a *BLOB* column of the previously executed *SELECT* query):

```
Dim st As New Stream
st.Type = adTypeBinary
st.Open
st.LoadFromFile "C:\test1.gif"
rec!pic = st.Read
```

Conversely, you can read a *BLOB* field from the table and store it in a file with *SaveToFile*:

```
Dim st As New Stream
st.Type = adTypeBinary
st.Open
st.Write rec!pic
st.SaveToFile "C:\test2.gif", adSaveCreateOverWrite
```

A complete example showing the use of these methods appears later in this chapter.

Determining the AUTO_INCREMENT Number After the Insertion of a Data Record

It often happens that after the insertion of a new data record into a table, you require the ID number of that record (that is, the value of the *AUTO_INCREMENT* column for the primary index). Unfortunately, this cannot be read from the *Recordset* with which the record was inserted. The solution to this conundrum is to determine the ID number via *SELECT LAST_INSERT_ID()*. To accomplish this, you would do well to add the following function to your program:

```
Private Function LastInsertedID() As Long
  Dim rec As New Recordset
  rec.CursorLocation = adUseClient
  rec.Open "SELECT LAST_INSERT_ID()", conn
  LastInsertedID = rec.Fields(0)
End Function
```

Bound Database Controls

Visual Basic offers several controls that can be bound directly to database queries (to *Recordset* objects). Within the control, the contents of the *Recordset* (or perhaps only of the currently active data record) are displayed. Such controls offer a great savings in effort in the representation of database queries. Some controls even offer the possibility of altering data directly. In the ideal case, one can program a database interface with a minimal amount of code (see Figure 19-4).

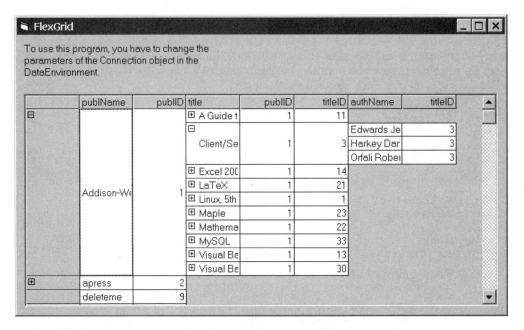

Figure 19-4. *Visual Basic example program with the MSHFlexGrid for representing data from the mylibrary database*

In reality, things do not always go so smoothly. In general, you must take care in your work with Connector/ODBC that for bound controls, too, you work with a client-side cursor. Furthermore, the alteration of data does not always function reliably, so that (except in well-tested special cases) one is advised not to use this feature.

Apart from that, the use of bound controls is independent of whether you use a Microsoft database system or MySQL as the data source. Additional information on using bound controls can be found in any book on database programming with Visual Basic.

Executing SQL Commands Directly

ADO *Recordsets* can simplify your dealings with query results, but it is often necessary to execute SQL commands directly. To do this, use the *Execute* method of the *Connection* object:

```
conn.Execute "INSERT INTO table (a, b) VALUES ('x', 'y')"
```

As with other programming languages, with Visual Basic you also run into the problem that you have to format various data in conformity with the rules of MySQL. In the following, you will find some auxiliary functions to help you in this task:

Floating-Point Numbers: With floating-point numbers you must take into account that Visual Basic normally formats such numbers according to the country for which the language has been customized (for example, in Germany one refers to Pi as 3,14159265 instead of 3.14159265). If your program is to function equally well everywhere in the known universe, you should transform your floating-point numbers into character strings with the Visual Basic function *Str*.

Date: The following *Format* instruction formats the date contained in *x* in accord with MySQL conventions:

```
Format(x, "'yyyy-mm-dd Hh:Nn:Ss'")
```

Character Strings: *Quote* places a backslash character before the backslash and before the single- and double-quote characters, and it replaces the byte code 0 with \0:

```
Function Quote$(tmp$)
  tmp = Replace(tmp, "\", "\\")
  tmp = Replace(tmp, """", "\""")
  tmp = Replace(tmp, "'", "\'")
  Quote = Replace(tmp, Chr(0), "\0")
End Function
```

Binary Data: *HexCode* transforms a byte array of arbitrary length into a hexadecimal character string of the form *0x0102031232*:

```
Function HexCode(bytedata() As Byte) As String
  Dim i As Long
  Dim tmp As String
  tmp = ""
  For i = LBound(bytedata) To UBound(bytedata)
    If bytedata(i) <= 15 Then
      tmp = tmp + "0" + Hex(bytedata(i))
    Else
      tmp = tmp + Hex(bytedata(i))
    End If
  Next
  HexCode = "0x" + tmp
End Function
```

You might use this function in the following way:

```
conn.Execute "INSERT INTO table (col) VALUES (" + HexCode(...) + ")"
```

HexCodeStr functions in principle like *Hexcode*, except that it expects data bytewise in a character string. Note, however, that Visual Basic character strings are UTF16 encoded, and not in the form UTF8, which is more usual under Unix:

```
Function HexCodeStr(bytedata As String) As String
  Dim i As Long, b As Long
  Dim tmp As String
  tmp = ""
  For i = 1 To LenB(bytedata)
    b = AscB(MidB(bytedata, i, 1))
    If b <= 15 Then
      tmp = tmp + "0" + Hex(b)
    Else
      tmp = tmp + Hex(b)
    End If
  Next
  HexCodeStr = "0x" + tmp
End Function
```

Example: authors Column for the titles Table

If you want to obtain a list of all books and their authors from the *mylibrary* database, it is necessary to formulate a relatively complex query with two *JOIN*s, a grouping, and the use of the *GROUP_CONCAT* aggregation function:

```
USE mylibrary
SELECT title,
  GROUP_CONCAT(authname ORDER BY authname SEPARATOR '; ') AS authors
FROM authors, titles, rel_title_author
WHERE authors.authID = rel_title_author.authID
AND   titles.titleID = rel_title_author.titleID
GROUP BY titles.titleID ORDER BY title
```

title	authors
A Guide to the SQL Standard	Darween Hugh; Date Chris
A Programmer's Introduction to PHP 4.0	Gilmore W.J.
Alltid den där Annette	Pohl Peter

...

If you need such queries frequently, it would be worthwhile to enlarge the *titles* table with a column *authors* containing the author names. Of course, this column contains redundant data, but it would simplify and speed up access to the database.

```
ALTER TABLE titles ADD authors VARCHAR(255)
```

The example program presented here (see Figure 19-5) shows how the *authors* column can be filled with data. For this, we simply run through all the *titles* records, determine the authors for each book, combine the authors into a character string, and store them. (The program assumes that the *titles* table has been extended to include the column *authors*.)

Figure 19-5. *Visual Basic example program for changing the titles table*

Variant 1: Changing Data with Read/Write Recordsets

All of the code is contained in the event procedure *Command2a_Click*. This procedure assumes that the global variable *conn* creates the connection to the database (*Connection* object).

In the program, two *Recordset*s are opened. One of them, *titles*, refers directly to the like-named table and enables changes to it (*LockingType=adLockOptimistic*). The second, *authors*, contains a list of all *titleID* values and their authors. The *Recordset* is sorted locally after being read in (property *Sort*), and apart from the database, in order not to put unnecessary demands on resources.

The following loop runs through all the *titleID* values of the *titles Recordset*. With *Find*, the associated authors in the *authors Recordset* are determined and joined into the character string *authors_str*. This character string is then stored:

```
' Example vb6\authors_for_titles\form1.frm
Private Sub Command2a_Click()
  Dim authors_str As String
  Dim titles As New Recordset
  Dim authors As New Recordset
  ' titles Recordset: read/write
  titles.CursorLocation = adUseClient
  titles.Open "SELECT titleID, authors FROM titles", _
              conn, adOpenStatic, adLockOptimistic
 ' authors Recordset: readonly, disconnected
  authors.CursorLocation = adUseClient
  authors.Open "SELECT titleID, authname " _
              "FROM authors, rel_title_author " & _
              "WHERE authors.authID=rel_title_author.authID", _
              conn, adOpenStatic, adLockReadOnly
  authors.Sort = "titleID, authname"
  Set authors.ActiveConnection = Nothing

  ' loop over all titles
  While Not titles.EOF
    authors_str = ""
    ' loop over all authors of this title
    authors.MoveFirst
    authors.Find "titleID=" & titles!titleID
    While Not authors.EOF
      If authors_str <> "" Then authors_str = authors_str + "; "
      authors_str = authors_str & authors!authName
      authors.MoveNext
      authors.Find "titleID=" & titles!titleID
    Wend
    ' save author list
    If authors_str <> "" Then
      titles!authors = authors_str
      titles.Update
    End If
    titles.MoveNext
  Wend
End Sub
```

Variant 2: Changing Data with conn.Execute

In our second variant, the *authors Recordset* is opened just as in variant 1. The structure of the loop is a bit different in how it finds all the authors of the current *titleID* value. The authors are stored temporarily in the variable *authors_str*.

What is new in comparison to variant 1 is the instruction *conn.Execute*, with which the list of authors is stored in the *titles* table with the help of an *UPDATE* command. The function *Quote* is necessary to ensure that the SQL command is correct even when the author name has special characters such as '.

```
Private Sub Command2b_Click()
  Dim authors_str, titleID
  Dim authors As New Recordset
```

```
' authors Recordset: client-side, readonly, disconnected
authors.CursorLocation = adUseClient
authors.Open "SELECT titleID, authname " & _
            "FROM authors, rel_title_author " & _
            "WHERE authors.authID=rel_title_author.authID " & _
            "ORDER BY titleID, authName", _
            conn, adOpenStatic, adLockReadOnly
authors.Sort = "titleID, authname"
Set authors.ActiveConnection = Nothing

' loop over all titles (titleID)
While Not authors.EOF
  titleID = authors!titleID
  authors_str = ""
  ' search for all authors associated with current titleID value
  authors_str = ""
  Do While Not authors.EOF
    ' jump to the next titleID from the inner loop
    If authors!titleID <> titleID Then
      Exit Do
    End If
    ' add author name to authors_str
    If Not IsNull(authors!authName) Then
      If authors_str <> "" Then authors_str = authors_str + "; "
      authors_str = authors_str & authors!authName
    End If
    authors.MoveNext
  Loop

  ' save author list
  If authors_str <> "" Then
    conn.Execute "UPDATE titles " & _
                "SET authors = '" & Quote(authors_str) & "'" & _
                "WHERE titleID=" & titleID
  End If
Wend
End Sub
' place \ before ' " and \, replace Chr(0) by \0
Private Function Quote(tmp)
  tmp = Replace(tmp, "\", "\\")
  tmp = Replace(tmp, """", "\""")
  tmp = Replace(tmp, "'", "\'")
  Quote = Replace(tmp, Chr(0), "\0")
End Function
```

Example: Adding a New Book Title

With the following example program you can store a new book title in the *mylibrary* database. The book title consists of the title itself, one or more authors, and a publisher (see Figure 19-6). The program does not test whether the authors or publisher already exists in the database. The goal of this program is simply to demonstrate the principal methods of inserting data into linked tables.

Figure 19-6. *Visual Basic example program for inserting a new book title*

Variant 1: Changing Data with Read/Write Recordsets

At the beginning of the procedure, four *Recordset* objects are opened, with whose help the data are to be stored. Without *LIMIT 1*, the *SELECT* statement would retrieve all matching *Recordset*s. But we are not interested in these (we want only to change data here), so this would be a waste of time. What we want is an ADO object pointing to this table, and to get one, we have to execute a *SELECT* statement. The use of *LIMIT 1* thus speeds things up for us. (If you would like to improve the efficiency of the code, you should define the four *Recordset* variables globally and open them in *Form_Load*. You thereby avoid the *Recordset*s having to be opened for each storage event.)

The commands for storing the data from the three text fields *txtPublisher*, *txtTitle*, and *txtAuthors* are easy to understand. Worthy of note is the use of the auxiliary function *LastInsertedID()*, described above, for determining the most recently added *AUTO_INCREMENT* value:

```
' example vb6\insert_new_title\form1.frm
Private Sub SaveData_WithRecordsets()
  Dim i&, titleID&, authID&, publID&
  Dim authors_array
  Dim authors As New Recordset, titles As New Recordset
  Dim publishers As New Recordset, rel_title_author As New Recordset
  ' open Recordsets
  authors.CursorLocation = adUseClient
  titles.CursorLocation = adUseClient
  publishers.CursorLocation = adUseClient
  rel_title_author.CursorLocation = adUseClient
  authors.Open "SELECT * FROM authors LIMIT 1", _
    conn, adOpenStatic, adLockOptimistic
  titles.Open "SELECT * FROM titles LIMIT 1", _
    conn, adOpenStatic, adLockOptimistic
  publishers.Open "SELECT * FROM publishers LIMIT 1", _
    conn, adOpenStatic, adLockOptimistic
  rel_title_author.Open "SELECT * FROM rel_title_author LIMIT 1", _
    conn, adOpenStatic, adLockOptimistic
```

```
    ' save publisher (if given)
    If Trim(txtPublisher) <> "" Then
      publishers.AddNew
      publishers!publName = Trim(txtPublisher)
      publishers.Update
      publID = LastInsertedID()
    End If

    ' save book title (perhaps with publID reference)
    titles.AddNew
    titles!Title = Trim(txtTitle)
    If publID <> 0 Then titles!publID = publID
    titles.Update
    titleID = LastInsertedID()

    ' save authors and make entries to rel_title_author table
    authors_array = Split(txtAuthor, ";")
    For i = LBound(authors_array) To UBound(authors_array)
      authors.AddNew
      authors!authName = Trim(authors_array(i))
      authors.Update
      authID = LastInsertedID()
      rel_title_author.AddNew
      rel_title_author!titleID = titleID
      rel_title_author!authID = authID
      rel_title_author.Update
    Next
End Sub
Private Function LastInsertedID()  ... see earlier code
```

Variant 2: Changing Data with conn.Execute

In our second variant, the code is more like that to which you are accustomed in MySQL programming with languages such as PHP or Perl: You need to cobble together the SQL commands painstakingly, taking care to treat special characters correctly. (For this, the auxiliary function *Quote* will be used.) The structure of the code is otherwise like that of the first variant:

```
Private Sub SaveData_WithSQLCommands()
  Dim i&, titleID&, authID&, publID&
  Dim authors_array
    ' save publisher (if specified)
  If Trim(txtPublisher) <> "" Then
    conn.Execute "INSERT INTO publishers (publName) " & _
                 "VALUES ('" & Quote(Trim(txtPublisher)) & "')"
    publID = LastInsertedID()
  End If

  ' save book title (with any publID reference)
  conn.Execute "INSERT INTO titles (title, publID) " & _
               "VALUES ('" & Quote(Trim(txtTitle)) & "', " & _
                        IIf(publID <> 0, publID, "NULL") & ")"
  titleID = LastInsertedID()
```

```
' save authors and make any entries in the rel_title_author table
authors_array = Split(txtAuthor, ";")
For i = LBound(authors_array) To UBound(authors_array)
  conn.Execute "INSERT INTO authors (authName) " & _
               "VALUES ('" & Quote(Trim(authors_array(i))) & "')"
  authID = LastInsertedID()
  conn.Execute "INSERT INTO rel_title_author " & _
               " (titleID, authID) " & _
               "VALUES (" & titleID & ", " & authID & ")"
  Next
End Sub
Private Function Quote$(tmp$)  ... see earlier code
```

Example: Storing an Image File in BLOB Format and Then Reading It

The following example program reads the file test.jpg from the current directory and stores it in a table (*Command2_Click*). In a second step, the binary data are read from the table and stored in the file test1.jpg (*Command3_Click*). As a visual check whether everything worked as it should have, the new file will be displayed in a *Picture* control (see Figure 19-7). For storing the image, at the beginning of the program a table is created as shown in the following code and then deleted at the end of the program.

Figure 19-7. *A photo is loaded from a BLOB field and displayed.*

```vb
' example vb6\blob\form1.frm
Option Explicit
Dim conn As Connection
Dim id As Long

' create connection to MySQL
Private Sub Command1_Click()
  Set conn = New Connection
  'Options: 16395 = 16384 + 8 + 2 + 1
  '  Don't Optimize Column Width + Return Matching Rows +
  '  Allow Big Results + Change BIGINT Columns to INT
  conn.ConnectionString = "Provider=MSDASQL;" + _
    "DRIVER={MySQL ODBC 3.51 Driver};" + _
    "Server=localhost;UID=root;PWD=uranus;" + _
    "database=mylibraryodbc;Option=16395"
  conn.Open
  ' create table
  conn.Execute "CREATE TABLE IF NOT EXISTS testpic " + _
    "(id INT NOT NULL AUTO_INCREMENT, pic MEDIUMBLOB, PRIMARY KEY (id))"
  Command2.Enabled = True
End Sub

' load file into a Stream object
' and store in the table testpic
Private Sub Command2_Click()
  Dim rec As New Recordset
  Dim fname As String
  Dim st As New Stream
  ' open file
  fname = App.Path + "\test.jpg"
  st.Type = adTypeBinary
  st.Open
  st.LoadFromFile fname

  ' store file in table
  rec.CursorLocation = adUseClient
  rec.Open "SELECT * FROM testpic LIMIT 1", conn, adOpenKeyset, _
    adLockOptimistic
  rec.AddNew
  rec!pic = st.Read
  rec.Update
  rec.Close
  st.Close

  ' note id (AUTO_INCREMENT number)
  id = LastInsertedID()
  Command3.Enabled = True
End Sub

' read BLOB from table and store in new file
Private Sub Command3_Click()
  Dim rec As New Recordset
  Dim fname As String
  Dim st As New Stream
  ' Stream object for the new file
fname = App.Path + "\test1.jpg"
  st.Type = adTypeBinary
  st.Open
```

```
' read BLOB into the Stream object
rec.CursorLocation = adUseClient
rec.Open "SELECT pic FROM testpic WHERE id = " & id, conn, _
   adOpenKeyset, adLockReadOnly
st.Write rec!pic
rec.Close

' store Stream in file
st.SaveToFile fname, adSaveCreateOverWrite
st.Close
' display file in picture control element
Picture1.Picture = LoadPicture(fname)
End Sub
```

Converter: Microsoft SQL Server to MySQL

If up to now you have managed a database with the Microsoft SQL Server (or the MSDE, that is, the Microsoft Data Engine) and are considering porting it to MySQL, there are two main ways of bringing your data into a MySQL database.

- Summon Access to your assistance. First, import the table into an empty Access database, and then export it to MySQL.

- Use the VBA/Visual Basic script mssql2mysql (developed in its first version by me). The program should generally enable a more exact copy of the database structure, since there is no intermediate Access step. The remainder of this section is related to this program. The program can also be seen as a further example of ADO database programming with MySQL, although for reasons of space we omit the source code.

Tip The current version of mssql2mysql can be found at http://www.kofler.cc/mysql/ mssql2mysql.html. Various other converters, both commercial and free of charge, between MySQL and a number of other databases can be found at http://solutions.mysql.com/software/. A worthwhile article on migration from Microsoft SQL Server to MySQL can be found at http://dev.mysql.com/ tech-resources/articles/migrating-from-microsoft.html.

Properties of mssql2mysql

- Freely obtainable (GPL)

- Copies an entire database, that is, all user-defined tables (structure, indexes, data)

- Automatically changes the name of a table or column if the name is not allowable in MySQL (for example, *My table* becomes *My_table*)

- Generates either a text file with SQL commands or executes the required commands directly on the MySQL server

Assumptions

- To execute the script, either a current VBA interpreter (e.g., in all components of Microsoft Office since Office 2000) or the programming language Visual Basic 6 must be available.

- The program requires the libraries ADO and SQLDMO. (SQLDMO allows the control of the Microsoft SQL server. The library is installed together with the SQL server.)

- If the converted database is not to be written into a text file (*.sql), but transmitted directly to a running MySQL server, then Connector/ODBC must also be installed.

The converter was most recently tested with SQL Server 2000, MySQL server 5.0.2, ADO 8, and Connector/ODBC 3.51.11.

Restrictions

- The converter ignores the following database characteristics: integrity rules, views, stored procedures, user-defined data type, and access privileges.

- MySQL allows only one *AUTO_INCREMENT* column per table, and that column must be defined as *PRIMARY KEY*. The converter does not check this condition. You must therefore change your SQL server as necessary before starting the script.

- SQL server *TIMESTAMP*s are incompatible with MySQL *TIMESTAMP*s and are therefore transformed into *TINYBLOB*s.

How to Use It

The text file mssql2mysql is available over the Internet at http://www.kofler.cc/mysql/mssql2mysql.html. To execute the code, use either Visual Basic 6 or a program with VBA 6 support (for example, Excel 2000, Word 2000, Access 2000).

Visual Basic 6: If you are working with Visual Basic 6, begin a new standard project and insert the entire code into the code window of a form. Then start the program by pressing F5.

VBA: If you are working with a VBA 6 compatible program, switch with Alt+F11 into the VBA development environment, insert a new, empty module, and copy the code into this module. Then with F5 open the dialog for macro execution and execute the procedure *main*.

Setting Parameters

All the parameters of the conversion process are controlled by a number of constants, which can be found at the beginning of the code. The first five constants describe the database on the Microsoft SQL server. The login to the database can be effected either via the security system integrated into Windows 2000/XP or by the explicit specification of user name and password:

```
Const MSSQL_SECURE_LOGIN = True 'login type (True for 2000/XP Security)
Const MSSQL_LOGIN_NAME = ""     'user name ("" for 2000/XP Security)
Const MSSQL_PASSWORD = ""       'password ("" for 2000/XP Security)
Const MSSQL_HOST = "mars"       'computer ("(local)" for localhost)
Const MSSQL_DB_NAME = "pubs"    'database name
```

OUTPUT_TO_FILE specifies whether the program should generate a text file with SQL commands or whether the commands should be executed at once. The file variant has the advantage that if problems arise, the text file can be directly edited. However, it has a drawback: The resulting text file uses the Windows character set *cp850* (corresponds mostly to *latin1*). If there are Unicode strings in the Microsoft SQL database that contain characters that are not *latin1* compatible, these characters are lost.

```
Const OUTPUT_TO_FILE = 0        '1 write file,
                                '0 execute SQL commands at once
```

If you have decided for *OUTPUT_TO_FILE=1*, you must specify the name of the resulting file in *OUTPUT_FILENAME*:

```
Const OUTPUT_FILENAME = "C:\export.sql"
```

With *OUTPUT_TO_FILE=0* you must specify all parameters so that a connection to MySQL can be created. For this there must be sufficient access privileges so that *CREATE DATABASE*, etc., can be executed:

```
Const MYSQL_USER_NAME = "root"    'user name
Const MYSQL_PASSWORD = "uranus" ' password
Const MYSQL_HOST = "localhost"  ' computer name or "localhost"
Const MYSQL_PORT = 3306          'MySQL port
```

Which of the following two commands is necessary depends on whether you are using Connector/ODBC 3.51 or 2.51:

```
Const MyODBCVersion = "MySQL ODBC 3.51 Driver"
Const MyODBCVersion = "MySQL"     'for 2.50.n
```

Finally, we mention a few conversion options:

NEW_DB_NAME enables the name of the new MySQL database to be given. If the constant remains empty, the new database keeps the same name as the SQL server database.

DROP_DATABASE specifies whether at the beginning of the conversion any existing MySQL database with the same name should be deleted.

MAX_RECORDS specifies how many records per table should be converted. Here 0 means that all data records should be converted. This option is practical for first carrying out a quick test and, for example, converting only ten records per table. Only after it is working without error is the entire database converted. (Otherwise, it could happen that after half an hour an error might occur on the last table.)

VARCHAR_MAX specifies the maximal length of *VARCHAR* columns. Columns with more characters are changed into *TEXT* columns. *VARCHAR_MAX* should have the value 255 for MySQL server versions up to 5.0.2. Newer MySQL server versions support longer *VARCHAR* columns up to 65,535 bytes. The maximum number of characters depends on the character set. If you use UTF8, then 32,000 is a sensible limit.

TABLE_ENGINE specifies the table type of the MySQL tables (InnoDB or MyISAM).

CHARSET gives the character set for the text columns in the tables.

COLLATION gives the desired sort order. If the field is empty, the default order of the selected character set is used.

```
Const NEW_DB_NAME = ""            'MySQL database name
Const UNICODE_TO_BLOB = False     'Unicode --> BLOBs?
Const DROP_DATABASE = True        'begin with DROP database?
Const MAX_RECORDS = 0             '0: convert all data
Const VARCHAR_MAX = 255           ' larger values only for MySQL-Server >= 5.0.3
Const TABLE_ENGINE = "InnoDB"     'MyISAM or InnoDB
Const CHARSET = "utf8"            'desired character set in the MySQL tables
Const COLLATION = ""              'empty for default sort order
```

VBMySQLDirect

The ADO programming based on Connector/ODBC introduced in the previous sections works, but it is not particularly efficient. If processing speed is more important to you than ADO compatibility, then you will find the library *VBMySQLDirect* introduced in this section an interesting alternative. This library offers Visual Basic programmers more direct access to MySQL. The classes *MYSQL_CONNECTION*, *MYSQL_RS*, *MYSQL_FIELD*, and *MYSQL_ERR* offer functionality similar to that of the ADO objects *Connection*, *Recordset*, *Field*, and *Error*, without, however, being compatible with them.

VBMySQLDirect itself consists of Visual Basic code and comes from the discontinued project *MyVbQL*. For this book, *VBMySQLDirect 1.0.2* was tested.

VBMySQLDirect builds on the MySQL client library libmySQL.dll. Access to the MySQL server via *MyVbQL* takes place according to the following scheme: Visual Basic ➤ *VBMySQLDirect* object library ➤ libmySQL.dll ➤ MySQL.

In comparison to ADO + Connector/ODBC, *VBMySQLDirect* code is generally faster. A further considerable advantage is that *VBMySQLDirect* is much less complex than ADO + Connector/ODBC. In other words, there are fewer functions, and they are generally less likely to cause errors. It is also quite practical that in distributing *VBMySQLDirect* programs, one does not have to include ADO libraries, which inflate the setup files considerably. Unfortunately, there are some drawbacks as well:

- *VBMySQLDirect* is not ADO compatible. It therefore takes some effort to convert existing ADO code to *VBMySQLDirect*.

- The *MYSQL_RS* object cannot be used as the data basis for bound database controls, which makes the use of ADO database controls in combination with *VBMySQLDirect* impossible. (On the *VBMySQLDirect* website you can find an additional library that creates a connection between *VBMySQLDirect* and the program Crystal Reports. This allows you to use this popular reporting tool with *VBMySQLDirect*.)

VBMySQLDirect is available free of charge under the *GNU Library General Public License*. However, *VBMySQLDirect* uses the library libmysql.dll, for which the stricter GPL holds. Thus for commercial applications the same rules hold as for Connector/ODBC programs: If you develop a program based on *VBMySQLDirect* that is not open source in the sense of GPL, then your customers must obtain a commercial license for the MySQL server.

Installation

An installation program for *VBMySQLDirect* is available at http://www.vbmysql.com/projects/vbmysqldirect/. During installation, the source code for *VBMySQLDirect* as well as some example projects are copied to the directory Programs\VBMySQLDirect. Furthermore, the libraries vbmysqldirect.dll and libmysql.dll are installed in the directory Windows/System32. Moreover, vbmysqldirect.dll is entered into the Windows registration database. Unfortunately, the version of libmysql.dll delivered with *VBMySQLDirect* 1.0.2 is relatively old (MySQL 4.1.n).

■**Caution** The installation of *VBMySQLDirect* can lead to incompatibilities with other programs that use `libmysql.dll`. For example, if you have installed PHP as described in Chapter 2, there are now two `libmysql.dll` files, one in the `Windows` directory, the other in `Windows\System32`.

The next time Apache is launched, it gives the DLL in `Windows/System32` precedence over the one in the `Windows` directory. Since PHP 5 requires a current version of `libmysql.dll` and not the old version of *VBMySQLDirect*, an error results.

The solution to the problem is to shut down Apache and rename the file `Windows\System32\libmysql.dll` or delete the file. After a restart of Apache, PHP again uses `Windows\libmysql.dll`. However, now *VBMySQLDirect* also uses this library. According to a posting in the *VBMySQLDirect* forum, the combination of *VBMySQLDirect* with recent versions of `libmysql.dll` has not been tested, but it should work. In my tests, no problems occurred.

Application

In order to use *VBMySQLDirect* in your own Visual Basic project you must simply create a reference to the library. You will find the library under the name *VBMySQL Direct v1.0* in the dialog PROJECT | REFERENCES. You can then use the four *MYSQL_xxx* objects as you would normal Visual Basic objects.

Example

Again we shall use as an example the program that stores a character string with all the authors belonging to a given book title in the *authors* column of the *titles* table.

For establishing the connection you create an object of type *MYSQL_CONNECTION* and pass the computer name, user name, password, and database name to the method *OpenConnection*:

```
' authors_for_titles_VBMySQLDirect\form1.frm
' create connection to MySQL
Dim conn As New MYSQL_CONNECTION
Private Sub Command1_Click()
  conn.OpenConnection "localhost", "root", "xxx", "mylibrary"
  Command2.Enabled = True
End Sub
```

MYSQL_RS objects are derived with the method *Execute* from the *MYSQL_CONNECTION* object. Access to individual fields of the current record is effected with *rs.Fields("columnName").Value* (instead of *rs!columnName*, as with ADO).

To alter data in *MYSQL_RS* objects, simply assign a new value to the *Value* property of the affected column and store the changes with the *Update* method. (You can also insert a new record with *AddNew* or delete one with *Delete*, but these are not demonstrated in our example.)

■**Caution** Be sure to close every *MYSQL_RS* object explicitly with *Close* after you are through with it. If you forget this, then the piece of memory for storing the object will never be released.

```
' change the titles table
Private Sub Command2_Click()
  Dim authors_str, titleID
  Dim titles As MYSQL_RS
  Dim authors As MYSQL_RS
  ' titles Recordset for a loop over all titles
  ' and for changing the authors column
  Set titles = conn.Execute( _
    "SELECT titleID, authors FROM titles")
  ' loop over all book titles
  While Not titles.EOF
    titleID = titles.Fields("titleID").Value
    ' authors recordset to read the authors of a title
    Set authors = conn.Execute( _
      "SELECT authname FROM authors, rel_title_author " & _
      "WHERE authors.authID=rel_title_author.authID " & _
      "  AND rel_title_author.titleID = " & titleID & " " & _
      "ORDER BY authName")
    ' loop over all authors
    authors_str = ""
    Do While Not authors.EOF
      ' assemble string with the author names
      If Not IsNull(authors.Fields("authName").Value) Then
        If authors_str <> "" Then authors_str = authors_str + "; "
        authors_str = authors_str & authors.Fields("authName").Value
      End If
      authors.MoveNext
    Loop
    authors.CloseRecordset
    ' save authors field in the titles recordset object
    If Len(authors_str) > 254 Then _
      authors_str = Left(authors_str, 254)
    titles.Fields("authors").Value = authors_str
    titles.Update
    titles.MoveNext
  Wend
  titles.CloseRecordset
End Sub
```

CHAPTER 20

■■■

Visual Basic .NET and C#

This chapter deals with programming MySQL applications with the languages Visual Basic 2005 (alias VB.NET 2) and C#. In both cases one uses the database library ADO.NET in combination with the MySQL driver Connector/Net.

■Note The examples presented in this chapter use, with few exceptions, VB.NET as the programming language. Friends of C# will find equivalent C# projects to most of these examples in the source code (www.apress.com).

All examples were developed with the VS.NET development environment; that is, we have used the usual default settings for libraries and imports.

It is basically true that MySQL programming with ADO.NET is not particularly MySQL-specific. Once the connection has been made, the rest is like any other ADO.NET program. The only major difference is that instead of the classes *OleDbXxx* and *SqlXxx* described in all the ADO.NET books, the largely equivalent classes *OdbcXxx* and *MySQLXxx* must be used.

Communication Between ADO.NET and MySQL

Many roads lead from ADO.NET to MySQL, regardless of whether you prefer to work with C# or VB.NET. The following list gives an overview:

Connector/ODBC + ODBC data provider: In this variant, communication takes place via ODBC. The interface between MySQL and ODBC is provided by Connector/ODBC. As data provider for ADO.NET, the ODBC data provider (name space *Microsoft.Data.Odbd*) is used. This data provider has been an integral component of ADO.NET since .NET 1.1 (Visual Studio 2003).

VB.NET/C# ➤ ADO.NET ➤ ODBC data provider ➤ Connector/ODBC ➤ MySQL

Connector/ODBC + OLEDB data provider: In this variant as well, communication takes place via ODBC. However, the access route to MySQL is now extended by an additional component, the OLEDB provider for ODBC.

VB.NET/C# ➤ ADO.NET ➤ OLEDB data provider ➤ OLEDB provider for ODBC ➤ Connector/ODBC ➤ MySQL

Managed data provider for ADO.NET: For efficient communication between ADO.NET and MySQL, it is best to use a special provider for ADO.NET.

VB.NET/C# ➤ ADO.NET ➤ MySQL data provider ➤ MySQL

The obvious advantage of such a provider is that the communication path is the shortest. This represents fewer compatibility problems between the individual layers and greater efficiency.

Moreover, such providers can provide MySQL-specific functions (such as support of the compressed communication protocol). These additional functions have the drawback of making difficult a later change of provider (or even the database system).

Fortunately, there is now a host of such providers. In February 2003 I found the following drivers on the Internet:

Connector/Net (GPL): This driver is the official .Net provider of the MySQL company. It is derived from the former ByteFX Provider: `http://dev.mysql.com/`.

MySQLDriverCS (Open Source, GPL): This driver is an open-source alternative to the official driver of MySQL: `http://sourceforge.net/projects/mysqldrivercs/`.

MySQLDirect .NET from CoreLab: This is yet another commercial driver: `http://crlab.com/mysqlnet/`.

It was impossible to test in full all the variants introduced here. I have tried out connections with the provider Connector/Net as well as with the combination Connector/ODBC + ODBC provider (see the following two sections).

■**Note** An additional option is to use, in place of ADO.NET, the old ADO library in VB.NET or C#. Thanks to the COM compatibility layer, this is possible in principle. ADO, however, is less efficient and secure than ADO.NET and does not fit in well with the .NET framework. For this reason we will not pursue this variant further.

Establishing a Connection with Connector/Net

Installing Connector/Net

The driver Connector/Net is an offshoot of the former ByteFX driver and is the official ADO.NET driver for MySQL supported by the firm MySQL. If you are unsure which driver to use, this one should be your first choice. The driver can be used free of charge under the GPL license, and can be downloaded from `http://dev.mysql.com`. If you are developing commercial projects, your customers must possess a commercial license for the MySQL server.

The ZIP archive contains a `*.msi` file that installs the driver together with various example files in the directory `Programs\MySQL\MySQL Connector Net n.n`. The actual driver—the library `MySql.Data.dll`—is then registered in the *global assembly cache* (GAC), which currently works only for the .NET framework 1.0 and 1.1.

Using the Connector/Net Library

In order to use Connector/Net in your project, you must create a reference to the libraries `System.Data.dll` and `MySql.Data.dll` with PROJECT | ADD REFERENCE. With the tested program version Visual Studio 2005 Beta 1 and Connector/Net 1.0.4, the registration of `MySql.Data.dll` in the GAC of the .NET framework 2.0 did not function. Therefore, the library `MySql.Data.dll` does not appear in the .NET dialog sheet. To establish a reference to the library, switch into the dialog sheet BROWSE and open the following file: `Programs\MySQL\MySQL Connector Net 1.0.4\bin\.NET 1.1\MySql.Data.dll`.

To avoid having to specify *MySql.Data.MySQLClient.xxx* repeatedly, you should place an *Imports* or *using* instruction at the beginning of your code:

```
Imports MySql.Data.MySqlClient  '  VB.NET
using MySql.Data.MySqlClient;   // C#
```

Establishing the Connection

The connection is now made with a *MySQLConnection* object. The string with connection data is made up of several pieces, which are separated by semicolons. Table 20-1 describes the most important parameters. Note that many parameters are accepted in various forms (e.g., *User Id* or *Uid* or *Username* or *User name*). A complete reference of all parameters in all forms together with the default values can be found in the online help for Connector/Net under the key word *ConnectionString*.

Table 20-1. *Connection Parameters of Connector/Net*

Parameter	Meaning
Data Source or *Hostname*	Hostname or IP address of the MySQL server.
Initial Catalog or *Database*	Name of the database.
User Id or *Username*	User name.
Password	Password.
Connection Timeout	Maximum time for connection creation before error is triggered (default 15 seconds).
Allow Batch	Tells whether more than one SQL command at a time can be executed (default *true*); commands must be separated by semicolons.

The code for creating a connection looks something like this:

```
Dim myconn As New MySqlConnection( _
  "Data Source=localhost;Initial Catalog=mylibrary;" + _
  "User ID=root;PWD=xxxxxx")
myconn.Open()
```

■**Note** An additional parameter is allowed in the connection string, one that is not mentioned in the official documentation and is apparently a relic of the ByteFX past history of the driver: *UseCompression=true* has the effect that communication between the program and the MySQL server is compressed. That can be useful with a very slow network connection. However, *UseCompression=true* assumes that the program contains a reference to the library ICSharpCode.SharpZipLib.dll. This library can be found in the installation of Connector/Net in the directory Programs\MySQL\MySQL Connector Net n.n.n\src.

Project Transfer (Setup Project)

In transferring a project to others, you must see to it that the library MySql.Data.dll is installed on the target computer (best is in the program's local directory).

VB.NET Example

The following example program creates a connection to the local MySQL server, obtains a sorted list of all publishers (*publishers* table from the *mylibrary* database), and displays it in a text field (see Figure 20-1).

Figure 20-1. *Connector/Net example program*

```vbnet
' example code vbnet\connector_net_intro
Imports MySql.Data.MySqlClient
Public Class Form1
  Dim myconn As MySqlConnection

  ' create connection
  Private Sub Button1_Click(...) Handles Button1.Click
    Try
      myconn = New MySqlConnection( _
          "Data Source=localhost;Initial Catalog=mylibrary;" + _
          "User ID=root;PWD=xxxxx")
      myconn.Open()
    Catch myerror As MySqlException
      MsgBox("Database connection error: " & myerror.Message)
      Me.Close()
    End Try
    Button2.Enabled = True
  End Sub

  ' execute SQL query, display result in text box
  Private Sub Button2_Click(...) Handles Button2.Click
    Dim com As MySqlCommand
    Dim dr As MySqlDataReader
    com = New MySqlCommand( _
      "SELECT publID, publName FROM publishers ORDER BY publName", _
      myconn)
    dr = com.ExecuteReader()
    While dr.Read()
      TextBox1.AppendText("id = " & dr!publID & _
        ",  name = " & dr!publName & vbCrLf)
    End While
    dr.Close()
  End Sub

  ' program end
  Private Sub Button3_Click(...) Handles Button3.Click
    Me.Close()
  End Sub
End Class
```

C# Example

The equivalent C# code looks like this:

```csharp
// example code csharp\connector_net_intro
using ...;
using MySql.Data.MySqlClient;

namespace connector_net_intro {
  partial class Form1 : Form {
    MySqlConnection myconn;
    public Form1() {
      InitializeComponent();
    }

    // create connection
    private void button1_Click(object sender, EventArgs e) {
      try {
        myconn = new MySqlConnection(
          "Data Source=localhost;Initial Catalog=mylibrary;" +
          "User ID=root;PWD=uranus");
        myconn.Open();
      }
      catch (MySqlException myerror) {
        MessageBox.Show("MySQL connection error: " + myerror.Message);
        this.Close();
      }
      button2.Enabled = true;
    }

    // execute SQL query, display result in text box
    private void button2_Click(object sender, EventArgs e) {
      MySqlCommand com;
      MySqlDataReader dr;
      com = new MySqlCommand(
        "SELECT publID, publName FROM publishers ORDER BY publName",
        myconn);
      dr = com.ExecuteReader();
      while (dr.Read())
        textBox1.AppendText("id = " + dr["publID"] +
          ", name = " + dr["publName"] + Environment.NewLine);
      dr.Close();
    }

    // program end
    private void button3_Click(object sender, EventArgs e) {
      this.Close();
    }
  }
}
```

Establishing the Connection with the ODBC Data Provider

Establishing the Connection

The connection looks very much as it did with ADO (see the previous chapter). The main difference is that now an *OdbcConnection* object is used, and the connection string can be passed to the constructor. The connection string is exactly the same as with ADO.

As a rule, the *Options* setting should be 3. This corresponds to the options *Don't optimize column width (1)* and *Return matching rows (2)*. The option *Change BIGINT into INT (16384)* is not required with ADO.NET.

```
' VB.NET
Dim odbcconn As New System.Data.Odbc.OdbcConnection( _
   "Driver={MySQL ODBC 3.51 Driver};Server=localhost;" + _
   "Database=mylibraryodbc;UID=root;PWD=uranus;Options=3")
odbcconn.Open()
```

```
// C#
OdbcConnection odbcconn = new System.Data.Odbc.OdbcConnection(
   "Driver={MySQL ODBC 3.51 Driver};Server=localhost;" +
   "Database=mylibraryodbc;UID=root;PWD=uranus;Options=3");
odbcconn.Open();
```

VB.NET Example

The following small program displays an alphabetic list of all publishers in *mylibrary.publishers* in a console window (see Figure 20-2). After the connection is established with *OdbcCommand*, a *SELECT* query is executed. The result is evaluated with an *OdbdDataReader* object in a loop.

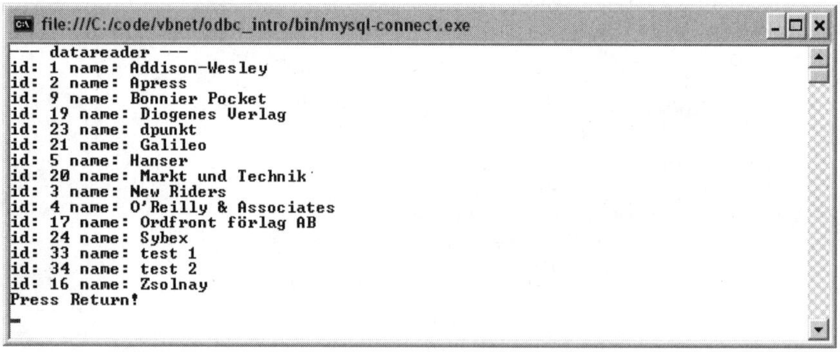

```
file:///C:/code/vbnet/odbc_intro/bin/mysql-connect.exe

--- datareader ---
id: 1 name: Addison-Wesley
id: 2 name: Apress
id: 9 name: Bonnier Pocket
id: 19 name: Diogenes Verlag
id: 23 name: dpunkt
id: 21 name: Galileo
id: 5 name: Hanser
id: 20 name: Markt und Technik
id: 3 name: New Riders
id: 4 name: O'Reilly & Associates
id: 17 name: Ordfront förlag AB
id: 24 name: Sybex
id: 33 name: test 1
id: 34 name: test 2
id: 16 name: Zsolnay
Press Return!
```

Figure 20-2. *ODBC example program*

```
' example vbnet/odbc_connectintro/module1.vb
Option Strict On
Imports System.Data
Imports MicrosoftSystem.Data.Odbc
```

```
Module Module1
  Dim odbcconn As OdbcConnection
  Sub Main()
    odbcconn = New OdbcConnection( _
      "Driver=MySQL ODBC 3.51 Driver;Server=localhost;" + _
      "Database=mylibrary;UID=root;PWD=xxxxx;Options=16387")
    odbcconn.Open()
    read_publishers_datareader()
    odbcconn.Close()
  End Sub

  ' example for OdbcDataReader
  Sub read_publishers_datareader()
    Dim com As OdbcCommand
    Dim dr As OdbcDataReader
    com = New OdbcCommand( _
      "SELECT publID, publName FROM publishers ORDER BY publName", _
      odbcconn)
    dr = com.ExecuteReader()
    While dr.Read()
      Console.WriteLine("id: {0} name: {1}", dr!publID, dr!publName)
    End While
    dr.Close()
  End Sub
End Module
```

C# Example

The equivalent C# code looks like this:

```
// example csharp\odbc_connect\Class1.cs
using System;
using System.Data.Odbc;

namespace odbc_connect {
  class mainclass         {
    [STAThread]
    static void Main(string[] args) {
      Odbctest tst = new Odbctest();
      tst.ReadPublishersDataset();
      Console.WriteLine("Return drücken");
      Console.ReadLine();
    }
  }
  class Odbctest {
    OdbcConnection odbcconn;

    public Odbctest() {      // use constructor to connect
      odbcconn = new OdbcConnection(
        "Driver={MySQL ODBC 3.51 Driver};Server=localhost;" +
        "Database=mylibrary;UID=root;PWD=xxxxx;Options=16387");
      odbcconn.Open();
    }
```

```
    public void ReadPublishersDataset() {
      OdbcCommand com = new OdbcCommand(
        "SELECT publID, publName FROM publishers ORDER BY publName",
        odbcconn);
      OdbcDataReader dr = com.ExecuteReader();
      while(dr.Read()) {
        Console.WriteLine("id: {0} name: {1}",
          dr["publID"], dr["publName"]);
      }
      dr.Close();
    }
  }
}
```

Programming Techniques

As I have already mentioned, all the remaining examples in this chapter assume that the MySQL
connection has been made with Connector/Net. *myconn* is an open *MySqlConnection* object that
refers to a suitable MySQL database.

If you use another provider, you must establish a reference to the appropriate library, change
the *Imports/using* instruction, replace *MySqlXxx* by *OdbcXxx* or the class name of the provider, and
adapt the connection string according to the provider's required syntax. Depending on the provider,
you may also have to make minor changes in the code (e.g., cast operators, parameter syntax in SQL
commands).

Executing SQL Commands (MySqlCommand)

To execute SQL commands, you need an *MySqlCommand* object. The basic *MySqlConnection* object
and the SQL command can be passed to the constructor or handled separately. (The latter is especially useful if you wish to execute several SQL commands with a single *MySqlCommand* object.)

There are three ways to execute SQL commands:

ExecuteNonQuery is used for all commands that do not immediately return a result (e.g.,
UPDATE, INSERT, DELETE):

```
Dim com As New MySqlCommand()
com.Connection = myconn
com.CommandText = "INSERT INTO table (colname) VALUES ('abc')"
com.ExecuteNonQuery()
```

ExecuteReader is used if you wish to execute a *SELECT* query and read the result with
MySqlDataReader (see the example somewhat later in this chapter).

ExecuteScalar is used when the command returns a single value (e.g., *SELECT COUNT(*)
FROM table*); an example follows shortly.

If an error occurs during the execution of an SQL command, a *MySqlException* occurs, which
can be caught with *Try/Catch*:

```
Try
   com.ExecuteNonQuery()
 Catch e As MySqlException
   MsgBox(e.Message)
   Stop
 End Try
```

In formulating an SQL command, you must heed the MySQL syntax rules: In character strings, the characters ', ", \, and 0-byte must be indicated by \', \", \\, and \0. Dates must also be correctly formatted (*2005-12-31 23:59:59*). You can save effort with *INSERT* and *DELETE* commands by using commands with parameters.

AUTO_INCREMENT Column (LAST_INSERT_ID)

The ID number of the last record inserted with *INSERT* can be determined with the command *SELECT LAST_INSERT_ID()*. The method *ExecuteScalar* just mentioned returns the ID number as a *Long* integer.

```
Dim n As Long
Dim com As New MySqlCommand()
com.Connection = myconn
com.CommandText = "INSERT INTO table (columns ...) VALUES (...)"
com.ExecuteNonQuery()
com.CommandText = "SELECT LAST_INSERT_ID()"
n = CLng(com.ExecuteScalar())
```

Commands with Parameters (MySql Parameters)

Parameters in SQL commands are indicated by *?name*. There are two variants. The first is to give the values directly with *Add("?name", data)* and then execute the command. This variant is especially well suited for commands that are to be executed only once:

```
Dim com1 As MySqlCommand
com1 = myconn.CreateCommand()
com1.CommandText = _
  "INSERT INTO authors (authName, authID, ts) VALUES(?name, ?id, ?ts)"
com1.Parameters.Add("?name", "authorname")
com1.Parameters.Add("?id", 12345)
com1.Parameters.Add("?ts", DateTime.Now())
com1.ExecuteNonQuery()
```

In the second variant, all the parameters are defined with their type. Here all the MySQL data types are available as elements of the *MySqlDbType* enumeration. Then the command is prepared for execution with *Prepare*. The assignment of a value takes place only in the second step, when the *Value* property of the *MySqlParameter* object is set.

This variant is good for commands that are to be executed more than once with maximum efficiency. If you have at least version 4.1 of the MySQL server, the SQL commands will be executed as prepared statements. This offers several advantages: somewhat greater speed, type checking of all passed data, and an optimal conversion of data into the relevant MySQL format. This works in particular for binary data (BLOBs).

```
' prepare command
Dim com2 As MySqlCommand
Dim pname, pid, pts As MySqlParameter
com2 = myconn.CreateCommand()
com2.CommandText = _
  "INSERT INTO authors (authName, authID, ts) VALUES(?name, ?id, ?ts)"
pname = com2.Parameters.Add("?name", MySqlDbType.VarChar)
pid = com2.Parameters.Add("?id", MySqlDbType.Int32)
pts = com2.Parameters.Add("?ts", MySqlDbType.Timestamp)
```

```
com2.Prepare()
' execute command for the first time
pname.Value = "test 124"
pid.Value = 124
pts.Value = DateTime.Now
com2.ExecuteNonQuery()
' execute command a second time
pname.Value = "test 125"
pid.Value = 125
pts.Value = DateTime.Now
com2.ExecuteNonQuery()
```

If you wish to pass the value *NULL* to a parameter, then use *DBNull.Value*:

```
com.Parameters(0).Value = DBNull.Value
```

The equivalent C# code to the listing above looks like this:

```
 // prepare command
MySqlCommand com2;
MySqlParameter pname, pid, pts;
com2 = myconn.CreateCommand();
com2.CommandText =
  "INSERT INTO authors (authName, authID, ts) VALUES(?name, ?id, ?ts)";
pname = com2.Parameters.Add("?name", MySqlDbType.VarChar);
pid = com2.Parameters.Add("?id", MySqlDbType.Int32);
pts = com2.Parameters.Add("?ts", MySqlDbType.Timestamp);
com2.Prepare();

// execute command for first time
pname.Value = "test 124";
pid.Value = 124;
pts.Value = DateTime.Now;
com2.ExecuteNonQuery();

// execute command for second time
pname.Value = "test 125";
pid.Value = 125;
pts.Value = DateTime.Now;
com2.ExecuteNonQuery();
```

Evaluating Individual SELECT Results (ExecuteScalar)

Queries such as *SELECT COUNT(*) FROM …* are a special case. They return a single record with only a single column. In this case, you can avoid the use of a *DataReader*. Instead, execute the SQL command specified in the *MySqlCommand* object with the method *ExecuteScalar*, which returns the result as an *Object*. In VB.NET you obtain with *CInt* the associated *Integer*. For strings, use the analogous *CStr*, and for dates and times, *Cdate*, etc.

```
Dim n As Integer
Dim com As New MySqlCommand("SELECT COUNT(*) FROM table", myconn)
n = CInt(com.ExecuteScalar())
```

In C# you have to use casting operators instead of these functions, for example, *(int)*, *(string)*, or *(DateTime)*:

```
DateTime dt;
com = new MySqlCommand("SELECT MAX(ts) FROM authors ", myconn);
dt = (DateTime) com.ExecuteScalar();
```

In many cases in C# it is necessary to use two casting operators: *com.ExecuteScalar()* in the following example returns an *object*, behind which, however, a *long* value is hiding. If you wish to store this value in an *int* variable, you must first convert *object* into *long* and then *long* into *int*. (The first casting operator, here *(long)*, is responsible for what in C# is called *unboxing*.)

```
int id;
com = new MySqlCommand("SELECT LAST_INSERT_ID()");
id = (int)(long)com.ExecuteScalar();
```

Reading SELECT Results (MySqlDataReader)

The *MySqlDataReader* class offers the simplest way of reading *SELECT* results. The *MySqlDataReader* does not support free navigation in the result list (hence only *forward only*). Nor are changes possible. In return, *MySqlDataReader* is frugal with resources and offers the most efficient path to *SELECT* results.

You obtain a *MySqlDataReader* when you execute an SQL command with the method *ExecuteReader*. *Read* reads the first, or next, record, and returns *True* or *False* depending on whether a record was found. The *MySqlDataReader* object should be explicitly closed with *Close* as soon as it is no longer needed. (Otherwise, it takes up memory.)

The following lines show how all records can be run through in a loop. The results are stored temporarily in a *StringWriter* object and then output to the console window.

```
Dim sstr As New IO.StringWriter
Dim com As New MySqlCommand( _
  "SELECT publID, publName FROM publishers", myconn)
Dim dr As MySqlDataReader = com.ExecuteReader()
While dr.Read()
  sstr.WriteLine("id: {0} name: {1}", dr!publID, dr!publName)
End While
Console.WriteLine(sstr)
sstr.Close()
dr.Close()
```

The *MySqlDataReader* offers no way of determining the number of records in advance. Thus you must count along as you read all the records, or else execute a *SELECT COUNT(*) ...* query.

Access to data fields: In VB.NET, access to data fields takes place in the form *dr!columnname*. As result you obtain *Object* data that you must convert into the actual data format with functions such as *CStr*, *CInt*.

In C#, the syntax is *dr["columnname"]*. The *object* results must be converted with casting operators into the actual data format.

As an alternative, you can read data with *GetByte(n)*, *GetDateTime(n)*, *GetInt32(n)*, etc., where *n* is the column number (0 for the first column).

Access to metadata: With the functions *GetName(n)* and *GetDataTypeName(n)* you can determine the column name and data type for each column. If you wish to know whether a query has returned any results at all, evaluate the property *dr.HasRows*. The number of columns in the result is returned by *dr.FieldCount*.

Special Data Types

NULL: Data fields that in the database contain *NULL* have in ADO.NET the value *System.DBNull*. There are various methods for testing for *NULL*:

```
If Convert.IsDBNull(dr!column) Then ...
If dr!column Is DBNull.Value Then ...
If dr.IsDBNull(columnnumber) Then ...
```

In using *SELECT* results (e.g., *stringvar = CStr(dr!textcolumn)*), you must always consider the case that the data field contains *NULL*: Then the VB.NET method *CStr* or the C# cast operator (*string*) leads to an error.

Dates: Date information (*DATE, TIMESTAMP*) is automatically transformed in ADO.NET into *Date* objects.

Times: Times (*TIME*) are transformed in ADO.NET into *TimeSpan* objects.

The *MySqlDateTime* data type: You can also process MySQL dates and times directly in the form of *MySqlDateTime* objects. To do so, use the *DataReader* method *GetMySqlDateTime*. From the resulting object you can then evaluate the components of the date and time with the properties *Day, Hour*, etc. The property *IsValidDate* tells whether the date is valid. (MySQL allows the storage of invalid dates, depending on the configuration, such as 31.2.2005.)

Fixed-point numbers: Fixed-point numbers (*DECIMAL*) are represented in ADO.NET by *Decimal* objects.

BIGINTs: In contrast to ADO, ADO.NET has no problems with 64-bit integers (*BIGINT*). Such numbers are represented in ADO.NET as *Long* numbers.

BLOBs: Binary data are represented in ADO.NET by *Byte* fields.

Character strings: In VB.NET and C#, character strings are coded in UTF16 (aka UCS2), a Unicode format in which each character is represented by 2 bytes. In transfer between ADO.NET and MySQL, the conversion takes place automatically into the character set of table.

Several SELECT Results

If you execute more than one SQL command at a time (*"SELECT 1;SELECT 2"*) or if you are using stored procedures, it can happen that you obtain several *SELECT* results. The *MySqlDataReader* gives by default access to only the first result. You can activate the additional results with the method *NextResult*, which returns *False* if there are no more results.

The following lines form a loop over all results (*Do*), over all records of each result (*While*), and over all columns of each record (*For*), and then the data are returned as a character string in the console window.

```
Dim i As Integer
Dim com As New MySqlCommand( _
  "SELECT * FROM authors LIMIT 3;SELECT COUNT(*) FROM authors;SELECT 1+2", _
  myconn)
Dim dr As MySqlDataReader = com.ExecuteReader()
Do
  Console.WriteLine("-----")
  While dr.Read()
    For i = 0 To dr.FieldCount - 1
      If dr.IsDBNull(i) Then
        Console.Write("NULL ")
      Else
        Console.Write(dr.GetString(i) + " ")
      End If
    Next
    Console.WriteLine()
  End While
Loop While dr.NextResult()
dr.Close()
```

DataSet, DataTable, MySqlDataAdapter

If you wish to navigate at will (backward as well as forward) through *SELECT* results and alter, delete, or insert new records, then you need a *DataSet* object and at least one *DataTable* contained therein. A *DataSet* helps in managing one or more *DataTables*. A *DataTable* is simply a table with data, usually the result of *SELECT* queries. *DataSet* and *DataTable* are general ADO.NET classes, and are independent of the provider. For this reason, there are no independent *MySqlDataTables*, *MySqlDataSets*, etc. However, for communication between the *DataSet* and the provider, a connection class is necessary, and it is precisely this task that is taken over by the *MySqlDataAdapter* object.

All the data contained in a *DataSet* are located in the memory of the ADO.NET program. When a *DataTable* contained in a *DataSet* is created on the basis of a *SELECT* query, all resulting records from the query are transmitted to the ADO.NET program. From this point on, you are processing the local copy of the data. The data stored on the MySQL server are updated only when the *Update* method for the *MySqlDataAdapter* is executed.

The following commands show how to fill a *DataTable* with the results of a *SELECT* query. As usual, you first create an *MySqlCommand* object for your SQL command. This object will be passed to an *MySqlDataAdapter*. The *SELECT* query is executed by the method *Fill* of the *MySqlDataAdapter*. The results are stored in the *DataSet*. For this, a new *DataTable* is created in the *DataSet*, which in this example is given the name *"test"*. You can now access this *DataTable* via *ds.Tables("name")*.

```
Dim com As New MySqlCommand("SELECT * FROM tablename", myconn)
Dim da As New MySqlDataAdapter(com)
Dim ds As New DataSet()                    'currently empty DataSet ds
da.Fill(ds, " dtname")                     'create DataTable "dtname" in ds
Dim dt As DataTable = ds.Tables("dtname")  'access to the DataTable
```

You can now access the data of the *DataTable* in the form of *dt.Row(rowno)!columnname*. Here, *Row(n)* returns a single record (class *DataRow*), and *Rows.Count* gives the number of records. A loop over all records can be formulated thus:

```
Dim row As DataRow
For Each row In dt.Rows  'loop over all records
  row!columnname = ...   'change data
Next
```

With *datarow.Delete* you can delete individual records. It is somewhat more complex to insert new records. For that, you first create a new record with *datatable.NewRow*, change its contents, and finally add it with *datatable.Rows.Add* to the *DataTable*:

```
Dim newrow As DataRow
newrow = dt.NewRow()
newrow!a_big_int = 12345
dt.Rows.Add(newrow)
```

As already mentioned, all changes in the *DataSet* are valid initially only locally (that is, in memory of the ADO.NET program). For the changes to be carried out in the MySQL database, you must execute the method *Update* for the *MySqlDataAdapter*. The update is carried out in a series of *INSERT*, *UPDATE*, and *DELETE* commands, which the *MySqlDataAdapter* sends to MySQL. However, the *MySqlDataAdapter* is not able to generate these commands. Therefore, first, before the *Update* method, a *MySqlCommandBuilder* object must be generated to take over this task. The following lines demonstrate how that is done:

```
' ... Code to change data in dt
Dim cb As New MySqlCommandBuilder(da)
Try
  da.Update(ds, "test")
Catch e As Exception
  Stop
End Try
```

If you wish to know which *UPDATE, INSERT,* and *DELETE* commands are being executed, you can find this out with *cb.GetInsert/Update/DeleteCommand()*.

What looks great in theory, is in practice hemmed in with limitations:

- Changes can be stored only if the *DataTables* contained in the *DataSet* come directly from a MySQL table. *DataTables* based on *SELECT* commands that include several tables (*JOIN*) or use aggregating functions (*GROUP BY*) cannot be updated. In this case, the *MySqlCommandBuilder* is incapable of determining the appropriate SQL commands.

  This limitation is not one of ADO.NET, but has to do with the fact that changes in such tables can often be interpreted in more than one way, and ADO.NET and the *CommandBuilder* are not clairvoyant.

- The change in a *DataSet* is strongly provider-dependent. While I have had good experiences with Connector/J, the ODBC provider often causes problems. The strong provider-dependence also means that you cannot count on your code functioning after a change of provider.

■**Tip** Not everything that looks technologically appealing is ready to be used in the real world. You should carry out exhaustive testing before using *DataSets* for changing data. You will be safe if you use *DataSets* primarily for reading data. To alter data, you should create the necessary SQL commands yourself and execute them with *MySqlCommand* objects (preferably using parameters).

An Example

In the following lines of code a *DataTable* is created in a *DataSet* with the results of the query *SELECT * FROM authors*. In the *For* loop, all the records whose author name begins with *test* are deleted.

```
Dim com As New MySqlCommand("SELECT * FROM authors", myconn)
Dim da As New MySqlDataAdapter(com)          'interface MySQL<-->DataSet
Dim cb As New MySqlCommandBuilder(da)        'necessary for updates
Dim ds As New DataSet()                      'currently empty DataSet
da.Fill(ds, "authors")                       'creates DataTable "authors" in ds
Dim dt As DataTable = ds.Tables("authors")   'access to the DataTable
Dim row As DataRow
For Each row In dt.Rows                       'loop over all records
  If LCase(Left(CStr(row!authName), 4)) = "test" Then    'alter data
    Console.WriteLine("delete author " & row!authName.ToString)
    row.Delete()
  End If
Next
Try
  da.Update(ds, "authors")
Catch e As Exception
  MsgBox(e.Message)
End Try
```

In C# the code looks like this:

```
MySqlCommand com;
MySqlDataAdapter da;
DataSet ds;
DataTable dt;
MySqlCommandBuilder cb;
com = new MySqlCommand("SELECT * FROM authors", myconn);
da = new MySqlDataAdapter(com);
cb = new MySqlCommandBuilder(da);
ds = new DataSet();
da.Fill(ds, "authors");
dt = ds.Tables["authors"];
foreach (DataRow row in dt.Rows) {
  if (row["authName"].ToString().Substring(0, 4).ToLower() == "test") {
    Console.WriteLine("delete author " + row["authName"].ToString());
    row.Delete();
  }
}
try {
  da.Update(ds, "authors"); }
catch (Exception e) {
  Console.WriteLine(e.Message); }
```

Auxiliary Methods

The class *MySqlHelper* contains some methods that make your work with Connector/Net simpler and more efficient:

ExecuteDataRow creates a connection to the MySQL server, executes a *SELECT* command, returns the first record of the *SELECT* result, and closes the connection to the MySQL server.

ExecuteReader creates a connection to the MySQL server, executes a *SELECT* command, returns the result as a *DataReader* object, and closes the connection to the MySQL server.

UpdateDataSet saves changes to a *DataSet* in the underlying database of the MySQL server. As with the two previous methods, a new connection to the MySQL server is created and then closed.

ExecuteScalar executes a *SELECT* command and returns the scalar result as an *Object*. This method can use an existing connection to the MySQL server or create a new connection and then close it.

ExecuteDataSet executes a *SELECT* command and returns the result as a *DataSet* object. As with *ExecuteScalar*, either an existing connection can be used or a new one created.

ExecuteNonQuery executes an SQL command that does not return a list of records as result. As with *ExecuteScalar*, either an existing connection can be used or a new one created.

Error-Handling

When errors occur in the execution of ADO.NET methods and properties, *Exceptions* are triggered. Such exceptional situations are usually processed with *Try-Catch* constructions.

If Connector/Net classes are directly responsible for the error, a *MySqlException* object is passed to the *Catch* block. In the case of errors for which the general classes of the *System.Data* namespace are responsible, the *Catch* block receives a *System.Data.DataException* object. In both cases the *Message* property provides more precise information about the error.

Windows.Forms and ASP.NET Controls

The .NET Framework offers a great number of controls for Windows and Internet applications (ASP.NET) that can be bound to *DataSet*s. This simplifies the representation and processing of lists and tables on the basis of query results.

A basic rule is that as long as you display only data with the controls, and don't try to alter the data, you may expect few problems. However, if you permit data updating, then you should test extensively what is possible. (Internally, data bound controls use *DataSet*s almost exclusively, and I have already referred to their possible *Update* problems.)

Space here does not suffice to introduce data bound controls and go into the details of their deployment. The following example program should at least provide a first impression of what can be done with them. The program contains a listbox with all publishers. When one is selected, a table field displays that publisher's titles (see Figure 20-3).

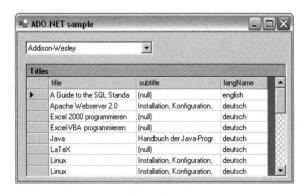

Figure 20-3. *ADO.NET example program*

```
' example program vbnet\datacontrols
Imports MySql.Data.MySqlClient
Public Class Form1
  Inherits System.Windows.Forms.Form
  ' Windows Forms Designer generated code ...

  Dim myconn As MySqlConnection
  Dim titlecommand As MySqlCommand
  Dim publparam As MySqlParameter

  Private Sub Form1_Load(...) Handles MyBase.Load
    ' create connection to database
    myconn = New MySqlConnection( _
      "Data Source=localhost;Initial Catalog=mylibrary;" + _
      "User ID=root;PWD=uranus")
    myconn.Open()

    'prepare command and parameters for title query and Parameter
    titlecommand = New MySqlCommand( _
      "SELECT title, subtitle, langName FROM titles, languages " + _
      "WHERE publID = ?publ AND titles.langID = languages.langID " + _
      "ORDER BY title", _
      myconn)
    publparam = titlecommand.Parameters.Add("?publ", MySqlDbType.Int32)
    titlecommand.Prepare()
```

```
    'fill ComboBox with a list of all publishers
    Dim com As New MySqlCommand( _
      "SELECT publID, publName FROM publishers ORDER BY publName", _
      myconn)
    Dim da As New MySqlDataAdapter(com)
    Dim ds As New DataSet()
    da.Fill(ds, "publishers")
    ComboBox1.DisplayMember = "publName"
    ComboBox1.ValueMember = "publID"
    ComboBox1.DataSource = ds.Tables("publishers")
  End Sub

  ' nw publisher selected --> create new DataSet with titles
  Private Sub ComboBox1_SelectedIndexChanged(...) _
      Handles ComboBox1.SelectedIndexChanged
    publparam.Value = ComboBox1.SelectedValue
    Dim ds As New DataSet()
    Dim da As New MySqlDataAdapter(titlecommand)
    da.Fill(ds, "titles")
    DataGrid1.DataSource = ds.Tables("titles")
  End Sub
End Class
```

Transactions

At the beginning of a transaction, execute the method *BeginTransaction* for the *MySqlConnection* object. As result, you obtain an *MySqlTransaction* object, with whose method *Commit* or *Rollback* you can end the transaction. For all commands that are executed within the confines of the transaction, the *Transaction* property must be set, either through the third parameter of the *MySqlCommand* constructor or through an explicit allocation of the *Transaction* property. The following lines show the usual way of proceeding:

```
Dim tr As MySqlTransaction
tr = myconn.BeginTransaction()
Dim com As New MySqlCommand("UPDATE ...", myconn, tr)
com.ExecuteNonQuery()
' ... additional commands of the transaction
tr.Commit()
```

Example: Storing New Titles in mylibrary

The example program of this section consists of a simple input mask in which you can input new book titles together with their authors and publishers. In the author field you may input more than one name, separated by semicolons. The publisher field is allowed to remain empty (in which case, the title is stored without a publisher). (See Figure 20-4.) In storing a new title, a check is made whether the authors and publisher are already known to the database, in which case the records already stored are used. There are no other plausibility checks or error-checking.

Figure 20-4. *Form for storing a new book title*

The program code is broken into two procdures. In *Form1_Load*, a number of *MySqlCommand* objects are initialized with *INSERT* and *SELECT* commands. These commands are then used when the procedure *btnSave_Click* is called for storing input:

```
' example vbnet\newtitleform
Option Strict On
Imports MySql.Data.MySqlClient
Public Class Form1
  Inherits System.Windows.Forms.Form
  ' Windows Forms Designer generated code ...
Dim mysqlConn As MySqlConnection
  Dim insertPublisherCom, insertAuthorCom, _
      insertTitleCom, insertRelAuthTitleCom, _
      selectPublisherCom, selectAuthorCom, _
      lastIDCom As MySqlCommand

  ' initialization tasks
  Private Sub Form1_Load(...) Handles MyBase.Load
    ' create connection to database
    mysqlConn = New MySqlConnection( _
      "Data Source=localhost;Initial Catalog=mylibrary;" + _
      "User ID=root;PWD=uranus")
    mysqlConn.Open()

    ' command for storing an author
    insertAuthorCom = New MySqlCommand( _
      "INSERT INTO authors (authName) VALUES (?authName)", mysqlConn)
    insertAuthorCom.Parameters.Add("?authName", MySqlDbType.VarChar)
    insertAuthorCom.Prepare()

    ' command for author search
    selectAuthorCom = New MySqlCommand( _
      "SELECT authID FROM authors WHERE authName = ?authName LIMIT 1", _
      mysqlConn)
    selectAuthorCom.Parameters.Add("?authName", MySqlDbType.VarChar)
    selectAuthorCom.Prepare()

    ' command for storing a title
    insertTitleCom = New MySqlCommand( _
      "INSERT INTO titles (title, publID) VALUES (?title, ?publID)", _
      mysqlConn)
    insertTitleCom.Parameters.Add("?title", MySqlDbType.VarChar)
    insertTitleCom.Parameters.Add("?publID", MySqlDbType.Int32)
    insertTitleCom.Prepare()
```

```
  ' command for storing a publisher
  insertPublisherCom = New MySqlCommand( _
    "INSERT INTO publishers (publName) VALUES (?publName)", mysqlConn)
  insertPublisherCom.Parameters.Add("?publName", MySqlDbType.VarChar)
  insertTitleCom.Prepare()

  ' command for publisher search
  selectPublisherCom = New MySqlCommand( _
    "SELECT publID FROM publishers WHERE publName = ?publName LIMIT 1", _
    mysqlConn)
  selectPublisherCom.Parameters.Add("?publName", MySqlDbType.VarChar)
  selectPublisherCom.Prepare()

  ' command for storing  rel_title_author enries
  insertRelAuthTitleCom = New MySqlCommand( _
    "INSERT INTO rel_title_author (titleID, authID) " + _
    "VALUES (?titleID, ?authId)", _
    mysqlConn)
  insertRelAuthTitleCom.Parameters.Add("?titleID", MySqlDbType.Int32)
  insertRelAuthTitleCom.Parameters.Add("?authID", MySqlDbType.Int32)
  insertRelAuthTitleCom.Prepare()

  ' command for determining LAST_INSERT_ID
  lastIDCom = New MySqlCommand( _
    "SELECT LAST_INSERT_ID()", mysqlConn)
End Sub

Private Sub btnSave_Click(...) Handles btnSave.Click
  Dim publID, titleID As Integer
  Dim result As Object
  Dim author, authors() As String

  ' Test whether input complete
  txtTitle.Text = Trim(txtTitle.Text)
  txtAuthors.Text = Trim(txtAuthors.Text)
  txtPublisher.Text = Trim(txtPublisher.Text)
  If txtTitle.Text = "" Or txtAuthors.Text = "" Then
    MsgBox("Please specify title and authors!")
    Exit Sub
  End If

  ' search for publisher or store new publisher
  If txtPublisher.Text <> "" Then
    ' does publisher already exist?
    selectPublisherCom.Parameters("?publName").Value = txtPublisher.Text
    result = selectPublisherCom.ExecuteScalar()
    If result Is Nothing Then
      insertPublisherCom.Parameters("?publName").Value = txtPublisher.Text
      insertPublisherCom.ExecuteNonQuery()
      publID = CInt(lastIDCom.ExecuteScalar())
    Else
      publID = CInt(result)
    End If
  End If
```

```
    ' store title
    insertTitleCom.Parameters("?title").Value = txtTitle.Text
    If publID > 0 Then
      insertTitleCom.Parameters("?publID").Value = publID
    Else
      insertTitleCom.Parameters("?publID").Value = DBNull.Value
    End If
    insertTitleCom.ExecuteNonQuery()
    titleID = CInt(lastIDCom.ExecuteScalar())

    ' store authors
    authors = Split(txtAuthors.Text, ";")
    insertRelAuthTitleCom.Parameters("?titleID").Value = titleID
    For Each author In authors
      ' does the author exist already?
      selectAuthorCom.Parameters("?authName").Value = author
      result = selectAuthorCom.ExecuteScalar()
      If result Is Nothing Then
        ' no, store new author
        insertAuthorCom.Parameters("?authName").Value = author
        insertAuthorCom.ExecuteNonQuery()
        insertRelAuthTitleCom.Parameters("?authID").Value = _
          CInt(lastIDCom.ExecuteScalar())
      Else
        ' yes, determine authID
        insertRelAuthTitleCom.Parameters("?authID").Value = CInt(result)
      End If
      'store  rel_title_authors entry
      insertRelAuthTitleCom.ExecuteNonQuery()
    Next

    MsgBox("Your input has been saved")
    txtTitle.Text = ""
    txtAuthors.Text = ""
    txtPublisher.Text = ""
  End Sub
End Class
```

Example: Storing an Image File in a BLOB and Then Reading It

The following example program reads the file test.jpg from the current directory and stores it in a table (*btnSave_Click*). In a second step, the binary data are read from the table, displayed in a *PictureBox* control element (see Figure 20-5), and saved to a second file test1.jpg (*btnLoad_Click*).

Figure 20-5. *Example of using images and binary data*

The program shows various programming techniques for reading and writing binary data from and to a database. For storing the image, the following table is created at the beginning of the program and then deleted at the end:

```
CREATE TABLE IF NOT EXISTS testpic
  (id INT NOT NULL AUTO_INCREMENT, pic MEDIUMBLOB, PRIMARY KEY (id))
```

Here is the program code:

```
' example code vbnet/blob_test
Option Strict On
Imports MySql.Data.MySqlClient
Imports System.IO
Public Class Form1
  Dim myconn As MySqlConnection
  Dim com As MySqlCommand
  Dim id As Integer

  ' create connection to MySQL server, create testpic table
  Private Sub btnConnect_Click(...) Handles btnConnect.Click
    Try
      myconn = New MySqlConnection( _
        "Data Source=192.168.80.128;Initial Catalog=mylibrary;" + _
        "User ID=root;PWD=uranus")
      myconn.Open()
```

```vb
        com = New MySqlCommand( _
          "CREATE TABLE IF NOT EXISTS testpic " + _
          "  (id INT NOT NULL AUTO_INCREMENT, " + _
          "   pic MEDIUMBLOB, PRIMARY KEY (id))", _
          myconn)
        com.ExecuteNonQuery()
        btnSave.Enabled = True
      Catch myerror As MySqlException
        MsgBox("Database connection error: " & myerror.Message)
        Me.Close()
      End Try
    End Sub

    ' load file test.jpg and store in the table testpic
    Private Sub btnSave_Click(...) Handles btnSave.Click
      Dim fs As FileStream
      Dim bindata As Byte()
      Dim picpara As MySqlParameter

      ' prepare INSERT command
      com = New MySqlCommand( _
        "INSERT INTO testpic (pic) VALUES(?pic)", myconn)
      picpara = com.Parameters.Add("?pic", MySqlDbType.MediumBlob)
      com.Prepare()

      ' read file into the byte field
    fs = New FileStream("test.jpg", FileMode.Open, FileAccess.Read)
      ReDim bindata(CInt(fs.Length))
      fs.Read(bindata, 0, CInt(fs.Length))
      fs.Close()

      ' execute INSERT, bindata as parameter
      picpara.Value = bindata
      com.ExecuteNonQuery()

      ' determine ID of the new record in testpic
      com.CommandText = "SELECT LAST_INSERT_ID()"
      id = CInt(com.ExecuteScalar())
      btnLoad.Enabled = True
    End Sub

    ' read BLOB, store as file test1.jpg and display in PictureBox1
    Private Sub btnLoad_Click(...) Handles btnLoad.Click
      Dim fs As FileStream
      Dim bindata As Byte()
      Dim ms As New MemoryStream

      ' execute SELECT command
      com = New MySqlCommand("SELECT pic FROM testpic WHERE id=" & id, myconn)
      bindata = CType(com.ExecuteScalar(), Byte())

      ' write Byte field in MemoryStream,
      ' create from this a new bitmap object
      ms.Write(bindata, 0, bindata.Length)
      PictureBox1.Image = New Bitmap(ms)
```

```vbnet
    ' write MemoryStream in FileStream as file test1.jpg
    fs = New FileStream("test1.jpg", FileMode.Create, FileAccess.Write)
    ms.WriteTo(fs)
    fs.Close()
  End Sub

  ' delete testpic table
  Private Sub btnEnd_Click(...) Handles btnEnd.Click
    com = New MySqlCommand( _
      "DROP TABLE IF EXISTS testpic ", myconn)
    com.ExecuteNonQuery()
    Me.Close()
  End Sub
End Class
```

PART 5

■ ■ ■

Reference

## CHAPTER 21

SQL Reference

This chapter gives an overview of the SQL operators, functions, and commands available under MySQL 5.0. My goal in organizing the information in this chapter was to give you, dear reader, a compact overview of the most important and useful syntactic variants.

This chapter is no substitute for the MySQL documentation, which provides not only the MySQL source code, but also the best, most complete, and most up-to-date reference for MySQL. No book could supersede this online reference. The great advantage of the MySQL documentation, its huge amount of information, is also its greatest drawback: important commands and syntax variants get lost amid the countless details, which for 90 percent of the cases are irrelevant. See `http://dev.mysql.com/doc/mysql/en/index.html`.

Please note that MySQL boasts countless extensions as well as, alas, certain shortcomings with respect to the ANSI-SQL/92 standard.

Syntax

We begin with a brief section describing the syntax of object names, character strings, dates and times, and binary data.

Object Names

Names of objects—databases, tables, columns, etc.—can be at most 64 characters in length. Permitted characters are all the alphanumeric characters of the character set used by MySQL as well as the characters _ and $. For practical reasons, however, it makes sense to restrict oneself to the alphanumeric ASCII characters together with the underscore character. There are two reasons for this:

- The coding of special characters depends on the character set. If the client and server are not in agreement on the character set, then access to objects might become problematic.

- The names of databases and tables can be stored in files, and it is not MySQL, but the operating system that is responsible for the naming rules for files. This can be yet another source of conflict (especially if databases must be exchanged among various operating systems).

Names with special characters and reserved words: Object names are normally not permitted to be the same as reserved SQL key words (*select*, *from*, etc.). Also, most special characters are not permitted in a name (-!%, etc.). Both restrictions can be gotten around, however, by putting the name in backward single quotes:

```
CREATE TABLE `special name` (`from` INT, `a!%` INT)
```

Compound names: Table names that do not refer to the current database must have the database name prefixed to them. Likewise, the name of a column must be extended by the name of the table and that of the database if the column name alone fails to provide a unique identification (such as in queries in which several like-named columns in different tables appear):

> **Table names:** *tablename* or *db.tablename*
>
> **Column names:** *colname* or *tblname.colname* or *dbname.tblname.colname*

Case Sensitivity

The following objects are listed according to whether they exhibit case sensitivity:

> **Case Sensitivity:** Database names (except under Windows), table names (except under Windows), alias names, variable names through MySQL 4.1.
>
> **No Case Sensitivity:** SQL commands and functions, column names, index names, variable names since MySQL 5.0.

Under Windows, MySQL is flexible with respect to case in the naming of databases and tables. The reason is that the operating system does not distinguish case in the naming of directories and files. Note, however, that case must be consistent within an SQL command. The following command will not function properly: *SELECT * FROM authors WHERE Authors.authName = "xxx"*.

Since MySQL 4.0, MySQL under Windows uses exclusively lowercase names in the creation of new databases and tables (regardless of how it is written in the *CREATE* command). This should simplify the migration of databases from Windows to Unix/Linux. This automatic transformation is the result of the option `lower_case_table_names`, which is set to 1 under Windows by default.

Character Strings

Character strings can be enclosed in single or double quotes. The following two expressions are equivalent in MySQL, though only the single-quote variant conforms to the ANSI-SQL/92 standard.

```
'character string'
"character string"
```

If a quotation mark should happen to be part of the character string, then there are various ways of expressing this:

```
"abc'abc"    means    abc'abc
"abc""abc"   means    abc"abc
"abc\'abc"   means    abc'abc
"abc\"abc"   means    abc"abc
'abc"abc'    means    abc"abc
'abc''abc'   means    abc'abc
'abc\"abc'   means    abc"abc
'abc\'abc'   means    abc'abc
```

Within a character string, the special characters provided by the prevailing character set are allowed, for example, äöüß if you are working with the default character set ISO-8859-1 (*latin1*). However, some special characters must be specially coded:

Quoting of Special Characters Within a String

\0	0 byte (Code 0).
\b	Backspace character (Code 8).
\t	Tab character (Code 9).
\n	Newline character (Code 10).
\r	Carriage return character (Code 13).
\"	Double quote (Code 34).
\'	Single quote (Code 39).
\\	Backslash (Code 92).

If x is not one of the above-mentioned special characters, then \x simply returns the character x. Even if a character string is to be stored as a BLOB (binary object), then the 0 character as well as the single quote, double quote, and backslash must be given in the form \0, \', \", and \\.

Instead of indicating special characters in character strings or BLOBs by the backslash escape character, it is often easier simply to specify the entire object using hexadecimal notation. MySQL accepts hex codes of arbitrary length in SQL commands in the following form: 0x4142434445464748494a.

However, MySQL is incapable of returning the result of a query in this form. (If you are working with PHP, then that programming language offers a convenient function for this purpose: *bin2hex*.)

■**Tip** If two character strings are to be concatenated, then you must use the function *CONCAT*. (The operators + and | | from other SQL dialects or programming languages will not serve the purpose.) In general, MySQL provides a broad range of functions for working with character strings.

Character Set and Sort Order

- The character string and sort order (*collation*) will be set independently of each other.

- Each table, and indeed each column within a table, can have its own character set and its own sort order.

- Unicode is now a possible choice for the character set (in formats UTF8 and UCS2 = UTF16).

In SQL commands one can specify the character set for every string. For this, you can use the function *CONVERT* or the cast operator _*characterset*. Here are two equivalent examples, demonstrating the internal Unicode encoding in the format UTF8:

```
SELECT HEX(CONVERT('ABCäöü' USING utf8))
   414243C3A4C3B6C3BC
SELECT HEX(_utf8 'ABCäöü')
   414243C3A4C3B6C3BC
```

In many cases, it can be necessary to specify the sort order as well as the character set. (This determines which characters are considered equivalent and how character strings are to be sorted.) For this, one has the syntax _*characterset* '*abc*' COLLATE *collname*. Here is an example:

```
SELECT _latin1 'a' = _latin1 'ä'
   0
SELECT _latin1 'a' COLLATE latin1_german1_ci =
       _latin1 'ä' COLLATE latin1_german1_ci
   1
```

Numbers

Decimal numbers are written with a period for the decimal point and without a thousands separator (thus 27345 or 2.71828). One may also use scientific notation (6.0225e23 or 6.626e-34) for very large or very small numbers.

MySQL can also process hexadecimal numbers prefixed by 0x or in the form *x'1234'*. Depending on the context, the number is interpreted as a character string or as a 64-bit integer:

```
SELECT 0x4142434445464748494a, x'4142434445464748494a'
       ABCDEFGHIJ                ABCDEFGHIJ
SELECT 0x41 + 0
       66
```

Automatic Transformation of Numbers and Character Strings

In carrying out an operation on two different data types, MySQL makes every attempt to find a compatible data type. Integers are automatically changed into floating-point numbers if one of the operators is a floating-point number. Character strings are automatically changed into numbers if the operation involves a calculation. (If the beginning of the character string cannot be interpreted as a number, then MySQL calculates with 0.)

```
SELECT '3.14abc' + 1
4.14
```

Date and Time

MySQL represents dates as character strings of the form *2005-12-31*, and times in the form *23:59:59*. With the data type *DATETIME* both formats are simply concatenated, yielding, for example, *2005-12-31 23:59:59*.

```
USE exceptions
SELECT * FROM test_date
```

id	a_date	a_time	a_datetime	a_timestamp
1	2005-12-07	09:06:29	2005-12-07 09:06:29	2005-12-07 09:06:29

■**Caution** Beginning with MySQL 4.1, the default setting of *TIMESTAMP*s has changed. They are returned from the server in the format *YYYY-MM-DD HH:MM:DD*. Through MySQL 4.0, the usual form was *YYYYMMDDHHMMDD*. Add a zero if you wish to use the old format (*SELECT ts+0 FROM table*).

Version 5.0 has introduced another important change. In *DATE* and *DATETIME* columns only valid dates are now accepted. (Older versions of MySQL made only a cursory validity check, which recognized *2005-02-45* as invalid, but not *2005-02-31*.) The date *'0000-00-00'* is a special case. This value is officially permitted in MySQL as a date.

In storing dates, MySQL is quite flexible: Both numbers (e.g., *20051231*) and character strings are accepted. Hyphens are allowed in character strings, or they can simply be done without. If a year is given but no century is specified, then MySQL automatically uses the range 1970—2069. Therefore, MySQL accepts the following character strings for a *DATETIME* column: *'2005 12 31'*, *'20051231'*, *'2005.12.31'*, and *'2005&12&31'*.

Binary Data

Binary data that are to be stored in *BLOB* fields are dealt with in SQL commands like character strings. (However, there are differences in sorting.)

Binary Numbers

Since version 5.0.3, MySQL supports the data type *BIT*. Binary numbers can be written in the form *b'110010'*.

Comments

There are three ways of supplying comments in SQL commands:

```
SELECT 1    #  comment
SELECT 1    /* comment */
SELECT 1    -- comment
```

Comments that begin with # or with — (there must be a space after the —) hold until the end of the line. Comments between /* and */ can extend over several lines, as in C. Nesting is not allowed.

If you wish to write SQL code that makes use of some of the peculiarities of MySQL yet remains compatible as much as possible with other dialects, a particular variant of the comment is often useful:

```
SELECT /*! STRAIGHT_JOIN */ col FROM table ...
```

With the MySQL-specific *SELECT* extension, *STRAIGHT_JOIN* will be executed only by MySQL; all other SQL dialects will consider this a comment.

A variant of this enables differentiation among various MySQL dialects:

```
CREATE /*!32302 TEMPORARY */ TABLE ...
```

In this case, the key word *TEMPORARY* is processed only if the command is executed by MySQL 3.23.02 or a more recent version.

Semicolons at the End of SQL Commands

Neither ANSI-SQL nor the SQL dialect of MySQL allows semicolons at the end of an instruction. This syntax rule holds as well for MySQL when a single command is to be executed. However, there are cases in which semicolons are necessary:

- If you execute commands with the MySQL command interpreter (that is, the program `mysql`), you must terminate commands with a semicolon.

- In defining stored procedures and triggers, commands must be separated by semicolons.

- Since MySQL 4.1 the client library has allowed for the execution of several commands at once, and here as well the commands must be separated by semicolons. PHP also provides for the *mysqli* method *multi_query*. With other APIs a *MULTI_STATEMENT* mode must be explicitly activated, in C, for example, with *mysql_real_connect(…, CLIENT_MULTI_STATEMENTS)*.

Operators

MySQL Operators

	Arithmetic Operators
+ - * /	Basic calculation.
%	Modulo (remainder on integer division).
DIV	Alternative division operator (from MySQL 4.1).
MOD	Alternative modulo operator (from MySQL 4.1).
	Bit Operators
|	Binary OR.
&	Binary AND.
~	Binary negation (inverts all bits).
<<	Shifts all bits left (implies multiplication by $2n$).
>>	Shifts all bits right (implies division by $2n$).
	Comparison Operators
=	Equality operator.
<=>	Equality operator that permits a *NULL* comparison.
!= <>	Inequality operator.
< > <= >=	Comparison operators.
IS [NOT] NULL	*NULL* comparison.
BETWEEN	Range comparison (e.g., *x BETWEEN 1 AND 3*).
IN	Set comparison (e.g., *x IN (1, 2, 3)* or *x IN ('a', 'b', 'c')*).
NOT IN	Set comparison (e.g., *x NOT IN ('a', 'b', 'c')*).
	Pattern Comparison
[NOT] LIKE	Simple pattern comparison (e.g., *x LIKE 'm%'*).
[NOT] REGEXP	Extended pattern comparison (e.g., *x REGEXP '.*x$'*).
SOUNDS LIKE	Corresponds to *SOUNDEX(a) = SOUNDEX(b)*, since MySQL 4.1.
	Binary Comparison
BINARY	Marks the operands as binary (e.g., *BINARY x = y*).
	Logical Operators
!, *NOT*	Negation.
||, *OR*	Logical OR.
&&, *AND*	Logical AND.
XOR	Logical exclusive OR (new since MySQL 4.0).
	Casting Operators (Since MySQL 4.1)
_charset 'abc'	The character set *charset* holds for *'abc'*.
_charset 'abc'COLLATE col	The character set *charset* and sort order *col* hold for *'abc'*.

Arithmetic Operators, Bit Operators

Arithmetic operators for which one of the operands is *NULL* generally return *NULL* as result. In MySQL, a division by zero also returns the result *NULL* (in contrast to many other SQL dialects).

Comparison Operators

Comparison operators normally return 1 (corresponding to *TRUE*) or 0 (*FALSE*). Comparisons with *NULL* return *NULL*. The two exceptions are the operators <=> and *IS NULL*, which even in comparison with *NULL* return 0 or 1:

```
SELECT NULL=NULL, NULL=0
  NULL, NULL
SELECT NULL<=>NULL, NULL<=>0
  1, 0
SELECT NULL IS NULL, NULL IS 0
  1, 0
```

In the case of string comparisons with <, <=, >, and >= with *BETWEEN* (and of course with all sort operators), the character set and sort order of the affected column come into play. For strings in quotes, the character set and sort order must be given explicitly. Comparisons of strings in different character sets is not permitted.

Pattern Matching with LIKE

MySQL offers two operators for pattern matching. The simpler, and ANSI-compatible, of these is *LIKE*. As with normal character string comparison, there is no case distinction. In addition, there are two wild cards:

LIKE Search Pattern

_	Placeholder for an arbitrary character.
%	Placeholder for arbitrarily many (including 0) characters (but not for *NULL*).
_	The underscore character _.
\%	The percent sign %.

Pattern Matching with REGEXP

Considerably wider scope in the formulation of a pattern is offered by *REGEXP* and the equivalent command *RLIKE*. The relatively complicated syntax for the pattern corresponds to the Unix commands grep and sed.

REGEXP Search Patterns

	Definition of the Pattern
abc	The string *abc*.
(abc)	The string *abc* (formed into a group) .
[abc]	One of the characters *a, b, c*.
[a-z]	A character in the range a to *z*.
[^abc]	None of these characters (but any other).
.	Any character.

Continued

REGEXP Search Patterns *(Continued)*

	Appearance of the Pattern
x	The expression *x* must appear once.
x|*y*	The expression *x* or *y* must appear once.
x?	The expression *x* may appear once (or not at all) .
*x**	The expression *x* may appear arbitrarily often (or not at all).
x+	The expression *x* may appear arbitrarily often, but at least once.
x{n}	The expression *x* must appear exactly *n* times.
x{,n}	The expression *x* may appear at most *n* times.
x{n,}	The expression *x* must appear at least *n* times.
x{n,m}	The expression *x* must appear at least *n* and at most *m* times.
^	Placeholder for the beginning of the string.
$	Placeholder for the end of the string.
x	Special character *x* (e.g., \\$ for $).

As with *LIKE*, there is no case distinction. Please note that *REGEXP* is successful when the search pattern is found somewhere within the character string. The search pattern is thus not required to describe the entire character string, but only a part of it. If you wish to encompass the entire character string, then you must use ^ and $ in the search pattern.

■**Tip** The above table contains only the most important elements of *REGEXP* patterns. A complete description can be obtained under Unix/Linux with `man 7 regex`. This can also be found on the Internet, for example, at `http://linux.ctyme.com/man/alpha7.htm`.

Binary Character String Comparison

Character strings are normally compared without case being taken into consideration. Thus *'a' = 'A'* returns *1* (true). If you wish to execute a binary comparison, then you must place *BINARY* in front of one of the operands. *BINARY* is a cast operator; that is, it alters the data type of one of the operands (in this case it changes a number or character string into a binary object). *BINARY* can be used both for ordinary character string comparison and for pattern matching with *LIKE* and *REGEXP*:

```
SELECT 'a'='A', BINARY 'a' = 'A', 'a' = BINARY 'A'
      1, 0, 0
```

Logical Operators

Logical operators likewise return 0 or 1, or *NULL* if one of the operands is *NULL*. This holds also for *NOT*; that is, *NOT NULL* again returns *NULL*.

Variables and Constants

MySQL supports a variety of variable types:

Ordinary variables (user variables): Such variables are identified by a prefixed @ character. They lose their definition at the end of the MySQL session.

System and server variables: Such variables contain states or attributes of the MySQL server. These variables are identified by two prefixed @ characters (e.g., *@@binlog_cache_size*).

Many system variables exist in two versions: one specific to the current connection (e.g., *@@session.wait_timeout*) and one global for the MySQL server (e.g., *@@global.wait_timeout*, with the default value for this variable).

Structured variables: These are a special case of system variables. MySQL uses such variables at this time only for defining additional MyISAM index caches.

Local variables and parameters within stored procedures: These variables are declared within stored procedures and are valid only there. They have no identifier, and so must have a name that makes them uniquely distinguishable from table and column names.

Through MySQL 4.1, MySQL variable names were case sensitive. However, starting with MySQL 5.0, these names are case insensitive. Thus *@name*, *@Name*, and *@NAME* all denote the same variable.

Variable Assignment

The following examples show several syntax variants for assigning values to variables. Note that *SET* uses the assignment operator =, while *SELECT* uses :=. The last variant, the assignment of several columns of a record to several variables, has been possible only since MySQL 5.0, and there only if the *SELECT* command returns exactly one record.

```
SET @varname = 3
SELECT @varname := 3
SELECT @varname := COUNT(*) FROM tabelle
SELECT COUNT(*) FROM tabelle INTO @varname
SELECT title, subtitle FROM titles WHERE titleID=... INTO @t, @st
```

Evaluating and Displaying Variables

Most variables can be evaluated with *SELECT*:

```
SELECT @varname
 3
SELECT @@binlog_cache_size
@@binlog_cache_size
         32768
```

In the case of system variables, you can use *SHOW VARIABLES* in addition to *SELECT*. This command has the advantage that it can display a list of variables all at once. The @@ identifier is absent.

```
SHOW VARIABLES LIKE 'b%'
```

Variable_name	Value
back_log	50
basedir	C:\Programs\MySQL\MySQL Server 5.0
binlog_cache_size	32768
bulk_insert_buffer_size	8388608

Remarkably, there exist system variables that can be evaluated only with *SELECT* (e.g., *@@autocommit*) or only with *SHOW VARIABLES* (e.g., *system_time_zone*).

Global System Variables versus System Variables at the Connection Level

In its system variables, MySQL distinguishes between *SESSION* and *GLOBAL* variables. *SESSION* variables are valid only for the current session (connection), while *GLOBAL* variables hold for the entire server.

```
SELECT @@wait_timeout              -- Session (connection level)
SELECT @@session.wait_timeout      -- Session (connection level)
SELECT @@global.wait_timeout       -- Global
```

System variables can also be changed. According to whether the change is only for the current connection or should be valid globally, the following syntax variants are available. Note that with *SET*, you may omit the two @ symbols. One cannot change system variables with *SELECT*.

```
SET @@wait_timeout = 10000          -- Session (connection level)
SET @@session.wait_timeout = 10000  -- Session (connection level)
SET SESSION wait_timeout = 10000    -- Session (connection level)
SET @@global.wait_timeout = 10000   -- Global
SET GLOBAL wait_timeout = 10000     -- Global
```

Variables at the global level can be changed by users possessing the *Super* privilege. When a global variable is changed, the new value holds for all new connections, but not for those already in existence.

Changes in *SESSION* variables, on the other hand, hold only until the end of the current connection. When a new connection is made, the global default value again holds.

Tip This book does not contain a complete description of all MySQL system variables. A complete list of *GLOBAL* and *SESSION* variables can be found in the MySQL documentation. You may end up at the key word *LOCAL*, which has the same meaning in this context as *SESSION*: http://dev.mysql.com/doc/mysql/en/system-variables.html.

Enlightenment on the contents of the variables can be found in the MySQL documentation at the following pages: http://dev.mysql.com/doc/mysql/en/server-parameters.html, http://dev.mysql.com/doc/mysql/en/set-option.html, and http://dev.mysql.com/doc/mysql/en/show-variables.html.

SET PASSWORD

The command *SET* can also be used to change the connection passwords. However, *PASSWORD* is not a variable!

```
SET PASSWORD = PASSWORD('xxx')
SET PASSWORD FOR user@hostname = PASSWORD('xxx')
```

SET has some special forms, which are described later in this chapter under the heading *SET*.

Structured Variables

With many system variables there is the possibility of creating more than one instance. The MySQL documentation calls these *structured variables*. They are addressed in the form *instancename.variablenname*. Indeed, an entire group of variables can be related to an instance. (In the nomenclature of object-oriented programming, one speaks simply of objects and properties.)

At present there is only one group of structured variables in MySQL, which serves for control of cache storage for MyISAM indexes: *key_buffer_size, key_cache_block_size, key_cache_division_limit,* and *key_cache_age_threshold.* These four variables determine the size and management of RAM in which indexes of MyISAM tables are temporarily stored.

After the start of the MySQL server there automatically exists an instance of this cache object, which has the name *default.* Using *SET @@default.key_buffer_size = …* you can set the size of the default cache. The shorthand *SET @@key_buffer_size=…* automatically refers to the instance *default.*

With the following command you can create an additional cache area:

```
SET @@mycache.key_buffer_size = n
```

Now *mycache* is a new instance of the cache. With *SET @@mycache.key_cache_xxx* you can set additional properties of the cache. Then you can assign individual indexes to the new cache with the command *CACHE INDEX.* To deactivate the cache, set its size to zero:

```
SET @@mycache.key_buffer_size = 0
```

■**Tip** The use of several index caches is useful only rarely for speed optimization. Further background information is available at http://dev.mysql.com/doc/mysql/en/myisam-key-cache.html, http://dev.mysql.com/doc/mysql/en/multiple-key-caches.html, and http://dev.mysql.com/doc/mysql/en/structured-system-variables.html.

Constants

Starting with version 4.1, MySQL recognizes the constants *TRUE* (1) and *FALSE* (0).

MySQL Data Types

MySQL Data Types

	Integers
TINYINT(m)	8-bit integer (1 byte); the optional value *m* gives the desired column width in *SELECT* results (*maximum display width*), but has no influence on the allowable range of numeric values.
SMALLINT(m)	16-bit integer (2 bytes).
MEDIUMINT(m)	24- bit integer (3 bytes).
INT(m), INTEGER(m)	32- bit integer (4 bytes).
BIGINT(m)	64- bit integer (8 bytes).
	Floating-Point Numbers
FLOAT(m, d)	Floating-point number, 8-place precision (4 bytes); the optional values *m* and *d* specify the desired number of places before and after the decimal point in *SELECT* results; the values have no influence over the way the number is stored.
DOUBLE(m, d)	Floating-point number, 16-place precision (8 bytes).
REAL(m, d)	Synonym for *DOUBLE.*
DECIMAL(p, s)	Fixed-point number, stored as string; arbitrary number of places (1 byte per digit + 2 bytes overhead); *p* specifies the entire number of places, where *s* is the number of places after the decimal point; default is *DECIMAL(10,0).*
NUMERIC, DEC	Synonyms for *DECIMAL.*

Continued

MySQL Data Types *(Continued)*	
	Date, Time
DATE	Date in the form *'2005-12-31'*, range *1000-01-01* to *9999-12-31* (3 bytes).
TIME	Time in the form *'23:59:59'*, range *+/-838:59:59* (3 bytes).
DATETIME	Combination of *DATE* and *TIME* in the form *'2005-12-31 23:59:59'* (8 bytes).
YEAR	Year in the range *1900–2155* (1 byte).
TIMESTAMP(m)	Date and time in the form *20051231235959* for times between 1970 und 2038 (4 bytes); the optional value *m* specifies the number of places in *SELECT* results; *m=8*, for example, has the effect that only year, month, and day are displayed.
	Character Strings
CHAR(n)	String with prescribed length, maximum 255 characters.
NATIONAL CHAR(n)	Unicode string (corresponds to *CHAR(n) CHARSET utf8* or *NCHAR(n)*).
VARCHAR(n)	String with variable length; maximum 255 characters through MySQL 4.1, and maximum 65,535 bytes since MySQL 5.0.3 for MyISAM tables, where the maximum number of characters depends on the character set.
NATIONAL VARCHAR(n)	Unicode string with variable length (corresponds to *NCHAR VARCHAR(n)*, *VARCHAR(n) CHARSET utf8*).
TINYTEXT	String with variable length, maximum 255 characters.
TEXT	String with variable length, maximum 2^{16}-1 characters.
MEDIUMTEXT	String with variable length, maximum 2^{24}-1 characters.
LONGTEXT	String with variable length, maximum 2^{32}-1 characters.
	Binary Data
TINYBLOB	Binary data with variable length, maximum 255 bytes.
BLOB	Binary data with variable length, maximum 2^{16}-1 bytes.
MEDIUMBLOB	Binary data with variable length, maximum 2^{24}-1 bytes.
LONGBLOB	Binary data with variable length, maximum 2^{32}-1 bytes.
	Geometric Data (Since MySQL 4.1)
GEOMETRY	A general geometric object; further geometric types are listed later in this chapter.
	Miscellaneous
ENUM	Enumeration of at most 65,535 strings (1 or 2 bytes).
SET	Enumeration of at most 255 strings (1 to 8 bytes).
BIT	Individual bits (since MySQL 5.0.3).
BOOL	Synonym for *TINYINT(1)*.

In the definition of columns (*CREATE TABLE, ALTER TABLE*), different options can be used for different columns. The following table summarizes these options. Note that not all options are suitable for all data types.

Attributes (Options) of the MySQL Data Types

NULL	Specifies that the column may contain the value *NULL*; this setting holds by default.
NOT NULL	Forbids the value *NULL*.
DEFAULT xxx	Specifies the default value *xxx* to be used if no other input value is specified. Even if you do not specify an explicit default value, MySQL itself uses one in many cases: *NULL* when it is permitted, otherwise 0 in numeric columns, an empty string with *VARCHAR*, the date *0000-00-00* with dates, the year *0000* with *YEAR* as well as the first element of an *ENUM* enumeration.
DEFAULT CURRENT_TIMESTAMP	Has the effect on *TIMESTAMP* columns that the current time is automatically stored when new records are inserted.
ON UPDATE CURRENT_TIMESTAMP	Has the effect on *TIMESTAMP* columns that when changes are made (*UPDATE*) the current time is automatically stored.
PRIMARY KEY	Defines the column as primary key.
AUTO_INCREMENT	Results in an automatically increasing number being inserted in the column; it can be used for only one column, with integer values; moreover, the options *NOT NULL* and *PRIMARY KEY* must be specified (instead of *PRIMARY KEY*, the column can be given a *UNIQUE* index).
UNSIGNED	Integers are stored without a sign; note that calculations are also made without signs.
ZEROFILL	Integers in *SELECT* results are left-filled with zeros to fill out their length (thus five-digit numbers such as 00123 and 01234).
BINARY	With *CHAR* and *VARCHAR* columns, comparison and sort operations are executed in binary. Hence uppercase letters are sorted before lowercase ones. This is more efficient, but less practical when results are to be displayed in alphabetical order.
CHARACTER SET name, [COLLATE sort]	With strings, gives the character set and optional sort order.
COMMENT text	Stores *text* as a comment on the column (since MySQL 4.1).
SERIAL	Since MySQL 4.1 is a synonym for *BIGINT NOT NULL AUTO_INCREMENT UNIQUE*.

Command Overview (Thematic)

In the section following this one, SQL commands will be listed in alphabetical order. As a supplementary aid to orientation, we provide here a systematic overview:

Database Queries, Data Manipulation

SELECT	Queries existing record (data search).
INSERT	Inserts new record.
REPLACE	Replaces existing record.
UPDATE	Changes existing record.
DELETE	Deletes selected records.
TRUNCATE TABLE	Deletes all records of a table.
LOAD DATA	Inserts records from a text file.
HANDLER	Reads records more efficiently than *SELECT* (since MySQL 4.0).

Transactions (Only with InnoDB Tables)

BEGIN or *START TRANSACTION*	Begins a group of SQL commands.
COMMIT	Confirms all executed commands.
ROLLBACK	Aborts executed commands.
SAVEPOINT	Places a marker within a running transaction.

Create Databases/Tables/Views, Change Database Schema

ALTER DATABASE	Makes changes to the database (since MySQL 4.1).
ALTER TABLE	Changes individual columns of a table, adds indexes, etc.
ALTER VIEW	Changes a view (since MySQL 5.0).
CREATE DATABASE	Creates a new database.
CREATE INDEX	Creates a new index for a table.
CREATE TABLE	Creates a new table.
CREATE VIEW	Creates a view (since MySQL 5.0).
DROP DATABASE	Deletes an entire database.
CREATE FUNCTION or *PROCEDURE*	Deletes a stored procedure (since MySQL 5.0).
DROP INDEX	Deletes an index.
DROP TABLE	Deletes an entire table.
DROP VIEW	Deletes a view (since MySQL 5.0).
RENAME TABLE	Renames a table.

Administration of Tables (General)

ANALYZE TABLE	Returns information on internal index management.
CHECK TABLE	Tests table file for consistency errors.
FLUSH TABLES	Closes all table files and then opens them.
LOCK TABLE	Blocks tables for (write) access by other users.
OPTIMIZE TABLE	Optimizes memory use in tables.
UNLOCK TABLES	Releases tables locked with *LOCK*.

Administration of MyISAM Tables

BACKUP TABLE	Copies table files into a backup directory.
CACHE INDEX	Assigns individual caches to table indexes.
LOAD INDEX INTO CACHE	Loads table indexes into the cache.
REPAIR TABLE	Attempts to repair defective table files.
RESTORE TABLE	Restores tables backed up with *BACKUP*.

Administration and Execution of Stored Procedures and Triggers (Since MySQL 5.0)

ALTER FUNCTION| PROCEDURE	Changes a stored procedure.
CALL	Calls a stored procedure.
CREATE FUNCTION| PROCEDURE| TRIGGER	Creates a stored procedure or trigger.
DROP FUNCTION| PROCEDURE| TRIGGER	Deletes a stored procedure or trigger.
SHOW CREATE FUNCTION| PROCEDURE	Displays the code of a stored procedure.
SHOW FUNCTION| PROCEDURE STATUS	Returns a list of all defined stored procedures.

Information on the Database Schema, Other Administrative Information

DESCRIBE	Same as *SHOW COLUMNS*.
EXPLAIN	Explains how a *SELECT* is executed internally.
SHOW	Displays information about databases, tables, views, fields, stored procedures, etc.

Administration, Access Privileges, etc.

FLUSH	Empties MySQL temporary storage and reads it in again.
GRANT	Grants additional privileges.
KILL	Ends a process.
REVOKE	Restricts access privileges.
RESET	Deletes the query cache or logging files.
SET	Changes the content of MySQL system variables.
SHOW	Displays the MySQL status, system variables, processes, etc.
USE	Changes the active database.

Replication (Master)

PURGE MASTER LOGS	Deletes old logging files.
RESET MASTER	Deletes all logging files.
SET SQL_LOG_BIN=0/1	Deactivates/activates binary logging.
SHOW BINLOG EVENTS	Returns a list of all entries in the active logging file (since MySQL 4.0).
SHOW MASTER LOGS	Returns a list of all logging files.
SHOW MASTER STATUS	Specifies the currently active logging file.
SHOW SLAVE HOSTS	Returns a list of all registered slaves (since MySQL 4.0).

Replication (Slave)	
CHANGE MASTER TO	Changes replication settings in `master.info`.
LOAD DATA FROM	Copies all tables from master to slave (since MySQL 4.0).
LOAD TABLE FROM	Copies a table from master to slave.
RESET SLAVE	Reinitializes `master.info`.
SH*OW SLAVE STATUS*	Displays content of `master.info`.
SLAVE START/STOP	Starts and stops replication.

Command Reference (Alphabetical)

In the following reference section, the following syntax is in force:

[option]: Optional parts of a command are shown in square brackets.

variant1 | variant2 | variant3: Alternatives are separated by the | character.

```
ALTER DATABASE [dbname] actions
```

Since MySQL 4.1, with *ALTER DATABASE* you can change global database attributes. The settings are stored in the file dbname/`db.opt`. Instead of *ALTER DATABASE* you can use the equivalent command *ALTER SCHEMA*. If *dbname* is missing, the command applies to the current database.

actions: Currently, two *actions* commands have been implemented.

[DEFAULT] CHARACTER SET charset specifies which character set the database should use by default. (In the definition of tables and columns a different character set can be specified.)

[DEFAULT] COLLATE collname specifies the default sort order.

```
ALTER FUNCTION/PROCEDURE name options
```

ALTER FUNCTION/PROCEDURE since MySQL 5.0 changes details of a stored procedure (SP). However, the command is incapable of changing the code of an SP; for that, you need to delete the SP (*DROP FUNCTION/PROCEDURE*) and then re-create it (*CREATE FUNCTION/PROCEDURE*).

options: *NAME newname* renames the stored procedure.

SQL SECURITY DEFINER/INVOKER changes the security mode of the SP (see *CREATE FUNCTION*).

COMMENT 'newcomment' changes the comment stored with the SP.

```
ALTER TABLE tblname tbloptions
```

ALTER TABLE can be used to change various details of the structure of a table. In the following, we present an overview of the syntactic variants.

In the syntactically simplest form that we shall show here, *ALTER TABLE* changes the table options. The possible options are described in *CREATE TABLE*. The command can be used, for example, to change the type of a table (e.g., from MyISAM to InnoDB).

Note that with many *ALTER TABLE* variants, the table must be re-created. To do this, MySQL creates a new table *X* with the new table properties, and then copies all the records into this new table. Then the existing table is renamed *Y*, and table *X* is renamed *tblname*. Finally, *Y* is deleted. On large tables, this can take considerable time and temporarily use a great deal of hard-disk space.

```
ALTER TABLE tblname ADD newcolname coltype coloptions [FIRST | AFTER existingcolumn]
```

This command adds a new column to a table. The definition of the new column takes place as with *CREATE TABLE*. If the position of the new column is not specified with *FIRST* or *AFTER*, then the new column will be the last column of the table.

The following example adds a new column *ts* with data type *TIMESTAMP* to the *authors* table:

```
ALTER TABLE authors ADD ts TIMESTAMP
```

```
ALTER TABLE tblname ADD INDEX [indexname] (indexcols ...)
ALTER TABLE tblname ADD FULLTEXT [indexname] (indexcols ...)
ALTER [IGNORE] TABLE tblname ADD UNIQUE [indexname] (indexcols ...)
ALTER [IGNORE] TABLE tblname ADD PRIMARY KEY (indexcols ...)
ALTER TABLE tblname ADD SPATIAL INDEX (indexcol)
```

These commands create a new index for a table. If no *indexname* is specified, then MySQL simply uses the name of the indexed column.

The optional key word *IGNORE* comes into play if several identical fields are discovered in the creation of a *UNIQUE* or primary index. Without *IGNORE*, the command will be terminated with an error, and the index will not be generated. With *IGNORE*, such duplicate records are simply deleted.

A spatial index for geometric data can be created starting with MySQL 4.1. The column *indexcol* must have data type *GEOMETRY* and the attribute *NOT NULL*.

```
ALTER TABLE tblname ADD [CONSTRAINT [fr_keyname]]
    FOREIGN KEY [c1_keyname]
    (column1) REFERENCES table2 (column2)
    [ON DELETE {CASCADE | SET NULL | NO ACTION | RESTRICT}]
    [ON UPDATE {CASCADE | SET NULL | NO ACTION | RESTRICT}]
```

This command defines a foreign key constraint. This means that the foreign key *tblname.column1* refers to *table2.column2*, and the table driver should ensure that no references point to nowhere.

This command results in two new indexes being created: the foreign key index for linking *column1* and *column2*, and, if it doesn't exist already, an ordinary index for *tablename.column1*.

Optionally, you can give these indexes names (*ci_keyname* and *fr_keyname*). If you are using a replication system, you should definitely do this; otherwise, it could happen that MySQL uses different names for the original and replicating databases. That can lead later to problems if you wish to delete the foreign key rules.

The optional *ON DELETE* and *ON UPDATE* clauses specify how the table driver is to react to damage to integrity on *DELETE* and *UPDATE* commands (see Chapter 8 for details). By default, the condition is *STRICT*, meaning that potential damage to integrity results in the command not being issued and an error message being triggered.

Currently (MySQL 5.0.*n*), foreign key constraints can be applied only to InnoDB tables. *column2* must be given an index and must be of the same data type as *column1*.

```
ALTER TABLE tblname ALTER colname SET DEFAULT value
ALTER TABLE tblname ALTER colname DROP DEFAULT
```

This command changes the default value for a column or table or deletes an existing default value.

```
ALTER TABLE tblname CHANGE oldcolname newcolname coltype coloptions
```

This command changes the default value for a column in a table or deletes an existing default value. The description of the column proceeds as with *CREATE TABLE*, which you may refer to. If the column name is to remain unchanged, then it must be given twice (that is, *oldcolname* and *newcolname* are identical). Even if *ALTER TABLE* is used only to change the name of a column, both *coltype* and *coloptions* must be completely specified.

```
ALTER TABLE tblname CONVERT TO
    CHARACTER SET  charset [COLLATE collname]
```

This command changes the character set and the optional sort order of all text columns of a table. This change affects not only the formal definition of the table, but its content as well: all text fields of the records are converted.

If you want to change only the definition of the table, and not its content, then you must change the affected column to a BLOB and then back into the desired text data type with the associated character set and sort order. This results in no change to the data, since MySQL leaves BLOB data untouched:

```
ALTER TABLE tblname CHANGE colname colname BLOB
ALTER TABLE tblname CHANGE colname colname VARCHAR(100) CHARACTER SET ...
```

If the text column is equipped with an index, you must first delete the index before the first *ALTER TABLE* command and then re-create it after the second *ALTER TABLE* command.

```
ALTER TABLE tblname DISABLE KEYS
ALTER TABLE tblname ENABLE KEYS
```

Since MySQL 4.0, *ALTER TABLE … DISABLE KEYS* has the effect that all *nonunique* indexes are no longer automatically updated with *INSERT, UPDATE,* and *DELETE* commands. *ALTER TABLE … ENABLE KEYS* restores activation and updating of indexes.

The two commands should be used for carrying out extensive revisions to tables in the most efficient manner possible. (The reconstruction of indexes with *ENABLE KEYS* costs considerably less time than the constant updating with each altered record.)

```
ALTER TABLE dbname.tblname DISCARD TABLESPACE
ALTER TABLE dbname.tblname IMPORT TABLESPACE
```

These two commands are suitable only for InnoDB tables whose data are located in their own files (MySQL server option innodb_file_per_table). In MySQL 5.0 it is not permitted to copy such files from one database directory into another or from one MySQL installation to another. The two *ALTER TABLE* variants enable, under certain circumstances, a *tablespace* file to be deactivated and later reactivated.

ALTER TABLE dbname.tblname DISCARD TABLESPACE deletes the table *tblname* and the underlying file dbname/tblname.ibd. The file tblname.frm is preserved. *ALTER TABLE dbname.tblname*

IMPORT TABLESPACE reactivates the file `dbname/tblname.ibd`. The file must be the result of a backup of the running MySQL installation that was carried out before the *DISCARD TABLESPACE* command.

Further details on these commands, for which there is hardly any useful practical application, can be found at `http://dev.mysql.com/doc/mysql/en/multiple-tablespaces.html`.

```
ALTER TABLE tblname DROP colname
ALTER TABLE tblname DROP INDEX indexname
ALTER TABLE tblname DROP PRIMARY KEY
ALTER TABLE tblname DROP FOREIGN KEY foreign_key_name
```

The first three commands delete a column, an index, or the primary index. The fourth command, since MySQL 4.0.13, deletes the specified foreign key constraint. You can determine with *SHOW CREATE TABLE* the *foreign_key_name* of the index to be deleted.

If you are using replication, you should avoid deleting *FOREIGN KEY* rules. The reason is that MySQL creates a special index when a *FOREIGN KEY* rule is defined. If you do not name this index explicitly, it can happen that different names are used for the original and replicated database.

```
ALTER TABLE tblname ENGINE tabletype
```

This command changes the type of the table (the table driver). Allowed table types include InnoDB and MyISAM. Note that a type change is possible only if the new table driver supports all the properties of the table. For example, the InnoDB table driver supports at present no full-text indexes. If you wish to transform a MyISAM table into an InnoDB table, you must first delete the full-text index (*ALTER TABLE tblname DROP indexname*).

```
ALTER TABLE tblname MODIFY colname coltype coloptions
```

This command functions like *ALTER TABLE … CHANGE* (see above). The only difference is that the column cannot be changed, and thus the name needs to be given only once.

```
ALTER TABLE tblname ORDER BY colname
```

This command re-creates the table and orders the data records by *colname*. If you frequently read records from the table ordered *colname*, this can increase efficiency a bit. The command has no influence over new or changed records, and is therefore useful only if few future changes to the table are expected.

```
ALTER TABLE tblname RENAME AS newtblname
```

This command renames the table (see also *RENAME TABLE*).

```
ALTER TABLE tblname TYPE tabletype
```

This command corresponds to *ALTER TABLE tblname ENGINE tabletype*.

```
ALTER [algoption] VIEW viewname [(columns)] AS command [chkoption]
```

ALTER VIEW changes the properties of a view. It has the same syntax as *CREATE VIEW*. *ALTER VIEW* offers no way to change the name of a view.

ANALYZE TABLE tablename1, tablename2, …

ANALYZE TABLE performs an analysis of the indexed values of a column. The results are stored, and in the future, this speeds up index access to data records a bit.

With MyISAM tables, the external program `myisamchk -a tblfile` can be used.

BACKUP TABLE tblname TO '/backup/directory'

BACKUP TABLE copies the files for the specified MyISAM table into a backup directory. The table can be re-created with *RESTORE TABLE*.

Under Unix/Linux, the backup directory for the account under which MySQL is executed must be writable.

BACKUP and *RESTORE* do not work for InnoDB tables. Both commands are considered *deprecated* and are best not used. Alternatives are external backup tools such as `mysqldump`, `mysqlhotcopy` or the InnoDB backup utility.

BEGIN

If you are working with transaction-capable tables, then *BEGIN* introduces a new transaction. The following SQL commands can then be confirmed with *COMMIT* or revoked with *ROLLBACK*. (All changes to tables are executed only via *COMMIT*.) Further information and examples on the topic of transactions can be found in Chapter 10.

Since MySQL 4.0.11, you can use the ANSI-conforming command *START TRANSACTION* instead of *BEGIN*.

CACHE INDEX indexspec1, indexspec2 … IN cachename

Since MySQL 4.1, *CACHE INDEX* determines in which cache area a MyISAM index is placed. The command can be used effectively only if first an additional cache area is created (see also the information on structured variables in this chapter).

indexspec: Specifies which MyISAM indexes are to have their caches changed. The following syntax is used for the index specification:

tablename [[INDEX\KEY] (indexname1, indexname2 …)]

If no index name is given, the command holds for all indexes in *tablename*.

cachename: denotes the cache instance in which the indexes are to be placed. Such an area must first be set up with *SET @@cachename.key_buffer_size=n* (*n* is the reserved area size in bytes).

CALL spname [parameter1, parameter2 …]

This command calls a stored procedure. *CALL* is designed only for user-defined procedures, not for user-defined functions, which must be called with ordinary SQL commands (e.g., with *SELECT*).

```
CHANGE MASTER TO variable1=value1, variable2=value2, …
```

With this command, the replication settings for slave are carried out. The settings are stored in the file master.info. The command can be used only for slave computers in a replication system, and it requires the *Super* privilege. It recognizes the following variable names:

MASTER_HOST specifies the hostname or IP number of the master computer.

MASTER_USER specifies the user name used for communication with the master computer.

MASTER_PASSWORD specifies the associated password.

MASTER_PORT specifies the port number of the master computer (normally 3306).

MASTER_LOG_FILE specifies the current logging file on the master computer.

MASTER_LOG_POS specifies the current read position within the logging file on the master computer.

```
CHECK TABLE tablename1, tablename2 … [ TYPE=QUICK ]
```

CHECK TABLE tests the internal integrity of the database file for the specified table. Any errors that are discovered are not corrected. With MyISAM tables, instead of this command, the external program myisamchk -m tblfile can be used.

```
COMMIT
```

COMMIT ends a transaction and stores all changes in the database. (Instead of executing *COMMIT*, you can cancel the pending changes with *ROLLBACK*.) *BEGIN/COMMIT/ROLLBACK* function only if you are working with transaction-capable tables. Further information and examples on transactions can be found in Chapter 10.

```
CREATE  DATABASE  [IF NOT EXISTS] dbname [options]
```

CREATE DATABASE generates the specified database. (More precisely, an empty directory is created in which tables belonging to the new database can be stored.) Note that database names are case sensitive. This command can be executed only if the user has sufficient access privileges to create new databases. Instead of *CREATE DATABASE* the equivalent command *CREATE SCHEMA* can be used.

options: Since MySQL 4.1, you can specify the default character set for a table:

[DEFAULT] CHARACTER SET charset [COLLATE collname].

The optional key word *DEFAULT* has no function (that is, it does not matter whether you specify it or not). With *COLLATE* you can select the sort order if there is more than one for the character set in question. If you do not specify the *CHARACTER SET*, then the default character set of the server is used.

CREATE FUNCTION name ([parameters]) RETURNS datatype [options] code

---

Since MySQL 5.0, *CREATE FUNCTION* creates a user-defined function (stored procedure) in the current database. Defining stored procedures requires the *Super* privilege and executing them requires the *Execute* privilege.

> *name*: Specifies the function name. It is allowed for a function and a procedure within a single database to have the same name (see *CREATE PROCEDURE*).

> *parameters*: Several parameters may be specified, separated by commas. Each parameter must be followed by its data type, e.g., *para1 INT, para2 BIGINT*.

> *datatype*: Gives the data type of the function's return value. All MySQL data types are allowed, e.g., *INT, DOUBLE, VARCHAR(n)*.

> *options*: The following options can be used in function definition:

> *LANGUAGE SQL*: Specifies the language of the stored procedure code. The only permissible *LANGUAGE* setting is currently SQL. This setting holds by default. Future versions of MySQL will offer the option of defining SPs in other programming languages (e.g., PHP).

> *[NOT] DETERMINISTIC*: An SP is considered deterministic if it always returns the same results with the same parameters. (SPs whose result depends on the content of the database are not deterministic.) By default, SPs are nondeterministic. Deterministic SPs can be executed particularly efficiently. (For example, it is possible to store the result for particular parameters in a cache.) Currently, however, the *DETERMINISTIC* option is ignored by the MySQL optimization functions.

> *SQL SECURITY DEFINER/INVOKER*: The *SECURITY* mode specifies the access privileges under which the SP should be executed. SPs that are defined with *SQL SECURITY DEFINER* have the same privileges as the MySQL user who defined the SP. This is the default security mode. SPs defined with the option *SQL SECURITY INVOKER* have the access privileges of the MySQL user who executed the SP.

> *COMMENT 'text'*: The comment text is stored together with the SP.

> *code*: The actual SP code is usually given in the form of an SQL command. If the SP consists of more than one command, they must be placed between *BEGIN* and *END* and separated by semicolons (details are in Chapter 13).

> Here is an example:

```
CREATE FUNCTION half(a INT) RETURNS INT
BEGIN
  RETURN a/2;
END
```

CREATE FUNCTION name RETURNS datatype SONAME libraryname

CREATE FUNCTION makes possible not only the definition of SPs, but also the binding of a function to an external library into MySQL. Such functions are called *user-defined functions*, or UDFs for short. Programming such functions in C or C++ requires a degree of background knowledge about how functions work in MySQL (and, of course, the requisite tools, like compilers). Further information can be found at http://dev.mysql.com/doc/mysql/en/extending-mysql.html and http://mysql-udf.sourceforge.net/.

```
CREATE [UNIQUE|FULLTEXT] INDEX indexname ON tablename (indexcols …)
```

CREATE INDEX enlarges an existing database to include an index. As *indexname*, the name of the column is generally used. *CREATE INDEX* is not a freestanding command, but merely an alternative form of *ALTER TABLE ADD INDEX/UNIQUE*, which you should see for details.

```
CREATE PROCEDURE name ([parameters]) [options] code
```

CREATE PROCEDURE creates, since MySQL 5.0, a user-defined procedure (stored procedure) in the current database. The definition of stored procedures requires the *Super* privilege, while execution requires the *Execute* privilege.

The syntax of this command is very similar to that of *CREATE FUNCTION*. However, unlike a function, a procedure cannot return a result directly. However, a *SELECT* command can be executed and parameters changed. For this reason, the syntax for the parameter list is a bit different from that of *CREATE FUNCTION*.

parameters: More than one parameter can be defined, and they are separated by commas. Each parameter is defined as follows:

[IN or OUT or INOUT] parametername datatype

The key words *IN*, *OUT*, and *INOUT* specify whether the parameter is only for input, only for output, or for data transport in both directions (default is *IN*). All MySQL data types are allowed, such as *INT*, *VARCHAR(n)*, *DOUBLE*.

Here is an example:

```
CREATE PROCEDURE half(IN a INT, OUT b INT)
BEGIN
  SET b=a/2;
END
```

```
CREATE [TEMPORARY] TABLE [IF NOT EXISTS]  tblname
  (colname1 coltype coloptions reference,
    colname2 coltype coloptions reference...
[ , index1, index2 ...]
  )
  [tbloptions]
```

CREATE TABLE generates a new table in the current database. If a database other than the current one is to be used, the table name can be specified in the form *dbname.tblname*. If the table already exists, an error message results. There is no error message if *IF NOT EXISTS* is used, but in this case, the existing table is not affected, and no new table is created.

With the key word *TEMPORARY* a temporary table is created. If a temporary table is created and a like-named, but not temporary, table already exists, the temporary table is created without an error message. The old table is preserved, but it is masked by the temporary table. If you want your temporary table to exist only in RAM (for increased speed), you must also specify *ENGINE = HEAP*.

The creation of regular tables requires the *Create* privilege. Since version 4.0, the creation of temporary tables requires the *Create Temporary Table* privilege.

colname: Name of the column.

coltype: Data type of the column. A list of all MySQL data types (*INT*, *TEXT*, etc.) appears earlier in this chapter.

coloptions: Here certain attributes (options) can be specified:

  NOT NULL | NULL

  UNSIGNED

  ZEROFILL

  BINARY

  DEFAULT defaultval | DEFAULT CURRENT_TIMESTAMP

  ON UPDATE CURRENT_TIMESTAMP

  AUTO_INCREMENT | IDENTITY

  PRIMARY KEY

  CHARACTER SET charset [COLLATE collname]

  COMMENT text

reference: MySQL provides various key words for the declaration of foreign keys in keeping track of referential integrity, e.g., *REFERENCES tblname (idcolumn)*. These key words are currently ignored, however (and with no error message). Even if you use InnoDB tables, the foreign key constraints for such tables must be specified within the confines of the index definition.

index: *KEY* or *INDEX* defines a usual index spanning one or more columns. *UNIQUE* defines a unique index (that is, in the column or columns, no identical values or groups of values can be stored). With both variants an arbitrary index name may be given for the internal management of the index. *PRIMARY KEY* likewise defines a *UNIQUE* index. Here, however, the index name is predefined: It is, not surprisingly, *PRIMARY*. With *FULLTEXT*, an index is declared for full-text search (in MySQL 4.0, only with MyISAM tables). Since MySQL 4.1, an index for *GEOMETRY* data can be created with *SPATIAL INDEX*; *indexcol* must be defined with the attribute *NOT NULL*.

KEY | INDEX [indexname] (indexcols ...)

UNIQUE [INDEX] [indexname] (indexcols ...)

PRIMARY KEY (indexcols ...)

FULLTEXT [indexname] (indexcols ...)

SPATIAL INDEX [indexname] (indexcol)

Foreign key constraints: If you are using InnoDB tables, here you can formulate foreign key constraints. The syntax is as follows:

[CONSTRAINT [fr_keyname]]

FOREIGN KEY [c1_keyname] (column1) REFERENCES table2 (column2)

 [ON DELETE {CASCADE | SET NULL | NO ACTION | RESTRICT}]

 [ON UPDATE {CASCADE | SET NULL | NO ACTION | RESTRICT}]

This means that *tblname.column1* is a foreign key that refers to *table2.column2*. More details can be found under *ALTER TABLE ... ADD FOREIGN KEY*.

tbloptions: Here various table options can be specified, though here we shall exhibit only the most important of them. Not all options are possible with every table type. Information on the different table types and their variants can be found in Chapter 8.

ENGINE = MYISAM | HEAP | INNODB

ROW_FORMAT= default | dynamic | static | compressed

AUTO_INCREMENT gives the initial value for the counter of an *AUTO_INCREMENT* column (e.g., 100000 if you wish to have six-digit integers). *CHECK_SUM=1* has the effect that a check sum is stored for each data record, which helps in reconstruction if the database is damaged. *PACK_KEYS=1* results in a smaller index file. This speeds up read access, but slows down changes. *DELAY_KEY_WRITE = 1* results in indexes not being updated each time a change to a record is made. Rather, they are updated every now and then.

AUTO_INCREMENT = n

CHECKSUM = 0 | 1

PACK_KEYS = 0 | 1

DELAY_KEY_WRITE = 0 | 1

With *COMMENT* you can save a brief text, for example, to describe the purpose of the table. The comment can be read with *SHOW CREATE DATABASE dbname*:

COMMENT= 'comment'.

Since MySQL 4.1, you can specify the character set and sort order for a table. (You can also set these parameters for a single column.) If no character set is specified, then the default character set for the table or that of the MySQL server is used:

[DEFAULT] CHARACTER SET charset [COLLATE collname].

The *CREATE TABLE* syntax contains some duplication. For example, a primary index can be declared in two different ways, either as an attribute of a column (*coloptions*) or as an independent index (*index*). The result is, of course, the same. It is up to you to decide which form you prefer.

MySQL has the property that in many cases changes the definition of a column, for example by providing a suitable *DEFAULT* value if none is specified (*silent column changes*; see also Chapter 9). For this reason it is recommended that after you create a table, you take a look at the actual MySQL table definition with *SHOW CREATE TABLE name*.

Here is an example:

```
CREATE TABLE test (id    INT NOT NULL AUTO_INCREMENT,
                   data  INT NOT NULL,
                   txt   VARCHAR(60),
                   PRIMARY KEY (id))
```

```
CREATE  [TEMPORARY]  TABLE  [IF NOT EXISTS]  tblname
  [(newcolname1 coltype coloptions reference,
    newcolname2 coltype coloptions reference …
    [ , key1, key2 …]
  )]
  [tbloptions]
  [IGNORE | REPLACE] SELECT …
```

With this variant of the *CREATE TABLE* command, a table is filled with the result of a *SELECT* command. The individual columns of the new table take their types from the data types of the *SELECT* command and thus do not have to be (and may not be!) declared explicitly.

Unfortunately, neither indexes nor attributes such as *AUTO_INCREMENT* are carried over from the old table. There can also be changes in column types, such as *VARCHAR* columns turning into *CHAR*.

If an index is to be created in the new table for individual columns (e.g., *PRIMARY KEY (id)*), then this can be specified. Moreover, there is the option of defining new columns (e.g., an *AUTO INCREMENT* column.

The key words *IGNORE* and *REPLACE* specify how MySQL should behave if several records with the same value are placed by the command into a *UNIQUE* column. With *IGNORE*, the existing record is retained, and new records are ignored. With *REPLACE* existing records are replaced by the new ones. If neither option is used, an error message results.

If a table is to be copied one to one, it is better to create the new table with *CREATE TABLE table2 LIKE table1* (since MySQL 4.1) and then copy in the data with *INSERT INTO table2 SELECT * FROM table1*.

Here is an example:

```
CREATE TEMPORARY TABLE tmp
  SELECT id, authName FROM authors WHERE id<20
```

```
CREATE [TEMPORARY] TABLE [IF NOT EXISTS] newtable LIKE oldtable
```

This command, since MySQL 4.1, creates a new, empty table *newtable* corresponding to the declaration of the existing table *oldtable*.

```
CREATE TRIGGER name time event
  ON tablename
  FOR EACH ROW code
```

CREATE TRIGGER defines SQL code that in the future will be executed automatically before or after particular database commands for the affected table. For each event only one trigger procedure is allowed. The execution of *CREATE TRIGGER* requires the *Super* privilege.

> *name*: Specifies the name of the trigger. Currently (MySQL 5.0.3) like-named triggers are allowed within a single database if they are defined for different tables. In future MySQL versions a trigger name must be unique for the entire database.

> *time*: BEFORE | AFTER

> Specifies whether the trigger code is to be executed before or after the trigger event.

> *event*: INSERT | UPDATE | DELETE

> Specifies for what database operations the trigger code is to be executed.

> *tablename*: Specifies for which table the trigger is defined.

> *code*: Gives the trigger code. The syntax is the same as for a stored procedure.

Here is an example:

```
CREATE TRIGGER test_before_insert
  BEFORE INSERT ON test FOR EACH ROW
BEGIN
  IF NEW.percent < 0.0 OR NEW.percent > 1.0 THEN
    SET NEW.percent = NULL;
  END IF;
END
```

```
CREATE [algoption] VIEW viewname [(columns)] AS command [chkoption]
```

CREATE VIEW creates, since MySQL 5.0, a *View*. This is a virtual table based on a *SELECT* command. If you wish to replace an existing *View*, execute the command in the form *CREATE OR REPLACE ....* The command requires the *Create View* privilege.

algoption: *ALGORITHM = UNDEFINED | MERGE | TEMPTABLE*

ALGORITHM tells how the *View* is to be represented internally. This option was not documented as this book was being completed. By default, MySQL always uses *UNDEFINED* (can be determined with *SHOW CREATE TABLE viewname*).

viewname: Specifies the name of the *View*. The same rules hold as for table names. The name of the *View* may not be the same as that of the table.

columns: The columns of a *View* have as a rule the same names and data types as the columns of the underlying table. With *columns* you can specify different names and data types. The syntax is the same as for *CREATE TABLE*.

command: Here you give a *SELECT* command. The data in the *View* are the result of this command.

chkoption: *WITH [CASCADED | LOCAL] CHECK OPTION*

WITH CHECK OPTION means that changes to the *View* records are allowed only if the *WHERE* conditions of the *SELECT* command are satisfied. *WITH CHECK OPTION* is of course relevant only if the *View* is changeable.

The variant *WITH LOCAL CHECK OPTION* affects *Views* that have been derived from other *Views*. *LOCAL* means that only the *WHERE* conditions of the *CREATE VIEW* command are considered, and not the *WHERE* conditions of higher-level *Views*.

The opposite effect is achieved with *WITH CASCADED CHECK OPTION*: Now the *WHERE* conditions of all higher-level *Views* are considered. If you specify neither *CASCADED* nor *LOCAL*, the default is *CASCADED*.

Here is an example:

```
CREATE VIEW v1 AS
  SELECT titleID, title, subtitle FROM titles
  ORDER BY title, subtitle
```

```
DELETE [deleteoptions] FROM tablename
  [WHERE condition]
  [ORDER BY ordercolumn [DESC]]
  [ LIMIT maxrecords ]
```

DELETE deletes the records in a table encompassed by *condition*.

deleteoptions: *LOW_PRIORITY, QUICK, IGNORE*

LOW_PRIORITY has the effect that the data records are deleted only when all read operations are complete. (The goal of this option is to avoid having *SELECT* queries unnecessarily delayed due to *DELETE* operations.)

QUICK has the effect that during deletion, an existing index is not optimized. This speeds up the *DELETE* command, but it can lead to a somewhat inefficient index.

IGNORE has the effect since MySQL 4.1 that the *DELETE* command is continued even if errors occur. All errors are converted to warnings, which can be read with *SHOW WARNINGS*.

condition: This condition specifies which records are to be deleted. For the syntax of *condition*, see *SELECT*.

ordercolumn: With *ORDER BY* you can first sort the data to be deleted. This makes sense only in combination with *LIMIT*, in order, for example, to delete the first or last ten records (according to some sort criterion).

maxrecords: With *LIMIT*, the maximum number of records that may be deleted is specified.

If *DELETE* is executed without conditions, then all records of the table are deleted (so be careful!). *DELETE* without conditions cannot be part of a transaction. If a transaction is open, it is closed with *COMMIT* before the *DELETE* command is executed. If you wish to delete large tables completely, it is more efficient to use the command *TRUNCATE*.

```
DELETE [deleteoptions]  table1, table2 … FROM table1, table2, table3 …
  [USING columns]
  WHERE conditions
```

This variant of *DELETE* (available since version 4.0) deletes records from tables *table1*, *table2*, etc., where the data of additional tables (*table3*, etc.) are considered in the search criteria.

After *DELETE*, all tables from which data are to be deleted must be specified. After *FROM*, all *DELETE* tables must appear, as well as any additional tables that serve only in formulating the search criteria.

deleteoptions: Here you can specify options as in a usual *DELETE* command.

columns: Here fields that link the tables can be specified (see also *SELECT*). This assumes that the linking field has the same name in both tables.

conditions: In addition to the usual delete criteria, here one may specify linking conditions (e.g., *WHERE table1.id = table2.forgeinID*).

```
DESCRIBE tablename [ columnname ]
```

DESCRIBE returns information about the specified table in the current database (or about a particular column of this table). Instead of *columnname*, a pattern with the wild cards _ and % can be given. In this case, *DESCRIBE* displays information about those columns matching the pattern. *DESCRIBE* returns the same information as *EXPLAIN* or *SHOW TABLE* or *SHOW COLUMN*.

```
DO selectcommand
```

DO is a variant of *SELECT* and has basically the same syntax. The difference between the two is that *DO* returns no results. For example, *DO* can be used for variable assignment, for which it is somewhat faster than *SELECT* (thus, for example, *DO @var:=3*).

```
DROP DATABASE [IF EXISTS] dbname
```

DROP DATABASE deletes an existing database with all of its data. This cannot be undone, so be careful! If the database does not exist, then an error is reported. This error can be avoided with an *IF EXISTS*.

In the execution of this command, all files in the directory dbname with the following endings are deleted, among others: .BAK, .DAT, .HSH, .ISD, .ISM, .MRG, .MYD, .MYI, .db, .frm, as well as the file db.opt.

```
DROP FUNCTION fnname
```

DROP FUNCTION deletes the specified stored procedure or deactivates an external auxiliary function that was made available to MySQL earlier with *CREATE FUNCTION*.

```
DROP INDEX indexname ON tablename
```

DROP INDEX removes an index from the specified table. Usually, *indexname* is the name of the indexed column, or else *PRIMARY* for the primary index.

```
DROP PROCEDURE  prname
```

DROP PROCEDURE deletes the specified stored procedure.

```
DROP [TEMPORARY] TABLE [IF EXISTS] tablename1, tablename2 … [options]
```

DROP TABLE deletes the specified (temporary) tables irrevocably. The option *IF EXISTS* avoids an error message if the tables do not exist.

Note that *DROP TABLE* automatically ends a running transaction (*COMMIT*).

DROP TEMPORARY TABLE (available since MySQL 4.1) deletes only temporary tables. In contrast to the ordinary *DROP TABLE* command, this one has no influence over running transactions.

> *options*: *RESTRICT* | *CASCADE*
>
> The two options *RESTRICT* und *CASCADE* are currently nonfunctional. They currently should simplify the porting of SQL code to other database systems.

```
DROP TRIGGER tablename.triggername
```

DROP TRIGGER deletes the specified trigger.

```
DROP VIEW [IF EXISTS] viewname1, viewname2 … [options]
```

DROP VIEW deletes the specified *Views* irrevocably. The same options are available as for *DROP TABLE*.

```
EXPLAIN tablename
```

EXPLAIN returns a table with information about all the columns of a table (field name, field type, index, default value, etc.). The same information can be determined as well with *SHOW COLUMNS* or *DESCRIBE*, or via an external program such as mysqlshow.

```
EXPLAIN SELECT selectcommand
```

EXPLAIN SELECT returns a table with information about how the specified *SELECT* command was executed. These data can help in speed optimization of queries, and in particular in deciding which columns of a table should be indexed. (The syntax of *selectcommand* was described under *SELECT*. An example of the use of *EXPLAIN SELECT* and a brief description of the resulting table can be found in Chapter 8.)

```
FLUSH flushoptions
```

FLUSH empties the MySQL internal intermediate storage. Any information not stored already is thereby stored in the database. The execution of *FLUSH* requires the *RELOAD* privilege.

flushoptions: Here one may specify which cache(s) should be emptied. Multiple options should be separated by commas.

DES_KEY_FILE: Reloads the key files for the functions *DES_ENCRYPT* and *DES_DECRYPT*.

HOSTS: mpties the host cache table. This is necessary especially if in the local network the arrangement of IP numbers has changed.

LOGS: Closes all logging files and then reopens them. In the case of update logs, a new logging file is created, whereby the number of the file ending is increased by 1 (*name.000003* ➤ *name.00004*). With error logs the existing file is renamed to name.old and a new error log file is created.

QUERY CACHE: Defragments the query cache so that it can use its memory more efficiently. The cache is not emptied. (If you wish to do this, execute *RESET QUERY CACHE*.)

PRIVILEGES: Reloads the privileges database *mysql* (corresponds to mysqladmin reload).

STATUS: Sets most status variables to 0.

TABLES: Closes all open tables.

TABLE[S] tblname1, tblname2, …: Closes the specified tables.

TABLES WITH READ LOCK: As above, except that additionally, *LOCK* is executed for all tables, which remains in force until the advent of a corresponding *UNLOCK table*.

USER_RESOURCES: Resets the counters for *MAX_QUERIES_PER_HOUR*, *MAX_UPDATES_PER_HOUR*, and *MAX_CONNECTIONS_PER_HOUR* (see *maxlimits* under *GRANT*).

Most *FLUSH* operations can also be executed through the auxiliary program *mysqladmin*.

```
GRANT privileges ON objects
  TO users [IDENTIFIED BY 'password']
  [REQUIRE ssloptions ]
  [WITH GRANT OPTION | maxlimits ]
```

GRANT helps in the allocation of access privileges to database objects.

ALTER, CREATE, CREATE TEMPORARY TABLES, CREATE VIEW, DELETE, DROP, EXECUTE, FILE, INDEX, LOCK TABLE, PROCESS, REFERENCES, RELOAD, REPLICATION CLIENT, REPLICATION SLAVE, SELECT, SHOW DATABASE, SHOW VIEW, SHUTDOWN, SUPER, UPDATE

If you wish to set all (or no) privileges, then specify *ALL* (or *USAGE*). (The second variant is useful if you wish to create a new MySQL user to whom as of yet no privileges have been granted.) The *Grant* privilege can be set only via *WITH GRANT OPTION*; that is, *ALL* does not include the *Grant* privilege.

If the privileges are to hold only for certain columns of a table, then specify the columns in parentheses. For example, you may specify *GRANT SELECT(columnA, columnB)*.

objects: Here databases and tables are specified. The following syntactic variants are available:

databasename.tablename	only this table in this database
databasename.spname	only this stored procedure
*databasename.**	all tables in this database
tablename	only this table in the current database
*	all tables of the current database
.	global privileges

Wild cards may not be used in the database names.

users: Here one or more (comma-separated) users may be specified. If these users are not yet known to the *user* table, they are created. The following variants are allowed:

username@hostname	only this user at *hostname*
'username'@'hostname'	as above, with special characters
username	this user at all computers
''@hostname	all users at *hostname*
''	all users at all computers

password: Optionally, with *IDENTIFIED BY*, a password in plain text can be specified. *GRANT* encrypts this password with the function *PASSWORD* before it is entered in the *user* table. If more than one user is specified, then more than one password may be given:

TO user1 IDENTIFIED BY 'pw1', user2 IDENTIFIED BY 'pw2', ...

ssloptions: If access to MySQL is to be SSL encrypted or if user identification is to take place with X509, you can specify the required information for establishing the connection here. The syntax is as follows:

REQUIRE SSL | X509 [ISSUER 'iss'] [SUBJECT 'subj'] [CIPHER 'ciph']

REQUIRE SSL means that the connection must be SSL encrypted (thus a normal connection is not permitted). *REQUIRE X509* means that the user must possess a valid certificate for identification that meets the X509 standard.

ISSUER specifies the required issuer of the certificate. (Without *ISSUER*, the origin of the certificate is not considered.)

SUBJECT specifies the required content of the certificate's *subject* field. (Without *SUBJECT*, the content is not considered.)

CIPHER specifies the required SSL encryption algorithm. (SSL supports various algorithms. Without this specification, all algorithms are allowed, including older ones that may have security loopholes.)

maxlimits: Here you can specify how many connections per hour the user is allowed to establish, as well as the number of *SELECT* and *INSERT/UPDATE/DELETE* commands. The default setting for all three values is 0 (no limit):

MAX_QUERIES_PER_HOUR n

MAX_UPDATES_PER_HOUR n

MAX_CONNECTIONS_PER_HOUR n

If the specified user does not yet exist and *GRANT* is executed without *IDENTIFIED BY*, then the new user has no password (which represents a security risk). On the other hand, if the user already exists, then *GRANT* without *IDENTIFIED BY* does not alter the password. (There is thus no danger that a password can be accidentally deleted by *GRANT*.)

It is impossible with *GRANT* to delete privileges that have already been granted (for example, by executing the command again with a smaller list of privileges). If you wish to take away privileges, you must use *REVOKE*.

GRANT may be used only by users with the *Grant* privilege. The user that executes *GRANT* may bestow only those privileges that he himself possesses. If the MySQL server is started with the option safe-user-create, then to create a new user, a user needs the *Insert* privilege for the table *mysql.user* in addition to the *Grant* privilege.

Since MySQL 5.0.3 *GRANT* can be used to create new users only by those with the *Create User* privilege.

```
HANDLER tablename OPEN [AS aliasname]
HANDLER tablename READ  FIRST|NEXT    [ WHERE condition  LIMIT n, m ]
HANDLER tablename READ indexname  FIRST|NEXT|PREV|LAST [ WHERE … LIMIT …]
HANDLER tablename CLOSE
```

Since MySQL 4.0.3, *HANDLER* enables direct access to MyISAM and InnoDB tables. This command can be used as a more efficient substitute for simple *SELECT* commands. This is particularly true if records are to be processed one at a time or in small groups.

The command is easy to use: First, access to a table is achieved with *HANDLER OPEN*. Then, *HANDLER READ* may be executed as often as you like, generally the first time with *FIRST*, and thereafter with *NEXT*, until no further results are forthcoming. The command returns results as with *SELECT ** (that is, all columns). *HANDLER CLOSE* terminates access.

HANDLER tablename READ reads the records in the order in which they were stored. On the other hand, the variant *HANDLER tablename READ indexname* uses the specified index. If you wish to use a primary index, you must use the form `primary`.

HANDLER was not conceived for use with typical MySQL applications, if for no other reason than that the code would be completely incompatible with every other database server. *HANDLER* is suitable for programming low-level tools (e.g., backup tools or drivers that simulate simple data access with a cursor). Note that *HANDLER* does not block tables (no locking), and therefore, the table can change while its data are being read.

HANDLER should not be used in stored procedures. Instead, use a cursor. *HANDLER* also has nothing to do with the command *DECLARE HANDLER*, which is used for error-handling in stored procedures.

```
HELP
HELP contents
HELP functionname
```

Since MySQL 4.1, *HELP* returns a brief help text. Instead of *HELP* the abbreviation *?* can be used.

```
INSERT [options1]  [INTO]  tablename [(columnlist)]
    VALUES (valuelist1), (…), …  [options2]

INSERT [options1]  [INTO]  tablename
    SET column1=value1, column2=value2 … [options2]

INSERT [options1]  [INTO]  tablename [ (columnlist) ]
    SELECT …
```

The *INSERT* command has the job of inserting new records into an existing table. There are three main syntax variants. In the first (and most frequently used) of these, new data records are specified in parentheses. Thus a typical *INSERT* command looks like this:

```
INSERT INTO tablename (columnA, columnB, columnC)
VALUES ('a', 1, 2), ('b', 7, 5)
```

The result is the insertion of two new records into the table. Columns that are allowed to be *NULL*, for which there is a default value, or which are automatically filled in by MySQL via *AUTO_IN* do not have to be specified. If the column names (i.e., in *columnlist*) are not given, then in *VALUES* all values must be given in the order of the columns.

With the second variant, only one record can be changed (not several simultaneously). Such a command looks like this:

```
INSERT INTO tablename SET columnA='a', columnB=1, columnC=2
```

For the third variant, the data to be inserted come from a *SELECT* instruction.

options1: The behavior of this command can be controlled with options:

IGNORE has the effect that the insertion of records with existing values is simply ignored for *UNIQUE KEY* columns. (Without this option, the result would be an error message.)

LOW_PRIORITY | DELAYED | HIGH_PRIORITY have influence over when the insertion operation is carried out.

In *LOW_PRIORITY* and *DELAYED*, MySQL delays its storage operation until there are no pending read accesses to the table. The advantage of *DELAYED* is that MySQL returns OK at once, and the client does not need to wait for the end of the saving operation. However, *DELAYED* cannot be used if then an *AUTO_INCREMENT* value with *LAST_INSERT_ID( )* is to be determined. *DELAYED* should also not be used if a *LOCK* was placed on the table. (The reason is this: For executing *INSERT DELAYED*, a new MySQL thread is started, and table locking uses threads in its operation.)

The records to be inserted are stored in RAM until the insertion operation has actually been carried out. If MySQL should be terminated for some reason (crash, power outage), then the data are lost.

HIGH_PRIORITY normally has no effect; that is, *INSERT* inserts the data at once. *HIGH_PRIORITY* is designed only for the case that the server was started with the option low-priority-updates. This option has the effect that *INSERT* commands are stored in LOW_PRIORITY mode. *HIGH_PRIORITY* overwrites this default setting.

options2: *ON DUPLICATE KEY UPDATE column1=value1, column2=value2 ...*

When a *UNIQUE* or *PRIMARY* index is violated during the insertion of new data, this option has the effect since MySQL 4.1 of replacing the existing record. If *id* is a *PRIMARY* column and an entry with *id=1* already exists, then

INSERT INTO tablename (id, data) VALUES (1, 10)

ON DUPLICATE KEY UPDATE data=data+10

has the same effect as

UPDATE tablename SET data=data+10 WHERE id=1.

Here *VALUE(columnname)* can be used in the column allocation. This function returns the value of the affected column. It is useful when a general *UPDATE* instruction is to be formulated for several records:

```
INSERT INTO tablename (id, data) VALUES (1, 10), (2, 15)
ON DUPLICATE KEY UPDATE data=data+VALUE(data)
```

Note that in using default values, there are special rules for *TIMESTAMP* and *AUTO_INCREMENT* values. (These rules hold for *UPDATE* commands as well.)

Columns with default values: If you want MySQL to use the default value for a column, then either do not specify this column in your *INSERT* command, or pass an empty character string (not *NULL*) as the value:

```
INSERT INTO table (col1, col2_with_default_value) VALUES ('abc', '')
```

TIMESTAMP columns: If you want MySQL to insert the current time in the column, then either omit this column in your *INSERT* command, or pass the value *NULL* (not an empty character string). It is also allowed to pass a character string with a timestamp value if you wish to store a particular value.

AUTO_INCREMENT columns: Here as well, either you don't pass the column, or you pass the value *NULL* if MySQL is to determine the *AUTO_INCREMENT* value itself. You may pass any other value that is not otherwise in use.

JOIN

JOIN is not actually an SQL command. This key word is mostly used as part of a *SELECT* command, to link data from several tables. *JOIN* will be described under *SELECT*.

KILL threadid

This command terminates a specified thread (subprocess) of the MySQL server. It is allowed only to those users who possess the *Super* privilege. A list of running threads can be obtained via *SHOW PROCESSLIST* (where again, this command assumes the *Process* privilege). Threads can also be terminated via the external program mysqladmin.

```
LOAD DATA  [ loadoptions ]  INFILE 'filename'  [ duplicateopt ]
  INTO TABLE tablename
  [ importopt ]
  [ IGNORE ignorenr LINES ]
  [ (columnlist) ]
```

LOAD DATA reads a text file and inserts the data contained therein line by line into a table as data records. *LOAD DATA* is significantly faster then inserting data by multiple *INSERT* commands.

Normally, the file *filename* is read from the server's file system, on which MySQL is running. (For this, the *FILE* privilege is required. For security reasons, the file must either be located in the directory of the database or be readable by all users of the computer.)

If the text file to be imported has characters outside the ASCII character set, you must set the character set of the text with *SET NAMES* before the command *LOAD DATA*.

loadoptions: LOCAL has the effect that the file *filename* on the local client computer is read (that is, the computer on which the command *LOAD DATA* is executed, not on the server computer). For this, no *FILE* privilege is necessary. (The *FILE* privilege relates only to the file system of the MySQL server computer.) Note that *LOAD DATA LOCAL* can be deactivated, depending on how the MySQL server was compiled and configured (option local-infile).

LOW PRIORITY has the effect that the data are inserted into the table only if no other user is reading the table.

CONCURRENT makes it possible in many cases for data to be inserted into a table and read out at the same time (by other clients). However, this works only for MyISAM tables and only when the new records are inserted exclusively at the end of the table file. The table file is not allowed to contain any free memory (holes). You can ensure this via *OPTIMIZE TABLE*.

filename: If a file name is given without the path, then MySQL searches for this file in the directory of the current database (e.g., *'bulk.txt'*).

If the file name is given with a relative path, then the path is interpreted by MySQL relative to the data directory (e.g., *'mydir/bulk.txt'*).

File names with absolute paths are taken without alteration (for example, *'/tmp/mydir/bulk.txt'*).

duplicateoptions: IGNORE | REPLACE determine the behavior of MySQL when a new data record has the same *UNIQUE* or *PRIMARY KEY* value as an existing record. With *IGNORE*, the existing record is preserved, and the new records are ignored. With *REPLACE*, existing records are replaced by the new ones. If neither of these options is used, then the result is an error message.

importoptions: Here is specified how the data should be formatted in the file to be imported. The entire *importoptions* block looks like this:

[FIELDS

  [TERMINATED BY 'fieldtermstring']

  [ENCLOSED BY 'enclosechar']

  [ESCAPED BY 'escchar']]

[LINES TERMINATED BY 'linetermstring']

fieldtermstring specifies the character string that separates the individual columns within the row (e.g., a tab character).

enclosechar specifies the character that should stand before and after individual entries in the text file (usually the single or double quote character for character strings). If an entry begins with this character, then that character is removed from the beginning and end. Entries that do not begin with the *enclosechar* character will still be accepted. The use of the character in the text file is thus to some extent optional.

escchar specifies which character is to be used to mark special characters (usually the backslash). This is necessary if special characters appear in character strings in the text file that are also used to separate columns or rows. Furthermore, MySQL expects the zero-byte in the form \0, where the backslash is to be replaced as necessary by *escchar* if a character has been specified for *escchar*).

linetermstring specifies the character string with which rows are to be terminated. With DOS/Windows text files this must be the character string ' \r\n'.

In these four character strings, the following special characters can be specified:

\0	0 byte
\b	backspace
\n	newline
\r	carriage return
\s	space
\t	tab
\'	single quote (')
\"	double quote (")
\\	backslash

Furthermore, the character strings can be given in hexadecimal form (e.g., *0x22* instead of '\"').

If no character strings are given, then the following is the default setting:

FIELDS TERMINATED BY '\t'   ENCLOSED BY "   ESCAPED BY '\\'

LINES TERMINATED BY '\n'

ignorenr: This value specifies how many lines should be ignored at the beginning of the text file. This is particularly useful if the first lines contain table headings.

columnlist: If the order of the columns in the text file does not exactly correspond to that in the table, then here one may specify which file columns correspond with which table columns. The list of columns must be set in parentheses: for example, *(firstname, lastname, birthdate).*

If *TIMESTAMP* columns are not considered during importation or if *NULL* is inserted, then MySQL inserts the actual time. MySQL exhibits analogous behavior with *AUTO_INCREMENT* columns.

LOAD DATA displays as result, among other things, an integer representing the number of warnings.

Starting with MySQL 4.1 you will can display all warnings and errors caused by *LOAD DATA* with the commands *SHOW WARNINGS* and *SHOW ERRORS.*

Instead of *LOAD DATA*, you can also use the program `mysqlimport`. This program creates a link to MySQL and then uses *LOAD DATA*. The inverse of *LOAD DATA* is the command *SELECT ... INTO OUTFILE.* With it you can export a table into a text file. Further information and concrete examples can be found in Chapter 14.

LOAD DATA FROM MASTER

This command since MySQL 4.0 copies all MyISAM tables from master to slave of a replication system. The tables of the *mysql* database are not copied. After copying, replication is begun on the slave (that is, the variables *MASTER_LOG_FILE* and *MASTER_LOG_POS* are set, which normally must be set with *CHANGE MASTER TO*).

This command can be used in many cases, in particular when no InnoDB tables are being used, for a convenient setting up of a replication system. It assumes that the replication user possesses the privileges *Select, Reload,* and *Super.*

LOAD INDEX INTO CACHE indexspec1, indexspec2 …

This command loads all specified indexes of MyISAM tables into the cache. This makes sense only in rare cases, such as carrying out repeatable benchmark tests.

indexspec: Specifies the MyISAM tables to be loaded. The following syntax is used:

tablename [[INDEX|KEY] (indexname1 …)] [IGNORE LEAVES]

Currently, the command loads all indexes of the table into the cache. Thus the specification of individual indexes will make sense only in the future. *IGNORE LEAVES* means that only a part of the index is to be loaded.

LOAD TABLE dbname.tablename FROM MASTER

This command copies a table in a replication system from master to slave, if the table does not yet exist there. The purpose of the command is actually to simplify debugging for MySQL developers. However, the command can possibly also be used for repairing a replication system after errors have been detected. The execution of the command requires that the replication user possess the privileges *Select, Reload,* and *Super. LOAD TABLE* works only for MyISAM tables.

LOCK TABLE table1 [AS aliasname] locktype, table2 [AS alias2] locktype, …

LOCK TABLE prevents other MySQL users from executing write or read operations on the specified tables. If a table is already blocked by another user, then the command waits (unfortunately, without a timeout value, thus theoretically forever) until that block is released.

Table *LOCK*s ensure that during the execution of several commands no data are changed by other users. Typically, *LOCK*s are necessary when first a *SELECT* query is executed and then tables are changed with *UPDATE*, where the results of the previous query are used. (For a single *UPDATE* command, on the other hand, no *LOCK* is necessary. Individual *UPDATE* commands are always completely executed by the MySQL server without giving other users the opportunity to change data.)

LOCK TABLE should not be used on InnoDB tables, for which you can achieve much more efficient locking using transactions and the commands *SELECT … IN SHARE MODE* and *SELECT … FOR UPDATE*.

Note that *LOCK TABLE* commands end a running transaction as with *COMMIT*. For future versions of MySQL there are InnoDB-specific *LOCK* variants planned that will be able to be executed outside of transactions.

locktype: In MySQL 5.0 there are four *LOCK* types available:

READ: All MySQL users may read the table, but no one may change anything (including the user who executed the *LOCK* command). A *READ LOCK* is allocated only when the table is not blocked by other *WRITE LOCK*s. (Existing *READ LOCK*s, on the other hand, are no hindrance for new *READ LOCK*s. It is thus possible for several users to have simultaneous *READ LOCK*s on the same table.)

READ LOCAL: Like *READ*, except that *INSERT*s are allowed if they do not change existing data records.

WRITE: The current user may read and change the table. All other users are completely blocked. They may neither change data in the blocked table nor read it. A *WRITE LOCK* is allocated only if the table is not blocked by other *LOCK*s (*READ* or *WRITE*). Until the *WRITE LOCK* is lifted, other users can obtain neither a *READ LOCK* nor a *WRITE LOCK*.

LOW PRIORITY WRITE: Like *WRITE*, except that during the waiting time (that is, until all other *READ* and *WRITE LOCK*s have been ended) other users may obtain on demand a new *READ LOCK*. However, this means as well that the *LOCK* will be allocated only when there is no other user who wishes a *READ LOCK*.

In future versions of MySQL there will presumably be two additional *LOCK* variants especially for InnoDB tables. These two variants are not yet officially documented, and so it is possible that the following description is inaccurate.

IN SHARE MODE: This *LOCK* type will have the same effect as *SELECT * FROM table* and will protect the entire table from changes by other connections. (*INSERT, UPDATE*, and *DELETE* commands of other connections are thus blocked until the end of the lock.)

There are two advantages over the *SELECT* command: The InnoDB table driver can execute locking more efficiently, and the *LOCK* command is compatible with other database systems (Oracle, PostgreSQL, etc.).

IN EXCLUSIVE MODE: This *LOCK* type is even more restrictive and blocks *SELECT* commands of other connections if this option is executed with the option *LOCK IN SHARE MODE* or *LOCK FOR UPDATE*.

Table *LOCK*s can increase the speed with which several database commands can be executed one after the other (of course, at the cost that other users are blocked during this time).

MySQL manages table *LOCK*s by means of a thread, where each connection is associated with its own thread. Only one *LOCK* command is considered per thread. (But several tables may be included.) As soon as *UNLOCK TABLES* or *LOCK* is executed for any other table, then all previous locks become invalid.

For reasons of efficiency, it should definitely be attempted to keep *LOCK*s as brief as possible and to end them as quickly as possible by *UNLOCK*. *LOCK*s end automatically when the current process ends (that is, for example, when the connection between server and client is broken).

OPTIMIZE TABLE tablename

OPTIMIZE TABLE removes, since MySQL 4.1.3, unused storage space from MyISAM and InnoDB tables and ensures that associated data in a data record are stored together.

OPTIMIZE TABLE should be regularly executed for tables whose contents are continually being changed (many *UPDATE* and *DELETE* commands). This speeds up data access. With MyISAM tables the database file is also made smaller. The *table space* of InnoDB tables, on the other hand, cannot in principle be made smaller.

PROCEDURE procname

MySQL can be extended with external procedures. Their code must be formulated in the C++ programming language. To use such functions in *SELECT* commands, the key word *PROCEDURE* must be used.

As an example of such a procedure, the MySQL program code contains the function *ANALYSE*. This procedure can be used to analyze the contents of a table in the hope of determining a better table definition. The function is called thus:

```
SELECT * FROM tablename PROCEDURE ANALYSE()
```

As with the creation of user-defined functions (UDFs; see *CREATE FUNCTION*), the programming of procedures requires a great deal of MySQL background knowledge. Further information can be found in the MySQL documentation: `http://dev.mysql.com/doc/mysql/en/extending-mysql.html`.

An elegant and much simpler alternative to UDFs is stored procedures, which have been available since MySQL 5.0.

PURGE MASTER LOGS TO 'hostname-bin.n'

This command deletes all binary logging files that are older than the file specified. Execute this command only when you are sure that the logging files are no longer needed, that is, when all slave computers have synchronized their databases. This command can be executed only on the master computer of a replication system, and only if the *Super* privilege has been granted. See also *RESET MASTER*.

RENAME TABLE oldtablename TO newtablename

RENAME TABLE gives a new name to an existing table. It is also possible to rename several tables, e.g., *a TO b, c TO d*, etc.

There is no command for giving a new name to an entire database. If you are using MyISAM tables, then to do so, you can stop the MySQL server, rename the database directory and then restart the server. Note that you may have to change access privileges in the *mysql* database. With InnoDB tables, you must make a backup (`mysqldump`) and then import the tables into a new database.

```
REPAIR TABLE tablename1, tablename2, … [ TYPE = QUICK ]
```

REPAIR TABLE attempts to repair a defective table file. With the option *TYPE = QUICK* only the index is re-created.

REPAIR TABLE can be used only with MyISAM tables. Instead of this command, you may also use the external program `myisamchk -r tblfile`. (If *REPAIR TABLE* does not return OK as result, then you might try `myisamchk -o`. This program offers more repair possibilities than *REPAIR TABLE*.)

```
REPLACE [INTO]
```

REPLACE is a variant of *INSERT*. The only difference relates to new records whose key word is the same as that of an existing record. In this case, the existing record is deleted and the new one is stored in the table. Since the behavior with duplicates is so clearly defined, *REPLACE* does not have the *IGNORE* option possessed by the *INSERT* command.

```
RESET MASTER
```

This command deletes all binary logging files including the index file `hostname-bin.index`. With this command, replication can be restarted at a particular time. For this, *RESET SLAVE* must be executed on all slave systems. Before the command is executed it must be ensured that the databases on all slave systems are identical to those of the master system. This command assumes the *reload* privilege.

If you wish to delete only old (no longer needed) logging files, then use *PURGE MASTER LOGS*.

```
RESET QUERY CACHE
```

This command deletes all entries from the query cache. It assumes the *reload* privilege.

```
RESET SLAVE
```

This command reinitializes the slave system. The contents of `master.info` (and with it the current logging file and its position) are deleted. The command assumes the *reload* privilege.

This command makes sense only if after some problems the databases are to be set up on the slave based on previous snapshots so that the slave system then can synchronize itself by replication, or when *RESET MASTER* was executed on the master system (so that all logging files are deleted there). In this case, first *SLAVE STOP* and then *SLAVE START* should be executed on the slave system.

```
RESTORE TABLE tblname FROM '/backup/directory'
```

RESTORE TABLE copies the files of the specified table from a backup directory into the data directory of the current database. *RESTORE TABLE* is the inverse of *BACKUP TABLE*.

BACKUP and *RESTORE* do not work for InnoDB tables. Both commands are considered *deprecated* and should not be used if possible. Alternatives are external backup tools such as `mysqldump`, `mysqlhotcopy`, and the InnoDB backup utility.

REVOKE privileges ON objects FROM users

REVOKE is the inverse of *GRANT*. With this command you can remove individual privileges previously granted. The syntax for the parameters *privileges*, *objects*, and *users* can be read about under the *GRANT* command. The only difference relates to the *Grant* privilege: To revoke this privilege from a user, *REVOKE* can be used in the following form: *REVOKE GRANT OPTION ON ... FROM ...*.

Although *GRANT* inserts new users into the *mysql.user* table, *REVOKE* is incapable of deleting this user. You can remove all privileges from this user with *REVOKE*, but you cannot prevent this user from establishing a connection to MySQL. (If you wish to take that capability away as well, you must explicitly remove the entries from the *user* database with the *DELETE* command.)

Please note that in the MySQL access system you cannot forbid what is allowed at a higher level. If you allow *x* access to database *d*, then you cannot exclude table *d.t* with *REVOKE*. If you wish to allow *x* access to all tables of the database *d* with the exception of table *t*, then you must forbid access to the entire database and then allow access to individual tables of the database (with exception of *d*). *REVOKE* is not smart enough to carry out such operations on its own.

ROLLBACK

ROLLBACK undoes the most recent transaction. (Instead of *ROLLBACK*, you can confirm the pending changes with *COMMIT* and thereby finalize their execution.) *BEGIN/COMMIT/ROLLBACK* work only if you are working with transaction-capable tables. Further information and examples on transactions can be found in Chapter 10.

ROLLBACK TO SAVEPOINT name

ROLLBACK ends the current transaction. All SQL commands executed since the specified *SAVEPOINT* are canceled. Commands before the *SAVEPOINT* are accepted. The command has been available since version 4.0.14.

SAVEPOINT name

This command sets, since MySQL version 4.0.14, a mark within the running transaction. With *ROLLBACK TO SAVEPOINT* the transaction can be aborted beyond this point. *SAVEPOINT*s are valid only within a transaction. They are deleted at the end of the transaction.

```
SELECT [selectoptions] column1 [[AS] alias1], column2 [[AS] alias2] ...
  [ FROM tablelist ]
  [ WHERE condition ]
  [ GROUP BY groupfield  [ASC |DESC] ]
  [ HAVING condition ]
  [ ORDER BY ordercolumn1 [DESC], ordercolumn2 [DESC] ... ]
  [ LIMIT [offset,] rows ]
  [ PROCEDURE procname]
  [ LOCK IN SHARE MODE  |   FOR UPDATE ]
```

SELECT serves to formulate database queries. It returns the query result in tabular form. *SELECT* is usually implemented in the following form:

```
SELECT column1, column2, column3 FROM table ORDER BY column1
```

However, there are countless syntactic variants, thanks to which *SELECT* can be used also, for example, for processing simple expressions.

```
SELECT HOUR(NOW( ))
```

Note that the various parts of the *SELECT* command must be given in the order presented here.

selectoptions: The behavior of this command can be controlled by a number of options:

DISTINCT | DISTINCTROW specify how MySQL should behave when a query returns several identical records. *DISTINCT* and *DISTINCTROW* mean that identical result records should be displayed only once. *ALL* means that all records should be displayed (the default setting).

Since MySQL 4.1, the sort order can also be specified for *DISTINCT* (which is also the basis for determining equivalence of character strings): The syntax is *DISTINCT column COLLATE collname*.

HIGH_PRIORITY has the effect that a query with higher priority than change or insert commands will be executed. *HIGH_PRIORITY* should be used only for queries that need to be executed very quickly.

SQL_SMALL_RESULT | SQL_BIG_RESULT specify whether a large or small record list is expected as result, and they help MySQL in optimization. Both options are useful only with *GROUP BY* and *DISTINCT* queries.

SQL_BUFFER_RESULT has the effect that the result of a query is stored in a temporary table. This option should be used when the evaluation of the query is expected to range over a long period of time and locking problems are to be avoided during this period.

SQL_CACHE and *SQL_NO_CACHE* specify whether the results of the *SELECT* command should be stored in the query cache or whether such storage should be prevented. By default, *SQL_CACHE* usually holds, unless the query cache is executed in demand mode (*QUERY_CACHE_TYPE=2*).

SQL_CALC_FOUND_ROWS has the effect that MySQL determines the total number of found records even if you limit the result with *LIMIT*. The number can then be determined with a second query *SELECT FOUND_ROWS( )*.

STRAIGHT_JOIN has the effect that data collected from queries extending over more than one table should be joined in the order of the *FROM* expression. (Without *STRAIGHT_JOIN*, MySQL attempts to find the optimal order on its own. *STRAIGHT_JOIN* bypasses this optimization algorithm.)

column: Here column names are normally given. If the query encompasses several tables, then the format is *table.column*. If a query is to encompass all the columns of the tables specified by *FROM*, then you can save yourself some typing and simply specify *. (Note, however, that this is inefficient in execution if you do not need all the columns.)

However, instead of column names, you may also use general expressions or functions, e.g., for formatting a column (*DATE_FORMAT(…)*) or for calculating an expression (*COUNT(…)*).

With *AS*, a column can be given a new name. This is practical in using functions such as *HOUR(column) AS hr*. The use of *AS* is optional. That is, *HOUR(column) hr* is syntactically correct (but not as readable).

Such an alias name can then be used in most of the rest of the *SELECT* command (e.g., *ORDER BY hr*). The alias name cannot, however, be placed in a *WHERE* clause.

Since MySQL 4.1, the desired sort order can be specified with *COLLATE* (e.g., *column COLLATE collname AS alias*).

tablelist: In the simplest case, there is simply a list (separated by commas) of all tables that are to be considered in the query. If no relational conditions (further below with *WHERE*) are formulated, then MySQL returns a list of all possible combinations of data records of all affected tables.

There is the possibility of specifying here a condition for linking the tables, for example in the following forms:

table1 LEFT [OUTER] JOIN table2 ON table1.xyID = table2.xyID

table1 LEFT [OUTER] JOIN table2 USING (xyID)

table1 NATURAL [LEFT [OUTER]] JOIN

An extensive list of the many syntactic synonyms can be found in Chapter 9, where the topic of links among several tables is covered in great detail.

Within *tablelist* an alias can be given for every table name. The key word *AS* is optional:

table1 [AS] t1, table2 [AS] t2

condition: Here is where conditions that the query results must fulfill can be formulated. Conditions can contain comparisons (*column1>10* or *column1=column2*) or pattern expressions (*column LIKE '%xy'*), for example. Several conditions can be joined with *AND*, *OR*, and *NOT*.

MySQL allows selection conditions with *IN*:

WHERE id IN(1, 2, 3) is equivalent to *WHERE id=1 OR id=2 OR id=3.*

WHERE id NOT IN (1,2) is equivalent to *WHERE NOT (id=1 OR id=2).*

Full-text search: Conditions can also be formulated with M*ATCH(col1, col2) AGAINST('word1 word2 word3').* Thereby a full-text search is carried out in the columns *col1* and *col2* for the words *word1*, *word2*, and *word3*. (This assumes that a full-text index for the columns *col1* and *col2* has been created.)

AGAINST also supports Boolean search expressions, for example, in the form *AGAINST('+word1 +word2 -word3' IN BOOLEAN MODE).* Here the plus sign represents a logical AND operation, while the minus sign means that the specified word may not appear in the record. The full syntax for search expressions can be found in Chapter 10.

***WHERE* versus *HAVING*:** Conditions can be formulated with *WHERE* or *HAVING. WHERE* conditions are applied directly to the columns of the tables named in *FROM*.

HAVING conditions, on the other hand, are applied only after the *WHERE* conditions to the intermediate result of the query. The advantage of *HAVING* is that conditions can also be specified for function results (for example, *SUM(column1)* in a *GROUP BY* query). Alias names can be used in *HAVING* conditions (*AS xxx*), which is not possible in *WHERE*.

Conditions that can be equally well formulated with *WHERE* or *HAVING* should be expressed with *WHERE*, because in that case, better optimization is possible.

groupfield: With *GROUP BY*, you can specify a group column. If the query returns several records with the same values for the group column, then these records are collected into a single new record. Along with *GROUP BY*, in the *column* part of the query so-called aggregate functions are usually placed, with which calculations can be made over grouped fields (e.g., *COUNT, SUM, MIN, MAX*).

By default, grouped results are sorted as though *ORDER BY* had been specified for the columns. Optionally, the sort order can be determined with *ASC* or *DESC*.

Since MySQL 4.1, the desired sort order can be given with *COLLATE* (e.g., *GROUP BY column COLLATE collname*).

ordercolumn: With *ORDER BY* several columns or expressions can be specified according to which the query result should be sorted. Sorting normally proceeds in increasing order (A, B, C, ... or 1, 2, 3, ...). With the option *DESC* (for *descending*) you have decreasing order.

[offset,] row: With *LIMIT* the query results can be reduced to an arbitrary selection. This is to be recommended especially when the results are to be displayed pagewise or when the number of result records is to be limited. The position at which the results are to begin is given by *offset* (0 for the first data record), while *row* determines the maximum number of result records.

procname: This enables the call of a user-defined procedure (see the description of *PROCEDURE*).

MySQL does not support the formulation *SELECT ... INTO table*, which is recognized in many other SQL dialects. In most cases you can get around this lack with *INSERT INTO ... SELECT ...* or *CREATE TABLE tablename ... SELECT ....*

Locking (InnoDB Tables)

If you use transactions, then the addition of *LOCK IN SHARE MODE* has the effect that all records found by the *SELECT* command will be blocked by a *shared lock* until the end of the transaction. This has two consequences: First, your *SELECT* query will not be executed until there is no running transaction that could change the result. Second, the affected records cannot now be changed by other connections (though they can be read with *SELECT*) until your transaction has ended.

FOR UPDATE is even more restrictive, blocking the found records with an *exclusive lock*. In contrast to a *shared lock*, other connections that execute *SELECT ... LOCK IN SHARE MODE* must now wait until the end of your transaction (of course, only if the same records are affected by *SELECT* queries).

SubSELECTs

Beginning with version 4.1, MySQL supports so-called *subSELECTs*. This means that the results of one query can flow into a condition of another. Examples of the use of *subSELECTs* can be found in Chapter 10. Here are the syntactic variants:

SELECT ... WHERE col = [ANY|ALL|SOME] (SELECT ...)

In this variant the second *SELECT* query must return a single value (one row and one column). This value is used for the comparison *col = ...* Other comparison operators are allowed as well, such as *col > ...* and *col <= ...* and *col <> ....*

SELECT ... WHERE col = ANY|SOME (SELECT ...)

Here the second *SELECT* query can return more than one value. *ANY* or the equivalent key word *SOME* results in all suitable values being considered. Then the entire query returns more than one result. *col = ANY ...* is the same as col *IN ...* (see below).

SELECT ... WHERE col = ALL (SELECT ...)

The expression *comparisonoperator ALL* has the value *TRUE* if the comparison is true for all the results of the second *SELECT* query or if the second *SELECT* query returns no results at all.

SELECT ... WHERE col [NOT] IN (SELECT ...)

With this variant, the second *SELECT* query can return a list of individual values. This list is then processed in the form *SELECT ... WHERE col IN (n1, n2, n3).* In place of *IN* one may also use *NOT IN*.

SELECT ROW(value1, value2 ...) = [ANY] (SELECT col1, col2 ...)

This query tests whether there exists a record that satisfies certain criteria. The result can be either 1 (true) or *NULL* (false). As comparison criterion there is not a single value, but a group of values. If the result record agrees with the *ROW* record, the entire query returns 1, otherwise *NULL*.

If the optional key word *ANY* or its synonym *SOME* is used, the second *SELECT* query can return more than one result. If at least one of these agrees with the *ROW* record, then the entire query returns 1.

SELECT ... WHERE [NOT] EXISTS (SELECT ...)

With this variant, the second query is executed for each record found from the first *SELECT* query. Only if this returns a result (at least one record) does the record from the first *SELECT* query remain in the result list. *EXISTS* constructions are as a rule useful only if the records of the two *SELECT* commands are linked with a *WHERE* condition.

SELECT ... FROM (SELECT ...) AS name WHERE ...

With this variant first the *SELECT* command in parentheses is executed. It returns a table that serves as the basis for the outer *SELECT* query. The outer *SELECT* command thus does not access a preexisting table, but instead the table that was the result of the previous *SELECT* command. Such tables are called *derived tables*. The SQL syntax prescribes that these tables must be named using *AS name*.

SELECT commands can be nested within one another. Such commands are difficult to read and understand, however. *SELECT* commands can also be placed in the *WHERE* condition of *UPDATE* or *DELETE* commands to decide which records should be altered or deleted.

```
SELECT [selectoptions] columnlist
 INTO @var1, @var2 ...
 [ FROM ... WHERE ... GROUP BY ... HAVING ... ORDER BY  ... LIMIT ... ]
```

With this variant of the *SELECT* command, all columns of the result record are stored, since MySQL 5.0, in the variables *var1*, *var2*, etc. This works only if the query returns exactly one record. (If necessary use *LIMIT 1*.)

INTO @var1, @var2 ... can also be placed at the end of the instruction. The following two examples are therefore equivalent:

```
SELECT title, subtitle INTO @mytitle, @mysub FROM titles WHERE titleID=1
SELECT title, subtitle FROM titles WHERE titleID=1 INTO @mytitle, @mysub
```

```
SELECT [selectoptions] columnlist
  INTO OUTFILE 'filename' exportopt
  [ FROM ... WHERE ... GROUP BY ... HAVING ... ORDER BY  ... LIMIT ... ]
```

With this variant of the *SELECT* command, the records are written into a text file. Here we describe only those options that are specific to this variant. All other points of syntax can be found under *SELECT*.

filename: The file is generated in the file system of the MySQL server. For security reasons, the file should not already exist. Moreover, you must have the *FILE* privilege to be able to execute this *SELECT* variant.

exportoptions: Here it is specified how the text file is formatted. The entire option block looks like this:

[FIELDS

  [TERMINATED BY 'fieldtermstring']

  [[OPTIONALLY] ENCLOSED BY 'enclosechar']

  [ESCAPED BY 'escchar']]

[LINES TERMINATED BY 'linetermstring']

fieldtermstring specifies the character string that separates columns within a line (e.g., a tab character).

enclosechar specifies a character that is placed before and after every entry, e.g., '123' with *ENCLOSED BY* ' \". With *OPTIONALLY*, the character is used only on *CHAR, VARCHAR, TEXT, BLOB, TIME, DATE, SET*, and *ENUM* columns (and not for every number format, such as *TIMESTAMP*).

escchar specifies the character to be used to mark special characters (usually the backslash). This is especially necessary when in character strings of a text file special characters appear that are also used for separating data elements.

If *escchar* is specified, then the escape character is always used for itself (\\) as well as for ASCII code 0 (\0). If *enclosechar* is empty, then the escape character is also used as identifier of the first character of *fieldtermstring* and *linetermstring* (e.g., \t and \n). On the other hand, if *enclosechar* is not empty, then *escchar* is used only for *enclosechar* (e.g., \"), and not for *fieldtermstring* and *linetermstring*. (This is no longer necessary, since the end of the character string is uniquely identifiable due to *enclosechar*.)

linetermstring specifies the character string with which lines are to be terminated. With DOS/Windows text files this must be the character string ' \r\n'.

In the four character strings, special characters can be specified, for example, \b for backspace. The list of permissible special characters can be found at the command *LOAD DATA*. Moreover, character strings can be given in hexadecimal notation (such as *0x22* instead of ' \").

As with *LOAD DATA* the following is the default setting:

FIELDS TERMINATED BY '\t' ENCLOSED BY '' ESCAPED BY '\\'

LINES TERMINATED BY '\n'

If you wish to input files generated with *SELECT … INTO OUTFILE* again into a table, then use *LOAD DATA*. This command is the inverse of *SELECT … INTO OUTFILE*. Further information and concrete application examples for both commands can be found in Chapter 14.

```
SELECT [selectoptions] column
   INTO DUMPFILE 'filename'
   [ FROM … WHERE … GROUP BY … HAVING … ORDER BY   … LIMIT … ]
```

SELECT … INTO DUMPFILE has, in principle, the same function as *SELECT … INTO OUTFILE* (see above). The difference is that here data are stored without any characters to indicate column or row division.

SELECT … INTO DUMPFILE is designed for saving a single BLOB object into a file. The *SELECT* query should therefore return precisely one column and one row as result. Should that not be the case, that is, if the query returns more than one data element, then usually (and for some strange reason not always) one receives an error message: *ERROR 1172: Result consisted of more than one row.*

```
(SELECT selectoptions) UNION [ALL] (SELECT selectoptions) unionoptions
```

Since MySQL 4.0 you can use *UNION* to unite the results of two or more *SELECT* queries. You thereby obtain a result table in which the results of the individual queries are simply strung together. The individual queries can affect different tables, though you must ensure that the number of columns and their data types are the same.

The optional key word *ALL* has the effect that duplicates (that is, results that arise in more than one *SELECT* query) appear in the end result with their corresponding multiplicity. Without *ALL*, duplicates are eliminated (as with *DISTINCT* in *SELECT*).

With *SELECT* commands, all options described earlier for selecting columns, setting sort order, etc., are permitted. With *unionoptions* you can also specify how the final result is to be sorted (*ORDER BY*) and reduced (*LIMIT*).

```
SET @variable1 = expression1, @variable2 = expression2 …
```

MySQL permits the management of one's own user variables. These variables are indicated by the @ symbol before the name. These variables are managed separately for each client connection, so that no naming conflicts can arise among clients. The content of such variables is lost at the end of the connection.

Instead of *SET*, one may also use *SELECT* for the assignment of user variables. The syntax is *SELECT @variable:=expression* (note that := must be used instead of =).

```
SET [options] [@@]systemvariable = expression
```

If the variable name has either no @ prefixed or two of them (@@), then *SET* is setting system variables.

options: MySQL distinguishes two levels of validity among system variables: *GLOBAL* (valid for the entire MySQL server) and *SESSION* (valid only for the current connection). The default setting is *SESSION*.

Instead of the options *GLOBAL* and *SESSION* you can prefix *global.* or *session.* to the variable names. Thus *SET GLOBAL name = …* is equivalent to *SET global.name = …*.

Variables at the global level can be changed only by users with the *Super* privilege. Global changes are valid only for new connections, not those already in existence.

```
SET [OPTION] option=value
```

SET can also be used to modify certain MySQL options as well as the password. Although the syntax looks the same as that for variable assignment, most of the options described here cannot be evaluated with *SHOW VARIABLES*. However, *SELECT @@name* works in most cases.

For example, with

```
SET SQL_LOW_PRIORITY_UPDATES = 0 / 1
```

it is possible to determine the order in which MySQL executes queries and change commands. The default behavior (1) gives priority to change commands. (This has the effect that a lengthy *SELECT* command will not block change commands, which are usually executed quickly.) With the setting 0, on the other hand, changes are executed only when no *SELECT* command is waiting to be executed.

Important SET Options

Here are the most important *SET* syntax variants, presented in alphabetical order:

SET AUTOCOMMIT = 0 or *SET AUTOCOMMIT = 1* switches the autocommit mode for transactions off or on. Autocommit mode holds only for transaction-capable tables (see Chapter 10).

SET CHARACTER SET 'csname' assigns the character set *csname* to the two session variables *character_set_client* and *character_set_result* and to the session variable *character_set_connection* the value of *character_set_database*. *SET CHARACTER SET DEFAULT* resets the three variables to their default settings. A description of *character_set_xxx* variables appears in Chapter 10.

SET FOREIGN_KEY_CHECKS = 0 or *1* deactivates or activates the checking of foreign key constraints (see also Chapter 8).

If you use replication, you can temporarily interrupt binary logging on the master system with *SET SQL_LOG_BIN =0* in order to make manual changes that should not be replicated. *SET SQL_LOG_BIN=1* resumes logging.

SET NAMES 'csname' is a variant of *SET CHARACTER SET*. The difference is that the character set *csname* is assigned to all three session variables *character_set_client*, *character_set_result*, and *character_set_connection*.

SET PASSWORD offers a convenient way of changing one's own password, sparing the comparatively difficult manipulation of the access tables in the *mysql* database:

```
SET PASSWORD = PASSWORD('some password')
```

If you have sufficient privileges, you can also set another user's password with *SET*.

```
SET PASSWORD FOR username@hostname = PASSWORD('newPassword')
```

SET SQL_QUERY_CACHE = 0|1|2|ON|OFF|DEMAND sets the mode of the query cache (see Chapter 14).

SET TRANSACTION ISOLATION LEVEL sets the isolation level for transactions. The setting holds for transaction-capable tables. Here is the syntax:

```
SET [SESSION|GLOBAL] TRANSACTION ISOLATION LEVEL
    READ UNCOMMITTED | READ COMMITTED |
    REPEATABLE READ | SERIALIZABLE
```

SET SESSION changes the transaction degree for the current connection, and *SET GLOBAL* for all future connections (but not the current one). If neither *SESSION* nor *GLOBAL* is specified, then the setting is valid only for the coming transaction. (Note that *SESSION* and *GLOBAL* in *SET TRANSACTION* have a somewhat different effect from that of *SET [@@]systemvariable*.)

The four isolation degrees are described in Chapter 10. With InnoDB tables, the default is *REPEATABLE READ*. The isolation degree can also be read from the variable *@@[global.]tx_isolation*.

Additional SET Options

The following list presents all the options that can be changed with *SET*:

```
SET BIG_TABLES = 0 | 1
SET CHARACTER SET character_set_name | DEFAULT
SET IDENTITY = #
SET INSERT_ID = #
SET LAST_INSERT_ID = #
SET LOW_PRIORITY_UPDATES = 0 | 1
```

```
SET MAX_JOIN_SIZE = value | DEFAULT
SET QUERY_CACHE_TYPE = 0 | 1 | 2
SET QUERY_CACHE_TYPE = OFF | ON | DEMAND
SET SQL_AUTO_IS_NULL = 0 | 1
SET SQL_BIG_SELECTS = 0 | 1
SET SQL_BUFFER_RESULT = 0 | 1
SET SQL_LOG_OFF = 0 | 1
SET SQL_LOG_UPDATE = 0 | 1
SET SQL_QUOTE_SHOW_CREATE = 0 | 1
SET SQL_SAFE_UPDATES = 0 | 1
SET SQL_SELECT_LIMIT = value | DEFAULT
SET TIMESTAMP = timestamp_value | DEFAULT
```

An explanation of these (mostly seldom used) setting options can be found in the MySQL documentation in the description of the *SET* command: `http://dev.mysql.com/doc/mysql/en/set-option.html`.

```
SHOW BINLOG EVENTS [IN logname] [FROM pos] [LIMIT offset, rows]
```

If this command is executed without options, then it returns the complete contents of the currently active binary logging file. The options allow for the specification of other logging files or for limiting the output. Note that this command can also be used to read the logging file of an external MySQL server.

```
SHOW CHARACTER SET [ LIKE pattern ]
```

Since MySQL 4.1, *SHOW CHARACTER SET* returns a list of all available character sets and their default sort orders.

```
SHOW COLLATION[ LIKE pattern ]
```

Since MySQL 4.1, *SHOW COLLATION* returns a list of all available sort orders.

```
SHOW COLUMN TYPES
```

In the future, *SHOW COLUMN TYPES* will return a list of all data types available for column definition in a table. (In the tested version 5.0.2 the resulting list was incomplete.)

```
SHOW [FULL] COLUMNS FROM tablename
    [ FROM databasename ]   [ LIKE pattern ]
```

SHOW COLUMNS returns a table with information on all columns of a table (field name, field type, index, default value, etc.). With *LIKE* the list of columns can be filtered with a search pattern with the wild cards _ and %. The optional key word *FULL* has the effect that the access privileges of the current user are also displayed on the columns. The same information can be obtained with *SHOW FIELDS FROM tablename*, *EXPLAIN tablename*, or *DESCRIBE tablename*, as well as with the external program mysqlshow. More detailed information can be found in the virtual table *information_schema.columns* (since MySQL 5.0).

`SHOW CREATE DATABASE tablename`

Since MySQL 4.1, *SHOW CREATE DATABASE* displays the SQL command with which the specified database can be re-created.

`SHOW CREATE FUNCTION/PROCEDURE name`

SHOW CREATE FUNCTION/PROCEDURE displays since MySQL 5.0 the SQL command with which the specified stored procedure can be re-created.

`SHOW CREATE TABLE name`

SHOW CREATE TABLE displays the SQL command with which the specified table or view can be re-created.

In the result of the command, all object names are set between backward single quotes, for example `tablename` or `columnname`. If you don't want this, then execute *SET SQL_QUOTE_SHOW_CREATE=0* beforehand.

`SHOW CREATE VIEW name`

SHOW CREATE VIEW displays the SQL command with which the specified view can be re-created. The command assumes the *Create View* privilege.

`SHOW DATABASES [ LIKE pattern ]`

SHOW DATABASES returns a list of all databases that the user can access. The list can be filtered with a search pattern with the wild cards _ and %. The same information can also be obtained with the external program `mysqlshow`.

For users possessing the *Show Databases* privilege, *SHOW DATABASES* returns a list of all databases, including those to which the user does not have access.

`SHOW [STORAGE] ENGINES`

Since MySQL 4.1, *SHOW ENGINES* displays a list of all table drivers (MyISAM, InnoDB, etc.) including information as to whether the driver is supported by the current MySQL version.

`SHOW [COUNT(*)] ERRORS [LIMIT [offset, ] count]`

Since MySQL 4.1, *SHOW ERRORS* returns a list of errors that were triggered by the execution of the most recent command. With *LIMIT* the result can be limited as with a *SELECT* command.

`SHOW FIELDS`

See *SHOW COLUMNS*.

SHOW FUNCTION STATUS [LIKE 'pattern']

This command returns since MySQL 5.0 a list of all functions (SPs). The list covers all databases. Optionally, the list can be reduced to all functions whose names satisfy a search pattern (where the SQL wild cards % and _ are allowed). A list of all procedures can be determined with *SHOW PROCEDURE STATUS*.

SHOW GRANTS FOR user@host

SHOW GRANTS displays a list of all access privileges for a particular user. It is necessary that *user* and *host* be specified exactly as these character strings are stored in the various *mysql* access tables. Wild cards are not permitted.

SHOW INDEX FROM table

SHOW INDEX returns a table with information about all indexes of the given table.

SHOW INNODB STATUS

SHOW INNODB STATUS returns information about various internal workings of the InnoDB table driver. The data can be used for speed optimization. More information can be found at http://dev.mysql.com/doc/mysql/en/innodb-tuning.html.

SHOW KEYS

See *SHOW INDEX*.

SHOW [BDB] LOGS

This command shows which BDB logging files are currently being used. (If you are not using BDB tables, the command returns no result.)

SHOW MASTER LOGS

This command returns a list of all binary logging files. It can be executed only on the master computer of a replication system.

SHOW MASTER STATUS

This command shows which logging file is the current one, as well as the current position in this file and which databases are excepted from logging (configuration settings binlog-do-db and binlog-ignore-db). This command can be used only on the master computer of a replication system.

SHOW PRIVILEGES

Since MySQL 4.1, this command returns a list of all available privileges with a brief description.

`SHOW PROCEDURE STATUS [LIKE 'pattern']`

This command returns, since MySQL 5.0, a list of all procedures (SPs). The list comprises SPs from all databases. Optionally, the list can be reduced to all procedures whose names match the pattern *pattern* (where the SQL wild cards % and _ are allowed). A list of all functions can be determined with *SHOW FUNCTION STATUS.*

`SHOW  [ FULL ]  PROCESSLIST`

This command returns a list of all running threads (subprocesses) of the MySQL server. If the *PROCESS* privilege has been granted, then all threads are shown. Otherwise, only the user's threads are displayed.

The option *FULL* has the effect that for each thread, the complete text of the most recently executed command is displayed. Without this option, only the first 100 characters are shown.

The process list can also be determined with the external command `mysqladmin`.

`SHOW SLAVE HOSTS`

This command returns a list of all slaves that replicate the master's databases. The command can be used only by the master computer of a replication system. It functions only for slaves for which the host name is specified in the configuration file explicitly in the form `report-host = hostname`.

`SHOW SLAVE STATUS`

This command provides information on the state of replication, including the display of all information about the file `master.info`. This command can be executed only on a slave computer in a replication system.

`SHOW STATUS`

This command returns a list of various MySQL variables that provide information on the current state of MySQL (for example, *Connections, Open_files, Uptime*). This same information can also be determined with the external program `mysqladmin`. A description of all variables can be found in the MySQL documentation under the command *SHOW STATUS*: `http://dev.mysql.com/doc/mysql/en/show-status.html`.

`SHOW TABLE STATUS  [FROM database] [LIKE pattern]`

SHOW TABLE STATUS returns information about all tables of the currently active or specified database: table type, number of records, average record length, *Create_time, Update_time*, etc. The same information can also be determined with the external program `mysqlshow`. With *pattern* the list of tables can be limited; the SQL wild cards % and _ are permitted in *pattern*.

`SHOW TABLE TYPES see also SHOW ENGINES`

Since MySQL 4.1, *SHOW TABLE TYPES* returns a list of all available table types (MyISAM, HEAP, InnoDB, etc.).

SHOW TABLES [FROM database] [LIKE pattern]

SHOW TABLES returns a list of all tables and *Views* of the current (or specified) database. Optionally, the list of all tables can be reduced to those matching the search pattern *pattern* (where the SQL wild cards % and _ are allowed). More information on the construction of individual tables can be obtained with *DESCRIBE TABLE* and *SHOW COLUMNS*. The list of tables can also be retrieved with the external program mysqlshow.

SHOW [options] VARIABLES [LIKE pattern]

This command returns a seemingly endless list of all system variables defined by MySQL together with their values (e.g., *ansi_mode, sort_buffer, tmpdir, wait_timeout*, to name but a very few). To limit the list, a pattern can be given (e.g., *LIKE 'char%'*).

Many of these variables can be set at launch of MySQL or afterwards with *SET*. The list of variables can also be recovered with the external command mysqladmin.

> *options*: Here you can specify *GLOBAL* or *SESSION*. *GLOBAL* has the effect that the default values valid at the global level are displayed. *SESSION*, on the other hand, results in the values being displayed that are valid for the current connection. The default is *SESSION*.

> An extensive description of the variables can be found in the MySQL documentation: http:// dev.mysql.com/doc/mysql/en/server-system-variables.html.

SHOW [COUNT(*)] WARNINGS [LIMIT [offset,] count]

Since MySQL 4.1, this command returns a list of all warnings that arose from the execution of the most recent command.

SLAVE START/STOP [IO_THREAD | SQL_THREAD]

These commands start and stop replication (we leave it to the reader to determine which is which). They can be executed only on the slave computer of a replication system.

By default, two threads are started for replication: the IO thread (copies the binary logging data from the master to the slave) and the SQL thread (executes the logging file's SQL command). With the optional specification of *IO_THREAD* or *SQL_THREAD*, these two threads can be started or stopped independently (which makes sense only for debugging).

START TRANSACTION

If you are working with transaction-capable tables (InnoDB), *START TRANSACTION* initiates a new transaction. The command is ANSI-99 conforming, but it has been available only since MySQL 4.0.11. In older versions, you must use the equivalent command *BEGIN*.

TRUNCATE TABLE tablename

TRUNCATE has the same functionality as *DELETE* without a *WHERE* condition; that is, the effect is that all records in the table are deleted. This is accomplished by deleting the entire table and then re-creating it. (This is considerably faster than deleting each record individually.)

TRUNCATE cannot be part of a transaction. *TRUNCATE* functions like *COMMIT*; that is, all pending changes are first executed. *TRUNCATE* can also be undone with *ROLLBACK*.

UNION see also SELECT UNION

With *UNION*, you can assemble the results of several *SELECT* queries.

UNLOCK TABLES

UNLOCK TABLES removes all of the user's *LOCK*s. This command holds for all databases (that is, it doesn't matter which database is the current one).

```
UPDATE [updateoptions] tablename SET col1=value1, col2=value2 ..
  [ WHERE condition ]
  [ ORDER BY columns ]
  [ LIMIT maxrecords ]
```

UPDATE changes individual fields of the table records specified by *WHERE*. Those fields not specified by *SET* remain unchanged. In *value* one can refer to existing fields. For example, an *UPDATE* command may be of the following form:

```
UPDATE products SET price = price + 5 WHERE productID=3
```

Warning: Without a *WHERE* condition, all data records in the table will be changed. (In the above example, the prices of all products would be increased by 5.)

updateoptions: Here the options *LOW PRIORITY* and *IGNORE* may be given. The effect is the same as with *INSERT*.

condition: This condition specifies which records are affected by the change. For the syntax of *condition* see *SELECT*.

columns: With *ORDER BY*, you can sort the record list before making changes. This makes sense only in combination with *LIMIT*, for example, to change the first or last ten records (ordered according to some criterion). This possibility has existed since MySQL 4.0.

maxrecords: With *LIMIT*, the maximum number of records that may be changed is specified.

```
UPDATE [updateoptions] table1, table2, table3
  SET table1.col1=table2.col2 ...
  [ WHERE condition ] [ ORDER BY columns ] [ LIMIT maxrecords ]
```

Since MySQL 4.0, *UPDATE* commands can include more than one table. All tables included in the query must be specified after *UPDATE*. The only tables that are changed are those whose fields were specified by *SET*. The link between the tables must be set with *WHERE* conditions.

USE databasename

USE turns the specified database into the default database for the current connection to MySQL. Until the end of the connection (or until the next *USE* command), all table names are automatically assigned to the database *databasename*.

Function Reference

The functions described here can be used in *SELECT* queries as well as in other SQL commands. We begin with a few examples. In our first example, we shall join two table columns with *CONCAT* to create a new character string. In the second example, the function *PASSWORD* will be used to store an encrypted password in a column. In the third example, the function *DATE_FORMAT* will be summoned to help us format a date:

```
SELECT CONCAT(firstname, ' ', lastname) FROM users
    Peter Smith
    ...
INSERT INTO logins (username, userpassword)
VALUES ('smith', PASSWORD('xxx'))
SELECT DATE_FORMAT(a_date, '%Y %M %e')
FROM exceptions.test_date
    2005 December 7
```

■**Tip** This section aims to provide only a compact overview of the functions available. Extensive information on these functions can be found in the MySQL documentation. Some of these functions have been introduced at various places in this book by way of example. See the Index for page numbers.

Arithmetic Functions

Arithmetic Functions	
ABS(x)	Calculates the absolute value (nonnegative number).
ACOS(x), *ASIN(x)*	Calculates the arcsin and arccos.
ATAN(x), *ATAN2(x, y)*	Calculates the arctangent.
CEILING(x)	Rounds up to the least integer greater than or equal to *x*.
COS(x)	Calculates the cosine; *x* is given in radians.
COT(x)	Calculates the cotangent.
DEGREES(x)	Converts radians to degrees (multiplication by 180/pi).
EXP(x)	Returns e^x.
FLOOR(x)	Rounds down to the greatest integer less than or equal to *x*.
LOG(x)	Returns the natural logarithm (i.e., to base *e*).
LOG10(x)&	Returns the logarithm to base 10.
MOD(x, y)	Returns the mod function, equivalent to *x* % *y*.
PI( )	Returns 3.1415927.
POW(x, y)	Returns x^y.
POWER(x, y)	Equivalent to *POW(x, y)*.
RADIANS(x)	Converts degrees into radians (multiplication by Pi/180).
RAND( )	Returns a random number between 0.0 and 1.0.
RAND(n)	Returns a reproducible (thus not quite random) number.
ROUND(x)	Rounds to the nearest integer.
ROUND(x, y)	Rounds to *y* decimal places.
SIGN(x)	Returns -1, 0, or 1 depending on the sign of *x*.

Arithmetic Functions

SIN(x)	Calculates the sine.
SQRT(x)	Calculates the square root.
TAN(x)	Calculates the tangent.
TRUNCATE(x)	Removes digits after the decimal point.
TRUNCATE(x, y)	Retains *y* digits after the decimal point (thus T*RUNCATE(1.236439, 2)* returns 1.23).

In general, all functions return *NULL* if provided with invalid parameters (e.g., *SQRT(-1)*).

Comparison Functions, Tests, Branching

Comparison Functions

COALESCE(x, y, z, …)	Returns the first parameter that is not *NULL*.
GREATEST(x, y, z, …)	Returns the greatest value or greatest character string.
IF(expr, val1, val2)	Returns *val1* if *expr* is true; otherwise, *val2*.
IFNULL(expr1, expr2)	Returns *expr2* if *expr1* is *NULL*; otherwise, *expr1*.
INTERVAL(x, n1, n2, …)	Returns 0 if *x<n1*; 1 if *x< n2*, etc.; all parameters must be integers, and *n1 < n2 < …* must hold.
ISNULL(x)	Returns 1 or 0, according to whether *x IS NULL* holds.
LEAST(x, y, z, …)	Returns the smallest value or smallest character string.
STRCMP(s1, s2)	Returns 0 if *s1=s2* in sort order, -1 if *s1<s2*, 1 if *s1>s2*. Since MySQL 4.0 the function takes into account the valid character set. By default the function no longer distinguished uppercase and lowercase (which is different from MySQL 3.32).

Tests, Branching

IF(expr, result1, result2)	Returns *result1* if *expr* is true; otherwise, *result2*.
CASE expr	Returns *result1* if *expr=val1*, returns *result2* if *expr=val2*.
WHEN val1 THEN result1 *WHEN val2 THEN result2* *ELSE resultn.*	If no condition is satisfied, then the result is *resultn*.
CASE *WHEN cond1 THEN result1* *WHEN cond2 THEN result2* *ELSE resultn* *END*	Returns *result1* if condition *cond1* is true, etc.

Type Conversion (Cast)

Type Conversion

CAST(x AS type)	Changes *x* into the specified type. *CAST* works with the following types: *BINARY, CHAR, DATE, DATETIME, SIGNED [INTEGER], TIME,* and *UNSIGNED [INTEGER]*.
CONVERT(x, type)	Equivalent to *CAST(x AS type)*.
CONVERT(s USING cs)	Represents the string *s* in the character set *cs* (since MySQL 4.1).

String Processing

Most character string functions can also be used for processing binary data. Since MySQL 4.1 (with Unicode support), the position and length specification functions such as *LEFT* and *MID* apply to characters, not bytes. MID*(column, 3, 1)* thus returns the third character, regardless of the character set that is defined for *column*.

Processing Character Strings

CHAR_LENGTH(s)	Returns the number of characters in *s*; *CHAR_LENGTH* works also for multibyte character sets (e.g., Unicode).
CONCAT(s1, s2, s3, ...)	Concatenates the strings.
CONCAT_WS(x, s1, s2,...)	Functions like *CONCAT*, except that *x* is inserted between each string; *CONCAT_WS(', ', 'a', 'b', 'c')* returns *'a, b, c'*.
ELT(n, s1, s2, ...)	Returns the *n*th string; *ELT(2, 'a', 'b', 'c')* returns *'b'*.
EXPORT_SET(x, s1, s2)	Creates a string from *s1* and *s2* based on the bit coding of *x*; *x* is interpreted as a 64-bit integer.
FIELD(s, s1, s2, ...)	Compares *s* with strings *s1, s2* and returns the index of the first matching string; *FIELD('b', 'a', 'b', 'c')* returns 2.
FIND_IN_SET(s1, s2)	Searches for *s1* in *s2*; *s2* contains a comma-separated list of strings; *FIND_IN_SET('b', 'a,b,c')* returns 2.
INSERT(s1, pos, 0, s2)	Inserts *s2* into position *pos* in *s1*; *INSERT('ABCDEF', 3, 0, 'abc')* returns *'ABabcDEF'*.
INSERT(s1, pos, len, s2)	Inserts *s2* at position *pos* in *s1* and replaces *len* characters of *s2* with the new characters; *INSERT('ABCDEF', 3, 2, 'abc')* returns *'ABabcEF'*.
INSTR(s, sub)	Returns the position of *sub* in *s*; *INSTR('abcde', 'bc')* returns 2.
LCASE(s)	Changes uppercase characters to lowercase.
LEFT(s, n)	Returns the first *n* characters of *s*.
LENGTH(s)	Returns the number of bytes necessary to store the string *s*; if multibyte character sets are used (e.g., Unicode), then *CHAR_LENGTH* must be used to determine the number of characters.
LOCATE(sub, s)	Returns the position of *sub* in *s*; *LOCATE('bc', 'abcde')* returns 2.
LOCATE(sub, s, n)	As above, but the search for *sub* begins only at the *n*th character of *s*.
LOWER(s)	Transforms uppercase characters to lowercase.
LPAD(s, len, fill)	Inserts the fill character *fill* into *s*, so that *s* ends up with length *len*; *LPAD('ab', 5, '*')* returns *'***ab'*.
LTRIM(s)	Removes spaces at the beginning of *s*.
MAKE_SET(x, s1, s2 ...)	Forms a new string in which all strings *sn* appear for which in *x* the bit *n* is set; *MAKE_SET(1+2+8, 'a', b', 'c', 'd')* returns *'a,b,d'*.
MID(s, pos, len)	Reads *len* characters from position *pos* from the string *s*; *MID('abcde', 3, 2)* returns *'cd'*.
POSITION(sub IN s)	Equivalent to *LOCATE(sub, s)*.
QUOTE(s)	Since MySQL 4.0, returns a string suitable for SQL commands; special characters such as ', ", \ are prefixed with a backspace.
REPEAT(s, n)	Joins *s* to itself *n* times; *REPEAT('ab', 3)* returns *'ababab'*.
REPLACE(s, fnd, rpl)	Replaces in *s* all *fnd* strings by *rpl*; *REPLACE('abcde', 'b', 'xy')* returns *'axycde'*.
REVERSE(s)	Reverses the string.
RIGHT(s, n)	Returns the last *n* characters of *s*.

Processing Character Strings

RPAD(s, len, fill)	Inserts the fill character *fill* at the end of *s*, so that *s* has length *len*; *RPAD('ab', 5, '*')* returns *'ab***'*.
RTRIM(s)	Removes spaces from the end of *s*.
SPACE(n)	Returns *n* space characters.
SUBSTRING(s, pos)	Returns the right part of *s* from position *pos*.
SUBSTRING(s, pos, len)	As above, but only *len* characters (equivalent to *MID(s, pos, len)*).
SUBSTRING_INDEX(s, f, n)	Searches for the *n*th appearance of *f* in *s* and returns the left part of the string up to this position (exclusive); for negative *n*, the search begins at the end of the string, and the right part of the string is returned; *SUBSTRING_INDEX('abcabc', 'b', 2)* returns *'abca'* *SUBSTRING_INDEX('abcabc', 'b', -2)* returns *'cabc'*
TRIM(s)	Removes spaces from the beginning and end of *s*.
TRIM(f FROM s)	Removes the character *f* from the beginning and end of *s*.
UCASE(s) / UPPER(s)	Transforms lowercase characters to uppercase.

Converting Numbers and Character Strings

ASCII(s)	Returns the byte code of the first character of *s*: thus *ASCII('A')* returns 65; see also *ORD*.
BIN(x)	Returns the binary code of *x*; *BIN(12)* returns *'1010'*.
CHAR(x, y, z, ...)	Returns the string formed from the code *x, y, ...*; *CHAR(65, 66)* returns *'AB'*.
CHARSET(s)	Since MySQL 4.1, returns the name of the character set in which *s* is represented.
CONV(x, from, to)	Transforms *x* from number base *from* to base *to*; *CONV(25, 10, 16)* returns the hexadecimal *'19'*.
CONVERT(s USING cs)	Since MySQL 4.1, represents the string *s* in the character set *cs*.
FORMAT(x, n)	Formats *x* with commas for thousands separation and *n* decimal places; *FORMAT(12345.678, 2)* returns *'12,345.68'*.
HEX(x)	Returns the hexadecimal code for *x*; *x* can be a 64-bit integer or (since MySQL 4.0) a character string; in the second case, each character is transformed into an 8-bit hex code; *HEX('abc')* returns *'414243'*.
INET_NTOA(n)	Transforms *n* into an IP address with at least four groups; *INET_NTOA(1852797041)* returns *'110.111.112.113'* *INET_ATON(ipadr)* transforms an IP address into the corresponding 32- or 64-bit integer; *INET_ATON('110.111.112.113')* returns 1852797041.
OCT(x)	Returns the octal code of *x*.
ORD(s)	Like *ASCII(s)*, returns the code of the first character, but functions also for multibyte character sets.
SOUNDEX(s)	Returns a string that should match similar-sounding English words; *SOUNDEX('hat')* and *SOUNDEX('head')* both return *'H300'*; extensive information on the SOUNDEX algorithm can be found in the book *SQL for Smarties* by Joe Celko.

Encryption of Character Strings and Password Management

AES_DECRYPT(crypt, key)	Decrypts *crypt* with the AES algorithm (Rijndael) and uses *key* for decryption.
AES_ENCRYPT(str, key)	Encrypts *str* using *key* for encryption.
DES_ENCRYPT(str [, keyno | keystr])	Encrypts *str* using the DES algorithm; available since MySQL 4.0 and only when MySQL is compiled with SSL functions; without the optional second parameter, the first key from the DES key file is used for encryption; optionally, the number or name of the key can be specified.
DES_DECRYPT(crypt [, keyno | keystr])	Decrypts *crypt* using the DES algorithm.
DECODE(crypt, pw)	Decrypts *crypt* using the password *pw*.
ENCODE(str, pw)	Encrypts *str* using *pw* as password; the result is a binary object that can be decrypted with *DECODE*.
ENCRYPT(pw)	Encrypts the password with the UNIX *crypt* function; if this function is unavailable, returns *ENCRYPT NULL*.
PASSWORD(pw)	Encrypts the password with the algorithm that was used for storing passwords in the *USER* table; the result is a 16-character string; note that since MySQL 4.1, *PASSWORD* uses stronger encryption and returns a string of 45 characters.
OLD_PASSWORD(pw)	Encrypts the password as for *PASSWORD* under MySQL 3.23.*n* and 4.0.*n*; available since MySQL 4.1.

Calculation of Check Sums

CRC32(s)	Since MySQL 4.1, computes a check (cyclic redundancy check value) for the string *s*.
MD5(str)	Computes the MD5 check sum for the string *str*.
SHA(str), SHA1(str)	Since MySQL 4.0, computes a 160-bit check sum using the SHA1 algorithm (defined in RFC 3174). SHA is considered more secure than MD5. The result is returned as a string containing a 40-digit hexadecimal code; SHA and SHA1 are synonyms.

Date and Time

Some of the following functions have been available only since MySQL 4.0 or 4.1.

Determining the Current Time

CURDATE()	Returns the current date, e.g., *'2005-12-31'*. Synonym: *CURRENT_DATE()*
CURTIME()	Returns the current time as a string or an integer, depending on the context, e.g., *'23:59:59'* or *235959* (integer). Synonym: *CURRENT_TIME()*
NOW()	Returns the current time in the form *'2005-12-31 23:59:59'*. Synonyms: *CURRENT_TIMESTAMP()*, *LOCALTIME()*, *LOCALTIME-STAMP()*, *SYSDATE()*
UNIX_TIMESTAMP()	Returns the current system time as a Unix timestamp (32-bit integer).
UTC_DATE()	Returns the date in Coordinated Universal Time.
UTC_TIME()	Returns the time in Coordinated Universal Time.
UTC_DATETIME()	Returns the date and time in Coordinated Universal Time.

Calculating, Formatting, and Transformation Functions

ADDDATE(d, n)	Adds *n* days to the starting time *d*.
ADDDATE(...)	Adds a time interval to the starting time *d* (see below). Synonym: *DATE_ADD()*
ADDTIME(d, t)	Adds the time *t* (*TIME*) to the starting time *d* (*DATETIME*).
CONVERT_TZ(d, tz1, tz2)	Converts the time *d* from the time zone *tz1* into the time zone *tz2*. The syntax for the given time zone depends on the operating system. Under Windows the time difference from UTC must be given (e.g., '+2:00'), while under Linux, after a configuration, you may use the name of the time zone (e.g., 'America/New_York'; see Chapter 10).
DATE(d)	Returns only the date portion of a *DATETIME* expression. (That is, the function removes the time portion.)
DATEDIFF(d1, d2)	Returns the number of days between *d1* and *d2*. The time portion is ignored in the calculation.
DATE_FORMAT(d, form)	Formats *d* according to formatting string *f*; see below.
DAYNAME(date)	Returns 'Monday', 'Tuesday', etc.
DAYOFMONTH(date)	Returns the day of the month (1 to 31).
DAYOFWEEK(date)	Returns the day of the week (1 = Sunday through 7 = Saturday).
DAYOFYEAR(date)	Returns the day in the year (1 to 366).
EXTRACT(i FROM date)	Returns a number for the desired interval.
EXTRACT(YEAR FROM '2003-12-31')	Returns 2003.
FROM_DAYS(n)	Returns the date *n* days after the year 0.
FROM_DAYS(3660)	Returns '0010-01-08'.
FROM_UNIXTIME(t)	Transforms the Unix timestamp number *t* into a date.
FROM_UNIXTIME(0)	Returns '1970-01-01 01:00:00'.
FROM_UNIXTIME(t, f)	As above, but with formatting as in *DATE_FORMAT*.
GET_FORMAT(...)	Returns predefined formatting code for *DATE_FORMAT* (see the table further below).
HOUR(time)	Returns the hour (0 to 23).
LAST_DAY(d)	Returns the last day of the month specified by the date *d*. *LAST_DAY('2005-02-01')* returns '2005-02-28'.
MAKEDATE(y, dayofyear)	Creates a *DATE* expression from the input of year and day.
MAKETIME(h, m, s)	Creates a *TIME* expression from the input for hours, minutes, and seconds.
MICROSECOND(d)	Returns the number of microseconds (0 to 999999).
MINUTE(time)	Returns the minute (0 to 59).
MONTH(date)	Returns the month (1 to 12).
MONTHNAME(date)	Returns the name of the month ('January', etc.).
PERIOD_ADD(s, n)	Adds *n* months to the start date, which must be specified in the form 'YYYYMM' (e.g., '200512' for December 2005).
PERIOD_DIFF(s, e)	Returns the number of months between the start and end dates. Both times must be given in the form 'YYYYMM'.
QUARTER(date)	Returns the quarter (1 to 4).

Continued

Calculating, Formatting, and Transformation Functions *(Continued)*

SECOND(time)	Returns the second (0 to 59).
SEC_TO_TIME(n)	Returns the time *n* seconds after midnight.
SEC_TO_TIME(3603)	Returns *'01:00:03'*.
STR_TO_DATE(s, form)	Interprets the string *s* according to the formatting code in *form*. *STR_TO_DATE* is the inverse function of *DATE_FORMAT*.
SUBDATE(d, n)	Subtracts *n* days from the starting time *d*.
SUBDATE(d,)	Subtracts a time interval from the starting time *d* (see below). Synonym: *DATE_ADD()*
SUBTIME(d, t)	Subtracts the time *t* (*TIME*) from the starting time *d* (*DATETIME*).
TIMESTAMP(s)	Returns the starting time given in the string as a *TIMESTAMP* value. TIMESTAMP('2005-12-31') returns '2005-12-31 00:00:00'.
TIMESTAMP(s, time)	Returns *s* + *time* as a *TIMESTAMP* value.
TIMESTAMPADD(i, n, s)	Adds *n* times the interval *i* (e.g., *MONTH*) to the starting time *s*.
TIMESTAMPDIFF(i, s, e)	Returns the number of intervals *i* between the start time *s* and the end time *e*. *TIMESTAMPDIFF(HOUR, '2005-12-31', '2006-01-01')* returns 24.
TIME_FORMAT(time, f)	Like *DATE_FORMAT*, but for times only. *TIME_TO_SEC(time)* returns the number of seconds since midnight.
TO_DAYS(date)	Returns the number of days since the year 0.
UNIX_TIMESTAMP(d)	Returns the timestamp number for the given date.
WEEK(date)	Returns the week number (1 for the week beginning with the first Sunday in the year).
WEEK(date, mode)	Returns the week number (0 to 53 or 1 to 53). The parameter *mode* determines the first day of the week and how a week is defined. For example, *mode=0* means that weeks begin on Sunday and that 1 is the first week in the new year. If *mode* is not specified, the server default setting holds (*default_week_format* in my.cnf/my.ini). A description of modes can be found at http://dev.mysql.com/doc/mysql/en/date-and-time-functions.html.
WEEKDAY(date)	Returns the day of the week (0 = Monday, 1 = Tuesday, etc.).
WEEKOFYEAR(date)	Returns the calendar week (1 to 53).
YEAR(date)	Returns the year.
YEARWEEK(date, mode)	Returns an integer or string, depending on context, that consists of the year number and week number. *mode* is set as in *WEEK*. *YEARWEEK('2005-12-31')* returns *200552*.

The functions for dates and times generally assume that the initial data are valid. Do not expect a sensible return value for input such as *'2005-02-31'*.

With all functions that return a time or a date (or both), the format of the result depends on the context. Normally, the result is a character string (e.g., *'2005-12-31 23:59:59'*). However, if the function is used within a numeric calculation, for example *NOW()+0*, then the result is an integer of the form *20051231235959*.

Intervals with *ADDDATE, SUBDATE, EXTRACT, TIMESTAMPADD*, etc.

ADDDATE (date, INTERVAL n i) adds *n* times the interval *i* to the starting date *date*. The permitted interval names are collected in the table following some examples. The third example shows how intelligently the function deals with ends of months (31.12 or 28.2):

ADDDATE('2005-12-31', INTERVAL 3 DAY) returns *'2006-01-03'.*

ADDDATE('2005-12-31', INTERVAL '3:30' HOUR_MINUTE) returns *'2005-12-31 03:30:00'.*

ADDDATE ('2005-12-31', INTERVAL 2 month) returns '2006-02-28'.

SUBDATE is like *ADDDATE*, but it subtracts the given interval *n* times.

EXTRACT extracts the given interval from the time: *EXTRACT(MONTH FROM '2005-12-31')* returns 12.

TIMESTAMPADD is like *ADDDATE*, but it uses a different syntax for specifying the interval: *TIMESTAMPADD(DAY, 5, '2005-12-31')* returns *'2006-01-05'.*

TIMESTAMPDIFF returns the difference between two times as a multiple of the given interval: *TIMESTAMPDIFF(DAY, '2005-12-31', '2006-02-15')* returns 46.

Intervals for ADDDATE, SUBDATE, EXTRACT, TIMESTAMPADD

MICROSECOND	*n*
SECOND	*n*
MINUTE	*n*
HOUR	*n*
DAY	*n*
MONTH	*n*
YEAR	*n*
SECOND_MICROSECOND	*'ss.mmmmmm'*
MINUTE_SECOND	*'mm:ss'*
HOUR_MINUTE	*'hh:mm'*
HOUR_SECOND	*'hh:mm:ss'*
DAY_HOUR	*'dd hh'*
DAY_MINUTE	*'dd hh:mm'*
DAY_SECOND	*'dd hh:mm:ss'*
YEAR_MONTH	*'yy-mm'*

Formatting Dates and Times

DATE_FORMAT(date, format) helps in representing dates and times in other formats than the usual MySQL format. Two examples illustrate the syntax:

DATE_FORMAT('2003-12-31', '%M %d %Y') returns *'December 31 2003'.*

DATE_FORMAT('2003-12-31', '%D of %M') returns *'31st of December'.*

Names of days of the week, months, etc., are always given in English, regardless of the MySQL language setting (*language* option).

STR_TO_DATE is the inverse function to *DATE_FORMAT*: *SELECT STR_TO_DATE('December 31 2005', '%M %d %Y')* returns *'2005-12-31'.*

Date Symbols in DATE_FORMAT, TIME_FORMAT, and FROM_UNIXTIME

%W	day of week	*Monday* to *Sunday*
%a	day of week abbreviated	*Mon* to *Sun*
%e	day of month	*1* to *31*
%d	day of month two-digit	*01* to *31*
%D	day of month with ending	*1st, 2nd, 3rd, 4th, …*
%w	day of week as number	*0* (*Sunday*) to *6* (*Saturday*)
%j	day in year, three-digit	*001* to *366*
%U	week number, two-digit (Sunday)	*00* to *52*
%u	week number, two-digit (Monday)	*00* to *52*
%M	name of month	*January* to *December*
%b	name of month abbreviated	*Jan* to *Dec*
%c	month number	*1* to *i*
%m	month number, two-digit	*01* to *12*
%Y	year, four-digit	*2002, 2003, …*
%y	year, two-digit	*00, 01, …*
%%	the symbol %	*%*

A few remarks about the week number are in order: *%U* returns 0 for the days from before the first Sunday in the year. From the first Sunday until the following Saturday, it returns 1, then 2, etc. With *%u* you get the same thing, with the first Sunday replaced by the first Monday.

Time Symbols in DATE_FORMAT, TIME_FORMAT, and FROM_UNIXTIME

%f	microseconds	000000 to 99999
%S or %s	seconds, two-digit	00 to 59
%i	minutes, two-digit	00 to 59
%k	hours (24-hour clock)	0 to 23
%H	hours, two-digit, 0 to 23 o'clock	00 to 23
%l	hours (12-hour clock)	1 to 12
%h or %I	hours, two-digit, to 12 o'clock	01 to 12
%T	24-hour clock	00:00:00 to 23:59:59
%r	12-hour clock	12:00:00 AM to 11:59:59 PM
%p	AM or PM	AM, PM

In order to avoid having to re-create frequently used formatting strings, since MySQL 4.1 you can get help from the function *GET_FORMAT.*

```
SELECT DATE_FORMAT(NOW(), GET_FORMAT(DATE, 'EUR'))
   31.12.2005
```

The following table summarizes the results of these functions and gives examples of the resulting formatting of dates and times.

GET_FORMAT Formatting Codes

GET_FORMAT(DATE, 'USA')	*'%m.%d.%Y'*	*12.31.2005*
GET_FORMAT(DATE, 'EUR')	*'%d.%m.%Y'*	*31.12.2005*
GET_FORMAT(DATE, 'ISO')	*'%Y-%m-%d'*	*2005-12-31*
GET_FORMAT(DATE, 'JIS')	*'%Y-%m-%d'*	*2005-12-31*
GET_FORMAT(DATE, 'INTERNAL')	*'%Y%m%d'*	*20051231*
GET_FORMAT(TIME, 'USA')	*'%h:%i:%s %p'*	*11:59:59 PM*
GET_FORMAT(TIME, 'EUR')	*'%H:%i:%s'*	*23:59:59*
GET_FORMAT(TIME, 'ISO')	*'%H:%i:%s'*	*23:59:59*
GET_FORMAT(TIME, 'JIS')	*'%H:%i:%s'*	*23:59:59*
GET_FORMAT(TIME, 'INTERNAL')	*'%H%i%s'*	*235959*
GET_FORMAT(DATETIME, 'USA')	*'%h:%i:%s %p %h:%i:%s %p'*	
GET_FORMAT(DATETIME, 'EUR')	*'%H:%i:%s %H:%i:%s'*	
GET_FORMAT(DATETIME, 'ISO')	*'%H:%i:%s %H:%i:%s'*	
GET_FORMAT(DATETIME, 'JIS')	*'%H:%i:%s %H:%i:%s'*	
GET_FORMAT(DATETIME, 'INTERNAL')	*'%H%i%s%H%i%s'*	

GROUP BY Functions

The following functions can be used in *SELECT* queries (frequently in combination with *GROUP BY*):

```
USE mylibrary
SELECT catName, COUNT(titleID) FROM titles, categories
WHERE titles.catID=categories.catID
GROUP BY catName
ORDER BY catName
catName                 COUNT(titleID)
Children's books            3
Computer books              5
Databases                   2
...
```

Since MySQL 4.1, the desired sort order can be specified in some aggregate functions, as in MAX(*column COLLATE collname*).

Aggregate Functions

AVG(expr)	Computes the average of *expr*.
BIT_AND(expr)	Performs a bitwise AND of *expr*.
BIT_OR(expr)	Performs a bitwise OR of *expr*.
BIT_XOR(expr)	Performs a bitwise XOR of *expr*.
COUNT(expr)	Returns the number of expressions *expr*.
COUNT(DISTINCT expr)	Returns the number of different *expr* expressions.
GROUP_CONCAT(expr)	Concatenates the strings (since MySQL 4.1). Here is the complete syntax for *expr*: *[DISTINCT] expr1, expr2 ... [ORDER BY column [DESC]] [SEPARATOR '...']*. *ORDER BY* sorts the strings before concatenating them. *SEPARATOR* specifies the separator character (by default a comma). Examples of *GROUP_CONCAT* can be found in Chapter 9.

Continued

Aggregate Functions *(Continued)*

MAX(expr)	Returns the maximum of *expr*.
MIN(expr)	Returns the minimum of *expr*.
STD(expr)	Computes the standard deviation of *expr*.
STDDEV(expr)	Like *STD(expr)*.
SUM(expr)	Computes the sum of *expr*.
VARIANCE(expr)	Computes the variance of *expr* (since MySQL 4.1).

Additional Functions

Miscellaneous

BIT_COUNT(x)	Returns the number of set bits.
COALESCE(list)	Returns the first element of the list that is not *NULL*.
LOAD_FILE(filename)	Loads a file from the local file system.

Administrative Functions

BENCHMARK(n, expr)	Executes *expr* a total of *n* times and measures the time elapsed.
CONNECTION_ID( )	Returns the ID number of the current database connection.
CURRENT_USER( )	Returns the name of the current user in the form in which authentication takes place (that is, with the IP number instead of the host name, e.g., *"radha@127.0.0.1"*).
DATABASE( )	Returns the name of the current database.
FOUND_ROWS( )	Returns since MySQL 4.0 the number of records found by a *SELECT LIMIT* query if in the *SELECT* command, the option *SQL_CALC_FOUND_ROWS* was used.
GET_LOCK(name, time)	Defines a lock with the name *name* for the time *time* (in seconds); see also Chapter 10.
IDENTITY( )	Since MySQL 4.0 equivalent to *LAST_INSERT_ID( )*.
IS_FREE_LOCK(name)	Tests whether the lock *name* is available; returns 0 if the lock is currently in use (thus before *GET_LOCK* was executed), otherwise, 1.
LAST_INSERT_ID( )	Returns the *AUTO_INCREMENT* number most recently generated within the current connection to the database.
RELEASE_LOCK(name)	Releases the lock *name*.
SESSION_USER( )	Equivalent to *USER( )*.
SYSTEM_USER( )	Equivalent to *USER( )*.
USER( )	Returns the name of the current user and associated host name (e.g., *"root@localhost"*).
VERSION( )	Returns the MySQL version number as a string.

GIS Data Types and Functions

The GIS data types and functions described here have been available since MySQL 4.1. The GIS data types collected in the following table can be used in the declaration of a table column (such as *INT* or *VARCHAR*). At present, these data types can be used only in MyISAM tables, and not in InnoDB tables. Optionally, geometric columns can be equipped with a *SPATIAL INDEX*, which is independent of the GIS data type used.

GIS Data Types	
GEOMETRY	Can accept any of the following data types.
POINT	Stores a single point. Example: *POINT(10 10)*.
MULTIPOINT	Stores a list of points. Example: *MULTIPOINT(10 10, 0 20, -3 2)*.
LINESTRING	Stores a line segment. Example: *LINESTRING(0 0, 1 1, 3 3)*.
MULTILINESTRING	Stores several line strings. Example: *MULTILINESTRING((0 0, 5 5), (10 10, 20 20, 40 20), (10 10, 2 0))*.
POLYGON	Stores a closed polygon, which is permitted to have holes. Example: *POLYGON((1 1, 9 1, 9 9, 1 9, 1 1), (3 3, 3 6, 6 6, 6 3, 3 3))*.
MULTIPOLYGON	Stores several polygons. Example: *MULTIPOLYGON(((0 0, 5 0, 5 5, 0 5, 0 0)), ((10, 10, 30 30, 30 10, 10 10)))*.
GEOMETRYCOLLECTION	Stores a list of arbitrary geometric objects. Example: *GEOMETRYCOLLECTION(POINT(100 100), POINT(10 10), LINESTRING (1 1, 100 1, 100 100))*.

Conversion Functions	
ASTEXT(geom)	Returns a geometric object as *well-known text*.
ASBINARY(geom)	Returns a geometric object as *well-known binary*.
GEOMFROMTEXT(txt [, srid])	Creates the MySQL-internal geometric format out of a *well-known text* (WKT) string. Optionally, an identifier for the coordinate system can be given, which is stored by MySQL but otherwise ignored.
GEOMFROMWKB(bindata)	Creates the MySQL-internal geometry format from binary data in WKB format.

General Geometric Functions (for All GIS Data Types)	
DIMENSION(g)	Returns the dimension of the object. Possible results are: 1 for empty objects, 0 for points (length = 0, area = 0), 1 for lines (length > 0, area = 0), 2 for polygons, etc. (length > 0, area > 0).
ENVELOPE(g)	Returns the bounding box of the geometric object (see below). The result has the data type *POLYGON*.
GEOMETRYTYPE(g)	Returns the type of the geometric object as a string: (*POINT, LINESTRING, POLYGON, …*).
SRID(g)	Returns the identifier of the coordinate system. (MySQL stores a coordinate system identifier for all geometric objects, but it does evaluate this information.)

POINT Functions

X(pt)	Returns the X coordinate.
Y(pt)	Returns the Y coordinate.

LINESTRING Functions (in Part Also MULTILINESTRING)

GLENGTH(ls)	Returns the length of the line as a floating-point number.
ISCLOSED(ls)	Returns 1 if the starting point is equal to the endpoint, otherwise 0.
NUMPOINTS(ls)	Returns the number of points that the line consists of.
STARTPOINT(ls)	Returns the first point (*POINT* object).
ENDPOINT(ls)	Returns the last point.
POINTN(ls, n)	Returns the *n*th point.

POLYGON Functions (in Part Also *MULTIPOLYGON*)

AREA(p)	Returns the area of the polygon as a floating-point number.
EXTERIORRING(p)	Returns the exterior ring of the polygon as a *LINESTRING* object.
INTERIORRINGN(p, n)	Returns the interior ring of the polygon as a *LINESTRING* object.
NUMINTERIORRINGS(p)	Returns the number of interior rings (holes).

GEOMETRYCOLLECTION Functions

GEOMETRYN(gc, n)	Returns the geometric object at location *n*.
NUMGEOMETRIES(gc)	Returns the number of objects in a collection.

The OpenGIS specification provides for the following analysis functions in two variants. The fast variant takes into account only the bounding box of the geometric object (*MBRname*, where *MBR* stands for *minimum bounding rectangle*). The precise variant, on the other hand, calculates with the complete geometric data (*name*). MySQL formally recognizes both variants, but internally they are identical, and only the bounding box is considered.

Analysis Functions for GIS Data Types

[MBR]CONTAINS(g1, g2)	Returns *TRUE*, if *g2* is completely contained in *g1*.
[MBR]WITHIN(g1, g2)	Returns *TRUE*, if *g1* is completely contained within *g2*. (*CONTAINS(a, b)* is equivalent to *WITHIN(b, a)*.)
[MBR]EQUAL(g1, g2)	Returns *TRUE* if *g1* and *g2* are equal.
[MBR]INTERSECTS(g1, g2)	Returns *TRUE* if *g1* and *g2* intersect.
[MBR]OVERLAPS(g1, g2)	Returns *TRUE* if *g1* and *g2* overlap.
[MBR]TOUCHES(g1, g2)	Returns *TRUE* if *g1* and *g2* touch each other.
[MBR]DISJOINT(g1, g2)	Returns *TRUE* if *g1* and *g2* neither overlap nor touch.

Language Elements for Stored Procedures and Triggers

You can place almost any SQL command or function described in this chapter in the code of a stored procedure or trigger. Furthermore, MySQL provides some additional language elements with which you can declare system variables and cursors, form loops and queries, and so on. The syntax of these language elements is summarized in the following tables.

Summary of Commands, Loops, and Queries

[blockname:] BEGIN
  DECLARE variables, cursors,
    conditions, handlers etc.; commands …;
END [blockname];
	BEGIN introduces a block of commands; *END* ends the block. First, variables, cursors, etc., can be declared within a block, followed by the SQL commands and additional language elements.

LEAVE blockname;	If the block has a name (*blockname*), then it can be exited early with *LEAVE*. Code execution is continued after *END blockname*.
RETURN result;	With functions, a result can be returned with *RETURN*. At the same time, code execution ends.

Queries

IF condition1 THEN
  commands …;
[ELSE IF condition2 THEN
  commands …;]
[ELSE
  commands …;]
END IF;
	IF/END IF creates a simple branch. Arbitrarily many *ELSE-IF* clauses are allowed, but only one terminating *ELSE* branch.

CASE expression
WHEN value1 THEN
  commands …;
[ELSE
  commands …;]
END CASE;
	CASE/END CASE helps to formulate case decisions with several variants in a more understandable manner. Arbitrarily many *WHEN* branches are allowed. (Each *CASE* can be formulated equivalently with *IF/END IF.*)

Loops

[loopname:] REPEAT *commands …;* *UNTIL condition* *END REPEAT [loopname];*	*REPEAT* loops are executed until the condition is satisfied (at least once).
[loopname:] WHILE condition DO *commands …;* *END WHILE [lpname];*	*WHILE* loops are executed while the condition is satisfied. If the condition is *FALSE* (0) before the first execution of the loop, the loop is not executed at all.
loopname: LOOP *commands …;* *END LOOP loopname;*	*LOOP/END LOOP* creates an infinite loop. It must be ended with *BREAK*.
LEAVE loopname;	Ends a loop prematurely.
ITERATE loopname;	Repeats the commands of the loop body one more time.

The following *DECLARE* instructions must be executed at the beginning of a code block and in the order given (that is, first variable declaration, then cursors, then conditions and handlers).

Variables, Cursors , Conditions, Handlers (DECLARE)	
DECLARE varname1, varname2, … datatype [DEFAULT value];	Declares the local variables *varname1, varname2,* etc. with a particular data type (e.g., *INT*). Optionally, a default value can be assigned. The variables can be used only within the block in which they are defined. Their names cannot coincide with those of a table or column.
DECLARE cursorname CURSOR FOR select-command;	Declares a cursor for step-by-step processing of the results of a *SELECT* command.
DECLARE name CONDITION FOR condition1, c2, c3 …;	Names one or more error conditions. There are several possibilities for specifying the error conditions: *SQLSTATE 'code'* *n* (MySQL error number) *SQLWARNING* *NOT FOUND* *SQLEXCEPTION*
*DECLARE CONTINUE	EXIT HANDLER FOR condition1, c2, c3 … command;*	Declares a handler for error-handling. With *CONTINUE* the code is simply continued, while with *EXIT* the current code block is exited. First, any *command* is executed. In addition to the above variants, for the error conditions a *CONDITION* is allowed.

The following table shows the application of a cursor.

Cursor Application	
DECLARE done INT DEFAULT 0;	Defines the variable for the handler.
DECLARE var1, var2 … datatype;	Declares the variables for the *SELECT* command.
DECLARE mycursor CURSOR FOR select command;	Declares the cursor.
DECLARE CONTINUE HANDLER FOR NOT FOUND SET done=1;	Declares a handler that becomes active after the last record is read.
OPEN mycursor;	Activates the cursor.
myloop: LOOP	
FETCH mycursor INTO var1, var2 …; *IF done=1 THEN LEAVE myloop; END IF;*	
END LOOP myloop;	Within the loop, reads the records of the *SELECT* command into the variables *var1, var2,* etc. If there are no further records, the handler assigns the value 1, and the loop is ended.
CLOSE mycursor;	Closes the cursor.

## CHAPTER 22

MySQL Tools and Options

This chapter is a reference for the options and functions of the most important MySQL tools. We discuss the server `mysqld`, the command interpreter `mysql`, and the administration tools `mysqladmin`, `myisamchk`, etc.

These tools have a number of common options, and they evaluate configuration files in the same manner. For this reason, the chapter begins with a section describing these common properties.

Overview

The common feature exhibited by the commands introduced in this section is that they are launched as external programs in a command window (Windows) or in a command shell (Unix/Linux). The entire operation of these programs is carried out in text mode and is therefore not what one would term excessively convenient. However, these commands are very well suited for execution in scripts in the automation of administrative tasks.

The following table provides an overview of the commands discussed in this section.

MySQL Server and Included Administrative Tools	
`mysqld`	Is the actual MySQL server. The program is usually not started directly, but under Windows as a system service, under Unix/Linux via an Init-V script with the help of `mysqld_safe`.
`mysqld_safe`	Should be used under Unix/Linux for a secure server launch.
`mysql`	Enables interactive execution of SQL commands.
`mysqladmin`	Assists in various administrative tasks (display status, reinput privileges, execute shutdown, etc.).
`mysqldump`	Saves contents of a MySQL database in a text file.
`mysqlimport`	Inputs data into a table from a text file.
`mysqlshow`	Displays information on databases, tables, and columns.
`myisamchk`	Checks the integrity of MyISAM table files and repairs them as necessary.
`myisampack`	Compresses MyISAM table files for more efficient read-only access.

Common Options and Configuration Files

A common feature of the programs described in this chapter is that there are certain options that can be used by almost all of the commands, and these options can be preset in a common configuration file, so as to save typing when the commands are invoked.

Common Options

Various options can be passed to all commands when they are executed. As is usual with Unix/Linux, commands can be prefixed with a hyphen (short form) or two hyphens (full option name). Please note that the short forms of options are case-sensitive.

Common Options of the MySQL Server (mysqld) and the MySQL Client Tools (mysql, mysqladmin, mysqldump, mysqlimport, etc.)

`--help`	Displays a brief operation introduction.
`--print-defaults`	Displays default values for options; default values can come from configuration files or system variables.
`--nodefaults`	Causes no configuration files to be read at startup.
`--defaults-file=filename`	Causes only this configuration file to be read at startup.
`--defaults-extra-file=filename`	First the global configuration file is read, and then `filename`, and finally (only under Unix/Linux), the user-specific configuration file.
`--port=n`	Specifies the TCP/IP port over which communication takes place (usually 3306).
`--socket=filename`	Specifies which socket file should be used for local communication between client and server (only under Unix/Linux; by default usually `/var/lib/mysql/mysql.sock`). If named pipes are used under Windows, then `socket` specifies the name of the named pipe (by default *MySQL*).
`--version`	Displays the version number of the program.

Common Options of the MySQL Client Tools

`-u un`	`--user=username`	Determines the user name for registration with MySQL.
`-p`	`--password`	Asks for input of password immediately after start of the command.
`-pxxx`	`--password=xxx`	Passes the password directly; in contrast to other options, there can be no space after `-p`; this is more convenient than interactive input of the password, but it represents a considerable security risk and thus should generally be avoided; under some operating systems, any user can see the password by looking at the process list.
`-h hn`	`--host=hostname`	Gives the name or IP number of the computer on which the server is running (assumed by default to be *localhost*, that is, the local computer).
	`--protocol=name`	Determines which protocol should be used for communication between client and server. Permissible settings are `tcp`, `socket`, `pipe`, and `memory`.
`-W`	`--pipe`	Uses a named pipe for communication with the MySQL server. Named pipes are available only for local connections under Windows 2000/XP if `my.ini` contains the option `enable-named-pipes`.
`-C`	`--compress`	Minimizes the data flow between client and server by making use of data compression.

Common Options of the MySQL Client Tools *(Continued)*	
`--default-character-set=name`	Specifies the character set for communication with the MySQL server (e.g., `latin1` or `utf8`).
`--character-sets-dir="dir"`	Specifies the directory in which the character set files are located (e.g., `"C:/Programs/MySQL/MySQL Server 5.0/share/charsets"`). This option is necessary only for the few character sets that were not precompiled into the client program.

For a connection to the MySQL server to be at all possible, the following two options must generally be used at the start of each client command:

```
> mysql -u username -p
Enter Password: xxxxxx
```

If MySQL is not yet password-secured, then this will work, of course, without a password being specified. Information on user and privilege management in MySQL can be found in Chapter 11.

■**Caution** If you execute MySQL commands under Windows and create a directory with options, then instead of the backslash you should use the forward slash (/). If the file name contains space characters, then put the entire path in quotation marks, as in the following example: `--basedir="C:/Programs/MySQL/MySQL Server 5.0/"`.

Setting Options in Configuration Files

If you observe that you are using particular options over and over, you can save these in options files for many of the commands covered in this section. The options are used by `mysql`, `mysqladmin`, `mysqld`, `mysqldump`, `mysqlimport`, `myisamchk`, `myisampack`, and `mysqld_safe`.

The following table collects the locations where the options files must be stored. At startup, all options files—those that exist already—are read in the order in which they are listed below. In the case of contradictory settings, the most recently read options file takes precedence. (Whether and what configuration files will be read depends on the options `--no-defaults`, `--defaults-file`, and `--defaults-extra-file`; see above.)

Validity	Windows	Unix/Linux
Global options	Current MySQL versions: `C:\Programs\MySQL\ MySQL Server n.n\my.ini` Old MySQL versions: `C:\my.cnf` or `Windows\ my.ini`	`/etc/my.cnf`
User-specific options (only for client programs)		`~/.my.cnf`
Server-specific options (only for `mysqld`)	`DATADIR\my.cnf`	`DATADIR/my.cnf`

The directory `DATADIR` is the default directory, which during compilation of MySQL is provided as data directory. Under Windows, this is normally `C:\mysql\data`, while under Unix/Linux, it is generally `/var/lib/mysql`. Note that `DATADIR` need not be the directory in which MySQL actually stores the database files. This directory is usually set when the MySQL server is launched with the option `--datadir`. However, access to the configuration file takes place before this option is evaluated.

The syntax of the file is based on the following pattern:

```
# Comment
[program name]
option1              # equivalent to: -option1
option2=abc          # equivalent to: --option2=abc
```

These options are divided into groups for each program. Instead of *program name*, you should specify the name of the program:

- Settings that are to be used by all programs other than mysqld are assigned to the group [client].

- Settings that relate only to the server are assigned to the group [mysqld]. (The group [server] is also used by mysqld.)

- Settings special to the program xyz are assigned to the group [xyz].

Here, *option* is the option name in long form, but without hyphens. (So, for example, the option —*host* in the configuration file becomes simply *host*.) If options expect parameters, then these are specified with =.

Let us see, finally, a concrete example of a configuration file:

```
# configuration file /etc/my.cnf (Unix/Linux) or my.ini (Windows)
# options for all MySQL tools
[client]
user=username
password=xxx
host=uranus.sol
# options for mysqldump
[mysqldump]
force
# options for mysql (command interpreter)
[mysql]
safe-updates
select_limit=100
```

■**Caution** Changes to configuration files are effective only after a restart of the program in question. This holds in particular for the MySQL server (thus for options in the group [mysqld]).

Please be sure that the options specified in the [client] section are truly supported by all MySQL tools. If a MySQL tool finds an unknown option in the [client] section, then the command is terminated with an error message.

If you wish under Unix/Linux to execute user-specific options settings in ~/.my.cnf and possibly specify passwords there, then ensure that no other users are able to read this file.

user$ **chmod 600 ~/.my.cnf**

If you specify Windows paths or directories in a configuration file, then you must use / or \\ instead of the backslash \. (In the Windows version of MySQL, the backslash is used as an escape character.)

Paths cannot be placed in quotation marks within a configuration file (even if the path contains space characters): basedir=C:/Programs/MySQL/MySQL Server 5.0/.

Please note that these rules are different from those that obtain a direct setting of options with --option =....

You can use the program my_print_defaults grp to determine the options set for [grp] in the configuration file. The program is particularly suited for use in custom scripts.

Memory Specifications

For options and variables that expect a memory specification, the letters K, M, and G may be used to denote kilobytes (1024 bytes), megabytes, and gigabytes. Thus the settings key_buffer_size=16M, key_buffer_size=16384K, and key_buffer_size=16777216 are equivalent.

Options in Environment Variables (aka System Variables)

An additional possibility for specifying options are environment variables at the level of the operating system. (Under Windows, these variables are usually known as system variables.)

The following table names the most important of these variables. To set such variables under Windows, you use the dialog for system control (see Figure 4-1). Under Linux you can define such variables in script files (e.g., in /etc/profile or ~/.profile) with export. Depending on which shell you use, you may use the command declare -x or setenv instead of export.

Import and Environment Variables for mysql, mysqladmin, mysqld, mysqldump	
MYSQL_TCP_PORT	Specifies the port number for the TCP/IP connection to MySQL (generally 3306).
MYSQL_UNIX_PORT	Specifies the socket file for local communication under Linux/Unix (e.g., /var/mysql.lock).
TMPDIR	Specifies the directory to be used for temporary files; this directory is also used for temporary tables.
USER	Specifies the user name.

Precedence

Option settings are read in the following order: environment variables, configuration files, options at program startup. In the case of contradictory settings, the last setting read takes precedence. For example, options at program startup supersede settings in environment variables.

Rules for Specifying Options

The following rules hold in the setting of options:

- A hyphen may replace an underscore in variable names (thus --variable-name=123 instead of --variable_name=123).

- Several forms are permitted for options that activate a particular function: A function is activated by --option, --option=1, --enable-option, and deactivated by --option=0, --disable-option, --skip-option.

  Note, however, that there are options like --skip-grant-tables for which skip is an integral part of the operator name. In this case, --enable-grant-tables and --grant-tables=0 do not function.

- There are MySQL server variables that can be changed by the user at run time specifically for the currently active connection. To do this, the user simply executes an SQL command like *SET read_buffer_size=16M*. For such variable names, an upper bound can be set at server start by prefixing --maximum, as in --maximum-read_buffer_size=32M.

- Every new version of MySQL offers new options. If you are writing a script and do not wish to prescribe a particular version of MySQL, you may use the new option --loose as a prefix (e.g., --loose-optionname=3). If the option exists, it will be properly set. On the other hand, if the program does not recognize the option, then the setting is ignored without an error message.

mysqld (Server)

The following lists, organized by topic, summarize the most-used mysqld options.

■**Tip** A complete reference to the long list of mysqld options can be obtained in mysqld --verbose --help. In the MySQL documentation there is unfortunately no unified description of all options. Instead, it is distributed among a number of sections (e.g., replication options, InnoDB options). The following addresses will lead you to the most important of these:

http://dev.mysql.com/doc/mysql/en/server-options.html

http://dev.mysql.com/doc/mysql/en/command-line-options.html

http://dev.mysql.com/doc/mysql/en/privileges-options.html

http://dev.mysql.com/doc/mysql/en/replication-options.html

http://dev.mysql.com/doc/mysql/en/innodb-start.html

The MySQL server is generally started as a service (Windows 2000/XP) or in an Init-V script via the script mysqld_safe (Unix/Linux). In such a case, it is impossible to specify options directly. Therefore, mysqld options are specified almost exclusively in configuration files. For this reason, in the following tables, the options are given in the manner in which they would appear in a configuration file (that is, without the prefixed --).

Two exceptions are the options --defaults-extra-file and --user:

- With --defaults-extra-file=filename, an additional configuration file can be specified that is read after all other configuration files.

- user=name specifies the Unix/Linux account under which mysqld is to be executed. For a change of account to take place at the start of MySQL, mysqld must be started by *root*. Normally, mysqld is started by the script mysqld_safe with --user =mysql.

Both options must be passed directly to mysqld or to the start script mysqld_safe. They cannot be specified in a configuration file.

Basic Settings

mysqld — Directories and Files	
basedir=path	Uses the given directory as base directory (installation directory).
character-sets-dir=path	Specifies the directory for the character set files.
datadir=path	Reads database files from the specified directory.
pid-file=filename	Specifies the file in which the process ID number should be stored (under Unix/Linux only); the file is evaluated by the Init-V script to terminate mysqld.
socket=filename	Specifies under Unix/Linux the file name mysql.sock generally /var/lib/mysql/mysql.sock. Under Windows, socket can be used to set the name of a named pipe (by default *MySQL*).
lower_case_table_names=1/0	Specifies whether in the creation of new directories and tables, lowercase should be used exclusively; under Windows the default setting is 1.

mysqld — Language Setting

character-set-server=name	Specifies the default character set for creating new databases and tables. The character set can also be set with the option default-character-set to ensure compatibility with older versions of MySQL. However, this option is considered deprecated.
collation-server=name	Specifies the default sort order for the creation of new databases and tables.
language=name	Specifies the language in which error messages, etc., are to be output.

mysqld — Communication, Network, Security

enable-named-pipes	Enables a connection under Windows 2000/XP between client and server with named pipes. The name of the named pipe is *MySQL* by default. It can be set with the option socket.
local-infile[=0]	Activates/deactivates the ability to process local files with *LOAD DATA LOCAL.*
myisam-recover[=opt1, opt2, ...]	Has the effect that at startup, all damaged MyISAM tables are automatically restored; the possible options are *DEFAULT, BACKUP, QUICK,* and *FORCE;* they correspond to the myisamchk options.
old-passwords	Passwords in the *mysql* database are encrypted as in MySQL 3.23 and 4.0 (by default, a new, more secure encryption is used since MySQL 4.1).
port=n	Specifies the port for TCP/IP communication (default is 3306).
safe-user-create	A user can create a new user with *GRANT* only if he has the *Insert* privilege for the table *mysql.user;* this is a supplementary security mechanism (the user also needs the *Grant* privilege to be able to execute *GRANT*).
shared-memory	Enables communication over *shared memory* (only under Windows).
shared_memory_base_name = name	Gives the *shared memory* storage block a name (by default *MYSQL*).
skip-grant-tables	Omits input of *mysql* database with access information; (caution: anyone can change any database).
skip-host-cache	A cache is not used to store the association between computer names and IP numbers.
skip-name-resolve	Suppresses the resolution of IP numbers into the corresponding host names, resulting in access control (table *mysql.user*) exclusively via IP numbers.
skip-networking	Permits only local connections over a socket file (Unix/Linux) or over named pipes and shared memory (Windows), not over TCP/IP; this increases security but excludes external connections over a network and excludes all Java clients (which use TCP/IP even in a local connection).
user=name	Specifies the Unix/Linux account under which mysqld is to be executed; for the switch to work after startup, mysqld must be started up from *root;* normally, mysqld is started via the script mysqld_safe with user=mysql.

mysqld — Memory Usage, Tuning, Query Cache

bulk_insert_buffer_size=n	Specifies how much memory is allocated for executing *INSERT* commands in which many records are simultaneously inserted (default 8MB).
key_buffer_size=n	Specifies how much RAM is reserved for index blocks (default 8MB).
join_buffer_size=n	Specifies how much memory is to be allocated for *JOIN* operations when there is no index for the *JOIN* columns (default 128KB).
max_heap_table_size=n	Specifies the maximum size of *HEAP* tables (default 16MB); if this size is exceeded, the table is stored in a temporary file instead of in RAM.
max_connections=n	Specifies the maximum number of simultaneous database connections (default 100).
query_cache_limit=n	Specifies the maximum size of a query result to be stored in the query cache (default 1MB).
query_cache_size=n	Specifies the size of the query cache (by default 0, meaning that the query cache is inactive).
query_cache_type=0/1/2	Specifies the mode in which query cache runs: 0, query cache is off; 1, query cache is on (default mode); 2, demand mode only for *SELECT SQL_CACHE*.
read_buffer_size=n	Specifies how much memory is reserved for each thread for reading sequential data from tables (default 128KB); the parameter can be set as needed with *SET SESSION read_buffer_size=n*.
read_rnd_buffer_size=n	Similar to read_buffer_size, but holds for the case that the records are to be output in a particular order, e.g., with *ORDER BY* (default 256KB).
sort_buffer=n	Specifies the size of the buffer for sorting (default 2MB); if the buffer is too small, a temporary file must be used.
table_cache=n	Specifies the maximum number of open tables (default 64).
tmp_table_size=n	Specifies the maximum size of temporary *HEAP* tables (default 32MB); if this size is exceeded, the tables are transformed to MyISAM tables and stored in a temporary file.

Logging, Replication

mysqld — Logging

log[=file]	Logs every connection as well as all SQL commands (general query log); if no file name is specified, then MySQL uses the file name hostname.log in the database directory.
log-slow-queries[=file]	Logs queries whose execution takes longer than the time specified in the variable *long_query_time* (slow query log).
long_query_time=n	Specifies the time limit for slow queries (default 10 seconds).
log-queries-not-using-indexes	Logs not only slow queries, but also all queries that are carried out without the use of an index (holds for log-slow-queries).
log-bin[=filename]	Logs all SQL commands that make a change in the data, in particular, all *INSERT*, *UPDATE*, and *DELETE* commands; a binary format is used (binary update log); as file name, filename.n or the default hostname.n is used, where n is a six-digit integer (the logging files are sequentially numbered).

mysqld — Logging *(Continued)*

`log-bin-index=filename`	Specifies the file name for the index file for binary logging. By default, the file has the same name as the binary logging files, but with ending `.index` instead of `.nnnnnn`.
`max_binlog_size=n`	Specifies the maximal size of a binary logging file (default 1GB). Before the size is exceeded, the MySQL server automatically provides a new file.
`binlog-do-db=dbname`	Limits binary logging to the specified database; changes in other databases are not logged; to specify more than one database, the option must be repeated in the configuration file, one database in each line.
`binlog-ignore-db=dbname`	Excludes the database from binary logging; changes in this database are not logged.
`sync-binlog=n`	Specifies how often the logging file should be written to the hard drive (synchronized). Here n gives the number of log write operations after which synchronization is to take place; n=1 is the most secure setting, but it makes binary logging very slow. By default the setting is n=0. The operating system looks after synchronization of the file.
`log-update[=file]`	Enables up through MySQL 4.1 an update log in text format. Beginning with MySQL 5.0 this form of logging is no longer supported. Use binary logging.
`log-error=file`	Specifies the file name for the error logging file (error log); this logging variant cannot be deactivated; if the option is not specified, MySQL uses the file name `hostname.err`.

mysqld — Replication (Master)

`server-id=n`	Assigns the server a unique ID number; *n* can be between 1 and 2^{31}.
`log-bin=name`	Activates binary logging. The logging files receive the specified names, to which a six-digit running integer is appended.
`binlog-do/ignore-db=dbname`	Logs only the specified databases or ignores the specified databases in logging.

mysqld — Replication (Slave)

`server-id=n`	Assigns a unique ID number to the server.
`log-slave-updates`	Executes logging on the slave so that the computer can be used to continue a replication chain ($A \blacktriangleright B \blacktriangleright C$).
`master-host=hostname`	Specifies the host name or IP address of the replication master; this setting is ignored once replication is set up if the file `master.info` exists.
`master-user=replicusername`	Specifies the user name for replication communication; ignored once `master.info` exists.
`master-password=pword`	Specifies the associated password; ignored if `master.info` exists.
`master-port=n`	Specifies the port number of the master server (default 3306); ignored if `master.info` exists.

Continued

mysqld — Replication (Slave) *(Continued)*

`master-connect-retry=n`	Specifies after how many seconds an attempt to reestablish a broken connection to the master can be made (default 60); ignored if `master.info` exists.
`master-ssl-xxx=xxx`	Enables the configuration of SSL communication between master and slave.
`read-only=0/1`	Specifies whether the slave server is also permitted to execute SQL commands independently (default setting 0) or whether it can execute SQL commands only from the master (1).
`relay-log-purge=0/1`	Specifies whether processed SQL commands are removed at once from the relay log files (default setting 1) or not (0).
`replicate-do-table=dbname.tablename`	Replicates only this table; to specify more than one table, the option must be repeated (each table requires its own line in the configuration file).
`replicate-wild-do-table=dbname.tablename`	Functions like `replicate-do-table` except that the wild card % is allowed to form a pattern (e.g., `test%.%` to replicate all tables of all databases whose name begins with `test`).
`replicate-do-db=dbname`	Replicates only this database.
`replicate-ignore-table=dbname.tablename`	Excludes this table from replication.
`replicate-wild-ignore-table=dbn.tablen`	Excludes these tables from replication.
`replicate-do-db=dbname`	Excludes this database from replication.
`replicate-rewrite-db=db1name->db2name`	Replicates the database `db1name` on the master under the name `db2name` on the slave.
`report-host=hostname`	Specifies the host name of the slave; this information is relevant only for the command *SHOW SLAVE HOSTS*, which allows on the master system the creation of a list of all slaves.
`slave_compressed_protocol=1`	Enables compressed communication between master and slave if both servers are capable of it.
`slave-skip-errors=n1,n2,… or all`	Continues replication even if errors *n1*, *n2*, etc., have occurred, or (with `all` regardless of any errors being triggered; under a correct configuration, no errors should occur on the slave due to SQL commands being executed (if an error occurs on the master, the command is not replicated); without `slave-skip-errors`, replication is stopped by an error and must be manually resumed.

InnoDB Configuration

mysqld — InnoDB — General Settings, Tablespace Files

`skip-innodb`	Specifies that the InnoDB table driver should not be loaded; useful to save memory when no InnoDB tables are to be used.
`innodb_file_per_table`	Creates an individual tablespace file for each new table instead of storing the table in the central tablespace (holds by default). This option has been available since MySQL 4.1.
`innodb_open_files=n`	Specifies the maximum number of files that the InnoDB table driver may have open at once (by default 300). If you use `innodb_file_per_table` and very many tables are open at once, this value should be increased.
`innodb_data_home_dir=p`	Specifies the InnoDB directory; all additional directory or file specifications are relative to the path p; by default, the InnoDB driver uses the MySQL data directory.
`innodb_data_file_path=ts`	Specifies the tablespace for all InnoDB tables; can involve more than one file; the size of each file must be specified in bytes, megabytes (M), or gigabytes (G); the names of the tablespace files are separated by semicolons; for the last of the tablespace files, the attribute autoextend and a maximal size (`max:n`) can be specified (e.g., `ibdata1:1G;ibdata2:1G:autoextend:max:2G`, by which `ibdata1` has size 1GB, `ibdata2` is set up with the same size and can grow as large as 2GB); instead of a file, the device name of a hard-drive partition can be given; in this case, the key word `newraw` must follow the exact size for initialization, and for further use, the key word `raw` (e.g., `/dev/hdb1:20Gnewraw` or `/dev/hdb1:20Graw`); the default setting since MySQL 4.0 is `ibdata1:10M:autoextend`.
`innodb_autoextend_increment=n`	Specifies by how many megabytes autoextend files should be enlarged (default 8MB). The setting does not hold for individual tablespace files, which in any case grow by smaller steps.
`innodb_lock_wait_timeout=n`	Specifies how long (in seconds) should be waited for the release of locks; after this time, the transaction is broken off with *ROLLBACK*; the setting is especially important when deadlocks develop that the InnoDB driver does not recognize; the default value is 50 seconds.
`innodb_fast_shutdown=0/1`	Specifies whether InnoDB should shut down as quickly as possible; in the default setting 1, InnoDB does not transfer the *INSERT* buffer into the tables; this process is repeated at the next start of the MySQL server (the setting 1 does not represent a risk, since the *INSERT* buffer is a component of the tablespace; thus no data can be lost; the setting 0 is more dangerous, since in a computer shutdown it could happen that InnoDB would not have enough time for its synchronization work and would be stopped in its tracks by the operating system).

mysqld — InnoDB — Logging

innodb_log_group_home_dir=lp	Specifies the directory for InnoDB logging files (ib_logfile0, 1, etc.); by default, the InnoDB driver uses the MySQL data directory.
innodb_log_files_in_group=n	Specifies how many logging files should be used (default is 2); the InnoDB table driver fills these files sequentially; when all files are full, the first is over-written with data, etc.
innodb_log_file_size=n	Specifies how large each logging file should be (default 5MB); the size specification uses M for megabytes and G for gigabytes.
innodb_flush_log_at_trx_commit=0/1/2	Determines when data should be written to the logging file and when these files should be synchronized (that is, when changes should be physically stored to the hard disk); the setting 0 means that the data are written and synchronized about once per second; the default setting 1 is more secure (save and synchronize after each *COMMIT*); a compromise is the setting 2, with writing after *COMMIT* and synchronization only about once per second.
innodb_flush_method=x	Under Unix/Linux, specifies how logging files are synchronized (i.e., how they are stored on the hard drive); choices are fdatasync, synchronization with *fsync( )* and O_DSYNC, synchronize with *O_SYNC( )*.
innodb_log_archive=1	Activates archive logging in the files ib_arch_log_n; this type of logging does not make sense when InnoDB is used together with MySQL (instead, use binary logging of the MySQL server).

mysqld — InnoDB — Buffer Settings and Tuning

innodb_buffer_pool_size=n	Specifies how much RAM should be used for table data and indexes (default 8MB); this parameter has considerable influence on speed and should be up to 80% of available RAM on computers used exclusively as MySQL/InnoDB database servers.
innodb_log_buffer_size=n	Specifies how much RAM should be used for writing the transaction logging files (default 1MB).
innodb_additional_mem_pool_size=n	Specifies how much RAM should be used for various internal management structures (default 1MB).
innodb_file_io_threads=n	Specifies how many threads for I/O operations, that is, for access to the hard drive, should be used (default 4).
innodb_thread_concurrency=n	Specifies how many threads InnoDB should use altogether (default 8).

Miscellaneous

mysqld — Miscellaneous	
`bind-address=ipadr`	Specifies the IP address that MySQL should use; this option is important if the computer is so configured that it uses several IP addresses.
`default-storage-engine=type`	Specifies the table type that new tables are to use if the type is not explicitly given (default is *MyISAM*). The default table type can also be set with `default-table-type`.
`default-timezone=name`	Sets the time zone for the MySQL server if it is to differ from the time zone of the local computer (see Chapter 14).
`ft_min_word_len=n`	Specifies the minimal word length for a full-text index; in the default setting 4, words with three or fewer letters are not included.
`max-allowed-packet=n`	Specifies the maximum packet size for data exchange between client and server; `max-allowed-packet` must be at least as large as the largest BLOB to be processed by client programs; default is 1MB.
`sql-mode=mode1,mode2,...`	Specifies the SQL mode in which the MySQL server should be run. This permits greater compatibility with other database systems to be achieved. Allowable settings include `ansi`, `db2`, `oracle`, `no_zero_date`, `pipes_as_concat` (see also Chapter 14).

■**Caution** If you specify an option in a configuration file that `mysqld` does not know about (for example, due to a silly typo), then the server cannot start up. So watch out!

mysqld_safe (Server Start)

Under Unix/Linux, the MySQL server is usually started by an Init-V script (e.g., /etc/init.d/mysqld or /etc/init.d/mysql). This script is automatically executed at the startup of the operating system. It does not directly launch the server, but instead, executes the script `mysqld_safe`. It is this script that starts the MySQL server.

The script `mysqld_safe` is started with *root* privileges. The MySQL server, on the other hand, is started with the privileges of a user designed for this purpose (normally with the name *mysql*).

After the start of the MySQL server, `mysqld_safe` continues to run until it is explicitly ended (e.g., with `mysqladmin shutdown`). If the MySQL server is ended unexpectedly due to a crash, then it is immediately restarted by `mysqld_safe`.

Usually, only a few options are passed to `mysqld_safe` (e.g., `--data-dir` and `--pid-file`), which transmit the script to the MySQL server `mysqld`. There are also some options specifically for `mysqld_safe`.

mysqld_safe — Options	
--core-file-size=n	Limits the size of the core file, which contains an image of the server after a crash and makes debugging possible; *n* must be given in bytes.
--ledir=dirname	Specifies the directory in which the MySQL server is located (by default /usr/sbin).
--mysqld=filename	Specifies the name of the MySQL server that is to be started (default mysqld).
--mysqld-version=suffix	Specifies an extension to the server name (e.g., max if mysqld-max should be started instead of mysqld).
--nice=n	Specifies the priority in which the mysqld process should be executed (man nice provides further information).

mysql_install_db (New Installation of the mysql Database)

Under Unix/Linux, the *mysql* database can be freshly installed with the script mysql_install_db. For this, the server must be stopped (the script then starts the server itself with the option --bootstrap) and the database *mysql* deleted.

```
root# /etc/init.d/mysql stop
root# rm -r /usr/lib/mysql/mysql
root# mysql_install_db
```

Among other things, the script must be executed in the same account as is used for executing the MySQL server (usually *mysql*). You can also execute mysql_install_db as *root*, in which case you must subsequently change the owner of the database directory mysql and the files contained therein:

```
root# mysql_install_db
root# chown mysql -R /var/lib/mysql/mysql
```

The script is generally executed automatically as a component of a new MySQL installation. The script is also suited to recreating the default state of the *mysql* database. Under Windows mysql_install_db is unavailable.

■**Caution** Depending on the network configurarion, the script enters the local host name without the domain name into the table *mysql.user*. The use of an abbreviated computer name can lead to login problems. It may be necessary to place the complete computer name manually in the *mysql.user* table (see also Chapter 11).

---

mysql_fix_privileges (Updating the mysql Database)

The *mysql* database for managing MySQL access privileges is being continually extended and improved. If you carry out a MySQL update and use the *mysql* database from a previous installation (see Chapter 14), you should execute the script mysql_fix_privileges, which updates the database, inserts new columns as necessary, etc. The single parameter that must be passed to the script is the MySQL *root* password.

After the script has been executed, there is generally some work that has to be done by hand, because the script does not always know whether certain new privileges should be set. In case of doubt, the script elects not to set, which is more secure, but for some MySQL users, it reduces their privileges with respect to previous versions of MySQL.

The script is available only under Unix/Linux. Under Windows you will find instead in the directory scripts a like-named *.sql file, which you can execute with mysql.

mysql_fix_extensions (Renaming MyISAM Files)

In transferring database directories with MyISAM tables from Windows to Unix/Linux, the problem sometimes occurs that the case (upper/lower) of the file identifier is incorrect. (Unix/Linux is case-sensitive, while Windows could use some case-sensitivity training.) MySQL expects, for example, *.frm, but *.MYI and *.MYD.

The Perl script mysql_fix_extensions solves this problem. The single parameter passed to the script is the name of the MySQL data directory, e.g., /var/lib/mysql or C:\mysql\data. There are no options.

mysql (SQL Command Interpreter)

The command interpreter mysql allows interactive execution of SQL commands. This program can also be run in batch mode for many administrative tasks, including the generation of HTML tables. The commands are input from a file with < file. All SQL commands can be used in this file. The commands must be followed by a semicolon. Comments are introduced with the character #. (All additional characters to the end of the line are then ignored.)

At the launch of mysql, numerous options can be specified. Furthermore, an optional database name can be given, in which case this database becomes the default database (corresponds to the command *USE databasename*).

---

mysql — Syntax

```
mysql [options] [databasename] [ < commands.sql]
```

---

mysql — General Options

-e cmd	--execute=cmd	Executes the given command(s); commands must be separated by semicolons and placed in quotation marks; then mysql is ended.
-i	--ignore-space	Recognizes functions even if there are spaces between function names and their parameters; with -i, for example, *SUM (price)* is allowed, while without the option it must be written *SUM(price)*.
-L	--skip-line-numbers	Displays error messages without line numbers; the line numbers otherwise displayed refer to the location at which the faulty SQL command is located in a batch file and is generally an aid in debugging.
-U	--i-am-a-dummy or --safe-updates	Permits *UPDATE* and *DELETE* commands only if the effective range is limited with *WHERE* or *LIMIT*; furthermore, there is a maximum number of query results from *SELECT* commands as well as a maximum number of *JOIN*s.

Continued

mysql — General Options *(Continued)*

-V	--version	Displays the version of mysql; mysql is then terminated.
	--tee=filename	Copies all input and output into the specified logging file; this option is allowed only if mysql is used in interactive mode (not in batch mode).
	--no-tee	Does not use logging (the default).

mysql — Formatting and Output Options

-B	--batch	Separates columns in tables by tab characters (instead of by spaces and lines); moreover, only results of queries are displayed, and no status information.
-E	--vertical	Lists the results of queries with columns displayed horizontally, one below the next (instead of with vertical columns, one next to the other); this option is particularly to be recommended if a query returns many columns but few rows (ideally only one); as with --batch, only results of queries are shown, and no status information.
-H	--html	Formats the results of queries as HTML tables; as with --batch, only results of queries are shown, and no status information.
-N	--skip-column-names	Leaves off column titles in the output of tables.
-r	--raw	In query results, outputs the characters 0-byte, tab, newline, and \ unchanged (normally, these characters are output as \0, \t, \n, and \\); this option is effective only in combination with --batch.
-s	--silent	Displays less status information than in normal mode; does not use costly table formatting.
-t	--table	Formats tables with lines and spaces (default setting).
-v	--verbose	Displays extensive status information, more than in normal mode.
-X	--xml	Formats the results of queries as an XML document.

mysql — Commands for Interactive Mode

\c	clear	Interrupts input of a command; \c can be given at the end of a command and leads to the entire input being simply ignored.
\e	edit	Calls the external editor named in the environment variable *EDITOR* and there enables a change in the command; this works only under Unix/Linux; after the return to mysql, the command given in the editor is not displayed in mysql, which makes this option somewhat confusing to use.
\g	go	Executes the command (equivalent to ; and Return).
\h	help	Displays a list of commands.
\p	print	Displays the entire current command on the screen.
\q	exit or quit	Terminates mysql (under Unix/Linux, this works also with Ctrl+D).
\r	connect	Terminates the current connection to MySQL and creates a new connection; optionally, a database name and host name of the MySQL server can be given (in that order).

mysql — Commands for Interactive Mode *(Continued)*		
\s	status	Displays status information about the MySQL server.
\T [fn]	tee [filename]	Logs all input and output into the specified file; if no file name is given, then the file name used in the previous tee command is used; if the file already exists, then the input and output are appended to the end of the file.
\t	notee	Ends tee; logging can be resumed at any time with tee or \T.
\u db	use database	Makes the given database the default database.
\#	rehash	Creates (only under Unix/Linux) an internal list of all mysql commands, the most important SQL key words, and all table and column names of the current database; in the sequel, the input of the initial letters suffices; with Tab the abbreviation is extended to the full key word.
\. fn	source filename	Executes the SQL commands contained in the file; the commands must be separated by semicolons.

mysqladmin (Administration)

Various administrative tasks can be accomplished with mysqladmin, such as creating new databases and changing passwords. There are several commands that can be passed to mysqladmin, which are then executed sequentially.

The names of mysqladmin commands can be abbreviated to the point where the name remains unique (e.g., flush-l instead of flush-logs, or k instead of kill).

Most mysqladmin commands can also be executed as SQL commands, for example, by *CREATE DATABASE, DROP DATABASE, FLUSH, KILL, SHOW*. These commands are given in parentheses in the lists below. There is additional information in the SQL reference in Chapter 21.

mysqladmin — Syntax
mysqladmin [options] command1 command2 …

mysqladmin — Options		
-f	--force	No warnings are displayed (e.g., with drop database); further commands are executed even after errors.
-i n	--sleep=n	Repeats the command every *n* seconds (for example, for regular display of status or for ping); mysqladmin now runs endlessly; under Unix/Linux, it can be terminated with Ctrl+C, under Windows, only by closing the command window.
-r	--relative	Displays, in combination with -i and the command extended-status, a change in the previous status.
-E	--vertical	Has the same effect as --relative, but changes are displayed in a single, very long, line.
-t n	--timeout=n	Sets the timeout time for establishing a connection to the server; if after *n* seconds no connection has been established, then mysqladmin is terminated.
-w n	--wait=n	Attempts *n* times to establish a connection to the MySQL server.

mysqladmin — Commands	
create dbname	Generates a new database (corresponds to *CREATE DATABASE*).
drop dbname	Deletes an existing database irrevocably (corresponds to *DROP DATABASE*).
extended-status	Displays countless status variables of the server (*SHOW STATUS*).
flush-hosts	Empties the host cache table (*FLUSH HOSTS*).
flush-logs	Closes all logging files and then reopens them (*FLUSH LOGS*); with update logs, a new file is created, where the number of the file terminator is increased by 1 (e.g., *file.003* ➤ *file.004*).
flush-status	Resets many status variables to 0 (*FLUSH STATUS*).
flush-tables	Closes all open tables (*FLUSH TABLES*).
flush-threads	Empties the thread cache.
flush-privileges	Reinputs the privileges database *mysql* (*FLUSH PRIVILEGES*).
kill id1, id2, …	Terminates the specified threads (*KILL*).
password newpassw	Changes the password of the current user; under Windows, this command often causes problems; one could use instead the SQL command *SET PASSWORD* (see Chapter 14).
ping	Tests whether a connection to the server can be established.
processlist	Displays all threads (*SHOW THREADS*).
reload	Reinputs the privileges database *mysql*.
refresh	Closes all tables and log files and then reopens them.
shutdown	Terminates the SQL server.
start-slave / stop-slave	Starts/stops a slave process for replication.
status	Displays some server status variables.
variables	Displays the system variables of the SQL server (*SHOW VARIABLES*).
version	Determines the version of the MySQL server.

mysqldump (Backup/Export)

With mysqldump, you get a long list of all SQL commands that are necessary to re-create a database exactly as it was. There are three syntax variants of mysqldump, depending on whether a database, several enumerated databases, or all databases managed by MySQL are to be stored. Only with the first variant can the output be limited to particular tables. As a rule, the output of mysqldump is sent to a file with > backupfile.sql.

mysqldump — Syntax
mysqldump [options] dbname [tables]
mysqldump [options] --databases [moreoptions] dbname1 [dbname2 ...]
mysqldump [options] --all-databases [moreoptions]

mysqldump — Options

--	--add-drop-table	Inserts a *DROP TABLE* command before every *CREATE TABLE*; when tables are read in, existing tables are deleted. This option is part of --opt and holds by default.
--	--add-locks	Inserts *LOCK TABLE* before the first *INSERT* command and *UNLOCK* after the last *INSERT* command; generally speeds up reading in a database; this option is part of --opt and holds by default. However, the option should not be used with InnoDB tables.
--	--all	Specifies all MySQL-specific options in the *CREATE TABLE* command.
-A	--all-databases	Saves all databases managed by MySQL; *CREATE DATABASE* and *USE* are placed in the backup file.
-B	--databases	Stores several databases.
—	--compatible=name	Determines with what database system or standard the backup should be compatible. Allowable settings are ansi, mysql323, mysql40, postgresql, oracle, mssql, db2, maxdb, no_key_options, no_table_options, no_field_options. It is allowed to have more than one key word, separated by commas.
--	--complete-inserts ●	Generates for each data record a separate *INSERT* command.
—	--create-options	Includes all MySQL-specific options in *CREATE* commands. This option is part of --opt and holds by default.
—	--default-character-set=name	Specifies the character set in which the backup file is to be created (by default UTF8).
--	--delayed-inserts	Creates *INSERT* commands with the option *DELAYED*.
-K	--disable-keys	Inserts *ALTER TABLE ... DISABLE KEYS* or *... ENABLE KEYS* before or after *INSERT* commands; indexes are thereby not updated until the end of the insertion process, which is faster.
-e	--extended-insert	Generates few *INSERT* commands with which several records can be inserted simultaneously (more efficient and reduces the size of the backup file). This option is part of --opt and holds by default.
-F	--flush-logs	Updates the logging files before the backup is begun.
-f	--force	Continues even after errors.
—	--hex-blob	Outputs the content of binary fields (BLOBs) in hexadecimal format.
-x	--lock-all-tables	Executes *LOCK TABLE READ* for the entire database. This ensures that during the entire backup no table can be changed. Note that --lock-tables does not offer this protection, but prevents changes only during the time in which a table is locked. At this time another table can be changed.

Continued

mysqldump — Options *(Continued)*

-l	--lock-tables	Executes a *LOCK TABLE READ* for every table before the data are read; this ensures that no data can be changed while mysqldump is running. This option is part of --opt and holds by default. The obvious drawback is that all write processes are blocked until mysqldump is done, which can take a while with large databases (with InnoDB tables, you should use --single-transaction instead of --lock-tables).
	--master-data [=n]	Adds a comment at the end of the output containing a *CHANGE MASTER* command. This command is suitable for replication on a slave system. If n=1 is passed as parameter, then the *CHANGE MASTER* command is added in a normal fashion (not as a comment), so that it is automatically executed when the backup is restored. This option also activates --lock-all-tables if --single-transaction is not used at the same time.
	--no-create-db	Creates no *CREATE DATABASES* commands. (These commands are created only if the option --all-databases or --databases is used.)
	--no-create-info	Creates no *CREATE TABLE* commands, but only the *INSERT* commands.
	--no-data	Creates no *INSERT* commands (but only *CREATE TABLE* commands in order to restore the database schema).
	--opt	Shorthand for the following options: --add-drop-table, --create-options, --add-locks, --disable-keys, --extended-insert, --lock-tables, --quick, --set-charset. In most cases, this is an optimal setting, for which reason it holds by default. If you don't wish this, you must use --skip-opt.
-q	--quick	Outputs results record by record without internal intermediate storage. This option is part of --opt and holds by default. Without this option, first the entire table is moved into RAM and then output; the advantage of --quick is the lower memory requirement; the disadvantage is that the MySQL server is generally blocked for a longer period of time; --quick should definitely be used for very large tables (when the entire table cannot be held in RAM of the local computer).
-Q	--quote-names	Encloses table and column names in single quotes (e.g., 'name').
	--set-charset	Changes the active character set at the start of mysqldump output, and at the end, the previously valid character set is restored. This option is part of --opt and holds by default. It can be deactivated with --skip-char-set.
	--skip-opt	Deactivates the default option --opt.
	--single-transaction	Results in all tables being read within a single transaction; this makes sense only when InnoDB tables are used, in which case this option ensures that no data are changed during output. This option deactivates --lock-tables.

mysqldump — Options *(Continued)*	
`-T dir   --tab=dir`	Writes the result directly into the specified directory, whereby for each table two files are created, one with the table structure (`*.sql`) and the second with the stored data in the format of the command *SELECT ... INTO OUTFILE* (`*.txt`).
`-w cnd   --where=condition`	Considers only data records that satisfy the *WHERE* condition *cnd* or *condition*; the entire option must be placed in quotation marks, e.g., `"-wprice>5"` or "`--where=ID=3`".
`-X       --xml`	Creates an XML file with the contents of the table (without information on the table structure).

mysqldump — Formatting Options (Only in Combination with —tab)	

`--fields-terminated-by`
`--fields-enclosed-by`
`--fields-optionally-enclosed-by`
`--fields-escaped-by`
`--lines-terminated-by`
	See Chapter 21: *SELECT ... INTO OUTFILE*.

If you are using `--tab`, then the second file (`tablename.txt`) contains the contents of the table directly (that is, not in the form of *INSERT* commands). This has several advantages: The resulting file is somewhat more compact, and a later importation can be executed significantly more quickly. (However, the operation is more complex, and only a single table can be handled.)

The options `--fields` and `--lines` should each be set in quotation marks. The following example shows how you can pass the double quote itself as a character to the option:

```
> mysqldump -u root -p --tab /tmp "--fields-enclosed-by=\"" ...
```

To reinput the file thus generated (`*.txt`) with `mysqldump`, you can use either the program `mysqlimport`, discussed in the following section, or the SQL command *LOAD DATA*.

mysqlimport (Text Import, Bulk Import)

With `mysqlimport`, it is possible to import specially formatted text files into MySQL tables. Here, `mysqlimport` represents merely an interface to the command *LOAD DATA*, described in detail in Chapter 14.

mysqlimport — Syntax
`mysqlimport [options] databasename filename`

---

mysqlimport — Options

-d	--delete	Deletes all existing records in the table before importation.
-i	--ignore	Ignores new records with an existing value for a *UNIQUE* or *PRIMARY KEY* column.
-L	--local	Reads the file from the local file system (not from that of the MySQL server).
-l	--lock-tables	Blocks the tables for all other clients during importation.
-r	--replace	Overwrites existing records with the same value in a *UNIQUE* or *PRIMARY KEY* column.
	--fields-terminated-by --fields-enclosed-by --fields-----optionally-enclosed-by --fields-escaped-by --lines-terminated-by	Affects special characters; see *LOAD DATA* in Chapter 21.

---

mysqlshow (Displaying Information)

With mysqlshow, you can quickly obtain an overview of the databases, tables, and columns managed by MySQL. Without parameters, the command returns a list of all databases managed by MySQL. With parameters, the command displays information on the specified database, table, or column.

---

mysqlshow — Syntax

```
mysqlshow [options] [databasename [tablename [columnname]]]
```

---

mysqlshow — Options

-i	--status	Displays additional status for tables (table type, average record length, etc.).

Example

```
> mysqlshow -u root -p
Enter password: xxx
Databases:
  books
  myforum
  mylibrary
  mysql
  test
  ...
> mysqlshow -u root -p mysql
Enter password: xxx
Database: mysql
Tables:
  columns_priv
  db
  host
  ...
```

```
> mysqlshow -u root -p mylibrary authors
Enter password: xxx
Database: mylibrary  Table: authors  Rows: 0
Field    Type        Collation          Null  Key  Default Extra  Privileges
authID   int(11)                              PRI          ...    ...
authName varchar(60) latin1_german1_ci       MUL                 ...
ts       timestamp                      YES        ...           ...
```

myisamchk (Repairing MyISAM Files)

With myisamchk you can check the integrity of MyISAM database files (name.MYD and name.MYI). Damaged files and indexes can be repaired as required.

The parameters of myisamchk are tables names. Here the complete file name is given (either without the ending or with the ending *.MYI). Depending on the options specified, however, both MyISAM files, that is, name.MYD and name.MYI, are analyzed or changed.

Please note that with myisamchk there are several options whose significance depends on whether the program is used simply for checking (without -r, -o, --recover, --saferecover) or for changing table files (with one of these options).

myisamchk — Syntax

myisamchk [options] tablename1 tablename2 …

myisamchk — Options (Analyze Table File Without -r or -o)

-c	--check	Checks the integrity of the table files; -c is the default option if no options are specified.
-e	--extend-check	Checks most thoroughly (and slowly).
-F	--fast	Checks only tables whose files were not properly closed.
-C	--check-only-changed	Checks only tables that were changed since the last check.
-f	--force	Restarts myisamchk with the option -r if errors are discovered.
-i	--information	Displays statistical information about the tables.
-m	--medium-check	Checks more thoroughly (and slowly) than with -c.
-U	--update-state	Marks a file as damaged if errors are discovered.
-T	--read-only	Does not change the file.

myisamchk — Options (Repair and Change Table File with -r or -o)

-B	--backup	Creates the backup file name.bak for name.myi.
-e	--extend-check	Attempts to re-create every data record; however, this usually leads to many records with incorrect or deleted data; moreover, the repair takes a long time; this option should be used seldom.
-f	--force	Overwrites temporary files.
-l	--no-symlinks	Follows no symbolic links (that is, only those files are repaired that are found under the actual file name; available only under Unix/Linux).
-o	--safe-recover	Like -r, but a different algorithm is used.

Continued

---

myisamchk — Options (Repair and Change Table File with -r or -o) *(Continued)*

-q	--quick	Only an index file is repaired; the actual file is left untouched.
-q -q		Has almost the same effect as -q, but the data file is unchanged if key fields are not unique.
-r	--recover	Attempts to re-create defective files.
-t p	--tmpdir=path	Uses the specified directory for temporary files.
-u	--unpack	Decompresses table files that were compressed with myisampack.

---

myisamchk — Other Options

-a	--analyze	Analyzes and stores the distribution of key fields in the indexes; this can speed up table access somewhat.
-A n	--set-auto-increment[=n]	Uses as start value for *AUTO INCREMENT* a number that is one greater than the highest value used so far, or else *n* (whichever is greater).
-d	--description	Displays various information about the table (record format and length, character set, indexes, etc.).
-R	--sort-records=idxnr	Sorts the records in the table file according to the specified index; the index is specified as a number (where this number can be determined first with -d); then nearby records in the index are located near each other in the table file as well; this can speed up access if records are frequently read in the order defined by the index.
-S	--sort-index	Sorts the blocks of the index file.

---

myisamchk — Variables for Memory Management

-O key_buffer_size=n	Specifies the size of the key buffer (default 512KB).
-O read_buffer_size=n	Specifies the size of the read buffer (default 256KB).
-O sort_buffer_size=n	Specifies the size of the sort buffer (default 2MB).
-O write_buffer_size=n	Specifies the size of the write buffer (default 256KB).

---

myisampack (Compressing MyISAM Files)

MyISAM database files (name.MYD) are compressed with myisampack. Thereby one can achieve drastic reductions in storage requirements for tables (often considerably more than one-half) and under some circumstances increased access speed to the data. However, the data can now no longer be changed.

myisampack — Syntax

```
myisampack [options] tablename1 tablename2 …
```

myisampack — Options

-b	--backup	Creates a backup name.old of the table file.
-f	--force	Executes the operation even if the resulting file is bigger than the original.
-j	--join='new_table_name'	Unites all tables specified into a single, large file; the tables must all have exactly the same column definitions.
-t	--test	Executes myisampack provisionally without actually changing any data.
-T p	--tmpdir=path	Uses the specified directory for temporary files.

■■■

## CHAPTER 23

API Reference

This chapter contains a reference to the APIs (application programming interfaces) that were introduced in this book for the programming languages PHP, Perl, Java, and C.

PHP API (mysql Interface)

Since PHP 5 two interfaces have been available for interacting with MySQL: the *mysql* functions and the *mysqli* classes and methods. This section gives a compact overview of the *mysql* functions and their parameters for access to MySQL databases. In the next section follows a reference to the *mysqli* interface.

First a few formal remarks to the following explanation of syntax:

- Square brackets in the left column indicate optional parameters.

- For all functions for which there is an enumeration over an index *n*, this index is in the range 0 to *nmax -1*.

- Examples of the application of these functions can be found particularly in Chapters 3 and 15. Further references can be found in the Index.

Establishing a Connection

$id = mysql_connect($host, $user, $pw);	Establishes a connection.
$id = mysql_connect($host, $user, $pw, $new_link, $client_flags);	As above, except that *new_link* specifies whether a new connection should be made if a similar connection already exists (default *false*); *client_flags* specifies whether particular connection properties should be used (e.g., *MYSQL_CLIENT_COMPRESS*); these two optional parameters have been available only since PHP 4.3.
$id = mysql_pconnect($host, $user, $pw [, $new_link [, $client_flags]]);	Establishes a persistent connection or attempts to reuse a still open connection of another PHP page.
mysql_change_user($newuser, $passw);	Changes the user name for the connection.
mysql_select_db($dbname);	Determines the default database.
mysql_close([$id]);	Closes the connection.

Generally, the specification *id* can be omitted as long as there is only one connection to MySQL and thus no possibility of confusion.

Administration

$result = mysql_list_dbs([$id]);	Determines a list of all known databases; the evaluation is like that of *SELECT* queries.
$result = mysql_list_tables($dbname [,$id]);	Determines a list of all tables of the database; the evaluation is like that of *SELECT* queries.
$result = mysql_list_fields($dbn, $tbln [,$id]);	Determines a list of all fields of the table; the evaluation is like that of *SELECT* queries.
mysql_create_db($dbname [,$id]);	Creates a new database.
mysql_drop_db($dbname [,$id]);	Deletes a database.

Error Evaluation

$n = mysql_errno([$id]);	Determines the number of the most recent error.
$txt = mysql_error([$id]);	Determines the error message.

Information Functions

$txt = mysql_get_client_info([$id]);	Returns a character string with the version number of the client library.
$txt = mysql_get_host_info([$id]);	Returns a character string that describes the connection with the server (including host name, e.g., *"localhost via TCP/IP"*).
$n = mysql_get_proto_info([$id]);	Returns an integer with the number of the communication protocol in use (e.g., 10).
$txt = mysql_get_server_info([$id]);	Returns a character string with the version number of the server (e.g., *"5.0.2-alpha-standard"*).
$n = mysql_thread_id([$id]);	Returns an integer with the thread number of the given connection.
$txt = mysql_stat([$id]);	Returns a character string with a brief status report on the server (e.g., *"Uptime: 24763 Threads: 1 Questions: 65 …"*).

Executing SQL Commands

[$result =] mysql_query($sql [, $id])	Executes an SQL command for the default database; if it is a *SELECT* command, the found records can be evaluated with *$result*.
[$result =] mysql_db_query($db, $sql [, $id]);	Executes a command for the database *db* (which becomes the default database for all further queries).
$result = mysql_unbuffered_query($sql [, $id]);	Functions in principle like *mysql_query*, but is designed only for *SELECT* queries; the difference between this and *mysql_query* is that found records remain at first on the server and are transferred only as needed; the number of found records can be determined only by running through all of them; *mysql_num_rows* cannot be used.
$sql = addslashes($s);	Replaces 0-bytes and the characters ', ", and \ in *$s* with the strings \0, \', \", and \\.
$sql = mysql_escape_string($s);	Functions like *addslashes*, but also replaces carriage return, line feed, and Ctrl+Z with the strings \n, \r, and \z.
$sql = mysql_real_escape_string($s [,$id]);	Functions like *mysql_escape_string*, but also considers the character set of the MySQL connection.

Output of *SELECT* Query Results

mysql_data_seek($result, $rownr);	Determines the active data record within the result.
$row = mysql_fetch_array($result);	Returns the next record of the result (or *false*); access to individual fields takes place with *row[n]* or *row['fieldname']*, where case sensitivity is enforced.
$row = mysql_fetch_assoc($result);	Functions like *mysql_fetch_array*, except that field access must be by column name; *row[n]* is not permitted.
$row = mysql_fetch_row($result);	Returns the next record of the result (or *false*); access to individual fields is via *row[n]*.
$row = mysql_fetch_object($result);	Returns the next record of the result (or *false*); access to individual fields is via *row->fieldname*.
$data = mysql_result($result, $rownr, $colnr);	Returns the contents of the field in row *rownr* and column *colnr*; this function is slower than the other functions in this list and should therefore be used only in particular cases (such as to read a single value, e.g., *SELECT COUNT(*)*).
mysql_free_result($result);	Frees the query result immediately (otherwise, not until the end of the script).

All of the above functions except for *mysql_treat_result()* treat *result* as a value that enables access to the list of data records from a *SELECT* query. Usually, all records are output one after the other with *mysql_fetch_array, mysql_fetch_row,* or *mysql_fetch_object*, with each subsequent execution of the function setting the next record as the active one. The active record can also be set with *mysql_data_seek*.

The three functions *mysql_fetch_array, mysql_fetch_row,* and *mysql_fetch_object* differ only in the way in which individual fields of a record are accessed: *row['fieldname'], row[n],* or *row->fieldname*. Of the three functions, *mysql_fetch_row* is the most efficient, but the difference in speed is negligible.

Metainformation on Query Results

$n = mysql_num_rows($result);	Determines the number of result records (*SELECT*).
$n = mysql_num_fields($result);	Determines the number of result columns (*SELECT*).
$n = mysql_affected_rows([$id]);	Determines the number of records that were changed by the last SQL command (*INSERT, UPDATE, DELETE, CREATE, ..., SELECT*).
$autoid = mysql_insert_id([$id]);	Determines the *AUTO_INCREMENT* value generated by the last *INSERT* command.
$txt = mysql_info([$id]);	Returns status information on the last command, e.g., *"Rows matched: 65 Changed: 65 Warnings: 0"*; `mysql_info` is designed only for commands that usually affect large numbers of records (*INSERT INTO, UPDATE, ALTER TABLE*, etc.).

Metainformation on the Fields (Columns) of Query Results

$fname = mysql_field_name($result, $n);	Returns the field name of column *n*.
$tblname = mysql_field_table($result, $n);	Returns the table name for column *n*.
$typename = mysql_field_type($result, $n);	Returns the data type of column *n* (e.g., *"TINYINT"*).
$length = mysql_field_len($result, $n);	Returns the maximum length of the column.
$lengths = mysql_fetch_length($result);	Returns a field with length information for all fields of the last-read data record (access with *lengths[n]*).
$flags = mysql_field_flags($result, $n);	Returns the attribute properties of a column as a character string (e.g., *"not_null primary_key"*); the properties are separated by spaces; evaluation is done most easily with *explode*.
$info = mysql_fetch_field($result, $n);	Returns information on column *n* as an object; evaluation proceeds with *info->name* (see the list below); note that *info* may contain, in part, properties other than *flags*.

Attributes of mysql_field_flags

---

auto_increment	Attribute *AUTO_INCREMENT*.
binary	Attribute *BINARY*.
blob	Data type *BLOB*, *TINYBLOB*, etc.
enum	Data type *ENUM*.
multiple_key	The field is part of a nonunique index.
not_null	Attribute *NOT NULL*.
primary_key	Attribute *PRIMARY KEY*.
timestamp	Attribute *TIMESTAMP*.
unique_key	Attribute *UNIQUE*.
unsigned	Attribute *UNSIGNED*.
zerofill	Attribute *ZEROFILL*.

Field Information for mysql_fetch_field

---

info->name	column name (field name).
info->table	name of the table from which the field comes.
info->max_length	maximum length of the field.
info->type	name of the data type of the field (e.g., *"TINYINT"*).
info->numeric	1 or 0, depending on whether the field contains numeric data.
info->blob, not_null, multiple_key, primary_key, unique_key, unsigned, zerofill	1 or 0; see list above for interpretation.

PHP-API (mysqli Interface)

In addition to the *mysql* interface described in the previous section, since PHP 5 the new *mysqli* interface has been available. Among its advantages are object-oriented programming, greater functionality, and support for new MySQL features (e.g., prepared statements).

The *mysqli* interface offers three classes:

mysqli: Objects of this class manage the connection to the MySQL server.

mysqli_result: Objects of this class contain the results of *SELECT* queries.

mysqli_stmt: Objects of this class enable the definition and execution of prepared statements.

The following syntax tables describe the most important properties and methods of the three classes. Here *$mysqli* is an object of the *mysqli* class, *$result* an object of the *mysqli_result* class, and *$stmt* an object of the *mysqli_stmt* class.

The mysqli Class

Establishing a Connection

$mysqli = new mysqli("servername", "user", "pw", "dbname");	Connection variant 1: The *mysqli* constructor creates the connection.
$mysqli = mysqli_init();* *$mysqli->options(...); *$mysqli->ssl_set("key", "cert", "ca", "capath", "cipher");* *$mysqli->real_connect("servername", "user", "pw", "dbname", portno, "socketfile", flags);*	Connection variant 2: The *mysqli* object is created with *mysqli_init.* Then you can set options, for example, in the form *$mysqli->options(MYSQLI_OPT_CONNECT_TIMEOUT, 10).* The actual creation of the connection finally takes place via *real_connect*, where the last three parameters are optional. Allowable flags include *MYSQLI_CLIENT_COMPRESS* and *MYSQL_CLIENT_SSL.*
$err = mysqli_connect_errno();	Tests whether an error has occurred during creation of the connection. The return value 0 means that the connection has succeeded.

mysqli — Executing SQL Commands

[$result =] $mysqli->query($sqlstring);	Executes an SQL command. With queries (*SELECT*), moreover, the entire result is transferred to the client and returned as a *mysqli_result* object.
$mysqli->real_query($sqlstring);	Executes an SQL command without transferring the result.

$sql = "sqlcmd1;cmd2;cmd3";
 $ok = $mysqli->multi_query($sql);
 if($ok)
  do {
   $result = $mysqli->store_result();
   ... process result
  while($mysqli->next_result());
	Executes several SQL commands. The first *SELECT* result can be determined at once with *store_result.* If there is more than one result, these must be activated with *next_result.* This method returns 0 if there are no more results or if an error occurred.

$stmt = $mysqli->prepare($sqlstring);	Prepares a parameterized SQL command and returns a *mysqli_stmt* object; the execution of the command and the evaluation of the result take place via the *mysqli_stmt* methods (see below).

---

mysqli — Important Methods

$mysqli->autocommit(0 / 1);	Sets the autocommit mode.
$mysqli->close();	Closes the connection.
$mysqli->commit();	Ends a transaction.
$str = $mysqli->escape_string($str);	Places a backslash in front of special characters in strings or replaces them with SQL-conforming character combinations.
$mysqli->rollback();	Aborts a transaction.

---

mysqli — Important Properties

$n = $mysqli->affected_rows;	Returns the number of records that were altered by the most recent SQL command (*INSERT, UPDATE, DELETE,* etc.).
$n = $mysqli->errno;	Returns the number of the last-occurring error.
$str = $mysqli->error;	Returns the most recent error message.
$str = $mysqli->info;	Returns a string with information about the last-executed SQL command (e.g., after an *UPDATE* command: *Rows matched: nnn Changed: nnn Warnings: nnn*).
$n = $mysqli->insert_id;	Determines the *AUTO_INCREMENT* value created by the last *INSERT* command.
$n = $mysqli->warning_count;	Returns the number of warnings that were triggered by the last SQL command.

mysqli_result Classes

mysqli_result — Important Methods

$result->close();	Releases memory occupied by an object.
$result->data_seek(n);	Makes record *n* the active record (*n=0* for the first record). This does not work if *query* was executed with the optional parameter *MYSQLI_USE_RESULT*.
$row = $result->fetch_array();	Returns the next record of the result (or *FALSE*). Access to individual fields takes place via *$row[n]* or *$row['fieldname']*, where case sensitivity is in force.
$row = $result->fetch_assoc();	Like *fetch_array*, except that access to fields can take place only in the form *$row['fieldname']*.
$meta = $result->fetch_fields();	Returns an array of objects that contain metadata on the columns. For example, *$meta[$n]->name* gives the name of a column.
$row = $result->fetch_row();	Like *fetch_array*, except that field access can take place only in the form *$row[n]*.
$row = $result->fetch_object();	Returns the next record of the result (or *FALSE*). Access to individual fields is via *$row->fieldname*, where case sensitivity is in force.

mysqli_result — Important Properties

$n = $result->affected_rows;	Returns the number of records that were most recently changed with *INSERT, DELETE,* or *UPDATE.*
$n = $result->field_count;	Returns the number of columns of the *SELECT* result.
$lenarray = $result->lengths;	Returns an array whose elements contain the number of characters of all columns of the record most recently read with *fetch_xxx.*
$n = $result->num_rows;	Returns the number of records in a *SELECT* result.

mysqli_stmt Class

mysqli_stmt — Important Methods

$stmt->bind_param('idsb...', $var1, $var2 ...);	Binds the parameters of an SQL command with the associated variables. For each variable the data type must be specified with a character: *i* = integer, *d* = double, *s* = string, *b* = binary (BLOB).
$stmt->bind_result($var1, $var2 ...);	Binds the columns of a *SELECT* result and the associated PHP variables. The method must be executed after *execute.*
$stmt->close();	Releases an object's memory.
$stmt->execute();	Executes an SQL command, where the parameters are passed via *$var1, $var2,* etc.
$stmt->fetch();	Transfers the next record of a *SELECT* result into the variables previously specified with *bind_result. fetch* returns *FALSE* if all records have been processed. *fetch* normally transfers each record individually from the server to the client, unless *store_result* was executed first.
$stmt->store_result();	Transfers all *SELECT* results to the client.

mysqli_stmt — Important Properties

$n = $stmt->affected_rows;	Returns the number of records that were changed by *INSERT, DELETE,* or *UPDATE.*
$n = $stmt->num_rows;	Returns the number of records in a *SELECT* result; this property can be used only if *store_result* was previously executed.

Perl DBI

This reference does not contain an exhaustive list of all *DBI* methods, functions, and attributes. We have included only those key words that are most relevant for everyday MySQL programming with Perl. A complete reference can be found in the *perldoc* documentation.

In this book we generally place Perl methods in parentheses to improve readability. However, Perl syntax allows the execution of methods without parentheses, as in *$dbh->disconnect.*

The following lines show the principles for building a Perl script file:

```
#!/usr/bin/perl -w
use DBI;                  # database access
use CGI qw(:standard);  # required only with CGI scripts
use CGI::Carp qw(fatalsToBrowser);  # only with CGI scripts
...                      # here follows the actual code
```

Common Variable Names

The Perl *DBI* module is object-oriented. Thus the key words introduced in this section relate in part to methods that can be applied to specific objects (which in Perl are generally called *handles*). In this reference the following variable names will be used for such objects:

Common Variable Names for *DBI* Handles		
$dbh	(database handle)	Represents the connection to the database.
$sth	(statement handle)	Enables evaluation of query results (with *SELECT* queries).
$h	(handle)	General handles, used in this section with methods that are available to *$dbh*, *$sth*, and *DBI*.
$drh	(driver handle)	Enables access to many administrative functions.

Establishing the Connection

The Connection	
use DBI();	Activates the DBI module.
$datasource = "DBI:mysql:dbname;" . *"host=hostname";*	Specifies database names and computer names; the database name may be omitted, but then at least the colon must be given.
$dbh = DBI->connect($datasource, $username, $password [, %attributes]);	Creates the connection to the database.

Within the *datasource* character string, further parameters—separated by semicolons—may be given. Details on these parameters can be found in Chapter 22.

Optional Parameters in the *datasource* Character String	
host=hostname	Specifies the name of the computer with the MySQL server (default *localhost*).
port=n	Specifies the IP port (default 3306).
mysql_compression=0/1	Compresses communication (default 0).
mysql_read_default_file=filename	Specifies the file name of the MySQL configuration file.
mysql_read_default_group=mygroup	Reads the group *[mygroup]* within the configuration (default group *[client]*).

A list with attributes can be passed as an optional fourth parameter of *connect.* You can supply these attributes either directly or in the form of an array variable:

```
$dbh = DBI->connect($source, $user, $pw, {Attr1=>val1, Attr2=>val2});
%attr = (Attr1=>val1, Attr2=>val2);
$dbh = DBI->connect($source, $user, $pw, \%attr);
```

To a great extent, these attributes can be read and changed with *$dbh* after the connection has been established:

```
$dbh->{'LongReadLen'} = 1000000;
```

The following table describes the most important *connect* attributes.

Optional *connect* Attributes ($*dbh* Attributes)

RaiseError=>0/1	Displays an error message and ends the program if the connection is not properly established (default 0)
PrintError=>0/1	Displays an error message but continues execution if the connection is not properly established (default 1)
LongReadLen=>n	Determines the maximum size of an individual data field in bytes (0: do not even read long fields)
LongTruncOK=>0/1	Specifies whether data fields that are too long should be truncated (1) or whether an error should be triggered (0)

Terminate the Connection

$dbh->disconnect();	Terminates connection to the database.

Executing SQL Commands, Evaluating SELECT Queries

Execute Queries Without Return of Data Records

$n = $dbh->do("INSERT ...");	Executes an SQL query without returning records; *$n* contains the number of records that were changed, *0E0* if no records were changed, *-1* if the number is unknown, or *undef* if an error has occurred.
$n = $dbh->do($sql, \%attr, @values);	Executes a parameterized query; *@values* contains values for the wild card expressed in the SQL command by *?*; these values are handled automatically with *quote()*; *%attr* can contain optional attributes (otherwise, specify *undef*).
$id = $dbh->{'mysql_insertid'};	Returns the *AUTO_INCREMENT* value of the last record to be inserted (caution: the attribute *mysql_insertid* is MySQL-specific).

Execute Queries with Return of Data Records

$sth = $dbh->prepare("SELECT ...");	Prepares an SQL query (generally *SELECT* queries); all further operations proceed with the help of the *statement handle*.
$sth->execute();	Executes the query.
$sth->execute(@values);	Executes a parameterized query; *@values* contains values for the wild card expressed in the SQL command by *?*.
$sth->fetchxxx();	Evaluates the results (see below).
$sth->finish();	Releases the resources of the statement handle.

If a query was executed with *prepare* and *execute* and a list of records was returned as result, then this list can be evaluated with a number of *fetch* methods.

Evaluating Lists of Data Records

@row = $sth->fetchrow_array();	Reads the next record into the array *@row*, if the end of the list is reached or if an error occurs, then *@row* contains an empty array; access to individual elements proceeds with *$row[n]* (where for the first column, *n=0*).
@row = $sth->fetch();	Equivalent to *fetchrow_array()*.
$rowptr = $sth->fetchrow_arrayref();	Equivalent to *fetchrow_array()*, but returns pointers to arrays (or *undef* if the end of the list of records is reached or an error occurs).
$row = $sth->fetchrow_hashref();	Reads the next record into the associated array *$row*, if the end of the list of records is reached or if an error occurs, then *$row* contains the value *undef*; access to individual elements proceeds with *$row->{'columnname'}*, where case sensitivity is enforced.
$result = $sth->fetchall_arrayref();	Reads all records and returns a pointer to an array of pointers to the individual records; access to individual elements proceeds with *$result->[$row][$col]*.
$result = $sth->fetchall_arrayref({});	As above, but the records are now associative arrays; access is via *$result->[$row]->{'columnname'}*.

Bind Variables to Columns (for *fetchrow_array*)

$sth->bind_col($n, \$var);	Binds the column *n* to the variable *$var* (where for the first column we have, exceptionally, *n=1*); the variable is automatically updated when the next record is read; *bind_col* must be executed after *execute*; the function returns *false* if an error occurs.
$sth->bind_columns(\$var1, \$var2, ...);	Equivalent to *bind_col*, except that variables are assigned to all columns of the query; make sure you have the correct number of variables.

Metainformation on SQL Commands

$n = $sth->{'NUM_OF_FIELDS'};	Returns the number of result columns (after *SELECT*).
$n = $sth->{'NUM_OF_PARAMS'};	Returns the number of parameters in queries with wild cards.
$sql = $sth->{'Statement'};	Returns the underlying SQL command.

Determine Column Names, Data Types, etc., of *SELECT* Results

$array_ref = $sth->{'NAME'};	Returns a pointer to an array with the names of all columns evaluation takes place with *@{$array_ref}[$n]*, where *n* ranges from 0 to *$sth->{'NUM_OF_FIELDS'}-1*.
$array_ref = $sth->{'NAME_lc'};	As above, but names in lowercase.
$array_ref = $sth->{'NAME_uc'};	As above, but names in uppercase.
$array_ref = $sth->{'NULLABLE'};	Specifies for each column whether *NULL* may be stored there (1) or not (0); if this information cannot be determined, then the array contains the value 2 for this column.
$array_ref = $sth->{'PRECISION'};	Specifies the precision in the sense of ODBC (the maximum column width).

Determine Column Names, Data Types, etc., of *SELECT* Results *(Continued)*

$array_ref = $sth->{'SCALE'};	Specifies the number of decimal places for floating-point numbers.
$array_ref = $sth->{'TYPE'};	Specifies the data type of all columns in the form of numerical values; the values relate to the ODBC standard; tests determined the following values: *CHAR: 12, INT: 4, TEXT/BLOB: -1, DATE: 9, TIME: 10, TIMESTAMP: 11, FLOAT: 7, DECIMAL: 3, ENUM/SET: 1.*

Shorthand Notation

@row = $dbh->selectrow_array($sql);	Corresponds to a combination of *prepare, execute,* and *fetchrow_array;* the result is an array of the first result data record; access to further records is not possible.
$result = $dbh->selectrow_array($sql);	As above, but *$result* contains the value of the first column of the first result record.
$result = $dbh->selectall_arrayref($sql);	Corresponds to *prepare, execute,* and *fetchall_arrayref;* for evaluation of *$result,* see *fetchall_arrayref.*

Marking Special Characters in Character Strings and BLOBs with the Backslash

$dbh->quote($data);	Prefixes the contents of *$data* between single quotes, prefixes \ and ' with \, and replaces 0-bytes with \0; if *$data* is empty (*undef*), then *quote()* returns the character string *NULL.*

Transactions

$dbh->{'AutoCommit'} = 0;	Deactivates autocommit mode. From now on, all SQL commands form transactions.
$dbh->commit();	Confirms a transaction.
$dbh->rollback();	Aborts a transaction.

Error Handling

Methods for Error Handling

$h->err();	Returns the error number of the last error (0: no error).
$h->errstr();	Describes the last error (empty string: no error).
DBI->trace($n [, $filename]);	Logs all internal data accesses and redirects output to *STDERR* or the given file; *n* specifies the degree of detail to be logged (0 deactivates logging, 1 gives a good idea, 15 logs everything).

Auxiliary Functions

DBI Functions

@bool = DBI::looks_like_a_number(@data);	Tests for each element in the array *@data* whether it is a number and returns *true* or *undef* in the result array.
$result = DBI::neat($data [, $maxlen]);	Formats the character string contained in *$data* in a form suitable for output; character strings are placed in single quotes; non-ASCII characters are replaced by a period; if the character string is longer than *$maxlen* characters (default 400), then it is truncated and terminated with ... .
$result = DBI::neat_list(\@listref, $maxlen, $sep);	As above, but for an entire array of data; the individual elements are separated by *$sep* (default ",,").

$dbh Methods

$ok = $dbh->ping();	Tests whether the connection to MySQL still exists and returns *true* or *false* accordingly.

MySQL-Specific Extension of the DBD::mysql Driver

If you use the *DBI* module for access to MySQL databases, then there are some supplementary functions available via *DBI* methods and attributes, of which we shall now describe some of the most important. The use of these functions can simplify programming and can make Perl programs more efficient. However, the code will no longer be portable; that is, a later change to another database system will require additional work.

Administrative Functions Based on a Separated Connection

$drh = DBI->install_driver('mysql');	Returns a driver handle.
$drh->func('createdb', $database, $host, $user, $password, 'admin');	Creates a new database; a new connection is used for this.
$drh->func('dropdb', $database, $host, $user, $password, 'admin');	Deletes a database.
$drh->func('shutdown', $host, $user, $password, 'admin');	Shuts down the MySQL server.
$drh->func('reload', $host, $user, $password, 'admin');	Reinputs all MySQL tables (including the *mysql* tables with privilege management).

Administrative Functions Within the Current Connection

$dbh->func('createdb', $database, 'admin');	Creates a new database.
$dbh->func('dropdb', $database, 'admin');	Deletes a database.
$dbh->func('shutdown', 'admin');	Shuts down the MySQL server.
$dbh->func('reload', 'admin');	Reinputs all MySQL tables.

$dbh Attributes

$info = $dbh->{'mysql_hostinfo'};	Returns a string with the connection data for the MySQL server (e.g., *192.168.80.128 via TCP/IP*).
$info = $dbh->{'mysql_info'};	After certain special SQL commands returns a character string with information about the command (e.g., after an *UPDATE* command: *Rows matched: 13 Changed: 13 Warnings: 0*).
$id = $dbh->{'mysql_insertid'};	Returns the *AUTO_INCREMENT* value of the last inserted record.
$n = $dbh->{'mysql_protoinfo'};	Returns the version number of the MySQL connection protocol (e.g., 10).
$info = $dbh->{'mysql_serverinfo'};	Returns a string with the version number of the MySQL server (e.g., *5.0.2-alpha-standard*).
$info = $dbh->{'mysql_stat'};	Returns a string with the server status (number of threads, open tables, etc.).
$threadid = $dhb->{'mysql_thread_id'};	Returns the thread ID number of the current connection to MySQL.

$sth Methods and Attributes

$sth->rows();	Returns after *SELECT* queries the number of data records found by *SELECT*; caution: this does not work if *$sth->{'mysql_use_result'}=1* holds.
$sth->{'mysql_store_result'}=1;	Activates *mysql_store_result*, so that with *SELECT* queries all results are stored temporarily on the client computer (default setting).
$sth->{'mysql_use_result'}=1;	Activates *mysql_use_result*, so that with *SELECT* queries only a single record is stored temporarily on the client.

$sth Attributes for Determining Metadata on *SELECT* Results

$ar_ref = $sth->{'mysql_is_auto_increment'};	Tells whether for the columns the *AUTO_INCREMENT* attribute holds. This and all additional attributes return a pointer to an array whose values give the status. Evaluation is with *@{$ar_ref}[$n]*, where *n* ranges from 0 to *$sth->{'NUM_OF_FIELDS'}-1*.
$ar_ref = $sth->{'mysql_is_blob'};	Tells whether the columns contain BLOBs.
$ar_ref = $sth->{'mysql_is_key'};	Specifies whether the columns are indexed.
$ar_ref = $sth->{'mysql_is_not_null'};	Specifies whether the attribute *NOT NULL* holds for the columns.
$ar_ref = $sth->{'mysql_is_num'};	Specifies whether numerical data are stored in the columns.
$ar_ref = $sth->{'mysql_is_pri_key'};	Specifies which columns are part of the primary index.
$ar_ref = $sth->{'mysql_max_length'};	Specifies the maximum column width of the query results.
$ar_ref = $sth->{'mysql_table'};	Specifies the underlying table names for all columns.
$ar_ref = $sth->{'mysql_type_name'};	Specifies the names of the data types for all columns.

JDBC (Connector/J)

In order to be able to access MySQL under Java, a JDBC driver for MySQL must be installed. This book assumes that you are using Connector/J version 3.*n*. If this assumption is satisfied, you can use numerous classes and methods of JDBC (Java Database Connectivity) with the names *java.sql.** and *javax.sql.**. The following tables assemble only the most important classes and methods of JDBC. There is simply no room for a complete reference to this complex database programming library.

Establishing a Connection

Connection with *DriverManager*

import java.sql.*;	Enables direct access to the JDBC base classes.
Class.forName("com.mysql.jdbc.Driver").newInstance();	Loads and registers Connector/J, the MySQL driver for JDBC.
Connection conn = DriverManager.getConnection ("jdbc:mysql://hostname/dbname", "username", "password");	Creates a connection to the database *dbname* on the computer *hostname*; in the connection string, a large number of additional optional parameters may be passed, the most important of which appear in two tables in Chapter 17.

Connection with DataSource (Since Java 2, Version 1.4)

import java.sql.*; *import javax.sql.*;*	Enables direct access to the JDBC base and extension classes.
com.mysql.jdbc.jdbc2.optional. MysqlDataSource ds = new com.mysql.jdbc.jdbc2.optional. MysqlDataSource(); *ds.setServerName("hostname");* *ds.setDatabaseName("dbname");* *Connection conn = ds.getConnection("username", "password");*	Creates an object of the class *com.mysql.jdbc.jdbc2. optional.MysqlDataSource*, sets the host and database names, and finally establishes the connection.
ds.setUrl("...");	To be used instead of *setServerName* and *setDatabaseName* for setting various connection parameters; the syntax of the connection string (URL) is the same as for *DriverManager.getConnection*.

Executing SQL Commands

SQL Commands (*Statement*)

Statement stmt = *conn.createStatement();*	Creates a *Statement* object, necessary to execute an SQL command.

Statement stmt =
conn.createStatement(
  java.sql.ResultSet.
   TYPE_FORWARD_ONLY,
  java.sql.ResultSet.
   CONCUR_READ_ONLY);
stmt.setFetchSize(
  Integer.MIN_VALUE);
	Defines a *Statement* object for forward only *ResultSets*.

Statement stmt =
conn.createStatement(
  java.sql.ResultSet.
   TYPE_SCROLL_SENSITIVE,
  java.sql.ResultSet.
   CONCUR_UPDATABLE);
	Defines a *Statement* object for a variable *ResultSet*.

int n = stmt.executeUpdate(*"INSERT ...");* *stmt.getWarnings();*	Executes *INSERT, UPDATE,* and *DELETE* commands. The return value gives the number of changed records. With *getWarnings* you can determine the warnings issued when the command was executed (equivalent to *SHOW WARNINGS*). This method returns an *SQLWarning* object until all warnings have been processed.
ResultSet res = stmt.executeQuery(*"SELECT ...");*	Executes a *SELECT* query and returns as result a *ResultSet* object.
stmt.addBatch("INSERT ..."); *stmt.addBatch("INSERT ...");* *int[] n = stm.executeBatch();*	Collects a number of SQL commands and executes them as a group; *executeBatch* returns an *int* field that specifies the number of changed records.

Determining *AUTO_INCREMENT* IDs After *INSERT* Commands

stmt.executeUpdate("INSERT ...");	The starting point for the following three variants.

ResultSet newid =
  stmt.getGeneratedKeys();
if(newid.next()) {
  int id = newid.getInt(1); }
	getGeneratedKeys returns a *ResultSet* object with the most recently generated ID number(s); normally, that is, after a usual *INSERT* command, *res* contains exactly one ID number that is read with *next()* and *getInt(1)*; *getGeneratedKeys* is available since Java 2, version 1.4.

long id = ((com.mysql.jdbc. *Statement)stmt).getLastInsertID();*	*getLastInsertID* also returns the ID number; however, the method is Connector/J-specific and not portable.

ResultSet newid =
  stmt.executeQuery(
   "SELECT LAST_INSERT_ID()");
if(newid.next()) {
  id = newid.getInt(1); }
	Here the ID number is returned with a separate SQL command; note that the command is executed in the same transaction.

Executing *PreparedStatments*

PreparedStatement pstmt =
  conn.prepareStatement(
   "INSERT ... (?, ?)");
	Declares an SQL command with two parameters indicated by question marks.

pstmt.setString(1, "O'Reilly"); *pstmt.setInt(2, 7878);*	Passes the parameter; there are numerous methods in addition to *setString* and *setInt*, e.g., *setNull, setDate, setTime, setFloat, setBinaryStream;* to these methods are passed the parameter number (beginning with 1) and the actual data.
int n = pstmt.executeUpdate(); *ResultSet res = pstmt.executeQuery();* *pstmt.addBatch();* *int n pstmt.executeBatch();*	Executes the command(s); the methods have the same meaning as for the *Statement* class.

Processing SELECT Results (ResultSet Class)

Changing *ResultSets*

res.deleteRow();	Deletes the active record.
res.updateXxx(n, data); *res.updateRow();*	First changes the specified columns of the active record and then stores the changes.
res.moveToInsertRow(); *res.updateXxx(n, data);* *res.insertRow();*	Inserts a new record, changes its columns, and then stores the changes.

Evaluating *ResultSet*

res.getInt(n); *res.getString(n);* *res.getBytes(n);* ...	Returns the data field of column *n* of the currently active record; instead of the column number (1 for the first column), the name of the column may be specified, e.g., *getDate("birthdate")*.
res.wasNull();	Tests whether the most recently read data field was *NULL*; this test is necessary with elementary Java data types that cannot store the value *NULL* and instead contain 0; *wasNull* offers the only way of distinguishing between 0 and *NULL*.
res.getBinaryStream(n);	Returns an *InputStream* object for bytewise reading of binary data.
res.getCharacterStream(n);	Returns a *Reader* object for characterwise reading of binary data.
res.getBlob(n);	Returns a *Blob* object for reading binary data.
res.getClob(n);	Returns a *Clob* object for reading binary data.

ResultSet Navigation

res.next();	Makes the next record in *ResultSet* the active record; the method returns *false* if there are no more records.
res.first();	Activates the first record; the method returns *false* if the *ResultSet* contains no records.
res.previous();	Activates the previous record.
res.last();	Activates the last record.
res.beforeFirst();	Places the record cursor before the first record; the *ResultSet* object is thereby in the same condition as immediately after *executeQuery*; now the first record can be activated with *next*.
res.afterLast();	Places the record cursor after the last record; *previous* activates the last record.
res.isFirst(); *res.isLast();*	Tests whether the current record is the first/last.
int n = res.getRow();	Returns the number of the active record (1 for the first record).
res.absolute(n);	Activates record *n*.

Metadata on *ResultSet*

ResultSetMetaData meta = res.getMetaData();	Returns a *ResultSetMetaData* object that gives information about the *SELECT* result.
meta.getColumnCount();	Returns the number of columns.
meta.getColumnName(i);	Returns the name (*String*) of column *i*.
meta.getColumnType(i);	Returns the data type of column *i*; the result is an *int* with one of the constants from *java.sql.Types*.
meta.getColumnTypeName(i);	Returns the name (*String*) of the data type of column *i*.
meta.IsNullable(i);	Tells whether the column may contain *NULL*.
meta.IsAutoIncrement(i);	Tells whether it is an *AUTO_INCREMENT* column.

Transactions

Transactions

conn.setAutoCommit(false);	Enables transactions (of course only if the MySQL tables are transaction-capable).
conn.commit();	Confirms all SQL commands executed in the current transaction and begins the next transaction.
conn.rollback();	Aborts the commands of the current transaction and begins a new one.

ADO.NET (Connector/Net)

The following tables summarize the most important classes and methods provided by Connector/J (that is, the library MySql.Data.dll). Visual Basic syntax is used.

Establishing a Connection, Connection Properties

Creating the Connection

Imports MySql.Data.MySqlClient	Enables convenient access to the Connector/Net classes.

Dim myconn As MySqlConnection
myconn = New MySqlConnection(_
  "Data Source=localhost;
  Initial Catalog=mylibrary;
  User ID=root;PWD=xxxxxx")
myconn.Open()
	Creates a connection to the MySQL server.

Methods and Properties of the *MySqlConnection* Class

BeginTransaction	Begins a transaction and returns a *MySqlTransaction* object (see below).
Close	Ends the connection.
ConnectionString	Contains the connection properties as a character string.
CreateCommand	Creates a *MySqlCommand* object.
Dispose	Releases memory used by the connection.
Ping	Tests whether the connection is active.
ServerThread	Contains the MySQL server thread number for the connection.
ServerVersion	Contains the MySQL version number as a string (e.g., *5.0.2-alpha-standard-log*).
State	Provides information about the state of the connection (data type *System.Data.ConnectionState*).

Executing and Evaluating SQL Commands

Executing SQL Commands (*MySqlCommand* Class)

Dim com As MySqlCommand *com = myconn.CreateCommand("sql")* *com = New MySqlCommand("sql", _* *myconn)*	Creates a *MySqlCommand* object in two different ways.
com.ExecuteNonQuery()	Executes an SQL command that returns no result (e.g., *UPDATE* or *INSERT*).
obj = com.ExecuteScalar()	Returns a single result (a scalar). *ExecuteScalar* is suitable only for *SELECT* queries that return exactly one row and one column. The return value of *ExecuteScalar* has the data type *Object* and must be transformed with a conversion function (e.g., *CInt*) or a cast operator (e.g., *(int)*) into the desired data format.
dr = com.ExecuteReader()	Returns a *MySqlDataReader* object (see below).
Dim n As Long *com.CommandText =* *"SELECT LAST_INSERT_ID()"* *n = CLng(com.ExecuteScalar())*	Returns the ID number (*AUTO_INCREMENT* column) of the last record inserted with *INSERT*.

Executing SQL Commands with Parameters (*MySqlParameter* Class)

Dim com As MySqlCommand
Dim p1, p2, p3 As MySqlParameter
com = myconn.CreateCommand()
com.CommandText = _
  "INSERT ... VALUES(?a, ?b, ?c)"
p1 = com.Parameters.Add("?a", _
  MySqlDbType.VarChar)
p2 = com.Parameters.Add("?b", _
  MySqlDbType.Int32)
...
com.Prepare()
	Prepares an SQL command with parameters. Each parameter is specified in the form *?name*. Then an associated *MySqlParameter* object must be created in which the desired data type of the parameter is specified. *Prepare* prepares the command for later execution.

p1.Value = ... *p2.Value = ...* *com.ExecuteXxx()*	Assigns values to the *Value* properties of the *MySqlParameter* object and then executes the command with the method *Execute* described above.

Evaluating SELECT Results (*MySqlDataReader* Class)

Dim dr As MySqlDataReader *dr = com.ExecuteReader()*	Executes a *SELECT* command and returns the result as a *MySqlDataReader* object. Access to the *SELECT* results takes place under *forward-only* and *read-only*.
dr.HasRows	Tests whether the *DataReader* contains any data.
dr.FieldCount	Returns the number of columns of the *DataReader*.

While dr.Read()
  n = CInt(dr!publID)
  s = CStr(dr!publName)
End While
	Outputs the *DataReader* row by row. *Read* returns *False* if there are no more records. Access to the columns of the current record takes place in VB.NET in the form *dr!columnname*, and in C# in the form *dr["columnname"]*. The return values have the data type *Object* and must be transformed into the actual data format using *Cdatatype* functions (VB.NET) or *(datatype)* cast operators.

dr.GetName(n)	Returns the name of column *n* (0 for the first column).
dr.GetDataTypeName(n)	Returns the name of the column's data type.
dr.IsDBNull(n)	Tests whether column *n* of the current record contains *NULL*.
dr.GetByte(n) *dr.GetBytes(n, ...)* *dr.GetChar(n)* *dr.GetDateTime(n)* *...*	Reads the data of column *n* directly. These methods are suitable in particular for processing binary data.
bool = dr.NextResult()	Activates the next *SELECT* result. The method returns *False* if there are no further results.
dr.Close()	Closes the *DataReader* and releases the data.

Altering Data in DataSet/DataTable

Application of *MySqlDataAdapter* and *MySqlCommandBuilder*

Dim da As New _
  MySqlDataAdapter(com)
 Dim ds As New DataSet()
 da.Fill(ds, "dtname")
 Dim dt As DataTable = _
  ds.Tables("dtname")
	Creates a *DataTable* on the basis of the SQL command *com* (*MySqlCommand*) and makes it available under the name *dtname* in a *DataSet*.

n = dt.Count	Determines the number of records in the *DataTable*.
Dim row As DataRow *For Each row In dt.Rows* *var = row!columnname* *Next*	Creates a loop over all records of a *DataTable*. In C# column access is in the form *dt["columnname"]*.
row.Delete()	Deletes the current record in *DataSet*.
row!columnname = ... *row.Update()*	Changes the current record in *DataSet*.
Dim newrow As DataRow *newrow = dt.NewRow()* *newrow!columnname = ...* *dt.Rows.Add(newrow)*	Creates a new record and stores it in *DataSet*.
Dim cb As New _ *MySqlCommandBuilder(da)* *da.Update(ds, "dtname")*	Stores the changes made locally in the *DataSet* permanently on the MySQL server. The *MySqlCommandBuilder* object provides the necessary SQL change commands.
cb.GetDeleteCommand() *cb.GetInsertCommand()* *cb.GetUpdateCommand()*	Returns the *DELETE*, *INSERT*, or *UPDATE* commands created by *MySqlCommandBuilder* as *MySqlCommand* objects. (The actual SQL code can be read from the property *CommandText*.)

Transactions

Transactions

Dim tr As MySqlTransaction *tr = myconn.BeginTransaction()*	Creates a *MySqlTransaction* object.
Dim com As New MySqlCommand(_ *"UPDATE ...", myconn, tr)* *com.ExecuteNonQuery()* *... further commands of the transaction*	Creates a *MySqlCommand* object and executes it in the framework of this transaction.
tr.Commit()	Confirms the transaction.
tr.Rollback()	Aborts the transaction.

C API

The following tables assemble the most important functions and structures of the C API.

Data Structures

Data Structures	
MYSQL *conn;	Structure with connection data.
MYSQL_RES *result;	Structure with the results of a *SELECT* query.
MYSQL_ROW row;	Pointer to the results of a row (i.e., of a data record).
MYSQL_ROW_OFFSET roffset;	Pointer to a record within the result list.
MYSQL_FIELD *field;	Structure for describing a column (column name, data type, number of digits, etc.); details in the next table.
MYSQL_FIELD_OFFSET foffset;	Offset within a record (0 for the first column, 1 for the second, etc.).
MYSQL_STMT *stmt;	Structure for processing prepared statements.
MYSQL_BIND bind[n];	Structure for describing the parameters of prepared statements.
MYSQL_TIME mytime;	Structure for passing date and time values in prepared statements.
my_ulonglong n;	64-bit integer; some of the MySQL functions described below return results of this data type.

In the further syntax tables, the variables *conn, result, row, field, roffset, foffset,* etc., will be used as if they had been declared in the above table. Note that *MYSQL_ROW* is already a pointer and is therefore declared without ***.

Elements of the *MYSQL_FIELD* Structure	
char *name;	Name of the column.
char *table;	Name of the table from which the column comes; if the column was computed or an *ALIAS* was used, then *table* points to a character string with the formula or the *ALIAS* name.
char *def;	Default value of the column or *NULL*.
enum enum_field_types type;	Data type of the column; these are the choices: *FIELD_TYPE_BLOB, FIELD_TYPE_DATE, FIELD_TYPE_DATETIME, FIELD_TYPE_DECIMAL, FIELD_TYPE_DOUBLE, FIELD_TYPE_ENUM, FIELD_TYPE_FLOAT, FIELD_TYPE_INT24, FIELD_TYPE_LONG, FIELD_TYPE_LONGLONG, FIELD_TYPE_NULL, FIELD_TYPE_SET, FIELD_TYPE_SHORT, FIELD_TYPE_STRING, FIELD_TYPE_TIME, FIELD_TYPE_TIMESTAMP, FIELD_TYPE_TINY, FIELD_TYPE_VAR_STRING, FIELD_TYPE_YEAR.*

Continued

Elements of the *MYSQL_FIELD* Structure *(Continued)*

unsigned int length;	Length of the column according to the column definition.
unsigned int max_length;	Maximal length of a column within the query result; the value is always 0 if you use *mysql_use_result()*.
unsigned int flags;	Additional information for describing the column: *AUTO_INCREMENT_FLAG,* *BINARY_FLAG,* *MULTIPLE_KEY_FLAG,* *NOT_NULL_FLAG,* *PRI_KEY_FLAG,* *UNIQUE_KEY_FLAG,* *UNSIGNED_FLAG,* *ZEROFILL_FLAG.*
unsigned int decimals;	Number of places after the decimal point in *DECIMAL* columns (e.g., 5 for *DECIMAL(10,5)*).

Data Structures for Prepared Statements

Elements of the *MYSQL_BIND* Structure

enum enum_field_types buffer_type;	Data type of the parameter; possible values are collected in the following table.
void *buffer;	Pointer to the buffer variable in which the data are passed.
unsigned long buffer_length;	Maximal buffer size (for strings/BLOBs).
unsigned long *length;	Actual length of the data passed (for strings/BLOBs).
my_bool *is_null;	Specifies whether *NULL* should be passed; in this case the contents of the buffer variable are not evaluated. Caution: *is_null* cannot be directly read; it is a pointer to the variable that contains the relevant information.
my_bool is_unsigned;	For integer data types specifies whether the value is to be interpreted as unsigned.
my_bool error;	Specifies whether an error has occurred in data transport (e.g., exceeding the maximum buffer size).

The following table summarizes the allowable settings for *buffer_type* in a *MYSQL_BIND* structure. The second column gives the matching MySQL data type and the best-fitting C data type.

enum_field_types (Settings)

MYSQL_TYPE_TINY	For MySQL *TINYINT* values *(C-Typ char)*.
MYSQL_TYPE_SHORT	For *SMALLINT* values *(short int)*.
MYSQL_TYPE_LONG	For *INT* values *(int)*.
MYSQL_TYPE_LONGLONG	For *BIGINT* values *(long long int)*.
MYSQL_TYPE_FLOAT	For *FLOAT* values *(float)*.
MYSQL_TYPE_DOUBLE	For *DOUBLE* values *(double)*.
MYSQL_TYPE_TIME	For *TIME* values *(MYSQL_TIME)*.
MYSQL_TYPE_DATE	For *DATE* values *(MYSQL_TIME)*.
MYSQL_TYPE_DATETIME	For *DATETIME* values *(MYSQL_TIME)*.

enum_field_types (Settings) *(Continued)*

MYSQL_TYPE_TIMESTAMP	For *TIMESTAMP* values *(MYSQL_TIME)*.
MYSQL_TYPE_STRING	For *CHAR* strings *(char *)*.
MYSQL_TYPE_VAR_STRING	For *VARCHAR* strings *(char *)*.
MYSQL_TYPE_TINY_BLOB	For *TINY_BLOB*s *(char *)*.
MYSQL_TYPE_BLOB	For *BLOB*s *(char *)*.
MYSQL_TYPE_MEDIUM_BLOB	For *MEDIUM_BLOB*s *(char *)*.
MYSQL_TYPE_LONG_BLOB	For *LONG_BLOB*s *(char *)*.

Elements of the *MYSQL_TIME* Structure

un*signed int year;*	Year.
unsigned int month;	Months.
unsigned int day;	Days.
unsigned int hour;	Hours.
unsigned int minute;	Minutes.
unsigned int second;	Seconds.
my_bool neg;	Boolean value that tells whether a negative value is involved (such as with a result of the function *TIME_DIFF*).
unsigned long second_part;	Microseconds; not used in MySQL 5.0.

Connection and Administration

Establishing a Connection

MYSQL *conn; *conn = mysql_init(NULL);*	Initializes the *MYSQL* data structure.
mysql_options(conn, option, "value");	Sets additional options for the connection; an *option* with one of the following values is passed: *MYSQL_OPT_CONNECT_TIMEOUT,* *MYSQL_OPT_LOCAL_INFILE,* *MYSQL_OPT_NAMED_PIPE,* *MYSQL_INIT_COMMAND,* *MYSQL_READ_DEFAULT_FILE,* *MYSQL_READ_DEFAULT_GROUP.* Many additional options are documented at http://dev.mysql.com/doc/mysql/en/mysql_options.html. With some options, *"value"* can be used to specify the desired value; for setting several options, the function must be called repeatedly; *mysql_options* must be exectued before *mysql_real_connect.*

Continued

Establishing a Connection *(Continued)*

mysql_real_connect(conn, "hostname", "username", "password", "dbname", portnum, "socketname", flags);	Makes a connection to the database and returns *NULL* in case of error; *flags* can contain a combination of the following values: *CLIENT_COMPRESS, CLIENT_FOUND_ROWS, CLIENT_IGNORE_SPACE, CLIENT_INTERACTIVE, CLIENT_LOCAL_FILES, CLIENT_MULTI_STATEMENTS, CLIENT_MULTI_RESULTS, CLIENT_NO_SCHEMA, CLIENT_ODBC, CLIENT_SSL.*
mysql_set_server_option(conn, option);	Changes server options for a long-term connection. Currently, only two values are accepted for server options: *MYSQL_OPTION_MULTI_STATEMENTS_ON, MYSQL_OPTION_MULTI_STATEMENTS_OFF.*
mysql_change_user(conn, "username", "password", "dbname");	Changes the user and the default database for an existing connection.
mysql_change_db(conn, "dbname");	Changes the default database; the function assumes that the user has access to the database.
mysql_ping(conn);	Tests whether the connection still exists; if not, the connection is recreated; returns 0 as result if an active connection exists.
mysql_close(conn);	Closes the connection.

Acquiring Information on the Current Connection

mysql_characterset_name(conn);	Returns a character string with the default character set of the connection.
mysql_get_client_info();	Returns a character string with information on the version of the client library in use (e.g., *"5.0.2"*).
mysql_get_server_info(conn);	Returns a string with the version of the server (e.g., *"5.0.2-alpha-standard"*).
mysql_get_host_info(conn);	Returns a string with information on the connection to the server (e.g., *"localhost via UNIX socket"*).
mysql_get_proto_info(conn);	Returns the version number (*unsigned int*) of the connection protocol, e.g., 10.
mysql_info(conn);	Returns a string with information on the execution of the last *INSERT, UPDATE, LOAD DATA,* or *ALTER TABLE* command (e.g., *"Rows matched: 3 Changed: 3 Warnings: 0"*).
mysql_stat(conn);	Returns a string with the server status (number of threads, number of open tables, etc.).
mysql_thread_id(conn);	Returns the number (*unsigned long*) of the thread that the current connection is processing on the server.

Adminstrative Functions

mysql_kill(conn, n);	Ends the thread specified by *n* (requires the *Process* privilege).
mysql_shutdown(conn);	Shuts down the server (execution requires the *Shutdown* privilege).

Error-Handling

mysql_errno(conn);	Returns the error number (*unsigned int*) for the most recently executed command (or 0 if there was no error).
mysql_error(conn);	Returns a string with the error message (or an empty string *""* if there was no error).
mysql_warning_count(conn);	Returns the number of warnings that the last command returned. To read the actual warnings, you must execute the command *SHOW WARNINGS.*

Executing and Evaluating SQL Commands

Execution of SQL Commands

mysql_query(conn, "SELECT …");	Executes the specified command and returns 0 if the server accepts the command without triggering an error.
mysql_real_query(conn, "SELECT … ", len);	Like *mysql_query*, except that the SQL command may now contain the 0-byte (e.g., to store BLOBs); for this, the length of the string must be specified explicitly.
mysql_affected_rows(conn);	Returns the number (data type *my_ulonglong*) of changed records after a *DELETE, INSERT,* or *UPDATE* command; the function does not return the number of results of a *SELECT* command.
mysql_insert_id(conn);	Returns the *AUTO_INCREMENT* value (data type *my_ulonglong*) of the last record created via *INSERT.*

Processing *SELECT* Results

result = mysql_store_result(conn);	Transfers all results from the server to the client and stores them in the *MYSQL_RES* structure.
result = mysql_use_result(conn);	Represents an alternative to *mysql_store_result*; the transfer of individual records is only prepared; no data are actually transferred.
mysql_num_fields(result);	Returns the number of columns of the result.
row = mysql_fetch_row(result);	Transfers the next record to a *MYSQL_ROW* structure; the function returns *NULL* if there are no further records available, i.e., if all records have already been processed.
row[n];	Returns a 0-terminated string with the content of column *n* of the current record; note that *row[n]* can contain *NULL*; if you are processing binary data with zero bytes, you must make the call with *mysql_fetch_lengths* to determine the size of the data field.
mysql_free_result(result);	Releases the result structure; if you are working with *mysql_use_result*, the result is only now released by the server.

Processing *SELECT* Results: Metainformation on Columns and Fields

mysql_fetch_lengths(result);	Returns for the current record an *unsigned long* field with the length of the result string in *row[n]*.
field = mysql_fetch_field(result);	Returns a description (*MYSQL_FIELD* structure) of the data type of a column; the first call returns the data for the first column, the next for the second column, etc.; the function returns *NULL* after all columns have been run through; the elements of the *MYSQL_FIELD* structure were described previously.
field = mysql_fetch_field_direct(result, n);	Returns a description of column *n* (0 for the first column, etc.).
mysql_fetch_fields(result);	Returns a description of all columns as a *MYSQL_FIELD* field.

The following functions can be used only if you are using *mysql_store_result* (and are not working with *mysql_use_result*).

Processing *SELECT* Results: Additional Functions for *mysql_store_result*

mysql_num_rows(result);	Returns the number of found records.
mysql_data_seek(result, n);	Moves the row cursor to record *n* (0 for the first record); then *mysql_fetch_row* must be executed to reinput data.
roffset = mysql_row_tell(result);	Returns a pointer (a sort of bookmark) to the current record.
mysql_row_seek(result, roffset);	Moves the row cursor to a particular location within the result list; then *mysql_fetch_row* must be executed to reinput data; *roffset* must be determined earlier with *mysql_row_tell*.

MULTI_STATEMENTS and MULTI_RESULTS Mode

mysql_real_connect(..., CLIENT_MULTI_STATEMENTS);	Activates the two *MULTI* modes at connection time.
mysql_set_server_option(conn, MYSQL_OPTION_ MULTI_-STATEMENTS_ON);	Activates the two *MULTI* modes at a later time.
mysql_query("command1; command2; command3");	Executes several commands separated by semicolons. The result of the first command can be processed as usual (*mysql_affected_rows*, *mysql_store_result*, etc.).
n = mysql_more_results(conn);	Tests whether there are more results (*n=1*).
n = mysql_next_result(conn);	Activates the next result. This can then be processed with the usual functions. The possible return values are these: *n=0* OK, there are more results, *n=-1* OK, but there are no more results, *n>0* error number.

Auxiliary Functions

n = mysql_real_escape_string (conn, dest, src, srclen);	Copies the string *src* into the string *dest* while replacing the special characters with \ character combinations (\0, \b, \t, \", \', etc.); *dest* is terminated with a 0-byte; *srclen* specifies the number of characters in *src*; *dest* must be previously initialized with a string of the appropriate length; to be able to copy a string full of special characters without error, *dest* must offer place for *srclen*2+1* characters; the function returns the number of characters in *dest* (without the 0-byte). If *"O'Reilly"* is copied, then afterward, *src* contains the string *O\'Reilly*, and *n* the value 9.
n = mysql_hex_string(to, from, len);	Changes every character of the string *from* into hexadecimal code and writes it to the buffer *to*. The resulting string in *to* ends with a 0-byte. It does not contain the characters 0x, which in MySQL indicate hexadecimal strings. You must insert 0x yourself when preparing the SQL command. *len* gives the length of the string in *from*. The buffer *to* must have length *len*2+1* characters. The function returns the length of the resulting string without the closing 0-byte.
destpt = strmov(dest, src);	Like *strcpy*, copies the string *src* to the string *dest*; the difference is in the return value, which points to the end of the string in *dest*; this makes it easy to construct a string from several pieces; to be able to use *strmov*, the files my_global.h and m_string.h must be included before mysql.h.

Prepared Statements

Preparing and Executing Prepared Statements

stmt = mysql_stmt_init(conn);	Returns a *MYSQL_STMT* structure.
mysql_stmt_prepare(stmt, sqlcmd, strlen(sqlcmd));	Initializes the *MYSQL_STMT* structure; *sqlcmd* is the string (*char[]*) with the SQL command to be executed.
mysql_stmt_bind_param(stmt, bind);	Declares the parameters for the SQL command; *bind* is a *MYSQL_BIND* field, where each field element describes a parameter.
mysql_stmt_execute(stmt);	Executes the SQL command. The parameters are read from the buffer variables given in *bind* and written there as well (*SELECT* results).
mysql_stmt_close(stmt);	Releases the memory for the *MYSQL_STMT* structure.

Evaluating *SELECT* Results of Prepared Statements

---

stmt = mysql_stmt_init(conn);	Returns a *MYSQL_STMT* structure.
mysql_stmt_prepare(stmt, sqlcmd, strlen(sqlcmd));	Initializes the *MYSQL_STMT* structure.
mysql_stmt_bind_result(stmt, bind);	Declares the result columns of the *SELECT* command; *bind* is a *MYSQL_BIND* field, where each field element describes a column.
mysql_stmt_execute(stmt);	Executes the SQL command.
mysql_stmt_store_result(stmt);	Transfers all results to the client and stores them in a buffer. Calling this function is optional. If you do not do so, the records remain on the server until the last record is read with *mysql_stmt_fetch.* Then *mysql_stmt_data_seek* is not available, and *mysql_stmt_num_rows* is available only after all records have been processed.
n = mysql_stmt_num_rows(stmt);	Returns the number of result records; *n* has the data type *my_ulonglong.*
mysql_stmt_fetch(stmt);	Reads the next record into the variables given by the *MYSQL_BIND* field. The function returns 0 if there are no further results.
mysql_stmt_data_seek(stmt, n);	Activates record *n.* The next call to *mysql_stmt_fetch* reads this record into the variables.
result = mysql_stmt_result_metadata(stmt);	Returns metainformation on the *SELECT* result. Details can then be determined with *mysql_num_fields, mysql_fetch_field,* etc.

PART 6

■ ■ ■

Appendixes

APPENDIX A

■■■

Glossary

This appendix contains a brief description of the most important notions from the world of databases and related areas.

Character Set: A character set is a specification that determines the set of codes used to represent the characters of a particular language or set of languages. Among the oldest character sets is the ASCII (American Standard Code for Information Interchange) character set, in which the letter A is coded by the integer 65.

Client: A client is a program that accesses a central service. In connection with databases, a client denotes a program that accesses a central database. The database is managed by another program, the database server.

Client/Server Architecture: Most modern database systems are based on a server that manages the data and executes SQL commands, and an arbitrary number of clients that access the server over a network. This concept is called client/server architecture. Alternatives to this model are file-server databases such as dBase and Access, in which all clients access the database file directly through a common file system. (This is quite inefficient when many users are trying to edit data simultaneously.)

Cluster: In information theory a cluster usually refers to a group of networked computers that work together on a common task. A database cluster is therefore a database system in which several computers provide a common database (particularly a large or fast or secure one).

Cursor: In MySQL a cursor enables step-by-step processing of query results (particularly in stored procedures). In the ADO library, cursor properties determine what processing options exist for the records of a *Recordset* object.

Data Dictionary: The MySQL Data Dictionary enables one to use *SELECT* queries to obtain information about the structure of databases and tables as well as other administrative data about the MySQL server. The MySQL server provides, since version 5.0, virtual *INFORMATION_ SCHEMA* tables.

Data Record: A data record, or simply *record*, is a row of a table.

Database: Generally speaking, a database is an ordered collection of data. In connection with MySQL, a database consists of a number of tables. In common usage, a database can also refer to an entire database system, that is, the program that manages the data. In MySQL, this program is called the database server (MySQL server).

Database Server: A database server is a program that permits access to databases over a network. The server is responsible for the management of the data and for the execution of SQL commands.

Derived Tables: These are tables that do not exist as such but are merely the result of a *SELECT* command. Derived tables are in fact nothing more than a variant of sub*SELECT*s, that is, nested *SELECT* commands.

Domain Name: The domain name denotes an entire network. A local network might consist of computers with the names *mars.sol, uranus.sol,* and *jupiter.sol,* in which case *mars, uranus,* and *jupiter* are computer names (*hostnames*), and *sol* is the domain name.

Domain Name Server (DNS): Internally, communication within a network takes place on the basis of IP numbers (e.g., 192.168.0.27). Since mere mortals do not keep track of such numbers very well, each computer also has a computer name, composed of host name and domain name (e.g., *uranus.sol*).

Whenever such a name is used, the running program must determine the associated IP number. Sometimes, the converse case arises, and for a given IP number, the computer name is required. In both situations, the domain name server provides the answer. (Small networks can get by without a DNS. In that case, the association between IP numbers and computer names is determined from static tables, under Unix/Linux in the file /etc/hosts.)

Foreign Key: A foreign key is a unique value (usually an integer) that refers to a particular column of another table. A foreign key thus creates a link (relation) between two tables.

Full-Text Index: A full-text index enables the search for several words in arbitrary order within a text. To make full-text search efficient, a special index is required, known as a full-text index.

Global Assembly Cache (GAC): This notion is specific to Microsoft. It describes a central directory of all *.dll files for .NET programs. In contrast to the Windows system directory, in the GAC, several different versions of a library can be installed simultaneously without leading to a conflict.

Host Name: The host name is the name of a computer valid over a network. If the complete name of the computer is *jupiter.sol,* then *jupiter* is the host name and *sol* the domain name.

Hot Backup: What makes a hot backup hot is that during the backup process, the database server can continue to run almost completely undisturbed. (During a normal backup, on the other hand, no changes in the data may be made.) Hot backups can currently be made in MySQL only with a commercial auxiliary program that works only for InnoDB tables.

Include File: An include file is a part of program code. It is read by the compiler (e.g., C) or during code execution (e.g., PHP).

Index: In database-speak, an index, or its synonym *key,* is an ordered list of the content of a table. An index serves primarily to speed up access to individual records: Instead of searching through all records, it suffices to search the index. Then, the desired record can be read directly. The use of an index is comparable to that of an index in a book.

InnoDB Tables: In MySQL, tables can be stored on the hard drive in more than one format, including MyISAM and InnoDB. InnoDB tables possess some additional functionality over MyISAM tables, such as transactions and foreign key constraints. The name InnoDB is derived from the name of the company Innobase, with DB being short for *database.*

Internet Service Provider (ISP): An ISP is a company that provides technical support and hosting of web sites. ISPs are used by commercial enterprises and private individuals who wish to maintain web sites on the Internet but do not themselves possess a permanent or sufficiently high-speed Internet connection. Be careful in your choice of ISP that it supports the programs presented in this book (Apache, PHP, MySQL, etc.). There are, of course, ISPs that offer Microsoft products instead.

Key: A key is an ordered index of a table. See also the entry of the synonym *Index.*

Logging: Logging refers to the recording of SQL commands in a file. The motivation for logging is usually to have available all the changes to the database made since the last backup so that the database can be re-created in the event of disaster. With MySQL, logging is also a prerequisite for replication.

MyISAM Tables: The MySQL server can store tables in various formats. The most important such format is called MyISAM, which stands for *indexed sequential access method*, referring to the method of access to data records within a file with the aid of an index. An alternative to MyISAM tables is InnoDB tables.

Named Pipes: Named pipes represent a mechanism whereby two programs can communicate under Windows 2000/XP. Data exchange takes place according to the principle of first in, first out (FIFO).

Normal Form: A database generally consists of a number of tables. A goal in the design of tables is to avoid redundancy. This goal is supported by particular rules. When the first *n* such rules are adhered to, the database is said to be in *n*th normal form.

Normalization: This term refers to the optimization of the database design to avoid redundancy. The goal is generally to achieve third normal form.

PHP: PHP is a script language for programming dynamic web sites. The program code is located in `*.php` files. These files are executed by the PHP interpreter at each access over the web server. The resulting HTML document is passed on to the web server.

Port: Network packets that are sent using the TCP/IP protocol are always addressed to a particular port. The port number is thus part of the address to which the packet is sent. Ports help in categorizing network traffic. For example, for data exchange between web browsers and web servers, port 80 is used. MySQL uses port 3306 by default.

Prepared Statements: These provide for a particularly efficient processing of SQL commands that differ only in the values of parameters. The entire SQL command is sent only once to the MySQL server, and thereafter only the varying parameters. This not only reduces the quantity of data that has to be transferred, but also spares the server the repeated analysis of the SQL command.

Primary Index (Primary Key): The primary index identifies each record of a table uniquely. Normally, the primary key field is an integer column. Whenever a new record is inserted, the database server determines a new, unique value for this column.

Privilege: In MySQL nomenclature, a privilege is a right to execute particular database operations (e.g., read or change data in a particular table).

Query: In database language, a query is generally a *SELECT* command. The syntax of this command is part of the language SQL (structured query language). SQL specifies how commands to the database server must be structured.

Query Cache: In many database applications, it happens that the same queries must be executed over and over. To speed up such queries, MySQL possesses, since version 4.0, a query cache, that is, temporary storage in which queries and their results can be stored. Queries thus stored can be answered much more rapidly than otherwise. However, this temporary storage must be deleted at each change in the underlying table.

Referential Integrity: Referential integrity holds if between linked tables, no reference points to nowhere. (For example, if referential integrity is satisfied for a library database, then there cannot exist a book title whose associated publisher does not exist in the database. On the other hand, if referential integrity has been damaged, then there might well be a publisher number in the titles table that does not exist in the publisher table.)

Many database systems can automatically check referential integrity when changes to a database are made. This requires the setting up of foreign key constraints, otherwise known as integrity rules. MySQL currently supports foreign key constraints only for InnoDB tables.

Relations: The most characteristic feature of relational databases is that a number of tables in a database can be linked based on their contents. These links are also called *relations*. The links are referenced in SQL commands by the *JOIN* operator or with *WHERE* conditions.

Replication: Through the process of replication, all changes to a database are carried out not on one, but on several database servers. Thus the same database exists on several servers. The advantages are increased security (if one server goes down) and greater speed (all servers can answer SQL queries, even if only one can make changes).

Schema: The schema (or *database schema*) describes the layout of a database, that is, the tables, their columns and data types, indexes, links between tables, etc.

 Server: A server is a central program that provides services or data to other programs (called *clients*). Examples of servers are the MySQL server (a database server) and Apache (a web server).

Socket File: A socket file enables communication under Unix/Linux between two programs. A socket file is not a real file, in that it contains no data and has length zero.

Local connections between a MySQL client and the MySQL server generally take place under Unix/Linux over a socket file, since this type of communication is more efficient than the network protocol TCP/IP. (An exception is Java clients, which do not support socket files.) The usual file name is /var/lib/mysql/mysql.sock. This file name can be set via the configuration file /etc/my.cnf.

Stored Procedures: A stored procedure is program code that is executed directly by the database server. Often, stored procedures are formulated in a programming language that extends SQL through the use of control structures (loops, branching, etc.). MySQL has supported stored procedures since version 5.0.

SubSELECTs: The nesting of several *SELECT* commands to form a query is called a sub*SELECT*. MySQL has supported such commands since version 4.1.

Tables: A table is a part of a database. The properties of a table are determined by its columns or fields (name and data type) and indexes. The rows of a table are also called data records. The MySQL server can store tables in several formats (e.g., MyISAM, InnoDB).

Timestamps: The data type *TIMESTAMP* is characterized by the fact that columns of this type store the current date and time each time a change is made.

Transactions: A transaction is a group of logically related SQL commands. Transaction-capable database systems are able to confirm all the commands of a transaction together or to abort them as a group. That is, a transaction is never only partially completed. Transactions thereby contribute to data security.

Transactions can also improve efficiency in that there is no longer the need to lock entire tables with *LOCK* during the execution of several SQL commands.

MySQL currently supports transactions only for InnoDB tables.

Triggers: This term refers to SQL code (stored procedures) that is automatically executed as a result of particular actions (e.g., upon an *UPDATE* or *INSERT* command). Triggers can be used, for example, to ensure that certain rules are followed in changing data. MySQL has supported triggers since version 5.0.

Unicode: Unicode is a character set in which every character is represented by a 16-bit integer. Thus almost all the special characters of the world's languages can be represented in this character set. MySQL supports the storage of Unicode character sets since version 4.1.

Within Unicode, there are various formats that specify the byte order of the 16-bit integer. Common formats are UTF8 (1 to 3 bytes, depending on the character code, avoids code 0) and UTF16 alias UCS2 (2 bytes for each character code).

Uniform Resource Locator (URL): This unwieldy term denotes Internet addresses (e.g., `http://www.kofler.cc/mysql/` or `ftp://ftp.mysql.com`). Additional information can be provided in a URL, such as variables or user names: `http://my.company/page.html?var=123`, `ftp://username.company/directory`.

Views: A view is an SQL query that enables a special view of several tables of a database. Views are used, for example, to enable simple access to particular parts of a table (e.g., for reasons of security if only part of a table is to be processed). MySQL has supported views since version 5.0.

Web Server: A web server is a program that makes HTML pages available over the Internet. The most popular web server today (current market share about 60 percent) is Apache.

■ ■ ■

The Files for this Book

The example files for this book are available as compressed files for download at the website www.apress.com. To decompress them under Windows, you can use, for example, WinZip (http://www.winzip.com/), while under Unix/Linux, you use the command unzip.

Trying Out the Example Programs

Note All the example programs will work only if the databases described in this book are activated and if you change the user names and passwords in the code so that they are accepted by your MySQL installation.

Additional information can be found in the various chapters of this book as well as in the readme file for the relevant example directories.

If you are having problems with PHP, test whether your PHP installation has the necessary *mysql* or *mysqli* interface available (see the first two sections of Chapter 15). Tips on error-handling are also to be found in those sections. Most of the examples assume PHP 5 and at least MySQL 4.1.

Updates, Errata, Links, Discussion Forum

A collection of MySQL links, a discussion forum for this book, and any updates and errata that come to my attention can be found at my web site: http://www.kofler.cc.

APPENDIX C

■■■

Bibliography

Rich Bowen et al. *Apache Server Unleashed*. SAMS, 2000.

Chris Date, Hugh Darwen. *A Guide to the SQL Standard*. Addison-Wesley Longman, 1998.

Paul DuBois. *MySQL*, second edition. Sams, 2003.

Paul DuBois. *MySQL Cookbook*. O'Reilly, 2002.

W. Jason Gilmore. *Beginning PHP 5 and MySQL*. Apress, 2004.

Cay S. Horstmann, Gary Cornell. *Core Java 2*, Volume II. Sun Microsystems Press/Prentice Hall, 1997.

Michael Kofler. *Definitive Guide to Excel VBA*, second edition. Apress, 2003.

Michael Kofler. *Linux: Installation, Configuration, and Use*, second edition. Addison-Wesley, 1999.

Michael Kofler. *Visual Basic Database Programming*. Addison-Wesley, 2001.

Laura Lemay. *Teach Yourself Perl in 21 Days*, third edition. SAMS, 1999.

Robert Orfali, Dan Harkey, Jeri Edwards. *Client/Server Survival Guide*, third edition. John Wiley & Sons, 1999.

Tobias Ratschiller, Till Gerken. *Web Application Development with PHP 4.0*. New Riders, 2000.

David Sceppa. *Microsoft ADO.NET (Core Reference)*. Microsoft Press, 2002.

Carsten Thomsen. *Database Programming with Visual Basic .NET*. Apress, 2002.

Luke Welling, Laura Thomson. *PHP and MySQL Web Development*. SAMS, 2001.

Index